The

MARRIAGE
BOOK

Edited by

LISA GRUNWALD AND STEPHEN ADLER

SIMON & SCHUSTER

New York   London   Toronto   Sydney   New Delhi

Simon & Schuster
1230 Avenue of the Americas
New York, NY 10020

First Simon & Schuster hardcover edition May 2015

SIMON & SCHUSTER and colophon are registered
trademarks of Simon & Schuster, Inc.

For information about special discounts for bulk purchases,
please contact Simon & Schuster Special Sales at
1-866-506-1949 or business@simonandschuster.com.

The Simon & Schuster Speakers Bureau can bring authors to your live event. For more
information or to book an event contact the Simon & Schuster Speakers Bureau
at 1-866-248-3049 or visit our website at www.simonspeakers.com.

Manufactured in the United States of America

1   3   5   7   9   10   8   6   4   2

Library of Congress Cataloging-in-Publication Data

The marriage book : centuries of advice, inspiration, and cautionary tales, from Adam and Eve to Zoloft /
edited by Lisa Grunwald and Stephen Adler. —First Simon & Schuster hardcover edition.
    pages   cm
Includes bibliographical references.
1. Marriage—Quotations, maxims, etc.   I. Grunwald, Lisa.   II. Adler, Stephen J.
        PN6084.M3M37   2015
306.81—dc23   2014034262

ISBN 978-1-4391-6965-0
ISBN 978-1-4391-6967-4 (ebook)

NOTE: Credits and permissions for source text and images are included on pages 519–34 and 535–36, respectively.

For Mildred and Norman Adler,
who got it right

CONTENTS

S

T

U

V

W

X

Y

Z

INTRODUCTION

Even at its very best, marriage is not for the faint of heart. It can be founded on love or property, faith or geopolitics, the urge to procreate or the unexpected realization that you already have. But no matter how or why it begins, marriage demands an improbable journey, the private, perilous, hopeful journey from *I* to *we*.

The route is by nature serendipitous, marked by rocky terrain and peaceful coves, murky troughs and dazzling summits. There will be unfamiliar languages and unaccustomed currency; treasured souvenirs and dirty laundry; things you lose by accident, and—as with any kind of travel—pleasures you could never have known just by looking at the pictures. Of course, the exact destination will be different for different travelers. But for most readers of this book, the ideal will probably be some version of a landscape filled with contentment and passion; help and forgiveness; honesty, patience, promises; and, let's not forget, love that never dies.

How do you plot your course? If you're not married, you might want to know what makes a marriage succeed or fail. Does everybody get cold feet? And how cold is cold enough so that you should pivot and flee? When people say marriage takes work, do they mean break-your-back, build-a-pyramid work, or do they mean be-a-grown-up-and-think-before-you-talk work?

If you are married, you might want to ponder the peculiar mathematics by which love can be spent and replenished at the same time; how it's possible to be thrilled, or at least delighted, by a body you've seen naked too many times to count; how to repair a hurt ego; how to understand failings but resist disdain; how to give without feeling used; how to need without being needy.

You won't find a single answer in this book; you will find hundreds. Countless writers—whether of books, movies, poetry, jokes, songs, letters, or fortune cookies—have had something to say about marriage. Grecian urns depicted it, as did Egyptian hieroglyphics and *Archie* comics. Google the word "marriage" and any other noun, and you'll find some connection. Marriage and "pasta." Marriage and "car." Marriage and "bathroom sink" (first hit: "Bathroom fixtures that will save your marriage"). In the pages that follow, you'll find proverbs and tweets, poetry and photographs, ads and cartoons, plays and sitcoms, movies and eulogies, and one memorable wedding toast, from Mel Brooks: "Never give your real name." What you'll find is an A to Z of some of the wittiest observations, as well as some of the wisest.

Is marriage a legal contract or a religious sacrament? A romantic ideal or society's bedrock? Look no further than yesterday's news for fervent debates about what the true purpose of the institution is, was, and should be. But this book is not a history of marriage and doesn't pretend to settle such questions. Rather, it is an attempt to capture the myriad ways in which marriage has been experienced and explained.

Over the ages (and these pages), marriage has been defined as a cage (Montaigne), a fruit (Finnish proverb), a tomb (Casanova), an ordeal (Joseph Campbell, but he meant it in a good way), a debt (Julia Ward Howe), and a dream (or rather a "dweam wiffim a dweam," *The Princess Bride*). Like love, death, and happiness, marriage seems to beg for a metaphor (see "a journey," six paragraphs up), and giving marital advice seems to be an almost atavistic need.

How-to books and how-to lists have abounded through time. Sometimes the titles seemed to say it all, like the 1886 *How to Be Happy Though Married*. Back in the thirteenth century, an Italian mother gave her daughter a list of a dozen prohibitions, beginning with the somewhat quixotic "Do not be joyful if he is sad, or sad if he is joyful." In 1902, a Pennsylvania wife compiled a set of twelve "commandments," including one involving the frequency of her husband's bathing, another the removal of his mother's cow. In 1936, the British author of *How to Be a Good Husband* cautioned in one of his many instructions: "Don't think that your wife has placed waste-paper baskets in the rooms as ornaments."

Naturally enough, one recurrent theme in marital advice has been what to look for in a husband or wife—and perhaps more frequently, what to avoid. In 1969, Martha Gellhorn, ex-wife of Ernest Hemingway, wrote to her son: "No woman should ever marry a man who hated his mother." An African proverb warned men against marrying women with bigger feet than their own. And sometime around 500 BC, a Hindu text advised: "[Do] not marry a girl who has red hair or an extra limb [or] is named after a constellation, a tree, [or] a river."

Weddings and wedding nights have been other popular topics. In these pages, you'll find a 1901 suggestion on what a best man should do with a groom's hat, Margaret Sanger's pragmatic suggestion that "a Pullman car is hardly . . . a proper setting for the first conjugal embrace," and W. F. Robie's solemn and surprising 1920 plea for honeymoon foreplay:

> Young husband . . . Don't say much; but slowly and carefully feel your way. Kiss without shame, for she desires it, your wife's lips, tongue, neck; and, as Shakespeare says: "If these founts be dry, stray lower where the pleasant fountains lie."

Indeed, what would marriage be without sex? (Just *marriage*, some couples might be quick to answer acerbically.) You'll find plenty of thoughts about sex under "S," naturally: how, when, and why it's a good idea to have it. Much of it is directed at women, with the assumption that they're the ones who have to keep things interesting. But back in 1829, no less a thinker than Honoré de Balzac addressed his advice, refreshingly, to husbands: "Just as ideas go on increasing indefinitely, so it ought to be with pleasures. . . . Every night should have its own menu."

When we started compiling this book, we thought it would be a compendium of only such direct advice. We were enchanted, as we certainly hope you will be, by the way that so many recognizable questions—and so many varied answers—have come down through the ages. But we soon realized that we were missing the kinds of insights that come not from rules or maxims but from experience and stories. In other words, to extend our marriage-as-journey metaphor, we wanted to produce an anthology that would be both a travel guide *and* a travelogue.

So when it came to looking at proposals, for example, we were amused by the trendy suggestions of contemporary "engagement planners," not very different in spirit from a 1907 advice column called "The Ticklish Art of Proposing Marriage." But how could any section on proposals exclude the unrivaled cluelessness of William Collins's approach to Elizabeth Bennet in *Pride and Prejudice*, or the half-romantic, half-cynical deal Rhett offers Scarlett in *Gone With the Wind*? Likewise, thinking about conflict, we found it fascinating to read the how-to rules for "fair fighting" that were offered at a Los Angeles marriage clinic back in 1969. But we also wanted a glimpse of famous fighters like Liz and Dick, Napoleon and Josephine, Ralph and Alice. And we couldn't forget the acid line of Martha to George in Edward Albee's *Who's Afraid of Virginia Woolf?*: "I swear, if you existed, I'd divorce you."

With the exception of Anne Morrow Lindbergh's suggestion in 1955 that spouses take separate vacations, we found little direct advice about the benefits of spending time apart. But a lot of inspiring entries were the result of just such separations. Despite his drinking and general debauchery, the poet Dylan Thomas, on his first trip to America, wrote to his wife with passionate longing:

> Why oh why did I think I could live, I could bear to live, I could think of living, for all these torturing, unending, echoing months without you, Cat, my life, my wife, my wife on earth and in God's eyes, my reason for my blood, breath, and bone.

Gladys Knight and the Pips sang it more succinctly in 1973: "I'll be with him / On that midnight train to Georgia / I'd rather live in his world / Than live without him in mine."

So often, the experiences we read about defied our expectations and may even have surprised the men and women who wrote about them. How poignant that, for all his many witty and wise instructions and aphorisms about marriage, Mark Twain was never more profound about the institution than when, after the death of his wife, he boarded a steamer from Naples to New York, and wrote in his journal:

> June 29. Sailed last night, at ten. The bugle called to breakfast. I recognized the notes, and was distressed. When I heard them last Livy heard them with me; now they fall upon her ears unheeded. The weather is beautiful, the sea is smooth and curiously blue. In my life there have been 68 Junes—but how vague and colorless 67 of them are contrasted with the deep blackness of this one.

And how shattering that the brilliant theoretical physicist Richard Feynman, a man who helped the world understand the nature of reality, would write a letter to his wife two years after her death and apologize for not having her current address.

Editing this book together supplied us with our own leg of a marital journey that began in 1987 with a blind date and a really good kiss. We got engaged just a few months after that, and phone calls from friends and relatives soon followed, with an understandable refrain of the three words "Are you sure?" And then, after a wedding most memorable for the way that even the flowers in Lisa's hair shook as her father tried to pilot her toward the center of the aisle, we began to receive our own share of marital advice:

- You don't have to tell each other every thought you have.
- Never go to bed angry.
- Combine your bank accounts.
- You can trash your own relatives, but never your spouse's.

- • Have a weekly date night.
- • Share your love with the people around you.

Some of this advice was truly helpful. Some of it we even followed. But one piece of advice we obviously ignored was:

- • Never work together.

Why did we tempt fate?

We thought it would be fun. Back on Valentine's Day in 1997, a flirtation with the notion of editing a collection of love letters evolved into the idea of telling the century's history in letters. *Letters of the Century: America, 1900–1999* was the result, and along the way, we reveled in the treasure hunt and the pride in a double byline. The book was enough of a success that it spawned another: *Women's Letters: America from the Revolutionary War to the Present*, and in finding the voices of those women in that research—so often frank and confiding—we ended up thinking that a book about marriage would offer further emotional and admittedly voyeuristic pleasures. Reading about other people's marriages, we figured, would be a lot like going to a series of dinner parties where the couples have a little too much to drink and you get to spend the ride home dishing about what's really going on with them.

Frankly, we anticipated that lifting the veil (or the covers) would reveal more lost illusions than fairy-tale moments. What surprised us was the persistence with which the crazy optimism of marriage kept coming through, and the extent to which some of the most distant examples—whether in time or place—held a personal resonance for us. The story of Rachel Calof, for example, seemed thoroughly remote at first: a Russian immigrant homesteader, she was the bride in an arranged marriage who wrote about making lunch for her new husband by gathering garlic, grass, and mushrooms from the untamed North Dakota land, making dough from flour and prairie water, and coffee from ground barley.

> Never was there a more delightful dinner than that one. The food was delectable and our shanty was filled with happiness. After we finished our meal, Abe insisted on knowing all the details of my accomplishment. As he listened, his gladness became tinged with a sadness that our condition was such that I was reduced to searching the prairie for food. But nothing could destroy the magic of that hour.

The struggle for the bare necessities of life was something we had luckily never had to experience during our marriage. But Rachel's journal entry struck a very personal chord. We were moved by the resilience with which she had faced the necessary tasks and by the pride she felt in making her spouse happy. Mostly we were reminded how the most sublime moments in a marriage can come at the most unexpected times. For us, it's never been garlic soup on the prairie, but eating Indian takeout while watching *Mad Men* on TV has come pretty close.

Then, too, unless you count the adulterous heroine in one of Lisa's novels (about whom Stephen has caught no end of flak), neither of us has had any personal experience with adultery. But this book's entries about famous cheaters—from Hester Prynne to Yves Montand ("I think a man can have two, maybe three affairs. . . . After that, you're cheating"), as well as the cheated—like Nora Ephron ("the man is capable of having sex with a venetian blind")—turned out to have personal resonance as well. As cautionary tales, those entries steered us back to the inspirational examples of the two great Homers: the Greek poet who described the fidelity of Penelope as she wove and unwove a burial shroud to keep her suitors at bay; and Homer Simpson, who, when faced with the temptation of a hotel tryst with an office colleague, answered the catcalls of a bellhop with "All I'm gonna use this bed for is sleeping, eating, and maybe building a little fort."

We are hopeful that readers of this book will be able to build or reaffirm their own marital credos from its pages. For what it's worth, here are ours:

We believe that "to love and honor" really means to support and, if necessary, forcibly extract the best of each other. Not always simple. It doesn't just mean remembering to inspire and cheer; it means remembering *what* to inspire and cheer—especially when your spouse falters or forgets. The great poet William Butler Yeats never got to marry the love of his life, but in 1909 he wrote a journal entry that perfectly described how a marriage could uphold this kind of promise:

> In wise love each divines the high secret self of the other and, refusing to believe in the mere daily self, creates a mirror where the lover or the beloved sees an image to copy in daily life.

When asked recently what he considered his greatest accomplishment to be, Stephen King said: "Staying married." We readily concede that many marriages go terribly, even tragically, wrong; that some should never have taken place; that many must end. But we also believe that the vow "as long as you both shall *love*" (which we heard at several weddings some years back) is not a vow but a timid, silly, New Age, cover-your-asses tautology. We believe in "as long as you both shall live"—in staying on the marriage journey if you possibly can. For all the probable detours and delays and wrong turns, the challenge and promise of this journey is perhaps best evoked by Tennyson in his 1867 poem "Marriage Morning":

Heart, are you great enough
For a love that never tires?
O heart, are you great enough for love?
I have heard of thorns and briers.
Over the thorns and briers,
Over the meadows and stiles,
Over the world to the end of it
Flash for a million miles.

EDITORS' NOTE

Given the nearly unlimited supply of information and commentary about marriage, our selection of entries for this volume was always going to be highly idiosyncratic. In our research, we tried to cast as wide a net as possible, conceding from the start that our choices would be dominated by text, by nonfiction, and by a decidedly Western perspective. We wanted examples from many media, centuries, and cultures, but because we were not attempting a history book, we felt free to ignore entries that might have filled out the historical or geographical picture but not met our other criteria. And our other criteria were extremely simple. Basically, the entries in this book had to do one of the following four things: advise us, inspire us, amuse us, or appall us.

We found treasures on eBay and Etsy, on Pinterest and HuffPo. With one former literature major and one former lawyer in the house, our bookshelves were their own happy hunting ground; add the fabulous ongoing liberal-arts educations of our children, and we didn't have to go far to find some of our favorite entries. Invariably a number of other anthologies proved extremely valuable, and we'd like to acknowledge—and recommend—several in particular: *The Oxford Book of Marriage*, edited by Helge Rubinstein; *A Letter Does Not Blush*, edited by Nicholas Parsons; and *The World's Greatest Letters*, edited by Michelle Lovric. Our search for material also led us through invaluable web databases, including the Ancient History Sourcebook, Early English Books Online, Gale's 19th Century U.S. Newspapers, Google Books, HathiTrust, and ProQuest.

Whatever the source, when we found a keeper, we tried to track it to its original context, as you'll see from the introductions to our entries. Sometimes that effort provided surprising results. The Internet is rife with sites dedicated to love, marriage, and weddings. But we soon discovered that a lot of the popular quotes they offer aren't quite what they seem. One favorite wedding toast, for example, attributed to Oliver Wendell Holmes, is: "Love is the master-key that opens the gates of happiness." Nice sentiment, except that the full quote turns out to be, "Love is the master-key that opens the gates of happiness, of hatred, of jealousy, and most easily of all, the gate of *fear.*" Likewise, Antoine de Saint-Exupéry is frequently cited for the romantic statement: "Love does not consist in gazing at each other but in looking together in the same direction." Turns out he wrote it not about marriage, nor even about relationships, but about society at large, and citizens' obligations to one another. The full quote? "Bound to our brothers by a common goal that is situated outside of ourselves, only then do we truly breathe; and our experience shows us that to love is not to look at each other but to look in the same direction."

Sadly, we sought in vain for proof that Queen Victoria had ever instructed her daughter to "lie still and think of England" during conjugal sex. Similarly, Margaret Mead is cited all over the Internet for having said: "One of the oldest human needs is having someone to wonder where you are when you don't come home at night." We loved the sentiment but couldn't find the source. And it turned out that Marabel Morgan, famous in the 1970s for advising women to greet their husbands wearing only Saran Wrap, never actually did so; it was a reader who got the idea from Morgan's other dress-up tips.

As to the texts: except where noted, the ellipses represent our own omissions. Occasionally, for clarity, we have substituted em dashes for ellipses in the excerpts. Except when clarity is deeply compromised, we have kept all original spellings and punctuation, however idiosyncratic or outmoded. In an effort to avoid cluttering the text, we have not used "sic," nor ellipses at the beginnings or ends of our entries, which often are taken from larger contexts; we are hopeful that in doing so, we have never misrepresented an author's meaning.

ADAM AND EVE

GENESIS 2:18-25

Like so much of the Bible, the appearance of Eve in Genesis, Chapter 2, is subject to debate: Hadn't God already created "male and female" in Chapter 1? Yet the verses below seem to portray the culmination of God's creation in the union of Adam and Eve as the very first husband and wife.

The writing of Genesis has been the source of waves of scholarly discussion that date the book to a multitude of points in the centuries before the birth of Christ.

And the Lord God said, It is not good that the man should be alone; I will make him an help meet for him.

And out of the ground the Lord God formed every beast of the field, and every fowl of the air; and brought them unto Adam to see what he would call them: and whatsoever Adam called every living creature, that was the name thereof.

And Adam gave names to all cattle, and to the fowl of the air, and to every beast of the field; but for Adam there was not found an help meet for him.

And the Lord God caused a deep sleep to fall upon Adam, and he slept: and he took one of his ribs, and closed up the flesh instead thereof;

And the rib, which the Lord God had taken from man, made he a woman, and brought her unto the man.

And Adam said, This is now bone of my bones, and flesh of my flesh: she shall be called Woman, because she was taken out of Man.

Therefore shall a man leave his father and his mother, and shall cleave unto his wife: and they shall be one flesh.

And they were both naked, the man and his wife, and were not ashamed.

JOHN MILTON
PARADISE LOST, 1674

John Milton (1608–1674) was hardly the first author—English or otherwise—to produce a literary retelling of Adam and Eve's fall. But *Paradise Lost* is, at more than ten thousand lines of free verse, certainly the longest version and generally viewed as the greatest. In Milton's rendition, Adam plays the clearly dominant male role, and yet when Eve eats the apple, Adam follows suit, led by the interdependent nature of their bond. The lines below are spoken by Adam after he realizes what Eve has done.

Among Milton's many other works were several treatises on divorce, way ahead of their time in suggesting that in addition to adultery and impotence, another acceptable reason for divorce might be incompatibility. Milton's first version of the epic was published in 1667.

O fairest of Creation, last and best
Of all God's Works, Creature in whom excell'd
Whatever can to sight or thought be form'd,
Holy, divine, good, amiable, or sweet!
How art thou lost, how on a sudden lost . . .
How can I live without thee, how forgo
Thy sweet Converse and Love so dearly join'd,
To live again in these wild Woods forlorn?
Should God create another *Eve*, and I
Another Rib afford, yet loss of thee
Would never from my heart; no no, I feel
The Link of Nature draw me: Flesh of Flesh,
Bone of my Bone thou art, and from thy State
Mine never shall be parted, bliss or woe.

MARK TWAIN
"EXTRACTS FROM ADAM'S DIARY," 1893

Samuel Clemens (1835–1910), a.k.a. Mark Twain (see Endings, pages 95–96), brought his signature style to a short, witty imagining of the Bible's first couple.

After all these years, I see that I was mistaken about Eve in the beginning; it is better to live outside the Garden with her than inside it without her.

H. L. MENCKEN
A BOOK OF BURLESQUES, 1916

Between his books, his columns, and his reviews, H. L. Mencken (1880–1956) left no shortage of caustic comments about marriage. Yet the author known as "the Sage of Baltimore" was by all accounts devoted to his wife, Sara, whom he married in 1930.
See Expectations, page 105; Jealousy, page 240, for more from Mencken.

Woman is at once the serpent, the apple—and the belly-ache.

JOHN PATRICK SHANLEY
MOONSTRUCK, 1987

In the Oscar-winning screenplay by John Patrick Shanley (1950–), Johnny Cammareri, dim-witted but well-intentioned, is beseeched for wisdom by his would-be mother-in-law.

ROSE: Listen, Johnny, there's a question I want to ask. I want you to tell me the truth—
          if you can. Why do men chase women?
JOHNNY: Well. There's the Bible story. God—God took a rib from Adam and made Eve.
          Now, maybe men chase women to get the rib back.

MICK STEVENS, 2012

A frequent contributor to *The New Yorker*, Mick Stevens caused a stir with this take on Adam and Eve. The magazine's popular Facebook page was temporarily shut down because the cartoon was judged to violate the social media site's nudity and sex guidelines, forbidding "naked 'private parts,' including female nipple bulges." The Facebook page was soon back up, but "Nipplegate" lingered online for some weeks as a topic of discussion.

"Well, it __was__ original."

ANNIVERSARIES

NATHANIEL HAWTHORNE
NOTE TO SOPHIA HAWTHORNE, 1843

Nathaniel Hawthorne (1804–1864) was thirty-eight when he married Sophia Peabody, who was thirty-two. Their ages (old for newlyweds at the time) did nothing to dampen their apparently childish glee: They used her diamond ring to engrave their names on their study window. They also shared a notebook in which they took turns recording their impressions and, as in the case below on the occasion of their first anniversary, writing love notes to one another.

For more Hawthorne, see Infidelity, pp. 204–5.

Dearest love,

I know not what to say, and yet cannot be satisfied without marking with a word or two this holiest anniversary of our life. But life now heaves and swells beneath me like a brimfull ocean; and the endeavor to comprise any portion of it in words, is like trying to dip up the ocean in a goblet. We never were so happy as now—never such wide capacity for happiness, yet overflowing with all that the day and every moment brings to us. Methinks this birth-day of our married life is like a cape [of land], which we have now doubled and find a more infinite ocean of love stretching out before us.

CLEMENTINE CHURCHILL
LETTER TO WINSTON CHURCHILL, 1909

Winston Churchill was already a respected member of Parliament when in 1908 he married Clementine Hozier (1885–1977). He was thirty-three; she was ten years his junior. Through his legendary career as orator, author, home secretary, lord of the admiralty, and wartime prime minister, he remained devoted to his "Kat" or "Clemmie Cat" (her nickname for him was "Pug," and they signed many of their letters with little drawings of dogs and cats). Their anniversary letters are one example of the loving gestures they extended to each other throughout a fifty-seven-year marriage in which they were often geographically separated but in which "too busy to write" never seemed to play a part.

Blenheim was the Churchill family estate. St. Margaret's, Westminster Abbey, was where the Churchills were married.

My Darling,

How I wish we were together today—It is just 5 o'clock—This time last year we were steaming out of Paddington on our way to Blenheim—The Pug was reading an account of the wedding presents in the Westminster aloud to the Kat!

Then the Pug embraced the Kat, but unfortunately another train was just passing us quite slowly & its occupants caught him in the very act—

My Beloved Winston I hope you are having a very happy holiday. I do long to see you again—Tell Eddie & Freddie that if they don't return you to me in the pink of health I will never forgive them. . . .

> Your most loving
> Clemmie Kat
> Miaow

WINSTON CHURCHILL
LETTER TO CLEMENTINE CHURCHILL, 1909

Churchill (1874–1965) was in Strasbourg on the couple's first anniversary.

My darling Clemmie,

A year to-day my lovely white pussy-cat came to me, & I hope & pray she may find on this September morning no cause—however vague or secret—for regrets. The bells of this old city are ringing now & they recall to my mind the chimes which saluted our wedding & the crowds of cheering people. A year has gone—& if it has not brought you all the glowing & perfect joy which fancy paints, still it has brought a clear bright light of happiness & some great things. My precious & beloved Clemmie my earnest desire is to enter still more completely into your dear heart & nature & to curl myself up in your darling arms. I feel so safe with you & I do not keep the slightest disguise. You have been so sweet & good to me that I cannot say how grateful I feel to you for your dear nature, & matchless beauty. Not please disdain the caresses of your devoted pug. . . .

> Always my own darling
> Clem-puss-bird
> Your loving husband
> W

WINSTON CHURCHILL
LETTER TO CLEMENTINE CHURCHILL, 1948

Churchill wrote this on the couple's fortieth anniversary.

My Beloved,

I send this token, but how little can it express my gratitude to you for making my life & any work I have done possible, and for giving me so much happiness in a world of accident & storm.

> Your ever loving and devoted
> husband
> W

RICHMOND LATTIMORE
"ANNIVERSARY," 1956

Best known for his translations of *The Iliad* and *The Odyssey*, Richmond Lattimore (1906–1984) was prolific as a poet, critic, and translator. In addition to serving in the U.S. Navy, he was a Rhodes Scholar, a PhD, and a professor at Bryn Mawr. He married Alice Bockstahler in 1935.

Where were we in that afternoon? And where
is the high room now, the bed on which you laid your hair,
as bells beat early in the still air?

At two o'clock of sun and shutters. Oh, recall
the chair's angle—a stripe of shadow on the wall—
the hours we gathered in our hands, and then let fall.

Wrist on wrist, we relive memory: shell of moon
on day-sky, two o'clock in lazy June—
and twenty years gone in an afternoon.

TENTH-ANNIVERSARY POSTCARD, CIRCA 1960

RONALD REAGAN
LETTER TO NANCY REAGAN, 1972

Whatever his reputation as an actor, governor, and, eventually, the fortieth president of the United States, Ronald Reagan (1911–2004) was also famously committed to his second wife, Nancy Davis (1921–), his fiercest defender and most ardent fan. He wrote this anniversary letter to her while he was governor of California.

My Darling Wife

This note is to warn you of a diabolical plot entered into by some of our so called friends—(ha!) calendar makers and even our own children. These and others would have you believe we've been married 20 years.

20 minutes maybe—but never 20 years. In the first place it is a known fact that a human cannot sustain the high level of happiness I feel for more than a few minutes—and my happiness keeps on increasing.

I will confess to one puzzlement but I'm sure it is just some trick perpetrated by our friends—(Ha again!) I can't remember ever being without you and I know I was born more than 20 mins ago.

Oh well—that isn't important. The important thing is I don't want to be without you for the next 20 years, or 40, or however many there are. I've gotten very used to being happy and I love you very much indeed.

Your Husband of 20 something or other.

W. S. MERWIN
"ANNIVERSARY ON THE ISLAND," 1988

William Stanley Merwin (1927–), the United States Poet Laureate in 2010, started his career with a bang when his first book of poems, *A Mask for Janus*, was awarded the Yale Series of Younger Poets prize in 1952 by W. H. Auden. The son of a Presbyterian minister, Merwin grew up in New Jersey and Pennsylvania but settled in Hawaii in 1976, a practicing Buddhist. Much of his poetry explores themes of nature, myth, and love. Merwin has been married to his third wife, Paula Schwartz, since 1983. They live atop a dormant volcano on a former pineapple plantation in Maui, presumably the island of this poem.

The long waves glide in through the afternoon
while we watch from the island
from the cool shadow under the trees where the long ridge
a fold in the skirt of the mountain
runs down to the end of the headland

day after day we wake to the island
the light rises through the drops on the leaves
and we remember like birds where we are
night after night we touch the dark island
that once we set out for

and lie still at last with the island in our arms
hearing the leaves and the breathing shore
there are no years any more
only the one mountain
and on all sides the sea that brought us

VICKI IOVINE
"SEVEN HABITS OF REALLY HAPPY WIVES," 1998

"Expect Him Not to Change" was the last of the seven "habits" that appeared in the author's article in *Redbook* magazine. Vicki Iovine (1954–), a onetime *Playboy* centerfold, has been the successful author of the Girlfriends' Guide books on everything from pregnancy to teenagers. Her marriage to music mogul Jimmy Iovine ended in 2009 after more than two decades.

Remember, you're adorable too, and you owe it to yourself to be happy as often as you can. If you're willing to put that off until he starts remembering your anniversary and giving you a gift he picked out himself that fits, is romantic, and costs a little more than it should have, then you're the sucker, girlfriend. Buy your own anniversary gift, give it to him to give you on your anniversary, and compliment him on his choice. Remember, the important thing is that you have an anniversary to celebrate.

H. DEAN RUTHERFORD
LETTER TO PATTIE RUTHERFORD, CIRCA 2012

Harvey Dean Rutherford (1932–) wrote this letter to his wife on their fifty-ninth anniversary. A former pastor in Oklahoma City, Rutherford is part of a large family of clergy. This letter was posted on the blog of his son, Dudley Clayton Rutherford, chief pastor of California's enormous Shepherd of the Hills Church.

Patsy Lou,

Happy 59th wedding anniversary! That old granddaddy clock has written on its face, "tempus fugit," which means "time flies." I knew it was quick, but now it seems like we're having Christmas three times a year. I am not absolutely sure that we will make it to our sixtieth, so

I'd better put some words on paper. Looking back, I now wonder why we had any reluctance at all to be married. The deep love I have struggled to define has now defined itself in time. We've lived together way too long to not know that we were made to live together. Living out the years with you keeps getting better. Once we figured out that we could not change each other, we became free to celebrate ourselves as we are. So my dear Trish-the-fish, we are gloriously together and it has never been dull company. It's kind of weird that we have been together for eight decades and yet still think of ourselves as young. There are plenty of moments when I find you to be that blushing and shy girl who took my cheap ring and name and then agreed to explore the world with me.

It's kind of weird that we have been together for eight decades and yet still think of ourselves as young.

We began to dream and work and love and worship. Sure, we only started with forty dollars and a fistful of promises, but we were wealthy. I can still remember that Georgia wedding 59 years ago today and oh my, how young we both were. We experienced the sweet warmth and love of youth. We felt that God had decorated the night sky with stars just for us. We drove every false and threatening thing out of our lives with simple truth and honesty. We have met 240 changing seasons and met each challenge. I still smile when I think, how wealthy we thought we were when we were really so very poor. And talk about money, those five children came along. I've almost forgotten how they got here or what it took to get them here. You can remind me later. But I've always known that they came from God and belonged to Him. And I remember my promise before they were ever born, that they would never take "first place" in my heart, the "first place" that you have always held. I love those once-upon-a-time "tax deductions," but I could never love them as much as I have loved you.

The other morning I was leaving the house and I found you in the kitchen, looking out the window while talking to Debbie on the phone. The morning sun fell across your hair and hands. I reached down and touched your hand, a hand made noble by its years of service and duty. I left that morning feeling like a king because you were mine.

I don't mean to sound morose, but I simply bring it to your attention that we will probably both not leave on the same day. The crispness of the fall air reminds us that we cannot have summer forever. Someday, all too soon one of us will be forced to test the shattering emptiness that we have seen transpire in the lives of couples who have gone on before us. One of us will go first but the other will celebrate our treasure, our union and love with a transcending joy. We will not sorrow not as those who have no hope. I walk so much slower now, and a little stooped. It's not because I'm tired or weary, but no one can walk fast, who is weighted down with great dreams and precious memories. My biggest apology is that I was never able to rebuke and turn back the wild, hurried pace of the years. There have been times when I actually dreamed that I might be the one person who could defeat old-age and remain in full health just for you. It was not to be. As I have repeated so many times: "Old 'Father Time' is still undefeated." Darn him!

Come walk with me my love. Just not too fast, we will not hurry, because there are still places to go, people to bless and vistas to see. We will continue to pace ourselves. And can I say it one more time with deep meaning and emphasis? "I love you." Happy 59th!!!

BED

JOHN HEYWOOD
PROVERB, 1546

Author of such epigrams as "the fat is in the fire" and "the more the merrier," British playwright and poet John Heywood (1497–1580) was a favorite of Henry VIII.

In house to kepe household when folkes will needes wed,
Moe thinges belonge than foure bare legges in a bed.

BEATRICE CAMPBELL, CIRCA 1934

The first actress to play Eliza Doolittle in *Pygmalion*, Mrs. Patrick Campbell (1865–1940) was George Bernard Shaw's friend and a famed correspondent of his (see Passion, page 334). *The New Yorker* writer Alexander Woollcott cited this as her definition of marriage.

Marriage is the result of the deep, deep longing for the double-bed after the hurly-burly of the chaise-longue.

B

MALLORY HOTEL POSTCARD, CIRCA 1940

When the Mallory Hotel in Portland, Oregon, wanted to attract romantic couples, it had a twenty-five-foot round bed custom made and promoted with this postcard. On the back, this description: "This unusual bed is entirely custom-built, including Beautyrest mattress—and box spring. Ideal for wedding nights, anniversaries or just sleeping!"

The Round Bed at the Mallory Hotel

ROBERT FARRAR CAPON
BED AND BOARD, 1965

Bed and Board was the first of twenty-seven books written by Robert Farrar Capon (1925–2013), an Episcopal priest who was vicar for a Port Jefferson, New York, congregation for nearly three decades. After a falling-out with the church surrounding his divorce from his wife of twenty-seven years, Capon devoted himself to writing, both about theology and cooking and, in the case of some of his most popular books, about both.

Capon's bestselling book was *The Supper of the Lamb*. He also wrote frequently about food and wine for the *New York Times* and *Newsday*.

I shall get to the Board and its adjuncts by and by. Table and rooftree, nursery and kitchen, even patio and rumpus room, will all have their turn. But the first must come first, and that is the Bed: the couple's initial piece of real estate. The things that come later in a marriage are, one way or another, extensions of this—added parcels, adjacent lots, buffer strips and subdivisions. The bed itself is their first soil, the uncrossed plain waiting for boundary and marker, for plough and seed. If this is well laid and planted, the rest will have order and comeliness; if not, they will be senseless bits of gerrymandering, spreading far and wide for reasons that have nothing to do with the good of the people of the land. The bed is the heart of home, the arena of love,

> The bed is the oldest, friendliest thing in anybody's marriage, the first used and the last left, and no one can praise it enough.

the seedbed of life, and the one constant point of meeting. It is the place where, night by night, forgiveness and fair speech return that the sun go not down upon their wrath; where the perfunctory kiss and the entirely ceremonial pat on the backside become unction and grace. [The bed] is the oldest, friendliest thing in anybody's marriage, the first used and the last left, and no one can praise it enough.

But there is mystery in it too. It is a strange piece of terrain, and finding ourselves in it is as unlikely as it is marvelous. We marry on attack or rebound. We come at each other for an assortment of pretty thin and transitory reasons. We ask, and are taken in matrimony; and in the haste of charge or retreat, we find ourselves thrown down into a very small piece of ground indeed. The marriage bed is a trench; adversity has made us bedfellows. I turn over at night. I try to see where I am and who is with me. It is not what I imagined at all. Where are the two triumphant giants of love I expected, where the conqueror smiling at conqueror? There are only the two of us, crouched down here under a barrage of years, bills and petty grievances, waiting for a signal which shows no sign of coming. Most likely we shall die in this trench. There is really no place else to go, so in the meantime we talk to each other. The sum and substance of what we manage to say, however, is "Well, here we are."

TONI MORRISON
JAZZ, 1992

Winner of the Nobel Prize for Literature, the Pulitzer Prize for Fiction, and numerous other honors, Toni Morrison (1931–) is a literary icon. Her sixth novel, *Jazz*, is set in Harlem during the twenties, tracing a story of love, adultery, and murder. In this passage, Morrison's narrator reflects on the main characters, Joe and Violet, as the dramatic storms in their marriage come to a seemingly quiet close.

It's nice when grown people whisper to each other under the covers. Their ecstasy is more leaf-sigh than bray and the body is the vehicle, not the point. They reach, grown people, for something beyond, way beyond and way, way down underneath tissue. They are remembering while they whisper the carnival dolls they won and the Baltimore boats they never sailed on. The pears they let hang on the limb because if they plucked them, they would be gone from there and who else would see that ripeness if they took it away for themselves? How could anybody passing by see them and imagine for themselves what the flavor would be like? Breathing and murmuring under covers both of them have washed and hung out on the line, in a bed they chose together and kept together never mind one leg was propped on a 1916 dictionary, and the mattress, curved like a preacher's palm asking for witnesses in His name's sake, enclosed them each and every night and muffled their whispering, old-time love. They are under the covers because they don't have to look at themselves anymore; there is no stud's eye, no chippie glance to undo them. They are inward toward the other, bound and joined by carnival dolls and the steamers that sailed from ports they never saw. That is what is beneath their undercover whispers.

BEGINNINGS

JULIA WARD HOWE
LETTER TO ANN ELIZA WARD, 1846

The future author of "The Battle Hymn of the Republic," Julia Ward Howe (1819–1910) had been married only three years when she sent these words of wisdom to her younger sister.

My poor dear little Ante-nuptial, I will write to you, and I will come to you, though I can do you no good—sentiment and sympathy I have none, but such insipidity as I have give I unto thee. . . . Dear Annie, your marriage is to me a grave and solemn matter. I hardly allow myself to think about it. God give you all happiness, dearest child. Some sufferings and trials I fear you must have, for after all, the entering into single combat, hand to hand, with the realities of life, will be strange and painful to one who has hitherto lived, enjoyed, and suffered, *en l'air*, as you have done. . . . To be happily married seems to me the best thing for a woman. Oh! my sweet Annie, may you be happy—your maidenhood has been pure, sinless, loving, beautiful—you have no remorses, no anxious thought about the past. You have lived to make the earth more beautiful and bright—may your married life be as holy and harmless—may it be more complete, and more acceptable to God than your single life could possibly have been. Marriage, like death, is a debt we owe to nature, and though it costs us something to pay it, yet are we more content and better *established* in peace, when we have paid it. A young girl is a loose flower or flower seed, blown about by the wind, it may be cruelly battered, may be utterly blighted and lost to this world, but the matron is the same flower or seed planted, springing up and bearing fruit unto eternal life.

ALFRED, LORD TENNYSON
"MARRIAGE MORNING," CIRCA 1867

Nearly twenty years after his own marriage to Emily Sellwood, Alfred, Lord Tennyson (1809–1892) wrote the lyrics for a song cycle by Arthur Sullivan (of Gilbert and Sullivan fame). "Marriage Morning" was the last section of "The Window; Or, The Song of the Wrens." The words weren't published until 1871 because, as Sullivan wrote in a letter, "[Tennyson] thinks they are too light, and will damage his reputation."

Light, so low upon earth,
You send a flash to the sun.
Here is the golden close of love,
All my wooing is done.
Oh, the woods and the meadows,
Woods where we hid from the wet,
Stiles where we stay'd to be kind,
Meadows in which we met!

B

Light, so low in the vale
You flash and lighten afar,
For this is the golden morning of love,
And you are his morning star.
Flash, I am coming, I come,
By meadow and stile and wood,
Oh, lighten into my eyes and my heart,
Into my heart and my blood!

Heart, are you great enough
For a love that never tires?
O heart, are you great enough for love?
I have heard of thorns and briers.
Over the thorns and briers,
Over the meadows and stiles,
Over the world to the end of it
Flash for a million miles.

KWEI-LI
LETTER TO HER HUSBAND, CIRCA 1886

Kwei-Li was the daughter of a Chinese viceroy and was about eighteen when, in an arranged marriage, she became the wife of a nobleman who was eventually governor of Jiangsu Province. Living in Suzhou, she wrote exquisitely to her husband while he was traveling the world with his master, Prince Chung.

Kwei-Li's letters were originally translated and published by a missionary's wife named Elizabeth Cooper. In her introduction to a new edition, Eileen Goudge concedes the possibility that Cooper, in the tradition of missionary writers, embellished or created the letters. Along with Goudge, however, we prefer to think that Kwei-Li was a real person.

Can I ever forget that day when first I came to my husband's people? I had the one great consolation of a bride, my parents had not sent me away empty-handed. The procession was almost a *li* in length and I watched with a swelling heart the many tens of coolies carrying my household goods. There were the silken coverlets for the beds, and they were folded to show their richness and carried on red lacquered tables of great value. There were the household utensils of many kinds, the vegetable dishes, the baskets, the camphor-wood baskets containing my clothing, tens upon tens of them; and I said within my heart as they passed me by, "Enter my new home before me. Help me to find a loving welcome." Then at the end of the chanting procession I came in my red chair of marriage, so closely covered I could barely breathe. My trembling feet could scarce support me as they helped me from the chair, and my hand shook with fear as I was being led into my new household. She stood bravely before you, that little girl dressed in red and gold, her hair twined with pearls and jade, her arms heavy with bracelets and with rings on each tiny finger, but with all her bravery she was frightened—frightened. She was away from her parents for the first time, away from all who loved her, and she knew if she did not meet with approval in her new home her rice-bowl would be full of bitterness for many moons to come.

After the obeisance to the ancestral tablet and we had fallen upon our knees before thine Honourable Parent, I then saw for the first time the face of my husband. Dost thou remember when first thou raised my veil and looked long into my eyes? I was thinking, "Will he find me beautiful?" and in fear I could look but for a moment, then my eyes fell and I would not raise them to thine again. But in that moment I saw that thou wert tall and beautiful, that thine eyes were truly almond, that thy skin was clear and thy teeth like pearls. I was secretly glad within my heart, because I have known of brides who, when they saw their husbands for the first time, wished to scream in terror, as they were old or ugly. I thought to myself that I could be happy with this tall, strong young man if I found favour in his sight, and I said a little prayer to Kwan-yin. Because she has answered that prayer, each day I place a candle at her feet to show my gratitude.

EERO SAARINEN
LETTER TO ALINE BERNSTEIN SAARINEN, 1954

Aline Bernstein Louchheim was an art critic for the *New York Times* when she interviewed the architect and designer Eero Saarinen (1910–1961) about the splash he had made with his General Motors center in Michigan. By all accounts—including Saarinen's, below—they fell hard. It would be the second marriage for both of them.

Saarinen would go on to design the Gateway Arch in St. Louis, the TWA terminal in New York, dozens of other buildings, and iconic furniture; Aline remained a successful author and, later, art critic on the *Today Show* and head of NBC's Paris news bureau.

I   FIRST I RECOGNIZED THAT YOU WERE VERY CLEVER

II   THAT YOU WERE VERY HANSOME

III   THAT YOU WERE PERCEPTIVE

IV	THAT YOU WERE ENTHUSIASTIC.
V	THAT YOU WERE GENEROUS.
VI	THAT YOU WERE BEAUTIFUL
VII	THAT YOU WERE TERRIBLY WELL ORGANIZED
VIII	THAT YOU WERE FANTASTICALLY EFFICIENT
IX	THAT YOU DRESS VERY VERY WELL
IIIA	THAT YOU HAVE A MARVELOUS SENSE OF HUMOR
X	THAT YOU HAVE A VERY VERY BEAUTIFUL BODY.
XI	THAT YOU ARE UNBELIEVABLY GENEROUS TO ME.
XII	THAT THE MORE ONE DIGS THE FOUNDATIONS THE MORE AND MORE ONE FINDS THE SOLIDEST OF GRANIT FOR YOU AND I TO BUILD A LIFE TOGETHER UPON. ◄— I KNOW THIS IS NOT A GOOD SENTENCE.

GROUCHO MARX
MEMOIRS OF A MANGY LOVER, 1963

Most famous of the famed Marx Brothers, Groucho Marx (1890–1977) was not only a stage, screen, radio, and television performer but also a determined author who published more than half a dozen books. The excerpt below is from his second autobiography and appeared in the chapter titled "On Polygamy (And How to Attain It)."

What attracted him to her? Her eyes? Her legs? Was it something mysteriously feminine about her that no other girl seemed to possess? She is young, cute, and romantic and her speech is fairly intelligent. As they get to know each other more intimately (I mean in a nice way, of course), they both discover that they are ecstatically happy when together and miserable when apart. And then, oh happy day, if she is smart enough not to spring her mother on him too unexpectedly, they will get married.

No matter how many married couples they know, some unhappy, some happy, it seems inconceivable that anything could ever mar the joy they presently find in each other. I am sure that if they ever had any doubts or misgivings about their future happiness, neither wild horses nor her father could drag them to the altar.

It is well known that young love is a temporary form of insanity and that the only cure for it is instant marriage.

ARMISTEAD MAUPIN
TALES OF THE CITY, 1978

Tales of the City was the first in a series of nine novels by the American author Armistead Maupin (1944–). The books are set in a San Francisco apartment house and feature memorably eccentric characters, including the landlady, Anna Madrigal, who recollects for a tenant this piece of advice.

The ellipses are the author's.

Mona . . . Lots of things are more binding than sex. They last longer too. When I was . . . little, my mother once told me that if a married couple puts a penny in a pot for every time they make love in the first year, and takes a penny out every time after that, they'll never get all the pennies out of the pot.

CHILDREN

AUGUST STRINDBERG
GETTING MARRIED, 1884

Swedish author August Strindberg (1849–1912) was exceptionally prolific and versatile over a span of three decades, writing plays, novels, short stories, histories, poems, and essays, many of them forging a path into modern theater and even modern thought. Yet Strindberg encountered severe controversy with only one of these works—a collection of short stories about marriage, for which he was tried (though eventually acquitted) on charges of blasphemy.

Though much of his work before and after was considered deeply misogynistic, *Getting Married* was marginally less an attack on women than it was a comment on society's roles for both sexes.

Since marriage, which is a human institution invented for purely practical purposes, is so frail and so full of stumbling-blocks, how is it that so many marriages hold together? They do so because both partners have one interest in common, the thing for which nature has always intended marriage, namely children. Man is in a state of perpetual conflict with nature, in which he is perpetually being vanquished. Take two lovers who want to live together, partly in order to enjoy themselves, partly for the sake of being in each other's company. They regard any talk of possible children as an insult. Long before a child arrives they discover that their bliss is not so heavenly after all, and their relationship becomes stale. Then a child is born. Everything is new again and now, for the first time, their relationship is beautiful, for the ugly egoism of the duet has vanished. A marriage without children is a sad affair, and is not a marriage at all. . . . Children are what holds a marriage together.

PATENT MEDICINE ADVERTISEMENT
ATCHISON DAILY GLOBE, 1896

Ah, Dr. Pierce's Favorite Prescription. Just a few of the dozen ingredients in this supposed elixir of female health, motherhood, and marital happiness were cinnamon, digitalis, opium, and alcohol. The appeal of being "truly married" was just one of many factors luring Americans to spend (according to a 1905 article in *Collier's*) an estimated $75 million a year on patent medicines.

A childless marriage cannot be a happy one. A healthy baby is the real jewel for which the wedding ring is only the setting. There is no place in Nature's economy for a childless marriage. Wedded couples that are childless are never truly married. A baby is the tie that binds. The baby is the pledge that makes husband and wife one in nature and in fact, and that teaches mutual self-sacrifice and sympathy. Thousands of couples are childless because of the wife's neglect of her health as a woman. Too few women fully appreciate the importance of keeping healthy and vigorous the organs upon which motherhood is dependent. As a consequence, they are weak where they should be strong, and motherhood is either an impossibility or a torturesome and dangerous ordeal. This is easily remedied.

The most wonderful medicine for women is Dr. Pierce's Favorite Prescription.

OLD JOKE

Sadie and Moishe go to see a lawyer.

"What can I do for you, folks?"

Moishe: "We want a divorce."

"Well, this is very odd. I mean, um, how old are you folks?"

"I'm ninety-three," Moishe says. "Wife's ninety-one. We've been married sixty-seven years."

"And you mean to tell me, after sixty-seven years of marriage, at your ages, you want a divorce?? Why now??"

"We wanted to wait 'til the kids were dead."

HENRY JAMES
WHAT MAISIE KNEW, 1897

In one of the most innovative of his twenty novels, Henry James (1843–1916) tells the story of a young girl who is the object of a custody battle between her obstinate parents, Ida and Beale Farange. After a judge rules that Maisie must live six months at a time with each parent, a distant relation offers to take her for the mother's half, arguing that the arrangement will offer the child at least some freedom from her parents' poisonous assessments of each other.

Told almost exclusively from Maisie's point of view, the novel prefigured some of the next century's stream-of-consciousness fiction and even its New Journalism.

Had [Maisie's parents] not produced an impression . . . that some movement should be started or some benelovent person should come forward? A good lady came indeed a step or two. She was distantly related to Mrs. Farange, to whom she proposed that, having children and nurseries wound up and going, she should be allowed to take home the bone of contention, and, by working it into her system, relieve at least one of her parents. This would make every time for Maisie, after her inevitable six months with Beale, much more of a change.

"More of a change?" Ida cried. "Won't it be enough of a change for her to come from that low brute to the person in the world who detests him most."

"No, because you detest him so much that you'll always talk to her about him. You'll keep him before her by perpetually abusing him."

Mrs. Farange stared. "Pray, then, am I to do nothing to counteract his villainous abuse of *me*?"

The good lady, for a moment, made no reply. Her silence was a grim judgment of the whole point of view. "Poor little monkey!" she at last exclaimed, and the words were an epitaph for the tomb of Maisie's childhood. She was abandoned to her fate. What was clear to any spectator was that the only link binding her to either parent was this lamentable fact of her being a ready vessel for bitterness, a deep little porcelain cup in which biting acids could be mixed. They had wanted her, not for any good they could do her, but for the harm they could, with her unconscious aid, do each other. She should serve their anger and seal their revenge, for husband and wife had been alike crippled by the heavy hand of justice, which, in the last resort, met on neither side their indignant claim to get, as they called it, everything.

C

VIRGINIA WOOLF
TO THE LIGHTHOUSE, 1927

To the Lighthouse is considered a modernist masterpiece and Virginia Woolf (1882–1941) a pioneer in stream-of-consciousness writing. The novel, set in Scotland and marked by scarce action and dense thought, takes place on two days, set a decade apart, in the life of the Ramsay family. Critics and biographers agree that Woolf began the novel as a study of her own problematic family. Like Woolf, the character of Lily Briscoe is an aspiring artist and determined observer. Like Woolf, too, she is childless.

So that is marriage, Lily thought, a man and a woman looking at a girl throwing a ball. That is what Mrs Ramsay tried to tell me the other night, she thought. For she was wearing a green shawl, and they were standing close together watching Prue and Jasper throwing catches. And suddenly the meaning which, for no reason at all, as perhaps they are stepping out of the Tube or ringing a doorbell, descends on people, making them symbolical, making them representative, came upon them, and made them in the dusk standing, looking, the symbols of marriage, husband and wife. Then, after an instant, the symbolical outline which transcended the real figures sank down again and they became, as they met them, Mr and Mrs Ramsay watching the children throwing catches.

JOAN WILLIAMS
"ARE CHILDREN NECESSARY TO A SUCCESSFUL MARRIAGE?," 1932

For most of recorded history, marriage was the social contract that created and protected the family unit. So the question posed by this *Times of India* headline was no doubt intended to be provocative, and dozens of readers' letters followed, representing both sides of the argument.

When two young people are engaged to be married, their sole purpose is to be happy in the love of each other, and their marriage can only be said to be successful if they are held together by this love, comradeship and mutual respect for each other. If on the other hand these qualities are missing, and it is only a matter of honourably playing the game for the sake of their children, then there is very likely much secret unhappiness and discontent between the two. . . .

    Children are certainly an added joy to marriage if both parents are healthy[,] happy and mutually long for them. If they can be brought up decently and will be an honour to the race they can be a blessing to marriage, but in no way are they the sole object of the marriage, they are simply an added blessing to what would still have been a perfectly happy marriage.

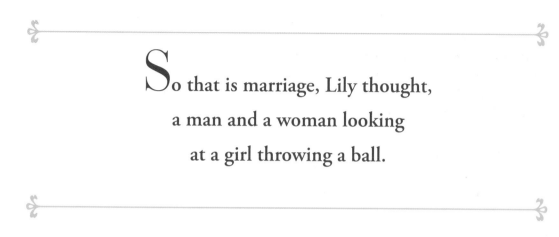

So that is marriage, Lily thought,

a man and a woman looking

at a girl throwing a ball.

DAVID LEVY
MATERNAL OVERPROTECTION, 1943

Decades before talk of the overinvolved "helicopter mom," Dr. David M. Levy (1892–1977) focused his research on the questionable effect of extremely protective mothers, offering numerous examples of children who were unusually aggressive, rebellious, demanding, and/or socially inept. Levy postulated that some of these problems might be mitigated if mothers gave less to their children—and got more from their husbands.

When husband and wife are sexually compatible and have social interests in common they thereby set up a number of conditions that operate against a mother-child monopoly. The fact that they have a life of their own as husband and wife withdraws certain time and energy from the parental relationship. A wife devoted to her husband cannot be exclusively a mother. In a more fundamental sense, the release of libido through satisfactory sexual relationship shunts off energy that must otherwise flow in other directions. . . . The child must bear the brunt of the unsatisfied love life of the mother. One might theoretically infer that a woman sexually well adjusted could not become overprotective to an extreme degree. Certainly she would not make the relationship to the child her exclusive social life.

C

DAVID GOODMAN
A PARENTS' GUIDE TO THE EMOTIONAL NEEDS OF CHILDREN, 1959

Sixteen years after Dr. Levy (see previous item) linked good sex and good mothering, Dr. David Goodman (1894–1971) was perfectly clear about what that link implied for husbands.

If you asked Mrs. Farnham where she found the energy to keep her home so clean, cook three good meals a day, and also romp and play with her three children, she would give you a merry smile and say: "That's my secret."

What was her secret?

Her secret was—well, her secret was greathearted Mr. Farnham, who knew how to make love to a woman.

A man who is a good lover to his wife is his children's best friend. His love upholds her spirit, gives her joy and enthusiasm. Child care is play to a woman who is happy. And only a man can make a woman happy. In deepest truth, a father's first duty to his children is to make their mother feel fulfilled as a woman.

ROBERT BENTON
KRAMER VS. KRAMER, 1979

The courtroom scene in the Oscar-winning film directed and written by Robert Benton (1932–) and based on Avery Corman's novel is one of its most wrenching. As portrayed by Meryl Streep and Dustin Hoffman, Joanna and Ted Kramer show the scars not only of their own marital break but also of a legal process that forces them to painful extremes. But in fighting for custody of his son—a battle rarely considered, let alone waged, in 1979—Ted Kramer also shows that a couple's passion to protect their children is sometimes the one part of a failed marriage that survives.

You know when you were talking, uh, I mean my wi—, my ex-wife, when she was talking before about how unhappy she was during our marriage, like, I guess most of what she said was probably true. There's a lot of things I didn't understand, a lot of things I'd do different if I could, just like I think there's a lot of things you wish you could change, but we can't. Some—things once they're done can't be undone. My, my wife, my—ex-wife, says that she loves Billy, and I believe she does, but I don't think that's the issue here; if I understand it correctly, what means the most here is what's best for our son, what's best for Billy. My wife used to always say to me, "Why can't a woman have the same ambitions as a man?" I think you're right, and maybe I've learned that much. But by the same token, I'd like to know what law is it that says that a woman is a better *parent*, simply by virtue of her sex? You know, I've had a lot of time to think about what it is that makes somebody a good parent. You know, it has to do with constancy, it has to do with, with, with patience, it has to do with listening to him, it has to do with pretending to listen to him when you can't even listen any more. It has to do with love, like, like, like, like she was saying. And I don't know where it's written that says that a woman has, has a corner on that market, that a, that a man has any less of those emotions than, than, than a woman does. Billy has a home with me. I've made it the best I could. It's not perfect, I'm not a perfect parent. Uh, sometimes I don't have enough patience and I forget that he's, uh, he's a little kid. But I'm there—I get up in the morning, and then we eat breakfast, and he talks to me and then we go to school, and at night we have dinner together and—and we talk then, and I read to him, and, and we've built a life together, and we love each other. If you destroy that, it may be irreparable. Joanna, don't do that, please. Don't do it twice to him.

JOSEPH CAMPBELL
THE POWER OF MYTH, CIRCA 1986

When television interviewer Bill Moyers sat down with scholar Joseph Campbell (1904–1987) for a series of one-on-one interviews in the last two years of Campbell's life, few could have predicted the extent to which the PBS series (and its companion volume) would become cultural touchstones. Enthusiastically expounding on his lifelong study of myth, Campbell urged audiences to follow their "bliss" and, more generally, to embrace mythic themes such as heroism, sacrifice, and transformation.

There are two completely different stages of marriage. First is the youthful marriage following the wonderful impulse that nature has given us in the interplay of the sexes biologically in order to produce children. But there comes a time when the child graduates from the family and the couple is left. I've been amazed at the number of my friends who in their forties or fifties go apart. They have had a perfectly decent life together with the child, but they interpreted their union in terms of their relationship through the child. They did not interpret it in terms of their own personal relationship to each other. Marriage is a relationship. When you make the sacrifice

C

in marriage, you're sacrificing not to each other but to unity in a relationship. . . . Marriage is not a simple love affair, it's an ordeal, and the ordeal is the sacrifice of ego to a relationship in which two have become one.

LOUIS C.K.
SHAMELESS, 2007

Louis C.K. (né Szekely, in 1967) has managed in his comic persona to combine anger, abjection, profanity, and scatology with winsome, often self-deprecating insight. Launched amid the stand-up comedy boom of the 1980s, his career included writing for David Letterman, Chris Rock, and Conan O'Brien before evolving into the series of successful one-man shows that began with *Shameless* and led the way to the television show *Louie*, of which he is star, producer, writer, and director.

Like the main character in *Louie*, the comedian has two daughters and is now divorced from their mother.

It's really the kids that do you in as a married couple. We have two kids, that's fucking stupid, don't do that. Because, you just, mainly what it does to a marriage is it just changes the way that you think about your spouse. Because when you're married, when you first get married, you have a relationship that's so important to you, and you're working on it together. But then you have a kid and you look at your kid and you go, holy shit, this is my child, she has my DNA, she has my name, I would *die* for her. And you look at your spouse and go, "Who the fuck are you? You're a stranger. Why do I take shit from you?"

. . . Having kids and being married, it's difficult, but one thing it's made me is, it's impossible for me to have any sympathy for single people. I just don't give a shit about single people. . . . You can die and it actually doesn't matter. It doesn't. Your mother will cry, whatever, but otherwise nobody gives a shit.

I can't die. I got two kids and my wife doesn't fucking work. So I don't get to die. I can't die. . . .

But so, single people, they complain. Like, we don't complain. When you ask a parent, "Hey, how's the family?" we go, "Great." That's all we ever say. It's never fucking great. But we say "great," 'cause we're never going to tell you, "Well, my wife assassinated my sexual identity and my children are eating my dreams." We don't fucking bother you with that. We just say, "Great."

But if you ask a single person how's it going, they're like, "Well, my apartment doesn't get enough southern light and the carpeting is getting a little moldy."

You know what you should do? Burn it down and kill yourself because nobody fucking cares.

"My girlfriend doesn't like the same music as me and she acts bored at parties." Well, fucking call her and say "fuck you" and hang up and leave her.

You can end that shit with a phone call.

I need a fucking gun and a plane ticket and bleach.

CHILDFREEEEE
"THE TOP 100 REASONS NOT TO HAVE KIDS (AND REMAIN CHILDFREE)," 2009

A blog started in 2007, *Childfreedom: Musings on the Childfree Lifestyle and Our Child-Centric Society*, featured a "Top 100" list of endorsements for the non-procreative life. The question of marital happiness without children hadn't changed since the 1932 *Times of India* column (see page 26). But the answers from blog creator "Childfreeeee" were far more numerous and considerably more strident. Here are the top dozen of her top hundred.

The blogger's profile had been viewed more than twelve thousand times as of this book's publication.

1.   You will be happier and less likely to suffer from depression.
2.   (Assuming you get married), you will have a happier marriage.
3.   You will have the capacity and time for meaningful, engaged, quality adult relationships.
4.   You will be able to save for a comfortable retirement.
5.   You are more likely to be an engaged and involved aunt or uncle because you are not jaded and worn down by your own kids.
6.   You can fully pursue and develop your career.
7.   You can fully pursue your educational goals.
8.   You can decorate your home as you wish with as many beautiful and/or breakable things as you wish and you will not have to child-proof your house.
9.   Your house will be free of junky, plastic kindercrap.
10.   Your spouse will get all the love and attention he/she deserves. You will come first in your spouse/partner's life.
11.   Your pets will get all the love and attention they deserve.
12.   You can eat whatever foods you wish at whatever time of the day you wish out in the open, whether it be a gourmet exotic meal, or chocolate chip cookies.

COMMUNICATION

OLD JOKE

I haven't spoken to my wife in years. I didn't want to interrupt her.

ROBERT LOUIS STEVENSON
"VIRGINIBUS PUERISQUE," 1876

A celebrated Scottish author in his time, Robert Louis Stevenson (1850–1894) is today internationally known for *Treasure Island, Strange Case of Dr. Jekyll and Mr. Hyde, A Child's Garden of Verses*, and for the willpower that enabled him to travel widely and write frequently despite recurring ill health. He married Fanny Van de Grift Osbourne in 1880 and became stepfather to her two children. "Virginibus Puerisque" (literally "for girls and boys") was an essay that originally appeared in the magazine *The Cornhill*.

A certain sort of talent is almost indispensable for people who would spend years together and not bore themselves to death. . . . And it is more important that a person should be a good gossip, and talk pleasantly and smartly of common friends and the thousand and one nothings of the day and hour, than that she should speak with the tongues of men and angels; for a while together by the fire, happens more frequently in marriage than the presence of a distinguished foreigner to dinner. That people should laugh over the same sort of jests, and have many a story of "grouse in the gun-room," many an old joke between them which time cannot wither nor custom stale, is a better preparation for life, by your leave, than many other things higher and better sounding in the world's ears. You could read Kant by yourself, if you wanted; but you must share a joke with some one else. You can forgive people who do not follow you through a philosophical disquisition; but to find your wife laughing when you had tears in your eyes, or staring when you were in a fit of laughter, would go some way towards a dissolution of the marriage.

FRIEDRICH NIETZSCHE
HUMAN, ALL TOO HUMAN, 1878

Friedrich Nietzsche (1844–1900) is often credited with planting the seeds of modern philosophical inquiry and sometimes assailed for providing—however unwittingly—the underpinnings of fascism. The prolific German philosopher was ill, either physically or mentally, for much of his life and never married. But he included maxims about many aspects of personal life in *Human, All Too Human*, one of his earliest works.

This was aphorism number 406, preceded by one called "Masks" and followed by one called "Girlish dreams."

Marriage as a long conversation.—When entering into a marriage one ought to ask oneself: do you believe you are going to enjoy talking with this woman up into your old age? Everything else in marriage is transitory, but most of the time you are together will be devoted to conversation.

ELLA CHEEVER THAYER
WIRED LOVE, 1880

Ella Cheever Thayer (1849–1925) subtitled her novel *A Romance of Dots and Dashes* and drew for it from her experience as a Boston telegraph operator. The passage below, so bizarrely prescient, was written just four years after Alexander Graham Bell's patent of the telephone.

We will soon be able to do everything by electricity; who knows but some genius will invent something for the especial use of lovers? something, for instance, to carry in their pockets, so when they are far away from each other, and pine for a sound of "that beloved voice," they will have only to take up this electrical apparatus, put it to their ears, and be happy. Ah! blissful lovers of the future!

EDITH WHARTON
THE AGE OF INNOCENCE, 1920

In much of her writing, Edith Wharton (1862–1937) evoked the manners and morals of the turn of the twentieth century—perhaps never more brilliantly than in her Pulitzer Prize–winning novel of New York society, *The Age of Innocence*. Newland Archer, dutiful fiancé and then husband to May Welland, is passionately and guiltily in love with her cousin, Ellen Olenska. This love is neither consummated with Ellen nor discussed with May, and it is only at the end of the book, in this memorable scene with his son Dallas, that it becomes clear to Newland how little his silence has succeeded in concealing anything.

Fanny is Dallas's fiancée. The line break and ellipsis are the author's.

Archer felt his colour rise under his son's unabashed gaze. "Come, own up: you and she were great pals, weren't you? Wasn't she most awfully lovely?"

"Lovely? I don't know. She was different."

"Ah—there you have it! That's what it always comes to, doesn't it? When she comes, *she's different*—and one doesn't know why. It's exactly what I feel about Fanny."

His father drew back a step, releasing his arm. "About Fanny? But my dear fellow—I should hope so. Only I don't see—"

"Dash it, Dad, don't be prehistoric! Wasn't she—once—your Fanny?"

Dallas belonged body and soul to the new generation. He was the first-born of Newland and May Archer, yet it had never been possible to inculcate in him even the rudiments of reserve. "What's the use of making mysteries? It only makes people want to nose 'em out," he always objected when enjoined to discretion. But Archer, meeting his eyes, saw the filial light under their banter.

"My Fanny—?"

"Well, the woman you'd have chucked everything for: only you didn't," continued his surprising son.

"I didn't," echoed Archer with a kind of solemnity.

"No: you date, you see, dear old boy. But mother said—"

"Your mother?"

"Yes: the day before she died. It was when she sent for me alone—you remember? She said she knew we were safe with you, and always would be, because once, when she asked you to, you'd given up the thing you most wanted."

Archer received this strange communication in silence. His eyes remained unseeingly fixed on the thronged sunlit square below the window. At length he said in a low voice: "She never asked me."

"No. I forgot. You never did ask each other anything, did you? And you never told each other anything. You just sat and watched each other, and guessed at what was going on underneath. A deaf-and-dumb asylum, in fact! Well, I back your generation for knowing more about each other's private thoughts than we ever have time to find out about our own.—I say, Dad,"

Dallas broke off, "you're not angry with me? If you are, let's make it up and go and lunch at Henri's. I've got to rush out to Versailles afterward."

Archer did not accompany his son to Versailles. He preferred to spend the afternoon in solitary roamings through Paris. He had to deal all at once with the packed regrets and stifled memories of an inarticulate lifetime.

After a little while he did not regret Dallas's indiscretion. It seemed to take an iron band from his heart to know that, after all, some one had guessed and pitied. . . . And that it should have been his wife moved him indescribably.

EVAN CONNELL
MRS. BRIDGE, 1959

Mrs. Bridge was the first novel published by Evan Connell (1924–2013), and it was both a critical and commercial success. In a spare but evocative voice, it tells the story of a midwestern American woman whose conventional marriage leads to a crisis of identity and a search for love. Connell would go on to write a companion novel, *Mr. Bridge*, in 1969, as well as nearly twenty other books, including the best-selling *Son of the Morning Star* in 1984.

As time went on she felt an increasing need for reassurance. Her husband had never been a demonstrative man, not even when they were first married; consequently she did not expect too much from him. Yet there were moments when she was overwhelmed by a terrifying, inarticulate need. One evening as she and he were finishing supper together, alone, the children having gone out, she inquired rather sharply if he loved her. She was surprised by her own bluntness and by the almost shrewish tone of her voice, because that was not the way she actually felt. She saw him gazing at her in astonishment; his expression said very clearly: Why on earth do you think I'm here if I don't love you? Why aren't I somewhere else? What in the world has gotten into you?

Mrs. Bridge smiled across the floral centerpiece—and it occurred to her that these flowers she had so carefully arranged on the table were what separated her from her husband—and said, a little wretchedly, "I know it's silly, but it's been such a long time since you told me."

Mr. Bridge grunted and finished his coffee. She knew it was not that he was annoyed, only that he was incapable of the kind of declaration she needed. It was so little, and yet so much.

C

BARRY LEVINSON
DINER, 1982

Barry Levinson (1942–) wrote and directed *Diner* more than two decades after the year in which it was set, but the film was hailed for the way it perfectly captured the bittersweet tensions lurking beneath the surface of relationships in 1959 urban America. In this scene, the recently married Shrevie Schreiber tries to reassure the soon-to-be married Eddie Simmons.

Beth is Shrevie's wife.

EDDIE:	Shreve, you happy with your marriage or what?
SHREVIE:	I don't know.
EDDIE:	What do you mean, you don't know? You don't know?
SHREVIE:	What?
EDDIE:	How could you not? You don't know. How could you not know?
SHREVIE:	I don't know. Beth is terrific and everything. But Jesus I don't know. I'll tell you a big part of the problem though when you get married—well, you know, when you're dating, everything is talking about sex, right? Where can we do it? You know, why can't we do it? Are your parents going to be out so, so we can do it? You know? Trying to get a weekend just so that we can do it.
EDDIE:	So you can do it.
SHREVIE:	Everything is just always talking about getting sex. And then planning the wedding, all the details.
EDDIE:	Details. Shit.
SHREVIE:	But then, when you get married, it's crazy, I don't know. I mean, you can get it whenever you want it. You wake up in the morning and she's there. And you come home from work and she's there. And so all that sex planning talk is over with. And so is the wedding planning talk 'cause you're already married.
EDDIE:	Right.
SHREVIE:	So, you know, I can come down here, we can bullshit the whole night away, but I cannot hold a five-minute conversation with Beth. I mean, it's not her fault, I'm not blaming her, she's great. It's—
EDDIE:	No, of course not.
SHREVIE:	It's just we got nothing to talk about. But it's good, it's good.
EDDIE:	It's good. It's nice, right? It's nice?

SHREVIE: Yeah, it's nice.

EDDIE: Right. Well, we always got the diner.

SHREVIE: Yeah, we always got the diner.

BRUCE ERIC KAPLAN, 1999

Bruce Eric Kaplan (1964–) had his first cartoons published in *The New Yorker* in 1991 and, with the signature BEK, has since contributed hundreds more. Book-length collections have followed, including *No One You Know* and *This Is a Bad Time*, and so has a career as a television writer for *Six Feet Under* and producer for *Six Feet Under* and *Girls*.

Kaplan also wrote an episode for the sitcom *Seinfeld* in which a fictionalized *New Yorker* cartoon editor reluctantly admits he doesn't understand one of the cartoons he's published.

"Sometimes I think he can understand every word we're saying."

C

JERRY SEINFELD
WHITE HOUSE TRIBUTE TO PAUL McCARTNEY, 2010

Comedian Jerry Seinfeld (1954–), star and co-creator of the nineties-defining sitcom *Seinfeld*, performed at the White House when Paul McCartney was given the Gershwin Prize for lifetime achievement. In his routine, Seinfeld suggested that the former Beatle's lyrics have paralleled his life stages, including what Seinfeld deemed marriage songs such as "The Long and Winding Road," "Fixing a Hole," and even "Let It Be."

It's a beautiful thing, marriage. It's two people, that's it. Trying to stay together without saying the words "I hate you." That is your goal. You never say those three words. You say other things. Things like, "Why is there never any Scotch tape in this house? Trying to tape something up down here!"

"Scotch" is "I." "Tape" is "hate." "House" is "you." But. It's an improvement.

CONFLICT

ELIZABETH SMITH SHAW
LETTER TO ABIGAIL ADAMS SMITH, 1786

Sister of Abigail Adams, Elizabeth Smith Shaw (1750–1815) had herself been married nine years when she offered this advice to her newly wed niece, Abigail "Nabby" Adams.

The woman who is *really* possessed of superior Qualities, or *affects* a Superiority over her Husband, betrays a pride which degrades herself, and places her in the most disadvantatious point of view. She who values domestick Happiness will carefully guard against, and avoid any little Contentions—the *Beginnings* of Evil—as she would a pestilential Disease, that would poison her sweetest comforts, and infect her every Joy. There is but one *kind* of Strife in the nuptial State that I can behold without horror, and that is who shall excell and who shall oblige the most.

"A LETTER OF ADVICE, FROM A FATHER TO HIS ONLY DAUGHTER, IMMEDIATELY AFTER HER MARRIAGE," 1822

The following letter, never definitively dated but alternately attributed to the patriot Patrick Henry; to Bishop James Madison, president of the College of William & Mary; and simply to "a father," was reprinted countless times (the version below was the earliest we could find). In 1834, the editors of the *Southern Literary Messenger* prefaced its own reprint by suggesting that the advice offered was admirable enough to warrant even an annual publication, urging all women—whether married or hoping to be—to heed it. Still, the editors added: "Let it not be understood, however, that we are believers in the doctrine, that the pleasures of the matrimonial voyage are wholly dependent upon the conduct of the lady. She is but the second in command, and still greater responsibilities rest upon him who stands at the helm and guides the frail bark of human happiness."

The first maxim, which you should impress most deeply upon your mind, is never to attempt to control your husband by opposition, by displeasure, or any other mark of anger. A man of sense, of prudence, of warm feelings, cannot, and will not bear an opposition of any kind, which is attended with an angry look or expressions.—The current of his affections is suddenly stopped; his attachment is weakened; he begins to feel a mortification the most pungent; he is belittled even in his own eyes; and be assured, the wife who once excites those sentiments in the breast of her husband, will never regain the high ground which she might, and ought to have retained— When he marries her, if he be a good man, he expects from her smiles, not frowns; he expects to find in her one who is not to control him, not to take from him the freedom of acting as his own judgment shall direct; but one who will place such confidence in him, as to believe that his own prudence is his best guide. Little things which, in reality, are mere trifles in themselves often produce bickerings and even quarrels. Never permit them to be a subject of dispute. Yield them with pleasure, with a smile of affection. Be assured that one difference outweighs them all, a thousand or ten thousand times. A difference, in reality, with your husband, ought to be considered as the greatest calamity, as one that is to be most studiously guarded against; it is a demon, which must never be permitted to enter a habitation, where all should be peace, unimpaired confidence and heartfelt affection. Besides, what can a woman gain by her opposition, or her differences?—Nothing. But she loses everything; she loses her husband's respect for her virtues; she loses his love, and with that, all prospects of future happiness.

THOMAS HILL
HILL'S MANUAL OF SOCIAL AND BUSINESS FORMS, 1879

Thomas Edie Hill (1832–1915) started out teaching penmanship, moved on to publishing Illinois's weekly *Aurora Herald*, and, in 1873, put out the first edition of *Hill's Manual of Social and Business Forms*. While subtitled "A Guide to Correct Writing" and offering diagrams of the proper way to hold a pen, the book also included tips on geography, cooking, poetry, and weddings. By 1879 (and as far forward as 1921), subsequent versions featured this marital advice, under the heading "Etiquette Between Husbands and Wives."

Let the rebuke be preceded by a kiss.
Do not require a request to be repeated.
Never should both be angry at the same time.
Never neglect the other, for all the world beside.
Let each strive to always accommodate the other.
Let the angry word be answered only with a kiss.
Bestow your warmest sympathies in each other's trials.
Make your criticism in the most loving manner possible.
Make no display of the sacrifices you make for each other.
Never make a remark calculated to bring ridicule upon the other.
Never deceive; confidence, once lost, can never be wholly regained.
Always use the most gentle and loving words when addressing each other.
Let each study what pleasure can be bestowed upon the other during the day.
Always leave home with a tender good-bye and loving words. They may be the last.
Consult and advise together in all that comes within the experience and sphere of each
individuality.
Never reproach the other for an error which was done with a good motive and with the best
judgment at the time.

Let the angry word be answered only with a kiss.

OGDEN NASH
"A WORD TO HUSBANDS," 1931

Ogden Nash (1902–1971) was not always this economical in his verse (see Wives, How to Keep, pages 492–93), but was frequently this blunt.

To keep your marriage brimming,
With love in the loving cup,
Whenever you're wrong, admit it;
Whenever you're right, shut up.

OLD JOKE

A man and woman had been married for more than sixty years. They had shared everything. They had talked about everything. They had kept no secrets from each other except that the little old woman had a shoe box in the top of her closet that she had cautioned her husband never to open or ask her about.

For all of these years, he had never thought about the box, but one day the little old woman got very sick and the doctor said she would not recover.

In trying to sort out their affairs, the little old man took down the shoe box and took it to his wife's bedside. She agreed that it was time that he should know what was in the box. When he opened it, he found two knitted dolls and a stack of money totaling $95,000.

He asked her about the contents.

"When we were to be married," she said, "my grandmother told me the secret of a happy marriage was to never argue. She told me that if I ever got angry with you, I should just keep quiet and knit a doll."

The little old man was so moved; he had to fight back tears. Only two precious dolls were in the box. She had only been angry with him two times in all those years of living and loving. He almost burst with happiness.

"Honey," he said, "that explains the dolls, but what about all of this money? Where did it come from?"

"Oh," she said, "that's the money I made from selling the dolls."

JAMES THURBER, 1932

The story goes that it was E. B. White who rescued a doodle drawn by James Thurber (1894–1961) of a seal on a rock. The seal was looking at two dots in the distance. The caption was "Hm, explorers." The drawing—like so many others that White had submitted to *The New Yorker*'s cartoon department on Thurber's behalf—was rejected, but eventually Thurber redrew the seal, turned the rock into a headboard when it didn't look enough like a rock, and wrote the caption that made the cartoon so funny and so famous.

"All right, have it your way—you heard a seal bark!"

A. P. HERBERT
"TWENTY-FIVE YEARS HAPPILY MARRIED," 1940

Novelist, playwright, lyricist, and member of Parliament, Sir Alan Patrick Herbert (1890–1971) also introduced the Matrimonial Causes Act of 1937, which allowed divorces to be granted without proof of adultery. London's *News Chronicle* printed this column on the occasion of his and his wife's twenty-fifth anniversary.

The Herberts were married for fifty-seven years, until his death.

It is customary, I know, for the happy pair on such occasions to let it be understood that for twenty-five years "We have never had a cross word." I am not going to be guilty of any such nonsense. We have had frightful rows. We are quite capable of having a frightful row tomorrow. But here we are!

Indeed, to me, the conception of two people living together for twenty-five years without having a cross word is absurd and suggests a lack of spirit only to be admired in the sheep. Where there is spirit there must be sparks.

EVELYN MILLIS DUVALL AND REUBEN HILL
"WAYS OF HANDLING CONFLICT," 1945

Sociologists Evelyn Millis Duvall (1906–1998) and Reuben Hill (1912–1985) collaborated on a textbook called *When You Marry* that was used in home economics programs for at least a decade. This was a quiz to enlighten couples about destructive versus productive approaches to conflict. Difficult though it may be to believe that any one of these statements was considered "productive," half were.

Ready for the answers? Destructive: 1, 3, 5, 8. Productive: 2, 4, 6, 7.

Which of the following excerpts suggest destructive and which productive quarreling?

1. "You aren't fit to be a mother, leaving the baby all week with strangers."
2. "Why didn't someone tell me marriage would be like this, cooking and ironing and scrubbing all day?"
3. "You will never amount to anything and neither will we as long as we depend on you to support us, you loafer."

C

4. "This is the last time I'm waiting for you for supper; after this you'll get your own or come on time."

5. "You aren't the man I married. What did I ever see in you? Oh, I could just die."

6. "You sit home all day reading or go out to some catty dame's bridge club and leave the house like a pig pen."

7. "Get a cookbook, sister, get a book and start studying. This is the last lousy meal I'm eating here, understand?"

8. "Darling, you must put on your rubbers. You aren't so young as you were."

CLIFFORD ADAMS
PREPARING FOR MARRIAGE, 1951

Clifford Adams (1902–1987) was a Penn State psychology professor and marriage counselor who predicted (correctly) that the U.S. divorce rate would reach roughly 50 percent by 1975. His advice (see also Grievances, pages 153–54) focused to a large extent on the reasons for unhappy marriages (such as differing religions, women's higher education, and Hollywood-fueled expectations), and he offered the following tips to help couples avoid conflict.

- Make sure you both get enough sleep, not just once in a while, but as a matter of routine.
- Get up early enough in the morning to insure a peaceful start on the day, including a leisurely breakfast and a margin for last-minute emergencies.
- Avoid racing with the clock, or forcing your mate to. Cut down on activities if need be—don't schedule your days too full.
- If either blows his top about some minor incident when tired or irritable, chances are he'll repent in a few minutes—if *you* keep still. But if you retort, you're inviting a battle. Silence is never more golden than when a quarrel is brewing.
- When a problem arises, wait for a suitable time to discuss it with the mate.
- When either comes home from work or is tired and harassed, the other's greeting should not include the day's bad news.
- In discussing an issue, stick to impersonal facts and avoid personalities. Blaming the mate, no matter how justified, is worse than useless.
- Remember that it takes two to start a quarrel—but only one to stop it. The more hurt or resentful you feel, the less you have to gain by going on with the argument.

THORNTON WILDER
THE MATCHMAKER, 1954

By now probably best known as the source material for the 1964 musical *Hello, Dolly!, The Matchmaker* was one of the most popular works by the novelist and playwright Thornton Wilder (1897–1975). The widowed hat shop owner Irene Molloy is the woman Horace Vandergelder intends to marry—despite the fact that matchmaker Dolly Levi has other plans for him. Minnie Fay is Molloy's younger assistant.

Wilder's original version of *The Matchmaker*, called *The Merchant of Yonkers*, ran for less than two months in 1938. That incarnation was itself based on an 1842 Austrian play and an 1835 British one-act comedy.

MINNIE:	But Mr. Vandergelder's not—
MRS. MOLLOY:	Speak up, Minnie, I can't hear you.
MINNIE:	—I don't think he's attractive.
MRS. MOLLOY:	But what I think he is—and it's very important—I think he'd make a good fighter.
MINNIE:	Mrs. Molloy!
MRS. MOLLOY:	Take my word for it, Minnie: The best of married life is the fights. The rest is merely so-so.
MINNIE:	*(Fingers in ears)* I won't listen.
MRS. MOLLOY:	Now Peter Molloy—God rest him!—was a fine arguing man. I pity the woman whose husband slams the door and walks out of the house at the beginning of an argument. Peter Molloy would stand up and fight for hours on end. He'd even throw things, Minnie, and there's no pleasure to equal that. When I felt tired I'd start a good blood-warming fight and it'd take ten years off my age; now Horace Vandergelder would put up a good fight; I know it. I've a mind to marry him.

C

THE HONEYMOONERS, 1955

The three-word refrain ("to the moon!") was featured in many an episode of the legendary TV show starring Jackie Gleason and Audrey Meadows. There were alternates ("Bang, zoom!" and "Pow, right in the kisser!"), always greeted by Meadows's perfectly deadpan face.

RALPH: You're goin' to the moon, Alice. Right to the moon!

ALICE: Yeah, and you're just the blimp to take me.

Audrey Meadows and Jackie Gleason

EDWARD ALBEE
WHO'S AFRAID OF VIRGINIA WOOLF?, 1962

Winner of the Tony and New York Drama Critics' Circle awards for best play, *Who's Afraid of Virginia Woolf?* was later immortalized in film with Richard Burton and Elizabeth Taylor playing the middle-aged, sulfurous, and alcoholic George and Martha. Edward Albee (1928–) created a portrait of modern marriage that was received as both shocking and admonitory, with one reviewer calling it an "incisive, inhuman drama." The following passage, from the second act, finds the two characters alone onstage, blaming and taunting each other not for the benefit of the younger couple who have been drawn into a hellish visit, but rather because they seem to have no other choice.

Martha's father is head of the college where George is an associate history professor. The ellipses are the author's.

MARTHA: . . . I sat there at Daddy's party, and I watched you . . . I watched you sitting there, and I watched the younger men around you, the men who were going to go somewhere. And I sat there and I watched you, and *you* weren't *there!* And it snapped! It finally snapped! And I'm going to howl it out, and I'm not going to give a damn what I do, and I'm going to make the damned biggest explosion you ever heard.

GEORGE: *(Very pointedly)* You try it and I'll beat you at your own game.

MARTHA: *(Hopefully)* Is that a threat, George? Hunh?

GEORGE: That's a threat, Martha.

MARTHA: *(Fake-spits at him.)* You're going to get it, baby.

GEORGE: Be careful, Martha . . . I'll rip you to pieces.

MARTHA: You aren't man enough . . . you haven't got the guts.

GEORGE: Total war?

MARTHA: Total.

C

GEORGE BACH AND PETER WYDEN
THE INTIMATE ENEMY, 1969

Clinical psychologist George Bach (1914–1986) is credited with originating the concept of "fair fighting" in the 1960s as part of his unconventional work at the Los Angeles group therapy institute that he founded. "People come to us to learn how to love," Bach wrote of his institute, "and we teach them how to fight." An advocate of greater sexual freedom, he nonetheless didn't share the view of many sixties' therapists that marriage was a failed institution not worth saving.

Coauthor Peter Wyden (1923–1998) was a prominent journalist and author.

The best way to get constructive results from intimate hostilities is to fight by appointment only. This may sound silly, but the more calmly and deliberately an aggressor can organize his thoughts before an engagement, the more likely it is that his arguments will be persuasive; that the fight will confine itself to one issue instead of ricocheting all over the intimate landscape; and that the opponent will feel compelled to come up with calm, constructive counterproposals. It's like negotiating a labor dispute well before the deadline, not after the union has voted to strike.

Surprisingly few couples realize this. . . .

Far too many fights become needlessly aggravated because the complainant opens fire when his partner really is in an inappropriate frame of mind or is trying to dash off to work or trying to concentrate on some long-delayed chore that he has finally buckled down to. Indeed, there are times when failure to delay—or to advance—the timing of a fight can have cataclysmic consequences. . . .

Making an advance appointment for a fight is particularly useful because mutually favored fight times are rare. There are morning fighters and evening fighters; partners who prefer to fight at cocktail time or bedtime or dinnertime, or only with (or only without) the children or others present. . . .

People tend to place fights where they feel territorially at home. The wife may fight most comfortably in the kitchen, the husband from behind the big desk in his office-fortress, the young man in his brand-new car.

A boat is a superb place for an intimate encounter, especially if one of the partners is fight-phobic, because fighting goes best where the combatants are isolated and find it hard to get away from each other. . . . Once partners are better informed about the why, when, and where of fighting, they are ready to consider what to fight about.

JOAN DIDION
O, THE OPRAH MAGAZINE INTERVIEW, 2005

C

Author Joan Didion (1934–) was married for thirty-nine years to the author John Gregory Dunne. His sudden death in 2003 inspired her to write a brilliant meditation on time, love, and mourning: *The Year of Magical Thinking*, which was published in 2005.

Didion has written novels including *Play It as It Lays* and *Democracy* as well as collections of essays and columns on social, political, and psychological subjects. Dunne wrote nonfiction books including *The Studio* and novels including *True Confessions*. Together they collaborated on screenplays. The interviewer was Sara Davidson.

DAVIDSON: As marriages go, I think you had a pretty great one. Do you feel that?

DIDION: Yeah, I do. Finally it was, which is not to say we thought it was great at every given moment. Each of us was mad at the other half the time.

DAVIDSON: Half?

DIDION: Maybe a quarter. A tenth of the time. In the early years, you fight because you don't understand each other. In later years, you fight because you do.

JAMES CARVILLE AND MARY MATALIN
CNN INTERVIEW, 2009

Democratic consultant James Carville (1944–) was known for his Cajun cockiness and his deft handling of Bill Clinton's 1992 presidential bid. Mary Matalin (1953–), a longtime Republican adviser, was his adversary on the campaign of incumbent George H. W. Bush. Separately, each was a political force to be reckoned with. Once they married (the year after the election), they were a walking (and frequently talking) example that ideological conflict need not be an obstacle to marital harmony.

Carville and Matalin have been frequent television and radio presences; both also teach and lecture. Carville consults on international campaigns. Matalin edits a Simon & Schuster imprint. The interviewer was John King.

KING: We asked people to text in a question for James and Mary. And here's what we got from Indiana: "Love you both. Can you show both houses of Congress your secret for compromise?"

MATALIN: Well, we're not a democracy. We're an enlightened MOM-archy. That's what we are.

CARVILLE: As long as one person is not arguing, there's nothing to argue about. I don't have a position on anything domestically. So I just say yes, and then go on and do it. I mean it. I would say the three ingredients to a successful marriage [are] surrender, capitulation, and retreat. If you've got those three things—

MATALIN: Spoken like a true liberal. What a martyr. Faith, family, and good wine. That's how we do it.

PHIL McGRAW
"MARRIAGE MELTDOWN," *DR. PHIL*, 2011

Starting in the late 1990s, when Oprah Winfrey introduced him as a regular guest on her talk show, Phil McGraw (1950–), a.k.a. Dr. Phil, dispensed relationship advice to TV audiences with a homey and straightforward, if occasionally scolding, air. The daytime *Dr. Phil* show, which began in 2002, proved extraordinarily popular in its own right as McGraw took on parents and children, siblings, in-laws, and of course husbands and wives. With episodes like the three-part "Marriage Meltdown," Dr. Phil joined a pop-culture tradition of finding, airing, and sometimes provoking marital blame.

MTV's *The Blame Game* ("Where broken-up couples go on trial to find out whose fault it really was") began in 1998 and ran for four seasons. The syndicated *Divorce Court* began in 1957 and has run, albeit in different incarnations, ever since.

ANNOUNCER: Who's to blame? Do you feel like your marriage is hanging on by a thread? Do you feel like divorce is your only option? Watch three couples go through an intensive relationship overhaul, as Dr. Phil challenges their commitment to each other and puts their marriage to the ultimate test!

DR. PHIL: *(To the three couples)* There are topics, and then there are issues. A husband can come home, kick the door open, say, "Why is the damn tricycle in the driveway again?" That's a topic. What's the issue that makes that so sensitive? That's what you've got to find out. Maybe it's that they haven't had any sex in two months, and he's frustrated about being rejected or hurt. I don't know. But I want to deal with issues. I don't care who said what to who at mother's front door two summers ago on the Fourth of July. If I look like I care, then let me get a different look on my face, because I don't. My goal is to give you guys an opportunity here where you can try to find a way to give yourself a chance to live in harmony.

IRONYDESIGNS, 2013

COVETING

BUDDHA
THE DHAMMAPADA, CIRCA 3RD CENTURY BC

One of the most familiar Buddhist texts, the *Dhammapada* is a collection of more than 400 sayings ranging in subject from flowers and evil to happiness and anger.

"Hell" in Buddhism is not an eternal destination but is, like other states of being, transient. Likewise, while there are no commandments, per se, in Buddhism, one of its central "Five Precepts" guides followers to refrain from sexual misconduct.

Four things does a reckless man gain who covets his neighbor's wife—demerit, an uncomfortable bed, thirdly, punishment, and lastly, hell.

There is demerit, and the evil way to hell: there is the short pleasure of the frightened in the arms of the frightened, and the king imposes heavy punishment; therefore let no man think of his neighbor's wife.

C

OTTO RANK
DIARY, CIRCA 1904

In his own version of the Ten Commandments (beginning with "Thou shalt have no God"), Austrian psychologist Otto Rank (1884–1939) took the biblical tenth commandment one step further.

Thou shalt not covet thy neighbor's wife, for there are plenty of others.

JIMMY CARTER
PLAYBOY INTERVIEW, 1976

Former Georgia governor Jimmy Carter (1924–) became the thirty-ninth president of the United States in the wake of the Watergate scandal, presenting himself as an outsider, an honest man of strong values and straight talk. His most unfortunate—and famous—example of the latter came about during the campaign, when he was interviewed by Robert Scheer for *Playboy* magazine. The article ran for a dozen pages, but the passage that follows was what people remembered. It was responsible for a 15 percent drop in Carter's poll numbers and for what was said to be a joke circulating at the White House: "He would have been all right if he'd just kept his heart in his pants."
Carter had married Rosalynn Smith, from his hometown of Plains, Georgia, in 1946.

I try not to commit a deliberate sin. I recognize that I'm going to do it anyhow, because I'm human and I'm tempted. And Christ set some almost impossible standards for us. Christ said, "I tell you that anyone who looks on a woman with lust has in his heart already committed adultery."

I've looked on a lot of women with lust. I've committed adultery in my heart many times. This is something that God recognizes I will do—and I have done it—and God forgives me for it. But that doesn't mean that I condemn someone who not only looks on a woman with lust but who leaves his wife and shacks up with somebody out of wedlock.

Christ says, Don't consider yourself better than someone else because one guy screws a whole bunch of women while the other guy is loyal to his wife. The guy who's loyal to his wife ought not to be condescending or proud because of the relative degree of sinfulness.

DEVOTION

THE DUNMOW OATH, 1510

Starting in the twelfth century, and intermittently since then, the custom in a British town called Dunmow was to bestow a "flitch" (a side) or sometimes a "gammon" (a hind leg) of bacon on married couples who convinced the town's prior that they had been married a year and a day without arguments, infidelities, or—waking or sleeping—regrets. The practice had many iterations, but the lines below comprise the oath that, as early as 1510, the winning couples swore while kneeling on pointed stones.

Some writers have suggested that this custom was the origin of the phrase "bringing home the bacon."

You shall swear by the Custom of our Confession
That you never made any Nuptial Transgression
Since you were married to your wife
By household brawles, or contentious strife
Or otherwise in bed or board
Offended each other in deed or word
Or since the Parish Clerk said Amen
Wished yourselves unmarried ag[ai]n
Or in a twelvemonth and a day

Repented not in thought any way

But continued true and in desire

As when you joined hands in the Holy Quire

If to these conditions without all fear

Of your own Accord you will freely swear

A Gammon of Bacon you shall receive

And beare it Hence with Love and Good Leave

For this is our Custom in Dunmow well known

Though the Sport be ours, the Bacon's your own.

CATHERINE OF ARAGON
LETTER TO HENRY VIII, 1536

The first wife of Henry VIII, Catherine of Aragon (1485–1536) was highly educated, devout, and at one point even a successful regent in Henry's absence. She also bore him six children, including two sons. Only their daughter Mary survived childhood, and Henry's two great desires—for a male heir and for the divorce that would allow him to marry his mistress, Anne Boleyn—led to his break with the Catholic Church. Catherine was banished from court and remained in exile until her death (probably from cancer). But she considered herself the rightful queen and stayed devoted until the end.

My most dear lord, king and husband,

The hour of my death now drawing on, the tender love I owe you forceth me, my case being such, to commend myself to you, and to put you in remembrance with a few words of the health and safeguard of your soul which you ought to prefer before all worldly matters, and before the care and pampering of your body, for the which you have cast me into many calamities and yourself into many troubles. For my part, I pardon you everything, and I wish to devoutly pray God that He will pardon you also. For the rest, I commend unto you our daughter Mary, beseeching you to be a good father unto her, as I have heretofore desired. I entreat you also, on behalf of my maids, to give them marriage portions, which is not much, they being but three. For all my other servants I solicit the wages due them, and a year more, lest they be unprovided for. Lastly, I make this vow, that mine eyes desire you above all things.

Katharine the Quene

SAMUEL JOHNSON
LETTER TO THOMAS LAWRENCE, 1780

Nearly three decades after the death of his wife, Elizabeth, in 1752, the great British author Samuel Johnson (1709–1784) still kept her wedding ring in a small wooden box, on the inside cover of which he had written "Eheu!" (Latin for *alas*). She had been twenty-one years older than Johnson and the subject of some contemporaneous ridicule. But this was his condolence letter to a friend, a doctor named Thomas Lawrence, upon the death of Lawrence's wife.
For more of Dr. Johnson, see Infidelity, page 203; Triumphs, page 430.

The loss, dear sir, which you have lately suffered, I felt many years ago, and know therefore how much has been taken from you and how little can be had from consolation. He that outlives a wife whom he has long loved, sees himself disjoined from the only mind that has the same hopes and fears and interest; from the only companion with whom he has shared much good or evil; and with whom he could set his mind at liberty to retrace the past or anticipate the future. The continuity of being is lacerated; the settled course of sentiment and action stopped; and life stands suspended and motionless, till it is driven by external causes into a new channel. But the time of suspense is dreadful.

JOHN BUTLER YEATS
LETTER TO OLIVER ELTON, 1917

Born in Ireland, educated at Trinity College Dublin, and trained as a barrister, John Butler Yeats (1839–1922) gave up law after a year for a career in painting. Several of his portraits—most notably of the Irish separatist John O'Leary—hang in the National Gallery of Ireland. Yeats was married in 1863 to Susan Pollexfen, whom he outlived by two decades. Together they had six children, including the poet William Butler Yeats (see Encouragement, page 83; Youth and Age, page 509).
Oliver Elton was a British literary scholar, author of many books of essays, criticism, and translation.

I am an old dusty sundried conservative in some things, marriage for instance. Marriage is the earliest fruit of civilization and it will be the latest. I think a man and a woman should choose each other for life, for the simple reason that a long life with all its accidents is barely enough for a man and a woman to understand each other; and in this case to understand is to love. The man who understands one woman is qualified to understand pretty well everything.

EZRA POUND
"THE RIVER-MERCHANT'S WIFE: A LETTER," 1917

There are many beautiful and, apparently, more accurately translated versions of this poem by the eighth-century Chinese writer Li Po (alternately spelled Li Bai, Li Bo, or—in the Japanese transliteration Pound used—Rihaku). Arguably, none is more transcendent than that of American poet Ezra Pound (1885–1972).

While my hair was still cut straight across my forehead
I played about the front gate, pulling flowers.
You came by on bamboo stilts, playing horse,
You walked about my seat, playing with blue plums.
And we went on living in the village of Chokan:
Two small people, without dislike or suspicion.

At fourteen I married My Lord you.
I never laughed, being bashful.
Lowering my head, I looked at the wall.
Called to, a thousand times, I never looked back.

At fifteen I stopped scowling,
I desired my dust to be mingled with yours
Forever and forever and forever.
Why should I climb the look out?

At sixteen you departed,
You went into far Ku-to-Yen, by the river of swirling eddies,
And you have been gone five months.
The monkeys make sorrowful noise overhead.
You dragged your feet when you went out.
By the gate now, the moss is grown, the different mosses,
Too deep to clear them away!
The leaves fall early this autumn, in wind.
The paired butterflies are already yellow with August

Over the grass in the West garden;
They hurt me.
I grow older.
If you are coming down through the narrows of the river Kiang,
Please let me know beforehand,
And I will come out to meet you,
As far as Cho-fu-Sa.

EDWARD VIII
ABDICATION SPEECH, 1936

Born to be king, Prince Edward (1894–1972) ruled Great Britain for only a year before abdicating so that he could marry the American divorcée Wallis Simpson. Edward made the following announcement by radio the day after Parliament endorsed his decision. Taking the throne, his younger brother, Albert, became George VI and named Edward the Duke of Windsor. No other British ruler had before or has since abdicated.

These paragraphs represent roughly half of Edward's speech.

At long last I am able to say a few words of my own. I have never wanted to withhold anything, but until now it has not been constitutionally possible for me to speak.

A few hours ago, I discharged my last duty as King and Emperor, and now that I have been succeeded by my brother, the Duke of York, my first words must be to declare my allegiance to him. This I do with all my heart.

You all know the reasons which have impelled me to renounce the throne. But I want you to understand that in making up my mind I did not forget the country or the empire, which, as Prince of Wales and lately as King, I have for twenty-five years tried to serve.

But you must believe me when I tell you that I have found it impossible to carry the heavy burden of responsibility and to discharge my duties as King as I would wish to do without the help and support of the woman I love.

And I want you to know that the decision I have made has been mine and mine alone. This was a thing I had to judge entirely for myself. The other person most nearly concerned has tried up to the last to persuade me to take a different course.

I have made this, the most serious decision of my life, only upon the single thought of what would, in the end, be best for all.

RICHARD FEYNMAN
LETTER TO ARLINE FEYNMAN, 1946

Richard Feynman (1918–1988) shared the 1965 Nobel Prize in Physics for his work on quantum electrodynamics. Unrivaled in his generation for his brilliance and innovation, he was also known for being witty, warm, and unconventional. Those last three qualities were particularly evident in this letter, which he wrote to his wife Arline nearly two years after her death from tuberculosis.

Feynman and Arline had been high school sweethearts and married in their twenties. Feynman's second marriage, in 1952, ended in divorce two years later. His third marriage, in 1960, lasted until his death.

D'Arline,

I adore you, sweetheart.

I know how much you like to hear that—but I don't only write it because you like it—I write it because it makes me warm all over inside to write it to you.

It is such a terribly long time since I last wrote to you—almost two years but I know you'll excuse me because you understand how I am, stubborn and realistic; & I thought there was no sense to writing.

But now I know my darling wife that it is right to do what I have delayed in doing, and that I have done so much in the past. I want to tell you I love you. I want to love you. I always will love you.

I find it hard to understand in my mind what it means to love you after you are dead—but I still want to comfort and take care of you—and I want you to love me and care for me. I want to have problems to discuss with you—I want to do little projects with you. I never thought until just now that we can do that together. What should we do. We started to learn to make clothes together—or learn Chinese—or getting a movie projector. Can't I do something now. No. I am alone without you and you were the "idea-woman" and general instigator of all our wild adventures.

When you were sick you worried because you could not give me something that you wanted to & thought I needed. You needn't have worried. Just as I told you then there was no real need because I loved you in so many ways so much. And now it is clearly even more true—you can give me nothing now yet I love you so that you stand in my way of loving anyone else—but I want you to stand there. You, dead, are so much better than anyone else alive.

I know you will assure me that I am foolish & that you want me to have full happiness & don't want to be in my way. I'll bet you are surprised that I don't even have a girl friend (except you, sweetheart) after two years. But you can't help it, darling, nor can I—I don't understand it, for I have met many girls & very nice ones and I don't want to remain alone—but in two or three meetings they all seem ashes. You only are left to me. You are real.

My darling wife, I do adore you.

I love my wife. My wife is dead.

Rich.

P.S. Please excuse my not mailing this—but I don't know your new address.

TAMMY WYNETTE AND BILLY SHERRILL
"STAND BY YOUR MAN," 1968

As a country-western singer/songwriter, Tammy Wynette (1942–1998) was a Nashville legend with more than twenty chart-topping songs and record sales of more than $100 million. Wynette had hits including "D-I-V-O-R-C-E," "I Don't Wanna Play House," and "'Til I Can Make It On My Own," so the loyalty-above-all point of "Stand By Your Man" was, despite its fame, hardly her only message. Wynette herself was married five times.

Country music producer Billy Sherrill (1936–) secured Wynette's first recording contract, convinced her to change her name from Wynette Byrd, and—according to legend—cowrote this, her most famous hit, with her in just fifteen minutes.

Sometimes it's hard to be a woman,
Giving all your love to just one man.
You'll have bad times and he'll have good times,
Doin' things that you don't understand.
But if you love him you'll forgive him,
Even though he's hard to understand.
And if you love him oh be proud of him,
'Cause after all he's just a man.

Stand by your man,
Give him two arms to cling to,
And something warm to come to
When nights are cold and lonely.

Stand by your man,
And tell the world you love him.
Keep giving all the love you can.

Stand by your man,
And show the world you love him.
Keep giving all the love you can.
Stand by your man.

TOM WOLFE
THE RIGHT STUFF, 1979

Gus Grissom was the second American to travel in space but, as memorably described by Tom Wolfe (1931–) in his National Book Award–winning account, the astronaut's fifteen-minute suborbital flight was controversial from the moment it ended. The fact that the capsule's hatch opened unexpectedly and the capsule sank meant that Grissom's welcome was considerably clouded by questions about whether he had been responsible. In Wolfe's novelistic telling, the upshot was that Gus's wife, Betty, would feel she'd been cheated out of the rewards she had expected in exchange for years of matrimonial sacrifice and devotion.

Grissom went on to a successful space mission in 1965, but died two years later in a fire during an Apollo 1 simulation. Except for those in brackets, the ellipses are Wolfe's.

Few wives seemed to believe as firmly as Betty did in the unofficial Military Wife's Compact. It was a compact not so much between husband and wife as between the two of them and the military. It was because of the compact that a military wife was likely to say *"We* were reassigned to Langley" . . . *we,* as if both of them were in the military. Under the terms of the unwritten compact, they were. The wife began her marriage—to her husband and to the military—by making certain heavy sacrifices. She knew the pay would be miserably low. They would have to move frequently and live in depressing, exhausted houses. Her husband might be gone for long stretches, especially in the event of war. And on top of all that, if her husband happened to be a fighter pilot, she would have to live with the fact that any day, in peace or war, there was an astonishingly good chance that her husband might be killed, *just like that.* In which case, the code added: *Please omit tears, for the sake of those still living.* In return for these concessions, the wife was guaranteed the following: a place in the military community's big family, a welfare state in the best sense, which would see to it that all basic needs, from health care to babysitting, were taken care of. And a flying squadron tended to be the most tightly knit of all military families. She was also guaranteed a permanent marriage, if she wanted it, at least for as long as they were in the service. Divorce—still, as of 1960—was a fatal step for a career military officer; it led to damaging efficiency reports by one's superiors, reports that could ruin chances of advancement.

And she was guaranteed one thing more, something that was seldom talked about except in comical terms. Underneath, however, it was no joke. In the service, when the husband moved up, the wife moved up. If he advanced from lieutenant to captain, then she became Mrs. Captain and now outranked all the Mrs. Lieutenants and received all the social homage the military protocol provided. And if her husband received a military honor, then she became the Honorable Mrs. Captain—all this regardless of her own social adeptness. Of course, it was well known that a gracious, well-spoken, small-talking, competent, sophisticated wife was a great asset to her husband's career, precisely because they were a team and *both* were in the service. At all the teas and socials and ceremonies and obligatory parties at the C.O.'s and all the horrible Officers Wives Club functions, Betty always felt at a loss, despite her good looks and intelligence. She always wondered if she was holding Gus back in his career because she couldn't be the Smilin' & Small-Talkin' Whiz that was required.

Now that Gus had been elevated to this extraordinary new rank—astronaut—Betty was not loath to receive her share, per the compact. It was as if . . . well, precisely because she had endured and felt out of place at so many teas and other small-talk tests, precisely because she had sat at home near the telephone throughout the Korean War and God knew how many hundreds of test flights wondering if the fluttering angels would be ringing up, precisely because her houses all that time had been typical of the sacrificial lot of the junior officer's wife, precisely because her husband had been away so much—it was as if precisely because that was the way things were, she fully intended to be the honorable Mrs. Captain Astronaut and to accept all the honors and privileges attendant thereupon. [. . .]

In the days after the flight Gus looked gloomier and gruffer than ever. He could manage an official smile when he had to and an official hero's wave, but the black cloud would not pass. Betty Grissom looked the same way after she and the two boys, Mark and Scott, joined Gus in Florida for the celebration. Some celebration . . . It was as if the event had been poisoned by the Gus-grim little secret. Betty also had the sneaking suspicion that everyone was saying, just out of earshot: "Gus blew it." But her displeasure was a bit more subtle than Gus's. They . . . NASA, the White House, the Air Force, the other fellows, Gus himself . . . were not keeping their side of the compact! Nobody could have looked at Betty at that time . . . this pretty, shy, ever-silent, ever-proper Honorable Mrs. Astronaut . . . and guessed at her anger.

They were violating the Military Wife's Compact!

BILL AND HILLARY RODHAM CLINTON
60 MINUTES INTERVIEW, 1992

In the heat of his first presidential campaign, Bill Clinton was accused by an Arkansas woman named Gennifer Flowers of having conducted a twelve-year-long affair with her. Together the Clintons sat down for a televised interview with *60 Minutes'* Steve Kroft, who grilled the candidate on the question of his fidelity. This exchange came near the end of the interview, when future first lady, senator, secretary of state, and presidential candidate Hillary Rodham Clinton (1947–) voiced her support for her husband.

See two entries above for the lyrics to Tammy Wynette's song.

KROFT:
[The] question of marital infidelity is an issue with a sizable portion of the electorate. According to the latest CBS News poll . . . fourteen percent of the registered voters in America wouldn't vote for a candidate who's had an extramarital affair.

BILL CLINTON:
I know it's an issue, but what does that mean? That means that eighty-six percent of the American people either don't think it's relevant to presidential performance or look at whether a person, looking at all the facts, is the best to serve.

KROFT:
I think most Americans would agree that it's very admirable that you've stayed together—that you've worked your problems out, that you seem to have reached some sort of an understanding and an arrangement.

BILL CLINTON:
Wait a minute, wait a minute, wait a minute. You're looking at two people who love each other. This is not an arrangement or an understanding. This is a marriage. That's a very different thing.

HILLARY CLINTON:
You know, I'm not sitting here some little woman standing by my man like Tammy Wynette. I'm sitting here because I love him, and I respect him, and I honor what he's been through and what we've been through together. And you know, if that's not enough for people, then heck, don't vote for him.

DIVORCE

BURGUNDIAN LAW
"OF DIVORCES," CIRCA 6TH CENTURY

The history of divorce may be even more abstruse than the history of marriage: There are divorces and divorce laws on record as far back as 1700 BC in Babylonia, as well as in ancient Egypt, ancient Greece, and ancient Rome. By the early part of the new millennium, Romans governed the lands (eventually areas of Germany, France, and Switzerland) where a tribe called the Burgundians settled and recorded these four simple rules.

Solidi were gold coins, originally issued by the Romans. In this context "put away" and "put aside" mean "leave."

1.   If any woman puts aside her husband to whom she is legally married, let her be smothered in mire.

2.   If anyone wishes to put away his wife without cause, let him give her another payment such as he gave for her marriage price, and let the amount of the fine be twelve solidi.

3.   If by chance a man wishes to put away his wife, and is able to prove one of these three crimes against her, that is, adultery, witchcraft, or violation of graves, let him have full right to put her away; and let the judge pronounce the sentence of the law against her, just as should be done against criminals.

4.   But if she admits none of these three crimes, let no man be permitted to put away his wife for any other crime. But if he chooses, he may go away from the home, leaving all household property behind, and his wife and their children may possess the property of her husband.

MIGUEL DE CERVANTES
"THE DIVORCE COURT JUDGE," CIRCA 1615

The legendary Spanish novelist Miguel de Cervantes (1547–1616) was not only the author of *Don Quixote*, but also of poems, short stories, and plays. He was probably least successful in the last endeavor, and it is unclear how many of his plays were performed during his lifetime.

But in his farce about an imagined divorce court, Cervantes anticipated a suggestion about marriage that was put forward by Mexican lawmakers as recently as 2012.

Mexican legislators rejected the proposal, and the archdiocese deemed it "absurd."

D

JUDGE:	Well, good people, what's your quarrel?
MARIANA:	Divorce, divorce, divorce. A thousand times divorce!
JUDGE:	Who from, madam? On what grounds?
MARIANA:	Who from? From this old crock here.
JUDGE:	On what grounds?
MARIANA:	I can't abide his peevish demands any longer. I refuse to look after his countless ailments all the time. My parents didn't bring me up to be a nurse and hand-maid. A very good dowry I brought this old bag of bones who's consuming my life. When he first got his hands on me, my face was as bright and polished as a mirror, and now it's as crumpled as a widow's veil. Please, your honor, unmarry me or I'll hang myself. Just look at the furrows I've got from the tears I shed every day that I'm married to this walking skeleton.

In well-ordered societies a marriage should be reviewed every three years, and dissolved or renewed like a rental agreement.

JUDGE:	Cry no more, madam. Cease your bawling and dry your tears. I'll see that justice is done.
MARIANA:	Let me cry, your honor. It's such a comfort. In well-ordered societies a marriage should be reviewed every three years, and dissolved or renewed like a rental agreement. It shouldn't have to last a lifetime and bring everlasting misery to both parties.
JUDGE:	If that policy were practical, desirable, or financially profitable, it would already be law.

"THE SALE OF WIVES"
WHITEHAVEN HERALD AND CUMBERLAND ADVERTISER, 1832

D

British citizens really did auction off their wives—even as late as the end of the nineteenth century. The practice was not legal, but it was widespread enough that upcoming "sales" were advertised, and usually held in public marketplaces, where onlookers—and potential bidders—would gather. This account was retold and republished throughout the nineteenth century. "Moore's melodies" refers to a collection of popular Irish songs by the poet Thomas ("Anacreon") Moore.

Joseph Thompson, a small farmer, renting between forty and fifty acres, lived at a village three miles from the city of Carlisle. He had been married about three years. He had no children. He and his wife could not agree. There was a continual soreness between the Montagues and Capulets, his family and hers. These three things made them resolve to part. So, on the 7th of April, early in the morning, Mr Thompson sent round the bellman to give notice that a man would sell his wife at twelve o'clock in the market. The odd announcement, of course, drew together a considerable mob. The lady placed herself upon a high oaken chair, with a halter of straw about her neck, and a large circle of relatives and friends around her. The husband-auctioneer stood beside her, and spoke, says my authority, nearly as follows:

"Gentlemen, I have to offer to your notice my wife, Mary Ann Thompson, otherwise Williamson, whom I mean to sell to the highest and fairest bidder. Gentlemen, it his her wish as well as mine to part for ever. She has been to me only a bosom-serpent. I took her for my comfort and the good of my house, but she became my tormentor, a domestic curse, a night invasion, and a daily devil. Gentlemen, I speak truth from my heart when I say may Heaven deliver us from troublesome wives. Avoid them as you would a mad dog, a loaded pistol, cholera morbus, Mount Etna, or any other pestilential phenomena in nature. Now I have shewn you the dark side of my wife, and her faults and failings, I will introduce the bright and sunny side of her, and explain her qualifications and goodness. She can read novels and milk cows; she can laugh and weep with the same ease that you could take a glass of ale when thirsty. Indeed, gentlemen, she reminds me of what the poet says of women in general—

> Heaven gave to women the peculiar grace,
> To laugh, to weep, and cheat the human race.

She can make butter, and scold the maid; she can sing Moore's melodies, and plait her frills and caps. She cannot make rum, gin or whisky; but she is a good judge of the quality from long ex-

D

perience in tasting them. I therefore offer her, with all her perfections and imperfections, for the sum of *fifty shillings*."

The reporter, I fancy, must have dressed up this speech. . . . It is difficult to believe that she had the kind of accomplishments mentioned in the speech, or that he really uttered this speech. He affirms that she did, however, and adds that the lady was a "spruce, lively damsel, apparently not exceeding twenty-three years of age. She seemed," he says, "to feel a pleasure at the exchange she was about to make." The sale took between an hour and a half and two hours. At last, Mrs Thompson was sold to Harry Mears, a pensioner, for one pound and a Newfoundland dog. The newly coupled pair left the city together, the mob huzzaing and cheering after them. Mr Thompson coolly took the straw-halter from off his old wife and put it on his new dog. He then betook himself to the nearest inn, and spent the remainder of the day there. No doubt, before the setting of the sun, the whole purchase-money of his wife had gone down his throat in drink. "He repeatedly exulted," says my authority, "in his happy release from bondage."

ELLEN COILE GRAVES
LETTER TO HENRY GRAVES, 1844

A Pennsylvania couple named Ellen Coile and Henry Graves married in 1841, but the bride left the groom just a year later, setting up a store in Philadelphia. He eventually sued her for divorce, noting that she had abandoned him. As part of her deposition to the court, she offered the following explanation.

This letter was written without punctuation but with spaces between sentences. We have added periods and capital letters. We have not corrected the misspellings.

Henry

I received your letter and in compliance with your request I send you this answer stating my feelings towards yourself. I thought that you was fully acquainted with me to know that you had no cause to imagine that I had for a moment entertained a thought of returning to you. It would be impossible for us to live *peaceble* together after what has occured and in connection with my feelings towards yourself which is that of perfect coldness. I do not and could not love you. I am not one of those lukewarm creatures who can bestow their affections upon all alike where they please. My affections spring spontaneously. I *cannot compel* myself to love where there is no congeniality of feeling. I did wrong very wrong in marrying you without feeling a sincere attachment but I believed you was capable of attaching me to you by kind and affectionate treatment. You encouraged me in this belief for you was not deceived in this respect. When I married you it was with the full determination of loving you which I believed to be an easy task. I was mistaken. I tried for three months as ardently as ever woman tried but each day devolved something calculated to turn me from you rather than win me to you. I gave up the task for I found it impossible. My punishment I think has paid for my indiscretion. I am sorry that you still love me and I trust that this letter will prove effectual in removing your unfortunate attachment for believe me that by me it can never be returned. And now let me remove every false hope by solemnly assuring you that you and I parted *forever* in this World. It is better that I should speak thus plainly than that you should encourage hopes that will only bring you disappointment. I wish you well sincerely from the bottom of my Heart. I should be glad to hear that you was Happyly married and successful in your Business. Mother sends her Love to you and the Family. Give my love to them likewise and

Believe me I am your Freind, Ellen Coile

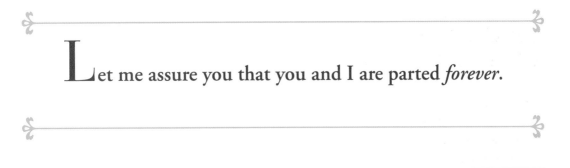

Let me assure you that you and I are parted *forever*.

JULES MICHELET
LOVE, 1859

Historian Jules Michelet (1798–1874), known for his nineteen-volume history of France, also wrote popular books about love, women, natural history, and religion.
Despite our best efforts, we have been unable to find a firsthand account of the following practice.

In Zurich, in the olden time, when a quarrelsome couple applied for a divorce, the magistrate never listened to them. Before deciding upon the case, he locked them up for three days in the same room, with one bed, one table, one plate, and one tumbler. Their food was passed into them by attendants who neither saw nor spoke to them. When they came out, at the end of the three days, neither of them wanted to be divorced.

EUGENE O'NEILL
LETTER TO AGNES BOULTON O'NEILL, 1927

Winner of the Nobel Prize in Literature and four-time recipient of the Pulitzer Prize for Drama, Eugene O'Neill (1888–1953) was in many ways the personification of the tortured, alcoholic author with a chaotic saga of home life and a haunting past. He had yet to write some of his greatest plays when he sent this letter to his second wife, Agnes Boulton.

O'Neill was married to his first wife, Kathleen Jenkins, for three years and, despite various separations, to his third wife, actress Carlotta Monterey, from 1929 until his death; she is the woman to whom he was referring in this letter.

I just got your cable a while ago, saying you understand. I wonder if you really do. Well, I will not beat about the bush but come to the point at once. I love someone else. Most deeply. There is no possible doubt of this. And the someone loves me. Of that I am as deeply certain. And under these circumstances I feel it is impossible for me to live with you, even if you were willing I should do so—which I am sure that you are not, as it would be even a greater degradation to your finer feelings than it would to mine to attempt, for whatever consideration there may be, to keep up the pretense of being husband and wife.

We have often promised each other that if one ever came to the other and said they loved someone else that we would understand, that we would know that love is something which cannot be denied or argued with, that it must be faced. And that is what I am asking you to understand and know now. I am sure that I could accept the inevitable in that spirit if our roles were reversed. And I know that you, if for nothing else than that you must remember with kindness our years of struggle together and that I have tried to make you happy and to be happy with you, will act with the same friendship toward me. After all, you know that I have always been faithful to you, that I have never gone seeking love, that if my love for you had not died no new love would have come to me. And, as I believe I said in my last letter, if you are frank and look into your own heart you will find no real love left for me in it. What has bound us together for the past few years has been deep down a fine affection and friendship, and this I shall always feel for you. There have been moments when our old love flared into life again but you must acknowledge that these have grown steadily rarer. On the other side of the ledger moments of a very horrible hate have been more and more apparent, a poisonous bitterness and resentment, a cruel desire to wound, rage and frustration and revenge. This has killed our chance for happiness together. . . .

I am not blaming you. I have been as much as you, perhaps more so. Or rather, neither of us is to blame. It is life which made us what we are.

My last letter did not mention being in love because, even if I were not so . . . entirely in love with someone else, I think we ought to end our marriage in order to give us both a chance, while we are both at an age when there still is a chance, to find happiness either alone or in another relationship. Soon it will be too late. And if in the end we have failed to give happiness to each other, then all the more reason why each of us owes the other another chance for it.

Looking at it objectively, I am sure freedom to do as you please will mean a lot to you. You can go to Europe, for instance, as you have always wished—live there or anywhere else you like. You can have the use of Spithead exclusively for the rest of your life as a permanent home. I will never go to Bermuda again. You can be reasonably sure, unless catastrophe beans me, that you will always have enough income from me to live in dignity and comfort. You know I am hardly a stingy person, that I will do anything that is fair, that I will want to do all I can for you. And, above all, you will have your chance of marrying someone else who will love you and bring you happiness. I am happy in my new love. I am certain that a similar happiness is waiting for you. It seems obvious to me that it must be.

When I say I am happy now, it is deeply true. My only unhappiness is what I expressed in my last letter—a bitter feeling of sadness when I think over all our years together and what the passage of time has done to us. At such moments I feel life-disgusted and hopeless. It gives me

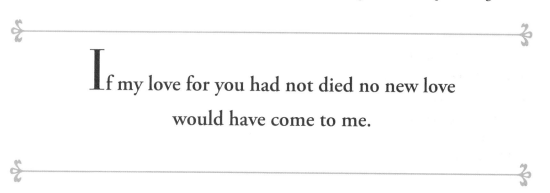

If my love for you had not died no new love would have come to me.

the intolerable feeling that it is perhaps not in the nature of living life itself that fine beautiful things may exist for any great length of time, that human beings are fated to destroy just that in each other which constitutes their mutual happiness. Fits of cosmic Irish melancholia, I guess! Otherwise I am strangely happy. Something new in me has been born. I tell you this in the trust that your friendship may understand and be glad and wish me luck—and set me free to live with that happiness.

I mean, divorce me. That is what we agreed we would do if the present situation ever occurred, isn't it?

DOROTHY THOMPSON
LETTER TO SINCLAIR LEWIS, 1938

A world-famous journalist, lecturer, radio commentator, and suffragist, Dorothy Thompson (1893–1961) was the model for Katharine Hepburn's hard-charging heroine in the movie *Woman of the Year* and, like that character, seemed more naturally suited to public than domestic life. Novelist Sinclair Lewis was the second and most famous of her three husbands and the only one with whom she had a child. By all accounts, their marriage, which began in 1928, was fractious at best, though they didn't divorce officially until 1942. Thompson never sent this letter.

Thompson's first marriage, to Hungarian writer Joseph Bard, lasted four years; her third, to artist Maxim Kopf, lasted fifteen, until his death. Lewis's given name was Harry; he was often called "Hal" (also "Red" for his hair). "Give me Vermont" was an allusion to the house he and Thompson shared there. "Your two children" referred to Lewis's son from a previous marriage and to Michael ("Mickey"), the son he and Thompson had together. The latter was sent to boarding school at the age of eight. Hamilton Fish Armstrong was editor of *Foreign Affairs*. Graham Hutton was an economist. "Faux [properly *faute*] de mieux" means *for lack of anything better*.

Hal:

If you think it's wicked—go ahead and get a divorce. I won't oppose it. I also won't get it. For God's sake, let's be honest. You left me, I didn't leave you. You want it. I don't. You get it. On any ground your lawyers can fake up. Say I "deserted" you. Make a case for mental cruelty. You can make a case. Go and get it.

What is "incredible" about my not writing? What is "incredible" is that I don't rush into the divorce court and soak *you* for desertion and "mental cruelty." I don't write because I don't know what to say to you. You have made it clear time on end that you dislike me, that you are bored with me, that you are bored with "situations and conditions. And reactions." You don't like my friends. You don't know my friends. You resent my friends. Shall I write you that I think Hamilton Armstrong has done a brilliant piece of journalism in his last book on the Munich conference? Or that Graham Hutton is in America and has a fascinating tale of Britain? . . . You are happy. Happier, you write, than you have been in years. I congratulate you. I am glad that you are happy. I happen not to be. I am not happy. I am not happy, because I have no home; because I have an ill and difficult child without a father. Because I have loved a man who didn't exist. Because I am widowed of an illusion. Because I am tremblingly aware of the tragedy of the world we live in.

I do not "admire and respect you." I have loved you. I do not admire your present incarnation or respect your present attitude toward anything. I did not like "Angela is 22" because

I think it is beneath the level of the author of "Arrowsmith" or of "It Can't Happen Here." I think it is a cheap concession to a cheap institution—the American Broadway Theater. I do not admire the people with whom you surround yourself. I am horrified, on your behalf, at the association of your name with that of Fay Wray. Why haven't I said so? Out of tact! Out of the feeling that a great man may allow himself indulgences. Out of the desire not to hurt someone who is sensitive. . . .

When I am with you I depress you. I am depressed. But I would rather be depressed than pretend that nothing really matters. I don't write to you because I can't lie to you. Maybe it is because I respect you, or maybe it is because I respect myself—somewhat. I think you have thrown down the sink the best things that life has ever offered you: the love of friends; of your wife; the pleasure in your sons. Your home. For what? For whisky and art? Where's the art, at long last? Or the whisky?

You say I am "brilliant." My dear Hal, I am "brilliant" faux de mieux. I am a woman—something you never took the trouble to realize. My sex is female. I am not insensitive. I am not stupid. I do not love you for your wit, or for "nostalgia"—my nostalgia antedates our marriage. I loved you, funnily enough, for your suffering, your sensitivity, your generosity, and your prodigious talent. I shall not reiterate my feelings, nor insist that I still love you. I do not even know you—the you of the present moment. I shall certainly not pursue you, I am a woman. If you want my friendship you have got to win it. If you care for anything more, you have got to woo it. If you don't—then you, be honest, as you advise me to be—and break this relationship finally and completely. Forget that I exist. Forget that Mickey exists. Wipe him out as a responsibility. Wipe me out as a memory. Be happy! Be free.

I, however, am not free. I can neither wipe out my memories, nor, above all, can I forget you, since you live with me, as the chief, perhaps the only tie I have to life, in the re-incarnation of yourself in your son. You have fathered a child, violent and frail, gifted, unbalanced, and charming, born to unhappiness, to ill-adjustment, to crazy joy and continual disappointment. Born to grow up in this tragic century. A sick, lovely, nerve-wracking, expensive child. He was conceived in a night that I remember, and you do not, and born in a night that I remember and that you[—]or do you? . . . There are things in my heart that you do not dream of, things that are compounded of passion and fury and love and hate and pride and disgust and tenderness and contrition[,] things that are wild and fierce[—]and you ask me to write you conventional letters because you are in "exile[.]" From what? From whom?

Give me Vermont. I want to watch the lilac hedge grow tall and the elm trees form, and the roses on the gray wall thicken, and the yellow apples hang on the young trees, and the sumac redden on the hills, and friends come, and your two children feel at home. Who knows?

Maybe some time you might come home yourself. You might go a long way and do worse. As a matter of fact and prophecy—you will.

d.

D

NEVADA POSTCARD, CIRCA 1940

Note the singular determination with which this divorcée is following the fabled custom of jettisoning her wedding ring from what became known in Reno, Nevada, as "The Bridge of Sighs." In 1906, the wife of the adulterous head of U.S. Steel was granted a much-publicized divorce there; the resulting gossip put Reno ahead of any other Nevada or U.S. city as the country's divorce destination. By 1931, when the "Severance Stay" to gain the required state residency was cut to six weeks, divorce became a lucrative industry and remained so during the Depression and for the next several decades. In the vernacular, "Going Reno" meant getting a divorce; columnist Walter Winchell called it getting "Reno-vated"; and in the 1940s "The Reno" was the name for a bra that was said to "separate and support."

EDWARD ALBEE
WHO'S AFRAID OF VIRGINIA WOOLF?, 1962

About Albee and this play, see Conflict, page 47. Ellipses in original.

MARTHA: I swear . . . if you existed I'd divorce you. . . .

WOODY ALLEN
"MY MARRIAGE," 1964

Eventually the writer and/or director of some half a hundred films (as well as being a successful playwright, actor, short story writer, and occasional jazz musician), Woody Allen (1935–) began his career as a teenager, selling jokes to newspaper columnists and, by nineteen, writing for television. In 1962, he and his childhood sweetheart, Harlene Rosen, divorced after six years of marriage, giving Allen not only his freedom but also a rich comic lode to mine for the stand-up career he pursued in the 1960s.

Allen's second marriage, to actress Louise Lasser, lasted from 1966 to 1970. His twelve-year relationship with actress Mia Farrow ended in 1992, when he left Farrow for her twenty-year-old adopted daughter, Soon-Yi Previn. Previn and Allen have been married since 1997. CONELRAD was an emergency broadcasting system begun during the Cold War.

It was partially my fault that we got divorced. I had a lousy attitude toward her. For the first year of marriage I had a bad—basically a bad attitude, I guess. I tended to place my wife underneath a pedestal all the time.

We used to argue and fight. We finally decided, we either take a vacation in Bermuda or get a divorce, one of the two things. And we discussed it very maturely, and we decided on the divorce, 'cause we felt that we had a limited amount of money to spend, ya know. A vacation in Bermuda is over in two weeks, but a divorce is something that you always have.

And I saw myself free again, living in the Village, ya know, in a bachelor apartment with a wood-burning fireplace and a shaggy rug, and on the walls one of those great Picassos by Van Gogh, and just great swinging—airline hostesses running amok in the apartment, ya know. And I got very excited, and I ran into my wife. She was in the next room at the time, listening to CONELRAD on the radio, ya know. I laid it right on the line with her, I came right to the point, I said "Quasimodo, I want a divorce."

NEIL SIMON
THE ODD COUPLE, 1965

With myriad awards (including a Pulitzer) for dozens of successful plays and films, Neil Simon (1927–) has been one of America's most productive and popular dramatists. *The Odd Couple*, one of his earliest works, is about two friends—one divorced, one recently separated—who share an apartment despite being temperamentally and hilariously unsuited. In this scene, the sportswriter slob Oscar Madison (played by Walter Matthau in both the play and its subsequent film adaptation) tries to explain his marriage to the neurotic neat freak Felix Ungar.

How can I help you when I can't help myself? You think *you're* impossible to live with? Blanche used to say, "What time do you want dinner?" And I'd say, "I don't know, I'm not hungry." Then at three o'clock in the morning, I'd wake her up and say "Now!" I've been one of the highest paid sports writers in the East for the past fourteen years—and we saved eight and a half dollars—in pennies! I'm never home, I gamble, I burn cigar holes in the furniture, drink like a fish and lie to her every chance I get and for our tenth wedding anniversary, I took her to the New York Rangers–Detroit Red Wings hockey game, where she got hit with a puck. And I *still* can't understand why she left me. That's how impossible *I* am.

"SHOULD THIS MARRIAGE BE SAVED?"
LADIES' HOME JOURNAL, 1970

Ladies' Home Journal launched the column "Can This Marriage Be Saved?" in 1953, and it has thrived since in various, book, TV, and digital formats. Seven years after Betty Friedan (see Freedom, pages 135–36) described the dilemma of the suburban housewife in *The Feminine Mystique*, the *Journal* printed the story of "Barbara," a thirty-three-year-old businessman's wife and mother of three. The story made it clear that women's perspectives were changing. "When she talked," the author of the article wrote, "she did not ask herself, 'Can My Marriage Be Saved?' She asked, instead, '*Should* My Marriage Be Saved?'"

Every morning my children and my husband leave the house, dressed and ready to spend the day outside. I am still in my nightgown, my teeth aren't brushed yet, and I have to go back to the breakfast dishes and the house. It makes me feel terrible, as if they were people but I am not. . . . When I was a girl, I wanted to do something important. First I wanted to be an explorer, and then a scientist. Then I got other ideas. I wanted to—it certainly seems really ridiculous now—I wanted to be a Congresswoman or Senator. Senator Barbara from Illinois, can you imagine? Me, who can't even get dressed in the morning?

My family got worried about all my crazy ideas. After a while, I stopped having those daydreams. I went to the state university, where I met my husband, Bill. He was very smart, ambitious and powerful. I couldn't believe he wanted to marry me. He was graduating, and he didn't want to wait for me to finish college; three years seemed too much. So, although I was a good student, I dropped out and got married. I was nineteen years old.

Being married was fun at first, except that I didn't know what to do with myself during the day and I was too scared to go out and get a job. My husband didn't want me to, anyway. Then the children came along and we moved out to the suburbs, and since then it's been, well, you know what it's like, cooking and shopping and washing diapers and picking up kids and bringing them home and arranging everything for everybody, all that sort of thing. . . .

At home he is very demanding. For example, he doesn't like the way laundries put starch in his shorts, so I have to iron them myself. He wants a gourmet dinner every night, so at five o'clock I make hot dogs and beans for the kids and at seven o'clock, veal *cordon bleu* with a dry white wine for me and Bill. He selects the wine, but I have to be sure it's perfectly chilled.

We don't have sex very often; he doesn't seem to want it. But when he does, I know I have to make myself available. I used to want him all the time. Now I don't feel that way anymore. These days it seems as if we either fight or don't talk with each other at all. Last year I went to a psychiatrist. He intimated that I had hidden masculine drives. This frightened me so I never went back.

Sometimes when I'm alone in the house I wander into the children's rooms and look at the piles of dirty underwear. I feel helpless and confused. I want to cry and can't decide which pile to pick up first. I ask myself, what shall I do with the rest of my life? . . . How would life be any better for me if I were divorced? I'd still have to do housework and take care of the children, but without even the little help I get from my husband. Get a job? What job? Where? . . .

Divorce means you have to put yourself back on the marketplace again, to fix yourself up to catch another husband. Divorce means nobody wants you. It means lawyers and fights and custody agreements.

The loneliness, how would I face it? Those awful nights by yourself with only the kids or maybe another woman for company. It takes a lot of courage to go anywhere as a single woman these days. Just the way waiters look at you in a restaurant if you haven't got a male escort makes me want to crawl back to my own house and home and husband, no matter how awful the situation there is.

RICHARD BURTON
LETTER TO ELIZABETH TAYLOR, 1973

D

Even factoring in the current age of electronic communication, there have been few if any romantic relationships more public than that of Richard Burton (1925–1984) and Elizabeth Taylor (1932–2011). They were each married to other people when they met and began an affair on the set of *Cleopatra* in 1963. They married each other the following year, and in a legendary, boozy, larger-than-life way, played out their affections and disaffections over the next decade before a world of breathless fans. Burton, a Welsh actor with an extraordinary gift for language, wrote Taylor this touching letter as their first attempt at marriage came to an end.

In her ensuing statement to the press, Taylor wrote: "I am convinced that it would be a good and constructive idea if Richard and I are separated for a while. Maybe we loved each other too much." They divorced in 1974, remarried in 1975, then divorced for good a year later. Taylor had six other husbands, four before Burton, two after. "His Eye is on the Sparrow" is a 1905 gospel hymn inspired by biblical verses in Matthew.

So My Lumps,

You're off, by God! I can barely believe it since I am so unaccustomed to anybody leaving me. But reflectively I wonder why nobody did so before. All I care about—honest to God—is that you are happy and I don't much care who you'll find happiness with. I mean as long as he's a friendly bloke and treats you nice and kind. If he doesn't I'll come at him with a hammer and clinker. God's eye may be on the sparrow but my eye will always be on you.

Never forget your strange virtues. Never forget that underneath that veneer of raucous language is a remarkable and puritanical LADY. I am a smashing bore and why you've stuck by me so long is an indication of your loyalty. I shall miss you with passion and wild regret.

You know, of course, my angelic one, that everything I (we) have is yours, so you should be fairly comfortable. Don't, however, let your next inamorata use it, otherwise I might become a trifle testy. I do not like the human race. I do not like his ugly face. And if he takes my former wife and turns her into stress and strife, I'll smash him bash him, laugh or crash him slash him trash him etc. Christ, I am possessed by language. Mostly bad. (Sloshed, d'yer think?) So now, have a good time. . . .

You may rest assured that I will not have affairs with any other female. Anybody after you is going to be disinteresting. I shall gloom a lot and stare morosely into unimaginable distances and act a bit—probably on the stage—to keep me in booze and butter. . . .

I'll leave it to you to announce the parting of the ways while I shall never say or write one word except this valedictory note to you. Try and look after yourself. Much love.

Elizabeth Taylor and Richard Burton, 1964

ROBIN WILLIAMS
THE TONIGHT SHOW, 1991

Comedian and actor Robin Williams (1951–2014) was married three times and divorced twice.

Divorce, from the old Latin word *divorcarum,* meaning having your genitals torn out through your wallet.

LEE LORENZ, 2006

Cartoonist Lee Lorenz (1933–) sold his first cartoon to *The New Yorker* in 1958 and has contributed some 1,700 more since. He served as the magazine's art editor from 1973 to 1993 and continued as its cartoon editor until 1997.

"Your wife gets the house, the car, the dog, your I.R.A., and ten thousand dollars a month.
In return, she acknowledges your right to exist."

CHRIS ROCK
"INTERCOURSE," 2007

In a career that started when he was seventeen, comedian Chris Rock (1966–) has traveled from stand-up comic to *Saturday Night Live* cast member to sitcom star, writer, director, and movie actor. Acerbic, profane, and hilarious, Rock has left few subjects—including world-famous icons—untouched.

Yo, marriage is tough, man. Marriage is real fucking tough, man. Marriage is so tough, Nelson Mandela got a divorce. Nelson Mandela got a fucking divorce. Nelson Mandela spent twenty-seven years in a South African prison, got beaten and tortured every day for twenty-seven years, and did it with no fucking problem. Made to do hard labor in 100-degree South African heat for twenty-seven years and did it with no problem. He got outta jail after twenty-seven years of torture, spent six months with his wife and said: "I can't take this shit no more!"

ANNELI RUFUS
"15 SIGNS YOU'LL GET DIVORCED," 2010

Anneli Rufus is the author of books and articles on subjects ranging from jealousy and travel to cooking and death. On the *Daily Beast* website, she presented the following list, based on conclusions presented either in scholarly journals or at national conferences, all within the previous decade.

1. If you're a woman who got married before the age of eighteen, your marriage faces a 48 percent likelihood of divorce within ten years.
2. If you're a woman who wants a child—either a first child or an additional child—much more strongly than your spouse does, your marriage is more than twice as likely to end in divorce as the marriages of couples who agree on how much they do or don't want a child.
3. If you have two sons, you face a 36.9 percent likelihood of divorce, but if you have two daughters, the likelihood rises to 43.1 percent.
4. If you're a man with high basal testosterone, you're 43 percent more likely to get divorced than men with low testosterone levels.

5.   If your child has been diagnosed with ADHD, you are 22.7 percent more likely to divorce before that child turns eight years old than parents of a child without ADHD.

6.   If you are currently married but have cohabited with a lover other than your current spouse, you are slightly more than twice as likely to divorce than someone who has never cohabited.

7.   If you didn't smile for photographs early in life, your marriage is five times more likely to end in divorce than if you smiled intensely in early photographs.

8.   If your child has died after the twentieth week of pregnancy, during labor, or soon after labor, you are 40 percent more likely to divorce than if you had not lost a child.

9.   If you're a woman who has recently been diagnosed with cancer or multiple sclerosis, your marriage is six times more likely to end in divorce than if your husband had been diagnosed with those diseases instead.

10.   If you're a Caucasian woman and you're separated from your spouse, there's a 98 percent chance that you'll be divorced within six years of that separation; if you're a Hispanic woman, the likelihood is 80 percent; if you're an African-American woman, the likelihood is 72 percent.

11.   If you're a dancer or choreographer, you face a 43.05 percent likelihood of divorce, compared with mathematicians, who face a 19.15 percent likelihood, and animal trainers, who face a 22.5 percent likelihood.

12.   If you're a farmer or rancher, you face only a 7.63 percent likelihood of divorce, joined by other low-risk occupations such as nuclear engineers, who face a 7.29 percent likelihood, and optometrists, who face a mere 4.01 percent likelihood.

13.   If either you or your spouse have suffered a brain injury, your marriage faces a 17 percent chance of ending in divorce.

14.   If you're an African-American woman, your first marriage has a 47 percent likelihood of ending in divorce within ten years; for Hispanic women, the likelihood is 34 percent; for Caucasian women, it's 32 percent; for Asian women, it's 20 percent.

15.   If you're a woman serving actively in the military, your marriage is 250 percent more likely to end in divorce than that of a man serving actively in the military.

NATALIE GREGG
"DIVORCE READINESS QUESTIONNAIRE," 2012

Blogger Natalie Gregg, self-described "Family lawyer, Entrepreneur and Mother of Two," contributed this questionnaire to the "Huff Post Divorce" section of the popular website.

If divorce is on your mind, here are 10 simple true-or-false questions to ask yourself before splitting:

1. True or False: In the last six months, my spouse has changed their exercise, dress and grooming regime to look younger or fitter.

2. True or False: I have not had sex with my spouse in over one month.

3. True or False: I suspect that my spouse is cheating.

4. True or False: I can't remember the last time sex was good.

5. True or False: I can't remember why I married my spouse in the first place.

6. True or False: I don't have access to the marital accounts, or the access that I have is very limited.

7. True or False: I am currently involved in a romantic relationship with someone other than my spouse.

8. True or False: My spouse has been diagnosed with a mental disorder/disease and fails to seek counseling or medical treatment.

9. True or False: My spouse has an addiction to drugs, alcohol, porn, gambling, shopping, etc. but fails to seek treatment to address the addiction.

10. True or False: We fight more than we laugh.

If you answered TRUE to 1 or 2 questions, you are probably in need of some marital counseling or a good, old-fashioned date night with your spouse that includes a heart-to-heart conversation.

If you answered TRUE to 2–5 questions, your marriage is salvageable but will take a lot of work. You need to ask yourself, "Does my desire to fix this marriage outweigh my exhaustion at trying to do so?" If so, then you should explore marital counseling. It is also advisable to consult with a lawyer just to ensure that you know your rights.

If you answered TRUE to more than 5 questions, contact a family attorney.

ENCOURAGEMENT

JEROME PAINE BATES
THE IMPERIAL HIGHWAY, 1880

One of several earnest meditations on how to live the good life, *The Imperial Highway* by Jerome Paine Bates (1837–1915) remained popular into the early twentieth century.

It is not so thankworthy for thee to cheer thy husband when he can cheer thee, or himself without thee, while the day of prosperity lasts [as it is] to play the sweet orator, and to make him merry when all other comforts have forsaken him.

W. B. YEATS
JOURNAL, 1909

One of the great poets in the English language, William Butler Yeats (1865–1939) used his journal to record fresh encounters, sketch out essays and poems, and—notably, for a man who never got to marry the love of his life (see Youth and Age, page 509)—ponder the mysteries of love.

In wise love each divines the high secret self of the other and, refusing to believe in the mere daily self, creates a mirror where the lover or the beloved sees an image to copy in daily life.

HENRY NEUMANN
MODERN YOUTH AND MARRIAGE, 1928

Henry Neumann (1882–1966) was a leader of the Society for Ethical Culture, a movement founded in 1876 by Felix Adler on the principle that ethics are independent of theology.

Disillusion, of course, enters in time. There are no full-grown perfect beings. Sooner or later the frailties are recognized. But there is in most people a better self which the fallible self hides; and the greatest privilege of the married life is to be the one who assists the other more and more to do justice to that better possibility.

KARL MENNINGER
LETTER TO A *LADIES' HOME JOURNAL* READER, 1930

Son of one physician and brother of another, Karl Menninger (1893–1990) helped establish the Menninger Sanitarium, a group practice in Topeka, Kansas. Focusing on psychiatry, Menninger authored more than a dozen books that had a significant influence on the perception of mental illness. In 1930, he began writing "Mental Hygiene in the Home," an advice column for *Ladies' Home Journal* that lasted only eighteen months but generated thousands of letters from readers, all of which Menninger is said to have answered. His demystification of psychiatry was quite ahead of its time, even if his advice was hardly progressive.

My dear Mrs. P.:

I read with care your letter of October 24 addressed to me in care of the *Ladies' Home Journal*.

What are the facts according to your own statement? First you married an ambitious, hardworking man who was well-liked. Secondly, he has given you the comforts of life, if not the luxuries. Thirdly, he recently worked hard to get a certain position which was, however, given to someone else who was personally preferred; fourth, this discouraged both him and you. Fifth, you suggested to him that he had better stop trying or hoping for a better position and take a job as a common laborer. Sixth, you are tired of poverty and feel cheated to have been given such a husband.

I am reciting these facts which you have given me because it will look and sound different to you coming from someone else. I think it will become perfectly obvious to you if you study over it, that you have been heartlessly cruel toward your husband. Instead of encouraging him, you have discouraged him; instead of boosting him a little when he met with a reverse which every man has to meet with in the battle of life, you gave him a further kick when he got home. Instead of loving him, it sounds to me as if you almost hated him. And why should you hate him? Because he didn't bring you the luxuries of life. I am quoting almost your own words.

Yes, I think you are dead wrong. I think you have the wrong attitude toward your husband entirely. I think it may be this disparagement of him, this unconscious depreciation of him, this doubt of his ability, and so forth which has been partly responsible for his not having more self-confidence and getting further ahead than he has. But your husband hasn't made a failure; he has failed in one particular as every man must do. Not once but many times if he ever amounts to anything. As a wife your duty is to do just the opposite from what you have done. You ought to love him more than ever. You ought to back him up, encourage him, reassure him, tell him that he has the stuff in him and next time he will be more successful, and so forth. This is the only way in the world for you to accomplish the thing which you say you want to accomplish. But the way you are treating your husband is the surest way in the world to achieve the things you say you cannot stand. I am a little surprised that your womanly intuition does not show you this.

The greatest privilege of married life is to be the one who assists the other to do justice to that better possibility.

Did you ever hear about Nathaniel Hawthorne's wife? Hawthorne was fired from his job and came home heartbroken and discouraged and in tears. His wife was sunshiny and happy and he was so afraid it would break her heart and make her cry that he didn't want to tell her. But finally he did. She burst into laughter and clapped her hands and he was amazed. But Darling, he said, how can you act that way, how can you be happy? Sweetheart, she said, now you will have time to write your book. And he sat down and wrote one of the most famous novels ever written, and certainly some of the finest literature ever created in the United States. . . . The point is that she encouraged him when he was so discouraged so that he was able to turn out a great piece of work, and turn defeat into success.

What you must do is to help your husband turn this little minor defeat into a greater success. But what it looks to me as if you were about to do is to turn his little defeat into a disaster for both of you. I think there is still time to change, but get busy.

F. SCOTT FITZGERALD
LETTER TO ZELDA FITZGERALD, 1934

Decadent, tragic, brilliant, and doomed, Scott Fitzgerald (1896–1940) and Zelda became the embodiment of the glittering 1920s and the tarnished 1930s. When Scott wrote this letter, Zelda was staying at one of the several sanitariums where she battled mental illness, with decreasing success, from the early thirties on. In one of his journals from that time, Fitzgerald wrote: "I left my capacity for hoping on the little roads that led to Zelda's sanitarium." Though he dictated this letter, it is one of his most poignant.

Anthony and Marjorie were among Zelda's siblings; Anthony had killed himself the year before. The pictures to which Scott refers were those shown in an exhibition of Zelda's paintings, one of her many attempts to forge an artistic identity of her own. Scott's reference to Zelda as a swan comes from the checklist she had designed for the exhibit, which featured a swan above the title "Parfois la Folie est la Sagesse" (sometimes madness is wisdom).

The thing that you have to fight against is defeatism of any kind. You have no reason for it. You have never had really a melancholy temperament, but, as your mother said: you have always been known for a bright, cheerful, extraverting attitude upon life. I mean *especially* that you share none of the melancholy point of view which seems to have been the lot of Anthony and Marjorie. You and I have had wonderful times in the past, and the future is still brilliant with possibilities if you will keep up your morale, and try to think that way. The outside world, the political situation, etc., is still gloomy and it *does* [a]ffect everybody directly, and will inevitably reach you indirectly, but try to separate yourself from it by some form of mental hygiene—if necessary, a self-invented one. . . .

There is no feeling of gloom on your part that has the *slightest* legitimacy. Your pictures have been a success, your health has been very much better, according to the doctors—and the only sadness is the living without you, without hearing the notes of your voice with its particular intimacies of inflection.

You and I have been happy: we haven't been happy just once, we've been happy a thousand times. The chances that the spring, that's for everyone, like in the popular songs, may belong to us too—the chances are pretty bright at this time because as usual, I can carry most of contemporary literary opinion, liquidated, in the hollow of my hand—and when I do, I see the swan floating on it and—I find it to be you and you only. But, Swan, float lightly because you are a swan, because by the exquisite curve of your neck the gods gave you some special favor, and even though you fractured it running against some man-made bridge, it healed and you sailed onward. Forget the past—what you can of it, and turn about and swim back home to me, to your haven forever and ever—even though it may seem a dark cave at times and lit with torches of fury; it is the best refuge for you—turn gently in the waters through which you move and sail back.

LADY BIRD JOHNSON
LETTER TO LYNDON JOHNSON, 1964

The Democratic convention was in full swing, but LBJ—wracked by terrible divisions within the nation—was hesitating about accepting the party's nomination when Lady Bird Johnson (1912–2007) sent him this note.

Her reference to *Time* magazine concerned that week's cover story, which, in a somewhat brutal and obvious comparison to Jacqueline Kennedy, had described the fifty-one-year-old first lady as "cast more in the pleasant image of a neat, busy suburban clubwoman than in the queenly mold of a jet-set Continental beauty. . . . Her nose is a bit too long, her mouth a bit too wide, her ankles a bit less than trim, and she is not outstanding at clotheshorseman-ship. She has a voice something like a brassy low note on a trumpet, and she speaks in a twanging drawl."

Beloved—

You are as brave a man as Harry Truman—or FDR—or Lincoln. You can go on to find some peace, some achievement amidst all the pain. You have been strong, patient, determined beyond any words of mine to express.

I honor you for it. So does most of the country.

To step out now would be wrong for your country, and I can see nothing but a lonely wasteland for your future. Your friends would be frozen in embarrassed silence and your enemies jeering.

I am not afraid of *Time* or lies or losing money or defeat.

In the final analysis I can't carry any of the burdens you talked of—so I know it's only *your* choice. But I know you are as brave as any of the thirty-five.

I love you always

Bird

E

ERNEST THOMPSON
ON GOLDEN POND, 1981

On Golden Pond, written by Ernest Thompson (1949–), was first produced as a Broadway play in 1979, then, two years later, as a film with dream casting. Katharine Hepburn was the feisty Ethel Thayer, and Henry Fonda her crotchety, more fragile husband, Norman. Oddly, it was the first and only time the two veteran actors worked together. Fonda died shortly thereafter, and Hepburn's shaking voice in this scene—a symptom of her neurological disorder, essential tremor—gave it unavoidable pathos.

Norman has gotten confused on his way to pick strawberries for lunch. Charlie is the town's mailman.

Henry Fonda and Katharine Hepburn

NORMAN: You want to know why I came back so fast? I got to the end of our lane. I couldn't remember where the old town road was. I went a little way in the woods, there was nothing familiar, not one damn tree. Scared me half to death. That's why I came running back here to you, to see your pretty face, I could feel safe, I was still me.

ETHEL:	You're safe, you old Poop. And you're definitely still you. Picking on poor old Charlie. After lunch, after we've gobbled up all those silly strawberries, we'll take ourselves to the old town road. We've been there a thousand times, darling. A thousand. And you'll remember it all. Listen to me, Mister. You're my knight in shining armor. Don't you forget it. You're going to get back up on that horse and I'm going to be right behind you, holding on tight, and away we're going to go, go, go!
NORMAN:	I don't like horses.
ETHEL:	Hah.
NORMAN:	You are a pretty old dame, aren't you? What are you doing with a dotty old son of a bitch like me?
ETHEL:	Well, I haven't the vaguest idea.

ENDINGS

ROMAN HUSBAND
"LAUDATIO TURIAE," 1ST CENTURY BC

Marriages that are ended by death, not divorce, sometimes provide the most extraordinary gifts of inspiration. Nothing is known about the author of this famous eulogy except that he was a wealthy Roman husband who lived during the reign of Augustus and apparently loved his wife very deeply. The eulogy was extraordinary for its length (just half the speech survived, and what follows below are only excerpts of that half), but even more so for the fact that the entire speech was inscribed on the wife's large tombstone.

The identity of the author's wife is also unknown, though some scholars have concluded from other sources that her name was Turia (hence "Laudatio Turiae," literally "the eulogy of Turia"). In ancient Rome, the Di Manes were considered spirits of the dead that could offer some protection in the afterlife.

Marriages as long as ours are rare, marriages that are ended by death and not broken by divorce. For we were fortunate enough to see our marriage last without disharmony for fully 40 years. I wish that our long union had come to its final end through something that had befallen me instead of you; it would have been more just if I as the older partner had had to yield to fate through such an event.

E

Why should I mention your domestic virtues: your loyalty, obedience, affability, reason-ableness, industry in working wool, religion without superstition, sobriety of attire, modesty of appearance? Why dwell on your . . . devotion to your family? You have shown the same at-tention to my mother as you did to your own parents. . . . It is your very own virtues that I am asserting, and very few women have encountered comparable circumstances. . . .

When you despaired of your ability to bear children and grieved over my childlessness, you became anxious lest by retaining you in marriage I might lose all hope of having children and be distressed for that reason. So you proposed a divorce outright and offered to yield our house free to another woman's fertility. Your intention was in fact that you yourself, relying on our well-known conformity of sentiment, would search out and provide for me a wife who was worthy and suitable for me, and you declared that you would regard future children as joint and as though your own, and that you would not effect a separation of our property which had hitherto been held in common, but that it would still be under my control and, if I wished so, under your administration: nothing would be kept apart by you, nothing separate, and you would thereafter take upon yourself the duties and the loyalty of a sister and a mother-in-law.

I must admit that I flared up so that I almost lost control of myself; so horrified was I by what you tried to do that I found it difficult to retrieve my composure.

. . . What desire, what need to have children could I have had that was so great that I should have broken faith for that reason and changed certainty for uncertainty? . . .

What you have achieved in your life will not be lost to me. The thought of your fame gives me strength of mind and from your actions I draw instruction so that I shall be able to resist Fortune. Fortune did not rob me of everything since it permitted your memory to be glorified by praise. But along with you I have lost the tranquility of my existence. When I recall how you used to foresee and ward off the dangers that threatened me, I break down under my calamity and cannot hold steadfastly by my promise.

Natural sorrow wrests away my power of self-control and I am overwhelmed by sorrow. I am tormented by two emotions: grief and fear—and I do not stand firm against either. When I go back in thought to my previous misfortunes and when I envisage what the future may have in store for me, fixing my eyes on your glory does not give me strength to bear my sorrow with patience. Rather I seem to be destined to long mourning.

The conclusions of my speech will be that you deserved everything but that it did not fall to my lot to give you everything as I ought; your last wishes I have regarded as law; whatever it will be in my power to do in addition, I shall do.

I pray that your Di Manes will grant you rest and protection.

WALTER RALEIGH
LETTER TO ELIZABETH THROCKMORTON, 1603

Sir Walter Raleigh (circa 1554–1618)—explorer, historian, at times one of Queen Elizabeth's most trusted courtiers—was imprisoned after her death in 1603 and found guilty of treason against her successor, James I. When Raleigh wrote this letter, he was in the Tower of London, expecting to be executed the following morning. King James spared him, but Raleigh remained jailed until 1616, when he was allowed to lead an expedition to South America—his second—in search of gold. After he attacked a Spanish outpost in Venezuela and returned to England, his death sentence was reinstated by James at the insistence of the Spanish ambassador. Raleigh was beheaded in 1618. His last words were addressed to his executioner: "Strike, man, strike!"

Many biographies of Raleigh have repeated the story that his severed, embalmed head was given to his wife, and that she kept it in a velvet bag for the rest of her life.

You shall now receive (my deare wife) my last words in these last lines. My love I send you that you may keep it when I am dead, and my councell that you may remember it when I am no more. I would not by my will present you with sorrowes (dear Besse) let them go to the grave with me and be buried in the dust. And seeing that it is not Gods will that I should see you any more in this life, beare it patiently, and with a heart like thy selfe.

First, I send you all the thankes which my heart can conceive, or my words can rehearse for your many travailes, and care taken for me, which though they have not taken effect as you wished, yet my debt to you is not the lesse: but pay it I never shall in this world.

Secondly, I beseech you for the love you beare me living, do not hide your selfe many dayes, but by your travailes seeke to helpe your miserable fortunes and the right of your poor childe. Thy mourning cannot availe me, I am but dust.

. . . When I am gone, no doubt you shall be sought for by many, for the world thinkes that I was very rich. But take heed of the pretences of men, and their affections, for they last not but in honest and worthy men, and no greater misery can befall you in this life, than to become a prey, and afterwards to be despised. I speake not this (God knowes) to dissuade you from marriage, for it will be best for you, both in respect of the world and of God. As for me, I am no more yours, nor you mine, death hath cut us asunder: and God hath divided me from the world, and you from me. . . .

I cannot write much, God he knows how hardly I steale this time while others sleep, and it is also time that I should separate my thoughts from the world. Begg my dead body which living was denied thee; and either lay it at Sherburne (and if the land continue) or in Exeter-Church, by my Father and Mother; I can say no more, time and death call me away.

The everlasting God, powerfull, infinite, and omnipotent God, That Almighty God, who is goodnesse it selfe, the true life and true light keep thee and thine: have mercy on me, and teach me to forgive my persecutors and false accusers, and send us to meet in his glorious King-dome. My deare wife farewell. Blesse my poore boy. Pray for me, and let my good God hold you both in his armes.

Written with the dying hand of sometimes thy Husband, but now alasse overthrowne.

Yours that was, but now not my own.

Walter Rawleigh

LADY SHIGENARI
LETTER TO KIMURA SHIGENARI, 1615

A Samurai warrior, Kimura Shigenari (1593–1615) led the charge in a fierce clan battle during a siege at Osaka. His wife (full name unknown) wrote this letter in anticipation of the battle. She had already killed herself by the time her husband was captured and beheaded.

I know that when two wayfarers take shelter under the same tree and slake their thirst in the same river it has all been determined by their karma from a previous life. For the past few years you and I have shared the same pillow as man and wife who had intended to live and grow old together, and I have become as attached to you as your own shadow. This is what I believed, and I think this is what you have also thought about us.

But now I have learnt about the final enterprise on which you have decided and, though I cannot be with you to share the grand moment, I rejoice in the knowledge of it. It is said that on the eve of his final battle, the Chinese general, Hsiang Yü, valiant warrior though he was, grieved deeply about leaving Lady Yü, and that (in our own country) Kiso Yoshinaka lamented his parting from Lady Matsudono. I have now abandoned all hope about our future together in this world, and, mindful of their example, I have resolved to take the ultimate step while you are still alive. I shall be waiting for you at the end of what they call the road to death.

I pray that you may never, never forget the great bounty, deep as the ocean, high as the mountains, that has been bestowed upon us for so many years by our lord, Prince Hideyori.

SULLIVAN BALLOU
LETTER TO SARAH BALLOU, 1861

Written from Camp Clark in Washington, DC, before the First Battle of Bull Run, this is one of the most famous letters of the Civil War. It is remarkable less for its sentiment, which has been expressed by countless husbands in countless wars, than for its extraordinarily poetic language (beautifully intoned by the actor Paul Roebling in Ken Burns's popular Civil War documentary; later set to music by Livingston Taylor). A lawyer and onetime member of the Rhode Island House of Representatives, Major Sullivan Ballou (1829–1861) had only been in the Union army for four weeks when he wrote this letter; he died twelve days later. Sarah, with whom he had two sons, died a widow at the age of eighty.

Several slightly different versions of the letter exist because many hand copies were made of the original, long since lost. Ballou had written another letter, earlier in the day, to Sarah, and wrote two more before the battle; those three were informative and chatty, with none of the foreboding in this, the famous one.

My dear Sarah,

The indications are very strong that we shall move in a few days—perhaps tomorrow. Lest I should not be able to write again, I feel impelled to write a few lines which will fall under your eye when I shall be no more. Our movement may be one of a few days duration and full of pleasure—and it may be one of severe conflict and death to me. Not my will but thine O God, be done. If it is necessary that I should fall on the battlefield for my country, I am ready. I have no misgivings about, or lack of confidence in the cause in which I am engaged, and my courage does not halt or falter. I know how strongly American Civilization now leans on the triumph of the Government and how great a debt we owe to those who went before us through the blood and sufferings of the Revolution. And I am willing—perfectly willing—to lay down all my joys in this life, to help maintain this Government and to pay that debt. But, my dear wife, when I know that with my own joys I lay down nearly all of yours, and replace them in this life with cares and sorrows—when, after having eaten for long years the bitter fruits of orphanage myself, I must offer it as their only sustenance to my dear little children—is it weak or dishonorable, while the banner of my purpose floats calmly and proudly in the breeze, that my unbounded love for you, my darling wife and children, should struggle in fierce, though useless, contest with my love of country?

I cannot describe to you my feelings on this calm summer night, when two thousand men are sleeping around me, many of them enjoying the last, perhaps, before that of death—and I, suspicious that Death is creeping behind me with his fatal dart, am communing with God, my country and thee.

E

I have sought most closely and diligently, and often in my breast, for a wrong motive in thus hazarding the happiness of those I loved and I could not find one. A pure love of country and of the principles I have often advocated before the people and "the name of honor that I love more than I fear Death" have called upon me and I have obeyed.

Sarah, my love for you is deathless, it seems to bind me with mighty cables that nothing but Omnipotence could break. And yet my love of Country comes over me like a strong wind and bears me irresistibly on with all those chains, to the battlefield.

The memories of all the blissful moments I have enjoyed with you come creeping over me, and I feel most grateful to God and you that I have enjoyed them for so long. And how hard it is for me to give them up and burn to ashes the hopes of the future years, when, God willing, we might still have lived and loved together and see our sons grown up to honorable manhood around us. I have, I know, but few and small claims upon Divine Providence, but something whispers to me—perhaps it is the wafted prayer of my little Edgar—that I shall return to my loved ones unharmed. If I do not, my dear Sarah, never forget how much I love you, and as my last breath escapes me on the battlefield, it will whisper your name. Forgive my many faults, and the many pains I have caused you. How thoughtless, how foolish I have often times been! How gladly I would wash out with my tears every little spot upon your happiness and struggle with all the misfortunes of this world to shield you, and your children from harm. But I cannot. I must watch you from the Spirit-land and hover near you, while you buffit the storm, with your precious little freight, and wait with sad patience, till we meet to part no more.

But O Sarah! if the dead can come back to this earth and flit unseen around those they loved, I shall always be near you—in the garish days and the darkest nights . . . amidst your happiest scenes and gloomiest hours—always, always, and if there be a soft breeze upon your cheek, it shall be my breath, or if the cool air fans your throbbing temple, it shall be my spirit passing by. Sarah, do not mourn me dead—think I am gone and wait for thee—for we shall meet again.

As for my little boys, they will grow as I have done, and never know a father's love and care. Little Willie is too young to remember me long, and my blue eyed Edgar will keep my frolics with him among the dimmest memories of his childhood. Sarah, I have unlimited confidence in your maternal care and your development of their characters, and feel that God will bless you in your holy work. Tell my two mothers, his and hers, I call God's blessing upon them. O Sarah, I wait for you there! Come to me, and lead thither my children.

Sullivan

MARK TWAIN
NOTEBOOK, 1904

Samuel Clemens (see Adam and Eve, page 3; Lasting, page 251) married Olivia Langdon in 1870. Through his literary successes, his financial peaks and valleys, the death of two children, and Livy's own illnesses, he remained devoted. When she died of heart failure in Florence, he wrote to a friend: "I am tired & old; I wish I were with Livy." He made these entries in his note-book as he prepared for and took the journey home.

The Clemenses' son, Langdon, had died in infancy; their three daughters were Clara, Susy (who died at twenty-four), and Jane, known as Jean. Ugo was the butler. The green tin box to which Clemens refers held some love letters, as well as a book he had used in his courtship of Livy. The other tin boxes were presumably receptacles for other keepsakes: 1870 was the year of the Clemenses' marriage, 1896 the year of Susy's death.

June 5. At a quarter past nine this evening, she that was the life of my life, passed to the relief of heavenly peace of death, after 22 months of unjust and unearned suffering. I first saw her near 37 years ago, and now I have looked upon her face for the last time. Oh, so unexpected!

June 6. At 12:20 P.M. I looked for the last time upon that dear face—and I was full of remorse for things done and said in the 34 years of married life that hurt Livy's heart.

June 7. . . . Fifty-four lamenting cablegrams have arrived—from America, England, France, Austria, Germany, Australia. Soon the letters will follow. Livy was beloved everywhere.

June 18. I got up in a chair in my room on the second floor and lost my balance and almost fell out. I don't know what saved me. The fall would have killed me; in my bereaved circumstances the world would have been sure it was suicide.

June 21. Left the villa. All arrived with the baggage at the Hôtel de la Ville. First day of the sad journey home.

June 26. When we were ready to leave the hotel at noon Jean was not well enough. We canceled all arrangements. Wait over till tomorrow at 1:20 P.M.

Our ship is the Prince Oscar. Our dear casket went on board at Genoa, yesterday.

June 27. Came down to Naples. Hôtel du Vesuve, good. The green tin box (1870) then the two black tin boxes (1896) all three now succeeded by the plain tin box (June 1904). After a little who will care for these so hallowed treasures?

How all values have shrunken.

June 29. Sailed last night, at ten. The bugle called to breakfast. I recognized the notes, and was distressed. When I heard them last Livy heard them with me; now they fall upon her ears unheeded.

This ship is the Prince Oscar, Hamburg American.

June 30. Clara keeps her bed and cannot bear to see any strangers.

The weather is beautiful, the sea is smooth and curiously blue.

In my life there have been 68 Junes—but how vague and colorless 67 of them are contrasted with the deep blackness of this one.

July 1. I cannot reproduce Livy's face in my mind's eye—I was never in my life able to reproduce a face. It is a curious infirmity—and now at last I realize that it is a calamity.

July 2. In these 34 years we have made many voyages together, Livy dear, and now we are making our last. You down below and lonely, I above with the crowd and lonely.

A MINER'S WIFE
LETTER, 1914

This anonymous letter was written after a mining accident in Whitehaven, England.

God took my man but I could never forget him he was the best man that ever lived at least I thought that, maybe it was just that I got the right kind of man. We had been married for 25 years and they were hard years at that, many a thing we both done without for the sake of the children. We had 11 and if I had him back I would live the same life over again. Just when we were beginning to stand on our feet I lost him I can't get over it when I think of him how happy he was that morning going to work and telling me he would hurry home, but I have been waiting a long time now. At night when I am sitting and I hear clogs coming down the street I just sit and wait hoping they are coming to my door, then they go right on and my heart is broke.

ERNEST COWPER
LETTER TO ELBERT HUBBARD II, 1916

Elbert Hubbard was extremely well known in his day as an author, advertising pioneer, editor, publisher, and a leader of the Arts and Crafts movement. After the sinking of the *Titanic*, he elegized a couple who had insisted on staying together as the ship sank ("You knew how to do three great things—you knew how to live, how to love and how to die"). Strangely, he and his second wife, Alice (see Friendship, pages 137–38), were on board the *Lusitania* when it was torpedoed by a German submarine just three years later. This was the description of their final moments, written to one of their children by a survivor, Toronto newsman Ernest Sedgwick Cowper (1883–1939).

Hubbard called Ernest "Jack" for *Jack Canuck*, the name of the newspaper for which he was working. During the sinking of the *Lusitania*, which took just twenty minutes, 1,196 of the ship's 1,960 passengers drowned.

I can not say specifically where your father and Mrs. Hubbard were when the torpedoes hit, but I can tell you just what happened after that. They emerged from their room, which was on the port side of the vessel, and came on to the boat-deck.

Neither appeared perturbed in the least. Your father and Mrs. Hubbard linked arms—the fashion in which they always walked the deck—and stood apparently wondering what to do. I passed him with a baby which I was taking to a lifeboat when he said, "Well, Jack, they have got us. They are a damn sight worse than I ever thought they were."

They did not move very far away from where they originally stood. As I moved to the other side of the ship, in preparation for a jump when the right moment came, I called to him, "What are you going to do?" and he just shook his head, while Mrs. Hubbard smiled and said, "There does not seem to be anything to do."

The expression seemed to produce action on the part of your father, for then he did one of the most dramatic things I ever saw done. He simply turned with Mrs. Hubbard and entered a room on the top deck, the door of which was open, and closed it behind him.

It was apparent that his idea was that they should die together, and not risk being parted on going into the water.

The blow to yourself and your sister must have been terrible, and yet, had you seen what I have seen, you would be greatly consoled, for never in history, I am sure, did two people look the Reaper so squarely in the eye at his approach as did your father and Mrs. Hubbard.

It was there that the philosopher shone.

Both showed that they had not been talking for talk's sake, or writing because it presented itself as a means of securing a livelihood. Both were philosophers, and both showed that they were each other's most apt pupils.

I don't believe that the prospect at that moment troubled them any more than it would have done had the call been to go to lunch instead of to tread the Valley of the Long Shadow.

If he wrote his philosophy, he certainly lived it to the last moment. He was a big man in life, but to my mind he is a vastly bigger man in death.

I suppose you have asked yourself the question; "Was it possible for them to have been saved? Did they really do all that could be done?" To this I would say they could do nothing more than was done, especially if they wanted to remain together, and apparently there was no intention on either side of separating.

HOWARD NEMEROV
"THE COMMON WISDOM," 1975

For his *Collected Poems*, in which this short verse appeared, Howard Nemerov (1920–1991) won the Pulitzer Prize, the National Book Award, and the Bollingen Prize.

Their marriage is a good one. In our eyes
What makes a marriage *good?* Well, that the tether
Fray but not break, and that they stay together.
One should be watching while the other dies.

EXPECTATIONS

SYDNEY OWENSON, LADY MORGAN
LETTER TO ALICIA LE FANU, 1812

Either because they don't want to tempt fate, or boast, or take the time, married people tend to comment less often upon expectations that have been met (or exceeded) than on those that haven't been. Of course, this phenomenon might also be explained by the possibility that marriage is simply more often disappointing than not. But in her somewhat gloating letter to her friend Alicia Le Fanu, the Irish author Sydney Owenson, Lady Morgan (circa 1776–1859), seemed to offer proof to the contrary.

Lady Morgan had made her first literary mark with her novel *The Wild Irish Girl* and was well established in society circles when she married the British doctor and essayist Sir Thomas Charles Morgan. Alicia Le Fanu was a novelist and playwright. Lord and Lady Abercorn were prominent British nobility who were hosting the newlyweds at their Irish castle. Argand lamps were the household oil lamps of the day. Glorvina was the fiery heroine of *The Wild Irish Girl*. Prunella was a kind of wool used in women's shoes, hence *leather and prunella* meant "nothing of consequence."

It is quite clear, that like all heroines, I no longer interest when I gain a husband.

Since you will not even ask me how I am, I will volunteer the information of my being as happy as being "loved up to my bent" (aye, and almost beyond it) can make me, and, indeed, so much is it true, "the same to-day, to-morrow, and for ever," that I can give you no other notice of my existence than that miraculous one of a man being desperately in love with his own wife, and she "nothing loath."

Though living in a palace, we have all the comfort and independence of home; besides bed-rooms and dressing-rooms, Morgan's study has been fitted up with all the luxury of a *joli boudoir* by Lady Abercorn (who neither spared her taste nor purse on the occasion). It is stored with books, music, and everything that can contribute to our use and amusement. Here "the world forgotten, and by the world forgot," we live all day, and do not join the family till dinner time, and as *chacun a son goût* is the order here, when we are weary of argand lamps and a gallery a hundred feet long in the evening—we retire to our own snuggery, where, very often, some of the others come to drink coffee with us. As to me, I am *every inch a wife,* and so ends that brilliant thing that was GLORVINA.

N. B.—I intend to write a book to explode the vulgar idea of matrimony being the tomb of love. Matrimony is the real thing and all before but "leather and prunella."

JOHANN WOLFGANG VON GOETHE, 1823

German author Johann Wolfgang von Goethe (1749–1832) was seventy-three when, according to his friend the German statesman Friedrich von Müller, he said what follows.

Love is something ideal, marriage is something real; and never with impunity do we exchange the ideal for the real.

CURRIER & IVES
THE DAY BEFORE MARRIAGE, 1847

"WHAT DO YOUNG MEN MARRY?," 1854

This anonymously written article was reprinted many times; the earliest version we've found appeared in the British weekly *Eliza Cook's Journal*.

Court plaister was an adhesive plaster used to cover small cuts. Empress Eugénie of France (married to Napoleon III) was a fashion icon of the day.

Some young men marry dimples, some ears; one I know married a beauty-spot made of court-plaister, while a second cousin of my wife's married an expression,—I believe an amiable expression.

It is difficult in the absence of any accurate statistics on the subject, to say, decidedly, which feature is most frequently sought in marriage. The rosiest, however, certainly lies between the eyes and the hair. The mouth, too, is occasionally married; the chin not so often.

Poor partners these, you will own, but what will you say to Will Carson, who actually married a blue ribbon—neither more nor less? It was employed to bind up some bonny brown hair. Will liked it, and, scorning all those antiquated saws which tell us that "Like blood, like good, and like ages, make the happiest marriages," and the counsel of a friend who advised him to seek a more suitable match, he clung honourably and firmly to the humble object of his affection, and married his bunch of blue ribbons.

Only the other day, a very sensible young fellow of my acquaintance fell over head and ears in love with a braid—*braid*, I believe, young ladies style that mass of hair that, descending from the forehead, forms a sort of mouse's nest over the ear. He was so far gone in his infatuation, that he became engaged to this braid, but the Eugénie mode of hair-dressing coming in just then, the charm was dissolved, and the match was happily broken off, and there is no present appearance of its being renewed.

What do young men marry? Why they marry all these, and many other bits and scraps of a *wife,* instead of the true thing. Some, more sagacious than the ordinary run, are not content with an eye, or a lip, but marry a set of teeth, a head of hair, and a neat foot and ankle, all at once. Some marry a fortune, and as Providence sends a female with it, they wed her too. Some marry a silk dress, and others a pretty bonnet, and yet others a pair of gloves. One youth was so fond of cards, that meeting with a girl whose mother was a good hand at whist, he married the lass, and so may be said to have married his mother-in-law.

So young men marry, and so they settle; and such as the marriage is, such is the after-life; and then, after wedding such features, or possessions, or attributes, or what not of females, they are surprised to find that, though married, they have no *wives*. He that would have a *wife* must marry a *woman.* If he can meet with one of equal social position, like education, similar disposition, kindred sympathies, and habits congenial to his own, let him marry. But let him beware of wedding an instep, of marrying a bust, however fair, or a neck, however swan-like, or a voice, however melodious.

EDWARD WHITTY
KNAVES AND FOOLS, 1857

Edward Whitty (1827–1860) was a British journalist and satirist. *Knaves and Fools: A Satirical Novel of London Life* took on the ruling class in fictional form.

Life is a desert. Profound thought! Marriage and mirage are the same thing, differently spelt. But does it do the caravan any harm to believe in water? When you are thirsty, the next best thing to having water, is to believe that you are going to have it. Live the mirage! Live marriage!

Marriage and mirage are the same thing, differently spelt.

HARRIET BEECHER STOWE
PINK AND WHITE TYRANNY, 1871

Harriet Beecher Stowe (1811–1896) published this work of fiction (subtitled "A Society Novel") roughly two decades after making her name—and possibly changing the course of U.S. history—with her antislavery novel *Uncle Tom's Cabin. Pink and White Tyranny* was comparatively light in subject matter, but through its main character—a girl who marries mainly for money—Stowe questioned the roles and expectations that society placed upon young women of the day.

The love that quickens all the nature, that makes a man twice manly, and makes him aspire to all that is high, pure, sweet, and religious,—is a feeling so sacred, that no unworthiness in its object can make it any less beautiful. More often than not it is spent on an utter vacancy. Men and women both pass through this divine initiation,—this sacred inspiration of our nature,—and find, when they have come into the innermost shrine, where the divinity ought to be, that there is no god or goddess there; nothing but the cold black ashes of commonplace vulgarity and selfishness. Both of them, when the grand discovery has been made, do well to fold their robes decently about them, and make the best of the matter. If they cannot love, they can at least be friendly. They can tolerate, as philosophers; pity, as Christians; and, finding just where and how the burden of an ill-assorted union galls the least, can then and there strap it on their backs, and walk on, not only without complaint, but sometimes in a cheerful and hilarious spirit.

GEORGE ELIOT
MIDDLEMARCH, 1874

She wanted her writing to be taken seriously, so Mary Ann Evans (1819–1880) adopted the pen name George Eliot. Under that pseudonym, she produced seven engaging realist novels and became one of the best-known authors of Victorian England. *Middlemarch*, which appeared in serial form starting in 1871, combines intricate plots and subplots, contemporaneous references, and meditations on society, politics, class, gender, and, memorably, marriage.

The fact is unalterable, that a fellow-mortal with whose nature you are acquainted solely through the brief entrances and exits of a few imaginative weeks called courtship, may, when seen in the continuity of married companionship, be disclosed as something better or worse than what you have preconceived. . . .

. . . How was it that in the weeks since her marriage, Dorothea had not distinctly observed but felt with a stifling depression, that the large vistas and wide fresh air which she had dreamed of finding in her husband's mind were replaced by ante-rooms and winding passages which seemed to lead nowhither? I suppose it was that in courtship everything is regarded as provisional and preliminary, and the smallest sample of virtue or accomplishment is taken to guarantee delightful stores which the broad leisure of marriage will reveal. But the door-sill of marriage once crossed, expectation is concentrated on the present. Having once embarked on your marital voyage, it is impossible not to be aware that you make no way and that the sea is not within sight—that, in fact, you are exploring an enclosed basin.

T. L. HAINES AND L. W. YAGGY
THE ROYAL PATH OF LIFE, 1881

Thomas Louis Haines (1844–?), was in the school supplies business and had served in the Michigan infantry during the Civil War. Living outside Chicago, he collaborated on several books with a neighbor, Levi W. Yaggy (1848–?), about whom we've been able to discover only that he was a Presbyterian church elder and that at one point he filed a patent for a portfolio that could carry anatomical charts.

Marriage is, to a woman, at once the happiest and saddest event of her life; it is the promise of future bliss, raised on the death of all present enjoyment. She quits her home, her parents, her companions, her occupations, her amusements—her everything upon which she has hitherto depended for comfort—for affection, for kindness, for pleasure. The parents by whose advice she has been guided, the sister to whom she has dared impart every embryo thought and feeling, the brother who has played with her, in turns the counselor and the counseled, and the younger children to whom she has hitherto been the mother and the playmate—all are to be forsaken in one instant; every former tie is loosened, the spring of every hope and action to be changed, and yet she flies with joy into the untrodden paths before her. Buoyed up by the confidence of requited love, she bids a fond and grateful adieu to the life that is past, and turns with excited hopes and joyous anticipations of the happiness to come. Then woe to the man who can blast such hopes—who can, coward-like, break the illusions that have won her, and destroy the confidence which his love inspired.

E very former tie is loosened, and yet
she flies with joy into the
untrodden paths before her.

E

BAMFORTH POSTCARD, EARLY 1900s

The British Bamforth Company became famous for its comic postcards, which poked fun at all sorts of twentieth-century fashions and institutions—marriage being high on the list.

H. L. MENCKEN
A BOOK OF BURLESQUES, 1916

For more Mencken, see Adam and Eve, page 3; Jealousy, page 240.

Strike an average between what a woman thinks of her husband a month before she marries him and what she thinks of him a year afterward, and you will have the truth about him in a very handy form.

GERMAINE GREER
THE FEMALE EUNUCH, 1970

Like Simone de Beauvoir with *The Second Sex* (see Work, page 495) and Betty Friedan with *The Feminine Mystique* (see Freedom, page 135), Australian author Germaine Greer (1939–) made a profound contribution to the late twentieth century's women's movement. In *The Female Eunuch*, Greer described the title figure as a woman who had essentially been stripped of her sexual awareness and societal power, and Greer blamed both sexes for preventing women from identifying their own goals. For modern women, Greer sought not just equality with men, but liberation from male definitions. The book was an international bestseller, a source of fervent debate, and a meditation on what Greer deemed the "myth" that the true adventure of a woman's life should be the pursuit and capture of a perfect husband.

The myth has always depended upon the riches, the handsomeness, the loveliness, the considerateness of a man in a million. There are enough women prepared to boast of having got a man in a million to persuade other women that their failure to find a man rich enough, handsome enough, skilled enough as a lover, considerate enough, is a reflection of their inferior deserts or powers of attraction. More than half the housewives in this country work outside the home as well as inside it because their husbands do not earn enough money to support them and their children at a decent living standard. Still more know that their husbands are paunchy, short, unathletic, and snore or smell or leave their clothes lying around. A very high proportion do not find bliss in the conjugal embrace and most complain that their husbands forget the little things that count. And yet the myth is not invalidated as a myth. There is always an extenuating circumstance, the government, high taxation, or sedentary work, or illness, or perhaps a simple mistake or a failure in the individual case, which can be invoked to explain its divergence from the mythical norm. Most women who have followed in the direction indicated by the myth make an act of faith that despite day-to-day difficulties they are happy, and keep on asserting it in the face of blatant contradiction by the facts, because to confess disappointment is to admit failure and abandon the effort. It never occurs to them to seek the cause of their unhappiness in the myth itself.

NENA O'NEILL AND GEORGE O'NEILL
OPEN MARRIAGE: A NEW LIFE STYLE FOR COUPLES, 1972

Open Marriage was a huge hit in the early seventies, with married authors Nena (1923–2006) and George O'Neill (1921–1980) advocating more communicative and flexible relationships, and room for individual experiences and growth. In passing—actually in just a few pages—they suggested that these experiences might even include sexual ones (see Sex, page 407), and the book became somewhat notorious for that. In its main message, however, it was far less inflammatory, and on the way to propounding a more dynamic state for relationships, the couple presented the following list, noting: "Every single one of these ideals, beliefs or expectations is false in one way or another, and practically impossible to attain, much less to sustain."

Unrealistic expectations, unreasonable ideals, and mythological beliefs of closed marriage.

- that it will last forever
- that it means total commitment
- that it will bring happiness, comfort and security
- that your mate *belongs* to you
- that you will have constant attention, concern, admiration and consideration from your mate
- that you will never be lonely again
- that your mate would rather be with you than with anyone else at all times
- that your mate will never be attracted to another person and will always "be true" to you
- that jealousy means you care
- that fidelity is a true measure of the love you have for one another
- that sex will improve with time if it isn't already the world-shaking experience it is supposed to be
- that good sex will in fact (if you can just get the positions right and learn the proper techniques) solve all your problems in marriage
- that all problems in marriage revolve around sex and love
- that you are not complete persons without becoming parents
- that the ultimate goal of marriage is having a child
- that having a child is the ultimate expression of your love for each other
- that having a child will bring new vitality to a sagging marriage or rescue a failing one

- that you will adjust to one another gradually without fights, arguments or misunderstandings
- that you don't love each other if there is conflict between you
- that any change in your mate will come gradually with the maturity of age
- that any other kind of change is disruptive and means loss of love
- that each of you plays a different part in marriage, a role for which you were biologically designed
- that you therefore have the right to expect one thing of a husband and another of a wife
- that sacrifice is a true measure of love
- and last, but most important, that the person you marry can fulfill all your needs, economic, physical, sexual, intellectual and emotional

---

HAYLEY NAVEY
"THE 5 BEST THINGS ABOUT BEING MARRIED," 2013

Hayley Navey was nineteen when she became pregnant and got engaged to a boyfriend she had first met in high school. In addition to blogging on *A Beautiful Exchange* about young motherhood, inspiration, faith, and daily life in Greensboro, North Carolina, she occasionally offered observations about marriage—including its unexpected joys.
The ellipses are the author's.

In case you haven't gathered from everything on this little blog, I really like being married. I hope that if you are married, you love it too and can understand where I'm coming from.

SEX

Is my mind in the gutter? Maybe. Either way, you married folk know I'm right. Having experienced this in the context that God designed, as well as outside of that context, I can say with full confidence that it is one of the greatest gifts He gives to married couples. It is a great act of service to your husband, along with all of the great emotional parts of being intimate. Sorry if it is still awkward to talk about S-E-X. Oh well.

COMING HOME

It's so nice to know that I will never go to bed alone. I am such a cuddly person and love that I have my amazing husband to curl up with after a long day. Call me a scaredy cat, but I can't sleep until he is home. I think he secretly has that same problem. Shhh!

DOING LIFE

Obviously, this is one of the main reasons you get married. I love my husband and love that we get to experience pretty much everything as a *team*. With each memory, he sees things differently. It's so nice when we talk about past times and I can throw out what I loved about it, then hear his perspective. I just love the conversations that begin with "Remember that time . . ."

GROWING

I hope that you have the privilege of being married to someone that makes you want to be a better person. From the very beginning, my husband has encouraged me to do more and be more. He is constantly guiding me and helping me along (even when I don't ask for it . . .). I can honestly say that I am a better person in Christ because of my husband being in my life. In the end, that's really all that it's about, right? Both of us getting closer to each other by getting closer to Him.

MY SHOULDER

When I've had a bad day or something has just really gotten under my skin, I know I can always go to my husband with it. Sometimes he will remind me that I shouldn't let things bother me so much. Sometimes he gets upset too and agrees with me. Sometimes he just quietly listens and recognizes that I just need someone to spill the beans to. He's the best best friend ever because I *know* that he is **never** going anywhere. I love that my heart is not as full on days that we don't see each other very much. It makes my day just to tell him about mine and hear about his.

FIDELITY

HOMER
THE ODYSSEY, CIRCA 8TH CENTURY BC

In writing his great saga, Homer (dates unknown) ensured that the name Penelope, wife of Odysseus, would become nearly synonymous with the word *fidelity*. Famously, while he is off fighting the Trojan War (and having literally epic troubles returning from it), she keeps a band of suitors at bay by saying she cannot consider marrying anyone until she has finished weaving her father-in-law's burial shroud. In the following passage, one of her suitors explains how she manages to draw that task out.

For three years now—and it will soon be four—
she has been breaking the hearts of the Akhaians,
holding out hope to all, and sending promises
to each man privately—but thinking otherwise.

Here is an instance of her trickery:
she had her great loom standing in the hall
and the fine warp of some vast fabric on it;

we were attending her, and she said to us:
"Young men, my suitors, now my lord is dead,
let me finish my weaving before I marry,
or else my thread will have been spun in vain.
It is a shroud I weave for Lord Laërtês,
when cold death comes to lay him on his bier.
The country wives would hold me in dishonor
if he, with all his fortune, lay unshrouded."
We have men's hearts; she touched them; we agreed.
So every day she wove on the great loom—
but every night by torchlight she unwove it;
and so for three years she deceived the Akhaians.

JOHN DRYDEN
"WHY SHOULD A FOOLISH MARRIAGE VOW," 1673

British poet laureate John Dryden (1631–1700), who married Lady Elizabeth Howard in 1663 and had three sons with her, wrote this as a song for his comedy *Marriage à la Mode*.

I.

Why should a foolish marriage vow,
Which long ago was made,
Oblige us to each other now,
When passion is decay'd?
We loved and lov'd, as long as we could,
'Till our love was lov'd out of us both;
But our marriage is dead,
When the pleasure is fled:
'Twas pleasure first made it an oath.

II.

If I have pleasure for a friend,
And further love in store,
What wrong has he, whose joys did end,

And who could give no more?
'Tis a madness that he should be jealous of me,
Or that I should bar him of another:
For all we can gain
Is to give ourselves pain,
When neither can hinder the other.

Can one always desire one's wife?

HONORÉ DE BALZAC
THE PHYSIOLOGY OF MARRIAGE, 1829

Between his novels, short stories, and essays, Honoré de Balzac (1799–1850) had a seemingly limitless number of observations to offer about marriage. The following is the first of several entries in this anthology (see Honeymoon, page 172; Power, pages 338–39; and Sex, page 401) from the famed French master who, at the outset of writing the ninety or so novels and short stories that comprised *La Comédie Humaine,* produced several lengthy meditations on marriage.

Love is the union of desire and tenderness, and happiness in marriage comes from a perfect understanding between two souls. And from this it follows that to be happy a man is obliged to bind himself by certain rules of honour and delicacy. After having enjoyed the privilege of the social laws which consecrate desire, he should obey the secret laws of nature which bring to birth the affections. If his happiness depends on being loved, he himself must love sincerely; nothing can withstand true passion.

But to be passionate is always to desire.

Can one always desire one's wife?

Yes.

It is as absurd to pretend that it is impossible always to love the same woman as to say that a famous artist needs several violins to play a piece of music and create an enchanting melody.

D. H. LAWRENCE
LADY CHATTERLEY'S LOVER, 1928

First published in Italy, *Lady Chatterley's Lover* wasn't available in England until 1932 and not printed in full until its 1959 U.S. edition. The novel, one of thirteen written by British author D. H. Lawrence (1885–1930), became infamous for its sexual explicitness. For Lawrence, fame remained after infamy subsided, one of the reasons being the complex portraits he drew of his characters' inner lives. In the scene below, Connie Chatterley's husband, the paralyzed and impotent Clifford, has just asked her to consider continuing a semblance of his aristocratic line by having a child with another man. At this moment, Connie is already having an affair with a writer named Michaelis.

The ellipses are the author's.

"Does it matter very much? Do these things really affect us very deeply . . . You had that lover in Germany . . . what is it now? Nothing almost. It seems to me that it isn't these little acts and little connections we make in our lives that matter so very much. They pass away, and where are they? Where . . . Where are the snows of yesteryear? . . . It's what endures through one's life that matters; my own life matters to me, in its long continuance and development. But what do the occasional connections matter? And the occasional sexual connections specially. If people don't exaggerate them ridiculously, they pass like the mating of birds. And so they should. What does it matter? It's the life-long companionship that matters. It's the living together from day to day, not the sleeping together once or twice. You and I are married, no matter what happens to us. We have the habit of each other. And habit, to my thinking, is more vital than any occasional excitement. The long, slow, enduring thing . . . that's what we live by . . . not the occasional spasm of any sort. Little by little, living together, two people fall into a sort of unison, they vibrate so intricately to one another. That's the real secret of marriage, not sex; at least not the simple function of sex. You and I are interwoven in a marriage. If we stick to that we ought to be able to arrange this sex thing, as we arrange going to the dentist; since fate has given us a checkmate physically there."

Connie sat and listened in a sort of wonder, and a sort of fear. She did not know if he was right or not. There was Michaelis, whom she loved; so she said to herself. But her love was somehow only an excursion from her marriage with Clifford; the long, slow habit of intimacy, formed through years of suffering and patience. Perhaps the human soul needs excursions, and must not be denied them. But the point of an excursion is that you come home again.

PAUL NEWMAN
PLAYBOY INTERVIEW, 1968

Paul Newman (1925–2008) was famous first as an actor (*The Hustler*, *The Sting*, *The Verdict*, and ten Academy Award nominations), then as a philanthropist (donating an estimated $250 million from sales of his Newman's Own food line). But he was also renowned for his marriage to actress Joanne Woodward, which lasted—despite their Hollywood roots—an exceptional fifty years.

In 1979, actor Roddy McDowall photographed Woodward for a book of portraits; during the session, Woodward said: "Someone once asked me what it was like to be married to the sexiest, most beautiful man in the world. I thought a minute and replied, 'Sexiness wears thin after a while and beauty fades, but to be married to a man who makes you laugh every day, ah, now that's a real treat!'" Just a decade into their marriage, this is what Newman said about Woodward.

PLAYBOY: To have remained married to the same woman for ten years is unusual enough in your profession, but to do so without rumors or gossip-column items even hinting at an extramarital affair in all that time is almost unique. How have you managed to resist the temptations?

NEWMAN: I know this is going to sound corny, but there's no reason to roam. I have steak at home; why should I go out for a hamburger?

RONALD REAGAN
LETTER TO MICHAEL REAGAN, 1971

A few days before Michael Reagan's wedding to Pamela Putnam, the future United States president wrote this letter to the son he had adopted with his first wife, Jane Wyman. The advice notwithstanding, Michael's marriage lasted only a year. His second marriage, to Colleen Sterns, endured.

Dear Mike:

You've heard all the jokes that have been rousted around by all the "unhappy marrieds" and cynics. Now, in case no one has suggested it, there is another viewpoint. You have entered into the most meaningful relationship there is in all human life. It can be whatever you decide to make it.

Some men feel their masculinity can only be proven if they play out in their own life all the locker-room stories, smugly confident that what a wife doesn't know won't hurt her. The truth is, somehow, way down inside, without her ever finding lipstick on the collar or catching a man in the flimsy excuse of where he was till three A.M., a wife does know, and with that knowing, some of the magic of this relationship disappears. There are more men griping about marriage who kicked the whole thing away themselves than there can ever be wives deserving of blame. There is an old law of physics that you can only get out of a thing as much as you put in it. The man who puts into the marriage only half of what he owns will get that out. Sure, there will be moments when you will see someone or think back on an earlier time and you will be challenged to see if you can still make the grade, but let me tell you how really great is the challenge of proving your masculinity and charm with one woman for the rest of your life. Any man can find a twerp here and there who will go along with cheating, and it doesn't take all

---

It does take quite a man to remain attractive to a woman who has heard him snore, seen him unshaven, and tended him while he was sick. Do that and you will know some very beautiful music.

---

that much manhood. It does take quite a man to remain attractive and to be loved by a woman who has heard him snore, seen him unshaven, tended him while he was sick, and washed his dirty underwear. Do that and keep her still feeling a warm glow and you will know some very beautiful music. If you truly love a girl, you shouldn't ever want her to feel, when she sees you greet a secretary or a girl you both know, that humiliation of wondering if she was someone who caused you to be late coming home, nor should you want any other woman to be able to meet your wife and know she was smiling behind her eyes as she looked at her, the woman you love, remembering this was the woman you rejected even momentarily for her favors.

Mike, you know better than many what an unhappy home is and what it can do to others. Now you have a chance to make it come out the way it should. There is no greater happiness for a man than approaching a door at the end of a day knowing someone on the other side of that door is waiting for the sound of his footsteps.

Love,

Dad

P.S. You'll never get in trouble if you say "I love you" at least once a day.

FRANK MULA
"THE LAST TEMPTATION OF HOMER," *THE SIMPSONS*, 1993

Despite his numerous shortcomings, Homer Simpson, the creation of cartoonist Matt Groening, manages to stay faithful to his wife, Marge. In the animated television series—the longest-running ever—Homer's greatest temptation comes in the shapely form of coworker Mindy Simmons. When the two attend a convention at the Capital City Plaza Hotel ("Legionnaires' Disease–Free since 1990"), they are shown their rooms by a bellhop.

BELLHOP: TV's there—bathroom's there—and there's your king-size bed for— *(Wolf-whistles, makes a cat noise, imitates a bed squeaking, purrs, pants, barks, howls, twiddles his lips.)* Hubba hubba!

HOMER: Stop that! I love my wife and family. All I'm gonna use this bed for is sleeping, eating, and maybe building a little fort.

MICHELLE OBAMA
EBONY INTERVIEW, 2006

Future U.S. president Barack Obama was still a freshman senator, and future first lady Michelle Obama (1964–) was still a hospital executive when she offered this comment in an interview titled "Not Just the Senator's Wife."

[I'm not worried about] some other woman pushing up on my husband. I never worry about things I can't affect, and with fidelity—that is between Barack and me, and if somebody can come between us, we didn't have much to begin with.

BLOGGERS
"IS FACEBOOK A CYBER THREAT TO YOUR MARRIAGE?," 2010

Full Marriage Experience is a blog written by Jason and Kelli Krafsky with an upbeat Christian perspective. In 2009, the couple posted advice about how to avoid some of the real-life marital threats that Facebook relationships were creating. The post was widely circulated, and these were some of the comments that later appeared in response to it.

In 2012, according to a British survey of divorce lawyers, the word *Facebook* had been mentioned in a third of the divorce cases filed the previous year. The ellipses are the author's.

ROSE: My husband and I have been married for 36 years. One year ago he was contacted by an old friend and neighbor on facebook. They became "friends" and started chatting. At first I was not concerned as she lives in New Zealand and we live in S. Africa. I soon became concerned at the time my husband spent chatting to her, supposedly about "old times." I picked up photos/cards and messages they sent to each other and approached him kindly saying it was hurting me and felt that he was becoming far too familiar for my liking. She was in a unhappy marriage and enjoyed his flattery and sweet talk. Then the sms's began followed by a daily phone call. Then the e-mails to and from his work address started. I was devastated. To cut a long story short we separated as a result. He was away from home for 5 months and during this time they became even more acquainted. After 5 months he came home and promised me it was all over and he was home for good. I later discovered that she had flown out to S. Africa and they had spent a three week holiday together. They had also got engaged and planned to get married. Well things went downhill from there and he moved out once again. He has since flown to New Zealand twice to be with her and we are busy with divorce proceedings. My heart is broken and at the moment I hate face book. If boundaries are not put in place and adhered to this will be the result.

MIKE: It's the same story on my end. My wife joined Facebook and was spending an incredible amount of time reconnecting with old friends and reading and sharing posts. Then, she found one of her high school sweethearts from 22 years ago. And yes, they were soon involved in an emotional affair. On May 17, 2010, she informed me that she wanted out of the marriage because she was involved with someone else. I soon discovered who he was and that it started with FB. She moved out and our divorce was final 3 weeks ago today on 10/6.

She walked away from her husband, her children, and her home for this guy. Only to find that after all of his sweet talking and promises, he was not going to leave his wife and kids as they had originally planned. I also contacted his wife and informed her of their infidelity. I was startled when she said . . . "He does this sh*t all the time. He's not going anywhere. It's just play time for him." So, here she is . . . No husband, children that don't want to see her, no home with a real white picket fence that I built for her, and no FB boyfriend (yet). She's lost her good girl reputation not only with my family and friends, but with her own family and friends as well.

18 years together. 13 years married. It just feels as if it was all for nothing.

Ya . . . I hate Facebook and the other social networking sites.

F

FOOD

FINNISH PROVERB

Love is a flower which turns into fruit at marriage.

GEORGE ROUTLEDGE
MANUAL OF ETIQUETTE, 1860

In addition to advice for newlyweds, the popular etiquette book by publisher George Routledge (1812–1888) included subjects as varied as how to organize a ball and how to carve a calf's head.

Not the least useful piece of advice—homely though it be—that we can offer to newly-married ladies, is to remind them that husbands are men, and that men must eat. We can tell them, moreover, that men attach no small importance to this very essential operation, and that a very effectual way to keep them in good-humour, as well as good condition, is for wives to study their husband's peculiar likes and dislikes in this matter. Let the wife try, therefore, if she have not already done so, to get up a little knowledge of the art of *ordering* dinner, to say the least of it. This task, if she be disposed to learn it, will in time be easy enough; moreover, if in addition she should acquire some practical knowledge of cookery, she will find ample reward in the gratification it will be the means of affording her husband.

"MARRIAGE AND COOKERY"
NEW-YORK TRIBUNE, 1890

F

Only one note to offer here: Blancmange is a cold dessert usually made with milk, sugar, and gelatin.

We don't know why it is, but Brooklyn men seem to be always getting into trouble . . .

This Fulton-street man was a widower, but did not appear to know enough to remain in that condition. He lived quietly with his sons and one or two servants. Last fall he hired a cook named Susannah Baumann. She proved to be a remarkably good cook, turning to pork and beans or blanc-mange with equal facility. Her pies were always done on the bottom, and as for her old-fashioned doughnuts, they were twisted poems, complicated as Browning, but palatable as Robert Burns. She was also sunny-tempered and open to conviction, and when her employer suggested another dash of salt in the chicken gravy, she complied with a smile. But did this Brooklyn man appreciate his treasure? Seemingly not—he married her. They were wedded in November. Are good cooks, then, so easy to obtain in Brooklyn? asks the New-Yorker. Not at all—they are no more numerous there than here. This foolish Brooklyn man simply thought that he could marry his cook and have her too.

We do not need to enlarge on what followed—it was the natural result. She no longer broiled the beefsteaks, but fried them over a slow fire. Boiled chicken gave place to something which had apparently been dried in the sun. Mutton chops she burned at the stake. As for pie and other forms of pastry, she refused to make them at all as involving too much labor. Her temper deteriorated and her voice grew harsh and severe. In April she insisted that her husband hire a cook, which he did. Last week the matter culminated. Susannah went away. The Brooklyn man had not, of course, since marrying her, given her any money—women not understanding the proper use of money. But when she went she took all the money that he had in the house ($300) and the jewelry belonging to himself and his sons. She wrote him a letter, which she posted in the iron letter-box on the corner. He got it the next day, and in it she told him that she had decided to endure his impudence no longer. She was going to Germany with a former lover, and in closing she hoped that these few lines would find him enjoying good health and reasonable prosperity. She expressed the hope that his heart would remain true to Susannah. Then she added pathetically, "Write soon," and that was all; and the Brooklyn man went around to the police station and told the whole story substantially as we have given it. For us to offer further comment would be mockery.

BRITISH POSTCARD, CIRCA 1912

BLANCHE EBBUTT
DON'TS FOR WIVES, 1913

British author Blanche Ebbutt wrote several small books of guidelines (see Husbands, How to Keep, pages 190–91; Wives, How to Keep, pages 490–91), some lofty, some very specific. Ebbutt's books were recently reissued and have been popular wedding gifts, but her identity remains a mystery.

Don't despise the domestic potato. There are a hundred appetising ways of cooking it; but unless you take it firmly in hand, it will arrive at table with the consistency of half-melted ice—mushy without, stony within. The boiled potato is the rock on which many a happy home barque has foundered.

RACHEL BELLA CALOF
MY STORY, 1936

Rachel Bella Calof (1876–circa 1952) was a Russian Jewish immigrant homesteader in North Dakota. Bride in an arranged marriage, she raised nine children; survived the harshest extremes of weather; made lamps out of mud, rags, and butter; and, as she remembered in the following passage from her memoir, found resourceful ways to feed her husband in the earliest days of their marriage.

Our water supply was so scant that I decided to find some usable water in some low place on the prairie where the snow melt might run together. I did discover such a place about a mile away. I carried two pailfuls from that place, but when I got back to the shack I saw that the water was full of worms and grass. The water would have to be boiled to be usable. The solution to the problem was not so easy as we had just run out of fuel. There was nothing with which to start a fire. I was determined though, and again went out into the prairie which held many provisions if one only knew where to look. I took with me only a rope and my huge belly.

    About two miles distant I came across a place where new grass was growing through a bed of dried-out grass. The dried grass was plentiful and looked dry enough to burn. I was delighted with my find. My pleasure, though was tempered with a certain dread. I knew little of the wild-life of this country, and I became fearful that I would encounter a snake in the beds of dried grass. I hesitated, but soon my stomach informed me how hungry I was, and the child within me needed food too. My husband labored in the field removing rocks and I knew that he too must be hungry. I needed that boiled water to prepare some kind of a meal and I said to myself, "Don't be a spoiled person. You must risk it. Even if there is a snake there, you must try." I stepped into the area. No snake bit me and soon I was enthusiastically gathering the dried grass. Quickly I gathered a great bundle and tied it into a compact bundle with my rope.

According to the sun it was already midmorning and Abe would be coming in from the field not long after noon. I had to get home quickly but the food left in the shack was only a little flour, some barley, some soured milk, and a little butter. A really daring idea came to me. I decided to spend a little more time looking around the place to see what else it might offer. Promptly, my further exploration brought results. I found what appeared to be wild garlic. . . . I enlarged my search area and before long I came across plants which unquestionably were wild mushrooms. Now I knew that some mushrooms were deadly poisonous. Still I thought that this was a good time to take a chance. I bit into one and held it in my mouth. It didn't burn or taste bad, so I swallowed it. I waited a while for something to happen. Nothing did, and I gathered an apronful of the mushrooms, and with my garlic and the bundle of dried grass on my shoulder, I started for home happy with my accomplishments and eager to see how I could put them to use.

Arriving at the shack, I immediately began my preparations. First I sieved the water through the fabric of a flour sack. I kneaded the dough and put it in the oven. I cleaned the mushrooms and steeped them in hot water. I then chopped up the garlic, put butter (we had our cow back) in the pan, and fried everything together. This meal made in large measure with food gathered from the wild prairie was simply delicious.

I should have mentioned that Abe had begun to dig a cellar in the dirt floor of the shack. . . . I was so excited in preparing this special meal that I nearly fell into the pit as I flew about the place, setting the table and making other preparations. We had no tea or coffee, but I ground up some barley, boiled it in water and so had, at least, a substitute coffee.

My husband would soon be coming through the door. I was so happy, truly in seventh heaven, and very proud. I had used my brains and my nerve and as a result my husband would soon sit down to a fine dinner, just the two of us alone.

Soon Abe arrived. It was evident that we liked one another, because when he came inside where I was, it was easy to see that he was glad to see me and we were happy to be together.

Never was there a more delightful dinner than that one. The food was delectable and our shanty was filled with happiness. After we finished our meal, Abe insisted on knowing all the details of my accomplishment. As he listened, his gladness became tinged with a sadness that our condition was such that I was reduced to searching the prairie for food. But nothing could destroy the magic of that hour. He kissed me and called me his good angel, and my contentment was complete knowing that he appreciated my devotion to him. I served the barley coffee in the cool outdoors and we spent another pleasant hour together before Abe returned to the field. So ended a charming interlude in the harshness of our lives. It was a great moment for us and its memory has been a sustaining treasure to me over the years.

ANNE MORROW LINDBERGH
GIFT FROM THE SEA, 1955

When he made the first nonstop solo flight across the Atlantic in 1927, Charles Lindbergh became one of the most famous men in the world. He married Anne Spencer Morrow two years later, and their marriage survived not only his renown and their many airplane flights but also the kidnapping and murder of their firstborn child. Anne Morrow Lindbergh (1906–2001) went on to have four more children and to publish several dozen books, including fiction, nonfiction, and poetry. *Gift from the Sea* was her most famous, staying on the *New York Times* bestseller list for eighty weeks. It remains, more than half a century later, a popular meditation on some of the particular challenges of being a woman.

Husband and wife can and should go off on vacations alone and also on vacations alone *together*. For if it is possible that woman can find herself by having a vacation alone, it is equally possible that the original relationship can sometimes be refound by having a vacation alone *together*. Most married couples have felt the unexpected joy of one of these vacations. How wonderful it was to leave the children, the house, the job, and all the obligations of daily life; to go out together, whether for a month or a weekend or even just a night in an inn by themselves. How surprising it was to find the miracle of the sunrise repeated. There was the sudden pleasure of having breakfast alone with the man one fell in love with. Here at the small table, are only two people facing each other. How the table at home has grown! And how distracting it is, with four or five children, a telephone ringing in the hall, two or three school buses to catch, not to speak of the commuter's train. How all this separates one from one's husband and clogs up the pure relationship. But sitting at a table alone opposite each other, what is there to separate one? Nothing but a coffee pot, corn muffins and marmalade. A simple enough pleasure, surely, to have breakfast alone with one's husband, but how seldom married people in the midst of life achieve it.

MARY KAY BLAKELY
"HERS," *THE NEW YORK TIMES*, 1981

Mary Kay Blakely (1948–) was an early contributor to *Ms.* magazine and the *New York Times*'s "Hers" column. The illustration that appeared with the piece below showed a bride walking a tightrope strung over a tub of ice cream. Blakely, now an associate professor of journalism at the University of Missouri, had two sons, in 1974 and 1975, and divorced in the early eighties, later writing in her book *American Mom*, "divorce is the psychological equivalent of a triple coronary bypass."

Brides are so happy they haven't noticed yet that the institution of marriage is designed to hold only one and a half persons. They don't immediately comprehend the multiple implications behind Norman Mailer's suggestion that the whole question of liberation boils down to one: "Who will do the dishes?" The same one who does the dishes also gets to be the half person.

In the case of "nontraditional" marriages, it can take a woman even longer to comprehend that she is the half person. Many intelligent couples like to believe they can balance the equation to an even three-quarters apiece. With a few liberating amendments—she gets to keep her job, maybe even her name, he helps with the dishes—they hope to even things out. So subtle is the shift from "bride" to "wife" that a woman convinced of her independence can miss it altogether.

I would certainly have remained oblivious to the myriad assumptions hidden in the institution of marriage had it not been for a woman named Agnes who rudely interrupted my bliss only six months after I became a bride.

I ran into Agnes at Hemingway's Moveable Feast, our neighborhood delicatessen in Chicago. We were returning from the bike paths along the lakefront, tennis sweaters draped cavalierly over our shoulders, looking like a couple who had just passed the screen test for an Erich Segal movie. We stopped at Hemingway's to find a treat to bring home. Newlyweds are fond of treats. After some deliberation, I selected a high-quality brand of butter-pecan ice cream and handed it to the man who was carrying our money in his wallet.

He looked at the price, something that had not occurred to me.

He handed it back, explaining that $1.95 was exorbitant for any ice cream, and besides, he didn't like butter-pecan. I gave it back to him, because what was $1.95 between friends and besides, he didn't have to eat any. We stood there for some time, passing the pint back and forth, straining for patience, he refusing to indulge an irresponsible purchase, I insisting it was none of his business. His patience was melting with the ice cream when he delivered his final opinion: There was no way he was going to pay $1.95 for a pint of ice cream just because it said on the bottom of the carton "Hand packed by Agnes." He was starting to hate Agnes.

We rode home in stony silence. Only six months before I had been the kind of self-actualized woman who could walk into just about any delicatessen and order whatever I wanted. Dimly, I realized that this sudden loss in opportunity had something to do with the vows I had taken. I didn't remember *ever* saying, "And I defer all ice cream judgments to you." That's when I first became aware that love is not only blind, it is also deaf. A woman in love can't possibly hear the varied assumptions packed between the promises and the vows. The "I do" that took approximately 10 minutes to pronounce will be followed by 10 incredulous years of asking, "I did?"

But I also knew that to challenge a husband's ice cream authority was to challenge the vast incomprehensible expectations built into the structure of marriage. To question an ice cream decision would lead irrevocably to questions about vacuuming. And children. And sexuality.

We thought we had a "nontraditional" marriage because we were largely unaware that the roles of "head of household" and "subservient spouse" had a pervasive influence on our own relationship. We didn't fully understand how much a husband's sense of entitlement and a wife's sense of duty affected our own decisions about economics and work and power.

The next day, on the way home from work, I stopped at Hemingway's and bought six pints of butter-pecan ice cream, all hand packed by Agnes. I had to get rid of the status of half wife, and it was the first step to becoming an unwife. My success as an unwife depended largely on the cooperation of an unhusband, and I knew that undoing our unspoken vows could well result in an unmarriage. For better or worse, I packed our small freezer full of butter-pecan ice cream.

KELLY OXFORD
TWEET, 2011

With more than half a million Twitter followers, Canadian author and humorist Kelly Oxford found fame through social media, and in the process earned a book contract that led to her 2013 bestselling *Everything Is Perfect When You're a Liar*.

Marriage is having someone to whisper "can you grab me some cereal?" to at 11 pm.

FREEDOM

MICHEL DE MONTAIGNE
"ON SOME VERSES OF VIRGIL," 1588

French essayist and philosopher Michel de Montaigne (1533–1592) had no shortage of observations about men and women—or about most subjects. His roughly 25,000-word essay, purporting to be about Virgil's poetry, was also about youth, age, temptation, sex, and marriage.

The fact that we see so few good marriages is a sign of its price and its value. If you form it well and take it rightly, there is no finer relationship in our society. We cannot do without it, and yet we go about debasing it. The result is what is observed about cages: the birds outside despair of getting in, and those inside are equally anxious to get out.

QUEEN VICTORIA
LETTER TO VICKY, THE PRINCESS ROYAL, 1858

Few women—royal or not—were as famously devastated by widowhood as was Great Britain's Queen Victoria (1819–1901), who dressed in black from the day of Prince Albert's death in 1861 until her own. Her devotion was legendary, but that did not stop her from writing to her oldest daughter about the lack of freedom that came with marriage—and particularly with pregnancy. Queen Victoria had nine children, most of whom married into European royalty. Princess Victoria, known as Vicky, was only seventeen when, at her mother's insistence, she married the future German emperor Friedrich III.

Now to reply to your observation that you find a married woman has much more liberty than an unmarried one; in one sense of the word she has,—but what I meant was—in a physical point of view—and if you have hereafter (as I had constantly for the first 2 years of my marriage)— aches—and sufferings and miseries and plagues—which you must struggle against—and enjoyments etc. to give up—constant precautions to take, you will feel the yoke of a married woman! Without that—certainly it is unbounded happiness—if one has a husband one worships! It is a foretaste of heaven. And you have a husband who adores you, and is, I perceive, ready to meet every wish and desire of your's. I had 9 times for 8 months to bear with those above-named enemies and real misery (besides many duties) and I own it tried me sorely; one feels so pinned down—one's wings clipped—in fact, at the best (and few were or are better than I was) only half oneself—particularly the first and second time. This I call the "shadow side" as much as being torn away from one's loved home, parents and brothers and sisters. And therefore—I think our sex a most unenviable one.

F

HENRIK IBSEN
A DOLL'S HOUSE, 1879

Norwegian playwright Henrik Ibsen (1828–1906) offered a critique of modern morality in *A Doll's House* that was shocking for its portrait of a disillusioning marriage and particularly for the play's lack of a happy ending. Torvald Helmer is the satisfied, upright lawyer, and Nora his seemingly frivolous wife. The events of the play reveal to Nora a less ethical side of her husband, even as they lead her to find a stronger self. The title echoes her telling him: "Our home's been nothing but a playpen. I've been your doll-wife here, just as at home I was Papa's doll-child." The dialogue below is from the last scene in the play. In 1905, the critic James Huneker would write: "that slammed door reverberated across the roof of the world."

NORA: Tomorrow I'm going home—I mean, home where I came from. It'll be easier up there to find something to do.

HELMER: Oh, you blind, incompetent child!

NORA: I must learn to be competent, Torvald.

HELMER: Abandon your home, your husband, your children! And you're not even thinking what people will say.

NORA: I can't be concerned about that. I only know how essential this is.

HELMER: Oh, it's outrageous. So you'll run out like this on your most sacred vows.

NORA: What do you think are my most sacred vows?

HELMER: And I have to tell you that! Aren't they your duties to your husband and children?

NORA: I have other duties equally sacred.

HELMER: That isn't true. What duties are they?

NORA: Duties to myself.

HELMER: Before all else, you're a wife and a mother.

NORA: I don't believe in that anymore. I believe that, before all else, I'm a human being, no less than you—or anyway, I ought to try to become one. . . .

HELMER: Oh, you think and talk like a silly child.

NORA: Perhaps. But you neither think nor talk like the man I could join myself to. When your big fright was over—and it wasn't from any threat against me, only for what might damage you—when all the danger was past, for you it was just as if nothing had happened. I was exactly the same, your little lark, your doll, that you'd have to handle with double care now that I'd turned out so brittle and frail. *(Gets up.)* Torvald—in that instant it dawned on me that for eight years I've been living here with a stranger, and that I'd even conceived three children—oh, I can't stand the thought of it! I could tear myself to bits.

HELMER: *(Heavily)* I see. There's a gulf that's opened between us—that's clear. Oh, but Nora, can't we bridge it somehow?

NORA: The way I am now, I'm no wife for you.

HELMER: I have the strength to make myself over.

NORA: Maybe—if your doll gets taken away.

HELMER: But to part! To part from you! No, Nora, no—I can't imagine it.

NORA: *(Going out, right)* All the more reason why it has to be. *(She reenters with her coat and a small overnight bag, which she puts on a chair by the table.)*

HELMER: Nora, Nora, not now! Wait till tomorrow.

NORA: I can't spend the night in a strange man's room.

HELMER: But couldn't we live here like brother and sister—

NORA: You know very well how long that would last. *(Throws her shawl about her.)* Good-bye, Torvald. I won't look in on the children. I know they're in better hands than mine. The way I am now, I'm no use to them.

HELMER: But someday, Nora—someday—?

NORA: How can I tell? I haven't the least idea what'll become of me.

HELMER: But you're my wife, now and wherever you go.

NORA: Listen, Torvald—I've heard that when a wife deserts her husband's house just as I'm doing, then the law frees him from all responsibility. In any case, I'm freeing you from being responsible. Don't feel yourself bound, any more than I will. There has to be absolute freedom for us both. Here, take your ring back. Give me mine.

HELMER: That too?

NORA: That too.

HELMER: There it is.

F

NORA:	Good. Well, now it's all over. I'm putting the keys here. The maids know all about keeping up the house—better than I do. Tomorrow, after I've left town, Kristine will stop by to pack up everything that's mine from home. I'd like those things shipped up to me.
HELMER:	Over! All over! Nora, won't you ever think about me?
NORA:	I'm sure I'll think of you often, and about the children and the house here.
HELMER:	May I write you?
NORA:	No—never. You're not to do that.
HELMER:	Oh, but let me send you—
NORA:	Nothing. Nothing.
HELMER:	Or help you if you need it.
NORA:	No. I accept nothing from strangers.
HELMER:	Nora—can I never be more than a stranger to you?
NORA:	*(Picking up her overnight bag)* Ah, Torvald—it would take the greatest miracle of all—
HELMER:	Tell me the greatest miracle!
NORA:	You and I both would have to transform ourselves to the point that—Oh, Torvald, I've stopped believing in miracles.
HELMER:	But I'll believe. Tell me! Transform ourselves to the point that—?
NORA:	That our living together could be a true marriage. *(She goes out down the hall.)*
HELMER:	*(Sinks down on a chair by the door, face buried in his hands.)* Nora! Nora! *(Looking about and rising.)* Empty. She's gone. *(A sudden hope leaps in him.)* The greatest miracle—?
	(From below, the sound of a door slamming shut)

HENRY WARD BEECHER
PROVERBS FROM PLYMOUTH PULPIT, 1887

Though the Protestant minister Henry Ward Beecher (1813–1887) became infamous when he was accused of adultery, he had already become famous for the wisdom he dispensed in sermons—and gathered for his book of proverbs.

Well-married, a man is winged—ill-matched, he is shackled.

VOLTAIRINE DE CLEYRE
"SEX SLAVERY," 1890

An American anarchist and poet, Voltairine de Cleyre (1866–1912) was an ardent opponent of marriage, believing it to be an enslaving institution. The passage below is from a speech she gave in defense of the imprisoned feminist Moses Harman, who, she said, had "looked beneath the word and saw the fact,—a prison more horrible than that where he is sitting now, whose corridors radiate over all the earth, and with so many cells, that none may count them."

It has often been said to me, by women with decent masters, who had no idea of the outrages practiced on their less fortunate sisters, "Why don't the wives leave?"

Why don't you run, when your feet are chained together? Why don't you cry out when a gag is on your lips? Why don't you raise your hands above your head when they are pinned fast to your sides? Why don't you spend thousands of dollars when you haven't a cent in your pocket? Why don't you go to the seashore or the mountains, you fools scorching with city heat? If there is one thing more than another in this whole accursed tissue of false society, which makes me angry, it is the asinine stupidity which with the true phlegm of impenetrable dullness says, "Why don't the women leave!" Will you tell me where they will go and what they shall do?

KATE CHOPIN
"THE STORY OF AN HOUR," 1894

Not nearly as militant as de Cleyre (above), Kate Chopin (1850–1904) wrote stories and novels that often portrayed the hidden strength of women, especially in the context of southern society. "The Story of an Hour" was one of her best-known works: economical and vivid in its narration, and—as a feminist fable—surprising. This is the story in its entirety.
Chopin herself married at twenty, had six children, and, after a dozen years, was left a widow in debt.

Knowing that Mrs. Mallard was afflicted with a heart trouble, great care was taken to break to her as gently as possible the news of her husband's death.

It was her sister Josephine who told her, in broken sentences; veiled hints that revealed in half concealing. Her husband's friend Richards was there, too, near her. It was he who had been in the newspaper office when intelligence of the railroad disaster was received, with Brently Mallard's name leading the list of "killed." He had only taken the time to assure himself of its truth by a second telegram, and had hastened to forestall any less careful, less tender friend in bearing the sad message.

She did not hear the story as many women have heard the same, with a paralyzed inability to accept its significance. She wept at once, with sudden, wild abandonment, in her sister's arms. When the storm of grief had spent itself she went away to her room alone. She would have no one follow her.

There stood, facing the open window, a comfortable, roomy armchair. Into this she sank, pressed down by a physical exhaustion that haunted her body and seemed to reach into her soul.

She could see in the open square before her house the tops of trees that were all aquiver with the new spring life. The delicious breath of rain was in the air. In the street below a peddler was crying his wares. The notes of a distant song which someone was singing reached her faintly, and countless sparrows were twittering in the eaves.

> When she abandoned herself, a little whispered word escaped her slightly parted lips. She said it over and over under her breath: "free, free, free!"

There were patches of blue sky showing here and there through the clouds that had met and piled one above the other in the west facing her window.

She sat with her head thrown back upon the cushion of the chair, quite motionless, except when a sob came up into her throat and shook her, as a child who has cried itself to sleep continues to sob in its dreams.

She was young, with a fair, calm face, whose lines bespoke repression and even a certain strength. But now there was a dull stare in her eyes, whose gaze was fixed away off yonder on one of those patches of blue sky. It was not a glance of reflection, but rather indicated a suspension of intelligent thought.

There was something coming to her and she was waiting for it, fearfully. What was it? She did not know; it was too subtle and elusive to name. But she felt it, creeping out of the sky, reaching toward her through the sounds, the scents, the color that filled the air.

Now her bosom rose and fell tumultuously. She was beginning to recognize this thing that was approaching to possess her, and she was striving to beat it back with her will—as powerless as her two white slender hands would have been.

When she abandoned herself a little whispered word escaped her slightly parted lips. She said it over and over under her breath: "free, free, free!" The vacant stare and the look of terror that had followed it went from her eyes. They stayed keen and bright. Her pulses beat fast, and the coursing blood warmed and relaxed every inch of her body.

She did not stop to ask if it were or were not a monstrous joy that held her. A clear and exalted perception enabled her to dismiss the suggestion as trivial.

She knew that she would weep again when she saw the kind, tender hands folded in death; the face that had never looked save with love upon her, fixed and gray and dead. But she saw beyond that bitter moment a long procession of years to come that would belong to her absolutely. And she opened and spread her arms out to them in welcome.

There would be no one to live for during those coming years; she would live for herself. There would be no powerful will bending hers in that blind persistence with which men and women believe they have a right to impose a private will upon a fellow-creature. A kind intention or a cruel intention made the act seem no less a crime as she looked upon it in that brief moment of illumination.

And yet she had loved him—sometimes. Often she had not. What did it matter! What could love, the unsolved mystery, count for in face of this possession of self-assertion which she suddenly recognized as the strongest impulse of her being!

"Free! Body and soul free!" she kept whispering.

Josephine was kneeling before the closed door with her lips to the keyhole, imploring for admission. "Louise, open the door! I beg, open the door—you will make yourself ill. What are you doing Louise? For heaven's sake open the door."

"Go away. I am not making myself ill." No; she was drinking in a very elixir of life through that open window.

Her fancy was running riot along those days ahead of her. Spring days, and summer days, and all sorts of days that would be her own. She breathed a quick prayer that life might be long. It was only yesterday she had thought with a shudder that life might be long.

She arose at length and opened the door to her sister's importunities. There was a feverish triumph in her eyes, and she carried herself unwittingly like a goddess of Victory. She clasped her sister's waist, and together they descended the stairs. Richards stood waiting for them at the bottom.

Some one was opening the front door with a latchkey. It was Brently Mallard who entered, a little travel-stained, composedly carrying his grip-sack and umbrella. He had been far from the scene of accident, and did not even know there had been one. He stood amazed at Josephine's piercing cry; at Richards' quick motion to screen him from the view of his wife.

But Richards was too late.

When the doctors came they said she had died of heart disease—of joy that kills.

FRENCH POSTCARD
"THE CHAINS OF MARRIAGE," 1906

BETTY FRIEDAN
THE FEMININE MYSTIQUE, 1963

Betty Friedan (1921–2006) was still living the life of suburban wife and mother when she sent out a questionnaire to fellow Smith College alumnae and was inspired by their answers to start researching the state of middle-class women in the United States. *The Feminine Mystique* was the bestselling book that resulted; the title referred to what she described as the aura of supposed fulfillment under which women in reality struggled to maintain their identities. Later a founder of the National Organization for Women, Friedan—like Simone de Beauvoir (see Work, page 495) and Greer (see Expectations, page 106)—was one of the pillars of twentieth-century feminism.

In her optimistic conclusion to *The Feminine Mystique*, Friedan wrote: "When their mothers' fulfillment makes girls sure they want to be women . . . they can stretch and stretch until their own efforts will tell them who they are. They will not need the regard of boy or man to feel alive. And when women do not need to live through their husbands and children, men will not fear the love and strength of women, nor need another's weakness to prove their own masculinity."

The problem lay buried, unspoken, for many years in the minds of American women. It was a strange stirring, a sense of dissatisfaction, a yearning that women suffered in the middle of the twentieth century in the United States. Each suburban wife struggled with it alone. As she made the beds, shopped for groceries, matched slipcover material, ate peanut butter sandwiches with her children, chauffeured Cub Scouts and Brownies, lay beside her husband at night—she was afraid to ask even of herself the silent question—"Is this all?"

For over fifteen years there was no word of this yearning in the millions of words written about women, for women, in all the columns, books and articles by experts telling women their role was to seek fulfillment as wives and mothers. Over and over women heard in voices of tradition and of Freudian sophistication that they could desire no greater destiny than to glory in their own femininity. Experts told them how to catch a man and keep him, how to breast-feed children and handle their toilet training, how to cope with sibling rivalry and adolescent rebellion; how to buy a dishwasher, bake bread, cook gourmet snails, and build a swimming pool with their own hands; how to dress, look, and act more feminine and make marriage more exciting; how to keep their husbands from dying young and their sons from growing into delinquents. They were taught to pity the neurotic, unfeminine, unhappy women who wanted to be poets or physicists or presidents. They learned that truly feminine women do not want careers, higher education, political rights—the independence and the opportunities that the old-fashioned feminists fought for. Some women, in their forties and fifties, still remembered painfully giving up those dreams, but most of the younger women no longer even thought about them. A thousand expert voices applauded their femininity, their adjustment, their new maturity. All they had to do was devote their lives from earliest girlhood to finding a husband and bearing children.

CLARE BOOTHE LUCE
A DOLL'S HOUSE 1970, 1970

Clare Boothe Luce (1903–1987) was a reporter, an editor, a congresswoman, a diplomat, and the wife of *Time* and *Life* cofounder Henry Luce. She is perhaps best known today as the author of the play *The Women*. Her one-act *A Doll's House 1970* was originally printed in *Life* magazine and performed a year later with the title *Slam the Door Softly*. Generally not considered one of her best efforts, it nonetheless captured the feminist spirit of the new decade, portraying a defiant, independent, modern-day Nora (see Ibsen, above) in the act of leaving her bewildered husband.

THAW: So nothing I've said—what little I've had a chance to say . . . *(She shakes her head.)*—you still intend to divorce me?

NORA: Oh, I never said I was divorcing you. I'm deserting you. So you can divorce me.

THAW: You do realize, Nora, that if a wife deserts her husband he doesn't have to pay her alimony?

NORA: I don't want alimony. But I do want severance pay.

FRIENDSHIP

MICHEL DE MONTAIGNE
"ON SOME VERSES OF VIRGIL," 1588

In 1565, Montaigne (see Freedom, page 127) married a woman named Françoise de la Chassaigne, who was the wealthy daughter of a fellow Bordeaux parliamentarian. They had six daughters together (only one of whom survived childhood), but their marriage was preceded by a relationship of apparently far greater intensity. Montaigne was twenty-four when he met

Étienne de la Boétie, another member of parliament, whom Montaigne would later immortalize in his essay "On Friendship." Holding this love up as the pinnacle, he wrote: "If you press me to tell why I loved him, I feel that this cannot be expressed, except by answering: Because it was he, because it was I."

Montaigne didn't marry until two years after La Boétie's death and didn't start writing until four years after that.

A good marriage, if such there be, rejects the company and conditions of love. It tries to reproduce those of friendship. It is a sweet association in life, full of constancy, trust, and an infinite number of useful and solid services and mutual obligations. No woman who savors the taste of it,

> Whom the nuptial torch with welcome light has joined,
> —Catullus

would want to have the place of a mistress or paramour to her husband. If she is lodged in his affection as a wife, she is lodged there much more honorably and securely. When he dances ardent and eager attention elsewhere, still let anyone ask him then on whom he would rather have some shame fall, on his wife or his mistress; whose misfortune would afflict him more; for whom he wishes more honor. These questions admit of no doubt in a sound marriage.

ELBERT HUBBARD
HOLLYHOCKS AND GOLDENGLOW, 1912

Author Elbert Hubbard (1856–1915) (see Ernest Cowper letter, page 97) was flamboyant in his opinions and restless in his twenty-year marriage to Bertha Crawford, with whom he had four children. His affair with a schoolteacher named Alice Moore lasted more than a dozen years and produced a daughter, who was for the most part raised by Moore's sister and brother-in-law. Eventually, Hubbard was sued by them for child support. Amid much scandal, he finally divorced his wife and married Alice in 1904. It was with Alice that he died during the sinking of the *Lusitania*.

A correspondent asks me this: "Do brilliant men prefer brilliant women?"

First, disclaiming the gentle assumption that I am brilliant, I say, yes.

The essence of marriage is companionship, and the woman you face across the coffee-urn every morning for ninety-nine years must be both able to appreciate your jokes and to sympathize with your aspirations. If this is not so, the man will stray, actually, or else chase the ghosts of dead hopes through the graveyard of his dreams.

. . . Brilliant men are but ordinary men who at intervals are capable of brilliant perfor- mances. . . . Your ordinary man who does the brilliant things would be ordinary all the time were it not for the fact that he is inspired by a woman. Great thoughts and great deeds are the children of married minds. . . .

Men and women must go forward hand in hand—single file is savagery. A brilliant man is dependent on a woman, and the greater he is the more he needs her. . . .

The only man who has no use for a woman is one who is not all there—one whom God has overlooked at the final inspection. The brilliant man wants a wife who is his chum, com- panion, a "good fellow" to whom he can tell the things he knows, or guesses, or hopes: one with whom he can be stupid and foolish—one with whom he can act out his nature. If she is stupid all the time, he will have to be brilliant, and this will kill them both. To grin and bear it is gradual dissolution; to bear it and not grin is death.

JOHN GOTTMAN AND NAN SILVER
THE SEVEN PRINCIPLES FOR MAKING MARRIAGE WORK, 1999

John Gottman (1942–) is a psychologist and author, one of the best known in the vast, clut- tered field of marital advice. In the 1990s, his research—based on couples' perceptions of one another—led him to create a system for predicting a marriage's success or failure, a system he has claimed to be 90 percent effective. In turn, those predictions led him to collaborate with author Nan Silver on their seminal bestselling work. Other books, as well as DVDs and TV appearances, have followed, as have a research organization (popularly known as "the Love Lab") and an institute where he and his wife, fellow psychologist Julie Gottman, offer training for other therapists and workshops for couples.

At the heart of my program is the simple truth that happy marriages are based on a deep friend- ship. By this I mean a mutual respect for and enjoyment of each other's company. These couples tend to know each other intimately—they are well versed in each other's likes, dislikes, personal- ity quirks, hopes, and dreams. They have an abiding regard for each other and express this fond- ness not just in the big ways but in little ways day in and day out.

Take the case of hardworking Nathaniel, who runs his own import business and works very long hours. In another marriage, his schedule might be a major liability. But he and his wife Olivia have found ways to stay connected. They talk frequently on the phone during the day. When she has a doctor's appointment, he remembers to call to see how it went. When he has a meeting with an important client, she'll check in to see how it fared. When they have chicken for dinner, she gives him both drumsticks because she knows he likes them best. When he makes blueberry pancakes for the kids Saturday morning, he'll leave the blueberries out of hers because he knows she doesn't like them. Although he's not religious, he accompanies her to church each Sunday because it's important to her. And although she's not crazy about spending a lot of time with their relatives, she has pursued a friendship with Nathaniel's mother and sisters because family matters so much to him.

If all of this sounds humdrum and unromantic, it's anything but. Through small but important ways Olivia and Nathaniel are maintaining the friendship that is the foundation of their love. As a result they have a marriage that is far more passionate than do couples who punctuate their lives together with romantic vacations and lavish anniversary gifts but have fallen out of touch in their daily lives.

Friendship fuels the flames of romance because it offers the best protection against feeling adversarial toward your spouse. Because Nathaniel and Olivia have kept their friendship strong despite the inevitable disagreements and irritations of married life, they are experiencing what is known technically as "positive sentiment override." This means that their positive thoughts about each other and their marriage are so pervasive that they tend to supersede their negative feelings. It takes a much more significant conflict for them to lose their equilibrium as a couple than it would otherwise. Their positivity causes them to feel optimistic about each other and their marriage, to assume positive things about their lives together, and to give each other the benefit of the doubt.

F

GRIEVANCES

WILLIAM DUNBAR
"UPON THE MIDSUMMER EVE, MERRIEST OF NIGHTS," 15TH CENTURY

William Dunbar (circa 1460–circa 1530) was a Scottish poet and priest notable for the versatility of his writing, which included elegies, hymns, and sermons as well as ribald lampoons and satires.

The speaker in this section of Dunbar's poem is one wife to another wife and a widow.

My husband was a whoremaster, the hugest in earth;
Therefore I hate him with my heart, so help me our Lord.
He is a young man, very lively, but not in the flower of youth,
For he is faded very far and enfeebled of strength.
He was as flourishing fresh within these few years,
But he is very greatly weakened and exhausted in labour.
He has been a lecher so long until his potency is lost,
His tool has become impotent, and lies in a swoon.
There was never a rest worse set than on that tired slug,
For after seven weeks' rest it will not strike once.

He has been wasted upon women before he chose me as his wife,

And in adultery in my time I have caught him often.

And yet he is as prancing with his bonnet at an angle,

And staring at the prettiest that dwell in the town,

As courtly of his clothes and combing of his hair,

As he that is more valiant in Venus' chamber.

He seems to be worth something, that nothing in the bedroom,

He looks as though he wants to be loved, though he's worth little,

He does as a doted dog that pisses on all the bushes,

And lifts his leg up high though he doesn't want to piss.

He has a look without lust and life without desire;

He has a form without force and appearance without power,

And fair words without reality, all useless in deeds.

He is for ladies in love a very lustful shadow,

But in private, at the deed, he shall be found drooping.

ALEXANDER POPE
"THE WIFE OF BATH, HER PROLOGUE, FROM CHAUCER," CIRCA 1704

The original "Wife of Bath's Tale" was Geoffrey Chaucer's, written in the fourteenth century in Middle English, and as famous for its prologue—in which the title character bawdily describes her five marriages—as for its message about women's desire for power over men. Chaucer's tale drew on works by previous writers and was in turn the inspiration for many others, including Dunbar's poem (above) and this one, by Alexander Pope (1688–1744), which in full ran some 150 lines.

If I but see a cousin or a friend,

Lord! how you swell and rage like any fiend!

But you reel home, a drunken beastly bear,

Then preach till midnight in your easy chair;

Cry, wives are false, and every woman evil,

And give up all that's female to the devil.

If poor (you say), she drains her husband's purse:

If rich, she keeps her priest, or something worse;

If highly born, intolerably vain,
Vapours and pride by turns possess her brain;
Now gaily mad, now sourly splenetic,
Freakish when well, and fretful when she's sick:
If fair, then chaste she cannot long abide,
By pressing youth attack'd on every side;
If foul, her wealth the lusty lover lures,
Or else her wit some fool-gallant procures,
Or else she dances with becoming grace,
Or shape excuses the defects of face.
There swims no goose so gray but soon or late
She finds some honest gander for her mate.
Horses (thou say'st) and asses men may try,
And ring suspected vessels ere they buy;
But wives, a random choice, untried they take,
They dream in courtship, but in wedlock wake.

"MARRIAGE AND HEALTH"
MILWAUKEE SENTINEL, 1893

This item ran as an editorial a few days after the case it described appeared in a New York courtroom. A month later, the matter was settled out of court, with Philip Scheyer paying Johanna Scheyer an extraordinary $18,000 in cash—the equivalent of about half a million dollars today. Headline writers around the country enjoyed themselves: "She Was Too Vivacious"; "Wife Laughed Too Much"; "Tired of His Young Wife."

We await with some interest the decision of Justice Burk of Harlem in the case brought by Mrs. Johanna Scheyer against her husband, Philip Scheyer, for abandonment. The case is peculiar from the nature of Mr. Scheyer's defense. He is a well-to-do cloakmaker, aged 50 years, who married a few months ago a tall brunette of 27 years "with luminous brown eyes and clear-cut features." In giving her testimony Mrs. Scheyer said she had not been in the house a week before he told her they must separate. "He told me I laughed too much and must behave myself differently." Later, while making another complaint of her too ready laugh, he averred that she was too good looking to be the wife of a man of his age and he offered to give her $8,000 if she would get a divorce. She refused, and when she insisted on knowing what her fault was he said: "Nothing; you are not at fault in any way." But still, after repeating his offer of $8,000, he left her.

The defense made by Mr. Scheyer is that his doctor told him he must separate from his wife or sink into hopeless melancholy. The doctor professed to have made an elaborate examination of his condition and to have discovered that the much laughing of the wife bore heavily on the spirits of the husband; and that as she seemed unable to control her cachinnatory impulses, the only hope was in a separation. It is probable that her alleged laugh is a giggle, in which case there is little reason to doubt the correctness of the doctor's diagnosis and prognosis.

Living with an irritable person is a kind of torture.

WILLIAM ROBINSON
SEXUAL PROBLEMS OF TO-DAY, 1912

With his frank and methodical approach to sexual problems, birth control, health, and behavior, New York urologist William J. Robinson (1867–1936) was a pioneer, brave enough to put the words *sex* or *sexual* into many of his titles, no small feat in an era still ruled by anti-obscenity laws. He was stern and quite specific in the following statement, and his later books, including the 1915 *Fewer and Better Babies*, were increasingly strident in support of eugenics.

No woman has a right to marry who has a bad odor from her mouth. It will end disastrously. It may not end in divorce—it often does—but it will surely cause coolness and marital infelicity, and the husband will be very apt to stray into by-paths. For which we should not be inclined to blame him too severely. There is no excuse for anybody, and particularly for a member of the lovely sex, to have a bad odor from the mouth (or from anywhere else). The worst and most obstinate case of bromopnea can be cured if the causes are diligently sought for and properly treated.

IRA WILE AND MARY DAY WINN
MARRIAGE IN THE MODERN MANNER, 1929

Psychiatrist and physician Ira Wile (1877–1943) and journalist Mary Day Winn (1888–1965) dedicated their book to "those who find increasing happiness in and through marriage." Enthusiastically, they offered the semi-radical idea that American wives, having had more education, independence, and earning power in the 1920s than ever before, should no longer be seen as housekeepers and mothers but might also be seen as partners. The authors enumerated plenty of traditional "don'ts" for wives (see Husbands, How to Keep, page 193), but in passages like the one below, husbands were nudged into a more reciprocal view of marriage.

In addition to working as a doctor and author, Wile spent six years as New York City's commissioner of education and was editor of several medical journals. Winn worked for the *New York Herald Tribune*.

G

The use of the home as a dumping-ground for business vexations may save [a husband's] business, but it is likely to wreck the home and condition the children. It wears down the wife's patience and exhausts her affection. One of the most fearful tortures ever invented was the steady, constant dripping of water on the head of a victim who had been tied so that he could not get away from it. People subjected to this method suffered only moderate physical pain, but they often became insane unless released in time, for each little drop caused a slight nervous shock and the effect was cumulative. Living with an irritable person is the same kind of torture; it causes a series of nervous shocks which can wear love down to nothingness. . . .

. . . If the husband carries his business troubles home every night, and the wife has saved her household worries to recount to him at the evening meal, that meal will not be a happy affair. Such a state of things, long continued, will eventually cause both wife and husband to dread the homecoming; each will have become for the other not a stimulant but a depressant.

OLD JOKE

Persky goes to the rabbi for counseling.

"Rabbi," he says. "I did a horrible thing. At dinner last night, I made this terrible Freudian slip."

"Well, tell me what you meant to say, and tell me what you said."

"I meant to say, 'Pass the butter, please.' What I said was, 'You bitch, you've ruined my life.' "

HOW TO BE A GOOD HUSBAND, 1936

This small British volume was originally published as *Do's and Don'ts for Husbands*. In the dedication, the anonymous author wrote: "The part which a husband must play in life is not exactly an easy one. He has definite obligations and numerous restrictions. Often he will be puzzled as to why things have gone wrong."

The following admonitions were among those appearing under the chapter called "Personal Habits."

Don't squeeze the tube of tooth paste from the top instead of from the bottom. This is one of the small things of life that always irritates a careful wife.

Don't think that your wife has placed waste-paper baskets in the rooms as ornaments. They are put there for you to use. Don't, however, utilise them for spent matches unless you are very well insured.

Don't get into the habit of storing up a lot of useless old stuff and then grumble for a week if your wife disposes of some of it. Every woman likes her house to be a home not a marine store depot.

Don't expect to be numbered among the good mannered if you use a nail file, comb or toothpick otherwise than in a dressing room.

GEORGE CRANE
"MARITAL RATING SCALE, HUSBAND'S CHART," 1939

Northwestern University's George W. Crane (1901–1995) was an MD and PhD who ran a counseling practice and matchmaking service, wrote an advice column called "The Worry Clinic," and devised a handy rating scale for husbands and wives. The lists were drawn from interviews Crane conducted with six hundred husbands and six hundred wives. While the items thus represented an early attempt at a scientific method for assessing marriages, Crane conceded that the points he assigned to various items were based on his personal judgment.

In computing the score, check the various items under DEMERITS which fit the husband and add the total. Each item counts one point unless specifically weighted, as in the parentheses. Then check the items under MERITS which apply. Now subtract the DEMERIT score from the MERIT score. The result is the husband's raw score. Interpret it according to this table:

RAW SCORES	INTERPRETATION
0–24	Very Poor (Failures)
25–41	Poor
42–58	Average
59–75	Superior
76 and up	Very Superior

G

DEMERITS

1. Stares at or flirts with other women while out with wife. (5)
2. Reads newspaper at the table.
3. Fails to come to table promptly when meal is ready.
4. Brings guests home for meals without warning wife.
5. Doesn't phone when late for dinner.
6. Compares wife unfavorably with his mother or other wives. (5)
7. Publicly praises bachelor days and regrets having married.
8. Criticizes wife in public. (5)
9. Belches without apology, or blows nose at table.
10. Leaves dresser drawers open.
11. Leaves shoes in living room.
12. Snores.
13. Careless in bathroom—leaves razor out or ring around tub.
14. Fails to bathe or change socks often enough.
15. Fails to brush teeth regularly or keep nails clean.
16. Dislikes to dress or shave on Sunday.
17. Hangs ties or clothes on doorknobs.
18. Picks teeth, nose, or sucks on teeth when in public.
19. Objects to wife's driving auto.
20. Uses profanity or vulgarity.
21. Blames wife for everything that goes wrong.
22. Complains of being too tired to go out at night with wife.
23. Is suspicious and jealous.
24. Uses alcohol. If ever drunk. (5)
25. Tells lies, not dependable. (5)
26. Angry if newspaper is disarranged.
27. Stubborn—rarely admits that he is wrong. Seldom apologizes. (5)

28.   Talks of efficiency of his stenographer or other women.

29.   Teases wife to fatness, slowness, etc.

30.   Tells embarrassing things about wife when out in public.

31.   Makes fun of wife's hats, clothes, cooking, housekeeping, etc.

32.   Smokes in bed.

33.   Calls "Where is—" without first hunting the object.

34.   Monopolizes radio on Sunday as for the baseball broadcasts.

35.   Dislikes children, or scolds them too harshly. (5)

36.   A chronic ailer or patent medicine addict.

37.   Writes on tablecloth with pencil.

38.   A chronic braggart or boaster.

39.   Argues with or curses other motorists.

40.   Will not help wife's relatives as much as his own.

41.   Rolls in bed covers—pulls them off wife.

42.   Eats onions, radishes or garlic before dates or going to bed.

43.   Addicted to gambling.

44.   Defers too much to mother, a "mama's boy." (5)

45.   Belittles wife's opinions, her judgment, or ability. (5)

46.   Opens his wife's mail.

47.   Boasts about his former girl friends or his conquests. (5)

48.   Leaves lights burning all over the house.

49.   Kisses wife just after her makeup has been applied.

50.   Too much a book worm—doesn't talk to wife enough when home.

MERITS

1.   Gives wife ample allowance or turns pay check over to her. (5)

2.   Courteous to wife's friends.

3.   Frequently compliments wife re looks, cooking, housekeeping, etc. (5)

4.   Remembers birthdays, anniversaries, etc. (5)

5.   Helps wife with dishes, caring for children, scrubbing.

6.   Polite and mannerly even when alone with his wife.

7.   Consults wife's opinion re business and social affairs.

8.   Has date with wife at least once per week. (5 per date)

9.   Reads newspaper, books or magazines aloud to wife.

10.   A good conversationalist.

11.   Steady worker and good provider. (5)

12.   Leaves car for wife on days she may need it.

13.   Handy about house re fixing, iron, vacuum, hanging pictures, etc.

14.   Enjoys taking wife along with him wherever he goes.

15.   Doesn't interfere with wife's correction of children.

16.   Carries adequate insurance for family. (5)

17.   Doesn't quarrel with wife before children or the public.

18.   Makes guests feel welcome—an interesting entertainer.

19.   Often tells wife he loves her. (5)

20.   Usually comes home with a smile.

21.   Shares his business and personal problems with her.

22.   Holds wife's coat and opens doors for her.

23.   Good humored in the morning.

24.   Even-tempered.

25.   Does not use tobacco.

26.   Interested in athletics.

27.   Writes often and lovingly when away from home.

28.   Plays with children or helps them with lessons. (5)

29.   Willing to go shopping with wife.

30.   Waits up for wife or calls for her at her party.

31.   Neat in appearance—shoes shined, hair cut, suit pressed.

32.   Attends church or urges children to attend Sunday school. (10)

33.   Attends parent-teacher meetings and educational lectures.

34.   Ambitious—works or studies to gain promotion.

35.   Surprises wife occasionally with candy, flowers, gifts.

36.   A fast and efficient worker, not the puttering sort.

37.   Willingly prepares own breakfast.

38.   Ardent lover—sees that wife has orgasm in marital congress. (20)

39.   Shows wife attention and affection in public. (5)

40.   Is a careful auto driver.

41.   Kind, but firm and the head of his household.

42.   Well liked by men, courageous—not a sissy.

43.   Is true to his wife. (10)

44.   Eats whatever is served without grumbling or criticism.

45.   His children are pleased at his arrival home. (5)

46.   Tries to keep wife equipped with modern labor saving devices. (5)

47.   Gives wife real movie kisses, not dutiful "peck" on the cheek.

48.   If wife is ill, phones from work to inquire about her.

49.   Neatly hangs up his clothes on hooks or hangers.

50.   Kisses wife when leaving for work or a trip.

G

GEORGE CRANE
"MARITAL RATING SCALE, WIFE'S CHART," 1939

In computing the score, check the various items under DEMERITS which fit the wife and add the total. Each item counts one point unless specifically weighted, as in the parentheses. Then check the items under MERITS which apply. Now subtract the DEMERIT score from the MERIT score. The result is the wife's raw score. Interpret it according to this table:

RAW SCORES	INTERPRETATION
0–24	Very Poor (Failures)
25–41	Poor
42–58	Average
59–75	Superior
76 and up	Very Superior

DEMERITS

1.   Slow in coming to bed—delays till husband is almost asleep.

2.   Doesn't like children. (5)

3.   Fails to sew on buttons or darn socks regularly.

4.   Wears soiled or ragged dresses and aprons around the house.

5.   Wears red nail polish.

6.   Often late for appointments. (5)

7.   Seams in hose often crooked.

8.   Goes to bed with curlers on her hair or much face cream.

9.   Puts her cold feet on husband at night to warm them.

10.   Is a back seat driver.

11.   Flirts with other men at parties or in restaurants. (5)

12.   Is suspicious and jealous. (5)

13.   Uses slang or profanity. (5)

14.   Smokes, drinks, gambles, or uses dope. (5)

15.   Talks about former boy friends or first husband.

16.   Squeezes tooth paste at the top.

17.   Reminds husband it is her money they are living on. (5)

18.   Tells family affairs to casual acquaintances, too talkative.

19.   A chronic borrower—doesn't keep stocked up.

20.   Slows up card game with chatter or gossip.

21.   Opens husband's personal mail.

22.   Frequently exceeds her allowance or family budget. (5)

23.   Eats onions, radishes, or garlic before a date or going to bed.

24.   Tells risque or vulgar stories. (5)

25.   Wears pajamas while cooking.

26.   Talks during movie, play or concert.

27.   Is more than 15 pounds overweight.

28.   Often whining and complaining.

29.   Discourteous to sales clerks and hired help.

30.   Shoulder straps hang over arms or slip is uneven and shows.

31.   Fails to wash top of milk bottle before opening it.

32.   Corrects husband's speech or actions before others. (5)

33.   Saves punishment of children for father at night. (5)

34.   Serves dinner but fails to sit down till meal is half over—then wants husband to wait for her.

35.   Wears pajamas instead of nightgown.

36.   Fails to bathe or brush teeth often enough. (5)

37.   Puts stockings to soak in wash basin.

38.   Serves too much from tin cans or the delicatessen store.

39.   Visits mother too often—a spoiled child.

40.   Is snobbish or too much concerned in "keeping up with the Jones."

41.   Dislikes husband's hobbies as fishing, baseball, etc.

42.   Tells lies—is not dependable. (5)

43.   Doesn't want to get up to prepare breakfast.

44.   Insists on driving the car when husband is along.

45.   Smokes in bed or has cigarette stained fingers.

46.   Cries, sulks or pouts too much.

47.   Makes evening engagements without consulting her husband.

48.   Talks too long on the phone.

49.   Is a gossip.

50.   Walks around the house in stocking feet.

MERITS

1.   A good hostess—even to unexpected guests.

2.   Has meals on time.

3.   Can carry on an interesting conversation.

4.   Can play a musical instrument, as piano, violin, etc.

5.   Dresses for breakfast.

6.   Neat housekeeper—tidy and clean.

7.   Personally puts children to bed.

8.   Never goes to bed angry, always makes up first. (5)

9.   Asks husband's opinions regarding important decisions and purchases.

10.   Good sense of humor—jolly and gay.

11.   Religious—sends children to church or Sunday school and goes herself. (10)

12.   Lets husband sleep late on Sunday and holidays.

13.   Encourages thrift—economical. (5)

14.   Laughs at husband's jokes and his clowning.

15.   Ambitious for her family—urges higher attainment.

16.   Belongs to parent-teacher club, or child study group.

17.   A good cook—serves balanced meals. (5)

18.   Tries to become acquainted with husband's business or trade.

19.   Greets husband at night with a smile.

20.   Has a pleasant disposition in the morning—not crabby.

21.   Keeps snacks in refrigerator for late eating.

22.   Likes educational and cultural things.

23.   Reacts with pleasure and delight to marital congress. (10)

24.   Faithful and true to husband. (10)

25.   Has pleasant voice—not strident.

26.   Has spunk—will defend her ideals and religion.

27.   Praises husband in public.

28.   Writes often and lovingly when away from husband.

29.   Writes to husband's parents regularly.

30.   Willing to assist husband at office or shop.

31.   Sympathetic—likes children and unfortunates. (5)

32.   Keeps hair neatly combed or shampooed and waved.

33.   Often comments on husband's strength and masculinity.

34.   Good seamstress—can make her own clothes or the children's clothes.

35.   Gives husband shampoo or manicure.

36.   Keeps husband's clothes clean and pressed.

37.   Bravely carries on during financial depression.

38.   Healthy or courageous and uncomplaining.

39.   Keeps self dainty, perfumed and feminine.

40.   Is of the same religion as her husband. (5)

41.   Has minor children to care for. (5 points per child)

42.   On friendly terms with neighbors.

43.   Fair and just in settling the children's quarrels with others.

44.   Likes to vacation with husband.

45.   An active member of some women's organization.

46.   Often tells husband she loves him. (5)

47.   Polite and mannerly even when alone with husband.

48.   Willing to get a job to help support the home.

49.   Praises marriage before young women contemplating it.

50.   Is unselfish and kind-hearted.

CLIFFORD ADAMS
PREPARING FOR MARRIAGE, 1951

Clifford Adams (see Conflict, page 44) posed the following question to several hundred married couples: "What changes would you make in your mate, if you could?" These were the answers from spouses identified as "unhappy."

CHANGES MENTIONED	BY HUSBANDS	BY WIVES
Strength of sex desire	43%	25%
[husbands wanting more, wives less]		
Mate's temper	35%	27%
Tendency to scold	24%	26%
Not showing affection	21%	19%
Lack of thriftiness	13%	10%

Carelessness in dress	12%	15%
Religious indifference	9%	16%
Serious-mindedness	7%	18%
Selfishness	7%	14%
Lack of talkativeness	4%	21%

G

OLIVER BUTTERFIELD
PLANNING FOR MARRIAGE, 1956

In his chapter "When Troubles Come," Dr. Oliver Butterfield (1891–1963) listed "Disgusting mannerisms" squarely between "Sexual abnormalities and obsessions" and "Drinking and drug addiction." A Methodist pastor, Butterfield wrote several books on love and marriage and was often quoted as an expert on both subjects.

Disgusting mannerisms of personal hygiene sometimes are the root of the disgust or repugnance which one mate develops for the other. . . .

One woman got to where she refused to sleep with her husband or to allow him any sexual privileges. He accused her of interest in other men and even had her examined by a psychiatrist because he considered her behavior such a radical change from her earlier romantic elopement and devotion to him. When given the opportunity to explain her side of the story she finally came out with the facts.

"Do you know why I don't sleep with him? Well, he stinks!"

JUDITH VIORST
LOVE AND SHRIMP, 1993

Renowned for her children's books, most notably *Alexander and the Terrible, Horrible, No Good, Very Bad Day,* Judith Viorst (1931–) has also written poetry, advice, and psychology books (including *Necessary Losses* and *Imperfect Control*). Her audience was identified as WAMMMs (White, Affluent, Middle-class, Middle-aged, Married Mothers) by a *Los Angeles Times* critic reviewing *Love and Shrimp,* a musical for which Viorst wrote the book and lyrics (Shelly Markham wrote the music). The following lines were half-sung, half-spoken by a character called simply "Woman 3."

(Sings.)

If I quit hoping he'll show up with flowers, and

He quits hoping I'll squeeze him an orange, and

I quit shaving my legs with his razor, and

He quits wiping his feet with my face towel, and

We avoid discussions like

Is he really smarter than I am, or simply more glib,

Maybe we'll make it.

(Speaks.)

Even if I had a PhD in psychology,

Even if I were a diplomatic whiz,

Even if I were Queen of the Charmers and more irresistibly sexual

Than whoever the current reigning sexpot is,

And even if I had a fortune to squander on payoffs,

And even if I had Mafia connections,

It still would be impossible for me to persuade my husband

To stop—please stop—the car, and ask for directions.

(Sings.)

If I quit looking to prove that he's hostile, and

He quits looking for dust on the tables, and

I quit inviting Lenore with the giggle, and

He quits inviting Maurice with the complex, and

We avoid discussions like

Suppose I died, which one of our friends would he marry,

Maybe we'll make it.

(Speaks.)

Even if I were collapsing from thirst and from hunger,

Even if I were reduced to darkest gloom,

Even if I observed, between sobs, that we should have arrived three hours ago

And the inn was going to give away our room,

And even if I revived all my marital grievances:

Old hurts and humiliations and rejections,

It still would be impossible for me to persuade my husband

To stop—just stop—the car, and ask for directions.

(Sings.)

If I quit clearing the plates while he's eating, and

He quits clearing his throat while I'm speaking, and

I quit implying I could have done better, and

He quits implying he wishes I had, and

We avoid discussions like

Does his mother really love him, or is she simply one of those over-possessive, devouring
     women who can't let go,

(Speaks.)

Even if I were to throw a full-scale temper tantrum,

Even if I were to call him an uncouth name,

Even if I were to not-so-gently note that, should we wind up getting divorced,

He would have nobody else but himself to blame,

And even if I, in a tone I concede is called screaming,

Enumerated his countless imperfections,

It still would be impossible for me to persuade my husband

To stop the goddamn car, and ask for directions.

(Sings.)

Maybe

Well, maybe

It's just possible

(Speaks.)

But not if he turns the heat down so low that one of these days—what does *he* care?—my
     thumbs will fall off.

And not if I turn the heat up so high that one of these days—that's what *he* says—his fillings
     will melt.

(Sings.)

Well, what the hell,

Even if we're thermostatically and navigationally

Incompatible

And even if I think we should call my father once a week,

And he thinks we should call my father once a year,

And even if I like a light in every room of the house,

And he likes to light the whole house with one 60-watt bulb,

And even if he says I play the music so low he can't hear it,

And I say he plays it so loud that it's wrecking my ear drums
And soon will be giving me brain damage,
Maybe we'll make it.
Maybe we'll make it.

FORTUNE COOKIE

Marriage lets you annoy one special person for the rest of your life.

G

HAPPINESS

JOSEPH ADDISON
"WEDLOCK'S AN ILL MEN EAGERLY EMBRACE," 1711

English author Joseph Addison (1672–1719) was admired for his essays, poetry, and plays. He wasn't nearly as successful at marriage, which he entered into in 1716 after courting the widowed Dowager Countess of Warwick for many years. The courtship had begun when Addison was tutoring her son, but—according to a biographical essay by Samuel Johnson—once married, she continued to treat Addison more as an employee than as an equal.

Those marriages generally abound most with love and constancy, that are preceded by long courtship. The passion should strike root, and gather strength before marriage be grafted on it. A long course of hopes and expectations fixes the idea in our minds, and habituates us to a fondness of the person beloved.

There is nothing of so great importance to us as the good qualities of one to whom we join ourselves for life; they do not only make our present state agreeable, but often determine our happiness to all eternity.

ELBERT HUBBARD
LOVE, LIFE & WORK, 1906

For background on Hubbard, see Friendship, page 137.

There are six requisites in every happy marriage; the first is Faith and the remaining five are Confidence.

H

ERNEST GROVES
MARRIAGE, 1933

A sociology professor at the University of North Carolina, Ernest R. Groves (1877–1946) was one of the first academics to offer a college course on marriage.

It is significant that the two words most commonly used to describe marriage success or failure are happy and unhappy. These terms are seldom employed by adults to describe other activities or other relationships. In the vocabulary of children, however, they appear frequently and are used to express judgment regarding both minor and major satisfactions and disappointments. . . . This fact suggests that the individual is likely to bring to the marriage relationship not only greater expectation and daydreaming than is carried to any other of his associations but that with this goes greater resistance to reconstruction of his expectations.

VIRGINIA WOOLF, CIRCA 1936

Despite her depressions and eventual suicide, Virginia Woolf (see Children, page 26) had moments of great marital joy. Even in her last note to her husband, Leonard, she wrote: "If anybody could have saved me it would have been you." According to a friend who later repeated it to Leonard, Woolf offered the comment below in answer to a question she herself had asked: What was the happiest moment in one's life?

I think it's the moment when one is walking in one's garden, perhaps picking off a few dead flowers, and suddenly one thinks: "My husband lives in that house, and he loves me."

LEWIS TERMAN
PSYCHOLOGICAL FACTORS IN MARITAL HAPPINESS, 1938

A developer of the Stanford-Binet IQ test, Lewis Terman (1877–1956) was a complex mixture of inquisitive scientist and didactic geneticist. He believed that IQ tests could not just reveal intelligence but also should influence the treatment of those who took them: better opportunities, schooling, and jobs for the "gifted," and opposite treatment for those who scored badly—even to include the sterilization of subjects then known as "feebleminded." Terman was also among the first psychologists to try to quantify happiness in marriage. As to the following list, he wrote: "The subject who 'passes' on all 10 of these items is a distinctly better-than-average marital risk. Any one of the 10 appears from the data of this study to be more important than virginity at marriage."

The 10 background circumstances most predictive of marital happiness are:

1.   Superior happiness of parents.
2.   Childhood happiness.
3.   Lack of conflict with mother.
4.   Home discipline that was firm, not harsh.
5.   Strong attachment to mother.
6.   Strong attachment to father.
7.   Lack of conflict with father.
8.   Parental frankness about matters of sex.
9.   Infrequency and mildness of childhood punishment.
10.   Premarital attitude toward sex that was free from disgust or aversion.

There are six requisites in every happy marriage; the first is Faith and the remaining five are Confidence.

NATIONAL FORUM POSTER, CIRCA 1940

Dr. Terman's *Psychological Factors in Marital Happiness* (see above) revealed the results of his study of 792 couples. A year later, Drs. Leonard Cottrell and Ernest Burgess published *Predicting Success or Failure in Marriage*, the result of their study of 526 couples in Illinois. A synthesis of their findings led to the creation of this poster for the National Forum, a Chicago-based private nonprofit that produced and sold educational posters and was directed by the Rev. Dr. William Russell Shull.

HOME

"THE HOUSEHOLDER OF PARIS"
THE GOOD WIFE'S GUIDE, CIRCA 1392

This advice book's author, popularly called "Le Ménagier de Paris," is unknown but was purported to be a husband writing to a much younger wife. The volume included recipes for meals and home remedies, as well as tips on conversation, sexual advice, and household hints. The passages below seem like a combination of sybaritic dream and pestilential nightmare.

Love your husband's person carefully. I entreat you to see that he has clean linen, for that is your domain, while the concerns and troubles of men are those outside affairs that they must handle, amidst coming and going, running here and there, in rain, wind, snow, and hail, sometimes drenched, sometimes dry, now sweating, now shivering, ill fed, ill lodged, ill shod, and poorly rested. Yet nothing represents a hardship for him, because the thought of his wife's good care for him upon his return comforts him immensely. The ease, joys, and pleasures he knows she will provide for him herself, or have done for him in her presence, cheer him: removing his shoes in front of a good fire, washing his feet, offering clean shoes and socks, serving plenteous food and drink, respectfully honoring him. After this, she puts him to sleep in white sheets and his nightcap, covered with good furs, and satisfies him with other joys and amusements, intimacies, loves, and secrets about which I remain silent. The next day, she has set out fresh shirts and garments for him.

. . . I urge you to bewitch and bewitch again your future husband, and protect him from holes in the roof and smoky fires, and do not quarrel with him, but be sweet, pleasant, and peaceful with him. Make certain that in winter he has a good fire without smoke, and let him slumber, warmly wrapped, cozy between your breasts, and in this way bewitch him. . . .

If you have a room or a floor in your dwelling infested with flies, take little sprigs of fern, tie them together with threads like tassels, hang them up, and all the flies will settle on them in the evening. Then take down the tassels and throw them outside. *Item,* close up your room firmly in the evening, leaving just one small opening in the eastern wall. At dawn, all the flies will exit through this opening, and then you seal it up. *Item,* take a bowl of milk and a hare's gall bladder, mix them together, and then set out two or three bowls of the mixture in places where the flies gather, and all that taste it will die. *Item,* otherwise, tie a linen stocking to the bottom of a pierced pot and set the pot in the place where the flies gather and smear the inside with honey, or apples, or pears. When it is full of flies, place a platter over the opening, then shake it. . . .

In this way, serve your husband and have him waited on in your house, protecting and keeping him from all irritations and providing him all the creature comforts that you can imagine. Rely on him for external matters, for if he is considerate, he will make even greater efforts and work harder than you could wish. If you do what is said here, he will always miss you and his heart will always be with you and your soothing ways, shunning all other houses, all other women, all other services and households. If you look after him in the way this treatise urges, in comparison with you, everything else will be dust. Your behavior should follow the example of those who traverse the world on horseback. As soon as they arrive home from a journey, they provide fresh litter for their horses up to their bellies. These horses are unharnessed and bedded down, given honey, choice hay, and ground oats, and are always better tended when they return to their own stables than anywhere else. If horses are made so comfortable, it makes good sense that a person should be treated similarly upon his return, particularly a lord at his own household.

WILLIAM ALCOTT
THE YOUNG WIFE, OR DUTIES OF WOMAN
IN THE MARRIAGE RELATION, 1838

A teacher, physician, and early proponent of strict vegetarianism, William Andrus Alcott (1798–1859) was also the author of more than a hundred books and pamphlets on health, home, and diet. His extremism about diet—he eschewed all animal products and even some vegetables ("radishes," he wrote, "are miserable things")—was matched by a conservatism in his view of marital roles and, in particular, the need for wives to instruct, to protect, and to keep a household healthy.

Alcott, cousin of the philosopher Bronson Alcott and Bronson's daughter, Louisa May Alcott, was referred to in a 1960s article as "The Least-Remembered Alcott," but his influence during his lifetime was considered substantial.

The importance of chemistry to the housewife, though admitted in words, seems, after all, but little understood. How can we hope to urge her forward to the work of ventilating and properly cleansing her apartments and her furniture, until she understands not only the native constitution of our atmosphere, but the nature of the changes which this atmosphere undergoes in our fire rooms, our sleeping rooms, our beds, our cellars, and our lungs? How can we expect her to cooperate, with all her heart, in the work of simplifying and improving cookery, simplifying our meals, and removing, step by step, from our tables, objectionable articles, or deleterious compounds, until she understands effectually the nature and results of fermentation, as well as of mastication and digestion? How can we expect her to detect noxious gases, and prevent unfavorable chemical changes, and the poisonous compounds which sometimes result, and which have again and again destroyed health and life, while she is as ignorant as thousands are, who are called housewives, of the first principles of chemical science? Would it not be to expect impossibilities?

If you do what is said here, he will always miss you.

H

PHOEBE CARY
"THE WIFE," 1854

Phoebe Cary (1824–1871), the younger of the two poets known as the Cary Sisters, tended to write lighter, wittier verse than her sister, Alice. "The Wife" was her takeoff on the well-known poem "A Death-Bed," by James Aldrich, which went: "Her suffering ended with the day, / Yet lived she at its close, / And breathed the long, long night away / In statue-like repose. / But when the sun in all his state / Illumed the eastern skies, / She passed through Glory's morning gate / And walked in Paradise!"

Neither Cary sister was married. Born in Ohio, they lived together in New York City, where they hosted a popular literary salon.

Her washing ended with the day,
Yet lived she at its close,
And passed the long, long night away,
In darning ragged hose.

But when the sun in all his state
Illumed the eastern skies,
She passed about the kitchen grate,
And went to making pies.

CHRISTOPHER MORLEY
"WASHING THE DISHES," 1917

American author Christopher Morley (1890–1957) was lighthearted and prolific in verse, fiction, and essays. He was also a judge for the Book-of-the-Month Club and an editor of several editions of *Bartlett's Familiar Quotations*. Ironically, one of his own best quotes never made it into that collection: "Read, every day, something no one else is reading. Think, every day, something no one else is thinking. Do, every day, something no one else would be silly enough to do."

Morley had been married—to Helen Booth Fairchild—for three years when he wrote this poem. They would have four children together. "Willow cup" refers to the popular eighteenth-century Blue Willow china pattern.

When we on simple rations sup
How easy is the washing up!
But heavy feeding complicates
The task by soiling many plates.

And though I grant that I have prayed
That we might find a serving-maid,
I'd scullion all my days, I think,
To see Her smile across the sink!

I wash, She wipes. In water hot
I souse each dish and pan and pot;
While Taffy mutters, purrs, and begs,
And rubs himself against my legs.

The man who never in his life
Has washed the dishes with his wife
Or polished up the silver plate—
He still is largely celibate.

One warning: there is certain ware
That must be handled with all care:
The Lord Himself will give you up
If you should drop a willow cup!

PHYLLIS McGINLEY
"THE 5:32," 1941

Phyllis McGinley (1905–1978) grew up in a family struggling through land speculation and farming in Oregon, Colorado, and Utah. At twenty-four she moved to New York, where she taught, wrote advertising jingles, and began contributing the kind of poetry generally known as "light verse" to magazines, especially *The New Yorker*. When in her thirties she married Bell Telephone executive Bill Hayden and moved to Westchester County, she embraced and described the joys of suburban living with lyricism and passion. Often dismissed by feminists as either hopelessly conservative or, worse, self-deluded, McGinley stayed true to her traditional values—as well as traditional rhyme and meter. She won the Pulitzer Prize for Poetry in 1961 and published eighteen books, including poetry, children's stories, and essays.

Hayden eventually retired from his job to help McGinley in her career, often saying, "There are 70,000 employees at the phone company, but only one Phyllis."

She said, If tomorrow my world were torn in two,
Blacked out, dissolved, I think I would remember
(As if transfixed in unsurrendering amber)
This hour best of all the hours I knew:

When cars came backing into the little station,
Children scuffing the seats, and the women driving
With ribbons around their hair, and the trains arriving,
And the men getting off with tired but practiced motion.

Yes, I would remember my life like this, she said:
Autumn, the platform red with Virginia creeper,
And a man coming toward me, smiling, the evening paper
Under his arm, and his hat pushed back on his head;

And wood smoke lying like haze on the quiet town,
And dinner waiting, and the sun not yet gone down.

PAT MAINARDI
"THE POLITICS OF HOUSEWORK," 1968

This essay was originally printed as a *New England Free Press* pamphlet, later in the magazine *Redstockings*, and it became part of the feminist canon. A decade and a half later, Pat Mainardi (1942–) became a PhD in art history, specializing in eighteenth- and nineteenth-century European art.

In addition to teaching at several colleges and universities, Mainardi has published articles and books on art and politics, as well as a history of marriage in nineteenth-century France. Italics and ellipsis in the original.

H

We women have been brainwashed more than even we can imagine. Probably too many years of seeing media-women coming over their shiny waxed floors or breaking down over their dirty shirt collars. Men have no such conditioning. They recognize the essential fact of housework right from the very beginning. Which is that it stinks.

Here's my list of dirty chores: buying groceries, carting them home and putting them away; cooking meals and washing dishes and pots; doing the laundry; digging out the place when things get out of control; washing floors. The list could go on but the sheer necessities are bad enough. All of us have to do these jobs, or get someone else to do them for us. The longer my husband contemplated these chores, the more repulsed he became, and so proceeded the change from the normally sweet considerate Dr. Jekyll into the crafty Mr. Hyde who would stop at nothing to avoid the horrors of—housework. As he felt himself backed into a corner laden with dirty dishes, brooms, mops and reeking garbage, his front teeth grew longer and pointier, his fingernails haggled and his eyes grew wild. Housework trivial? Not on your life! Just try to share the burden.

So ensued a dialogue that's been going on for several years. Here are some of the high points.

"I don't mind sharing the housework, but I don't do it very well. We should each do the things we're best at."

Meaning: Unfortunately I'm no good at things like washing dishes or cooking. What I do best is a little light carpentry, changing light bulbs, moving furniture. *(How often do you move furniture?)*

Also meaning: Historically the lower classes (Blacks and women) have had hundreds of years doing menial jobs. It would be a waste of manpower to train someone else to do them now.

Also meaning: I don't like the dull stupid boring jobs, so you should do them.

"I don't mind sharing the work, but you'll have to show me how to do it."

Meaning: I ask a lot of questions and you'll have to show me everything, every time I do it because I don't remember so good. Also, don't try to sit down and read while I'm doing my jobs because I'm going to annoy hell out of you until it's easier to do them yourself.

"We used to be so happy!" (said whenever it was his turn to do something)

Meaning: I used to be so happy.

Meaning: Life without housework is bliss. No quarrel here. Perfect agreement.

"We have different standards, and why should I have to work to your standards? That's unfair."

Meaning: If I begin to get bugged by the dirt and crap, I will say "This place sure is a sty" or "How can anyone live like this?" and wait for your reaction. I know that all women have a sore called *guilt over a messy house* or *housework is ultimately my responsibility.* If I rub this sore long and hard enough it'll bleed and you'll do the work. I can outwait you.

Also meaning: I can provoke innumerable scenes over the housework issue. Eventually, doing all the housework yourself will be less painful to you than trying to get me to do half.

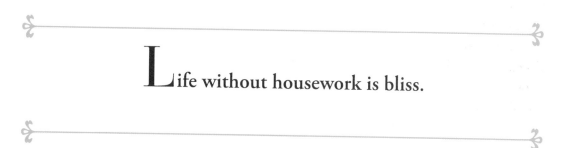

Life without housework is bliss.

"I've got nothing against sharing the housework, but you can't make me do it on your schedule."

Meaning: Passive resistance. I'll do it when I damn well please, if at all. If my job is doing dishes, it's easier to do them once a week. If taking out laundry, once a month. If washing the floors, once a year. If you don't like it, do it yourself oftener, and then I won't do it at all. . . .

"Housework is too trivial to even talk about."

Meaning: It's even more trivial to do. Housework is beneath my status. My purpose in life is to deal with matters of significance. Yours is to deal with matters of insignificance. You should do the housework.

"In animal societies, wolves, for example, the top animal is usually a male even where he is not chosen for brute strength but on the basis of cunning and intelligence. Isn't that interesting?"

Meaning: I have historical, psychological, anthropological and biological justification for keeping you down. How can you ask the top wolf to be equal?

"Women's Liberation isn't really a political movement."

Meaning: The Revolution is coming too close to home.

Also meaning: I am only interested in how I am oppressed, not how I oppress others. Therefore the war, the draft and the university are political. Women's Liberation is not.

"Man's accomplishments have always depended on getting help from other people, mostly women. What great man would have accomplished what he did if he had to do his own housework?"

Meaning: Oppression is built into the system and I as the white American male receive the benefits of this system. I don't want to give them up.

DIXIE CUP ADVERTISEMENT
LADIES' HOME JOURNAL, 1970

The ad showed a middle-aged, disgruntled man lying in bed while, in the background, a woman stands at a kitchen sink, surrounded by towers of presumably dirty glasses.

A woman's place is next to her husband. Not next to her sink.

If he wanted a glass washer, he'd have married one. But he wanted a wife. A woman. You.

And where *are* you? At the sink as usual. Washing those endless stacks of glasses your kids dirty up all day.

So put a Dixie Kitchen Dispenser above your sink. Then you'll have time on your hands instead of dishwater.

Time to paint pictures. Bake a peach pie. Or snuggle up to your husband and watch TV.

With a Dixie Kitchen Dispenser and Cups, you can stop being a glass washer. And start being a wife.

Try finding a marriage counselor for under $1.00.

A Dixie Kitchen Dispenser will get you together again.

HONEYMOON

BRITISH MEZZOTINTS
THE HONEY-MOON AND *SIX WEEKS AFTER MARRIAGE*, 1777

HONORÉ DE BALZAC
THE PHYSIOLOGY OF MARRIAGE, 1829

Balzac himself (see Fidelity, page 113) didn't marry until the woman with whom he had corresponded for decades was finally widowed and accepted his proposal. He died just five months later.

The fate of the house hangs on the first night.

GEORGE NAPHEYS
THE PHYSICAL LIFE OF WOMAN, 1869

An innovator in offering a frank and scientific approach to sex education, Dr. George Napheys (1842–1876) dedicated much of his short life to researching and writing books that were intended to be more useful and accurate than either the backyard gossip or dubious pamphlets of his day. *The Physical Life of Woman* sold nearly 150,000 copies in its first three years and inspired the Rev. Henry Ward Beecher (see Freedom, page 130) to write: "Every mother should have this book, nor should she suffer a child to be married without the knowledge which this work contains." That praise notwithstanding, Napheys was exactly wrong about a woman's time of greatest infertility and was on extraordinarily dubious ground in his comments about the differences between blondes and brunettes.

The initiation into marriage, like its full fruition, maternity, is attended with more or less suffering. Much, however, may be done to avert and to lessen the pain which waits upon the first step in this new life. For this purpose, regard must be had to the selection of the day. We have said that a time about midway between the monthly recurring periods is best fitted for the consummation of marriage. As this is a season of sterility, it recommends itself on this account, in the interest of both the mother and offspring. The first nuptial relations should be fruitless, in order that the indispositions possibly arising from them shall have time to subside before the appearance of the disturbances incident to pregnancy. One profound change should not too quickly succeed the other. About the tenth day after menstruation should therefore be chosen for the marriage ceremony.

It sometimes happens that marriage is consummated with difficulty. To overcome this, care, management, and forbearance should always be employed, and anything like precipitation and violence avoided. Only the consequences of unrestrained impetuosity are to be feared. In those rare cases in which greater resistance is experienced than can be overcome by gentle means, the existence of a condition contrary to nature may be suspected. Violence can then only be productive of injury, and is not without danger. Medical art should be appealed to, as it alone can afford assistance in such an emergency.

Although the first conjugal approaches are ordinarily accompanied by slight flooding, a loss of blood does not always occur. Its absence proves nothing. The appearance of blood was formerly regarded as a test of virginity . . . [but] it is now well known that widows, and wives long separated from their husbands, often have a like experience. The temperament is not without its influence. In those of lymphatic temperament, pale blondes, who often suffer from local discharge and weakness, the parts being relaxed, there is less pain and little or no haemorrhage. In brunettes, who have never had any such troubles, the case is reversed. The use of baths, unguents, etc., by the young wife, however serviceable they might prove, is obviously impracticable. This great change sometimes also produces swelling and inflammation of the glands of the neck.

H

Only the consequences of unrestrained impetuosity are to be feared.

Marital relations ordinarily continue during the first few weeks to be more or less painful. General constitutional disturbance and disorders of the nervous system often result. These troubles are all increased by the stupid custom of hurrying the bride from place to place, at a time when the bodily quiet and the mental calmness and serenity so desirable to her should be the only objects in view. Too frequent indulgence at this period is a fruitful source of various inflammatory diseases, and often occasions temporary sterility and ill-health. The old custom requiring a three days' separation after the first nuptial approach was a wise one, securing to the young wife the soothing and restoring influence of rest. Nothing was lost by it, and much gained.

EDWARD HARDY
HOW TO BE HAPPY THOUGH MARRIED: BEING A HANDBOOK TO MARRIAGE BY A GRADUATE IN THE UNIVERSITY OF MATRIMONY, 1886

The "though" in the title may seem ironic, but there wasn't much humor to be found in this volume by the Rev. Edward John Hardy (1849–1920). A British chaplain who served with his country's armed forces in various foreign outposts, he approached his subject with stereotypical Victorian cultural and religious convictions, stressing compromise and mutual respect. But he showed particular attention to the way marriages started, writing: "In matrimony, as in so many other things, a good beginning is half the battle." By that reasoning, it followed that the best beginning would be the best honeymoon.

[The honeymoon] certainly ought to be the happiest month in our lives; but it may, like every other good thing, be spoiled by mismanagement. When this is the case, we take our honeymoon like other pleasures—sadly. Instead of happy reminscences, nothing is left of it except its jars.

You take, says the philosophical observer, a man and a woman, who in nine cases out of ten know very little about each other (though they generally fancy they do), you cut off the woman from all her female friends, you deprive the man of his ordinary business and ordinary pleasures, and you condemn this unhappy pair to spend a month of enforced seclusion in each other's society. If they marry in the summer and start on a tour, the man is oppressed with a plethora of sight-seeing, while the lady, as often as not, becomes seriously ill from fatigue and excitement.

A newly-married man took his bride on a tour to Switzerland for the honeymoon, and when there induced her to attempt with him the ascent of one of the high peaks. The lady, who at home had never ascended a hill higher than a church, was much alarmed, and had to be carried by the guides with her eyes blindfolded, so as not to witness the horrors of the passage. The bridegroom walked close to her, expostulating respecting her fear. He spoke in honeymoon whispers; but the rarefaction of the air was such that every word was audible. "You told me, Leonora, that you always felt happy—no matter where you were—so long as you were in my company. Then why are you not happy now?" "Yes, Charles, I did," replied she, sobbing hysterically; "but I never meant above the snow line." It is at such times as these that awkward angles of temper make themselves manifest, which, under a more sensible system, might have been concealed for years, perhaps for ever.

SHEET MUSIC COVER, 1909

H. W. LONG
SANE SEX LIFE AND SANE SEX LIVING, 1919

An early advocate of eugenics who wrote that "if the breeding of human beings were as carefully managed as that of horses and cattle, the results would be no less remarkable," Harland William Long (1869–1943) was a practicing physician and notably even more candid in his advice about sex than William J. Robinson (see Grievances, page 144; Sex, page 403).

Long's book was one of many volumes targeted by Boston's Watch and Ward Society, a particularly rabid antivice organization that, spanning the nineteenth and twentieth centuries, censored the books, plays, and pastimes it deemed objectionable; the group was responsible for the accuracy and the allure of the phrase "Banned in Boston."

Both [bride and bridegroom] must be *taught* to *"Know what they are about"* before they engage in the sexual act, and be able to meet each other sanely, *righteously, lovingly,* because they both *desire* what each has to give to the other; in a way in which neither claims any *rights,* or makes any *demands* of the other—in a word, in *perfect concord* of agreement and action, of which mutual love is the inspirer, and *definite knowledge* the directive agent.

Such a first meeting of bride and bridegroom will be no raping affair. There will be no shock in it, no dread, no shame or thought of shame; but as perfectly as two drops of water flow together and become one, the bodies and souls of the parties to the act will mingle in a unity the most perfect and blissful that can ever be experienced by human beings in this world. This is no dream! It is a most blessed reality, which all normally made husbands and wives can attain to, if only they are properly *taught and educated*, if only they will learn how to reach such blissful condition.

MARGARET SANGER
HAPPINESS IN MARRIAGE, 1926

Like Long (above), Margaret Sanger (1879–1966) had some choice words for the way sex could go right or wrong on the honeymoon night. The mother of the birth-control movement, arrested eight times for distributing information about contraception, Sanger was downright pragmatic when it came to what she called the "alone at last" moment.

The custom of the wedding journey offers both advantages and disadvantages. Too often decisions concerning the bridal night are determined by train schedules and such exigencies. It should be obvious to all sensible people that a Pullman car is hardly suitable for the consummation of romance or a proper setting for the first conjugal embrace.

ISABEL HUTTON
THE SEX TECHNIQUE IN MARRIAGE, 1932

The chapter on "Preparation for Marriage" advised engaged couples to consider money, race, nationality, "feeblemindedness," and the possible effects of illnesses from syphilis to insanity as reasons to question or cancel their plans. But for couples who managed to run the gauntlet, Scottish physician Isabel Emslie Hutton (1887–1960) offered less radical advice on honeymoon sleeping arrangements.

The place where the honeymoon is to be spent should be well considered, for the impression it makes is very important and means a good deal to a sensitive woman. If possible it should be beautiful and quiet, but not so isolated that the young couple will be thrown entirely on their own resources. There must be something in the way of walking, games, or other entertainment. It is a great mistake to do a long tour or to travel about, and far more sensible to arrange to stay quietly in one place for most of the time. The accommodation should be as good as the man can

> Having separate beds in the early days makes it much easier both for the woman and the man.

afford, and carefully chosen; if possible there should be a dressing-room for the man, and at first perhaps the best arrangement is to have two beds. Probably this is the most healthy and practical plan to follow throughout, but whatever husband and wife decide to do later on, will depend on their individual temperaments.

Having separate beds in the early days makes it much easier both for the woman, who is thus introduced more gradually to the conditions of married life, and for the man because he has not the intimate physical contact which is so sexually exciting for him, especially at this time.

These things may seem too small to mention, but to a sensitive woman they may make just all the difference between the beginnings of a happy married life and an unhappy one.

JOHN LENNON AND YOKO ONO, 1969

For fans of the Beatles, Yoko Ono was an enigma from the start. With her conceptual art, sitar-like voice, and overall etherealness, she was a constant source of press coverage and speculation. When she married John Lennon (1940–1980) in 1969, the couple invited reporters and photographers to their "Bed-In," where their honeymoon suite was decked out with signs for peace. The event was immortalized in a bevy of iconic photographs, and in John Lennon and Paul McCartney's subsequent "Ballad of John and Yoko," featuring the lines, "The newspeople said, 'Say, what're you doing in bed?' / I said, 'We're only trying to get some peace.'"

H

IAN McEWAN
ON CHESIL BEACH, 2007

Set at an English Channel resort in 1962, the thirteenth book of fiction by Ian McEwan (1948–) tells the story of two virgins, Edward and Florence, on their honeymoon. Their love is not in question, but it turns out that they have vastly different desires: he to experience, at last, the wonders of sex; she to avoid it at all costs. Their two needs collide, finally—and, for their marriage, fatally—in this passage.

Prompted by her laughter, he moved closer to her again and tried to take her hand, and again she moved away. It was crucial to be able to think straight. She started her speech as she had rehearsed it in her thoughts, with the all-important declaration.

"You know I love you. Very, very much. And I know you love me. I've never doubted it. I love being with you, and I want to spend my life with you, and you say you feel the same way. It should all be quite simple. But it isn't—we're in a mess, like you said. Even with all this love. I also know that it's completely my fault, and we both know why. It must be pretty obvious to you by now that . . ."

She faltered; he went to speak, but she raised her hand.

"That I'm pretty hopeless, absolutely hopeless at sex. Not only am I no good at it, I don't seem to need it like other people, like you do. It just isn't something that's part of me. I don't like it, I don't like the thought of it. I have no idea why that is, but I think it isn't going to change." . . .

"I've thought about this carefully, and it's not as stupid as it sounds. I mean, on first hearing. We love each other—that's a given. Neither of us doubts it. We already know how happy we make each other. We're free now to make our own choices, our own lives. Really, no one can tell us how to live. Free agents! And people live in all kinds of ways now, they can live by their own rules and standards without having to ask anyone else for permission. Mummy knows two homosexuals, they live in a flat together, like man and wife. Two men. In Oxford, in Beaumont Street. They're very quiet about it. They both teach at Christ Church. No one bothers them. And we can make our own rules too. It's because I know you love me that I can actually say this. What I mean, it's this—Edward, I love you, and we don't have to be like everyone, I mean, no one, no one at all . . . no one would know what we did or didn't do. We could be together, live together, and if you wanted, really wanted, that's to say, whenever it happened, and of course it would happen, I would understand, more than that, I'd want it, I would because I want you to be happy and free. I'd never be jealous, as long as I knew that you loved me." . . .

He made a noise between his teeth, more of a hiss than a sigh, and when he spoke he made a yelping sound. His indignation was so violent it sounded like triumph. "My God! Florence. Have I got this right? You want me to go with other women! Is that it?"

She said quietly, "Not if you didn't want to."

"You're telling me I could do it with anyone I like but you."

She did not answer.

"Have you actually forgotten that we were married today? We're not two old queers living in secret on Beaumont Street. We're man and wife!"

The lower clouds parted again, and though there was no direct moonlight, a feeble glow, diffused through higher strata, moved along the beach to include the couple standing by the great fallen tree. In his fury, he bent down to pick up a large smooth stone, which he smacked into his right palm and back into his left.

He was close to shouting now. "With my body I thee worship! That's what you promised today. In front of everybody. Don't you realize how disgusting and ridiculous your idea is? And what an insult it is. An insult to me! I mean, I mean"—he struggled for the words—"how you!"

HUSBANDS, HOW TO GET

JOHN ADAMS
DIARY, 1761

American independence was still fifteen years away when the future U.S. president John Adams (1735–1826) wrote this draft of a letter that scholars believe was intended to be published as an essay. The nieces were a literary device, and though the tone of the letter is mature and instructive, Adams himself had yet to marry the famous Abigail.

"Bundling" was a common practice of the time, wherein an unmarried couple was allowed in a bed together, wrapped tightly in blankets, sometimes with a board placed between them, so that they could talk and be intimate without having sex.

Dear Nieces.

You remember that I wrote you a new Years Address, about two Years since, containing some few Articles of Advice that I then thought would pass with Propriety, considering the Relation between us, from me to you. You are at least two Years older, than you were then, and from a careful observation of your Conduct, I have found few Occasions of Blame, and from your Conversation, and a frequent Inspection of your Compositions, I have reason to think your time has been in general, and in Comparison of the rest of your own sex, not ill improved.

But there are numberless Particulars that . . . will . . . be I hope no unacceptable Present, for the Year 1761.

The first relate to the Delicacy of your own Persons and Houses . . . the very general Complaint of british Ladies is that their Teeth, Necks, Hair, Perspiration and Respiration, Kichens and even Parlors are no cleaner nor sweeter than they should be. And the same ground of Complaint is in America. For my own Part, tho not very attentive to my own Person, nothing is so disgustful and loathsome to me, and almost all our sex are of my mind, as this Negligence. My own Daughters, whenever they shall grow to Years of Discretion, I am determined to throw into a great Kettle and Boil till they are clean, If I ever find them half so nasty as I have seen some. . . .

2. The next Article is that of Dress. It may be just[ly] considered, as the Principal Design of a young Lady from her Birth to her Marriage, to procure and prepare herself for a worthy Companion in Life. This I believe is modestly enough expressed. Now the finest face, and shape, that ever Nature formed, would be insufficient to attract and fix the Eye of a Gentleman without some Assistance and Decoration of Dress. And I believe an handsome shoe, well judged Variety of Colours, in Linnen, Laces &c., and even the Rustling of silks has determined as many Matches as any natural features, or Proportions or Motions. Hes a fool that is determined wholly by either or by both, but even a wise man will take all these, as well as others less, into Consideration. . . .

3. The 3d is [a] sense of Elegance. . . .

Neither rich furniture nor dress, nor Provisions, without this, will ever please.

The 4th is Behaviour in mixed Companies. I would not have you Pedants in Greek and Latin nor the Depths of science, nor yet over fond to talk upon any Thing. When your opinion is asked, give it. When you know any Thing, that the Company are at a loss for, disclose it. But what I mean is this. Attend to the Conversation of Gentlemen even when News, Politicks, Morals, Oeconomy, nay even when Literature and science but beyond the fathom of your Line make the subject: do not attempt to turn the Conversation to Billy's Prattle—To the Doggs, or Negroes or Catts, or to any little contemptible tittle tattle of your own.

5thly. Observations of Mankind, or what is called the World. As the House is your Theatre of Action, an Attentive Observation of Domestic Characters should be your Rule. You are in all Probability in some future Part of your Life, to have Husbands. Remark carefully the Behaviour of other Wifes, wherever you go, to their Husbands, but distinguish well between Propriety of Behaviour and the Contrary. . . .

6thly. Under this Head of Conversation with the World falls naturally enough . . . Conversation with some Person of the other Sex alone: and this before Marriage And even

Courtship. Our illustrious young Monarck, indeed, will probably be married by Proxy to some Princess abroad, that he never saw: and this is for Reasons of State, no doubt necessary. . . .

And it seems, by what I see and hear, that Persons of Rank and figure even in this Province, are desirous that their Daughters should be married to Men who never saw them, by their prevailing Practice of concealing them from all Males, till a formal Courtship is opened. This Practice must proceed either from deplorable folly, an Awkward Imitation of Majesty, or else from a Consciousness of their Daughters futility and a Dread to expose them.

But be it remembered that no Man that is free and can think, will rush blindfold, into the Arms of any such Ladies, who, tho it is possible they may prove Angells of Light, may yet more probably turn out Haggs of Hell.

You must therefore associate yourselves in some good Degree, and under certain Guards and Restraints, even privately with young fellows. And, tho Discretion must be used, and Caution, yet on [considering] the whole of the Arguments on each side, I cannot wholly disapprove of Bundling.

"ADVICE TO UNMARRIED LADIES"
NEW-YORK DAILY GAZETTE, 1789

The article was not signed.

If you have blue eyes—languish.

    If black eyes—leer.

    If you have a pretty foot, wear short petticoats.

    If you are in the least *doubtful* as to that point—let them be rather long.

    If you have good teeth—don't forget to laugh now and then.

    If you have bad ones—you must only simper.

    While you are young—sit with your face to the light.

    When you are a little advanced—sit with your back to the window.

    If you have pretty hands and arms—play on the lute.

    If they are rather clumsy—work tapestry.

    If you have a bad voice—always speak in a low tone.

    If you have the finest voice in the world—never speak in a high tone.

    If you dance well—dance but seldom.

    If you dance ill—never dance at all.

If you sing well—make no previous excuses.

If you sing indifferently—hesitate not a moment when you are asked; for few people are judges of singing, but every one is sensible of a desire to please.

If in conversation you think a person wrong—rather hint a difference of opinion, than offer a contradiction.

If you find a person telling an absolute falsehood, let it pass over in silence—it is not worth your while to make any one your enemy by proving him a liar.

Never touch the sore place in any one's character—for be assured, whoever you are, you have a sore place in your own; and woman is a flower that may be blasted in a moment.

It is always in your power to make a friend by smiles—but a folly to make enemies by frowns.

If you dance well—dance but seldom.
If you dance ill—never dance at all.

When you have an opportunity to praise—do it with all your heart.

When you are forced to blame—appear, at least, to do it with reluctance.

If you are envious of another woman—never shew it but by allowing her every good quality and perfection except those she really possesses.

If you wish to let all the world know you are in love with a particular man—treat him with formality; and every one else with ease and freedom.

Make it a rule to please all—and never appear insensible to any desirous of pleasing or obeying you, however aukwardly it may be executed.

If you are disposed to be pettish or insolent—it is better to exercise your ill humours on your dog, your cat, or your servant, than your friends.

If you would preserve beauty—rise early.

If you would preserve esteem—be gentle.

If you would obtain power—be condescending.

If you would live happy—endeavor to promote the happiness of others.

DOROTHY DIX
COLUMN, 1922

Elizabeth Meriwether (1861–1951) was twenty-one when she married George Gilmer and still in her early twenties when she had to face the fact that he was both physically and mentally ill. Though the couple never divorced, she spent a great deal of time away from him. Hired by the New Orleans *Daily Picayune* in 1894, she started by writing obituaries, but a year later, as "Dorothy Dix," she introduced the weekly advice column for which she became internationally famous, eventually reaching an estimated sixty million readers through syndication in more than 250 newspapers.

Dix is sometimes confused with Dorothea Lynde Dix, a nineteenth-century social activist. In fact, the columnist chose her byline because she had always liked the name "Dorothy" and because "Dick" was the name of a former slave who had loyally saved the family's silver during the Civil War.

Mother didn't approve of bobbed hair, of high water-skirts, and bare knees, of jazz, of shimmying, of the eternal gadding of her flapper daughter, and she waged a ceaseless but futile fight against them.

"Aw, lay off, Ma," protested the girl. "Come up to date! This is 1922, instead of 1892. What do you expect me to do? Sit up of an evening in the parlor with a fellow, and show him the family photograph album, and feed him on chocolate cake like you used to do?

"I am having my day. You had yours, though I'll tell the world it must have been some punk day for a girl in your time."

"Oh, I don't know that life was so altogether unendurable in the remote ages to which you refer so pityingly," replied mother. "The girls in those times had their amusements, and life had its compensations even if we stayed in our own front yards instead of jumping all the bars as you do.

. . . "You speak with scorn of our simple amusements. It is true that we had no jazz then, and were so ignorant that we did not even suspect that cow bells and tin pans, and kitchen pots were musical instruments that ravished the senses when beaten upon by a husky hand, but every girl then played upon the piano, and she was a mighty poor performer who couldn't put on the soft pedal, and hand out gooey, sentimental stuff until she got a man so doped up that he would be proposing before he knew it. There is nothing in jazz that makes a man think about home and mother. It makes him want to go out and be free, and wild, and untrammeled. Put that in your cigarette and smoke it.

. . . "You modern girls are wise about many things, but you don't know your a b c's about how to handle men.

"In proof whereof," concluded mother, "in your day you run after men that you can't catch, and in my day we coyly eluded men who pursued us, captured us, and married us."

"Some day," said the flapper.

FRANK LOESSER
"MARRY THE MAN TODAY," 1949

For its unforgettable music, perfect structure, and lively characters, *Guys and Dolls* is often cited as the best musical of all time. The basic plot—inspired by Damon Runyon's stories of the New York underworld—involves two supposedly hard-boiled gamblers and the women they can't resist. Frank Loesser (1910–1969) wrote both the music and lyrics. "Marry the Man Today" is the duet sung at the end of the show by the two female leads.

Guy Lombardo was a popular bandleader; Rogers Peet was a men's clothing store.

Marry the man today
Trouble tho' he may be
Much as he likes to play
Crazy and wild and free.
Marry the man today
Rather than sigh and sorrow,
Marry the man today
And change his ways tomorrow.

Marry the man today
Maybe he's leaving town
Don't let him get away
Hurry and track him down
Counterattack him and
Marry the man today
Give him the girlish laughter
Give him your hand today
And save the fist for after.

Slowly introduce him to the better things

Respectable, conservative and clean

Reader's Digest!

Guy Lombardo!

Rogers Peet!

Golf!

Galoshes!

Ovaltine!

But marry the man today

Handle it meek and gently

Marry the man today and train him subsequently.

NUNNALLY JOHNSON
HOW TO MARRY A MILLIONAIRE, 1953

When it was originally released, *How to Marry a Millionaire* was as notable for its cast and story as it was for the fact that it was one of the first movies made in CinemaScope, the wide-screen format intended to attract an increasingly home-bound TV audience. The pros and cons of the technology supplied much of the focus for reviews in the *New York Times* and *The New Yorker*. The actual plot of the movie was seen as less revolutionary. Written by Nunnally Johnson (1897–1977), the comedy starred Lauren Bacall, Marilyn Monroe, and Betty Grable as three models who rent an upscale apartment in an effort to snare upscale husbands.

Schatze Page was played by Bacall, Loco Dempsey by Monroe.

SCHATZE:	Well, to put it simply, the idea is this. If you had your choice of everybody in the world, which would you rather marry, a rich guy or a poor one?
LOCO:	I think I'd rather marry a rich one.
SCHATZE:	All right, then, where would you be more likely to meet a rich one? In a walk-up on Amsterdam Avenue, or in a joint like this?
LOCO:	Well, I should say in a joint like this.
SCHATZE:	Okay then, that's it. We're all working steady, so we throw everything we make into the kitty and get a little organization into this marriage caper. Class address, class background, class characters. To be specific about it, nothing under six figures a year.

LOCO:	I've never heard anything so intelligent in my life.
SCHATZE:	Well, if you wanna catch a mouse, you set a mouse trap. So, all right, we set a bear trap. Now all we've got to do, is one of us has got to knock off a bear.
LOCO:	You mean marry him?
SCHATZE:	If you don't marry him, you haven't caught him, he's caught you.

HELEN ANDELIN
THE FASCINATING GIRL, 1969

Helen Andelin (1920–2009) was in her early forties, married for two decades, and the mother of eight children when she started teaching marriage classes in Fresno, California. Responding in part to the popularity of the new feminism, she offered an emphatically traditional alternative, asserting that women could achieve marital happiness only if they learned what men really wanted from women and then did everything they could to embody it. The popularity of the classes first led Andelin to write *Fascinating Womanhood*, which reportedly sold four hundred thousand copies in its self-published version and more than a million when Random House took over. The book spawned a grassroots movement in which other women were trained to teach Fascinating Womanhood classes. Five years after her first book's success, Andelin produced *The Fascinating Girl*, which told unmarried women how to get the guy.

The Fascinating Womanhood movement offered a religious element in its pro-patriarchy arguments but distanced even some Christian conservatives, who objected to Andelin's Mormon orthodoxy.

In theory, all obstacles out of the way, a man proposes. It is not always as simple as this, however. The man may find that unless he has a particular reason to hurry things along, it is easier to procrastinate the important step and keep things as they are. This may go on for months, with nothing resolved and the girl wondering all the time how serious the man's feelings for her are.

If this is the case, the girl can bring him to action. . . . [One way] of making it easy for him to act is to get him in a *romantic and sentimental frame of mind.*

Few men propose in a mood of cold and calculating reason. The girl should endeavor, therefore, to arouse in him the opposite moods—a feeling of warm, impulsive emotion, or of dreamy, drifting surrender to sentiment. In such a mood, reason is subdued and the impulse to speak out is unopposed. The manner of awakening these sentimental moods is accomplished by *creating romantic situations*. A number of suggestions are given here.

BE ALONE

The first thing to avoid is a third person. No man ever becomes romantic while other people are around. When more than two are present the conversation and the atmosphere become entirely matter-of-fact. . . .

A COZY WINTER EVENING

The atmosphere can be even more suggestive of sentiment if it is winter and the wind is howling outside and sleet is dashing against the window. How cozy and comforting it is for the girl and the boy, sitting before an open fire with the lights dimmed, to sit and dream. The man may feel that he would like for this to continue forever. There cannot be obstacles, he feels, when life is easy and peaceful as this. How easy for him to succumb to his desire and forget his fears. . . .

WATER: LAKES, RIVERS, THE OCEAN

Even in broad daylight, the effect of water is often spell-binding, especially upon those who may live daily in a crowded city. Night, water and romance are inseparable. Have you ever noticed how young people are inclined to spend their vacations or holidays on or near water? There is a reason. Nothing is more soothing, more calculated to subdue fears and draw a man and woman close to each other than a night scene on the water, with the moon and stars shining on the ripples, the gentle lap of waves upon a beach or against a boat, and the mysterious blackness of a distant shoreline. Many men have innocently taken a girl on a boating excursion at night and returned to find themselves engaged.

PARKS AND GARDENS

A stroll through some beautiful garden, or in the hills or mountains, or in the woods, can often superinduce the atmosphere desired. There is nothing like getting back to nature to encourage a man to follow nature's impulse to take a mate for himself. . . .

RESTAURANTS THAT ENCOURAGE ROMANCE

. . . Restaurants to avoid are those that are crowded. A small one may be better than a large busy one. Avoid the dazzling white restaurants, the gay and glittering kind, and the casinos. These don't suggest coziness and contentment; their atmosphere discourages all thought of home and marriage.

A picnic lunch in the woods, in a private park or by a river can be just as comfortable and cozy as a restaurant. Give the man time enough to absorb the atmosphere and time enough to let it penetrate deeply. Never hurry through a picnic in the woods.

HUSBANDS, HOW TO KEEP

OVID
THE ART OF LOVE, CIRCA 1 BC

The Roman poet Ovid (43 BC–17 AD), though intended by his father to have a public life, instead began a successful writing career with four popular volumes, all about love. Of them, the *Ars Amatoria* remains the most famous and is considered by some scholars to be responsible for Ovid's eventual banishment from Rome by the emperor Augustus. Others point to an unnamed indiscretion that may have involved Augustus's granddaughter. Whatever the case, Ovid was married three times.

You must sometimes keep your lover begging and praying and threatening before your door. Sweet things are bad for us. Bitters are the best tonic for the jaded appetite. More than one ship has sailed to perdition with a following wind. What makes men indifferent to their wives is that they can see them when they please. So shut your door and let your surly porter growl, "There's no admittance here!" This will renew the slumbering fires of love.

AN ITALIAN MOTHER
ADVICE TO HER DAUGHTER, CIRCA 1300

The author is anonymous, and the book, originally called *The Twelve Warnings That Must Be Given to His Daughter When Her Mother Sends Her to Her Husband*, was apparently translated from the Italian and first published in 1885.

Avoid anything that might annoy him; do not be joyful if he is sad, or sad if he is joyful. Try to find out the dishes he prefers; and if your taste does not agree with his, do not let him see it. If your husband is asleep, sick, or tired, do not disturb him; if you must do so, do it gently. Do not rob your husband, lend his goods, or give them away. Do not be too curious about his affairs; but if he confides in you, keep his secrets. Be good to his family and friends. Do not do anything important without seeking his advice. Do not ask him to do impossible things or things that would damage his honor or position. Be attractive, fresh, clean, and modest in appearance, and chaste in behavior. Do not be too familiar with servants. Do not go out too often; the man's domain is outside, whereas the woman's is in the home. Do not speak too much, for silence is a sign of modesty and chastity. Finally and most important, do not make your husband jealous.

"BROTHER JONATHAN'S WIFE'S ADVICE TO HER DAUGHTER ON THE DAY OF HER MARRIAGE"
NEW ENGLAND FARMER, 1833

H

"Brother Jonathan" was, as far back as the Revolutionary War, a kind of Uncle Sam figure, meant to represent the average American. His character went through a number of evolutions, but by the early nineteenth century, he was often a prudent moralizer.

You will be mistress of your own house, and observe the rules in which you have been educated. You will endeavor, above all things, to make your *fireside* the most agreeable place for the man of your choice. Pleasantry and a happy disposition will ever be considered as necessary to this important end; but a foolish fondness is disgusting to all. Let reason and common sense ever guide: these, aided by a pleasant, friendly disposition, render life happy; and without these, it is not desirable. Remember your cousin Eliza. She married with the brightest prospects; but, from her petulant, peevish, and complaining disposition, and negligence, every thing went wrong; and her home became a place of disquietude to her husband. To avoid this, he sought a place to pass away vacant time, where, associated with those more wicked than himself, he contracted the habit of intemperance, and all was lost—and poor Eliza was thrown on the charity of her friends.

BLANCHE EBBUTT
DON'TS FOR WIVES, 1913

This is a sampling of the hundreds of recommendations contained in British author Blanche Ebbutt's small guidebook (see Food, page 122).

Don't think that there is any satisfactory substitute for love between husband and wife. Respect and esteem make a good foundation, but they won't do alone.

Don't think that, because you have married for love, you can never know a moment's unhappiness. Life is not a bed of roses, but love will extract the thorns.

Don't expect your husband to have all the feminine virtues as well as all the masculine ones. There would be nothing left for *you* if your other half were such a paragon.

Don't worry about little faults in your husband which merely amused you in your lover. If they were not important then, they are not important now. Besides, what about yours?

Don't vegetate as you grow older if you happen to live in the country. Some women are like cows, but there is really no need to stagnate. Keep both brain and body on the move.

Don't omit to pay your husband an occasional compliment. If he looks nice as he comes in dressed for the opera, tell him so. If he has been successful with his chickens, or his garden, or his photography, compliment him on his results. Don't let him have to fall back on self-esteem all the while for want of a little well-directed praise.

Don't say, "I told you so," to your husband, however much you feel tempted to.

Don't nag your husband. If he won't carry out your wishes for love of you, he certainly won't because you nag him.

Don't "manage" your husband too visibly. Of course, he may require the most careful management, but you don't want your friends to think of him as a hen-pecked husband. Above all, never let him think you manage him.

Don't say bitter things when you are angry. They not only sting at the time, but they eat their way in and are remembered long after *you* have forgotten them.

Don't be everlastingly trying to change your husband's habits, unless they are *very* bad ones. Take him as you find him, and leave him at peace.

Don't spend all the best years of your life pinching and saving unnecessarily, until you are too old to get any pleasure out of your money.

Don't be shy of showing your love. Don't expect him to take it for granted. A playful caress as you pass his chair, an unexpected touch on the shoulder, makes all the difference between merely *knowing* that you care for him and actually *feeling* it.

Don't try to excite your husband's jealousy by flirting with other men. You may succeed better than you want to. It is like playing with tigers and edged tools and volcanoes all in one.

Don't let your husband wear a violet tie with grass-green socks. If he is unhappily devoid of the colour sense, he must be forcibly restrained, but—

Don't be sarcastic about your husband's taste in dress. Be gently persuasive and train his sense of fitness.

Don't be a household martyr. Some wives are never happy unless they are miserable, but their husbands don't appreciate this peculiar trait. The woeful smile is most exasperating.

BRITISH POSTCARD, EARLY 1900s

The caption reads: "When he deserves it, kiss him."

IRA WILE AND MARY DAY WINN
MARRIAGE IN THE MODERN MANNER, 1929

In their chapter on "Holding a Husband," the authors (see Grievances, page 145) describe seven types of unsuccessful wives: the wives who are too weepy, too demonstrative, too jealous, too controlling, too clingy, too comforting, and too seductive. The authors home in, below, on the weepy variety.

A husband's relation to his wife is threefold: he wants a physical mate, a satisfying social companion and, usually, a housekeeper. The perfect wife is the one who can be all three. If she cannot completely fulfil every one of these wants, or if she has ceased to do so, he is likely to look elsewhere for fulfilment. If she does not satisfy him physically, he may find a mistress. If they are sexually well mated but she is beneath his intellectual level, he may contract a morganatic marriage with his business, using that as his intellectual outlet, or become a chronic clubman, or a golf enthusiast, or even a saxophone player. Who can say that our great business preëminence is not, to some extent at least, a by-product of the large number of unhappy marriages which our divorce-rate seems to indicate?

There are many unions in which the wife falls down in one or more of these relationships but which do not end in divorce. Such a situation does not necessarily mean that the husband has ceased to love his wife, or that he wants their life together to come to an end. He may find her perfectly satisfactory as mother and home-maker, and be content to get his sexual satisfaction elsewhere, as is the case in so many French marriages. It is when the husband finds another mate who satisfies him as both a physical and a social companion that the marriage is in extreme jeopardy.

Few women, however, unless sexually cold, will be content with a half-way or one third ownership. They will want the marriage to be a success on every plane. Some of them fail to make it so because they do not realize that marriage is a partnership into which each should be willing to put all his capital constantly and to take out only small dividends until the business is a going concern.

A wife who fails in this way is the one who weeps on the slightest pretext. She tries to tie her husband with water, to hold his love by making his attitude toward her one of continual emotional outpouring. She endeavors to overcome indifference by arousing pity and anxiety. She weeps if he refuses her a fur coat; she cries if he stays late at the office. Obeisance has been paid to this type of woman by a restaurant in the down-town district of a southern city, which puts up boxes called by the men who buy them "Hush darlings." They contain hot fried oysters and other delights, and are designed as peacemakers for men working late at their offices. On the top of each box is printed "Hush, darling. Look what I brought you from Schmidt's."

HAL DAVID
"WIVES AND LOVERS," 1963

Hal David (1921–2012) wrote these lyrics for a movie by the same name; the song was the hit, recorded by, among others, Dionne Warwick, Frank Sinatra, Ella Fitzgerald, and Jack Jones, who won a 1964 Grammy for his version.

The composer was David's usual partner, Burt Bacharach, with whom David wrote dozens of other hits of the sixties and seventies, notably "Walk On By," "I Say a Little Prayer," and "What's New Pussycat?"

Hey, little girl, comb your hair, fix your make-up,
Soon he will open the door.
Don't think because there's a ring on your finger
You needn't try anymore.

For wives should always be lovers, too.
Run to his arms the moment he comes home to you.
I'm warning you.

Day after day there are girls at the office
And men will always be men.
Don't send him off with your hair still in curlers.
You may not see him again.

For wives should always be lovers, too.
Run to his arms the moment he comes home to you.
He's always here.

Hey, little girl, better wear something pretty,
Something you'd wear to go to the city,
And dim all the lights, pour the wine, start the music.
Time to get ready for love.
Oh, time to get ready, time to get ready,
Time to get ready for love.

MARABEL MORGAN
THE TOTAL WOMAN, 1973

Like Helen Andelin the decade before (see Husbands, How to Get, pages 187–88), Marabel Morgan (1937–) offered wives not just personal instruction and a bestselling book, but eventually an entire movement—with similar themes. A born-again Christian who quoted the Bible often in her hugely popular book and its several sequels, Morgan believed that marital happiness came from wives submitting to, usually while cosseting, their husbands. She was famously credited with the suggestion that wives might pique their husbands' interest by greeting them after a long day's work wearing only Saran Wrap. In fact, that particular ploy was a suggestion made by one of Morgan's many readers, but Morgan herself had gotten the ball rolling with a number of other strategies, some suggested in this passage.

Marabel married Charles Morgan, an attorney, in 1964; they had two daughters.

Take a few extra moments for that bubble bath tonight. If your husband comes home at 6:00, bathe at 5:00. I know it sounds ludicrous if you have two little ones and four hungry mouths to feed by 6:07. That's my situation, but the bubble bath is part of my schedule anyway. Let the little ones' eyes gaze if they must, but treat yourself to a warm, sweet-smelling, relaxing bath. In preparing for your six o'clock date, lie back and let go of the tensions of the day. Think about that special man who's on his way home to you. . . .

One morning, Charlie remarked about the pressures of the day that lay ahead of him. All day I remembered his grim face as he drove away. Knowing he would feel weary and defeated, I wondered how I could revive him when he came home.

For an experiment I put on pink baby-doll pajamas and white boots after my bubble bath. I must admit that I looked foolish and felt even more so. When I opened the door that night to greet Charlie, I was unprepared for his reaction. My quiet, reserved, non-excitable husband took one look, dropped his briefcase on the doorstep, and chased me around the dining-room table. We were in stitches by the time he caught me, and breathless with that old feeling of romance. Our little girls stood flat against the wall watching our escapade, giggling with delight. We all had a marvelous evening together, and Charlie forgot to mention the problems of the day.

Have you ever met your husband at the front door in some outrageously sexy outfit? I can hear you howl, "She's got to be kidding. My husband's not the type, and besides, we've been married twenty-one years!"

Nope, I'm not kidding, *especially* if you've been married twenty-one years. Most women dress to please other women rather than their own husbands. Your husband needs you to fulfill his daydreams.

I have heard women complain, "My husband isn't satisfied with just me. He wants lots of women. What can I do?" You can be lots of different women to him. Costumes provide variety without him ever leaving home. I believe that every man needs excitement and high adventure at home. Never let him know what to expect when he opens the front door; make it like opening a surprise package. You may be a smoldering sexpot, or an all-American fresh beauty. Be a pixie or a pirate—a cowgirl or a showgirl. Keep him off guard.

H

INDIVIDUALITY

RAINER MARIA RILKE
LETTER TO EMANUEL VON BODMAN, 1901

The mystical, existentialist streak in the writings of Austro-Hungarian poet Rainer Maria Rilke (1875–1926) has ensured their continued popularity, as has his eloquent affirmation of the solitary life of the writer, especially in his posthumously published *Letters to a Young Poet*. After a love affair with a married intellectual (formerly courted by Friedrich Nietzsche, coincidentally), Rilke married a sculptor named Clara Westhoff with the hopes he expressed in this letter. They had a daughter eight months later, and separated amicably the following year.

Emanuel von Bodman was a poet and friend of Rilke from Munich.

What matters in marriage, as I feel it, is not to create a swift communion by tearing down and overcoming all barriers, but a good marriage is more one in which each appoints the other guardian of his loneliness and shows him thus the greatest confidence he has to bestow. A joint life for two people is an impossibility, and, where it seems to exist, it is a limitation, a reciprocal agreement which robs one or both partners of his or their fullest freedom and development. But, presupposing the realization that between the nearest people there must exist boundless distances, there arises the possibility of the growth of a wonderful life side by side when it proves feasible to love the distance between them in that it gives them the ability to see one another always in their entirety against a vast sky.

KAHLIL GIBRAN
THE PROPHET, 1923

Creator of poetry, short stories, novels, paintings, and sculptures, Lebanese author and artist Kahlil Gibran (1883–1931) is by far best known for having written *The Prophet*, a collection of poetic and spiritual meditations offered by Almustafa, a fictional holy man, as his parting wisdom to followers. The messages of *The Prophet* are just universal enough to have appealed to an enormous and continuing audience in more than forty languages. In 2008, writing in *The New Yorker*, Joan Acocella pointed out that Gibran is the third-bestselling poet of all time (behind only Shakespeare and Lao-Tzu). The book hit the mainstream amid the counterculture movement of the 1960s, and has been sustained by New Age and nonsectarian readers ever since, which may be one reason that several of its passages have become popular readings at wedding ceremonies.

Then Almitra spoke again and said, And what of Marriage, master?
    And he answered saying:

You were born together, and together you shall be forevermore.
You shall be together when the white wings of death scatter your days.
Aye, you shall be together even in the silent memory of God.
But let there be spaces in your togetherness,
And let the winds of the heavens dance between you.

Love one another, but make not a bond of love:
Let it rather be a moving sea between the shores of your souls.
Fill each other's cup but drink not from one cup.
Give one another of your bread but eat not from the same loaf.
Sing and dance together and be joyous, but let each one of you be alone,
Even as the strings of a lute are alone though they quiver with the same music.

Give your hearts, but not into each other's keeping.
For only the hand of Life can contain your hearts.

And stand together yet not too near together:
For the pillars of the temple stand apart,
And the oak tree and the cypress grow not in each other's shadow.

MARLEY KLAUS
"25 YEARS," 2012

Marley Klaus (1957–) is a writer and former *60 Minutes* producer who in 2006 began a blog called *The Heathen Learns*, dedicated to learning about the seven major religious traditions. She and her husband—film, TV, and theater director Kevin Dowling—married in 1987 and have two sons.

When I see that look on Kevin's face just after my dad walked me up the aisle, it makes me want to cry. I cannot tell you how many times I have seen that look and heard the words that

Kevin Dowling and Marley Klaus

come with it. That look is one of the reasons we are still together today. It's also what almost did us in.

There's this idea about romantic love, about finding your "soul mate" as that man of mine surely is, that makes us think that our lives should be entwined, enmeshed, our happiness entrusted to another. I think that idea does more to undermine good relationships than almost any other. The underbelly of that notion is: so, if I'm not happy—and who is all the time?—it is my partner's responsibility to at least try to make me feel better, happier.

I won't speak for other people but, in our determination to put how we felt about each other into practice, we kinda got it wrong for a while. In the misguided attempt to make the other happier, we contorted ourselves and our lives into painful and unrecognizable pretzel shapes—or felt guilty when we didn't or couldn't. We thought we were responsible *for* each other instead of *to* each other. The result? We had about two years of hell that stripped our relationship right down to its foundation. I remember standing on a street, looking across the top of a car at him and thinking: I am willing to lose this but I am not willing to not be myself anymore.

I was lucky. He was braver and more determined than I was. He took the first steps to break our dynamic. At the time, it felt like he was retreating to his corner to work on his own issues, but it gave me the room to do the same. I would never, ever, ever want to go through that again (have I said "never" and "ever" enough?) however, the new relationship that was built on what remained, that foundation, that look, is everything I ever wanted and more.

Boy, I love you, I admire you, I like you and I'm grateful for you and to you for our quarter century together. . . .

What we now know is that marriage isn't about two becoming one, but about learning how to be yourself in the presence of another. That, to me, to us, is the secret of a marriage worth having.

INFIDELITY

EXODUS 20:14

The seventh commandment.

Thou shalt not commit adultery.

JOHN WINTHROP
DIARY, 1644

Biblical injunctions informed many of the early laws of Puritan Massachusetts, including the capital law against adultery: "If any person committeth Adultery with a mar[r]ied or espoused wife, the Adulterer and Adulteresse shall surely be put to death." In the following passage from his journal, John Winthrop (1588–1649), first governor of the Massachusetts Bay Colony, detailed one of the rare cases on record in which the penalty was actually carried out.

At this court of assistants one James Britton, a man ill affected both to our church discipline and civil government, and one Mary Latham, a proper young woman about 18 years of age, whose father was a godly man and had brought her up well, were condemned to die for adultery, upon a law formerly made and published in print. It was thus occasioned and discovered. This woman, being rejected by a young man whom she had an affection unto, vowed she would marry the next that came to her, and accordingly, against her friends' minds, she matched with an ancient man who had neither honesty nor ability, and one whom she had no affection unto. Whereupon, soon after she was married, divers young men solicited her chastity, and drawing her into bad company, and giving her wine and other gifts, easily prevailed with her, and among others this [James] Britton. But God smiting him with a deadly palsy and fearful horror of conscience withal, he would not keep secret, but discovered this, and other the like with other women, and was forced to acknowledge the justice of God that having often called others fools, etc., for confessing against themselves, he was now forced to do the like. The woman dwelt now in Plymouth patent, and one of the magistrates there, hearing she was detected, etc., sent her to us.

. . . The woman proved very penitent, and had deep apprehension of the foulness of her sin, and at length attained to hope of pardon by the blood of Christ, and was willing to die in satisfaction to justice. The man also was very much cast down for his sins, but was loth to die, and petitioned the general court for his life, but they would not grant it, though some of the magistrates spake much for it, and questioned the letter, whether adultery was death by God's law now. . . .

They were both executed, they both died very penitently, especially the woman, who had some comfortable hope of pardon of her sin, and gave good exhortation to all young maids to be obedient to their parents, and to take heed of evil company.

GEORGE MACKENZIE
MORAL GALLANTRY, 1667

Known as "Bloody Mackenzie" for his unyielding prosecution of a group of Scottish religious protesters, Sir George Mackenzie (1636–1691) was most famous as a lawyer. But years before his legal maneuvers led to the deaths of thousands of his countrymen, he had begun his career writing about such topics as solitude, heraldry, and, in the case below, the moral imperatives of the married gentleman.

Today's thesauruses equate the words *slut* and *strumpet*, but clearly the latter was once considered a more depraved version of the former.

Whoring renders men contemptible, whilst it tempts them to embrace such as are not only below themselves in every sense, but such as are scarce worthy to serve these handsomer Ladies, whom they either do, or may lawfully enjoy. Doth not this Vice persuade men to ly in Cottages with Sluts, or (which is worse) Strumpets, to lurk in corners, to fear the encounter of such as know them [?]. . . .

There is no Vice whereby gallantry is more stain'd, then by breach of promise, which becomes yet more Sacrilegious, when Ladies are wrong'd by it. . . .

. . . And though such as are guilty of Whoring, do justifie their debordings by a love to that glorious Sex, yet by this pretext they are yet more unjust and vicious then their former guilt made them; for by roaving amongst so many, they intimat that they are not satisfied with their first choice; and that not only there are some of that Sex, but that there is none in it who deserves their intire affection.

WILLIAM WYCHERLEY
THE COUNTRY-WIFE, 1675

A classic Restoration comedy by William Wycherley (circa 1640–1715), *The Country-Wife* features characters with names like Mr. Horner, Old Lady Squeamish, and the relatively serious Mr. Dorilant, who nonetheless has one of the best lines in the play.

A mistress should be like a little country retreat near the town, not to dwell in constantly, but only for a night and away, to taste the town the better when a man returns.

SAMUEL JOHNSON, 1768

Dr. Samuel Johnson (see Devotion, page 55; Triumphs, page 430) would have been a legendary literary figure even without becoming the subject of the biography written by James Boswell. But Boswell's *The Life of Samuel Johnson, LL.D.*, first published in 1791, made the older man more vivid—and more casually quotable—than his own writings could ever have done. Johnson's earlier musings on "the heinousness of the crime of adultery" were captured by Boswell in the following passage.

Confusion of progeny constitutes the essence of the crime; and therefore a woman who breaks her marriage vows is much more criminal than a man who does it. A man, to be sure, is criminal in the sight of God; but he does not do his wife a very material injury, if he does not insult her: if, for instance, from mere wantonness of appetite, he steals privately to her chambermaid. Sir, a wife ought not to greatly resent this. I would not receive home a daughter who had run away from her husband on that account. A wife should study to reclaim her husband by more attention to please him. Sir, a man will not, once in a hundred instances, leave his wife and go to a harlot, if his wife has not been negligent of pleasing.

GEORGE SAND
JACQUES, 1833

Notorious for a string of famous lovers including Frédéric Chopin, Prosper Mérimée, and Alfred de Musset, French author George Sand (1804–1876, née [with several variations] Amantine-Lucille-Aurore-Dupin) was a popular and controversial author whose more than three dozen novels often questioned the social conventions of the day. Famously, she wrote: "There is only one happiness in life, and that is to love and be loved." Even in her first novel, *Indiana*, Sand defended the right of women to leave their husbands in search of that happiness. In *Jacques*, she wrote in the voice of the jilted but resigned husband.

No human creature can command love, and no one is guilty for feeling or for losing it. It is falsehood that debases a woman. That which constitutes adultery is not the hour that she accords to her lover: it is the night that she afterward passes in the arms of her husband. Oh! I should hate my wife, and I should indeed become ferocious, if to my lips she had offered lips still warm from another's kisses, and had passed, unblushing, from his embrace to mine. She would have become hideous to me from that day, and I would have crushed her as I would a caterpillar that I should find in my bed. But such as she is, pale, depressed, suffering all the anguish of a timorous conscience, incapable of lying, and ever ready to confess to me her involuntary fault, I can only pity and regret her.

NATHANIEL HAWTHORNE
THE SCARLET LETTER, 1850

Hester Prynne, probably the most famous adulteress in American literature, is best known for the initial *A* that she is forced to wear as punishment for her infidelity but that she embroiders artfully and exhibits without the expected Puritan shame. Her creator, Nathaniel Hawthorne (see Anniversaries, page 5), based his celebrated novel on a 1658 Plymouth Colony law that, like the Massachusetts Bay law (see John Winthrop, page 201), was rarely recorded as having been enforced, but stated: "whosoever shall commit Adultery shall be severely punished by Whipping . . . and likewise to wear two Capital letters viz A D cut out in cloth and sewed on their uppermost Garments."

The baby in Hester's arms is named Pearl and is the product of the adulterous affair that ultimately proves the undoing of both Hester's husband and her lover.

The door of the jail being flung open from within, there appeared, in the first place, like a black shadow emerging into the sunshine, the grim and grisly presence of the town-beadle, with a sword by his side, and his staff of office in his hand. This personage prefigured and represented in his aspect the whole dismal severity of the Puritanic code of law, which it was his business to administer in its final and closest application to the offender. Stretching forth the official staff in his left hand, he laid his right upon the shoulder of a young woman, whom he thus drew forward; until, on the threshold of the prison-door, she repelled him, by an action marked with natural dignity and force of character, and stepped into the open air, as if by her own free will. She bore in her arms a child, a baby of some three months old, who winked and turned aside its little face from the too vivid light of day; because its existence, heretofore, had brought it acquainted only with the gray twilight of a dungeon, or other darksome apartment of the prison.

When the young woman—the mother of this child—stood fully revealed before the crowd, it seemed to be her first impulse to clasp the infant closely to her bosom; not so much by an impulse of motherly affection, as that she might thereby conceal a certain token, which was wrought or fastened into her dress. In a moment, however, wisely judging that one token of her shame would but poorly serve to hide another, she took the baby on her arm, and, with a burning blush, and yet a haughty smile, and a glance that would not be abashed, looked around at her townspeople and neighbors. On the breast of her gown, in fine red cloth, surrounded with an elaborate embroidery and fantastic flourishes of gold-thread, appeared the letter A. It was so artistically done, and with so much fertility and gorgeous luxuriance of fancy, that it had all the effect of a last and fitting decoration to the apparel which she wore; and which was of a splendor in accordance with the taste of the age, but greatly beyond what was allowed by the sumptuary regulations of the colony. . . .

. . . Her attire, which, indeed, she had wrought for the occasion, in prison, and had modelled much after her own fancy, seemed to express the attitude of her spirit, the desperate recklessness of her mood, by its wild and picturesque peculiarity. But the point which drew all eyes, and, as it were, transfigured the wearer,—so that both men and women, who had been familiarly acquainted with Hester Prynne, were now impressed as if they beheld her for the first time,—was that SCARLET LETTER, so fantastically embroidered and illuminated upon her bosom. It had the effect of a spell, taking her out of the ordinary relations with humanity, and enclosing her in a sphere by herself.

JOHN GRAHAM
OPENING ARGUMENT IN THE MURDER TRIAL OF DANIEL SICKLES, 1859

U.S. Congressman Daniel Sickles (1819–1914) was in Lafayette Square, within sight of the White House, when he fatally shot his young wife's lover, the District of Columbia DA, Philip Barton Key II. The ensuing trial featured a two-day opening by John Graham, who argued, in the alternative, that his client should be acquitted because of a biblical mandate to protect the weaker sex and/or because he had been defending his property and/or because he had been rendered temporarily insane by the discovery of adultery, "the greatest wrong that can be committed upon a human being."

The trial represented the first time that temporary insanity was used as a murder defense. The jury took barely an hour to acquit Sickles, who went on to become a major general in the Union army and to win the Medal of Honor.

Gentlemen, you would have thought, from this opening, that the learned counsel for the Government was describing a case of the most deliberate homicide—and yet the case, he was describing, was the case of a man, who, while acting from a sense, and under the influence of a sense, of right, was nevertheless, no doubt, at that particular juncture, entirely bereft of his reason. . . .

. . . [The question to ask is] whether the case is one of pardonable or excusable unsoundness of mind, or of wanton or ungovernable passion; whether the defendant, not being to blame for the provocation, the frenzy, or its results, can be holden for a crime? This point is regarded as one of the most important items in this prosecution. We mean to say, not that Mr. Sickles labored under any insanity consequent upon an established, permanent mental disease, but that the condition of his mind, at the time of the commission of the act in question, was such, as to render him legally unaccountable, *as much so,* as if the state of his mind had been produced by a mental disease.

THE MOTION PICTURE PRODUCTION CODE, 1930

Starting in 1922, lawyer and former Republican National Committee chairman Will Hays (1879–1954) was given a yearly salary of $100,000—roughly a million in today's dollars—to head the Motion Picture Producers and Distributors of America (later the Motion Picture Association of America), an organization formed by the movie industry to regulate itself and thus avoid government censorship. By 1930, the Hays Code, as it came to be known, included a list of "Don'ts and Be Carefuls" that forbade showing, among other things, miscegenation, drug trafficking, white slavery, ridicule of the clergy, and nudity "in fact or in silhouette." It also included the following rules regarding adultery.

PLOT MATERIAL:

1)   The triangle that is the love of a third party by one already married, needs careful handling, if marriage, the sanctity of the home, and sex morality are not to be imperiled.

2)   Adultery as a subject should be avoided:

    (a) [Adultery] is never a fit subject for comedy. Thru comedy of this sort, ridicule is thrown on the essential relationships of home and family and marriage, and illicit relationships are made to seem permissible, and either delightful or daring.

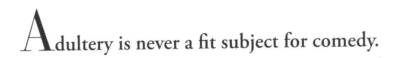

Adultery is never a fit subject for comedy.

(b) Sometimes adultery must be counted on as material occurring in serious drama. In this case:

1) It should not appear to be justified;

2) It should not be used to weaken respect for marriage;

3) It should not be presented as attractive or alluring.

JOHN LEVY AND RUTH MUNROE
THE HAPPY FAMILY, 1938

The Happy Family was a popular advice book that dealt with marriage and childrearing and went through ten printings in its first decade alone. One reason for the book's success was the imprimatur of Dr. John Levy (1897–1938), an associate professor of clinical psychiatry at Columbia University. Later editions, following Levy's death, were updated by his coauthor and widow, Sarah Lawrence psychology professor Dr. Ruth Munroe (1903–1963).

A great many people in our hypocritical society attempt to reconcile monogamy with freedom by pretending to the former while actually enjoying the latter. In practice this solution appears to work as well and as badly as any other. It is based on the theory that what people don't know won't hurt them. . . . The extramarital adventure frequently seems to its chief actor quite irrelevant to his marriage. He knows that it is transitory and unimportant, or at least wholly distinct from his family responsibilities. He feels perfectly capable of handling the situation himself without harm to anyone. . . . The erring husband maintains the rules of monogamy for the rest of the world while he orders his own life as he thinks best. He protects his wife from unnecessary pain by concealing his own freedom.

The husband usually feels, moreover, that his sexual conduct is his own affair. As a mature man he does not have to give an account of himself to his wife or to anyone else. Reticence about his love life is a mark of independence and self-sufficiency.

Sometimes this procedure works very well. I suspect, however, that it works well only in those marriages which are fundamentally sound anyway. A man who is genuinely fond of his wife, thoroughly responsible as a husband, and well integrated as a personality can handle hidden deviations from monogamy adequately. If the marriage is already disturbed, however, or if the man is himself very much upset by his behavior, the results of concealment are often as unhappy as they are unexpected.

U.S. POSTCARD, CIRCA 1943

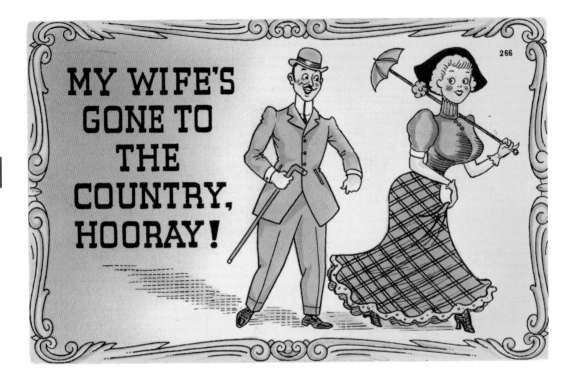

MIKE NICHOLS AND ELAINE MAY
"ADULTERY," 1960

In addition to their extraordinary separate successes in film, theater, and television, Mike Nichols (1931–2014) and Elaine May (1932–) are still remembered more than half a century after their performing partnership ended as among the most sublime and influential comics in America. Their overnight Broadway hit, *An Evening with Mike Nichols and Elaine May*, was based largely on sketches that they first improvised. The show album included the sketch "Adultery," which presented the same scene—set in a hotel lobby—in America, England, and France, and which can be recited, verbatim, by at least one editor of this anthology.

NICHOLS: Louise, where were you? I've been going out of my mind!

MAY: Darling, don't yell at me. Please.

NICHOLS:	Darling, to be doing this terrible thing and to be late on top of it!
MAY:	I'm sorry.
NICHOLS:	No, we mustn't.
MAY:	Please don't yell at me.
NICHOLS:	Oh, Louise, I feel so awful.
MAY:	Oh, God, what kind of a person must I be to do a thing like this?
NICHOLS:	I don't know. I'm sick, I'm physically sick, with guilt.
MAY:	Oh, God. Guilty? I tell you.
NICHOLS:	I know.
MAY:	I've never felt just so rotten.
NICHOLS:	I know.
MAY:	And just, just, just dirty.
NICHOLS:	I know. I know. All right, all right! Just think how I feel, will you? Will you think how I feel?
MAY:	Oh do I know!
NICHOLS:	George is my best friend!
MAY:	Your best friend!
NICHOLS:	He's my best friend.
MAY:	He's my husband!
NICHOLS:	Oh!
MAY:	One, one of the sweetest, gentlest people—oh—
NICHOLS:	He's a saint!
MAY:	Oh, what a good person he is!
NICHOLS:	No, he's a saint! He's a saint! He's a saint! The man is a saint!
MAY:	You're right. He's a saint!
NICHOLS:	He happens to be the only saint I know.
MAY:	Yes.
NICHOLS:	He's a kind—
MAY:	Isn't he?
NICHOLS:	A loving—
MAY:	Oh, you don't know—
NICHOLS:	Trusting—
MAY:	Trusting. You don't know.
NICHOLS:	I know!

MAY:	You don't know how he trusts me. He trusts me. I couldn't do it if he didn't trust me.
NICHOLS:	I know.
MAY:	I can't—I feel rotten. I can't, I can't, it's too much to take in the end, you know.
NICHOLS:	Oh, Louise, it's just awful.
MAY:	You know, I'd like to just kill myself, and you know? I'm too weak even for that. Isn't that funny? I'm too weak even for that!
NICHOLS:	Do you want to know how bad I feel? Do you want to know how bad I feel? Listen! If I hadn't rented that room already, I'd say forget it!

YVES MONTAND
OUI MAGAZINE INTERVIEW, 1973

Yves Montand (1921–1991) was famous for his appearances in both French and American films and was also the irresistibly sophisticated singer on several dozen record albums. He was married for thirty-four years, until the death of his wife, the actress Simone Signoret, and he had numerous mistresses, including Edith Piaf, Shirley MacLaine, and, most famously, Marilyn Monroe.

I think a man can have two, maybe three affairs while he is married. But three is the absolute maximum. After that, you're cheating.

TOM STOPPARD
THE REAL THING, 1982

One of the most celebrated and prolific of modern playwrights, Sir Tom Stoppard (1937–) was still in his late twenties when the success of one of his first plays, *Rosencrantz and Guildenstern Are Dead*, introduced audiences to what became a signature blend of intellectualism, humor, and occasional absurdity. Works including *Travesties*, *Jumpers*, and *Arcadia* followed, along with numerous projects for television, radio, and film. In *The Real Thing*, Stoppard created a protagonist (Henry) who is a famous playwright and whose extramarital affair with an actress (Annie) breaks up both their marriages. In the second act, which takes place two years after the first, Henry suspects Annie of infidelity and tears up their home, looking for proof.

ANNIE: You should have put everything back. Everything would be the way it was.

HENRY: You can't put things back. They won't go back. Talk to me. I'm your chap. I know about this. We start off like one of those caterpillars designed for a particular leaf. The exclusive voracity of love. And then not. How strange that the way of things is not suspended to meet our special case. But it never is. I don't want anyone else but sometimes, surprisingly, there's someone, not the prettiest or the most available, but you know that in another life it would be her. Or him, don't you find? A small quickening. The room responds slightly to being entered. Like a raised blind. Nothing intended, and a long way from doing anything, but you catch the glint of being someone else's possibility, and it's a sort of politeness to show you haven't missed it, so you push it a little, well within safety, but there's that sense of a promise almost being made in the touching and kissing without which no one can seem to say good morning in this poncy business and one more push would do it. Billy. Right?

ANNIE: Yes.

HENRY: I love you.

ANNIE: And I you. I wouldn't be here if I didn't.

HENRY: Tell me, then.

ANNIE: I love you.

HENRY: Not that.

ANNIE: Yes, that. That's all I'd need to know.

HENRY: You'd need more.

ANNIE: No.

HENRY: I need it. I can manage knowing if you did but I can't manage not knowing if you did or not. I won't be able to work.

ANNIE: Don't blackmail.

HENRY: You'd ask me.

ANNIE: I never have.

HENRY: There's never *been* anything.

ANNIE: Dozens.

HENRY: In your head.

ANNIE: What's the difference? For the first year at least, every halfway decent looking woman under fifty you were ever going to meet.

HENRY: But you learned better.

ANNIE:	No, I just learned not to care. There was nothing to keep you here so I assumed you wanted to stay. I stopped caring about the rest of it.
HENRY:	I care. Tell me.
ANNIE:	(*Hardening*) I did tell you. I spent the morning talking to Billy in a station cafeteria instead of coming straight home to you and I fibbed about the train because *that* seemed like infidelity—but all you want to know is did I sleep with him first?
HENRY:	Yes. Did you?
ANNIE:	No.
HENRY:	Did you want to?
ANNIE:	Oh, for God's sake!
HENRY:	You can ask me.
ANNIE:	I prefer to respect your privacy.
HENRY:	I have none. I disclaim it. Did you?
ANNIE:	What about your dignity, then?
HENRY:	Yes, you'd behave better than me. I don't believe in behaving well. I don't believe in debonair relationships. "How's your lover today, Amanda?" "In the pink, Charles. How's yours?" I believe in mess, tears, pain, self-abasement, loss of self-respect, nakedness. Not caring doesn't seem much different from not loving. Did you? You did, didn't you?

RICHARD TAYLOR
HAVING LOVE AFFAIRS, 1982

A philosopher with an abiding interest in virtue ethics, Richard Taylor (1919–2003) taught at Brown, Columbia, and Rochester universities, gave frequent guest lectures, wrote books on ethics and beekeeping (his avocation), and, in one of his most unconventional works, not only praised the joys of adultery but set out a series of marital rules intended to make it more practical.

The joy of a love affair is that someone seems to love you who does not have to, or who, in fact, positively should not. . . .

. . . It is very doubtful whether there can be found in any human experience anything as totally fulfilling as being loved in this way—intensely, intimately, and gratuitously. No one should say that it is bad, just because it is so easily condemned and so dangerous. It is still the ultimate joy that everyone wants more than anything else. The most vehement condemnations of it seem to come from those who have abandoned hope of experiencing it, and who therefore represent it to themselves as something base in order to assuage their own sense of deprivation. A person involved in such a love affair—overwhelming, forbidden, explosively dangerous—can think to himself, with some truth at least, that here is one person in the world who cares for him for no ulterior reason at all, who has nothing to gain by it and very much to lose, but who does nevertheless love. The feelings, together with this thought, are so totally intoxicating that those who have never experienced them, and especially those who have given up hope of them and perhaps taken complacent pride in this deprivation, should withhold their condemnation of others.

This does not mean that love affairs are better than marriage, for they seldom are. Love between married persons can, in the long run, be so vastly more fulfilling that none but the hopelessly romantic could suggest otherwise. . . .

It is nevertheless true that the joys of illicit and passionate love, which include but go far beyond the mere joys of sex, are incomparably good. And it is undeniable that those who never experience love affairs, and who perhaps even boast of their faultless monogamy year in and year out, have really missed something. Virtuous they may be—even this can be questioned—but truly blessed they are not quite. Such a person lives in a kind of lifelong total eclipse, or a house without windows. He is like someone who has never heard a nocturne of Chopin's, tasted caviar, or beheld the Alps—except that what he has missed is something with which these tepid things do not even begin to compare.

NORA EPHRON
HEARTBURN, 1983

Nora Ephron (1941–2012) had already made her name as a magazine columnist with several bestselling collections when she published her first and only novel, treating the grim facts of her marriage to journalist Carl Bernstein with signature bite and humor. *Heartburn* would become a movie starring Meryl Streep and Jack Nicholson, and Ephron would go on to add producer, director, and playwright to her already brilliant career as screenwriter and essayist.

When Mark finally came home, I was completely prepared. I had rehearsed a speech about how I loved him and he loved me and we had to work at our marriage and we had a baby and we were about to have another—really the perfect speech for the situation except that I had misapprehended the situation. "I am in love with Thelma Rice," he said when he arrived home. That was the situation. He then told me that although he was in love with Thelma Rice, they were not having an affair. (Apparently he thought I could handle the fact that he was in love with her but not the fact that he was having sex with her.) "That is a lie," I said to him, "but if it's true"—you see, there was a part of me that wanted to think it was true even though I knew it wasn't: the man is capable of having sex with a venetian blind—"if it's true, you might as well be having an affair with her, because it's free." Some time later, after going on saying all these lovey-dovey things about Thelma, and after saying he wouldn't give her up, and after saying that I was a shrew and a bitch and a nag and a kvetch and a grouse and that I hated Washington (the last charge was undeniably true), he said that he nonetheless expected me to stay with him. At that moment, it crossed my mind that he might be crazy.

DIANA, PRINCESS OF WALES
BBC INTERVIEW, 1995

Perhaps the most public marriage of the twentieth century was that of Britain's Prince Charles (1948–) and Lady Diana Spencer (1961–1997), and one of the most public infidelities was that of Charles and Camilla Parker Bowles (1947–). In an interview with the BBC's Martin Bashir, Diana discussed both topics. Having separated in 1992 after eleven years of marriage, Charles and Diana divorced in 1996, a year before her death in a car accident.

Charles was said (albeit in the tabloid *Daily Mail*) to have once asked his wife: "Do you seriously expect me to be the first Prince of Wales in history not to have a mistress?" He and Parker Bowles married in 2005.

BASHIR: Around 1986, again according to the biography written by Jonathan Dimbleby about your husband, he says that your husband renewed his relationship with Mrs. Camilla Parker Bowles. Were you aware of that?

DIANA: Yes I was, but I wasn't in a position to do anything about it.

BASHIR: What evidence did you have that their relationship was continuing even though you were married?

DIANA: Oh, a woman's instinct is a very good one.

BASHIR: Is that all?

DIANA: Well, I had, obviously I had knowledge of it.

BASHIR: From staff?

DIANA: Well, from people who minded and cared about our marriage, yes.

BASHIR: The Prince of Wales, in the biography, is described as a great thinker, a man with a tremendous range of interests. What did he think of your interests?

DIANA: Well, I don't think I was allowed to have any. I think that I've always been the eighteen-year-old girl he got engaged to, so I don't think I've been given any credit for growth. And, my goodness, I've had to grow.

BASHIR: What effect did that have on you?

DIANA: Pretty devastating. Rampant bulimia, if you can have rampant bulimia, and just a feeling of being no good at anything and being useless and hopeless and failed in every direction.

BASHIR: And with a husband who was having a relationship with somebody else?

DIANA: With a husband who loved someone else, yes.

BASHIR: You really thought that?

Well, there were three of us in this marriage.

DIANA: Uh, uh. I didn't think that, I knew it.

BASHIR: How did you know it?

DIANA: By the change of behavioural pattern in my husband; for all sorts of reasons that a woman's instinct produces; you just know. It was already difficult, but it became increasingly difficult.

BASHIR: In the practical sense, how did it become difficult?

DIANA: Well, people were—when I say people, I mean friends, on my husband's side— were indicating that I was again unstable, sick, and should be put in a home of some sort in order to get better. I was almost an embarrassment.

BASHIR: Do you think he really thought that?

DIANA: Well, there's no better way to dismantle a personality than to isolate it.

BASHIR: So you were isolated?

DIANA: Uh, uh, very much so.

BASHIR: Do you think Mrs. Parker Bowles was a factor in the breakdown of your marriage?

DIANA: Well, there were three of us in this marriage, so it was a bit crowded.

BILL CLINTON
GRAND JURY TESTIMONY, AUGUST 17, 1998

Six years after Bill Clinton dodged assertions by Gennifer Flowers about a lengthy affair (see Devotion, page 62), another allegation—that he had had a sexual relationship with White House intern Monica Lewinsky—was harder to refute. A 1994 investigation, originally intended to explore the Clintons' finances, was expanded to include the Lewinsky situation. The president's grand jury testimony was memorable for his definitional acrobatics (including the oft-quoted statement "It depends upon what the meaning of the word 'is' is") as well as his parsing of the phrase *sexual relationship*.

Clinton ultimately conceded in a televised address that he had had "a relationship with Miss Lewinsky that was not appropriate." He was formally impeached by the House of Representatives on charges of perjury and obstruction of justice but was acquitted by the Senate. The questioner was prosecutor Robert Bittman. Robert Bennett was Clinton's attorney.

BITTMAN: And you remember that Ms. Lewinsky's affidavit said that she had had no sexual relationship with you. Do you remember that?

CLINTON: I do.

BITTMAN: And do you remember in the deposition that Mr. Bennett asked you about that. This is at the end of the—towards the end of the deposition. And you indicated, he asked you whether the statement that Ms. Lewinsky made in her affidavit was—

CLINTON: Truthful.

BITTMAN: —true. And you indicated that it was absolutely correct.

CLINTON: I did. . . . I believe at the time that she filled out this affidavit, if she believed that the definition of sexual relationship was two people having intercourse, then this is accurate. And I believe that is the definition that most ordinary Americans would give it.

If you said Jane and Harry have a sexual relationship, and you're not talking about people being drawn into a lawsuit and being given definitions, and then a great effort to trick them in some way, but you are just talking about people in ordinary conversations, I'll bet the grand jurors, if they were talking about two people they know, and said they have a sexual relationship, they meant they were sleeping together; they meant they were having intercourse together.

So, I'm not at all sure that this affidavit is not true and was not true in Ms. Lewinsky's mind at the time she swore it out.

STEPHANY ALEXANDER
"TOP 10 WAYS ON HOW TO CATCH A CHEATING HUSBAND," 2009

The list below appeared on the popular website "WomanSavers," which was created by relationship guru Stephany Alexander as a "date screening service."

1.   Set a trap. Cheating husbands usually cheat when their wife is out of town. Tell your husband that you are leaving for a couple of days and then wait, listen and watch. Place a recording surveillance device in your bedroom or near the phone and then listen. Park in a friend's car with a hat and sunglasses on and follow his car or wait for someone to come to the house. Keep a camera, binoculars and a cell phone with you. Cheating husbands usually take their affair out for dinner and a rendezvous while you are gone. Give your cheating husband lots of space to make a mistake. Your husband will leave cheating signs unknowingly. Make sure you are "busy" or out of the house a lot while you are investigating. Take a long nap under your bed at lunch or in the evening or place a long-recording digital tape recorder which is voice activated under the bed. This wouldn't work if you have children or a dog.

2.   Watch his cell phone. If he protects his cell phone with a password, unexpectedly ask to borrow his cell phone to make an important call. Then make a fake call, pressing as many buttons of his call log as possible to note any strange calls. Go to the bathroom with phone if at all possible. Watch whether his cell phone is always turned off when with you or whether he takes unusually long to phone you back. Note the times, dates and length of any suspicious calls. Press the re-dial on the phone or *69. This is an effective way to find out who they've been calling.

3.   Place a long-recording digital tape recorder under your cheating husband's car seat every morning and then listen to it when you are alone. Please check the laws in your city or state to make sure it is legal to record someone in your car if they are borrowing it. The same goes for a GPS tracking device which tracks everywhere your husband's car goes. GPS tracking devices are now made the size of a pack of chewing gum so they are easy to hide.

4.   Monitor your husband's computer usage. Does he use the computer late at night or for an unusual amount of time? Cheating husbands frequently utilize free email services such as hotmail, msn, yahoo, gmail, hushmail, etc. Check his internet web browser history for warning signs. If you suspect your husband is cheating, you can install a

keystroke logger which will log every keystroke your husband types, including his passwords. There are many good ones currently for sale.

5. If your cheating husband is frequenting any dating sites, create a fake profile on-line of someone you think your husband would be attracted to and then start flirting. Many wives have successfully used this technique.

6. Be careful of your cheating husband's close friends who may cover for him because of loyalty feelings. Even if they don't approve of your husband's cheating ways, they may still cover for his cheating by providing an alibi for him.

7. Set booby traps in your house. If you think your cheating husband may be bringing someone into your home while you are traveling or out, set some traps. Put on a clean set of sheets and then place a crumb on the bedspread. Make sure that a dog or cat doesn't move it. Then check to see if the crumb is still in the same place after your return.

8. Get your girlfriends to help. Sign up a willing acquaintance or girlfriend to hit on your husband at a pre-determined location to see if he will bite. It is helpful if she carries a tape recorder in her purse so you may hear him.

9. Monitor your husband's driving habits for a month. Watch for increase in gas receipts and monitor the car's odometer to see if there are extra unexplained miles on the car. Monitor the time he leaves for work and the time he comes home. You should be able to establish a pattern by keeping a calendar and noting the times. If your husband claims to be working late, check paycheck stubs to verify his overtime. If your husband explains a late return home as a result of having to drive out of town on business, yet the mileage on the car indicates less than ten miles driven, you'll have caught your cheating husband in a lie which may be due to his adultery.

10. Paper signs of a cheating husband can include unexplained receipts, more frequent ATM withdrawals, and unexplained credit card charges. Note any strange dates and times. Is there a restaurant charge when he should have been at work? Check his business deductions if possible.

Monitor your husband's driving habits for a month.

If you have tried some of the above tips on how to catch a cheating husband and have been unsuccessful, try playing your poker face. Pretend like you know something and give him 24 hours to come clean or else. However, only resort to this after you have tried all other means because if you accuse him, your husband will know you are on to him, deny any wrong doing and cover his cheating tracks better next time.

WENDY PLUMP
"A ROOMFUL OF YEARNING AND REGRET," 2010

Wendy Plump originally wrote this article for the *New York Times*' "Modern Love" column. Her book on the same subject, *Vow: A Memoir of Marriage (and Other Affairs)*, was published in 2013.

Not long ago, the friend of a friend spent the night in a hotel room, which is sometimes what you do when you find out your spouse has been having a yearlong affair. His flight was sadly predictable—it's all many of us are capable of after discovering such a betrayal—though I am sure he now realizes that mere movement is not a fix for that kind of agony.

I know this for two reasons: No. 1, I have had an affair; No. 2, I have been the victim of one. When you unfurl these two experiences in the sunlight for comparison, and measure their worth and pain, the former is only marginally better than the latter. And both, frankly, are awful.

I recently offered my cheated-upon view of things to my acquaintance, who has returned every night for a week to that hotel because he cannot bear to look at his wife. A couple of years ago I offered the other side to a friend when she was considering having an affair.

Start, I suggested to her, by picturing yourself in the therapist's office with your betrayed husband after you've been found out (and you will be found out). You will hear yourself saying you cheated because your needs weren't being met. The spark was gone. You were bored in your marriage. Your lover understands you better. One or another version of this excuse will cross your lips like some dark, knee-jerk Hallmark-card sentiment.

I'm not saying these feelings aren't legitimate, just that they don't legitimize what you're doing. If you believed they did, your stomach wouldn't drop on your way out the door to your lover's. You wouldn't feel the need to shower before climbing into the marital bed after a liaison. You wouldn't feel like a train had struck you in the back when your son asked why you forgot his lacrosse game the other day.

When you miss a family function because of work, you get over it. When you miss a family function because you were in a hotel room with your lover, you feel breathless with misery.

The great sex, by the way, is a given. When you have an affair you already know you will have passionate sex—the urgency, newness and illicit nature of the affair practically guarantee that.

What you don't know, or perhaps what you don't allow yourself to think about, is that your life will become an unbearable mix of yearning and regret because of it. It will be difficult if not impossible to be in any one place with contentment.

This is no way for an adult to live. When you're with your lover, you'll be working on your alibi and feeling loathsome. When you're with your spouse, you'll be dying to return to your love nest. When you are at home, everything in your life will look just a little bit out of register—the furniture, the food in your refrigerator, your children, your dog—because you've detached yourself from your normal point of reference, and it now belongs to a reality you've abandoned.

> This is no way for an adult to live. When you're with your lover, you'll be working on your alibi and feeling loathsome. When you're with your spouse, you'll be dying to return to your love nest.

You will be pulled between two poles, one of obligation and responsibility, the other of pleasure and escape, and the stress of these opposing forces will threaten to split you in two.

I met the man I cheated with early in my marriage. He was the beautiful twin brother of a friend, something like a young Errol Flynn. I was entranced. My husband traveled a lot and I took advantage of that, finding myself at my lover's apartment often. But at home with my husband during those ragged months, I was anxious and ill at ease. I should have been focusing on our new house, our new jobs, but my inability to resist the pull of the affair ruined all of that. I could not concentrate on our coupled life and frankly did not care to.

I knew I needed to stop it, but didn't have the will to do so on my own. I had to enlist my husband, to tell him so that we could battle this together. So I admitted to the affair one evening after dinner.

Almost 20 years after that confession I can still remember how the whole world narrowed down to the two of us sitting there, that new truth congealing between us.

Once the affair is out in the open, you will strive mightily to justify yourself. You will begin many sentences with the phrase, "I never meant to—" But one look at the hollow-eyed, defeated form of your spouse will remind you that such a claim is beside the point. You can both get over this, yes. But the innocence will have gone out of your union and it will seem as if a bone has been broken and healed, but one that rain or cold weather can set to throbbing again.

So, now take the other side. You discover your cheating spouse, as I once did, and what you experience is not far removed from post-traumatic stress. It is a form of shock. As your mind struggles to accommodate this wrenching reality, you won't be able to sleep or focus. Your fight-or-flight mechanism will go haywire. You will become consumed with where your spouse is at any moment, even if you see him in the pool with your children.

You will lose your appetite. Stress will blow out your metabolism. You will torture yourself with details known and imagined. You will fit together the mysteries of his daily patterns like a wicked puzzle. Every absence or unexplained late night or new habit or sudden urge to join a gym, for instance, will suddenly make horrible sense. You will wonder why you were so stupid.

But as the writer Paul Theroux says in one of his travelogues, "It is very easy to plant a bomb in a peaceful, trusting place." That is what the cheating spouse has done. Then detonated it.

Sooner or later your illicit, once-beloved object of affection will become tawdry, wearying. You will come to long for simple, honest pleasures like making dinner with your sons or going out to the movies without having to look over your shoulder.

On the other side, your spouse's philandering will cease to torment you and instead the whole episode will leave you disgusted and bored and desirous to get out. You will just want to be with someone who does what he says he is going to do, goes where he says he is going to go, and can be found any time you need him because he is not hiding.

I say all this by way of hope, believe it or not. Affairs are one of the adult world's few disasters that can be gotten over, with a lot of time and kindness. It has to burn out of you over months and months, flaming up and then subsiding as you get used to the fact.

A great deal of comfort will come from your friends, many of whom will offer advice— hate him, leave him, move on—that you should listen to politely and then reject. After all, the consequences of your decisions will be visited upon you, not your friends. They will be only too happy to amplify your confusion, listen to you cry, and then get into the car and drive home to their own intact families.

In the end your marriage may not need to be trashed, though mine was. The affairs metastasized in our relationship from the inside out. By the time all was said and done, there was little left to save. Our marriage had become like a leaf eaten away by caterpillars, where the petiole and midrib remain with some ghostly connective tracery in between. Not enough to hold even a drop of rain.

I look at my parents and at how much simpler their lives are at the ages of 75, mostly because they haven't marred the landscape with grand-scale deceit. They have this marriage of 50-some years behind them, and it is a monument to success. A few weeks or months of illicit passion could not hold a candle to it.

If you imagine yourself in such a situation, where would you fit an affair in neatly? If you were 75, which would you rather have: years of steady if occasionally strained devotion, or something that looks a little bit like the Iraqi city of Fallujah, cratered with spent artillery?

From where I stand now, it all just looks like a cheap hotel room, whether you're in that room to have an affair or to escape from the discovery of one.

And despite the sex and the excitement, or the drama and the fix of everyone's empathetic attention, there is no view from this room that is worth having.

READERS' COMMENTS
THE NEW YORK TIMES, 2010

The vast majority of responses to Wendy Plump's "Modern Love" column (above) praised the writing, the insights, and/or the frankness, and in general affirmed Plump's views about the devastating effects of infidelity. Several readers, however, expressed opposite views.

"BELLA TERRA," ALBUQUERQUE, NEW MEXICO

. . . An affair is not always—rarely is—a rejection of one's spouse. Affairs happen because we are human. If a marriage is only about maintaining fidelity in the bedroom—maybe that's a main problem with the marriage? I do have one caveat: if affairs are repetitive and/or blatant, it's probably time to end the marriage.

"ANNE," CALIFORNIA

. . . As well written as this piece is—the "You Will" format is ridiculous. Every human being's experiences are different. This is a fatalistic American POV. I had an affair with a man who had been unhappy for years with his wife. I was in a marriage where I was lonely and neglected. We had known each other since college. We left our partners. And have been happy together for years now. Was it expensive? Difficult? Yes. And worth every freaking dime and difficult moment. Call it selfish, but we may only walk this way once. Being happy is the most valuable commodity in our lives. And we owe it to ourselves to be true to that.

"JM21," NEW YORK

Having an affair was one of the best things I ever did. It gave me the courage to leave a bad marriage and reminded me that I was worthy of love and would be loved again. I haven't a single regret about my actions; however, I somewhat resent being told that I should.

CHRISTOPHER RYAN AND CACILDA JETHÁ
SEX AT DAWN, 2010

A studious and comprehensive volume about human relationships, *Sex at Dawn* reexamined the long-held assumption that males—whether humans or other primates—have a greater tendency toward promiscuity than females because of the need to increase their chances of reproduction. The researchers found persuasive evidence that females are just as wanton as males, and that, for both genders, monogamy is a far cry from the natural human state that so many anthropologists, psychologists, and moralists have asserted it to be. Christopher Ryan and Cacilda Jethá, a married psychologist and psychiatrist, relied on primate research and cross-cultural anthropology to conclude that humans—much like the bonobo, our closest ape relative—began as foragers who worked cooperatively and shared sex partners freely.

Recall that the total number of monogamous primate species that live in large social groups is precisely *zero*—unless you insist on counting humans as the one and only example of such a beast. The few monogamous primates that do exist (out of hundreds of species) all live in the treetops. Primates aside, only 3 percent of mammals and one in ten thousand invertebrate species can be considered sexually monogamous. Adultery has been documented in *every* ostensibly monogamous human society ever studied, and is a leading cause of divorce all over the world today. . . .

Think about that. *No* group-living nonhuman primate is monogamous, and adultery has been documented in *every* human culture studied—including those in which fornicators are routinely stoned to death. In light of all this bloody retribution, it's hard to see how monogamy comes "naturally" to our species. Why would so many risk their reputations, families, careers—even presidential legacies—for something that runs *against* human nature?

IN-LAWS

PLUTARCH
ADVICE TO THE BRIDE AND GROOM, 1ST CENTURY

Best known for his *Parallel Lives*, the Greek historian Plutarch (circa 46–120) also wrote what has become known as the *Moralia*, a collection of essays and dialogues on ethical, literary, and political matters. His *Advice to the Bride and Groom* contained both prescriptions (see Oneness, page 322) and, as in the case below, descriptions.

In the African city of Leptis, the custom is for the bride, the day after her marriage, to send a message to her husband's mother, asking for a pot. The mother-in-law refuses, and says she does not have one. This is to ensure that the bride knows from the start the stepmotherliness of a mother-in-law, and so is not angry or upset if something worse follows later. Recognizing this, the wife must seek to palliate the cause. This is a mother's jealous rivalry for her son's love. The only way to cure this is to secure the husband's love privately, but not attempt to loosen or weaken his love for his mother.

JUVENAL
"THE WAYS OF WOMEN," 2ND CENTURY

Little is known about the life of Decimus Junius Juvenalis (circa 55–circa 127), but his writings, particularly his sixteen satires, were extremely influential. They took on subjects as varied as daily life in Rome, homosexuality, health, money, power, and, in the case of his sixth and longest satire, the general corruption of Roman women.

All chance of domestic harmony is lost while your wife's mother is living. She gets her to rejoice in despoiling her husband, stripping him naked. She gets her to write back politely and with sophistication when her seducer sends letters. She tricks your spies or bribes them. Then when your daughter is feeling perfectly well she calls in the doctor Archigenes and says that the blankets are too heavy. Meanwhile, her lover, in hiding shut off from her, impatient at the delay, waits in silence and stretches his foreskin. Maybe you think that her mother will teach her virtuous ways—ones different from her own? It's much more productive for a dirty old lady to bring up a dirty little girl.

COTESWORTH PINCKNEY
THE WEDDING GIFT, TO ALL WHO ARE ENTERING THE MARRIAGE STATE, 1848

Scion of a prominent South Carolina family of planters and politicians, Charles Cotesworth Pinckney (1812–1898) chose instead the life of an Episcopal priest. In this marriage manual (see also Secrets, page 385), he offered wide-ranging advice to newlyweds.

The solemnization of matrimony and the union of two hearts, as man and wife, does not of necessity constitute the union of the families of each party. This fact is deserving of deep consideration, inasmuch as it is not a rare occurrence that conjugal happiness, if not entirely broken up, is deranged to a degree almost tantamount, by the jealousies of the two families.

The delegating to you of the authority which a mother exercises over a son till his marriage—an indefinable authority, which every good mother exercises over a good son—has probably never once flashed across the mind of your mother-in-law. She will consider him to the latest moment as her peculiar property, granted to her by the laws of nature; a being whom she has reared and nourished, and trained up to her own mind, and whose daily progress she has watched with the most zealous affection. She will, therefore, regard with instinctive jealousy every estrangement of that affection which has existed from the birth of her offspring.

Now there are two points of view in which you must contemplate those feelings of affection, each of which will present to you a favorable view. First, you must bear in mind the affections of a mother for her offspring. If she were a worthless woman, and not fit to be entrusted with the care and training of a child, she would not possess these jealous feelings of attachment. Secondly, you may rest assured that if a strong attachment exists between a mother and her son, it prognosticates favorably for your future happiness; for an affectionate son rarely, if ever, makes a bad husband. It may be said, then, that if you wish to obtain a partner in every way desirable as the companion of your future life, you must expect a jealousy on the part of his mother on your taking him from the home of his first and best friend.

Seeing that such feelings are to be expected, you must exercise your utmost circumspection, as happiness is the prize. We have before observed that a good mother must merit your esteem; endeavor, therefore, to engage her affections as the mother of your husband, and engage her affections also as a senior whose experience is worth having. As a chief means of obtaining this end, form a resolution in your own mind to be pleased with her, and you will find that in this almost wholly consists the art of making yourself acceptable.

A&P TRADE CARD, 1885

The A&P food stores popularized the "trade card" in the nineteenth century—usually adorned with romantic or sentimental images, but occasionally with something a little more biting.

EDWARD HARDY
HOW TO BE HAPPY THOUGH MARRIED: BEING A HANDBOOK TO MARRIAGE BY A GRADUATE IN THE UNIVERSITY OF MATRIMONY, 1885

For more Hardy, see Honeymoon, page 174. Here he is quoting an unnamed clergyman.

Neither member of a conjugal partnership should listen to a single word of criticism of the other member from any relative whatever, even should the words of wisdom drop from the lips of father, mother, brother, or sister. The rules of the new society need not extend beyond these two, for there would be nothing in the conduct of members in good standing to require other special attention.

"ADVICE TO YOUNG WIVES"
CHICAGO DAILY TRIBUNE, 1895

Some excellent advice to a young wife consists of an earnest exhortation to preserve discreet silence with respect to family members.

Always remember that what you learn about your husband's family is to be kept to yourself; that when you married him and took his name you became one of the family, and the little trouble, the little skeleton, is not to be discussed with the members of the family in which you were born. To your sister it may mean nothing that some trouble has come to your husband's brother. You may tell it to her in secrecy, and it may seem of so little importance that she will repeat it to her sister-in-law, and gradually what was meant to be kept quiet is told all round the neighborhood. The art of keeping to yourself what you hear on each side of the house is one that you must cultivate, for it means the keeping of peace. Surely, you would not wish to hurt your husband, yet you will do it if you cannot keep quiet. When you enter his mother's house, anything that is told to you in confidence must be forgotten when you leave it, unless, indeed, it is discussed with your husband, and the same rule will apply to your own family. Don't imagine that every little frown, every little disagreeable word is meant for you, and do not retail in your husband anything unpleasant that may have happened when you were visiting at his mother's house. Think that she is your mother, too, and give her the privilege of speaking to you as your mother does. I know it isn't always easy to have fault found with one when one is trying to do one's best, but think over what is said, if there is anything helpful in it.

"ADVICE TO PROSPECTIVE MOTHERS-IN-LAW"
THE BALTIMORE SUN, 1908

Remember, first of all, mesdames, that a son-in-law, however silly he may look in his wedding gauds, with his hair clipped short and his cheeks depilitated to the verge of mayhem, is nevertheless a human being, with rights specifically guaranteed by the Constitution of the United States. . . . He may resemble, in complexion and mentality, a lobster, and you may have to support him, but he is still a man, and as such he is legally and biologically superior to all other domestic animals. To kill him is murder, to scorn him is sinful, and to rile him is unwise.

Strange as it may seem, it is not your duty to regulate his conduct. If he is of a boisterous nature and occasionally laughs too loud, you are not to blame. If he smokes cigarettes and acquires an orange-peel tint, you are not held responsible. If he belongs to the Elks and comes home from a Lodge of Sorrow with vine-leaves in his hair, you will be served with no subpoenas. If he sneaks off every Saturday night to go to a burlesque show, the sin is upon his own head. . . .

Your son-in-law is willing to submit to a good deal of bossing from your daughter, for he knows that she loves him, and every man regards the acts of any woman who loves him with toleration, because he has great respect for her taste and good sense. But in your own case there is no such palliative. He is well aware that you look upon him, not with affection, but with suspicion: that his sudden arrest on any charge, from selling liquor without a license to bigamy, would not surprise you in the least. Therefore, he is restless and ill at ease beneath your gaze. When you enter the room he starts. When you fix a fishy eye upon him and frown, a lump arises in his throat and he is flabbergasted.

You should treat him in a far more humane and diplomatic manner. Give him a free rein. Keep away from him as much as possible, and when you meet him by accident greet him with a smile. Do not assume an air of familiarity in your relations with him, for no man with proper self-respect likes his mother-in-law to address him by his first name.

BRITISH PROVERB

There is but one good mother-in-law, and she is dead.

HOW TO BE A GOOD HUSBAND, 1936

See Grievances, page 146, for more advice from this anonymously written British handbook.

When your mother-in-law departs, and your wife gives a sigh of relief, don't duplicate the expression of relief. Be absolutely passive for, while your wife may cast stones at her own people, she will thoroughly resent it if you take a hand at the game, also. It is a privilege of hers, not yours.

ELEANOR ROOSEVELT
THIS IS MY STORY, 1937

Seen by many historians as the ultimate meddling mother-in-law, Sara Roosevelt had persuaded her son, Franklin, to wait a year before announcing his engagement to Eleanor Roosevelt (1884–1962), his fifth cousin once removed. Then, in a master stroke of passive-aggression, Sara made their wedding gift the design and construction of a double town house in Manhattan—where she would live alongside the couple. Though there were separate entrances, a number of the rooms on several floors could be joined by pocket doors. "You were never quite sure when she would appear, day or night," Eleanor wrote in a magazine years later, and in her autobiography, she recalled her feelings about her new home.

The night before the wedding, Sara wrote in her journal about her twenty-three-year-old son, the future president: "This is Franklin's last night at home as a boy."

I did not know quite what was the matter with me, but I remember that a few weeks after we moved into the new house in East 65th Street I sat in front of my dressing table and wept, and when my bewildered young husband asked me what on earth was the matter with me, I said I did not like to live in a house which was not in any way mine, one that I had done nothing about and which did not represent the way I wanted to live. Being an eminently reasonable person, he thought I was quite mad and told me so gently, and said I would feel different in a little while and left me alone until I should become calmer.

I pulled myself together and realized that I was acting like a little fool, but there was a good deal of truth in what I said.

G.I. ROUNDTABLE SERIES
CAN WAR MARRIAGES BE MADE TO WORK?, 1944

Between 1943 and 1945, the Division of Information and Education of the U.S. Army collaborated with the American Historical Association to produce a series of pamphlets called "Constructing a Postwar World." The subjects varied from the international (*What Is the Future of Italy?*, *How Shall Lend-Lease Accounts Be Settled?*) to the very domestic, including advice for the everyman protagonist, "Private Puzzled."

The authoritative voice of the pamphlets was due in part to the fact that none of them was signed by an individual. Nonetheless, records show that at least the first draft of *War Marriages* was written by University of Minnesota sociology professor Clifford Kirkpatrick, and that the series' advisory board featured professors from top-ranking universities, including Arthur M. Schlesinger at Harvard.

Know the girl's parents before they become your parents-in-law. This may not be easy, for they may be placed on exhibition, best foot forward. In the romantic tradition of marriage, they may not seem to count, but generally they do at least appear upon the scene. In a sense you marry them in order to get the girl. All comic-strip ideas aside, parents-in-law are important because they have claims and emotional demands to make upon their children. From what has been said it follows that your father-in-law may be the kind of person you are *supposed* to be. If you don't like that kind of person or can't be that kind of person, it may be just too bad.

Furthermore, the girl's parents give some idea of what she now is or is going to become. By breeding and upbringing she is a product of her parents. Suppose the mother at fifty is silly and kittenish. The daughter has a girlish gaiety suitable to one who is young and pretty, but later on will she be like her mother? Suppose the mother at fifty is a bore—the daughter may have a better start than you realize, with only some twenty-five years to go. Look at the girl's parents for a dim preview of the future. Remember that the personalities of both parents are interwoven under the girl's skin. She may resemble them. She may exert herself to avoid resemblance. She may carry within her the strain of their disagreements and conflicts.

If it is important for the man to know the girl's parents, it is perhaps even more important for the girl to know his parents, particularly his mother. Generally he fits in better with her parents than she does with his.

EVELYN AND SYLVANUS DUVALL
SAVING YOUR MARRIAGE, 1954

Founded in 1935, the Public Affairs Committee was a nonprofit organization that published pamphlets offering advice on social, family, and health problems, with titles ranging from "So You Think It's Love!" to "Caring for Your Feet." Having written frequently about marriage, Evelyn Duvall (see Conflict, pages 43–44) teamed up with her husband, the Rev. Sylvanus Duvall (1900–1997), to survey more than five thousand spouses and report that three in four couples claimed they had trouble with in-laws. The Duvalls suggested diplomacy, respect, confrontation, love, and, if all that failed . . .

The pamphlet series was edited for many years by Maxwell Stewart, who also worked as an editor at *The Nation* and wrote some dozen economics books.

Some families have solved very difficult problems by helping "Mother" to find a job; a real job where she can feel wanted and worthy. A social agency may help in suggesting a useful program for the mother who has to give up her own home.

If you have done your best and still can not handle the problem, you may have to resort to more stringent measures. The simplest of these is escape. You move to another part of the

> If you have done your best and still cannot handle the problem, you may have to resort to more stringent measures. The simplest of these is escape.

town, or another city. If you cannot do this, you may have to face it where you are. Arguments with in-laws need not be fatal and may clear the air. The important thing is to make your own position clear. In any case, you may need assistance. Marriage counselors may help you to see your problems more clearly, and guide you in your actions.

In the last analysis, in-laws are people. Adjustments with them are basically the same as in any interpersonal relationships.

DANNY ARNOLD
"MOTHER, MEET WHAT'S HIS NAME," *BEWITCHED*, 1964

Partly inspired by the play *Bell, Book and Candle*, about a man who falls in love with a witch, the television series *Bewitched* ran for eight seasons. With an ever-flustered mortal husband (Darrin Stephens) and his loving witch wife (Samantha) determined to live a normal life, the series also featured a supernaturally intrusive mother-in-law. As played to campy perfection by the classical actress Agnes Moorehead, Endora never got over her initial conviction that her daughter had made a terrible mistake.

Producer/director/comedian Danny Arnold (1925–1995) wrote the season-one episode in which mother-in-law and son-in-law meet for the first time.

ENDORA: . . . You were saying?

DARRIN: Our firm handles some rather large accounts. *(He offers to light her cigarette.)*

ENDORA: Thank you, I have a light. *(The cigarette lights itself.)*

SAMANTHA: Mother, Darrin's firm is one of the largest advertising agencies in the world, and Darrin's one of its top executives.

ENDORA: That sounds very exciting. Samantha, may I have that ashtray, please.

SAMANTHA: Oh, yes, certainly. *(Samantha hands the ashtray to Endora.)* And Darrin is responsible for all of the creative designs for the campaigns.

ENDORA: What on earth did you do that for?

SAMANTHA: Do what?

ENDORA: You carried that ashtray to me. Don't tell me you've forgotten how to levitate.

SAMANTHA: Of course I haven't forgotten, Mother. It's just that Darrin prefers that I don't do any of that stuff anymore.

ENDORA: Why do you object to my daughter being herself, young man?

DARRIN: I don't object, Mrs.—

ENDORA: You'll never be able to pronounce it. Just call me Endora.

DARRIN: I like Samantha the way she is, Endora. She doesn't need any of that other nonsense.

ENDORA: Nonsense?

SAMANTHA: Darrin doesn't mean anything—Darrin, please—

DARRIN: I mean we don't need those powers of hers. We can handle things by ourselves.

ENDORA: Oh you think so, do you?

DARRIN: I don't mean to be disrespectful, but we want to live normal lives.

ENDORA: What is normal to you, young man, is to us asinine. Samantha is what she is and that you cannot change.

SAMANTHA: Mother, I made the decision myself.

ENDORA: Yes, I know. A decision I do not approve.

DARRIN: Samantha and I can handle our problems by ourselves. They're nobody else's business.

SAMANTHA: Darrin, please!

ENDORA: Are you threatening me?

DARRIN: Not exactly.

SAMANTHA: Darrin, please understand! Mother means well.

ENDORA: Don't you worry, my poor baby, your mother will see to it that you're treated properly.

DARRIN: I have every intention of treating her properly, without any help or interference from you.

ENDORA: Young man! *(She raises her arms to cast a spell.)*

SAMANTHA: Mother, don't!

ENDORA: Very well. (*To Darrin*) Just consider yourself lucky that you are not, at this moment, an artichoke.

JEALOUSY

EURIPIDES
MEDEA, 431 BC

In Greek myth, Medea was the wife of Jason and his divine assistant in taking the golden fleece—and with it, the power of rule—from her father. In the play by Euripides (circa 484–406 BC), however, "Medea" became *jealousy* personified. Having discovered Jason's infidelity with the daughter of Corinth's king, Medea exacts her revenge by murdering the king and his daughter, as well as both the sons she's had with Jason.

MEDEA: O Zeus, and Justice, child of Zeus, and sungod's light, now will I triumph o'er my foes, kind friends; on victory's road have I set forth; good hope have I of wreaking vengeance on those I hate. . . . A servant of mine will I to Jason send and crave an interview; then when he comes I will address him with soft words, say, "this pleases me," and "that is well," even the marriage with the princess, which my treacherous lord is celebrating, and add "it suits us both, 'twas well thought out"; then will I entreat that here my children may abide, not that I mean to leave them in a hostile land for foes to flout, but that I may slay the king's daughter by guile. For I will send them with gifts in their hands, carrying them unto the bride to save them from banishment, a robe of finest wool and a chaplet of gold. And if these ornaments she take and put them on, miserably shall she die, and likewise everyone who touches her; with such fell poisons will I smear my gifts. And here I quit this theme; but I shudder at the deed I must do next; for I will slay the children I have borne; there is none shall take them from my toils; and when I have utterly confounded Jason's house I will leave the land, escaping punishment for my dear children's murder . . . Never shall he see again alive the children I bore to him, nor from his new bride shall he beget issue, for she must die a hideous death, slain by my drugs. . . .

CHORUS: O lady, wilt thou steel thyself to slay thy children twain?

MEDEA: I will, for that will stab my husband to the heart.

FRANCIS BACON
"OF MARRIAGE AND SINGLE LIFE," 1612

Famous and influential as a statesman, author, scientist, and philosopher, Sir Francis Bacon (1561–1626) left no shortage of pronouncements on subjects ranging from the universal to the specific.

Bacon wrote this essay on marriage a decade before his own.

It is one of the best Bonds, both of Chastity and Obedience, in the Wife, if She think her Husband Wise; which She will never doe, if She finde him Jealous.

ALEXANDER BROME
"TO A JEALOUS HUSBAND," 1664

A British attorney and popular satirical poet, Alexander Brome (1620–1666) seemed in this ditty to be making a simple argument: If she's going to cheat, she's going to cheat.

In vain thou shutt'st thy doors by day, in vain,
Windows by night, thy wife's lust to restrain;
For if a woman only chaste will be
In watch and ward, she has no chastity.

ELIZA HAYWOOD
THE FEMALE SPECTATOR, 1745

It was known as "amatory fiction" in the days when Eliza Haywood (circa 1693–1756) pioneered what we now call the romance novel, and she wrote a lot of it. Though details of her personal life are few and contradictory, it is known that Haywood was an actress in Ireland and England before she began writing. Throughout the early eighteenth century, she supported herself—and, apparently, her two children—by writing novels and plays, in many of which she thinly veiled society's scandals. In 1728, Alexander Pope (see Grievances, pages 142–43) brutally mocked her in his epic *The Dunciad*, but she reemerged in 1744 with *The Female Spectator*, the first periodical written for women by a woman.

To be jealous without a Cause, is such an Injury to the suspected Person as requires the utmost Affection and Good-Nature to forgive; because it wounds them in the two most tender Parts, their Reputation and Peace of Mind; lays them under Restraints the most irksome to Human Nature, or in a manner obliges them to Measures which are the Destruction of all Harmony.

Those few therefore who truly love, are in Possession of the Object of their Wishes, and yet suffer this poisonous Passion to disturb the Tranquility of their Lives, may be compar'd to Misers that pine amidst their Stores, and are incapable of enjoying a present Plenty through the Fears of future Want.

That Desire of prying into every thing a Husband does, and even into his very Thoughts, appears to me rather a childish Fondness than a noble generous Passion; and tho' it may be pleasing enough to a Man in the first Months of his Marriage, will afterwards grow tiresome and insipid to him, as well as render both of them ridiculous to others.

We may depend on this, that the most innocent persons in the world, in some humours, or unguarded moments, may happen to say or do something which might not be altogether pleasing to us to be informed of—how mad a thing then is it to seek our occasions of disquiet! Yet this too many women are ingenious in doing, and afterwards no less industrious in throwing fresh matter on the mole-hill they haved discovered, till they raise it to a mountain—trifles perhaps too light to retain any place in the husband's memory, and no sooner over than forgotten, or if of consequence enough to be remembered by him, are thought on with remorse, are revived by reproaches, and made to seem less faulty than they are, by the wife's attempting to represent them as more so.

. . . Jealousy is the worst Rack the Heart that harbours it can possibly sustain.

NAPOLEON BONAPARTE
LETTER TO JOSEPHINE, 1796

Right up there with Scott and Zelda or Liz and Dick, Napoleon Bonaparte (1769–1821) and Josephine were as famous for their friction as they were for their love. Only days after their wedding, Napoleon was in Italy leading the French army, which did nothing to keep him from sending Josephine a barrage of letters, some adoring, some suspicious, and this one—written within a year of their marriage—clearly a bit of each.

Both spouses had affairs, and tempers, but their marriage continued despite all obstacles until Napoleon was forced to recognize that Josephine could never give him an heir. "I want to marry a womb," he reportedly said—and a "royal womb" at that. In 1810, he divorced Josephine and several months later married Marie-Louise of Austria, the future mother of Napoleon II (ironically heir only to the collapsed First French Empire). But according to one witness, the last words on the emperor's deathbed were "France, armée, tête d'armée, Joséphine," i.e., "France, army, head of the army, Josephine."

J

I love you no longer; on the contrary, I detest you. You are a wretch, very clumsy, very stupid, a Cinderella. You never write to me; you do not love your husband. You know what pleasure your letters give him, and you never write him even six miserable lines!

Pray, madam, what do you do all day? What important affairs have you that take up all the time in which you might be writing to your husband?

What affection stifles and pushes on one side the love, the tender, constant love, that you have experienced from him? Who can be this marvellous being—this new lover who absorbs all

> Josephine, beware! One fine night I shall break open the doors and be with you.

your time, tyrannizes over your days, and prevents you from thinking of your husband? Josephine, beware! One fine night I shall break open the doors and be with you.

In truth, my dearest, I am uneasy at having no news from you. Write me four pages filled with those nice, kind things that are such a pleasure to my heart. I hope that ere long I shall seize you in my arms, and cover you with a million burning kisses—burning as though they came from the equator.

MARY BAKER EDDY
SCIENCE AND HEALTH, 1875

Christian Science founder Mary Baker Eddy (1821–1910) devoted an entire chapter of her defining work to marriage, which she considered a binding contract.

Jealousy is the grave of affection; mistrust where confidence is due touches with mildew the flowers of Eden, and scatters to the four winds the leaves of love.

THE REAL TOLERANCE, 1913

Written anonymously, this British volume was dedicated to "Those who can understand" and was filled with aphorisms in categories such as "Friendship," "Pleasure," and "Sinners." In the foreword, the author wrote that the book was "an attempt to show how the true Charity, set forth in all Divine Philosophies, may be adjusted to the spirit of the age and brought to bear on the manifold circumstances of Life." These were among the author's injunctions about tolerance in marriage.

O you who strive after perfection and high love! unto you I say: if sometime you discover your wife loves another man, yet because of your children or the law you are unable to permit her to live with or marry this man, even if she desire to do so, then it beho[o]ves you to invite him to your house and treat him as your friend: for by so doing you will render two human beings happy instead of miserable; you will also save them from deceiving you, and will call forth unto yourself their grateful love.

O you who yearn after true magnanimity, unto you I say: if your wife has a child by another man, then do not give vent to your anger, but strive to love and care for that child as truly as if it were your own, for verily the man who is incapable of loving that which is not his own flesh and blood is still the slave of vanity.

Wise indeed is that woman who, knowing herself to be no longer possessed of bodily attraction, sympathetically suffers her husband to enjoy the embraces of another woman—treating that woman as her friend—for having lost the physical unity, which some day must inevitably pass away, she not only retains, but magnifies the mental unity, which is the greatest and most enduring love.

O you who are a passionless woman and find the sexual embraces of your husband irksome to you, so much so that you would fain deny him your body, unto you I say: drive him not to deceitfulness nor into the loveless arms of a harlot, but allow him the passion of some noble woman, and sanctify the relationship by the balm of your friendship; for it beho[o]ves nobody to deny unto another that which they cannot or will not give themselves. . . .

Fortunate is the man who can implicitly *trust* his wife, but infinitely more fortunate is he who *need* not trust his wife, in that he has uprooted the sense of possession, which is the mother of most misery.

O you who would be a noble husband, if your wife fall in love with another man, and you, in your resentment, are tempted to deny her the enjoyment of that love, then I say unto you: put your own selfish thought away; for in denying her that love towards the other man you only awaken her hatred towards yourself, while in permitting it you awaken her gratitude and greater devotion.

H. L. MENCKEN
A BOOK OF BURLESQUES, 1916

For more Mencken, see Adam and Eve, page 3; Expectations, page 105.

The way to hold a husband is to keep him a little bit jealous. The way to lose him is keep him a little bit more jealous.

"DECLARES HER HUSBAND WAS JEALOUS OF DOG"
PITTSBURGH POST-GAZETTE, 1916

The specter of marital jealousy, as suggested by the court case of Lillian Pulitzer (1885–?), was not always due to the presence of another man or woman.

Pulitzer obtained her divorce in Reno in 1918.

New York, Nov. 14—Supreme Court Justice Young of Westchester county yesterday transferred for trial from Westchester to this county the separation action brought by Mrs. [Lillian] Hearne Pulitzer against Walter Pulitzer, nephew of Joseph Pulitzer, late multi-millionaire publisher.

Mrs. Pulitzer alleges in her complaint that her husband showed signs of being jealous over her regard for her bulldog during her early married life, and abused the dog out of spite. Pulitzer denies the charges.

RICHARD BEN CRAMER
JOE DIMAGGIO, 2000

The marriage of Hollywood and baseball royalty in January of 1954 had the makings of a fairy tale, though as it turned out, more Grimm than Disney. Joe DiMaggio's intense discomfort with Marilyn Monroe's fame and sexual allure created obstacles from the start, resulting in raging fights and, at times, physical abuse. As told by writer Richard Ben Cramer (1950–2013), the breaking point came on September 14, just eight months after the wedding, when Marilyn filmed the famous subway-grate scene for the movie *The Seven Year Itch*, with an enraged DiMaggio as witness. Monroe filed for divorce the following month. DiMaggio, who never married again, sent roses to Marilyn's crypt several times a week for two decades after her death in 1962.

Natasha Lytess was Monroe's acting coach. Milton Greene was a photographer best known for his portraits of the star.

It was the need of the columnists that brought Joe out to watch Marilyn work. Walter Winchell (as he would later recall) knew it would make a good story. The studio had publicized a night scene with Marilyn, the papers trumpeted the news: "Miss Monroe's costume," Hearst's *Journal-American* announced, "is expected to be more revealing than the one she wore yesterday to stop the traffic." On a Wednesday at midnight, about fifteen hundred newsmen and fans, pro photographers and snapshot amateurs, turned out on Lexington Avenue, at 52nd Street, in front of the Trans-Lux Theater. But Winchell needed more than a street scene. (Everyone would have that.) That's why he hunted up Joe, who was having a couple of quiet belts with [a friend], in the bar of the St. Regis Hotel. Winchell wanted Joe to come with him to watch Marilyn strut her stuff.

Joe didn't think it was a good idea. "It would make her nervous, and it would make me nervous, too."

But Winchell insisted. "Oh, come on, Joe. I have to be there. It might make some copy for me."

The scene they went to witness would produce one of the most famous screen images in history—Marilyn Monroe, in simple summer white, standing on a subway grating, cooling herself with the wind from a train below. But what sent Joe DiMaggio into a fury was the scene around the scene. Fans were yelling and shoving at police barricades as the train (actually a wind machine manned beneath the street by the special effects crew) blew Marilyn's skirt around her ears. Each time it blew, the crowd would yell, "Higher!" "More!" Her legs were bare from her high heels to her thin white panties. Photographers were stretched out on the pavement, with their lenses pointed up at his wife's crotch, the glare of their flashbulbs clearly outlining the shadow of her pubic hair. "What the hell is going on here?" Joe growled. The director, Billy Wilder, would recall "the look of death" on DiMaggio's face. Joe turned and bulled his way through the crowd—on his way back to the bar—with the delighted Winchell trotting at his heels.

That night, there was a famous fight in Marilyn and Joe's suite on the eleventh floor of the St. Regis. It was famous because none of the guests on that floor could sleep. And famous because Natasha Lytess was so alarmed by Marilyn's cries that she went next door to intervene. (Joe answered the door, and told her to get lost.) It was famous because the following morning Marilyn told her hairdresser and wardrobe mistress that she had screamed for them in the night. ("Her husband got very, very mad with her, and he beat her up a little bit," said the hairdresser, Gladys Whitten. "It was on her shoulders, but we covered it up, you know.") And famous because Milton Greene's wife, Amy, came to visit at the suite the following day (to try on Marilyn's mink), and was appalled to see bruises all over her friend's back.

And the fight would stay famous—as the end of Joe and Marilyn's famous marriage.

GINA BARRECA
"JEALOUSY: HOW DO YOU SOLVE A PROBLEM LIKE MEDEA?," 2009

Regina Barreca (1957–) teaches literature, creative writing, and feminist literary theory at the University of Connecticut while writing books and articles on such topics as gender, power, and politics. This passage comes from her edgy take on jealousy, which appeared in *Psychology Today* and began: "Jealous? I was born jealous; I needed no apprenticeship."

Jealousy makes detectives, clairvoyants, and thieves of us all. We track down private papers; we imagine encounters in gruesome detail and construct passionate conversations; we purloin letters, phone bills, and e-mails; we decode their passwords, the retrieval code for their answering machines, their journal entries. When their phones are busy, we call the other numbers to see if indeed we can make the connection—are they talking to the one we *fear*? We drive by to see if lights are on, if cars are in driveways; we walk by offices to see if doors are open or shut; we go through trash; we go through credit card statements. We go through hell.

KNOWING

VICTOR HUGO
LETTER TO ADÈLE FOUCHER, 1821

Considered one of the greatest masters of French literature, Victor Hugo (1802–1885) wrote poems, plays, and novels, most famously *Les Misérables* and *The Hunchback of Notre-Dame*. He fell in love with Adèle Foucher, a childhood friend, and married her in 1822, the year after his disapproving mother's death. They eventually had five children and countless infidelities, but his certainty about their rightness for each other was expressed in numerous lengthy, portentous, and occasionally pretentious letters.

When two souls, which for a longer or a shorter time have sought each other amidst the crowd, at length find each other; when they perceive that they belong to each other; when, in short, they comprehend their affinity, then there is established between them a union, pure and ardent as themselves, a union begun upon earth in order that it may be completed in heaven. This union is *love*; real and perfect love, such love as very few men can adequately conceive; love which is a religion, adoring the being beloved as a divinity; love that lives in devotion and ardor, and for which to make great sacrifices is the purest pleasure. It is such love as this that you inspire in me, and it is such love that you will some day assuredly feel for me, even though, to my ever-present grief, you do not do so now. Your soul is formed to love with the purity and ardor of the angels, but it may be that only an angel can inspire it with love, and when I think this I tremble.

WILLIAM FAULKNER
GO DOWN, MOSES, 1942

In the connected series of short stories that was published as *Go Down, Moses*, William Faulkner (1897–1962) tells the tale of Lucas Beauchamp, a mixed-race descendant of a prominent Mississippi family. In his increasingly obsessive search for the family's fabled buried treasure—and the legitimacy that he feels will go with it—Lucas alienates his wife, Molly. In the section of the book called "The Fire and the Hearth," her divorce proceedings turn out to be the only way to get him to give up his search.

"The Fire and the Hearth" refers to the fire that Lucas, despite everything, has kept burning in the couple's home since the day they married.

Husband and wife did not need to speak words to one another, not just from the old habit of living together but because in that one long-ago instant at least out of the long and shabby stretch of their human lives, even though they knew at the time it wouldn't and couldn't last, they had touched and become as God when they voluntarily and in advance forgave one another for all that each knew the other could never be.

CANDICE BERGEN
KNOCK WOOD, 1984

Actress Candice Bergen (1946–) was thirty-three and had never been married when she and the French film director Louis Malle began dating. In Bergen's autobiography, she wrote that it took a while before they shook off their habitual mistrust and allowed the relationship to become romantic. They married the following year, and were married until Malle's death in 1995.

Here I was, in our late-night conversations, invariably curled up in the overstuffed armchair opposite his place on the sofa. Never daring, never dreaming to sit next to him on the couch. It took Louis to close the chasm. To take the risk. One night, he asked me quietly, smiling softly, "Candy, can I hold you?" And I smiled and said emphatically, "*Oh yes.*"

I felt like a small frightened animal who had spent its life curled up in the back of a cave snarling at intruders when, suddenly, someone turned on the light and said, "It's okay, it's safe—you can come out now." And from then, everything was simple, and I thought, So *this* is the point. I *understand*. Now it all makes sense.

BEN AFFLECK AND MATT DAMON
GOOD WILL HUNTING, 1997

Good Will Hunting starred Ben Affleck (1972–) and Matt Damon (1970–) and won them the 1997 Academy Award for Best Original Screenplay. The story, about a disenfranchised mathematical genius named Will Hunting (played by Damon), featured Robin Williams (see Divorce, page 78) as a down-to-earth psychotherapist named Sean Maguire, whose challenge is to help Will learn how to embrace both life and love.

K

WILL: So, when did you know, like, that she was the one for you?

SEAN: October 21st, 1975.

WILL: Jesus Christ. You know the fuckin' day?

SEAN: Oh yeah. 'Cause it was game six of the World Series. Biggest game in Red Sox history.

WILL: Yeah, sure.

SEAN: My friends and I had, you know, slept out on the sidewalk all night to get tickets.

WILL: You got tickets?

SEAN: Yep. Day of the game. I was sittin' in a bar, waitin' for the game to start, and in walks this girl. Oh it was an amazing game, though. You know, bottom of the eighth Carbo ties it up at a six–six. It went to twelve. Bottom of the twelfth, in stepped Carlton Fisk. Old Pudge. Steps up to the plate, you know, and he's got that weird stance.

WILL: Yeah, yeah.

SEAN: And BAM! He clocks it, you know. High fly ball along the left field line! Thirty-five thousand people, on their feet, yellin' at the ball, but that's not because of Fisk. He's wavin' at the ball like a madman.

WILL: Yeah, I've seen—

SEAN: He's going, "Get over! Get over! Get OVER!" And then it HITS the foul pole. OH, he goes apeshit, and 35,000 fans, you know, they charge the field, you know?

WILL: Yeah, and he's fuckin' bowlin' police out of the way!

SEAN: Goin', "God! Get out of the way! Get 'em away!" Banging people—

WILL: I can't fuckin' believe you had tickets to that fuckin' game!

SEAN: Yeah!

WILL: Did you rush the field?

SEAN: No, I didn't rush the fuckin' field. I wasn't there.

WILL: What?

SEAN: No. I was in a bar havin' a drink with my future wife.

WILL: You missed Pudge Fisk's home run?

SEAN: Oh, yeah.

WILL: To have a fuckin' drink with some lady you never met?

SEAN: Yeah, but you shoulda seen her; she was a stunner.

WILL: I don't care if fucking—

SEAN: Oh, no, no, she lit up the room.

WILL: I don't care if Helen of Troy walks in the room, that's game six!

SEAN: Oh, Helen of Troy—

WILL: Oh my God, and who are these fuckin' friends of yours they let you get away with that?

SEAN: Oh—they had to.

WILL: W-what'd you say to 'em?

SEAN: I just slid my ticket across the table and I said, "Sorry, guys, I gotta see about a girl."

WILL: "I gotta go see about a girl"?

SEAN: Yeah.

WILL: That's what you said? And they let you get away with that?

SEAN: Oh, yeah. They saw in my eyes that I meant it.

WILL: You're kiddin' me.

SEAN: No, I'm not kiddin' you, Will. That's why I'm not talkin' right now about some girl I saw at a bar twenty years ago and how I always regretted not going over and talking to her. I don't regret the eighteen years I was married to Nancy. I don't regret the six years I had to give up counseling when she got sick. And I don't regret the last years when she got really sick. And I sure as hell don't regret missin' the damn game. That's regret.

WILL: Wow—. Woulda been nice to catch that game, though.

SEAN: I didn't know Pudge was gonna hit a homerun.

GREG BEHRENDT AND LIZ TUCCILLO
HE'S JUST NOT THAT INTO YOU, 2004

Colleagues from behind the scenes of the TV show *Sex and the City* (see Unmarried, page 442), Greg Behrendt (1963–) and Liz Tuccillo (1962–) published their instantly bestselling, brutally frank, and funny-but-wise advice book after an office conversation in the writers' room. With Behrendt lending his male point of view to a meeting filled with women, Tuccillo was inspired to realize that knowing when a man wasn't right for marriage might be considerably easier than knowing when he was.

Just remember this. Every man you have ever dated who has said he doesn't want to get married or doesn't believe in marriage, or has "issues" with marriage, will, rest assured, someday be married. It just will never be with you. Because he's not really saying he doesn't want to get married. He's saying he doesn't want to get married *to you*. There is nothing wrong with wanting to get married. You shouldn't feel ashamed, needy, or "unliberated" for wanting that. So make sure from the start that you pick a guy who shares your views for the future, and if not, move on as quickly as you can. Big plans require big action.

Marriage is a tradition that has been somewhat imposed on us, and therefore has a lot of critics. Be that as it may, if someone is as against marriage as you are for it, please make sure there aren't other things going on besides he's just not that into the institution.

> Dear Greg,
>
> I've been dating a guy since I was twenty-three. I'm twenty-eight now. We started talking about marriage two years ago, and he said he wasn't ready. So we moved in together to help him get "ready." We talked about it recently and he said that he still wasn't ready. He reminded me that we're young and we still have a lot of time and there's no need to rush. In a way, he's right. I'm only twenty-eight and people get married much later these days. And sometimes it takes longer for guys to grow up than girls. So I want to be understanding, but I'm just not sure how long I'm supposed to wait. Does he need more time or is he just not that into marrying me?
>
> Danielle

Dear Waiting at the Altar,

He's right. Why rush? It's only been five years. He's going to know you so much better after ten. And you have all the time in the world, right? You know, in case after ten years he decides he's *still* not ready. I hate to tell you this, but here's why he feels rushed: He's still not sure you're the one. Yep, my lovely, I know it's hard to hear, but better to hear it now than ten years from now. So you can stay with him and continue to audition for the part of his lucky wife, or you can go find someone who doesn't need a decade or two to realize you're the best thing that ever happened to him.

MARVIN HAMLISCH AND TERRE BLAIR HAMLISCH
INTERVIEWS, 2012

Composer of the musical *A Chorus Line* and the soundtrack to *The Way We Were*, *The Sting*, and some forty other films, Marvin Hamlisch (1944–2012) was the winner of Emmy, Grammy, Oscar, Tony, and Golden Globe awards, as well as a Pulitzer Prize. He was a child prodigy who auditioned for and was accepted by Juilliard at the age of six. But despite his classical training, he was drawn to the world of songwriting, where his exuberance as a composer and sometime performer only enhanced his early success. In his forties, he encountered some professional setbacks and considerable pressure and self-doubt. But he also met his future wife, Terre Blair, then a TV reporter. A recent documentary intercut interviews in which each separately narrated the tale of their unusual courtship.

TERRE:	I was living in Los Angeles, and the lady that came in to help clean my house said "I think this is terrible, that you're not married" and said, "My sister's working for somebody who seems fairly nice."
MARVIN:	Out of the blue, I start talking to a girl on the phone that I was set up with, you know, on a phone conversation, and all of the sudden, that put the smile on my face.
TERRE:	The first time that we spoke on the phone I asked him where he was, and he said, "Oh, I'm in Virginia somewhere and I'm buying summer shirts on sale." And I tuned in that night and he was at the White House. Who does that? Who doesn't brag? And that was what hooked me.
MARVIN:	You know, here's a person I'm speaking to on the phone for many, many months. I have not met her. We're just discussing life and us.

TERRE: We spoke on the phone sometimes four hours, six hours. Sometimes we fell asleep with the phone in our hand.

MARVIN: If you can talk on a daily basis with someone for hours on the phone and you still are looking forward to the next conversation, then you got something.

TERRE: We had spoken on the phone for months and months, and then Marvin said, "Well, why don't we meet?" And so I flew east and went to the hotel and he was standing outside [my hotel room] door and I was very, very nervous because I had never met him in person. So, I had this questionnaire and I put the questionnaire on the outside of the door that said "Fill out the questionnaire before entering." And [it] said: "Do you love the girl behind the door? Is the girl behind the door the most beautiful person in the world to you? Does the girl behind the door spell her name with an E or an I? And does the girl behind the door love her Marvin with her whole heart?" He answered all the questions right. And then he said, um, sight unseen, "Will you marry me?"

MARVIN: I just was able to see her with that other part of me. You know. Where I didn't need to see her with [my eyes]. I needed to see her with [my heart].

TERRE: I said yes.

K

LASTING

MARK TWAIN
NOTEBOOK, 1894

Samuel Clemens (see Adam and Eve, page 3; Endings, page 95–96) had been married twenty-four years when he wrote this in his notebook.

Love seems the swiftest, but is the slowest of all growths. No man or woman really knows what perfect love is until they have been married a quarter of a century.

WARD JUST
"HONOR, POWER, RICHES, FAME, AND THE LOVE OF WOMEN," 1973

Ward Just (1935–) is a novelist and essayist whose focus has often been power, whether in politics or passion. He titled his 1973 novella (and the collection that later contained it) after a quote from a Sigmund Freud lecture about the roots of the artist's neuroses: "He desires to win honour, power, wealth, fame and the love of women; but he lacks the means for achieving these satisfactions." Here the narrator, a Washington lawyer named Wylie, has just had lunch with his friend Charlie, a married stockbroker.

As he was paying the check and we were preparing to leave, he said an extraordinary thing. "Of course, once you clear away the underbrush, women's liberation and hedonism and the rest of it, the heart of the problem is the death of romantic love. Marriage can't sustain it. Could once maybe, but not now. Maybe it never could. And we both know that we're romantic animals. If you don't get it one place you'll get it another. Try to suppress the impulse and you'll dry up like a prune. Indulge it and you'll end up in a motel somewhere with a teen-ager." He carefully signed the check and put it in the center of the table, the pencil placed just so across it, diagonally. "There's nothing in the contract that says it has to dry up, but it does—and I have a hunch that the reasons are identical to the ones that keep the marriage together. Civility, compromise, and a suppression of rage."

OLD JOKE

My wife and I have the secret to making a marriage last. Two times a week, we go to a nice restaurant. A little wine, good food. She goes Tuesdays, I go Fridays.

STANLEY KUNITZ
"ROUTE SIX," 1978

No American poet had the longevity and few the critical acclaim of Stanley Kunitz (1905–2006), whose seven decades of writing culminated in his being named the United States Poet Laureate at the age of ninety-five. Countless other honors had preceded this one, as had his devotion as professor, book editor, poetry ambassador, and, not incidentally, gardener. Kunitz was married and divorced twice; his third marriage, to the artist Elise Asher, lasted from 1958 until her death two years before his.

The city squats on my back.
I am heart-sore, stiff-necked,
exasperated. That's why
I slammed the door,
that's why I tell you now,

in every house of marriage
there's room for an interpreter.
Let's jump into the car, honey,
and head straight for the Cape,
where the cock on our housetop crows
that the weather's fair,
and my garden waits for me
to coax it into bloom.
As for those passions left
that flare past understanding,
like bundles of dead letters
out of our previous lives
that amaze us with their fevers,
we can stow them in the rear
along with ziggurats of luggage
and Celia, our transcendental cat,
past-mistress of all languages,
including Hottentot and silence.
We'll drive non-stop till dawn,
and if I grow sleepy at the wheel,
you'll keep me awake by singing
in your bravura Chicago style
Ruth Etting's smoky song,
"Love Me or Leave Me,"
belting out the choices.

Light glazes the eastern sky
over Buzzards Bay.
Celia gyrates upward
like a performing seal,
her glistening nostrils aquiver
to sniff the brine-spiked air.
The last stretch toward home!
Twenty summers roll by.

JAMES WOLCOTT
"NOISES ON," 2005

Best known as the longtime *Vanity Fair* culture and media critic, James Wolcott (1952–) has also published one novel, two nonfiction books (the recent one a memoir), articles for *The New Yorker*, and a blog for *Vanity Fair* that covers television, film, theater, books, and just about anything else, including the occasional peek into his own life. This essay appeared in an anthology of men's writings about love and relationships.

Wolcott is married to Laura Jacobs, a fellow *Vanity Fair* contributing editor.

Sporadic infighting kept things hopping under our own roof, before and after we moved out of The Heights into an actual house with porch, haunted garage, the whole bit. The dialogue sometimes varied, but the sound effects were consistent: my parents' raised voices, punctuated by the rattle of car keys palmed off the kitchen table—slam of the screen door, slam of the car door—squeal of tires as the angrier of the two tore off to the American Legion or another of the fine drinking establishments along Route 40 (with free fistfights in the parking lots on weekends). One night, between jingle of keys and slammeth of door, my father ventured upstairs to make a dramatic announcement. This was unlike him, to take time out from a busy battle royal to address the junior partners. His voice was low and grave. "I'm leaving your mother, moving out of the house," he said. "Look after your brothers." I was the oldest of three brothers (another brother and sister would join the family album later). My father's tone carried such a toll of finality that one of the younger ones began crying as soon as the car left the driveway. And I remember assuring him in classic gruff-sergeant older-brother manner, *Ohhhh, he's not going anywhere, he'll be back, go to sleep.* My father wasn't given to bluffing; in his own mind he may have reached a grim decision, yet the precocious critic in me (I must have been eleven or twelve then) didn't buy his exit speech for a sec—he was hanging his words a little too heavy, overweighting them for scare effect. He had committed the crime of hokeyness. My parents murdering each other, sure, that I could believe back then. But divorce? Nah, never happen. And it never did. Forty-some years later, these two former combatants are still together, sober for more than two decades, and getting along better than they ever did, fond of each other in ways they never were before, back when the furniture seemed to levitate. Family get-togethers today are as calm as Quaker services. My parents didn't confront their demons, they outlasted them, tuckered them out. That wouldn't work for everybody, but it worked for them.

The same pattern holds for the rest of the clan, some of whose marriages once resembled mutual-destruction pacts—Apache dances without the dancing—while others seemed to grow moss up the sides through sheer mutual tedium. But then what bystander, even a close relative, knows what truly goes on inside anyone's marriage? Each marriage is a country unto itself, with its own lingo, customs, unwritten regulations, secret passwords, telepathic powers, and historical landmarks (the picnic table under the one shade tree at Denny's where they first held hands). All I know is that nearly all of the marriages in my family have so far gone the marathon distance. I have one uncle, he and his wife are in their eighties now. Last time my mother mentioned him I was amazed this uncle was still above earth. I figured this crusty character had long since been discontinued due to heavy taxation of the liver. Back in the day, this uncle's favorite form of greeting—which he extended to everyone, friends, strangers, and kids alike—was to flip his blunt middle finger. That was how he said hello. He could be driving by—you'd wave at him— he'd flip the bird. Little memories like that stay with you through the years. Today he's lame and near blind, as is his wife, both of them falling apart and yet *still together*, looking after each other as best they can. Hit after hit to their health, an accumulation of wreckage, and the two of them are still hanging tough.

L

GARRISON KEILLOR
"HOW TO IMPROVE YOUR MARRIAGE IN JUST ONE DAY," 2006

Off and on (mostly on) since 1974, Garrison Keillor (1942–) has been host of the weekly public-radio show *A Prairie Home Companion*, during which he offers his folksy, funny, and often profound tales of the fictional town of Lake Wobegon, Minnesota, where, as he repeatedly puts it, "all the women are strong, all the men are good looking, and all the children are above average." Keillor has written novels and a screenplay set in the same all-American location, and from 2005 to 2010, a weekly newspaper column, in which this article appeared.
Married twice before, Keillor wed violinist Jenny Lind Nilsson in 1995.

Every marriage has its ups and downs. There are the days when you look at your spouse and hear choirs humming Alleluias and there are the days when you wonder, "Who are you and what is your stuff doing in my house?" Those are the days when you play golf. Fishing works, too, or writing sonnets or digging post holes. It keeps the two of you apart for a few hours and usually that's all you need.

I have an after-dinner speech about marriage that is 15 minutes long and somewhat funny. ("The rules for marriage are the same as for a lifeboat. No sudden moves, don't crowd the other person, and keep all disastrous thoughts to yourself.") As a thrice-married guy, one feels an obligation to share such insights.

So I found myself in a cab to LaGuardia to catch a plane to Atlanta to give the speech. (I was in New York to speak at the Edith Wharton Society but not about marriage since she had a miserable one.) The cab stops at the tollbooth on the Triborough Bridge, and I hand the cabbie a $5 bill for the toll, and he waves it away and gives the man in the booth a $50 bill, which turns out to be counterfeit. "Not just counterfeit," the toll-taker says. "It's lousy counterfeit." The $50 bill is confiscated, forms are filled out, I pay the toll and we get to LaGuardia thirty minutes before flight time. I give the driver $25 for a $23.75 fare and he yells, "Why take it out on me?" Because you knew the bill was counterfeit, that's why. I'm no rube. I didn't just fall off the cabbage wagon.

I dash to the plane. I am flying to Atlanta to speak at a benefit luncheon, and I dislike benefits because you have to endure other people's gratitude, which can be exhausting. This sounds ungracious but it's true. You go speak for free to a banquet of the Episcopal Promise Keepers of Poughkeepsie or the Honorary Society of Menomonie Economists or the Scandinavian Skin-Diving School in Schenectady and thirty people tell you what a wonderful thing you're doing and it wears you out. If one person would tell you a joke instead, you would throw your arms around him in gratitude.

I get on the plane and I'm in seat 8D on one of those toy jets that airlines have introduced, which are designed for groups of fourth-graders. The seats are hard on the vertically gifted such as myself, so that when the man in 7D reclines his seat, it almost kills me. If Abraham Lincoln were sitting in 8D, he would give up on that "malice toward none" concept and club 7D on the top of his little bald head. But I bite my tongue, and I also do not shoot my neighbor in 8C, a piggish fellow in an expensive sweater and tasseled shoes, snarfling his lunch while poring over the *Wall Street Journal* and poking me with his elbow as he eats. I come from a part of America where people apologize if they poke and make sure not to do it again. He comes from a part of America where you push your way up to the trough and elbow other people out of the way.

The benefit luncheon in Atlanta is not a happy time. It is an organization of Very Rich People Helping Wretched People Without Having To Be In The Same Room With Them, and it's full of alpha males of the sort you see strutting around airports with cell phones clipped to their ears hollering at somebody in Cincinnati and gushy women who tell you they adore your television show and never miss it on Sunday night, even though it's radio and it's Saturday. I give my 15-minute speech, which suddenly isn't amusing at all, and the president of Very Rich People gives me a hideous Lucite plaque in gratitude for my generosity, which I deposit in a trash bin at the airport, and I fly home to Minnesota, and there is my elegant wife waiting at the curb in her car.

It is so good to see her. We've been married ten years and surely we have problems, but at the moment I cannot think of a single one. We drive through the streets of St. Paul and there is no place I would rather be. Misery is the secret of happiness in marriage. Go make yourself miserable and then come home.

BILLY GRAHAM
NEWSWEEK INTERVIEW, 2006

Next to the nine popes who have spanned his lifetime, the minister Billy Graham (1918–) has probably been the most recognizable Christian leader of the twentieth and twenty-first centuries. A deep believer in the power of prayer and repentance, Graham in this interview lamented some limitations of aging, but counted his sixty-three-year marriage to Ruth Bell among the blessings. She died the following year.

At night we have time together; we pray together and read the Bible together every night. It's a wonderful period of life for both of us. We've never had a love like we have now—we feel each other's hearts.

OLIVIA HARRISON
INTERVIEW, *GEORGE HARRISON: LIVING IN THE MATERIAL WORLD*, 2011

Olivia Harrison (1948–) was the second wife of George Harrison, the Beatle known for his quiet demeanor, sharp cheekbones, sharp wit, and commitment to Eastern religion. In Martin Scorsese's documentary about the late musician, the filmmaker interviewed Olivia, with whom George had been married—despite any number of twists and turns—for thirty years.

Sometimes people say, you know, "What's the secret of a long marriage?"

It's like, "You don't get divorced."

And I think, you know, you go through challenges in your marriage, and here's what I found. First time we had a big hiccup in the road, I, you know, you go through things, and you go, "Wow, there is a reward at the end of it." There's this incredible reward. You love each other more. You learn something, you let go of something, you get—those hard edges get softened. You know, you're that block of stone and life shapes you and takes away those hard edges.

QUEEN ELIZABETH AND PRINCE PHILIP, 1947 AND 2007

L

STEPHEN KING
"PROUST QUESTIONNAIRE," *VANITY FAIR*, 2013

Stephen King (1947–) is the author of more than fifty novels and is considered the modern master of the horror genre. He married Tabitha Spruce in 1971.

Q: What do you consider your greatest achievement?
A: Staying married.

LEAP

JOHN HEYWOOD
PROVERB, 1546

At least one source, the online British *Phrase Finder*, claims that "look before you leap" originated not with horsemanship, but indeed with marriage—and this proverb.

And though they seeme wives for you never so fit,
Yet let not harmfull haste so far out run your wit:
But that ye harke to heare all the whole summe
That may please or displease you in time to cumme.
Thus by these lessons ye may learne good cheape
In wedding and all things to looke ere ye leap.

NINETEENTH-CENTURY RHYME

Some wed for gold and some for pleasure,
And some wed only at their leisure,
But if you wish to wait and weep,
When e'er you wed,
Look well before you leap.

"THE SILENT PROPOSAL," 1908

A British tradition holds that women may propose to men only on Leap Year.

W. H. AUDEN
"LEAP BEFORE YOU LOOK," 1940

The editors of this volume are extremely partial to this poem, because we asked Lisa's brother to read it at our wedding. Given the fact that we had met less than a year before, it seemed fitting for us. Most critics agree that W. H. Auden (1907–1973) wrote the poem not only as a general endorsement of risk taking but as a love poem to the American poet Chester Kallman.

Auden married Erika Mann, daughter of the German novelist Thomas Mann, so that she could attain a British passport and escape the Nazis. But it was his relationship with Kallman that he referred to as a marriage, and it lasted for several decades—though not always on sexual terms—until Auden's death.

The sense of danger must not disappear:
The way is certainly both short and steep,
However gradual it looks from here;
Look if you like, but you will have to leap.

Tough-minded men get mushy in their sleep
And break the by-laws any fool can keep;
It is not the convention but the fear
That has a tendency to disappear.

The worried efforts of the busy heap,
The dirt, the imprecision, and the beer
Produce a few smart wisecracks every year;
Laugh if you can, but you will have to leap.

The clothes that are considered right to wear
Will not be either sensible or cheap,
So long as we consent to live like sheep
And never mention those who disappear.

Much can be said for social savoir-faire,
But to rejoice when no one else is there
Is even harder than it is to weep;
No one is watching, but you have to leap.

A solitude ten thousand fathoms deep
Sustains the bed on which we lie, my dear:
Although I love you, you will have to leap;
Our dream of safety has to disappear.

WEDDING IN CROATIA, 2012

The leap was by a just-married couple, the photographs by Zvonimir Barisin.

LEGALITIES

MESOPOTAMIAN MARRIAGE CONTRACT, 2200 BC

The bride, a slave, attained her freedom through this marriage; the groom attained a bride. This apparently accounted for the difference in penalties if either of them wanted out.

If Bashtum to Rimum, her husband, shall say, "You are not my husband," they shall strangle her and cast her into the river. If Rimum to Bashtum, his wife, shall say, "You are not my wife," he shall pay ten shekels of money as her alimony.

I take thee to be my wife for the term of five months.

EGYPTIAN MARRIAGE CONTRACT, 200 BC

Among the many discoveries made in Luxor in the early part of the twentieth century was this marriage contract. It was written in demotic, the Egyptian vernacular of that period, and inscribed on an *ostracon*, or pottery shard. Historians suggest that the idea of a trial marriage may have been rooted in the importance of children in Egyptian life and thus of a wife's early pregnancy.

The *stater* was an early Greek coin. The word *ostracon* derived from the practice Athenians had of writing the names of outcast citizens on shards of pottery—hence the word *ostracism*.

I take thee, Taminis, daughter of Pamonthis, into my house to be my lawful wife for the term of five months. Accordingly I deposit for you in the Temple of Hathor the sum of four silver stater, which will be forfeited to you if I dismiss you before the conclusion of the five months, and besides this my banker shall do something for you. But if you leave me on your own account before the end of the five months, the above sum which I have deposited shall be refunded to me.

WOLFGANG AMADEUS MOZART
LETTER TO LEOPOLD MOZART, 1781

Rumors that Wolfgang Amadeus Mozart (1756–1791) had been carrying on an inappropriate relationship with Constanze Weber, at whose family's house he had been boarding, were circulating throughout Vienna and Salzburg in the autumn and winter of 1781. In this unctuous letter to his ever-critical father, Mozart explained that the rumors were the reason that Constanze's guardian had insisted Mozart sign what was in effect a prenuptial agreement.

Mozart and Constanze (he alternated between spelling her name with a C and a K) were married the following year and remained so until his death.

But let me talk now about the Marriage contract, or rather the written assurances of my honorable intentions concerning the girl; you do know, don't you, that they have a guardian because—unfortunately for the family and also for me and my Konstanze—the father is no longer living—and this guardian, who doesn't even know me, must have gotten an earful about me by such servile and loudmouthed gentlemen as Herr Winter:—that one must beware of me—that I had no secure income; that I was too intimate with her—that I might jilt her—and that the girl would be done for in the end, etc.; all this stuff wafted like a bad odor into the guardian's nose—because Constanze's mother, who knows me and my honest behavior, allowed all this to be said without saying anything that would put it right.—Yet, my entire association with them consisted in my—living there—and afterward in my visiting there every day.—No one ever saw me with her outside the house.—But this guardian filled the mother's ears with stories about me for so long until she finally told me about it and asked that I have a talk with him myself, because he was supposed to come by the house in a few days.—He came—I spoke with him—the result was (because I did not explain things as clearly as he had wished) that he told the mother to forbid all association between me and her daughter until I had settled the matter in writing.—The mother told him: his entire association with her consists in coming to my house and—I can't forbid him my house—he is too good a friend for that—a friend to whom I am obliged in many ways.—I am satisfied and I trust him—you must work out an agreement with him yourself.—So then he forbade me to have anything to do with the girl until I acknowledged my relationship in writing. So what other recourse did I have?—to give him a written contract or—never to see the girl again—but if you love honorably and truly, can you forsake the one you love?—could not the mother, could not my beloved herself, come up with ugliest interpretation of my conduct?—Such was my situation! So, I drew up a document in which I stated *that I obligated myself to marry Mad.elle Constance Weber within the time of 3 years; if it should prove impossible for me to do so owing to a change of mind, she would be entitled to receive from me 300 gulden a year.*—Nothing in the world was easier for me to write—because I knew I would never have to pay these 300 gulden—for I shall never forsake her—and even if I should be so unfortunate as to undergo a change of mind—I should be glad that I can liberate myself for a mere 300 gulden—and Konstanze, as I know her, would be too proud to let herself be bought off.—

But what did this heavenly girl do as soon as her guardian had left?—She demanded that her mother give her the document—then said to me—*dear Mozart! I don't need any written assurances from you; I believe what you say;* and she tore up the writ.—This gesture endeared my Konstanze to me even more.—and because she tore up the contract and the guardian gave his Parole d'honneur to keep this matter to himself, my mind, dearest father, was somewhat put at ease when I thought about you.—For I am not worried about obtaining your consent to get married when the time comes, for the only thing the girl lacks is money—and I know how reasonable you are in such matters. So will you forgive me?—I do hope so!—in fact, I don't doubt it at all.

L

FREDERICK DOUGLASS
FINSBURY CHAPEL SPEECH, 1846

Since America's colonial days, slave marriages had been prohibited, and even when they occurred, they were rarely taken into consideration by owners. It was not until the end of the Civil War, when the Thirteenth Amendment abolished slavery, that marriage between African-Americans was legally recognized by the United States. Twenty years before—in the midst of his improbable, eloquent, and hugely influential career as an abolitionist—the former slave Frederick Douglass (circa 1818–1895) made this argument in a speech at Finsbury Chapel in England.

Interracial marriage was not legally protected throughout the United States until the 1967 Supreme Court ruling in *Loving v. Virginia.*

The marriage institution cannot exist among slaves, and one sixth of the population of democratic America is denied its privileges by the law of the land. What is to be thought of a nation boasting of its liberty, boasting of its humanity, boasting of its christianity, boasting of its love of justice and purity, and yet having within its own borders three millions of persons denied by law the right of marriage? . . . If any of those three million find for themselves companions, and prove themselves honest, upright, virtuous persons to each other, yet in these cases—few as I am bound to confess they are—the virtuous live in constant apprehension of being torn asunder by the merciless man-stealers that claim them as their property.

HENRY BLACKWELL AND LUCY STONE MARRIAGE PROTEST, 1855

Suffragist Lucy Stone (1818–1893) kept her name when she married abolitionist Henry Blackwell (1825–1909), and in the marriage ceremony they created, they gave voice both to their mutual devotion and to their shared rejection of the marital laws that still deprived women of so much freedom and financial equality. Heartily endorsing the unconventional contract, Unitarian minister Thomas Wentworth Higginson presided over the wedding, later stating: "I never perform the marriage ceremony without a renewed sense of the iniquity of our present system of laws, in respect to marriage;—a system by which 'man and wife are one, and that one is the husband.' It was with my hearty concurrence, therefore, that the following protest was read and signed, as part of the nuptial ceremony."

While we acknowledge our mutual affection, by publicly assuming the sacred relationship of husband and wife, yet in justice to ourselves and a great principle, we deem it a duty to declare that this act on our part implies no sanction of, nor promise of voluntary obedience to, such of the present laws of marriage as refuse to recognize the wife as an independent rational being, while they confer upon the husband an injurious and unnatural superiority, investing him with legal powers which no honorable man would exercise, and which no man should possess.

We protest especially against the laws which give to the husband

1. The custody of his wife's person.
2. The exclusive control and guardianship of their children.
3. The sole ownership of her personal, and use of her real[,] estate, unless previously settled upon her, or placed in the hands of trustees, as in the case of minors, lunatics, and idiots.
4. The absolute right to the product of her industry.
5. Also against laws which give to the widower so much larger and more permanent an interest in the property of his deceased wife, than they give to the widow in that of her deceased husband.
6. Finally, against the whole system by which "the legal existence of the wife is suspended during marriage," so that in most States she neither has a legal part in the choice of her residence, nor can she make a will, nor sue or be sued in her own name, nor inherit property.

We believe the personal independence and equal human rights can never be forfeited, except for crime; that marriage should be an equal and permanent partnership, and so recognized by law; that until it is so recognized, married partners should provide against the radical injustice of present laws, by every means in their power.

We believe that where domestic difficulties arise, no appeal should be made to legal tribunals under existing laws, but that all difficulties should be submitted to the equitable adjustment of arbitrators mutually chosen.

Thus reverencing Law, we enter our earnest protest against rules and customs which are unworthy of the name, since they violate justice, the essence of all Law.

ALBERT EINSTEIN
LETTER TO MILEVA MARIĆ, 1914

L

Unquestionably the most famous and influential scientist of the twentieth century, Albert Einstein (1879–1955) was considerably less impressive as a husband. He married a fellow scientist named Mileva Marić in 1903 despite his parents' objections. But after a decade in which he composed some of his most brilliant papers and moved from a Swiss patent office to increasingly prestigious academic posts, their marriage foundered. In Berlin, Einstein began an affair with a cousin, Elsa Löwenthal, to whom he wrote in 1913: "I treat my wife as an employee whom I cannot fire." After persuading Mileva to move their family to Berlin, he laid down the following conditions for continuing the marriage. She agreed at first, but a few months later, they separated and later divorced.

Marić and Einstein had two sons, and also had a daughter, Lieserl, before their marriage; she is said to have had scarlet fever, but whether she died or was put up for adoption remains unknown.

CONDITIONS.

A. You will make sure
   1. that my clothes and laundry are kept in good order;
   2. that I will receive my three meals regularly *in my room*;
   3. that my bedroom and study are kept neat, and especially that my desk is left for *my use only*.

B. You will renounce all personal relations with me insofar as they are not completely necessary for social reasons. Specifically, you will forego
   1. my sitting at home with you;
   2. my going out or traveling with you.

C.   You will obey the following points in your relations with me:
1.   you will not expect any intimacy from me, nor will you reproach me in any way;
2.   you will stop talking to me if I request it;
3.   you will leave my bedroom or study immediately without protest if I request it.
D.   You will undertake not to belittle me in front of our children, either through words or behavior.

ISADORA DUNCAN
MY LIFE, 1927

The renowned dancer Isadora Duncan (1877–1927) was as unconventional in her private life as she was in her approach to ballet. Rejecting the idea of marriage, she had two children (by two different men) out of wedlock. In 1922, she did marry Russian poet Sergei Yesenin so that he could legally come to the United States.

Both of Duncan's children died with their nanny in a 1913 car accident. Three years after their marriage, Yesenin returned to the Soviet Union, where he committed suicide.

Any intelligent woman who reads the marriage contract, and then goes into it, deserves all the consequences.

MARGARET MARSHALL
MASSACHUSETTS SUPREME JUDICIAL COURT DECISION, 2003

The case was *Goodridge v. Department of Public Health*; the venue was the Supreme Judicial Court of Massachusetts. The ruling, written for the 4–3 majority by Chief Justice Margaret Hilary Marshall (1944–), was the first of its kind in the United States and held it unconstitutional for the state to deny equal marriage rights to same-sex couples. The arguments were many, some harking back to the *Loving v. Virginia* ruling that protected interracial marriage, but at the heart of the decision were several paragraphs that have frequently been used since in wedding ceremonies—both gay and straight.

As of this writing, thirty-six other states and the District of Columbia had legalized same-sex marriage, and in June of 2013, the U.S. Supreme Court, by a vote of 5–4, had struck down a key section of the Defense of Marriage Act, meaning that the federal government must acknowledge and protect the rights and benefits of same-sex couples legally married in their states.

Marriage is a vital social institution. The exclusive commitment of two individuals to each other nurtures love and mutual support; it brings stability to our society. For those who choose to marry, and for their children, marriage provides an abundance of legal, financial, and social benefits. In return it imposes weighty legal, financial, and social obligations. The question before us is whether, consistent with the Massachusetts Constitution, the Commonwealth may deny the protections, benefits, and obligations conferred by civil marriage to two individuals of the same sex who wish to marry. We conclude that it may not. The Massachusetts Constitution affirms the dignity and equality of all individuals. It forbids the creation of second-class citizens. In reaching our conclusion we have given full deference to the arguments made by the Commonwealth. But it has failed to identify any constitutionally adequate reason for denying civil marriage to same-sex couples. . . .

The decision whether and whom to marry is among life's momentous acts of self-definition.

Without question, civil marriage enhances the "welfare of the community." It is a "social institution of the highest importance." French v. McAnarney, supra. Civil marriage anchors an ordered society by encouraging stable relationships over transient ones. It is central to the way the Commonwealth identifies individuals, provides for the orderly distribution of property, ensures that children and adults are cared for and supported whenever possible from private rather than public funds, and tracks important epidemiological and demographic data.

Marriage also bestows enormous private and social advantages on those who choose to marry. Civil marriage is at once a deeply personal commitment to another human being and a highly public celebration of the ideals of mutuality, companionship, intimacy, fidelity, and family. "It is an association that promotes a way of life, not causes; a harmony in living, not political faiths; a bilateral loyalty, not commercial or social projects." Griswold v. Connecticut, 381 U.S. 479, 486 (1965). Because it fulfills yearnings for security, safe haven, and connection that express our common humanity, civil marriage is an esteemed institution, and the decision whether and whom to marry is among life's momentous acts of self-definition.

JONATHAN RAUCH
"GAY MARRIAGE IS GOOD FOR AMERICA," 2008

Conservative columnist Jonathan Rauch (1960–) published this argument for same-sex marriage the week that California's state supreme court first allowed the marriage of gay couples. Rauch, a longtime contributor to *National Journal* and *The Atlantic*, went on to write a memoir about growing up gay, *Denial: My 25 Years Without a Soul*.

The AIDS quilt, conceived in 1985, commemorates victims of the disease with hand-sewn panels from friends and family. By 1996, the last time it could be displayed in one place, the quilt was large enough to cover the National Mall in Washington, DC.

More ceremonies will follow, at least until November, when gay marriage will go before California's voters. They should choose to keep it. To understand why, imagine your life without marriage. Meaning, not merely your life if you didn't happen to get married. What I am asking you to imagine is life without even the possibility of marriage.

Re-enter your childhood, but imagine your first crush, first kiss, first date and first sexual encounter, all bereft of any hope of marriage as a destination for your feelings. Re-enter your first serious relationship, but think about it knowing that marrying the person is out of the question.

Imagine that in the law's eyes you and your soul mate will never be more than acquaintances. And now add even more strangeness. Imagine coming of age into a whole community, a whole culture, without marriage and the bonds of mutuality and kinship that go with it.

What is this weird world like? It has more sex and less commitment than a world with marriage. It is a world of fragile families living on the shadowy outskirts of the law; a world marked by heightened fear of loneliness or abandonment in crisis or old age; a world in some respects not even civilized, because marriage is the foundation of civilization.

This was the world I grew up in. The AIDS quilt is its monument.

Few heterosexuals can imagine living in such an upside-down world, where love separates you from marriage instead of connecting you with it. Many don't bother to try. Instead, they say same-sex couples can get the equivalent of a marriage by going to a lawyer and drawing up paperwork—as if heterosexual couples would settle for anything of the sort.

Even a moment's reflection shows the fatuousness of "Let them eat contracts." No private transaction excuses you from testifying in court against your partner, or entitles you to Social Security survivor benefits, or authorizes joint tax filing, or secures U.S. residency for your partner if he or she is a foreigner. I could go on and on.

Marriage, remember, is not just a contract between two people. It is a contract that two people make, as a couple, with their community—which is why there is always a witness.

Two people can't go into a room by themselves and come out legally married. The partners agree to take care of each other so the community doesn't have to. In exchange, the community deems them a family, binding them to each other and to society with a host of legal and social ties.

This is a fantastically fruitful bargain. Marriage makes you, on average, healthier, happier and wealthier. If you are a couple raising kids, marrying is likely to make them healthier, happier and wealthier, too. Marriage is our first and best line of defense against financial, medical and emotional meltdown. It provides domesticity and a safe harbor for sex. It stabilizes communities by formalizing responsibilities and creating kin networks. And its absence can be calamitous, whether in inner cities or gay ghettos. . . .

America needs more marriages, not fewer, and the best way to encourage marriage is to encourage marriage, which is what society does by bringing gay couples inside the tent.

MUSLIM INSTITUTE AND ISLAMIC SHARI'AH COUNCIL
MUSLIM MARRIAGE CONTRACT, 2008

With 1.25 billion Muslims living in dozens of countries, contemporary Islamic marriage practices naturally differ widely. In many places, details of the marriage are still arranged between the groom and a male guardian of the bride, known as the walee, to prevent premarital interactions, and polygamy is permissible as authorized by the Qur'an. However, in an effort to create a marriage contract complying with both Islamic religious law (Shari'ah), and British law, Muslim leaders in Great Britain collaborated in 2008 to produce a modern marriage contract that barred polygamy and made the walee optional.

"Security of gaze" refers to the Islamic admonition that men and women should lower their eyes to avoid sexual temptation.

MUTUAL RIGHTS AND OBLIGATIONS

Marriage is a union for life having mutually inclusive benefits and fulfillment for the contracting parties including the following:

- Preservation of chastity and security of gaze
- Companionship inside and outside home
- Emotional and sexual gratification
- Procreation and raising of any children by mutual consultation

- Agreement to live together in a mutually agreed country and establish their matrimonial home therein
- Working collectively towards the socio-economic welfare and stability of the family
- Maintaining their individual property rights but contributing to the welfare of the family according to their capacity
- Maintaining social contacts with family and friends mutually beneficial for the family
- Managing their individual activities/roles inside and outside the home by mutual consultation

OBLIGATIONS OF THE HUSBAND

In addition to the mutual duties and obligations, the husband undertakes not to:

- Abuse his wife/child(ren) verbally, emotionally, physically, or sexually
- Desert/be absent from the marital home for more than 60 days unless by mutual agreement
- Withhold economic contribution towards his wife/family
- Sexually transmit disease or other transmissible diseases
- Misuse/interfere with the wife's property

OBLIGATIONS OF THE WIFE

In addition to the mutual duties and obligations, the wife undertakes not to:

- Abuse her husband/child(ren) verbally, emotionally, physically, or sexually
- Desert/be absent from the marital home for more than 60 days unless by mutual agreement
- Sexually transmit disease or other transmissible diseases
- Misuse/interfere with the husband's property

SPECIAL CONDITIONS

- Both parties reserve the right to amend/alter the contract through mutual written agreement

- Both parties undertake to stay loyal to each other and never to engage in extramarital affairs with the oppos[ite] or same sex
- The husband is not to enter into formal or informal nikah (Muslim marriage) contract in the UK or abroad with another woman, as it is unlawful under the laws of England and Wales as well as the Scottish legal system
- The husband is to procure separate/independent accommodation from shared or parental abode
- The husband delegates his power of divorce (talaq al-tafwid) to his wife
- Details of any additional special conditions mutually agreed upon by bride

LOOKS

XENOPHON
ON HOUSEHOLD MANAGEMENT, 4TH CENTURY BC

Like Plato, the Greek philosopher Xenophon (circa 430–circa 350 BC) recorded conversations with Socrates that purportedly showed the master's interests, beliefs, and, not incidentally, his methods of dialogue. In this excerpt from Xenophon's book *On Household Management* (*Oeconomicus*), Socrates describes a conversation he had with an Athenian farmer named Ischomachus.

Ischomachus then said, "One time, Socrates, I saw that she had covered her face with white lead, so that she would seem to have a paler complexion than she really had, and put on thick rouge, so that her cheeks would seem redder than in reality, and high boots, so that she would seem taller than she naturally was.

"So I said, 'Tell me, my dear, would you consider me more worthy of your love as a partner in our shared wealth, if I told you what I was worth, and didn't boast that I had more than I actually had, and didn't hide anything from you, or if I tried to deceive you by saying that I had more than I in fact had, and showed you counterfeit money and necklaces of gold plate and said that they were real?'

"She interrupted me at that point and said, 'Don't say such things; don't become that sort of man, because if you did, I couldn't love you from my heart.' I replied: 'Haven't we come together, my dear, as partners in each other's bodies?' She replied: 'At least so people say.' 'Then tell me,' I said, 'if I would seem to you to be a more worthy bodily partner, if I cared for myself and tried to make myself more healthy and strong, and because of that were in reality healthy-looking, or if I smeared myself with vermilion and put flesh colour on my eyes and presented myself to you and made love to you deceiving you and presenting you with vermilion to see and touch rather than my own skin.' 'I would not,' she said, 'enjoy touching vermilion as much as your own skin and I do not enjoy looking at flesh colour as much as your own and I would not enjoy seeing your eyes covered with make-up as in good health.'

"'Don't think then, my dear,'" Ischomachus told me he said, 'that I enjoy the colour of white lead more than the colour of your own skin, but just as the gods made horses prefer horses and cattle prefer cattle, and sheep sheep, so human beings prefer the natural human body. You might successfully fool someone outside the household by this kind of deception, but insiders always get caught when they try to deceive one another. For they can be found out when they get up in the morning before they have time to prepare or they are caught out by sweat or put to the test by tears and exposed completely by washing.'"

"What, by the gods," I asked, "was her response to that?" "What else than that," he said, "she never put on make-up again, but tried to present herself with a clean face and suitably dressed. And she asked me if I could advise her how she might look beautiful in reality, and not just appear to be beautiful."

L

THOMAS MORE
UTOPIA, 1516

Famous for his judgment, erudition, and stubborn refusal to recognize Henry VIII as head of the Anglican Church, Sir Thomas More (1478–1535) was tried for treason and beheaded, but he was ultimately canonized by the Catholic Church. His most tangible legacy is the novel *Utopia*, in which, while imagining the ideal society, he took on subjects of both public and private life, including the role of looks in the importance of choosing one's spouse.

According to John Aubrey's *Brief Lives*, More allowed his future son-in-law (and biographer) William Roper to choose which of More's daughters to marry, somewhat along the *Utopian* principle described below; More supposedly led Roper to the bed where the daughters were sleeping on their backs, pulled off their sheet, watched them turn over, and allowed Roper to pat his preferred bride-to-be on the backside.

In choosing marriage partners, [the inhabitants of Utopia] solemnly and seriously follow a custom which seemed to us foolish and absurd in the extreme. Whether she is a widow or a virgin, the bride-to-be is shown naked to the groom by a responsible and respectable matron;

and, similarly, some respectable man presents the groom naked to his future bride. We laughed at this custom and called it absurd; but they were just as amazed at the folly of all other nations. When men go to buy a colt, where they are risking only a little money, they are so suspicious that though he is almost bare they won't close the deal until the saddle and blanket have been taken off, lest there be a hidden sore underneath. Yet in the choice of a mate, which may cause either delight or disgust for the rest of their lives, people are completely careless. They leave all the rest of her body covered up with clothes and estimate the attractiveness of a woman from a mere handsbreadth of her person, the face, which is all they can see. And so they marry, running great risk of hating one another for the rest of their lives, if something in either's person should offend the other. Not all people are so wise as to concern themselves solely with character; even the wise appreciate physical beauty, as a supplement to a good disposition. There's no question but that deformity may lurk under clothing, serious enough to make a man hate his wife when it's too late to be separated from her. When deformities are discovered after marriage, each person must bear his own fate, so the Utopians think everyone should be protected by law beforehand.

L

PROVERB

Chuse a Wife rather by your Ear, than your Eye.

SIR WALTER RALEIGH
"ADVICE TO HIS SON," 1702

On a different note from Thomas More, Sir Walter Raleigh (see Endings, pages 91–92) advised his son not to be too persuaded by a woman's appearance.

The . . . greatest care ought to be in the choice of a Wife, and the only danger therein, is beauty, by which all Men in all ages, wise and foolish, have been betrayed. And though I know it vain to use reasons or arguments, to disswade thee from being captivated therewith, there being few or none, that ever resisted that Witchery; yet I cannot omit to warn thee, as of other things, which may be thy ruin and destruction. For the present time, it is true, that every Man prefers his fantasie in that appetite, before all other worldly desires, leaving the care of honour, credit, and safety in respect thereof: But remember, that though these affections do not last, yet the bond of Marriage dureth to the end of thy life; and therefore better to be born withal in a Mistress, than in a Wife, for when thy humour shall change, thou art yet free to chuse again, (if thou give thy self that vain liberty.) Remember, secondly, That if thou marry for Beauty, thou bindest thy self all thy life for that, which perchance will never last nor please thee one year; and when thou hast it, it will be to thee of no price at all, for the degree dieth when it is attained, and the affection perisheth, when it is satisfied.

MARGARET GRAVES DERENZY
A WHISPER TO A NEWLY-MARRIED PAIR, FROM A WIDOWED WIFE, 1824

The title page said the author was anonymous, but the book was in fact written by Margaret Graves Derenzy (circa 1778–1829). Hardly a widow, the Irish-born writer had married a Major Derenzy when she was sixteen but been abandoned a few years later, when he eloped with his mistress. The experience undoubtedly informed the part of Derenzy's advice book in which she addressed the unheeding adulterers of the world: "Welcome hell! Welcome flames! Welcome devils!" But her bitterness did not stop her from urging wives to be careful in their daily habits and to see the overall challenge of marriage as keeping a husband from his natural tendency to stray.

Derenzy's book became extremely popular in the latter half of the nineteenth century and went through twenty-eight editions.

There is not an hour in the day in which a man so much likes to see his wife dressed with neatness, as when she leaves her bed-room, and sits down to breakfast. At any other moment, *vanity* stimulates her efforts at the toilette, for she expects to see and to be seen; but at this retired and early hour, it is for the very sake of cleanliness, for the very sake of pleasing her husband, that she appears thus neat and nice. Some one says, "A woman should never appear untidily or badly dressed, when in the presence of her husband." While he was your lover, what a sad piece of business if he caught you dressed to disadvantage!—"O dear, there he is, and my hair all in papers; and this frightful unbecoming cap! I had no idea he would have been here so early; let me off to my toilette!" But now that he is your husband, "Dear me, what consequence? My object is gained; my efforts to win him, and all my little manoeuvres to captivate, have been successful, and it is very hard if a woman is to pass her life in endeavouring to please *her husband!*" I remember greatly admiring a lady who lived among the mountains, and scarcely saw any one but her husband. She was rather a plain woman; and yet when she sat to breakfast each morning, and all the day long, her extreme neatness and attention to the niceness of her appearance, made her quite an agreeable object; and her husband loved her, and would look at her with more pleasure than at a pretty woman dressed soiled and untidily: for believe me, those things (though your husband appears not to notice them, nor perhaps is he himself conscious of the cause) strongly possess the power of pleasing or displeasing.

JOHN MATHER AUSTIN
A VOICE TO THE MARRIED, 1847

A Universalist minister and descendant of Cotton Mather, John Mather Austin (1805–1880) wrote several books of instruction early in his life and was later known as a defender of abolition and women's rights. His first marriage, to Sarah Somerdyke, lasted twenty-seven years and produced twelve children, four of whom survived him. He married twice more after Sarah's death, going on as well to become paymaster in the Union army and, later still, a newspaper editor.

Personal appearance is too often the only qualification which has any influence in choosing a companion. A young man meets in society a lady of prepossessing appearance. Her fair complexion, regular features, and symmetrical form make a deep impression upon him. He soon becomes very assiduous in his attentions—calls frequently upon her at her residence, and becomes more and more enraptured with the beauty of her person, and the pleasing vivacity of her manners. The young lady is flattered by his devotion—and being pleased with his person and manners, very naturally strives to exhibit her most attractive qualities, and to be as engaging as possible. Thus a courtship commences, and is carried on to the consummation of matrimony. Neither party sees the other, except under the most favorable circumstances—when they are *prepared* for company, and when they make their best appearance. If the thought of each other's disposition ever enters their minds, their captivated imaginations are ready to whisper that the inward person corresponds with the outward, and that one possessing so much personal beauty, must necessarily be everything desirable in moral and intellectual characteristics. Under this pleasing hallucination, and in entire ignorance of each other's actual tastes, habits, and dispositions, the irrevocable vows are plighted, and the indissoluble knot is tied!

CHARLOTTE BRONTË
JANE EYRE, 1847

In *Jane Eyre*, one of the most popular British novels of the nineteenth century, Charlotte Brontë (1816–1855) presented a protagonist who was strong, moral, and yearning for love—all things common to the author, who nonetheless turned down three marriage proposals until, just a year before her death, she accepted that of Arthur Bell Nicholls. In the novel, Jane's employer and love interest, Edward Rochester, explains how he ended up marrying the woman who would later go mad, be confined to his attic, and ultimately set fire to his house.

Blanche Ingram is a socialite with designs on Rochester.

When I left college, I was sent out to Jamaica, to espouse a bride already courted for me. My father said nothing about her money; but he told me Miss Mason was the boast of Spanish Town for her beauty: and this was no lie. I found her a fine woman, in the style of Blanche Ingram: tall, dark, and majestic. Her family wished to secure me, because I was of a good race; and so did she. They showed her to me in parties splendidly dressed. I seldom saw her alone, and had very little private conversation with her. She flattered me, and lavishly displayed for my pleasure her charms and accomplishments. All the men in her circle seemed to admire her and envy me. I was dazzled, stimulated: my senses were excited; and being ignorant, raw, and inexperienced, I thought I loved her. There is no folly so besotted that the idiotic rivalries of society, the prurience, the rashness, the blindness of youth, will not hurry a man to its commission. Her relatives encouraged me: competitors piqued me: she allured me: a marriage was achieved almost before I knew where I was. Oh, I have no respect for myself when I think of that act!—an agony of inward contempt masters me. I never loved, I never esteemed, I did not even know her. I was not sure of the existence of one virtue in her nature: I had marked neither modesty nor benevolence, nor candour, nor refinement in her mind or manners—and, I married her: gross, groveling, mole-eyed blockhead that I was!

EMILY WARD
LETTER TO SALLIE WARD LAWRENCE, 1849

Sallie Ward was the belle of the ball in her native Louisville, recalled in later years as "the most splendid creature this country has ever produced." She was accustomed to adoration, fine clothes, and makeup. Her new husband, Timothy Bigelow Lawrence, insisted she give up the cosmetics, which he and his Boston circle rejected as unhealthy. Sallie wrote home in abject misery. The excerpt below is part of the feisty response from her mother, Emily Flournoy Ward (1810–1874). But despite Emily's advice, discovery of Sallie's continued use of makeup led to confrontations with her husband, backsliding, tears, and finally, just a year after her marriage, divorce.

Sallie Ward went on to marry three more times. The inscription suggested for her tombstone by a Kentucky humorist was "At Last She Sleeps Alone." Her devotion to appearance extended even past her death. Her funeral instructions called for her to be wrapped in a white satin shroud and buried in a lavender casket draped in white satin.

I am going to write you a real war letter. You say you are acting by Mr. Lawrence's command, and you are unhappy by so doing. Then let me advise you in this case; seem to obey, but do as you please. If you use proper caution he can never know it. You say I can imagine your appearance now; yes, Sallie, I can, and nothing to object to either. You are better looking without complexion than with too much. This I have always said. But if you think differently, then do what would make you happy. You could not be less so, I should judge, under any circumstances. Then never fear Mr. Lawrence's anger; it could not be more enduring. Now, dear Sallie, if you would take the right means, he could never discover it. You must begin with caution, and keep it up. The most delicate tinge possible is all you want. If you have no more, defy the opinion of the universe, the commands of Mr. Lawrence, and every one else. Stick to it with some of your mother's spunk. Could you be worse off than now? You are miserable now; could you be more so then?

B. G. JEFFERIS AND J. L. NICHOLS
SAFE COUNSEL: SEARCH LIGHTS ON HEALTH, 1897

Benjamin Grant Jefferis (1851–1929) was a Canadian physician who teamed up with professor and publisher James Lawrence Nichols (1851–1895) in Chicago to write a series of practical books about health and home life. In *Safe Counsel*, there were sections on personal hygiene and letter writing, tight-lacing and "all the different kinds of baths," and—in the following section—what women like in men.

Above all other qualities in man, woman admires his intelligence. Intelligence is man's woman captivating card. This character in woman is illustrated by an English army officer, as told by O. S. Fowler, betrothed in marriage to a beautiful, loving heiress, summoned to India, who wrote back to her:

"I have lost an eye, a leg, an arm, and been so badly marred and begrimmed besides, that you never could love this poor, maimed soldier. Yet, I love you too well to make your life wretched by requiring you to keep your marriage-vow with me, from which I hereby release you. Find among English peers one physically more perfect, whom you can love better."

She answered, as all genuine women must answer:

"Your noble mind, your splendid talents, your martial prowess which maimed you, are what I love. As long as you retain sufficient body to contain the casket of your soul, which alone is what I admire, I love you all the same, and long to make you mine forever."

RAFAEL DE LEON
"UGLY WOMAN," 1934

In 1963 it was a *Billboard* chart topper sung by Jimmy Soul as "If You Wanna Be Happy." But with somewhat different words, the original song, called "Ugly Woman," was written and performed by Trinidadian calypso singer Hubert R. Charles, a.k.a. Rafael Arias Cairi Llama de Leon, a.k.a. The Roaring Lion (1908–1999).

De Leon's recording is scratchy at best, and transcriptions of the lyrics vary. But we have it on Trinidadian authority that "Du-du," as in the expression "du-du darling," means *love*.

L

If you want to be happy and live a king's life
Don't ever make a pretty woman your wife.
If you want to be happy and live a king's life
Don't ever make a pretty woman your wife.
All you gotta do is just what I say
And you will be jolly, merry, and gay.
Therefore from a logical point of view
Always marry a woman uglier than you.

A pretty woman makes her husband look small
And can very often cause his downfall.
As soon as she marries, there and then she'll start
To do the things that will break his heart.
And when you really think she belongs to you
She callin' somebody else du-du.
Therefore from a logical point of view
Always marry a woman uglier than you.

LOVE

1 CORINTHIANS 13:1-8

This may be one of the most popular readings used at Christian weddings, but it is not quite as straightforward as it seems. It is part of a letter written by the Apostle Paul to members of the Christian community he had founded when he was a missionary in Corinth, Greece. Having left there to live in Turkey for a number of years, he got wind of the fact that divisions had broken out among the members. In his letter, Paul's goal was apparently to refocus the Corinthians on Christ's teachings, and Paul's definitions of love, below, while perfectly noble for marriage, were actually given as a contrast to the fractious, internecine squabbles of which he had learned.

Many Bible translations, including the original King James Version, use the word *charity* instead of *love*.

1 Though I speak with the tongues of men and of angels, but have not love, I have become sounding brass or a clanging cymbal.

2 And though I have the gift of prophecy, and understand all mysteries and all knowledge, and though I have all faith, so that I could remove mountains, but have not love, I am nothing.

3 And though I bestow all my goods to feed the poor, and though I give my body to be burned, but have not love, it profits me nothing.

4 Love suffers long and is kind; love does not envy; love does not parade itself, is not puffed up;

5 does not behave rudely, does not seek its own, is not provoked, thinks no evil;

6 does not rejoice in iniquity, but rejoices in the truth;

7 bears all things, believes all things, hopes all things, endures all things.

8 Love never fails. . . .

PROVERB

Marry first, and love will follow.

WILLIAM SHAKESPEARE
SONNET 116, 1609

The life of William Shakespeare (1564–1616) has been the subject of endless speculation, and his 154 sonnets are among the reasons. More than a third of the poems—including Sonnet 116—are thought to have been written to a man, but whether the relationship was sexual or platonic, autobiographical or fictional, remain open questions. Some critics see echoes of religious, rather than romantic, love, in the opening quatrain. None of this speculation, however, has kept these fourteen lines from being read at uncountable wedding ceremonies and held up for centuries as a guideline for marital happiness.

Among the few facts known about Shakespeare's private life: He married Anne Hathaway when he was eighteen and she was already pregnant; they had three children together, two of whom survived to adulthood.

Let me not to the marriage of true minds
Admit impediments; love is not love
Which alters when it alteration finds
Or bends with the remover to remove.
O, no, it is an ever-fixèd mark
That looks on tempests and is never shaken;
It is the star to every wand'ring bark,
Whose worth's unknown, although his height be taken.
Love's not Time's fool, though rosy lips and cheeks
Within his bending sickle's compass come;
Love alters not with his brief hours and weeks,
But bears it out even to the edge of doom.
If this be error, and upon me proved,
I never writ, nor no man ever loved.

Let me not to the marriage of true minds
Admit impediments.

WILLIAM PENN
SOME FRUITS OF SOLITUDE, 1682

Born in England in 1644, William Penn was a Quaker convert who was frequently published, often imprisoned for expressing his views, and eventually best known as founder of Pennsylvania, which he named for his father. By the time of Penn's death in 1718, he had married twice, fathered sixteen children, and written more than a thousand maxims, including quite a few about marriage.

73.   Never marry but for Love; but see that thou lov'st what is *lovely.*

74.   If Love be not thy *chiefest* Motive, thou wilt soon grow weary of a Married State, and *stray* from thy Promise, to search out thy Pleasures in *forbidden* Places.

75.   Let not Enjoyment lessen, but augment Affection; it being the basest of Passions *to like when we have not, what we slight when we possess.*

76.   It is the Difference betwixt *Lust* and *Love*, that this is fixt, that volatile. Love grows, Lust wastes by Enjoyment: And the Reason is, That one springs from an *Union of Souls, and the other from an Union of Sense.*

77.   They have divers Originals, and so are of different Families: That *inward* and *deep*, this superficial; This transient, and that Permanent.

78.   They that Marry for Mony cannot have the true Satisfaction of Marriage; the requisite means being wanting. . . .

86.   But in Marriage do thou be wise; prefer the *Person* before Mony; *Vertue* before Beauty, the *Mind* before the Body: Then thou hast a Wife, a Friend, a Companion, a *Second Self;* one that bears an equal Share with thee in all thy Toyls and Troubles.

87.   Chuse one that Measures her Satisfaction, Safety and Danger, by thine; and of whom thou art sure, as of thy secretest Thoughts: A *Friend* as well as a Wife, which indeed a Wife implies: For she is but *half* a Wife that is not, or is not capable of being *such* a Friend.

88.   *Sexes* make no Difference; since in Souls there is *none*: And they are the Subjects of Friendship.

89.   He that minds a Body and not a Soul, has not the better Part of that Relation; and will consequently want the noblest Comfort of a Married Life.

ELIZABETH BARRETT BROWNING
SONNET 43, *SONNETS FROM THE PORTUGUESE*, CIRCA 1845

Married to fellow poet Robert Browning, Elizabeth Barrett Browning (1806–1861) became famous for the forty-four love poems she wrote him during their courtship. The title of the collection—with its suggestion that the poems had been translated—was an attempt to keep their authorship private. Originally they were called *Sonnets From the Bosnian*.

How do I love thee? Let me count the ways.
I love thee to the depth and breadth and height
My soul can reach, when feeling out of sight
For the ends of Being and Ideal Grace.
I love thee to the level of every day's
Most quiet need, by sun and candle-light.
I love thee freely, as men strive for Right;
I love thee purely, as men turn from Praise.
I love thee with the passion put to use
In my old griefs, and with my childhood's faith.
I love thee with a love I seemed to lose
With my lost saints,—I love thee with the breath,
Smiles, tears of all my life!—and, if God choose,
I shall but love thee better after death.

EDWARD LEAR
"THE OWL AND THE PUSSY-CAT," 1871

Limericks were just an obscure form of light verse before Edward Lear (1812–1888) popularized them. Among his many published short poems, "The Owl and the Pussy-Cat" was one of his most famous—and certainly among his most joyful.

Lear coined many words and phrases, including *runcible spoon*, which is sometimes defined as a kind of spoon with sharp edges.

I
The Owl and the Pussy-Cat went to sea
In a beautiful pea-green boat,

They took some honey, and plenty of money,
Wrapped up in a five-pound note.
The Owl looked up to the stars above,
And sang to a small guitar,
"O lovely Pussy! O Pussy, my love,
What a beautiful Pussy you are,
You are,
You are!
What a beautiful Pussy you are!"

II

Pussy said to the Owl, "You elegant fowl!
How charmingly sweet you sing!
O let us be married! too long we have tarried:
But what shall we do for a ring?"
They sailed away, for a year and a day,
To the land where the Bong-tree grows,
And there in a wood a Piggy-wig stood
With a ring at the end of his nose,
His nose,
His nose,
With a ring at the end of his nose.

III

"Dear Pig, are you willing to sell for one shilling
Your ring?" Said the Piggy, "I will."
So they took it away, and were married next day
By the Turkey who lives on the hill.
They dined on mince, and slices of quince,
Which they ate with a runcible spoon;
And hand in hand, on the edge of the sand,
They danced by the light of the moon,
The moon,
The moon,
They danced by the light of the moon.

CLARA ELSENE PECK
PHRASES, MAZES, AND CRAZES OF LOVE, 1904

The epigrams were collected by the poet Minna Thomas Antrim, but the illustrations, by Clara Elsene Peck (1883–1968), brought particular charm to the team's lively volume.

EMMA GOLDMAN
"MARRIAGE AND LOVE," 1911

Emma Goldman (1869–1940) was a Lithuanian immigrant who came to the United States in her teens and soon became a leading player among numerous anarchists, socialists, and radical laborers. By the first decade of the century, she had founded a magazine called *Mother Earth* and had become a popular lecturer on political, literary, and social subjects. "Free love" was one of her signature topics, and in this essay, she offered her argument against the institution of marriage.

Goldman herself never married but was involved for many years with fellow anarchist Alexander Berkman, whom she encouraged in his plot to assassinate the industrialist Henry Clay Frick. Berkman was sentenced to twenty-two years for the shooting (which Frick survived), but no sufficient evidence was found to try Goldman.

Love, the strongest and deepest element in all life, the harbinger of hope, of joy, of ecstasy; love, the defier of all laws, of all conventions; love, the freest, the most powerful moulder of human destiny; how can such an all-compelling force be synonymous with that poor little State and Church-begotten weed, marriage?

Free love? As if love is anything but free! Man has bought brains, but all the millions in the world have failed to buy love. Man has subdued bodies, but all the power on earth has been unable to subdue love. Man has conquered whole nations, but all his armies could not conquer love. Man has chained and fettered the spirit, but he has been utterly helpless before love. High on a throne, with all the splendor and pomp his gold can command, man is yet poor and deso-

How can such an all-compelling force as love be synonymous with that poor little State and Church-begotten weed, marriage?

late, if love passes him by. And if it stays, the poorest hovel is radiant with warmth, with life and color. Thus love has the magic power to make of a beggar a king. Yes, love is free; it can dwell in no other atmosphere. In freedom it gives itself unreservedly, abundantly, completely. All the laws on the statutes, all the courts in the universe, cannot tear it from the soil, once love has taken root. If, however, the soil is sterile, how can marriage make it bear fruit? It is like the last desperate struggle of fleeting life against death. . . .

In our present pygmy state love is indeed a stranger to most people. Misunderstood and shunned, it rarely takes root; or if it does, it soon withers and dies. Its delicate fiber can not endure the stress and strain of the daily grind. Its soul is too complex to adjust itself to the slimy woof of our social fabric. It weeps and moans and suffers with those who have need of it, yet lack the capacity to rise to love's summit.

Some day, some day men and women will rise, they will reach the mountain peak, they will meet big and strong and free, ready to receive, to partake, and to bask in the golden rays of love. What fancy, what imagination, what poetic genius can foresee even approximately the potentialities of such a force in the life of men and women. If the world is ever to give birth to true companionship and oneness, not marriage, but love will be the parent.

WILLIAM ROSE
GUESS WHO'S COMING TO DINNER, 1967

Interracial marriage in 1967 was still a shocking proposition, and state laws forbidding it were only struck down by the U.S. Supreme Court that year. The answer to the famously ironic title of the film written by William Rose (1914–1987) was Dr. John Wade Prentice Jr. (played by Sidney Poitier), a black physician engaged to marry a young white woman named Joanna Drayton. The story brings both sets of would-be in-laws together with the couple for an evening of intense dialogue and debate. This speech, delivered by Spencer Tracy as Matt Drayton, occurs at the film's conclusion and seems to settle the question of marriage with the answer of love. It memorably moved Katharine Hepburn, perhaps both as Tracy's life partner and as her character, Christina, to tears.

"His Reverence" is family friend Monsignor Mike Ryan. Tillie is the family's long-employed black cook. Tracy, who was dying, was denied insurance by the production company; the filming only took place when Hepburn and director Stanley Kramer agreed to put their salaries in escrow so that, if necessary, another actor could be hired for Tracy's part. As it turned out, he made it through the filming—and died seventeen days later.

Now it became clear that we had one single day in which to make up our minds as to how we felt about this whole situation. So what happened? My wife typically enough decided to simply ignore every practical aspect of the situation, and was carried away in some kind of a romantic haze which made her in my view totally inaccessible to anything in the way of reason. . . .

Now Mr. Prentice, clearly a most reasonable man, says he has no wish to offend me but wants to know if I'm some kind of a "nut." And Mrs. Prentice says that like her husband I'm a burnt-out old shell of a man who cannot even remember what it's like to love a woman the way her son loves my daughter. And strange as it seems, that's the first statement made to me all day with which I am prepared to take issue. Because I think you're wrong. You're as wrong as you can be.

I admit that I hadn't considered it, hadn't even thought about it. But I know exactly how he feels about her, and there is nothing, absolutely nothing that your son feels for my daughter that I didn't feel for Christina. Old? Yes. Burnt-out? Certainly. But I can tell you, the memories are still there—clear, intact, indestructible. And they'll be there if I live to be a hundred and ten. Where John made his mistake I think was attaching so much importance to what her mother and I might think. Because in the final analysis it doesn't matter a damn what we think. The only thing that matters is what they feel, and how much they feel, for each other. And if it's half of what we felt—that's everything.

As for you two and the problems you're going to have, they seem almost unimaginable, but you'll have no problem with me, and I think that when Christina and I and your mother have some time to work on him, you'll have no problem with your father, John. But you do know, I'm sure you know, what you're up against. There'll be a hundred million people right here in this country who will be shocked and offended and appalled at the two of you, and the two of you will just have to ride that out, maybe every day for the rest of your lives. You can try to ignore those people, or you can feel sorry for them and for their prejudices and their bigotry and their blind hatreds and stupid fears, but where necessary you'll just have to cling tight to each other and say, "Screw all those people!"

Anybody could make a case, and a hell of a good case, against your getting married. The arguments are so obvious that nobody has to make them. But you're two wonderful people who happened to fall in love and happen to have a pigmentation problem, and I think that now, no matter what kind of a case some bastard could make against your getting married, there would be only one thing worse, and that would be if—knowing what you two are, knowing what you two have, and knowing what you two feel—you didn't get married.

Well, Tillie, when the hell are we gonna get some dinner?

WOODY ALLEN
LOVE AND DEATH, 1975

Many of the films of Woody Allen (see Divorce, page 73) are send-ups of genre pieces, and one of his earliest, *Love and Death*, offers a pastiche of great Russian fiction, with its tradition of complex emotional relationships and philosophical exploration. The following deadpan exchange is between cousins Natasha, played by Jessica Harper, and Sonja, played by Diane Keaton.

NATASHA: It's a very complicated situation, cousin Sonja. I'm in love with Alexei. He loves Alicia. Alicia's having an affair with Lev. Lev loves Tatiana. Tatiana loves Simkin. Simkin loves me. I love Simkin, but in a different way than Alexei. Alexei loves Tatiana like a sister. Tatiana's sister loves Trigorian like a brother. Trigorian's brother is having an affair with my sister, who he likes physically, but not spiritually.

SONJA:	Natasha, it's getting a little late.
NATASHA:	The firm of Mishkin and Mishkin is sleeping with the firm of Taskov and Taskov.
SONJA:	Natasha, to love is to suffer. To avoid suffering, one must not love. But then one suffers from not loving. Therefore, to love is to suffer. Not to love is to suffer. To suffer is to suffer. To be happy is to love. To be happy, then, is to suffer, but suffering makes one unhappy. Therefore, to be unhappy one must love, or love to suffer, or suffer from too much happiness. I hope you're getting this down.
NATASHA:	I never want to marry. I just want to get divorced.

ALAIN DE BOTTON
"WHY BOOKS DO NOT PREPARE US FOR REAL LOVE," 2011

Born in Switzerland and living in London, Alain de Botton (1969–) has written extensively and philosophically on love, art, literature, and travel. Lecturer, radio commentator, and founder of a London enterprise called the School of Life, he became popular for books including *How Proust Can Change Your Life* and for a weekly *BBC News Magazine* column, in which the following passage appeared.

We are taught to imagine that romantic love might be akin to Christian love, a universal emotion that would allow us to declare "I will love you for everything that you are." A love without conditions or boundaries, a love that is the embodiment of acceptance.

But the arguments that even the closest couples experience are a reminder that Christian love does not well survive the transition into the bedroom. Its message seems more suited to the universal than the particular, to the love of all men for all women, to the love of two companions who will not hear each other clipping their toe-nails.

Married love teaches us that we bring all of ourselves into a marriage—anxiety, boredom, free-floating sadness and alarm. I continue sometimes to feel unhappy about my work, to worry about my future and to be disappointed with myself and with my friends. Except that now, rather than sharing my sorrows, I tend to blame the person who lives beside me for them. My wife isn't just a witness to my problems; on a bad day, she can sadly end up being held responsible for them.

MATH

ARTHUR SCHOPENHAUER
"OF WOMEN," 1851

German philosopher Arthur Schopenhauer (1788–1860), a renowned pessimist who focused on the continual thwarting of the human will, believed fervently in the inherent weakness of women. This passage was a building block of Schopenhauer's argument for polygamy, which he contended would spare women the fate to which monogamy condemned so many: to be left unmarried and unprotected, vulnerable to the lure of prostitution, and ultimately even less equal to men than they naturally were.

The laws of marriage prevailing in Europe consider the woman as the equivalent of the man—start, that is to say, from a wrong position. In our part of the world where monogamy is the rule, to marry means to halve one's rights and double one's duties. Now, when the laws gave women equal rights with man, they ought to have also endowed her with a masculine intellect. But the fact is, that just in proportion as the honors and priveleges which the laws accord to women exceed the amount which nature gives, is there a diminution in the number of women who really participate in these priveleges, and all the remainder are deprived of their natural rights by just so much is given over and above their share.

SAMUEL BUTLER
LETTER TO ELIZA MARY ANN SAVAGE, 1884

British author Samuel Butler (1835–1902) always gets credit for this quote about essayist Thomas Carlyle and his wife, Jane. The comment is alternately interpreted as a reference to the Carlyles' well-known belligerence and to the often-rumored platonic nature of their marriage. Butler's witticism was in fact the answer to the question in a letter from Eliza Savage, a set-up line if ever there was one: "Are you not glad that Mr. and Mrs. Carlyle were married to one another, and not to other people?"

Yes, it was very good of God to let Carlyle and Mrs. Carlyle marry one another and so make only two people miserable instead of four.

OSCAR WILDE
THE IMPORTANCE OF BEING EARNEST, 1895

Married with two children, Irish writer Oscar Wilde (1854–1900) was arrested and imprisoned for "gross indecency" just seven weeks after the triumphant London opening of *The Importance of Being Earnest*. The charge concerned Wilde's presumed affair with Alfred Douglas, son of the Marquess of Queensbury, whom the playwright had sued for libel. The arrest effectively ended the play's run and destroyed Wilde's playwriting career. But wife Constance Lloyd—while changing her own and their children's names and denying Wilde parental rights—remained married to him.

In the play's first act, Algernon and Jack reveal that each has created a useful fictional persona who allows for certain freedoms: Jack is "Earnest" in town and "Jack" in the country; Algernon has a sick friend named Bunbury whose constant brushes with death demand a lot of quick exits for bedside visits.

ALGERNON: Nothing will induce me to part with Bunbury, and if you ever get married, which seems to me extremely problematic, you will be very glad to know Bunbury. A man who marries without knowing Bunbury has a very tedious time of it.

JACK: That is nonsense. If I marry a charming girl like Gwendolen, and she is the only girl I ever saw in my life that I would marry, I certainly won't want to know Bunbury.

ALGERNON: Then your wife will. You don't seem to realize, that in married life three is company and two is none.

AMBROSE BIERCE
THE DEVIL'S DICTIONARY, 1911

A journalist, short-story writer, and dark satirist, Ambrose Gwinnett Bierce (1842–circa 1913) was a longtime columnist for San Francisco–area newspapers, including William Randolph Hearst's *Examiner*. His marriage was a messy one that ended in divorce and was followed by his ex-wife's suicide. His own life ended mysteriously sometime after December 26, 1913, when he was covering the Mexican Revolution. All things considered, the definition of marriage in the satirical lexicon for which he is best known was relatively benign.

Marriage, n. The state or condition of a community consisting of a master, a mistress and two slaves, making in all, two.

IAN FLEMING
DIAMONDS ARE FOREVER, 1956

Author of the hugely popular James Bond novels, Ian Fleming (1908–1964) brought his World War II experience in Britain's naval intelligence service to the creation of the irresistible Agent 007. The books—as well as the two dozen movies they spawned—could be counted on for intricate plots, outlandish contraptions, and outrageously named "Bond girls," including Pussy Galore, Holly Goodhead, and, in the scene below, the stunning diamond smuggler Tiffany Case.

In 1952, Fleming married Ann Charteris after their affair was discovered by her then-husband, the second Viscount Rothermere. They remained married until his death twelve years later.

"Are you married?" She paused. "Or anything?"

"No. I occasionally have affairs."

"So you're one of those old-fashioned men who like sleeping with women. Why haven't you ever married?"

"I expect because I think I can handle life better on my own. Most marriages don't add two people together. They subtract one from the other."

MONEY

HÉLOÏSE
LETTER TO ABELARD, 12TH CENTURY

Peter Abelard was a renowned French philosopher, Héloïse d'Argenteuil (circa 1098–1164) the niece of Notre Dame's Canon Fulbert. Smitten with the much younger Héloïse, Abelard arranged to be hired as her live-in teacher. They became lovers, conceived a child, then married secretly—but were forced apart after Fulbert had Abelard castrated. Héloïse ended up in a nunnery. Their story has stood for centuries as an emblem of enduring, unrepentant love in the face of family and societal disapproval, brutal retribution, and ultimate separation. Though apart, they remained married and began a long, passionate correspondence.

'Tis not Love, but the Desire of Riches and Honour, which makes Women run into the Embraces of an indolent Husband. Ambition, not Affection, forms such Marriages. I believe indeed they may be followed with some Honours and Advantages, but I can never think that this is the Way to enjoy the Pleasures of an affectionate Union, nor to feel those secret and charming Emotions of Hearts that have long strove to be united. These Martyrs of Marriage pine always for larger Fortunes, which they think they have lost. The Wife sees Husbands richer than her own, and the Husband Wives better portioned than his. Their interested Vows occasion Regret, and Regret produces Hatred. They soon part, or always desire it. This restless and tormenting Passion punishes them for aiming at other Advantages by Love than Love itself.

EDITORIAL
THE NATIONAL ADVOCATE, 1817

Universal concepts: the search for a wife, the search for a fortune, the use of advertising in pursuit of both. Personal ads date as far back as the 1700s.

We perceive in a Boston paper, that a young gentleman, in easy circumstances, advertises for a wife; his description of her qualities is interesting enough, and combine almost every advantage calculated to make the marriage state agreeable: doubtless conceiving, that which his descriptive powers were awakened, it would be well enough to give the picture a high and fanciful coloring; but he spoils all by saying, that she must possess a fortune of from ten to twenty thousand dollars. Now, under favour, a wife such as he describes would be a fortune in herself. He also has omitted to describe *his* qualities and attainments, doubtless considering that his, having "a fine house furnished," is a sufficient inducement, and having the cage he can easily get the bird. There is something new in this mode of advertising for a wife in the same manner as we would for a farm or a valet; and, on the score of sentiment, there is not much to be admired. The success of the "young gentleman" may be considered very problematical.

SAMUEL TAYLOR COLERIDGE
TABLE TALK, 1824

Perhaps best known for his poems "Kubla Khan" and "The Rime of the Ancient Mariner," Samuel Taylor Coleridge (1772–1834) was well enough established as a literary critic, poet, and biographer, even during his life, to have fragments of his sayings collected and published in the book *Table Talk*. His statement below notwithstanding, Coleridge was unhappily married for many years, with part of the strain due to the tension between financial income and literary output.

Show me one couple unhappy merely on account of their limited circumstances, and I will show you ten who are wretched from other causes.

"A FATHER'S ADVICE TO HIS DAUGHTER,"
PENNSYLVANIA INQUIRER AND NATIONAL GAZETTE, 1843

These words of advice, often reprinted in newspapers, were, as was typical of the genre, written anonymously.

Your mother was a woman of family: I had a large fortune; these were the sole considerations that influenced our parents to join us together. I have lost my fortune, she has lost her rank; forgot by her family: what doth it signify to her that she was born a lady? In the midst of our distress, the union of our hearts made up for every thing; the conformity of our tastes made us choose this retirement. We live happy in our poverty; each is to the other a friend and companion. [You are] our common treasure; we thank the Almighty for giving [you], and taking away every thing else.

You see, my dear child, whither Providence hath brought us. Those considerations which occasioned our marriage are vanished, and that which was accounted as nothing makes all our happiness. . . .

. . . You never saw our prosperity; you were born after we failed in the world. You have made our poverty pleasing to us, and we have shared in it without pain. Never, child, seek for that wealth which we thank Heaven for taking from us; we never tasted happiness until we lost our riches.

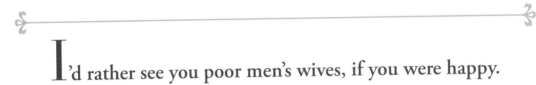

I'd rather see you poor men's wives, if you were happy.

LOUISA MAY ALCOTT
LITTLE WOMEN, 1868

With four daughters and an absent husband, Marmee March is the moral center of family life in the small-town New England house where *Little Women* is set. The novel's author, Louisa May Alcott (1832–1888), based much of the bestselling book on her own childhood experiences. The idea expressed here by Marmee to her daughters—that love and virtue should outshine money and position—was one of the central themes of the book.

To be loved and chosen by a good man is the best and sweetest thing which can happen to a woman; and I sincerely hope my girls may know this beautiful experience. It is natural to think of it, Meg; right to hope and wait for it, and wise to prepare for it; so that, when the happy time comes, you may feel ready for the duties and worthy of the joy. My dear girls, I *am* ambitious for you, but not to have you make a dash in the world—marry rich men merely because they are rich, or have splendid houses, which are not homes because love is wanting. Money is a needful and precious thing—and, when well used, a noble thing—but I never want you to think it was the first or only prize to strive for. I'd rather see you poor men's wives, if you were happy, beloved, contented, than queens on thrones, without self-respect and peace.

ELIZABETH CADY STANTON
HISTORY OF WOMAN SUFFRAGE, 1882

When Elizabeth Cady (1815–1902) married Henry Brewster Stanton in 1840, she persuaded their minister, Hugh Maire, to omit one traditional word from their vows. In her autobiography, she would recall: "I obstinately refused to obey one with whom I supposed I was entering into an equal relation." She had learned early, from working in her father's congressional office, about the unequal rights of women under the law, and her lifelong pursuit of women's equality led to the very front lines of the suffrage movement and the first wave of feminism in the United States.

In Ashfield, Mass., . . . a married woman was severely injured by a defective sidewalk. Her husband sued the corporation and recovered $13,000 damages. And those $13,000 belong to him *bona fide;* and whenever that unfortunate wife wishes a dollar of it to supply her needs she must ask her husband for it; and if the man be of a narrow, selfish, niggardly nature, she will have to hear him say, every time:

"What have you done, my dear, with the twenty-five cents I gave you yesterday?"

Isn't such a position, I ask you, humiliating enough to be called "servitude"?

M

ANNIE SWAN
COURTSHIP AND MARRIAGE AND THE
GENTLE ART OF HOME-MAKING, 1894

Whether using her given name or the pen names David Lyall or Mrs. Burnett-Smith, the Scottish writer Annie Shepherd Swan (1859–1943) published some two hundred novels and short stories, as well as contributing frequently to England's increasingly popular women's magazines. Swan was also a poet, journalist, advice-book author, and lecturer. She married James Burnett Smith in 1883 and, ironically, in light of the following passage, supported him financially in his quest to become a doctor.

There is a type of husband—unfortunately rather common—who begrudges his wife, whatever her character and disposition, every penny she spends, even though it is spent primarily for his own comfort, and who has never in his life cheerfully opened out to her his purse, whatever he may have done with the thing he calls his heart. This is a very serious matter, and one which presses heavily on the hearts of many wives. It is hard for a young girl, who may in her father's house have had pocket money always to supply her simple needs, to find herself after marriage practically penniless—having to ask for every penny she requires, and often to explain minutely how and where it is to be spent. I have known a man who required an absolute account of every halfpenny spent by his wife, and who took from her change of the shilling he had given her for a cab fare. We must pray, for the credit of the sex, that there are few so lost to all gentlemanly feeling, to speak of nothing else; but it is certain that, through thoughtlessness as much as stinginess often, many sensitive women suffer keenly from this form of humiliation. It ought not to be. If a woman is worthy to be trusted with a man's honour, which is supposed to be more valuable to him than his gold, let her likewise be trusted with a little of the latter, without having to crave it and answer for it as a servant sent on an errand counts out the copper change to her master on her return. There are many little harmless trifles a woman wants, many small kindnesses she would do on the impulse of the moment, had she money in her purse; and though she may sometimes not be altogether wise, she is blessed in the doing, and nobody is the poorer. However small a man's income, there are surely a few odd shillings the wife might have for her very own, if only to gratify her harmless little whims, and to make her feel that she sometimes has a penny to spare.

M

CARL REINER, R. S. ALLEN, HARVEY BULLOCK
"BANK BOOK 6565696," *THE DICK VAN DYKE SHOW*, 1962

Graduating from his on- and offstage roles as contributor to the Sid Caesar shows, Carl Reiner (1922–) went on to co-write and direct *The Dick Van Dyke Show*, a beloved staple of 1960s sitcoms that ran for five seasons. Rob Petrie, played by Dick Van Dyke, is happily married to Laura (Mary Tyler Moore) and can't fathom why she's felt the need to keep a separate and secret bank account.

This episode appeared in the series' second season, the only show written by Harvey Bullock (1921–2006) and R. S. Allen (1924–1981), collaborators on a number of other TV series, including *The Flintstones*.

ROB: I would like to know . . . what is wrong with the money in our joint account?

LAURA: Well, that's our account and our money. This is my money.

ROB: *Your* money?

LAURA: Yes, Rob. I want some money that's mine, to spend on anything I want. It's important to me. I don't want everything coming from you.

ROB: And where did you get this money?

LAURA: From you.

ROB: Well, isn't it all the same thing then? Either you get money from me or you get money from that, which came from me.

LAURA: No, Rob, it's completely different. I put this money in a little at a time. At first, it's from you. But then after it lies around for a while I forget that it came from you and then it's from me!

          (Rob gives Laura a look.)

LAURA: You just don't understand! *(Laura cries.)*

ROB: Oh boy. Honey, look, I want to understand, but you've got to help me a little bit. Just give me a hint. The first word. *(Laura continues to cry.)* The first letter. Honey, please!

LAURA: All right I'll tell you. And then I hope you'll be satisfied that you've just ruined everything! That money is for you!

ROB: For me?

LAURA: I wanted to buy you something for your birthday.

ROB: Well, you already bought me something for my birthday. Don't tell me that shirt cost—

LAURA: Oh, no Rob, this money isn't for now. It's for two or three or four years from now. Whenever I've saved up enough money to buy you that stupid sports car you've been drooling over. . . . I wanted to buy you an important present.

ROB: An important—Well, honey it's a wonderful thought, but it's a little bit crazy. Where'd you ever get an idea like that?

LAURA: From my mother.

ROB: Your mother!

LAURA: She saved for years and then on their twenty-fifth wedding anniversary, she bought my father a big important present.

ROB: What did she get him?

LAURA: His own room.

ROB: His own room!

LAURA: Well, I mean a den with a pool table and a beer dispenser, and now you've ruined it!

ROB: Aw, honey, no I haven't ruined it. Look, all I've done is forced you to tell me something that makes me very, very happy that I'm married to you. As a matter of fact, now that I know, it's going to be a lot easier for you.

M

LAURA:	How?
ROB:	Well, from now on when you ask me for extra money, I'm going to be a pretty soft touch.
	(She cries again.)
ROB:	Honey, what's the matter?
LAURA:	You're laughing at me.
ROB:	Honey, look, I'm not laughing at you. The only reason I'm being frivolous is because I'm so touched and embarrassed by the whole thing and if I didn't joke about it, I'd—
LAURA:	You'd what?
ROB:	Well, I'd probably put my arms around you and hug you so hard that I'd break two or three of your ribs.
LAURA:	Oh, please try.

ELIZABETH HARDWICK
"AMATEURS: JANE CARLYLE," 1972

Elizabeth Hardwick (1916–2007) wrote short stories and novels but was best known as a critic and essayist. Liberal and emphatic, she was one of the founders of the *New York Review of Books*, where many of her works appeared. The following comes from an article she wrote about the Carlyles (see Math, page 294).

Hardwick was married to the poet Robert Lowell for more than two decades, until their divorce in 1970. In her *New York Times* obituary, Christopher Lehmann-Haupt described the marriage, with Lowell's many adulterous and manic-depressive episodes, as "restless and emotionally harrowing." Harriet Ashburton was a friend and flatterer of Thomas Carlyle.

When Jane Carlyle was cleaning and sweeping and keeping the accounts within discreet limits she certainly did not set a price upon her actions. But, of course, there was a hidden price. It was that in exchange for her work, her dedication, her special, if somewhat satirical, charms, Carlyle would, as an instance, not go out to Lady Ashburton when she would rather he stayed at home. This is the unspoken contract of a wife and her works. In the long run wives are to be paid in a peculiar coin—consideration for their feelings. And it usually turns out this is an enormous, unthinkable inflation few men will remit, or if they will, only with a sense of being overcharged.

RALPH GARDNER JR.
"ALPHA WOMEN, BETA MEN," *NEW YORK* MAGAZINE, 2003

The assumption that husbands were the chief family breadwinners in the United States was no longer a given when Ralph Gardner Jr. (1953–) set out to explore the possible effects of women's increasing emergence as higher earners. In 2013, the Pew Research Center would report that, based on its analysis of U.S. Census Bureau figures, women were the sole or primary breadwinners in 40 percent of households with children under the age of eighteen. Of these, 37 percent, or some five million, were married with higher incomes than their husbands.

In addition to his magazine work, Gardner writes the daily "Urban Gardner" column for the *Wall Street Journal*.

Anna, a public-relations executive, saw her relationship with her Web-designer husband collapse as she became more and more successful and he floundered. In the last year of their marriage, she earned $270,000 while he brought in $16,000.

"He never spent money that wasn't his in an extravagant way," she says while taking therapeutic sips of a Sea Breeze at Tribeca Grill on a recent evening. "But by not helping, he was freeloading."

She felt unable to confront him. "We were really dysfunctional," she admits. "We acted as if we were a two-income family. He was in denial, and I was sort of protecting him. He'd pay for groceries. He was running up credit-card debt to make it appear he had more money."

While they may have been able to avoid the truth while she was off at work during the day, it came back to haunt them at night. "Sexuality is based on respect and admiration and desire," says Anna. "If you've lost respect for somebody, it's very hard to have it work. And our relationship initially had been very sexual, at the expense of other things."

"Sex was not a problem for him," she goes on. "It was a problem for me. When someone seems like a child, it's not that attractive. In the end, it felt like I had three children."

"The minute it becomes parental, it becomes asexual," agrees Betsy. "A friend of mine who works and makes money and whose husband doesn't told me one day that he was taking $100-an-hour tennis lessons," she recalls. "She said to him, 'You are not in the $100-an-hour category.' She had to spell it out for him. It was totally parental." . . .

It's not as if these women ever expected their husbands to support them completely—at least a lot of them didn't. It's just that it never occurred to them that they might be the ones doing all the heavy lifting. And as hip and open-minded as they like to think they are, they were, after all, raised on the same fairy tale as the rest of us—the one where Prince Charming comes to the rescue of Sleeping Beauty.

TERRY MARTIN HEKKER
"PARADISE LOST (DOMESTIC DIVISION)," 2006

In 1977, Terry Martin Hekker was living with her husband, a South Nyack, New York, judge, and their five children when she wrote an article for the *New York Times* celebrating her role as a traditional housewife. Two years later, she earned the outrage of working women all over the country when she expanded her theme in the book *Ever Since Adam and Eve*. Lectures, television appearances, and magazine columns followed. And then, when she was sixty-two, her husband left. She received her divorce papers on what would have been their fortieth anniversary. Her subsequent book was called *Disregard First Book*.

Sitting around my kitchen with two friends who had also been dumped by their husbands, I figured out that among the three of us we'd been married 110 years. We'd been faithful wives, good mothers, cooks and housekeepers who'd married in the 50's, when "dress for success" meant a wedding gown and "wife" was a tenured position.

Turns out we had a lot in common with our outdated kitchen appliances. Like them we were serviceable, low maintenance, front loading, self-cleaning and (relatively) frost free. Also like them we had warranties that had run out. Our husbands sought sleeker models with features we lacked who could execute tasks we'd either never learned or couldn't perform without laughing.

Like most loyal wives of our generation, we'd contemplated eventual widowhood but never thought we'd end up divorced. And "divorced" doesn't begin to describe the pain of this process. "Canceled" is more like it. It began with my credit cards, then my health insurance and checkbook, until, finally, like a used postage stamp, I felt canceled too.

I faced frightening losses and was overwhelmed by the injustice of it all. He got to take his girlfriend to Cancun, while I got to sell my engagement ring to pay the roofer. When I filed my first nonjoint tax return, it triggered the shocking notification that I had become eligible for food stamps.

The judge had awarded me alimony that was less than I was used to getting for household expenses, and now I had to use that money to pay bills I'd never seen before: mortgage, taxes, insurance and car payments. And that princely sum was awarded for only four years, the judge suggesting that I go for job training when I turned 67. Not only was I unprepared for divorce itself, I was utterly lacking in skills to deal with the brutal aftermath.

I read about the young mothers of today—educated, employed, self-sufficient—who drop out of the work force when they have children, and I worry and wonder. Perhaps it is the right choice for them. Maybe they'll be fine. But the fragility of modern marriage suggests that at least half of them may not be.

Regrettably, women whose husbands are devoted to their families and are good providers must nevertheless face the specter of future abandonment. Surely the seeds of this wariness must have been planted, even if they can't believe it could ever happen to them. Many have witnessed their own mothers jettisoned by their own fathers and seen divorced friends trying to rear children with marginal financial and emotional support.

These young mothers are often torn between wanting to be home with their children and the statistical possibility of future calamity, aware that one of the most poverty-stricken groups in today's society are divorced older women. The feminine and sexual revolutions of the last few decades have had their shining victories, but have they, in the end, made things any easier for mothers?

I cringe when I think of that line from my Op-Ed article about the long line of women I'd come from and belonged to who were able to find fulfillment as homemakers "because no one had explained" to us "that the only work worth doing is that for which you get paid." For a divorced mother, the harsh reality is that the work for which you do get paid is the only work that will keep you afloat.

M

NAMES

MARY RICHARDSON WALKER
LETTER TO AN UNKNOWN RECIPIENT, 1838

The embodiment of the pioneer woman, Mary Richardson Walker (1811–1897) claimed that she had decided by the age of ten to become a missionary. She was twenty-six when the American Board of Missions, generally uncomfortable about sending single women west, set her up with Elkanah Walker. The couple agreed to marry within the first two days of knowing each other. In her diary, she wrote: "I saw nothing particularly interesting or disagreeable in the man." Her lack of enthusiasm notwithstanding, Mary remained married to Elkanah for the rest of her long life.

Nothing gives me such a solitery feeling as to be called Mrs. Walker. It would sound so sweet to have some one now & then call [me] Mary or by mistake say Miss Richardson. But that expression Mrs. W. seems at once to indicate a change unlike all other changes. My father, my mother, my brothers, my sisters all answer to the name Richardson. The name W. seems to me to imply a severed branch. Such I feel myself to be—

EDITORIAL
RALEIGH REGISTER, 1850

We notice the marriage of Mr. Day to Miss Field, which presents this singular anomaly, that although he won the Field, she gained the Day.

"MEN, WOMEN, AND AFFAIRS"
SPRINGFIELD SUNDAY REPUBLICAN, 1901

This editorial offered the first modern suggestion that there should be a women's honorific that, like "Mr." for men, did not reveal or imply marital status. "Ms." came into common use in the 1970s after Gloria Steinem made it the title for her monthly magazine. It wasn't until 1972 that "Ms." was approved by the U.S. Government Printing Office; among the last holdouts, the *New York Times* didn't adopt "Ms." until 1986.

There is a void in the English language which, with some diffidence, we undertake to fill. Every one has been put in an embarrassing position by ignorance of the status of some woman. To call a maiden Mrs is only a shade worse than to insult a matron with the inferior title Miss. Yet it is not always easy to know the facts. When an author puts on the title page of a book Marion Smith, it is not even possible to be certain of the sex of the writer, and it is decidedly awkward for a reviewer to repeat the name in full over and over again. It would be a convenience if explanatory titles were added to the signature, but it seems to be regarded as "bad form." Signatures to letters also cause no end of trouble to correspondents. The "Miss" or "Mrs" sometimes added in brackets are but an awkward makeshift, and often it is taken for granted that the recipient of the letter will remember the proper style of the writer, when, as a matter of fact he does nothing of the sort. Now, clearly, what is needed is a more comprehensive term which does homage to the sex without expressing any views as to their domestic situation, and what could be simpler or more logical than the retention of what the two doubtful terms have in common. The abbreviation "Ms" is simple, it is easy to write, and the person concerned can translate it properly according to circumstances. For oral use, it might be rendered as "Mizz," which would be a close parallel to the practice long universal in many bucolic regions, where a slurred Mis' does duty for Miss and Mrs alike.

BÜLBÜL, 1979

Chicago native Genevieve Leland Guracar (1936–) used the name Bülbül, which means "nightingale" in Turkish, when she began her work as a cartoonist in the 1970s. Since then, her focus has continued to be women's issues, though a recent retrospective anthology has included cartoons about politics, employment, aging, health, and education.

In a 1984 interview, Guracar said: "In Middle Eastern poetry a *bülbül* is a bird of protest. I took it as a pen name when my family suffered for my outspoken opinions."

REDDIT USERS
"WILL YOU/HAVE YOU HYPHENATED YOUR LAST NAME?," 2011

The question was submitted by a reddit user called "ohbehave123" on the subreddit /r/twox chromosomes. Below is a sampling of the 149 answers and comments that followed.

BESTNANNYEVER: I always thought it would be sweet to come up with a new last name together and have both people change their names.

FOUXDEFAFA: A friend of mine got married a few years ago and he and his fiance did this. Essentially, they took their last names and combined them to make a new last name . . . Miller + Johnson = Millson. Pretty cool idea, though their last names fit together particularly well. Some people might not be so lucky

LAIKAFROMSPACE: Mine is British, very British. His is *very* Ukrainian. The end result of this would be hilarious: Billifrychuk? Onofrilliham?

KATIE_CAT_EYES: My surname is very Polish. His is very Ukrainian. All the combinations we've thought of sound like bodily functions. I don't have any desire to keep my name, and neither does he, so we've been going through the family tree to find something that works.

PUNKY_GRIFTER: That is what my partner and I are planning to do, I refuse to choose between my father's last name or my husband's, I want to start my clan.

ANAMATRONIX: I know I'm keeping mine for professional reasons, I have already published work under my maiden name and it's important not to have people get confused when searching after my work.

LYCHIZZLE: I will only take a man's last name if it begins in Y. So my initials will be SPY

ARISEFAIRMOON: If I marry someone whose last name starts with X my initials will be SEX. The search is on.

XSCIENTIST: I never asked my wife to change her name, since my name is quite ethnic, and very unrelated to her ethnicity. She is not particularly attached to her name (hates her father, etc), and totally loves my parents. A few months after we married, she suddenly told me she was taking on my name because she felt she was closer to our family than her own. It was very touching, and meant a lot to me. I still would never have pressured her either way.

BELLASTELLA: I decided a long time ago i would only change my name if i thought my husband's name was cooler.

NEIL PATRICK HARRIS
RADIO INTERVIEW, 2013

Best known for his role as Barney Stinson in the TV show *How I Met Your Mother*, Neil Patrick Harris (1973–) had been engaged for nearly seven years to fellow actor David Burtka when he spoke to Ryan Seacrest about one of the benefits getting married would bring. The couple married in Italy, with their two children beside them, in 2014.

I'd rather call him my husband than my partner! I think partner is such a weird name for a same-sex significant other. It sounds like we're either business partners or cowboys.

NEWLYWEDS

WILLIAM HOGARTH
MARRIAGE À LA MODE, 1743

William Hogarth (1697–1764) was an English painter and engraver known best—despite his continual attempts at being viewed as a serious portraitist—for his insightful, usually satirical, pictorial commentaries on society. *Marriage à la Mode* was a popular six-part work that the artist painted in oils and later re-created as engravings. The second image in the series, called "Shortly after the Marriage," shows a pair of newlyweds still awake past one in the morning after an evening apparently spent apart. The room is a mess, the husband debauched, the wife despairing, and their employee fleeing the scene in dismay.

BOB EUBANKS AND CONTESTANTS
THE NEWLYWED GAME, CIRCA 1972

Part game show, part reality show, in some ways an immediate parody-in-the-making, *The Newlywed Game*, hosted by the ever-cheerful Bob Eubanks, was on the air in its initial incarnation from 1966 to 1974. It featured four newlywed couples, with wives and husbands given the chance to predict what their spouses would say in answer to questions that ranged from the straightforward (like favorite color) to the obviously suggestive, such as the one below.

"Making whoopee" was the show's signature euphemism for *sex* at a time when networks would have censored more direct references. Nevertheless, one of the show's most infamous moments, aired in 1977, included a wife's answer to the question "Where is the weirdest place you have ever had the urge to make whoopee?" Her answer—aired but bleeped out—turned out to be not geographical but anatomical.

EUBANKS:	Last of our ten-point questions. Ladies, will your husband say he treats whoopee-making more like an occupation, a hobby, or a chore? Kathy?
KATHY:	What is "whoopee"?
EUBANKS:	"What is 'whoopee'?" Is that what she said, "What is 'whoopee'?"
KATHY:	Yes.
EUBANKS:	No one has ever asked me "What is 'whoopee'?" before.
KATHY:	I figured that. That's why I wanted to ask you.
EUBANKS:	I think it's—(He shields his face from the camera and whispers to her.)
KATHY:	Oh my goodness. What were the three again?
EUBANKS:	An occupation, a hobby, or a chore.
KATHY:	Oh, a hobby, I guess.
EUBANKS:	A hobby. Thank you. Bertha?
BERTHA:	A hobby.
EUBANKS:	Hobby. Chris?
CHRIS:	I'd say a hobby, 'cause it's like his drums, you know?
EUBANKS:	No, I didn't know that. Yes. Lynn?
LYNN:	I'd have to say like a chore.
EUBANKS:	A chore. Sorry. Twenty-five-point bonus question. Girls, what will your husband say is his favorite contact sport? Bertha?
BERTHA:	Basketball.
EUBANKS:	Basketball. Chris?
CHRIS:	Football.

EUBANKS:	Football. Lynn?
LYNN:	Football.
EUBANKS:	Football. Kathy?
KATHY:	Whoopee.

THE DON'T SWEAT GUIDE FOR NEWLYWEDS, 2003

Don't Sweat the Small Stuff—and It's All Small Stuff became a number one bestseller in 1997 and was eventually published in 135 countries. Its author, who parlayed that success into a hugely lucrative cottage industry, was Richard Carlson, a psychotherapist who used to sign his letters with the phrase "Treasure Yourself." His several dozen spin-offs included advice books for parents, bosses, teenagers, and, in the case of the above example, newlyweds. Carlson's wife, Kristine, wrote several of the books as well, and after Richard's death in 2006 at the age of forty-five, she continued to spread his live-in-the-moment message through both traditional and web formats, including guidebooks published by the Don't Sweat Press.

It's a good guess that if you've been trying unsuccessfully to change things about your partner since the wedding, right about now, you're pretty frustrated. Guess what? People don't change just because you married them.

Choosing to accept someone else for exactly who they are can liberate you from preconceptions. When you make a conscious choice to truly accept your new husband or wife, to understand that those little behaviors that drive you crazy are simply part of the person that you fell in love with, you can finally free yourself of your efforts to change them. Giving up this task will relieve you of the tension that has probably built up between you and your partner because of the pressure that you've put upon him or her to change.

OBJECTIONS

PROVERB

Why buy a cow when the milk is so cheap?

FRANCIS BACON
"OF MARRIAGE AND SINGLE LIFE," 1612

Sir Francis Bacon (see Jealousy, page 236) lined up the pros and cons of marriage in his oft-quoted essay. Though he opened with the objection below, he proceeded to note that "those that have Children should have greatest care of future times, unto which, they know, they must transmit their dearest pledges."

He that hath Wife and Children hath given Hostages to Fortune; For they are Impediments to great Enterprises, either of Vertue, or Mischiefe. Certainly, the best workes, and of greatest Merit for the Publike, have proceeded from the unmarried or Childlesse Men, which, both in Affection and Meanes, have married and endowed the Publike.

GIACOMO CASANOVA
HISTORY OF MY LIFE, 1797

Perhaps history's most famous seducer, Venice's Giacomo Casanova (1725–1798) was at various times an abbot, soldier, gambler, legal assistant, musician, and Freemason. He left sexual conquests in his path all over Europe, while getting into and out of trouble—and prison—as he enraged authorities with his libertine behavior and alleged blasphemies. Unmarried and ultimately worn down by illness and isolation, he embarked late in life on an autobiography that originally ran to twelve volumes but was much abridged upon publication.

The first speaker is Pauline, Casanova's young lover, referring to the way the couple was pretending to be married while entertaining Sophie, his daughter from a previous relationship. Sophie has just left Casanova's home and is on her way to see her mother.

"I laugh to think of [Sophie] telling her [mother] that she found you at table with your wife."

"She will not believe it, for she knows too well that marriage is the sacrament I detest."

"Why?"

"Because it is the tomb of love."

VICTORIA WOODHULL
"WHAT I OPPOSE IN MARRIAGE," *BOSTON INVESTIGATOR*, 1876

Victoria Claflin Woodhull (1838–1927) was a suffragist and fierce advocate of rights for women to marry, divorce, bear children, and even engage in prostitution without interference from the government. She was also the first woman to run for United States president, in 1872. She was fifteen when she married for the first time, and was divorced twice before she was forty. Her third marriage—to a British banker—lasted eighteen years, until his death.

A union between two persons of opposite sex, that is enforced by law is, in my view, nothing more or less than prostitution. I maintain stoutly and always that men have no right to make a law that shall take away the power of woman to control her own body. It may be denied that marriage, as a legal institution, does do this; but we have only to remember that, if a woman refuse the use of her body to her husband, the law gives him a divorce. Now here is a fact that cannot be escaped, and to which I desire to pin all those who pretend that they "do not agree with Mrs. Woodhull." Under this liberty, the law is simply a license for husbands to compel their wives to their desires, whether it be the wish of their wives or not. This is perhaps a rough view to take of the "divine institution"; but it is a true one nevertheless. For purely legal marriage I have the utmost horror; and it seems to me that every pure-hearted woman should regard it in the same way. . . .

But this is not my principal objection to legal marriage. If women, with their eyes wide open, prefer to obtain a living by selling themselves into such slavery, they have a perfect right to do so, and I should content myself with attempting to point out the terrible degradation of the condition. But when the evils do not stop with the two contracting parties, when by the relations entered into or maintained for any motive other than love they produce children to curse the future, then I have a right to do something more than merely to call attention to the debasement. I have the right to protest in the name of a common humanity against the breeding and rearing of children under such improper conditions. I have the right to say to men and women who are only legally married, that they have no right to bear children to curse the world and to be burdens to themselves and society.

AUGUST STRINDBERG
GETTING MARRIED, 1884

August Strindberg (see Children, pages 23–24), was still married to his first wife, Siri, when he published *Getting Married* and was consequently accused of blasphemy. After his trial and acquittal, his marriage broke up, and he lost custody of his four children. He had two short, unhappy marriages after that, leaving him deeply bitter and making the observations he had offered in the preface, below, seem all the more poignant.

The reasons for an unhappy marriage are many. The first lies in the nature of marriage itself. Two human beings, and what is more, beings of opposite sexes, are incautious enough to promise to stick together for the rest of their lives.

Thus marriage is based on an impossibility. One partner develops in one direction, the other in another, and their marriage breaks up. Or one of the two remains stationary, while the other develops, and they drift apart. Incompatibility between husband and wife may arise when two strong spirits clash, and realize that no compromise is possible unless one partner gives way. This makes them hate their bonds. If they were free they would adjust to each other, now they will not, for to do so would be a surrender of personality. Finally they may reach a position where, in order to keep their identity uncontaminated, and prompted by an instinctive impulse of self-preservation, each grows to hate what the other thinks. To contradict becomes a necessity as if it were a guarantee that each would be able to keep themselves and their thoughts intact. This situation, that the world finds so hard to explain, is one that often arises. They once loved each other, they shared the same views, but suddenly this inexplicable antipathy breaks out, and all that is left is a couple who cannot agree.

J. D. SALINGER
FRANNY AND ZOOEY, 1961

With his short stories about the Glasses, J. D. Salinger (1919–2010) created an eccentric and wholly vivid Manhattan family. In this scene—memorably set in the bathroom of the clan's apartment—Zooey, the youngest son, is told by his mother that she wishes he would get married.

He gave an explosive sound, mostly through the nose, of either laughter or the opposite of laughter. Mrs. Glass quickly and anxiously leaned forward to see which it was. It was laughter, more or less, and she sat back relieved. "Well, I *do*," she insisted. "Why *don't* you?"

Relaxing his stance, Zooey took a folded linen handkerchief from his hip pocket, flipped it open, then used it to blow his nose once, twice, three times. He put away the handkerchief, saying, "I like to ride in trains too much. You never get to sit next to the window any more when you're married."

PHILIP ROTH
PORTNOY'S COMPLAINT, 1969

Winner of the Pulitzer Prize, the National Book Award, and the PEN/Faulkner Award, Philip Roth (1933–) has published many novels exploring secular Jewish life in suburban twentieth-century America. But it was *Portnoy's Complaint*, with its graphic language and memorable images of both solitary and promiscuous sexual acts, that established Roth's fame.
The entire book takes the form of a monologue in the voice of Alexander Portnoy as he addresses a psychoanalyst.

Please, let us not bullshit one another about "love" and its duration. Which is why I ask: how can I marry someone I "love" knowing full well that five, six, seven years hence I am going to be out on the streets hunting down the fresh new pussy—all the while my devoted wife, who has made me such a lovely home, et cetera, bravely suffers her loneliness and rejection? How could I face her terrible tears? I couldn't.

LARRY DAVID
"THE ENGAGEMENT," *SEINFELD*, 1995

The television series known as "the show about nothing" was in fact about four unrepentantly self-centered Manhattanites who talked, worked, dated, and spent an inexplicable number of hours in a coffee shop, all while dissecting the minutiae of 1990s manners. *Seinfeld*, which starred the comedian Jerry Seinfeld playing a comedian named Jerry Seinfeld, ran from 1989 to 1998. Sixty-two of its 180 episodes, including "The Engagement," were written by head writer, executive producer, and co-creator Larry David (1947–).

Kramer, played by Michael Richards, is Jerry's idiosyncratic, iconoclastic next-door neighbor, referred to at one point in the series as a "hipster doofus." George is Jerry's oldest friend.

JERRY:	Hey. Well, I had a very interesting lunch with George Costanza today.
KRAMER:	Really.
JERRY:	We were talking about our lives, and we both kind of realized: We're kids. We're not men.
KRAMER:	So then you asked yourselves, "Isn't there something more to life?"
JERRY:	Yes, we did!
KRAMER:	Yeah, well let me clue you in on something. There isn't.
JERRY:	There isn't?
KRAMER:	Absolutely not. I mean, what are you thinking about, Jerry, marriage? Family?
JERRY:	Well—
KRAMER:	They're prisons. Manmade prisons. You're doing time! You get up in the morning, she's there. You go to sleep at night, she's there. It's like you've got to ask permission to, to—to use the bathroom. "Is it all right if I use the bathroom now?"
JERRY:	Really.
KRAMER:	Yeah, and you can forget about watching TV while you're eating.
JERRY:	I can?
KRAMER:	Oh yeah! You know why? Because it's dinnertime. And you know what you do at dinner?
JERRY:	What?
KRAMER:	You talk about your day. "How was your day today? Did you have a good day today or a bad day today? Well, what kind of day was it?" "Well, I don't know. How 'bout you? How was your day?"

0

JERRY:	Boy.
KRAMER:	It's sad, Jerry. It's a sad state of affairs.
JERRY:	I'm glad we had this talk.
KRAMER:	Oh, you have NO idea!

ELIZABETH GILBERT
EAT, PRAY, LOVE, 2006

One of the biggest bestsellers of the early twenty-first century, *Eat, Pray, Love* was, as the subtitle put it, "one woman's search for everything." A successful freelance writer who had been married for six years, Elizabeth Gilbert (1969–) left her husband, traveled the world, and, through her travelogue—and its subsequent film adaptation starring Julia Roberts—became a kind of beacon of female independence. Some critics found her troubles rarefied, and her reasons for wanting divorce obscure, but millions of readers enjoyed her writing style and reveled vicariously in her quest.

Gilbert married again in 2007 and subsequently wrote *Committed: A Skeptic Makes Peace with Marriage*.

I don't want to be married anymore.

I was trying so hard not to know this, but the truth kept insisting itself to me.

I don't want to be married anymore. I don't want to live in this big house. I don't want to have a baby.

But I was supposed to want to have a baby. I was thirty-one years old. My husband and I—who had been together for eight years, married for six—had built our entire life around the common expectation that, after passing the doddering old age of thirty, I would want to settle down and have children. By then, we mutually anticipated, I would have grown weary of traveling and would be happy to live in a big, busy household full of children and homemade quilts, with a garden in the backyard and a cozy stew bubbling on the stovetop . . . I kept waiting to want to have a baby, but it didn't happen. . . .

I don't want to be married anymore.

In daylight hours, I refused that thought, but at night it would consume me. What a catastrophe. How could I be such a criminal jerk as to proceed this deep into a marriage, only to leave it? We'd only just bought this house a year ago. Hadn't I wanted this nice house? Hadn't I loved it? So why was I haunting its halls every night now, howling like Medea? Wasn't I proud of all we'd accumulated—the prestigious home in the Hudson Valley, the apartment in Manhattan, the eight phone lines, the friends and the picnics and the parties, the weekends spent roaming the aisles of some box-shaped superstore of our choice, buying ever more appliances on credit? I had actively participated in every moment of the creation of this life—so why did I feel like none of it resembled me? Why did I feel so overwhelmed with duty, tired of being the primary breadwinner and the housekeeper and the social coordinator and the dog-walker and the wife and the soon-to-be mother, and—somewhere in my stolen moments—a writer?

I don't want to be married anymore.

ONENESS

PLATO
THE SYMPOSIUM, CIRCA 385 BC

In his dialogue *The Symposium*, Plato described a party at which a number of his fellow philosophers gathered for the purpose of discussing the mystery of love and the sexes. Seven of those present made long speeches, but when it came to Aristophanes, he got the hiccups and passed his turn. Eventually the conversation moved back around to him. Whether his statements were satire—or, for that matter, whether Plato was offering up some comic relief—have remained sources of debate. Yet the idea of the missing half is often ascribed to Plato as a sincere one.

Each of us when separated, having one side only, like a flat fish, is but the indenture of a man, and he is always looking for his other half. . . .

. . . Suppose Hephaestus, with his instruments, to come to the pair who are lying side by side and to say to them, "What do you people want of one another?" they would be unable to explain. And suppose further, that when he saw their perplexity he said: "Do you desire to be wholly one; always day and night to be in one another's company? for if this is what you desire, I am ready to melt you into one and let you grow together, so that being two you shall become one, and while you live a common life as if you were a single man, and after your death in the world below still be one departed soul instead of two—I ask whether this is what you lovingly desire, and whether you are satisfied to attain this?"—there is not a man of them who when he heard the proposal would deny or would not acknowledge that this meeting and melting into one another, this becoming one instead of two, was the very expression of his ancient need. And the reason is that human nature was originally one and we were a whole, and the desire and pursuit of the whole is called love.

PLUTARCH
ADVICE TO THE BRIDE AND GROOM, 1ST CENTURY

For Plutarch, see also In-laws, page 224.

Philosophers distinguish three classes of bodies: those made up of separate units, like a fleet or an army; those made of units connected together, like a house or a ship; and those which have a natural unity, such as animals have. A marriage between lovers has this natural unity; a marriage for money or children is made of units connected together; a marriage based simply on the pleasure of sleeping together is made of separate units, and should be called cohabitation rather than a shared life.

Scientists tell us that liquids mix completely: so should the bodies, resources, friends, and connections of a married couple. The Roman lawgiver forbade married couples to give or receive presents from each other. This was not to stop them sharing, but to make them think everything their common property.

HONORIUS OF AUTUN
SERMON, 12TH CENTURY

As a theologian, he was apparently quite popular because he offered his sermons and many of his writings in accessible prose. But few biographical details have been discovered about Honorius Augustodunensis (1080–1154), except that he may have come from Autun in France. What has become clear to scholars is that in emphasizing mutual love as a happy condition for marriage, he was well ahead of his time.

Let husbands love their wives with tender affection; let them keep faith with them in all things. . . . In the same way, women should love their husbands deeply, fear them, and keep faith with a pure heart. Let them agree in everything good, like a pair of eyes.

Scientists tell us that liquids mix completely: so should the bodies, resources, friends, and connections of a married couple.

ALFRED, LORD TENNYSON
"THE PRINCESS," 1847

"The Princess" (subtitled "A Medley") tells the story of Ida, betrothed to a prince since child-hood but now self-exiled to an all-women's college and determined to live a life without men. Bent on fulfilling his destiny, the prince and two friends enter the school disguised as women, gradually learning a new point of view. The following verses are spoken by the prince, near the poem's climax.

For background on Tennyson, see Beginnings, page 17.

Seeing either sex alone
Is half itself, and in true marriage lies
Nor equal, nor unequal: each fulfils
Defect in each, and always thought in thought,
Purpose in purpose, will in will, they grow,
The single pure and perfect animal,
The two-cell'd heart beating, with one full stroke,
Life.

EDWARD CARPENTER
LOVE'S COMING OF AGE, 1896

An English author and maverick social activist, Edward Carpenter (1844–1929) argued that civilization was the enemy of true humanity. He was in favor of socialism, rural craftsmanship, a return to nature, vegetarianism, women's rights, and uncloseted homosexuality. *Love's Coming of Age* portrayed success in marriage as a near impossibility but one that, if attempted at all, could only be based on what he called "an amalgamated personality."

Despite the punishing Victorian era—and the contemporaneous trial and arrest of Oscar Wilde—Carpenter managed to sustain a homosexual relationship with a man named George Merrill from roughly 1891, when they met, until Merrill's death in 1928.

That there should exist one other person in the world towards whom all openness of interchange should establish itself, from whom there should be no concealment; whose body should be as dear to one, in every part, as one's own; with whom there should be no sense of Mine or Thine, in property or possession; into whose mind one's thoughts should naturally flow, as it were to know themselves and to receive a new illumination; and between whom and oneself there should be a spontaneous rebound of sympathy in all the joys and sorrows and experiences of life; such is perhaps one of the dearest wishes of the soul. It is obvious, however, that this state of affairs cannot be reached at a single leap, but must be the gradual result of years of intertwined memory and affection. For such a union Love must lay the foundation, but patience and gentle consideration and self-control must work unremittingly to perfect the structure. . . . There falls a sweet, an irresistible, trust over their relation to each other, which consecrates as it were the double life, making both feel that nothing can now divide; and robbing each of all desire to remain, when death has indeed (or at least in outer semblance) removed the other.

ELINOR GLYN
THREE THINGS, 1915

The British author and screenwriter Elinor Sutherland Glyn (1864–1943) would eventually be best known for her romantic, sometimes scandalous, works of fiction, most famously the short story "It," which, as a film, starred Clara Bow as "the 'It' girl." *Three Things* was a collection of some of Glyn's early magazine articles. In the introduction, she explained: "to me there seem to be just three essentials to strive after in life. Truth—Common Sense and Happiness."

Glyn herself was immortalized in the Rodgers and Hart song "My Heart Stood Still": "I read my Plato. Love, I thought a sin,/But since your kiss I'm reading Missus Glyn!"

No marriage can be certain of continuing happy which has been entered into in the spirit of taking a lottery ticket. But most marriages could be fairly happy if both man and woman looked the thing squarely in the face and made up their minds that they would run together in harness as two well-trained carriage horses, both knowing of the pole, both pulling at the collar and not overstraining the traces, both taking pride in their high stepping and their unity of movement. How much more dignified than to make a pitiful exhibition of incompatibility like two wild creatures kicking and plunging, and finally upsetting the vehicle they had agreed to draw?

ROBERT FROST
"THE MASTER SPEED," 1936

Often crusty and world-weary in his life and poetry, the great New England poet Robert Frost (1874–1963) also could be sentimental at times. This poem, written as a wedding present for his daughter Irma, is famous for its evocative last line. Frost married Elinor White in 1895 and, enduring the loss of four of their six children and his wife's chronic heart problems, remained married to her until her death in 1938.

The last line of this poem is carved into the Frost family gravestone, under Elinor's name.

0

No speed of wind or water rushing by
But you have speed far greater. You can climb
Back up a stream of radiance to the sky,
And back through history up the stream of time.
And you were given this swiftness, not for haste
Nor chiefly that you may go where you will,
But in the rush of everything to waste,
That you may have the power of standing still—
Off any still or moving thing you say.
Two such as you with such a master speed
Cannot be parted nor be swept away
From one another once you are agreed
That life is only life forevermore
Together wing to wing and oar to oar.

JOHN STEINBECK
LETTER TO GWYNDOLYN STEINBECK, 1943

The author most famously of the novels *Of Mice and Men* and *The Grapes of Wrath*, John Steinbeck (1902–1968) was married three times: the first time for twelve years; the second for five; and the third for eighteen, until his death. His first wife, Carol, is thought to have had a great impact on his early writing career. His second wife, Gwyn, a singer, became resentful of his success and was combative, competitive, and unfaithful. His third wife, Elaine, was reportedly the perfect fit: calming, uncompetitive, and thoroughly constant in her companionship. And yet this beautiful letter, surprisingly enough, was written to Wife Number Two.

Steinbeck was in London, working as a war correspondent, when he wrote this.

Darling, you want to know what I want of you. Many things of course but chiefly these. I want you to keep this thing we have inviolate and waiting—the person who is neither I nor you but us. It's a hard thing this separation but it is one of the millions of separations at home and many more millions here. It is one hunger in a great starvation but because it is ours it overshadows all the rest, if we let it. But keep waiting and don't let it be hurt by anything because it is the one really precious thing we have. Later we may have others but so far it is a single unit—and you have the keeping of it for a little while. You say I am busy, as though that wiped out my end, but it doesn't. You can be just as homesick and lost when you are busy. I love you beyond words, beyond containing. Remember that always when the distance seems so great and the time so long. It will not be so long, my dear.

I want you to keep this thing we have inviolate and waiting—the person who is neither I nor you but us.

SYLVIA PLATH
LETTER TO AURELIA PLATH, 1956

American poet Sylvia Plath (1932–1963) published one novel (the autobiographical *The Bell Jar*) and one book of poetry (*The Colossus*) before killing herself, at the age of thirty, a year after separating from her husband, the poet Ted Hughes. The two were living in London and had married just months before Plath wrote this letter to her mother. By all accounts Hughes and Plath shared both poetry and passion. They had two children but eventually had to battle her depressions and his adultery.

Sylvia Plath is the only poet to have won a Pulitzer Prize posthumously. The ellipses appear in the collection of Plath's letters.

Have been back here exactly a week and am going through the most terrible state, but stoically, and will somehow manage. It is the longest I have ever been away from Ted and somehow, in the course of this working and vital summer, we have mystically become one. I can appreciate the legend of Eve coming from Adam's rib as I never did before; the damn story's true! That's where I belong. Away from Ted, I feel as if I were living with one eyelash of myself only. It is really agony. We *are* different from most couples; for we share ourselves perhaps more intensely at every moment. Everything I do with and for Ted has a celestial radiance, be it only ironing and cooking, and this *increases* with custom, instead of growing less . . . Perhaps, most important, our writing is founded in the inspiration of the other and grows by the proper, inimitable criticism of the other, and publications are made with joy of the other. What wife shares her husband's dearest career as I do? . . . I need no sorrow to write; I have had, and, no doubt will have enough. My poems and stories I want to be the strongest female paean yet for the creative forces of nature, the joy of being a loved and loving woman; that is my song.

KURT VONNEGUT
CAT'S CRADLE, 1963

In his fourth novel, *Cat's Cradle*, American author Kurt Vonnegut (1922–2007) created not only a fictional Caribbean island but also a religion, a language, a flag, a currency, and an apocalypse to go with it.

In the Republic of San Lorenzo, Bokonon is the cofounder of the religion Bokononism, which he secretly proceeds to help outlaw in order to ensure its success. The book is narrated by a writer named John, one of the only survivors at the end of the book. A "karass" is a unit of cosmically linked people.

The seating on the airplane, bound ultimately for San Lorenzo from Miami, was three and three. As it happened—"As it was *supposed* to happen"—my seatmates were Horlick Minton, the new American Ambassador to the Republic of San Lorenzo, and his wife, Claire. They were white-haired, gentle, and frail. . . .

They were lovebirds. They entertained each other endlessly with little gifts: sights worth seeing out the plane window, amusing or instructive bits from things they read, random recollections of times gone by. They were, I think, a flawless example of what Bokonon calls a *duprass,* which is a *karass* composed of only two persons.

"A true *duprass,*" Bokonon tells us, "can't be invaded, not even by children born of such a union."

I exclude the Mintons, therefore, from my own *karass* . . . The Mintons' *karass* was a tidy one, composed of only two. . . .

Bokonon tells us, incidentally, that members of a *duprass* always die within a week of each other. When it came time for the Mintons to die, they did it within the same second.

GABRIEL GARCÍA MÁRQUEZ
LOVE IN THE TIME OF CHOLERA, 1985

The fourth novel by Colombian Nobel Prize–winner Gabriel García Márquez (1927–2014) explored the intense power of love in the midst of war and ravaging disease. In this passage, he describes the long marriage of Fermina Daza and Dr. Juvenal Urbino, who together represent one side of the novel's decades-long love triangle.

In the end they knew each other so well that by the time they had been married for thirty years they were like a single divided being, and they felt uncomfortable at the frequency with which they guessed each other's thoughts without intending to, or the ridiculous accident of one of them anticipating in public what the other was going to say. Together they had overcome the daily incomprehension, the instantaneous hatred, the reciprocal nastiness and fabulous flashes of glory in the conjugal conspiracy. It was the time when they loved each other best, without hurry or excess, when both were most conscious of and grateful for their incredible victories over adversity. Life would still present them with other mortal trials, of course, but that no longer mattered: they were on the other shore.

OPPOSITES

SAMUEL TAYLOR COLERIDGE
TABLE TALK, 1824

For background on Coleridge, see Money, page 297.

You may depend upon it, that a slight contrast of character is very material to happiness in marriage.

THOMAS HILL
HILL'S MANUAL OF SOCIAL AND BUSINESS FORMS, 1879

For background on Hill, see Conflict, page 40.

PECULIARITIES SUITABLE FOR EACH OTHER.

Those who are neither very tall nor very short, whose eyes are neither very black nor very blue, whose hair is neither very black nor very red,—the mixed types—may marry those who are quite similar in form, complexion and temperament to themselves.

Bright red hair and a florid complexion indicate an excitable temperament. Such should marry the jet-black hair and the brunette type.

The gray, blue, black or hazel eyes should not marry those of the same color. Where the color is very pronounced, the union should be with those of a decidedly different color.

The very corpulent should unite with the thin and spare, and the short, thick-set should choose a different constitution.

The thin, bony, wiry, prominent-featured, Roman-nosed, cold-blooded individual, should marry the round-featured, warm-hearted and emotional. Thus the cool should unite with warmth and susceptibility.

The extremely irritable and nervous should unite with the lymphatic, the slow and the quiet. Thus the stolid will be prompted by the nervous companion, while the excitable will be quieted by the gentleness of the less nervous.

The quick-motioned, rapid-speaking person should marry the calm and deliberate. The warmly impulsive should unite with the stoical.

The very fine-haired, soft and delicate-skinned should not marry those like themselves; and the curly should unite with the straight and smooth hair.

The thin, long-face should marry the round-favored; and the flat nose should marry the full Roman. The woman who inherits the features and peculiarities of her father should marry a man who partakes of the characteristics of his mother; but in all these cases where the type is not pronounced, but is, on the contrary, an average or medium, those forms, features and temperaments may marry either.

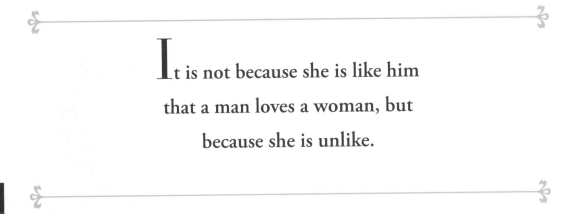

It is not because she is like him
that a man loves a woman, but
because she is unlike.

NELSON SIZER AND H. S. DRAYTON
HEADS AND FACES, AND HOW TO STUDY THEM, 1885

The late nineteenth century was a fine time for both phrenology and physiognomy, the studies, respectively, of the skull and the face. Authors such as Nelson Sizer (1812–1897) and Henry Drayton (1839–1923) popularized the ideas, some going back as far as Aristotle, that the character, and in some cases the future, could be known through such study. When it came to marital partners, the authors were firm in their belief that opposites not only do, but in fact should, attract.

There can be no harmony without some difference; there may be difference without harmony. It is not because she is like him that a man loves a woman, but because she is unlike. For the same reason she loves him. The more womanly the woman, the greater her power over men; in proportion as she approaches the masculine in person or character does she repel the other sex. So a woman admires manliness, strength, force in men, and contemns effeminacy, weakness, supineness, whenever she finds it in masculine dress. In the matter of physique, nature inclines us to select our opposites; the dark-haired, swarthy man, is inclined to admire the light-haired, blonde woman; the lean and spare admire the stout or plump; the plain man generally admires and associates with the fair and beautiful woman; and on the other hand, we find plain and apparently unattractive women, so far as face and proportion are concerned, united to handsome, striking men. Nature abhors extremes, and gives an impulse to the production of harmony and

Fig. 181. HARMONIOUS MAN.   Fig. 182. HARMONIOUS WOMAN.

proportion; would make the husband and wife not counterparts but complements, that the results which appear in their children be intermediate, symmetrical, and therefore an improvement on either parent. The temperaments, unless they are nicely combined on each side, so that the organization is well balanced and the character as finely proportioned as the mind is harmoniously developed, should be different; too close a similarity in special, one-sided constitution should be avoided.

PASSION

WILLIAM WORDSWORTH
LETTER TO MARY WORDSWORTH, 1810

The English Romantic poet William Wordsworth (1770–1850) had a love affair in France with a woman named Annette Vallon in 1792. He was back in England when war broke out between France and England the following year, and he didn't see the daughter he had fathered until the brief Peace of Amiens in 1802 allowed him to visit France again. After squaring things with Annette, he returned to England to marry his childhood friend Mary Hutchinson. They had five children together, three of whom they outlived. Wordsworth, as is evident from this and other letters, did not save all his poetry for his poems.

Every day every hour every moment makes me feel more deeply how blessed we are in each other, how purely how faithfully how ardently, and how tenderly we love each other; I put this last word last because, though I am persuaded that a deep affection is not uncommon in married life, yet I am confident that a lively, gushing, thought-employing, spirit-stirring, passion of love, is very rare even among good people. I will say more upon this when we meet, grounded upon recent observation of the condition of others. We have been parted my sweet Mary too long, but we have not been parted in vain, for wherever I go I am admonished how blessed, and almost peculiar a lot mine is.

FRIEDRICH NIETZSCHE
DAYBREAK, 1881

For background on Nietzsche, see Communication, page 33.

We ought not to be permitted to come to a decision affecting our life while we are in the condition of being in love, nor to determine once and for all the character of the company we keep on the basis of a violent whim: the oaths of lovers ought to be publicly declared invalid and marriage denied them: the reason being that one ought to take marriage enormously more seriously! so that in precisely those cases in which marriages have hitherto taken place they would henceforth usually not take place!

GEORGE BERNARD SHAW
ON MARRIAGE, 1908

Well known for his writings about theater, music, politics, economics, and society, the Irish author George Bernard Shaw (1856–1950) is often cited as one of the world's greatest playwrights. Through his semi-comic works—most famously *Arms and the Man*, *Major Barbara*, and *Pygmalion*—Shaw presented the human condition with a mixture of irresistible wit and profound social insight. Those same elements were evident in one of his early plays, *On Marriage*, and particularly in the lengthy introduction he wrote to it.

After numerous flirtations, as well as passionate correspondences that he called "paper courtships," Shaw had a long but reportedly platonic marriage with a fellow member of the socialist Fabian Society, Charlotte Payne-Townsend, as well as several affairs and some passionate correspondence with other men's wives.

The [marriage] service was really only an honest attempt to make the best of a commercial contract of property and slavery by subjecting it to some religious restraint and elevating it by some touch of poetry. But the actual result is that when two people are under the influence of the most violent, most insane, most delusive, and most transient of passions, they are required to swear that they will remain in that excited, abnormal, and exhausting condition continuously until death do them part. And though of course nobody expects them to do anything so impossible and so unwholesome, yet the law that regulates their relations, and the public opinion that regulates that law, is actually founded on the assumption that the marriage vow is not only feasible but beautiful and holy, and that if they are false to it, they deserve no sympathy and no relief.

WILLIAM FAULKNER
"WHAT IS THE MATTER WITH MARRIAGE?," 1925

William Faulkner (see Knowing, page 244) was twenty-seven, unmarried, and struggling to support himself as a writer when he sent in his response to the contest question "What Is the Matter with Marriage?" The *New Orleans Item-Tribune* printed his answer, paid him ten dollars, and ran a photograph of him captioned, "Poet, philosopher, student of life." In 1929, he married Estelle Oldham. The couple remained married, despite his alcoholism and many affairs, until Faulkner's death.

The first frenzy of passion, of intimacy of mind and body, is never love. That is only the surf through which one must go to reach the calm sea of real love and peace and contentedness. Breakers may be fun, but you cannot sail safely through breakers into port. And surely married people do want to reach some port together—some haven from which to look backward down golden years when mutual tolerance has removed some of the rough places and time has blotted out the rest.

If people would but remember that passion is a fire which burns itself out, but that love is a fuel which feeds its never-dying fire, there would be no unhappy marriages.

C. S. LEWIS
THE PILGRIM'S REGRESS, 1933

Clive Staples Lewis (1898–1963) didn't publish the first book of *The Chronicles of Narnia* series until 1950. Both before and after those children's classics, the Irish author was primarily a Christian theologian who produced dozens of works about religion while teaching at Oxford and Cambridge. *The Pilgrim's Regress* was Lewis's first novel and a representation of his own path toward Christianity.

Like John Bunyan's seventeenth-century *Pilgrim's Progress*, Lewis's novel describes the voyage of an everyman (named John) through a landscape of symbolic characters including Mother Kirk, Wisdom, and Mr. Sensible. John is questioning his faith when the hermit named History urges him to trust its authenticity. The last sentence is from Exodus.

"Have you not heard men say, or have you forgotten, that [spiritual craving] is like human love?" asked the hermit.

"What has that to do with it?"

"You would not ask if you had been married, or even if you had studied generation among the beasts. Do you not know how it is with love? First comes delight: then pain: then fruit. And then there is joy of the fruit, but that is different again from the first delight. And mortal lovers must not try to remain at the first step: for lasting passion is the dream of a harlot and from it we wake in despair. You must not try to keep the raptures: they have done their work. Manna kept, is worms."

JOHN MICHAEL HAYES
REAR WINDOW, 1954

Starring Jimmy Stewart as a maverick photographer whose badly broken leg has landed him in a wheelchair, *Rear Window*, written by John Michael Hayes (1919–2008) and directed by Alfred Hitchcock, made neighborhood detectives of Jeff Jefferies (Stewart); his girlfriend, Lisa Fremont (Grace Kelly); and his insurance-company nurse, Stella (Thelma Ritter). Early on in the film, Jeff tries to persuade Stella that Lisa isn't the right woman for him to marry.

JEFF: No, she's just not the girl for me.

STELLA: Yeah, she's only perfect.

JEFF: She's too perfect. She's too talented. She's too beautiful. She's too sophisticated. She's too everything but what I want.

STELLA: Is what you want something you can discuss?

JEFF: What? Well, it's very simple, Stella. She belongs to that rarefied atmosphere of Park Avenue, you know, expensive restaurants and then the literary cocktail parties—

STELLA: People with sense belong wherever they're put.

JEFF: Can you imagine her tramping around the world with a camera bum who never has more than a week's salary in the bank? If she was only ordinary.

STELLA: You never gonna get married?

JEFF: I'll probably get married one of these days. But when I do, it's going to be to someone who thinks of life not just as a new dress and a lobster dinner and the latest scandal. I need a woman who's willing to go anywhere and do anything and love it. So the honest thing for me to do is just call the whole thing off and let her find someone else.

STELLA: Yup, I can hear you right now. Get out of my life, you perfectly wonderful woman, you're too good for me. Look, Mr. Jefferies, I'm not an educated woman, but I can tell you one thing. When a man and woman see each other and like each other, they oughta come together—wham!—like a couple of taxis on Broadway, and not sit around analyzing each other like two specimens in a bottle.

JEFF: There's an intelligent way to approach marriage.

STELLA: Intelligence! Nothing has caused the human race so much trouble as intelligence. Ha, modern marriage!

JEFF: Now, we've progressed emotionally—

STELLA: Baloney! Once, it was: See somebody, get excited, get married. Now, it's: Read a lot of books, fence with a lot of four-syllable words, psychoanalyze each other until you can't tell the difference between a petting party and a civil service exam.

POWER

WILLIAM SHAKESPEARE
THE TAMING OF THE SHREW, CIRCA 1592

The basic plot: Younger sister Bianca has eager suitors; father forbids her to marry before older sister Katharina does. Problem: Katharina is a shrew. This famous final speech of hers, supposed proof of her "taming," has given generations of critics fodder for debate: Is she being sincere in her submissiveness, or utterly sarcastic? Joseph Papp, who directed Meryl Streep in the role in 1978, wrote: "Shakespeare says quite plainly that if two people are really in love, the issue of who does what for whom does not exist."

Froward means "wayward" or "difficult." *Vail your stomachs* means "swallow your pride." *Boot* means "profit."

I am ashamed that women are so simple
To offer war where they should kneel for peace,
Or seek for rule, supremacy, and sway
When they are bound to serve, love, and obey.

Why are our bodies soft and weak and smooth,
Unapt to toil and trouble in the world,
But that our soft conditions and our hearts
Should well agree with our external parts?
Come, come, you froward and unable worms!
My mind hath been as big as one of yours,
My heart as great, my reason haply more,
To bandy word for word and frown for frown;
But now I see our lances are but straws,
Our strength as weak, our weakness past compare,
That seeming to be most which we indeed least are.
Then vail your stomachs, for it is no boot,
And place your hands below your husband's foot,
In token of which duty, if he please,
My hand is ready; may it do him ease.

HONORÉ DE BALZAC
THE MARRIAGE CONTRACT, 1835

P

Another part of *La Comédie Humaine* (see Fidelity, page 113; Honeymoon, page 172; Sex, page 401), *The Marriage Contract* features a naïve daughter (Natalie); a wealthy, smitten suitor (Paul de Manerville); and a strong-willed, calculating mother (Madame Evangelista) for whom Natalie's marriage is the surest way to reclaim the wealthy lifestyle that has diminished since Monsieur Evangelista's death. This is Madame Evangelista's prenuptial advice to Natalie.

Marriage lasts a lifetime, and a husband is not a man like other men. Therefore, never commit the folly of giving yourself into his power in anything. Keep up a constant reserve in your speech and in your actions. You may even be cold to him without danger, for you can modify coldness at will. Besides, nothing is more easy to maintain than our dignity. The words, "It is not becoming in your wife to do thus and so," is a great talisman. The life of a woman lies in the words, "I will not." They are the final argument. Feminine power is in them, and therefore they should only be used on real occasions. But they constitute a means of governing far beyond that of argument or discussion. I, my dear child, reigned over your father by his faith in me. If your husband believes in you, you can do all things with him. To inspire that belief you must make him think that you understand him. Do not suppose that that is an easy thing to do. A woman can always make a man think that he is loved, but to make him admit that he is understood is far more difficult. I am bound to tell you all now, my child, for to-morrow life with its complications, life with two wills which *must* be made one, begins for you. Bear in mind, at all moments, that difficulty. The only means of harmonizing your two wills is to arrange from the first that there shall be but one; and that will must be yours.

Where despotic command is exercised, confusion, disobedience, and rebellion generally prevail.

JOHN MATHER AUSTIN
A VOICE TO THE MARRIED, 1847

As a minister, Austin (see Looks, page 278) wrote and preached in favor of abolitionism, prison reform, and—somewhat implausibly in light of the advice below—women's rights.

Although ultimate authority is vested in the husband, yet it should be his desire, his study, in all his conduct, to keep this circumstance from view as much as possible. Instead of constantly asserting his authority, and seeking opportunities to exhibit it, he should endeavor to act towards his wife, so far as practicable, as though he had no power superior to her own. He should exercise rule in a manner so gentle, so mild, so unseen, that those who are swayed by it, shall be unconscious of its existence. Delicacy, propriety, love for his companion, desire for domestic tranquility and peace, all urge him to pursue this course.

There are two methods in which the husband can make known his will—the one is in the form of a *command*—the other in that of a *request*. In the great majority of cases, the latter course is altogether the most successful manner of securing compliance. . . . Where despotic command is exercised, confusion, disobedience, and rebellion most generally prevail; for fear cannot produce so perfect an obedience from a rational being as love.

GEORGE ELIOT
ROMOLA, 1863

For Eliot's background, see Expectations, page 103. *Romola* was the author's fourth novel, a historical work set in fifteenth-century Florence. Romola, the erudite daughter of a classics scholar, falls in love with and marries Tito Melema, an Italian scholar who comes to Florence after a shipwreck, but whose increasing ambition makes him less and less desirable to his wife.

Romola's touch and glance no longer stirred any fibre of tenderness in her husband. The good-humoured, tolerant Tito, incapable of hatred, incapable almost of impatience, disposed always to be gentle towards the rest of the world, felt himself becoming strangely hard towards this wife whose presence had once been the strongest influence he had known. With all his softness of disposition, he had a masculine effectiveness of intellect and purpose which, like sharpness of edge, is itself an energy, working its way without any strong momentum. Romola had an energy of her own which thwarted his; and no man, who is not exceptionally feeble, will endure being thwarted by his wife. Marriage must be a relation either of sympathy or of conquest.

A MARRIED MAN
"THE MARRIAGE INJUNCTION TO OBEY," 1886

On June 2, Grover Cleveland married Frances Folsom in the Blue Room of the White House, and a few days later, the *St. Louis-Globe Democrat* ran a letter from "A Married Lady," complaining that the president should have traveled to Folsom's native Buffalo, New York, instead of having her come to Washington. "In my judgment," the woman wrote, "[Folsom] sacrificed, to a certain extent, the dignity of her sex." What follows is the opinion, printed the following day, of one male reader.
"The good old days of St. Paul" is a reference to the biblical injunction "wives, submit yourselves unto your own husbands."

You ask the ladies of St. Louis and the West to give you their opinion of the propriety of the omission of the injunction to "obey" from the recent marriage ceremony in Washington. Let me tell you the reason. I have been married ten years. My wife promised at the altar to obey me. Has she done it? Yes, whenever it suited her to obey me she has obeyed me. I think clergymen omit "obey" because it has been found by experience that it's no use to put in. The good old days of St. Paul have passed away. My wife and I live very happily together. We get along first rate, but if I should remind her of her marriage vow to obey her husband, I think there would be a fuss in our house, and I don't want that; so, if there is any "obeying" done, I do it myself.

The injunction that women shall obey their husbands is a dead letter, and that's why the preachers don't mention it. I am sorry, but " 'Tis true, 'tis pity, and pity 'tis 'tis true."

JOHN UPDIKE
COUPLES, 1968

Poet and essayist, critic and short-story writer, John Updike (1932–2009) produced twenty-three novels, many of which explored modern relationships. *Couples* was his fifth.

Every marriage tends to consist of an aristocrat and a peasant. Of a teacher and a learner.

NIA VARDALOS
MY BIG FAT GREEK WEDDING, 2002

As screenwriter and star, Nia Vardalos (1962–) lovingly created the character of Toula Portokalos, a thirty-year-old woman trying to break away from the expectations of her traditional Greek-American family. Step one—convincing Toula's father to let her take a college course—provided her mother, Maria (played by Lainie Kazan), the opportunity to explain wifely power.

MARIA: Toula, Toula, come on, Toula. I know what you want. Come. Don't you worry. I'm gonna talk to him.

TOULA: Ma, Dad is so stubborn. What he says goes. "Ah, the man is the head of the house!"

MARIA: Let me tell you something, Toula. The man is the head, but the woman is the neck. And she can turn the head any way she wants.

PROPOSALS

MARTIN MARTIN
A LATE VOYAGE TO ST. KILDA, 1698

Every marriage proposal involves the risk of rejection. But, as documented by the late-seventeenth-century travel writer Martin Martin (?–1718), one fabled Scottish approach to popping the question created physical peril as well. Climbing up and balancing on the "mistress stone" in the archipelago of St. Kilda was apparently a test both of rock-climbing agility (and thus of food-gathering ability in difficult terrain) and also a show of gallantry, both necessary before marriage. Drily, the author noted that when a native offered him a chance to try the feat, "I told him [that if I did it] the performance would have a quite contrary effect upon me, by robbing me both of my life and mistress at the same moment."

In the face of the rock, south from the town, is the famous stone, known by the name of the Mistress-stone; it resembles a door exactly, and is in the very front of this rock, which is twenty or thirty fathom perpendicular in height, the figure of it being discernible about the distance of a mile: upon the lintel of this door, every bachelor-wooer is, by an ancient custom, obliged in honour to give a specimen of his affection for the love of his mistress, and it is thus: he is to stand on his left foot, having the one half of it over the rock, he then draws the right foot towards the left, and in this posture bowing, puts both his fists further out to the right foot; after he has performed this, he has acquired no small reputation, being ever after accounted worthy the finest woman in the world: they firmly believe this achievement is always attended with the desired success.

Every bachelor-wooer is obliged in honour to give a specimen of his affection for the love of his mistress.

The Mistress Stone

PERSONAL AD
BOSTON EVENING POST, 1759

Sadly, there is no record of whether this proposal ever succeeded or, for that matter, attracted any answers at all.

Four hundred pounds in 1750 is the equivalent of about 60,000 pounds, or $100,000, today.

To the Ladies. Any young Lady between the Age of Eighteen and twenty three of a Midling Stature; brown Hair, regular Features and a Lively Brisk Eye; Of Good Morals & not Tinctured with anything that may Sully so Distinguishable a Form possessed of 3 or 400£ entirely her own Disposal and where there will be no necessity of going Through the tiresome Talk of addressing Parents or Guardians for their consent: Such a one by leaving a Line directed for A. W. at the British Coffee House in King Street appointing where an Interview may be had will meet with a Person who flatters himself he shall not be thought Disagreeable by any Lady answering the above description. N.B. Profound Secrecy will be observ'd. No trifling Answers will be regarded.

JANE AUSTEN
PRIDE AND PREJUDICE, 1813

"It is a truth universally acknowledged, that a single man in possession of a good fortune, must be in want of a wife." With that, one of the most famous opening lines in all literature, Jane Austen (1775–1817) set out to tell the story of the Bennet clan, a gentrified family living in a rural township outside London. Of the five Bennet daughters (all of whom their mother fervently wishes to marry off), Elizabeth, the second oldest, is the most independent. Unworried about the possibility of spinsterhood, and unmoved by the potential for financial security, she can scarcely stifle her amusement as a pompous and earnest clergyman, William Collins, does his best to entreat her.

Longbourn is the Bennets' home. The wealthy Lady Catherine de Bourgh is the noblewoman who is Collins's patron and, incidentally, the aunt of Elizabeth's future husband.

The next day opened a new scene at Longbourn. Mr. Collins made his declaration in form. Having resolved to do it without loss of time, as his leave of absence extended only to the following Saturday, and having no feelings of diffidence to make it distressing to himself even at the moment, he set about it in a very orderly manner, with all the observances which he supposed a regular part of the business. On finding Mrs. Bennet, Elizabeth, and one of the younger girls together, soon after breakfast, he addressed the mother in these words,

"May I hope, Madam, for your interest with your fair daughter Elizabeth, when I solicit for the honour of a private audience with her in the course of this morning?"

Before Elizabeth had time for anything but a blush of surprise, Mrs. Bennet instantly answered,

"Oh dear!—Yes—certainly.—I am sure Lizzy will be very happy—I am sure she can have no objection.—Come, Kitty, I want you up stairs." And gathering her work together, she was hastening away, when Elizabeth called out,

"Dear Ma'am, do not go.—I beg you will not go.—Mr. Collins must excuse me.—He can have nothing to say to me that any body need not hear. I am going away myself."

Almost as soon as I entered the house I singled you out as the companion of my future life.

"No, no, nonsense, Lizzy.—I desire you will stay where you are."—And upon Elizabeth's seeming really, with vexed and embarrassed looks, about to escape, she added, "Lizzy, I *insist* upon your staying and hearing Mr. Collins."

Elizabeth would not oppose such an injunction—and a moment's consideration making her also sensible that it would be wisest to get it over as soon and as quietly as possible, she sat down again, and tried to conceal by incessant employment the feelings which were divided between distress and diversion. Mrs. Bennet and Kitty walked off, and as soon as they were gone Mr. Collins began.

"Believe me, my dear Miss Elizabeth, that your modesty, so far from doing you any disservice, rather adds to your other perfections. You would have been less amiable in my eyes had there *not* been this little unwillingness; but allow me to assure you that I have your respected mother's permission for this address. You can hardly doubt the purport of my discourse, however your natural delicacy may lead you to dissemble; my attentions have been too marked to be mistaken. Almost as soon as I entered the house I singled you out as the companion of my future life. But before I am run away with by my feelings on this subject, perhaps it will be advisable for me to state my reasons for marrying—and moreover for coming into Hertfordshire with the design of selecting a wife, as I certainly did."

The idea of Mr. Collins, with all his solemn composure, being run away with by his feelings, made Elizabeth so near laughing that she could not use the short pause he allowed in any attempt to stop him farther, and he continued:

"My reasons for marrying are, first, that I think it a right thing for every clergyman in easy circumstances (like myself) to set the example of matrimony in his parish. Secondly, that I am convinced it will add very greatly to my happiness; and thirdly—which perhaps I ought to have mentioned earlier, that it is the particular advice and recommendation of the very noble lady

---

If what I have said can appear to you in the form of encouragement, I know not how to express my refusal in such a way as may convince you of its being one.

---

whom I have the honour of calling patroness. Twice has she condescended to give me her opinion (unasked too!) on this subject; and it was but the very Saturday night before I left Hunsford— between our pools at quadrille, while Mrs. Jenkinson was arranging Miss de Bourgh's foot-stool, that she said, 'Mr. Collins, you must marry. A clergyman like you must marry.—Chuse properly, chuse a gentlewoman for *my* sake; and for your *own*, let her be an active, useful sort of person, not brought up high, but able to make a small income go a good way. This is my advice. Find such a woman as soon as you can, bring her to Hunsford, and I will visit her.' . . . This has been my motive, my fair cousin, and I flatter myself it will not sink me in your esteem. And now nothing remains for me but to assure you in the most animated language of the violence of my affection. To fortune I am perfectly indifferent, and shall make no demand of that nature on your father, since I am well aware that it could not be complied with; and that one thousand pounds in the 4 per cents, which will not be yours till after your mother's decease, is all that you may ever be entitled to. On that head, therefore, I shall be uniformly silent; and you may assure yourself that no ungenerous reproach shall ever pass my lips when we are married."

It was absolutely necessary to interrupt him now.

"You are too hasty, Sir," she cried. "You forget that I have made no answer. Let me do it without farther loss of time. Accept my thanks for the compliment you are paying me. I am very sensible of the honour of your proposals, but it is impossible for me to do otherwise than decline them."

"I am not now to learn," replied Mr. Collins, with a formal wave of the hand, "that it is usual with young ladies to reject the addresses of the man whom they secretly mean to accept, when he first applies for their favour; and that sometimes the refusal is repeated a second or even a third time. I am therefore by no means discouraged by what you have just said, and shall hope to lead you to the altar ere long."

"Upon my word, Sir," cried Elizabeth, "your hope is rather an extraordinary one after my declaration. I do assure you that I am not one of those young ladies (if such young ladies there are) who are so daring as to risk their happiness on the chance of being asked a second time. I am perfectly serious in my refusal.—You could not make *me* happy, and I am convinced that I am the last woman in the world who would make *you* so.—Nay, were your friend Lady Catherine to know me, I am persuaded she would find me in every respect ill qualified for the situation."

"Were it certain that Lady Catherine would think so," said Mr. Collins, very gravely— "but I cannot imagine that her ladyship would at all disapprove of you. And you may be certain that when I have the honour of seeing her again I shall speak in the highest terms of your modesty, economy, and other amiable qualifications."

"Indeed, Mr. Collins, all praise of me will be unnecessary. You must give me leave to judge for myself, and pay me the compliment of believing what I say. I wish you very happy and very rich, and by refusing your hand, do all in my power to prevent your being otherwise. In making me the offer, you must have satisfied the delicacy of your feelings with regard to my family, and may take possession of Longbourn estate whenever it falls, without any self reproach. This matter may be considered, therefore, as finally settled." And rising as she thus spoke, she would have quitted the room, had not Mr. Collins thus addressed her,

"When I do myself the honour of speaking to you next on this subject I shall hope to receive a more favourable answer than you have now given me; though I am far from accusing you of cruelty at present, because I know it to be the established custom of your sex to reject a man on the first application, and perhaps you have even now said as much to encourage my suit as would be consistent with the true delicacy of the female character."

"Really, Mr. Collins," cried Elizabeth, with some warmth, "you puzzle me exceedingly. If what I have hitherto said can appear to you in the form of encouragement, I know not how to express my refusal in such a way as may convince you of its being one."

"You must give me leave to flatter myself, my dear cousin, that your refusal of my addresses is merely words of course. My reasons for believing it are briefly these:—It does not appear to me that my hand is unworthy your acceptance, or that the establishment I can offer would be any other than highly desirable. My situation in life, my connections with the family of De Bourgh, and my relationship to your own, are circumstances highly in my favour; and you should take it into farther consideration that in spite of your manifold attractions, it is by no means certain that another offer of marriage may ever be made you. Your portion is unhappily so small that it will in all likelihood undo the effects of your loveliness and amiable qualifications. As I must therefore conclude that you are not serious in your rejection of me, I shall chuse to attribute it to your wish of increasing my love by suspense, according to the usual practice of elegant females."

"I do assure you, Sir, that I have no pretension whatever to that kind of elegance which consists in tormenting a respectable man. I would rather be paid the compliment of being believed sincere. I thank you again and again for the honour you have done me in your proposals, but to accept them is absolutely impossible. My feelings in every respect forbid it. Can I speak plainer? Do not consider me now as an elegant female intending to plague you, but as a rational creature speaking the truth from her heart."

"You are uniformly charming!" cried he, with an air of awkward gallantry; "and I am persuaded that when sanctioned by the express authority of both your excellent parents, my proposals will not fail of being acceptable."

To such perseverance in wilful self-deception Elizabeth would make no reply, and immediately and in silence withdrew; determined, that if he persisted in considering her repeated refusals as flattering encouragement, to apply to her father, whose negative might be uttered in such a manner as must be decisive, and whose behaviour at least could not be mistaken for the affectation and coquetry of an elegant female.

CHARLOTTE BRONTË
JANE EYRE, 1847

This is the climactic scene of *Jane Eyre* (see Looks, page 279), in which Jane and Rochester finally make their feelings clear to each other. Jane is the first to speak.

"Do you think I can stay to become nothing to you? Do you think I am an automaton? a machine without feelings? and can bear to have my morsel of bread snatched from my lips, and my drop of living water dashed from my cup? Do you think, because I am poor, obscure, plain, and little, I am soulless and heartless? You think wrong! I have as much soul as you, and full as much heart! And if God had gifted me with some beauty, and much wealth, I should have made it as hard for you to leave me, as it is now for me to leave you. I am not talking to you now through the medium of custom, conventionalities, nor even of mortal flesh; it is my spirit that addresses your spirit; just as if both had passed through the grave, and we stood at God's feet, equal—as we are!"

"As we are!" repeated Mr. Rochester—"so," he added inclosing me in his arms, gathering me to his breast, pressing his lips on my lips; "so, Jane!"

"Yes, so, sir," I rejoined; "and yet not so; for you are a married man, or as good as a married man, and wed to one inferior to you—to one with whom you have no sympathy—whom I do not believe you truly love; for I have seen and heard you sneer at her. I would scorn such a union; therefore I am better than you—let me go!"

"Where, Jane? to Ireland?"

"Yes—to Ireland. I have spoken my mind, and can go anywhere now."

"Jane, be still; don't struggle so, like a wild, frantic bird that is rending its own plumage in its desperation."

"I am no bird; and no net ensnares me; I am a free human being, with an independent will; which I now exert to leave you."

Another effort set me at liberty, and I stood erect before him.

"And your will shall decide your destiny," he said; "I offer you my hand, my heart, and a share of all my possessions."

"You play a farce, which I merely laugh at."

"I ask you to pass through life at my side—to be my second self, and best earthly companion."

"For that fate you have already made your choice, and must abide by it."

"Jane, be still a few moments; you are over-excited; I will be still too."

A waft of wind came sweeping down the laurel-walk, and trembled through the boughs of the chestnut; it wandered away—away—to an indefinite distance—it died. The nightingale's song was then the only voice of the hour; in listening to it, I again wept. Mr. Rochester sat quiet, looking at me gently and seriously. Some time passed before he spoke; he at last said—

"Come to my side, Jane, and let us explain and understand one another."

"I will never again come to your side; I am torn away now, and cannot return."

"But, Jane, I summon you as my wife; it is you only I intend to marry."

I was silent; I thought he mocked me.

"Come, Jane—come hither."

"Your bride stands between us."

He rose, and with a stride reached me.

"My bride is here," he said, again drawing me to him, "because my equal is here, and my likeness. Jane, will you marry me?"

M. W. MOUNT
"THE TICKLISH ART OF PROPOSING MARRIAGE," 1907

Subtitled "Many Difficulties Encountered Both By Man and Maid," this advice column ran in the *New York Tribune*. Over several decades, its author, Mary ("May") Wilkinson Mount (circa 1866–1942), wrote for numerous publications on numerous subjects including homes and gardens, cooking, clothes, and of course love and marriage.

Numbers of men persistently make their offers of marriage in theatres and opera houses. Perhaps the romance upon the stage prompts them to speak; perhaps some phrase uttered by the stage hero fits so well into their sentiments that they immediately repeat it—with necessary additions. Perhaps the soft strains of a love song stir them into the mood for proposing, and they just offer themselves to the most handy woman without considering that she might not prove so handy in the years to come. Whatever their inscrutable reasons may be, thousands of Romeos have courted their Juliets in the seats before the lime lights and been as unconscious of how their expressions might be interpreted as that the girl is ardently wishing herself anywhere but just in that place. No womanly woman likes to see the most sacred moments of her life pinned up, as it were, upon the drop curtain for a whole audience to look at. . . .

No matter how prosaic the woman[,] she likes to be wooed amid proper surroundings. She likes to have her proposals without an audience—especially if she means to accept them. She doesn't fancy the suitor who shows entire disregard for her sentiments in this respect, but takes what chances he may at the first opportunity and proposes in the street. Now, how can a girl listen comfortably to an offer of marriage while prosaically walking down Broadway? Yet many of them have to make their decisions on the eventful matter of future happiness on that unromantic thoroughfare. Perhaps men fancy that in case of a refusal the open street permits them a graceful and immediate means of retreat.

GEORGE S. KAUFMAN, MORRIE RYSKIND, BERT KALMAR, AND HARRY RUBY
ANIMAL CRACKERS, 1930

No matter the medium or the character name, Groucho Marx (see Beginnings, page 20) was always Groucho Marx: wisecracking, fast-talking, lascivious, yet endearing. In *Animal Crackers* (the second of the Marx Brothers' stage shows adapted for film), he played Captain Spaulding, perpetually ruffling the feathers of the grande dame of second bananas, Margaret Dumont (here playing Mrs. Rittenhouse).

George S. Kaufman (1889–1961) and Morrie Ryskind (1895–1985) had collaborated on the Marx Brothers' *The Cocoanuts*; songwriters Bert Kalmar (1884–1947) and Harry Ruby (1895–1974) would work on several other Marx Brothers movies as well. Mrs. Whitehead (played by Margaret Irving) is one of the guests at a party in Spaulding's honor.

CAPTAIN SPAULDING:	Well, whadaya say, girls, are we all going to get married?
MRS. RITTENHOUSE:	All of us?
CAPTAIN SPAULDING:	All of us.
MRS. WHITEHEAD:	But that's bigamy!
CAPTAIN SPAULDING:	That's big of me, too. It's big of all of us. Let's be big for a change. I'm sick of these conventional marriages! One woman and one man was good enough for your grandmother. But who wants to marry your grandmother? Nobody! Not even your grandfather. Think! Think of the honeymoon! Strictly private! I wouldn't let another woman in on this. Well, maybe one or two, but no men. I may not go myself.

P

MARGARET MITCHELL
GONE WITH THE WIND, 1936

A million copies of *Gone With the Wind* sold within the first six months of its publication, and author Margaret Mitchell (1900–1949) won the Pulitzer Prize for Fiction the following year. Whether through the novel or the 1939 film starring Vivien Leigh and Clark Gable, audiences were enthralled by the coquettishness and resilience of Scarlett O'Hara and the brashness and charm of her suitor, Rhett Butler.

Scarlett, having married her first husband, Charles, for spite and her second husband, Frank, for money, is still officially in mourning when Rhett comes to pay her a visit.

He was actually asking her to marry him; he was committing the incredible. Once she had planned how she would torment him should he ever propose. Once she had thought that if he ever spoke those words she would humble him and make him feel her power and take a malicious pleasure in doing it. Now, he had spoken and the plans did not even occur to her, for he was no more in her power than he had ever been. In fact, he held the whip hand of the situation so completely that she was as flustered as a girl at her first proposal and she could only blush and stammer.

"I—I shall never marry again."

"Oh, yes, you will. You were born to be married. Why not me?"

"But Rhett, I—I don't love you."

"That should be no drawback. I don't recall that love was prominent in your other two ventures."

"Oh, how can you? You know I was fond of Frank!"

He said nothing.

"I was! I was!"

"Well, we won't argue that. Will you think over my proposition while I'm gone?"

"Rhett, I don't like for things to drag on. I'd rather tell you now. I'm going home to Tara soon and India Wilkes will stay with Aunt Pittypat. I want to go home for a long spell and—I—I don't ever want to get married again."

"Nonsense. Why?"

"Oh, well—never mind why. I just don't like being married."

"But, my poor child, you've never really been married. How can you know? I'll admit you've had back luck—once for spite and once for money. Did you ever think of marrying—just for the fun of it?"

"Fun! Don't talk like a fool. There's no fun being married."

"No? Why not?"

A measure of calm had returned and with it all the natural bluntness which brandy brought to the surface.

"It's fun for men—though God knows why. I never could understand it. But all a woman gets out of it is something to eat and a lot of work and having to put up with a man's foolishness—and a baby every year."

He laughed so loudly that the sound echoed in the stillness and Scarlett heard the kitchen door open.

"Hush! Mammy has ears like a lynx and it isn't decent to laugh so soon after—hush laughing. You know it's true. Fun! Fiddle-dee-dee!"

"I said you'd had bad luck and what you've just said proves it. You've been married to a boy and to an old man. And into the bargain I'll bet your mother told you that women must bear 'these things' because of the compensating joys of motherhood. Well, that's all wrong. Why not try marrying a fine young man who has a bad reputation and a way with women? It'll be fun."

"You are coarse and conceited and I think this conversation has gone far enough. It's—it's quite vulgar."

"And quite enjoyable too, isn't it? I'll wager you never discussed the marital relation with a man before, even Charles or Frank."

She scowled at him. Rhett knew too much. She wondered where he had learned all he knew about women. It wasn't decent.

Why not try marrying a fine young man who has a bad reputation and a way with women? It'll be fun.

"Don't frown. Name the day, Scarlett. I'm not urging instant matrimony because of your reputation. We'll wait the decent interval. By the way, just how long is a 'decent interval'?"

"I haven't said I'd marry you. It isn't decent to even talk of such things at such a time."

"I've told you why I'm talking of them. I'm going away tomorrow and I'm too ardent a lover to restrain my passion any longer. But perhaps I've been too precipitate in my wooing."

With a suddenness that startled her, he slid off the sofa onto his knees and with one hand placed delicately over his heart, he recited rapidly:

"Forgive me for startling you with the impetuosity of my sentiments, my dear Scarlett—I mean, my dear Mrs. Kennedy. It cannot have escaped your notice that for some time past the friendship I have had in my heart for you has ripened into a deeper feeling, a feeling more beautiful, more pure, more sacred. Dare I name it you? Ah! It is love which makes me so bold!"

"Do get up," she entreated. "You look such a fool and suppose Mammy should come in and see you?"

EVELYN WAUGH
LETTER TO LAURA HERBERT, 1936

With novels such as *Decline and Fall* and *Scoop*, British author Evelyn Waugh (1903–1966) established himself in the 1930s as a journalist, satirical novelist, and trenchant social commentator. The longer work *Brideshead Revisited*, which he published in 1945, was more solemn and earned him even greater respect, fame, and, eventually, pay. Having converted to Catholicism, he was still awaiting the grant of an annulment of his first marriage when he wrote this wonderful letter of proposal. Laura Herbert was nineteen at the time, and Waugh was thirty-two. They remained married until his death.

Waugh's marriage to Laura's cousin, Evelyn Gardner (yes, Evelyn and Evelyn), had ended with the revelation that she had been having an affair. The annulment was necessary (and eventually granted) under the rules of the Catholic Church. "Wop" is a derogatory term for an Italian.

Tell you what you might do while you are alone at Pixton. You might think about me a bit & whether, if those wop priests ever come to a decent decision, you could bear the idea of marrying me. Of course you haven't got to decide, but think about it. I can't advise you in my favour because I think it would be beastly for you, but think how nice it would be for me. I am restless & moody and misanthropic & lazy & have no money except what I earn and if I got ill you would starve. In fact it's a lousy proposition. On the other hand I think I could reform & become quite strict about not getting drunk and I am pretty sure I should be faithful. Also there is always a fair chance that there will be another bigger economic crash in which case if you had married a nobleman with a great house you might find yourself starving, while I am very clever and could probably earn a living of some sort somewhere. Also though you would be taking on an elderly buffer, I am one without fixed habits. You wouldn't find yourself confined to any particular place or group. Also I have practically no living relatives except one brother whom I scarcely know. You would not find yourself involved in a large family & all their rows & you would not be patronized & interfered with by odious sisters-in-law & aunts as often happens. All these are very small advantages compared with the awfulness of my character. I have always tried to be nice to you and you may have got it into your head that I am nice really, but that is all rot. It is only to you & for you. I am jealous & impatient—but there is no point in going into a whole list of my vices. You are a critical girl and I've no doubt that you know them all and a great many I don't know myself. But the point I wanted to make is that if you marry most people, you are marrying a great number of objects & other people as well, well if you marry me there is nothing else involved, and that is an advantage as well as a disadvantage. My only tie of any kind is my work. That means that for several months each year we shall have to separate or you would have to share some very lonely place with me. But apart from that we could do what we liked and go where we liked—and if you married a soldier or stockbroker or member of parliament or master of hounds you would be more tied. When I tell my friends that I am in love with a girl of 19 they look shocked and say "wretched child" but I don't look on you as very young even in your beauty and I don't think there is any sense in the line that you cannot possibly commit yourself to a decision that affects your whole life for years yet. But anyway there is no point in your deciding or even answering. I may never get free of your cousin Evelyn. Above all things, darling, don't fret at all. But just turn the matter over in your dear head.

BILLY WILDER AND I. A. L. DIAMOND
SOME LIKE IT HOT, 1959

One of the best filmmakers of the twentieth century, Billy Wilder (1906–2002) had already collaborated with I. A. L. Diamond (1920–1988) on *Love in the Afternoon* when they teamed up again—as cowriters, with Wilder as director—for *Some Like It Hot*. In addition to showcasing a transcendent Marilyn Monroe, the film offered the bonus of Tony Curtis and Jack Lemmon dressing in drag to join an all-girl band and escape Prohibition-era mobsters. In the scene below, Jerry (played by Lemmon) has just returned from a night with millionaire Osgood Fielding III (Joe E. Brown) and has been improbably but unforgettably swept away.

Some Like It Hot was loosely adapted from a French film called *Fanfare d'Amour*. Wilder and Diamond remained screenwriting partners for thirty years, until Diamond's death. As writer/director, especially early in his career, Wilder had many hits, including *Double Indemnity*, *The Lost Weekend*, *Sunset Boulevard*, and *Sabrina*. Beinstock is the manager of the band that Joe and Jerry have joined.

(Jerry, still in his evening gown, is stretched out on his bed, gaily singing LA CUMPARSITA and accompanying himself with a pair of maracas. Joe appears over the railing of the balcony, steps through the window into the room.)

JOE:	*(Exuberant)* Hi, Jerry. Everything under control?
JERRY:	Have I got things to tell you!
JOE:	What happened?
JERRY:	*(Beaming)* I'm engaged.
JOE:	Congratulations. Who's the lucky girl?
JERRY:	I am.
JOE:	WHAT?

JERRY:	*(Brimming over)* Osgood proposed to me. We're planning a June wedding.
JOE:	What are you talking about? You can't marry Osgood.
JERRY:	*(Getting up)* You think he's too old for me?
JOE:	Jerry! You can't be serious!
JERRY:	Why not? He keeps marrying girls all the time!
JOE:	But you're not a girl. You're a guy! And why would a guy want to marry a guy?
JERRY:	Security.
JOE:	Jerry, you better lie down. You're not doing well.
JERRY:	Look, stop treating me like a child. I'm not stupid. I know there's a problem.
JOE:	I'll say there is!
JERRY:	His mother—we need her approval. But I'm not worried—because I don't smoke.
JOE:	Jerry—there's another problem.
JERRY:	Like what?
JOE:	Like what are you going to do on your honeymoon?
JERRY:	We've been discussing that. He wants to go to the Riviera—but I kind of lean towards Niagara Falls.
JOE:	Jerry, you're out of your mind! How are you going to get away with this?
JERRY:	I don't expect it to last, Joe. I'll tell him the truth when the time comes.
JOE:	Like when?
JERRY:	Like right after the ceremony.
JOE:	Oh.
JERRY:	Then we get a quick annulment—he makes a nice settlement on me—and I keep getting those alimony checks every month.
JOE:	Jerry,
JERRY:	Olé!
JOE:	Jerry, Jerry listen to me, listen to me—there are laws—conventions—it's just not being done!
JERRY:	Shh! Joe!—this may be my last chance to marry a millionaire!
JOE:	Jerry, Jerry—will you take my advice—forget about the whole thing, will ya?—just keep telling yourself you're a boy. You're a boy.
JERRY:	I'm a boy—
JOE:	That's the boy.
JERRY:	I'm a boy—I'm a boy—I wish I were dead—I'm a boy—*(slaps his wig down on the desk)*. Boy oh boy am I a boy. Now, what am I going to do about my engagement present?

JOE: What engagement present?

(Jerry picks up a jewel box, opens it, hands it to Joe.)

JERRY: Osgood gave me a bracelet.

(Joe takes Beinstock's glasses out of his pocket, examines the bracelet through one of the lenses.)

JOE: Hey—these are real diamonds.

JERRY: Of course they're real. What do you think, my fiancé is a bum?

Joe E. Brown and Jack Lemmon

RICHARD CURTIS
FOUR WEDDINGS AND A FUNERAL, 1994

After decades as a successful British TV writer (*Blackadder, Mr. Bean*), Richard Curtis (1956–) made the jump to film, writing the hugely successful romantic comedy *Four Weddings and a Funeral.* In this scene, the somewhat shaggy, self-deprecating, and smitten Charles (played by Hugh Grant) tries and fails to make his case to his beloved—but already engaged—Carrie (played by Andie MacDowell).

The "recent shopping excursion" was for Carrie's wedding gown. *The Partridge Family* was a popular American sitcom in the seventies about a mother and children who form a rock band.

CHARLES: Um, Look. Sorry, sorry. I just, um—well, this is a really stupid question and, particularly in view of our recent shopping excursion, but, eh, I just wondered if by any chance, um, eh, I mean obviously not, because I am just some git who's only slept with nine people. But I, I just wondered, eh, I really feel, um, eh—in short, to recap in a slightly clearer version, eh, in the words of David Cassidy, in fact, um, while he was still with the Partridge Family, eh, "I think I love you." And, eh—I just wondered whether by any chance you wouldn't like to—Um, eh, ah—No. No. No, of course not. I'm an idiot. He's not. Excellent. Excellent. Fantastic. Lovely to see you. Sorry to disturb. Better get on—Fuck!

CARRIE: That was very romantic.

CHARLES: Well, I thought it over a lot, you know. I wanted to get it just right.

STEPHEN LILLEY
"HOW TO PROPOSE ON THE YANKEE STADIUM BIG SCREEN," 2011

More than a hundred years after Mary Wilkinson Mount (see page 350) warned men not to be careless about how they proposed, the combination of YouTube videos gone viral and reality TV shows like *The Bachelor* had made a simple ring and question far too simple for some. An article in the *Omaha World Herald* noted that recent proposals had included staging a fake arrest for murder and a production number in an IKEA store. And for the truly public proposal—

1.   Call guest services at Yankee Stadium at 718-579-4464.

2.   Inform the customer service representative you speak with that you will be proposing

at Yankee Stadium. Provide them with the exact date of the game you will be attending where the proposal will take place. You will also need to provide the first and last name of the person you will be proposing to.

3.   Pay the $10 special message fee by credit card over the phone (for a message appearing on the center field scoreboard). Once paid, you will be informed of exactly when your message will appear on the big screen. Watch the scoreboard during that inning for your message to appear and be prepared to propose when it does.

4.   Pay the $100.00 message fee by credit card over the phone (for a message appearing on the Zales Fan marquee in right-center field). If you are paying by check, that check must be made out to "New York Yankees Foundation." Once paid, you will be informed of exactly when your message will appear on the fan marquee. Watch the scoreboard during that inning for your message to appear and be prepared to propose when it does.

Inform the customer service representative you speak with that you will be proposing at Yankee Stadium.

SARAH PEASE
"THE PROPOSAL PLANNER," *BRILLIANT EVENT PLANNING* WEBSITE, 2013

Even the sports-arena approach had paled for some, and thus the business of engagement planning was born. In New York City, Brilliant Event Planning not only offered services for wedding planning but for proposal planning as well, and owner Sarah Pease, a former banking executive, gave a few examples and a few free tips on the company's website. The charges were $500 for a first consultation and up to $50,000 for a top-of-the-line proposal.

Before you get down on one knee, here are five important facts about marriage proposals that you should know.

Fact 1:   75% of women are disappointed with their marriage proposal story.

Fact 2:   Less than 10% of women say that they'd like to be proposed to at a sporting event.

Fact 3:   More than 75% of women agree that the "surprise factor" is important in a marriage proposal.

Fact 4:   The first thing everyone asks when you're engaged—"How did he propose?"

Fact 5:   Sarah Pease, The Proposal Planner™ is proud to have a 100% marriage proposal success rate!

Our marriage proposal planning process focuses on three major areas: design, organization and coordination. Using this approach, we're able to incorporate the unique elements of your history together with the logistical aspects involved with pulling off such an important surprise!

AN EXAMPLE FROM THE WEBSITE

Parvinder wanted a thoughtful and fun proposal, so that's exactly what we planned for him! He told Luvleen that they were part of a scavenger hunt competition with other couples, but what she didn't know was that all of the stops on the scavenger hunt were actually places of significance to them. Their first stop was the Museum of Natural History followed by stops at various other special NYC locations. In addition to going to these memorable spots, there were gifts at each stop on the scavenger hunt that reminded her of their relationship. The last "task" separated the couple, which gave Parvinder a chance to meet us at a private rooftop. When Luvleen finally arrived at the rooftop, she was greeted by a sea of rose petals in vibrant hues, a candlelit tree, tons of votive candles and, because she loves Bollywood, music from the most romantic part of her favorite movie was playing in the background. Parvinder then read her a letter he wrote and proposed! After she said yes they enjoyed a party with their closest friends and family on the rooftop. Congratulations, Parvinder and Luvleen!

QUALMS

HEINRICH HEINE
THOUGHTS AND FANCIES, 19TH CENTURY

Author Heinrich Heine (1797–1856) converted from Judaism to Protestantism in the hopes of pursuing an academic career (then forbidden to Jews in Germany). Later, he married Crescence Eugénie Mirat in a Catholic church but, rumors to the contrary, did not convert again.

The music at a marriage procession always reminds me of the music of soldiers entering on a battle.

VIRGINIA CARY HUDSON
O YE JIGS & JULIPS!, 1904

Virginia Cary Hudson (1894–1954) was just ten when she wrote a number of essays describing life in her hometown of Versailles, Kentucky. Several years after her death, the essays were published in several small volumes, the first of which, quoted here, sold more than a million copies.

I guess walking slow getting married is because it gives you time to maybe change your mind.

THE UNHAPPY FOOL AND THE "BINTEL BRIEF" EDITOR
THE JEWISH DAILY FORWARD, 1908

A celebrated feature in the *Jewish Daily Forward*, "A Bintel Brief" (literally "a bundle of letters") was an advice column, written in Yiddish, answering the queries of recent Jewish immigrants.

Dear Editor,

I ask you to give me some advice in my situation.

I am a young man of twenty-five, sixteen years in America, and I recently met a fine girl. She has a flaw, however, that keeps me from marrying her. The fault is that she has a dimple in her chin, and it is said that people who have this lose their first husband or wife.

At first I laughed at the idea, but later it began to bother me. I began to observe people with dimpled chins and found out that their first husbands or wives had really died prematurely. I got so interested in this that whenever I see someone with this defect I ask about it immediately, and I find out that some of the men have lost their first wives, and some of the women's first husbands are dead.

This upset me so that I don't know what to do. I can't leave my sweetheart. I love her very much. But I'm afraid to marry her lest I die because of the dimple. I've questioned many people. Some say it's true, others laugh at the idea.

Perhaps you, too, will laugh at me for being such a fool and believing such nonsense, but I cannot rest until I hear your opinion about it. I want to add that my sweetheart knows nothing about this.

Respectfully,

The Unhappy Fool

ANSWER:

The tragedy is not that the girl has a dimple in her chin but that some people have a screw loose in their heads! One would need the knowledge of a genius to explain how a dimple in the chin could drive a husband or wife to the grave. Does the angel of death sit hiding in the dimple? It seems to us that it is a beauty spot, and we never imagined it could house the Devil!

It's tragic humor to find such superstition in the world today. It's truly shameful that a young man who was brought up in America should ask such questions. To calm him, we wish to tell him we know many people with such dimples who have not lost their first husbands or wives, but live out their years together in great happiness.

FRANZ KAFKA
DIARY, 1913

The diaries of the Prague-born writer Franz Kafka (1883–1924) reflect the troubled personal life of the man who made literary history with the novella *The Metamorphosis* and the novel *The Trial*. Rejected by parents who disapproved of his unremunerative vocation, Kafka suffered through failed relationships, demanding office jobs, and poor health. As he wrote the passage below, he was contemplating marriage to Felice Bauer ("F." in his diary), to whom he was engaged twice before they split for good in 1917. He never married.

Neither Gustave Flaubert nor Franz Grillparzer—both of whom were of great literary and personal interest to Kafka—ever married, though both had lengthy relationships with women. Author Max Brod, Kafka's closest friend, got married the same year Kafka wrote this journal entry.

SUMMARY OF ALL THE ARGUMENTS FOR AND AGAINST MY MARRIAGE

1. Inability to endure life alone, which does not imply inability to live, quite the contrary, it is even improbable that I know how to live with anyone, but I am incapable, alone, of bearing the assault of my own life, the demands of my own person, the attacks of time and old age, the vague pressure of the desire to write, sleeplessness, the nearness of insanity—I cannot bear all this alone. I naturally add a "perhaps" to this. The connection with F. will give my existence more strength to resist.

2. Everything immediately gives me pause. Every joke in the comic paper, what I remember about Flaubert and Grillparzer, the sight of the nightshirts on my parents' beds, laid out for the night, Max's marriage. Yesterday my sister said, "All the married people (that we know) are happy, I don't understand it," this remark too gave me pause, I became afraid again.

3. I must be alone a great deal. What I accomplished was only the result of being alone.

4. I hate everything that does not relate to literature, conversations bore me (even if they relate to literature), to visit people bores me, the sorrows and joys of my relatives bore me to my soul. Conversations take the importance, the seriousness, the truth out of everything I think.

5. The fear of the connection, of passing into the other. Then I'll never be alone again.

6. In the past, especially, the person I am in the company of my sisters has been entirely different from the person I am in the company of other people. Fearless, powerful, surprising, moved as I otherwise am only when I write. If through the intermediation of my wife I could be like that in the presence of everyone! But then would it not be at the expense of my writing? Not that, not that!

7. Alone, I could perhaps some day really give up my job. Married, it will never be possible.

AMELIA EARHART
LETTER TO GEORGE PUTNAM, 1931

If this letter from aviatrix Amelia Earhart (1897–1937) to publisher George Palmer Putnam just before their wedding clearly expressed her qualms, it didn't change his determination. He had already proposed to Earhart five times before. Eventually Putnam would call this letter "brutal in its frankness but beautiful in its honesty." And when asked why he had let Earhart fly solo across the Atlantic the first time, he wrote in *Redbook* magazine: "When the person who happens to be my wife wants very much to do something, she doesn't have to get my permission— her husband's royal sanction—any more than I have to get her permission if I want to fly down to Washington or take a lady to lunch." They were still married six years later, when her plane disappeared over the Pacific Ocean.

Dear GPP,

There are some things which should be writ before we are married—things we have talked over before—most of them.

You must know again my reluctance to marry, my feeling that I shatter thereby chances in work which means most to me. I feel the move just now as foolish as anything I could do. I know there may be compensations but have no heart to look ahead.

On our life together I want you to understand I shall not hold you to any [medieval] code of faithfulness to me nor shall I consider myself bound to you similarly. If we can be honest I think the difficulties which arise may best be avoided should you or I become interested deeply (or in passing) in anyone else.

Please let us not interfere with each others' work or play, nor let the world see our private joys or disagreements. In this connection I may have to keep some place where I can go to be myself, now and then, for I cannot guarantee to endure at all times the confinement of even an attractive cage.

I must exact a cruel promise, and this is that you will let me go in a year if we find no happiness together.

I will try to do my best in every way and give you that part of me you know and seem to want.

A. E.

STEPHEN SONDHEIM
"GETTING MARRIED TODAY," 1970

For more than sixty years, Stephen Sondheim (1940–) has been an unrivaled force in the world of musical theater, writing some of its most brilliant songs, sparking some of its most passionate debates, and winning all of its most coveted awards. Quite a number of his greatest lyrics have been about marriage, and choosing among them for this book was a challenge. This song is from the musical *Company* and features a panic-stricken would-be bride, Amy, singing about her clueless would-be groom, Paul, while an imperturbable choir girl with a church-ready soprano voice brings a sense of occasion to the hysteria.

AMY

Pardon me, is everybody there?
Because if everybody's there,
I want to thank you all for coming to the wedding.
I'd appreciate your going even more,
I mean, you must have lots of better things to do,
And not a word of it to Paul.
Remember Paul? You know, the man I'm gonna marry,
But I'm not, because I wouldn't ruin
Anyone as wonderful as he is—

But I thank you all
For the gifts and the flowers.
Thank you all,
Now it's back to the showers.
Don't tell Paul,
But I'm not getting married today.

CHURCH LADY

Bless this day, tragedy of life,
Husband yoked to wife.
The heart sinks down and feels dead
This dreadful day.

AMY

Listen, everybody.

Look, I don't know what you're waiting for.

A wedding, what's a wedding?

It's a prehistoric ritual

Where everybody promises fidelity forever,

Which is maybe the most horrifying word I ever heard,

And which is followed by a honeymoon

Where suddenly he'll realize

He's saddled with a nut

And want to kill me, which he should.

So listen,

Thanks a bunch,

But I'm not getting married.

Go have lunch,

'Cause I'm not getting married.

You've been grand,

But I'm not getting married.

Don't just stand

There, I'm not getting married!

And don't tell Paul,

But I'm not getting married today.

Go!

Can't you go?

Why is no-

Body listening?

Goodbye!

Go and cry

At another person's wake.

If you're quick,

For a kick

You could pick

Up a christening,

But please,
On my knees,
There's a human life at stake!

Listen, everybody, I'm afraid you didn't hear,
Or do you want to see a crazy lady
Fall apart in front of you?
It isn't only Paul who may be ruining his life, you know,
We'll both of us be losing our identities—
I telephoned my analyst about it
And he said to see him Monday,
But by Monday I'll be floating
In the Hudson with the other garbage.

It's a prehistoric ritual,

Where everybody promises fidelity forever,

Which is maybe the most horrifying word I ever heard.

I'm not well,
So I'm not getting married.
You've been swell,
But I'm not getting married.
Clear the hall,
'Cause I'm not getting married.
Thank you all,
But I'm not getting married.
And don't tell Paul,
But I'm not getting married today!

JENNIFER GAUVAIN
"THE SHOCKING TRUTH FOR THIRTY PERCENT
OF DIVORCED WOMEN," 2011

Jennifer Gauvain (1972–), a licensed clinical social worker, sent out a survey and based her article on nearly a thousand responses. This column ran on the *Huffington Post*'s divorce page. Gauvain is the coauthor, with Anne Milford, of the book *How Not to Marry the Wrong Guy*.

Amid a chorus of critics who shout "hindsight bias" or "selective memory," I stand firm. If you take 10 divorced women and ask them whether they believed on their wedding day that they were marrying the right guy for the right reasons, seven of them would say yes and three will confess they had serious doubts *long before walking down the aisle*. That's the shocking truth for 30 percent of divorced women.

These women have very clear, distinct memories of the doubts, issues and concerns that existed in the relationship all along. They can also tell you exactly what they were feeling before they walked down the aisle. For example:

I was avoiding my dad's eyes as I waited with him at the end of the aisle. I did not want to hear any "pearls of wisdom." Instead I paid attention to the photographer. I simply could not look at my dad because I knew I was making a mistake.

I felt like I was dying a thousand deaths. I just wanted to get the whole thing over with.

By the time they made it to the ceremony, they felt it was too late to turn back. While their insides told them to run, their outsides marched down the aisle. They saw problems and ignored them. However, every single one of them put the blame for ignoring the problems and issues squarely on their own shoulders. The problem is not that their fiancé was a bad guy—*the problem was that they ignored the problems!*

Why would smart women do this? They cited many of the same reasons:

- Age: The self-imposed biological clock is starting to tick a little louder.
- "Marriage will instantly make the relationship better."
- "It's my last chance to get married and no one else will come along."
- "If it doesn't work out I can always get a divorce."

You can be critical, point your finger and shake your head. Judgment aside, "these women" are your sisters, daughters, and friends. Maybe even you. Their common—yet misguided—

belief is that they are better off with the wrong guy than being alone. It doesn't matter how self-actualized, independent or liberal-minded they are.

So what's the answer? When in doubt, don't!

JUSTIN LAVNER, BENJAMIN KARNEY, THOMAS BRADBURY "DO COLD FEET WARN OF TROUBLE AHEAD?," 2012

The *Oxford English Dictionary* dates the term "cold feet" to an 1893 Stephen Crane novel, also offering earlier synonyms, among them "sheepness" (which has nothing to do with farming) and "arghness" (which has nothing to do with pirates). By whatever name, apprehension before marriage is a phenomenon often noted but, until recently, never scientifically studied. In 2012, psychologists at UCLA published the results of their investigation into the relationship between pre-wedding jitters and post-wedding woes. This was the abstract for their report.

Are the doubts that people feel before marriage signs of impending difficulties or normative experiences that can be safely ignored? To test these opposing views, we asked 464 recently married spouses whether they had ever been uncertain about getting married and then compared 4-year divorce rates and marital satisfaction trajectories among those partners with and without premarital doubts. Doubts were reported by at least one partner in two-thirds of couples. Women with premarital doubts had significantly higher four-year divorce rates, even when controlling for concurrent marital satisfaction, the difficulty of their engagement, history of parental divorce, premarital cohabitation, and neuroticism. Among intact couples, men's and women's doubts predicted less satisfied marital trajectories. Premarital doubts appear to be common but not benign, suggesting that valid precursors of marital distress are evident during couples' engagements.

Doubts were reported by at least one partner in two-thirds of couples.

RINGS

COLLEY CIBBER
THE DOUBLE GALLANT; OR, THE SICK LADY'S CURE, 1707

A British actor, playwright, and theater manager, Colley Cibber (1671–1757) was renowned for playing popular foppish roles, writing widely derided poetry, and stitching together plays from any number of other sources.

In 1743, Cibber became the main character in Alexander Pope's *The Dunciad.*

Oh, how many torments lie in the small circle of a wedding-ring.

PROVERB

As your wedding-ring wears, your cares will wear away.

BENJAMIN FRANKLIN
"RULES AND MAXIMS FOR PROMOTING MATRIMONIAL HAPPINESS," 1730

Author, printer, inventor, and Founding Father Benjamin Franklin (1706–1790) wrote the article from which these lines were taken when he was a just-married twenty-four-year-old. It was subsequently, frequently, and anonymously reprinted by various British and American publications for many years.

For more Franklin, see also When, page 466; Why, page 477.

Always wear your wedding ring, for therein lies more virtue than usually is imagined. If you are ruffled unawares, assaulted with improper thoughts, or tempted in any kind against your duty, cast your eyes upon it, and call to mind, who gave it you, where it was received, and what passed at that solemn time.

ROBERT KEMP PHILP
ENQUIRE WITHIN UPON EVERYTHING, 1856

With the heading "Love's Telegraph," this was fact number 2,032 of 3,031 in the most popular of the many reference books compiled by Robert Kemp Philp (1819–1882). Other topics ranged from ringworm and the hyphen to baked eels and the management of blackbirds.

Between 1856 and 1888, *Enquire Within* sold more than a million copies.

If a gentleman wants a wife, he wears a ring on the *first* finger of the left hand; if he is engaged, he wears it on the *second* finger; if married, on the *third*; and on the fourth, if he never intends to be married. When a lady is not engaged, she wears a hoop or diamond on her *first* finger; if engaged, on the *second*; if married, on the *third*; and on the fourth, if she intends to die a maid.

A JEWELER
"MEN'S MARRIAGE RINGS," 1889

The "lady" described in this letter to the editor of the *St. Louis Globe-Democrat* was at least half a century ahead of her time. According to social historian Vicki Howard, an attempt on the part of U.S. jewelers and retailers had been organized in the 1920s to push the idea of a male engagement ring. While that never took, a 1940s effort capitalized on the sentimentality of the war and postwar years, and, spurred by print ads, newsreels, and movies, Americans began to see men's wedding rings as the norm, not the exception.

A lady came into our store the other day and asked whether we carried in stock "rings for married men." The question surprised me, and the lady continued: "Is there nothing in the line of rings for gentlemen to wear that would indicate that they are married? If not, there ought to be. As soon as a lady is married custom requires that she wear a ring of prescribed form, which is in the nature of a badge. It signifies 'hands off,' or 'taken.' A man is not required to wear any such insignia of his estate. If they did, perhaps there would not be so many wounded hearts lying around. When a gentleman approached a lady she could readily determine whether or not he is in or out of the matrimonial market and demean herself accordingly. Such a custom would put an end to the male married flirt in society, who has a wife who is rarely heard of."

HARRIET LANE
THE BOOK OF CULTURE, 1922

Though the De Beers company, with its virtual monopoly on the world's diamonds, is often blamed (or credited) with making the diamond engagement ring seem a necessity before marriage in the late 1930s, the Sears, Roebuck catalogue had offered them as far back as the late nineteenth century. But in this 1922 manual of etiquette, it was clear that they were not yet the only acceptable choice.

R

With regard to the engagement ring, finest and most considerate courtesy demands that the suitor consult the girl's taste and not his own in its selection. He may, however, buy the ring without consulting her if he sees fit. All precious stones have their meanings: the diamond, which symbolizes purity and perfection, is a most graceful tribute to the bride-to-be; and so is the sapphire, the blue stone of perfect faith and trustfulness. The ruby is a token of the giver's passion, his ardent love for the one to whom it is given; but pearls, emblems of tears, and the opal, the stone of ill luck, are to be avoided.

WILLIAM MANCHESTER
THE DEATH OF A PRESIDENT, 1967

Author of a favorable 1964 book about John F. Kennedy's first year and a half in office, historian William Manchester (1922–2004) was commissioned by the president's widow and brother Robert to pen the official account of the assassination. Tracing the paths of Lee Harvey Oswald and Kennedy before the shooting, Manchester re-created the events of November 22, 1963, in dramatic detail, including this moment in the emergency room at Parkland Memorial Hospital.

Despite objections from the Kennedy camp before publication, and continuing controversy about accuracy afterwards, the book became Manchester's bestselling work. Vernon O'Neal (Manchester had it as "Oneal") was the funeral director who came to the hospital. He said later that he, and not an orderly, had been the one to place Jackie's ring on JFK's finger. Patrick was the Kennedy son who had died within days of being born. Kenny O'Donnell was White House appointments secretary, had organized the Dallas visit, and was in the motorcade, directly behind the president's car, when the shooting took place. Sergeant Robert Dugger was the ranking police officer at the hospital.

[Mrs. Kennedy] was right behind Oneal. Crossing the passage, she continued to ponder what she could put with the President, and she had the odd feeling of reliving a moment in her own past. She remembered: it had been at her father's funeral. That had been the first time she had seen anyone dead, and she had been heartbroken. That day she had been wearing a bracelet; it was a graduation present from him. He had been so proud of her the day he had given it to her, and standing by his coffin she had unfastened it on impulse and placed it in his hand. She wanted to do the same thing now. But what could it be? Until this summer he had carried a St. Christopher medal, fashioned as a bill clip. She had given it to him when they were married, and it would have been appropriate now. It wasn't here, however. They had put it in the little coffin with Patrick. Afterward the President had asked her for another one, so on their tenth wedding anniversary, when he had presented her with a slim ring set with green emerald chips, she had given him a medal of gold. It would be here in his billfold; Kenny or one of the nurses could find it. Then she changed her mind. The new St. Christopher's, she decided, would be wrong. It was only two months old. It hadn't been with him long enough to be really a part of him. Besides, it was his, not hers. It already belonged to him. It couldn't be a gift twice.

Suddenly she thought of her wedding ring. Nothing had ever meant so much to her. Its very plainness made it dear. Unlike the circlet set with emeralds, it was unadorned. It was, in fact, a man's wedding band. The President had bought it in a hurry in Newport just before their wedding. There hadn't even been time to put the date in; she had taken it to a jeweler and had that done later. The ring would be exactly right—provided she could get it off. She attempted to unfasten the left glove and couldn't even work the snap.

They were inside the room now. Apart from the disinfectant and the blistering artificial light overhead, the place was much altered; it was nearly immaculate and almost empty. The audience of a half-hour ago had dispersed. Oneal was there, leaning over his burnished coffin, adjusting it on its truck. O'Donnell stood in the doorway. Sergeant Dugger had followed her across the threshold. He looked competent, and drawing herself up she held her wrist toward him. He understood. He found the snap with his thumbnail and unpeeled the glove.

She moved to the President's side and lifted his hand. An orderly succeeded in working the ring over Kennedy's knuckle with cream, and she looked down tenderly. She yearned to be alone with him. If only these people would go away. They would never leave her, of course; she knew that. They would be frightened for her and of what she might do, terrified of unspoken and nameless perils. To ask them would only upset them, so she withdrew in silence. In the passage she asked Ken, "The ring. Did I do the right thing?"

He said, "You leave it right where it is."

DEBRA WINGER
ESQUIRE INTERVIEW, 1986

Talented, temperamental, Method-driven, Oscar-nominated actress Debra Winger (1955–) married actor Timothy Hutton in 1986.

Winger and Hutton divorced in 1990; she has been married to director Arliss Howard since 1996.

I will say, candidly, that the sexiest thing in the world is to be totally naked with your wedding band on.

R

SECOND MARRIAGES

YIDDISH PROVERB

When two divorced people marry, four people get into bed.

WILLIAM PAINTER
"MARRIAGE OF WIDOW AND WIDOWER," 1566

For the three volumes that eventually comprised *The Palace of Pleasure*, William Painter (circa 1540–1594) translated and anthologized stories from Italy and France that became the basis for numerous Elizabethan plays, including several of Shakespeare's. In his tale of a man who had been married twenty times and a woman twenty-two, Painter questioned whether even twice was one time too many.

I woulde wishe all my frendes that be widowes, to folow the noble Romaine matrone and widowe called Annia, who (when her frendes and familiers exhorted her to marie againe, because She was yong and beautifull) aunswered that she would not. "For," quoth she, "if it be my fortune to have a good husband, as I had before, I shall still be afraied, lest death should take him away: but if it be my chaunce to matche with one that is evill, howe can I be able quietly to beare that, having had so good a husbande before." Declaringe thereby, that being ones well matched, great heede ought to be taken, how to chose the nexte, leaste in making hastie choise, leasure for repentaunce should follow.

NOËL COWARD
PRIVATE LIVES, 1930

Sir Noël Coward (1899–1973) was a playwright, actor, director, songwriter, and filmmaker, known in every sphere for his worldly wit. In *Private Lives*, one of his best-known comedies, he introduces us to Elyot and Amanda, a divorced couple each of whom happens to be honeymooning with a new spouse (Sibyl is Elyot's bride) in adjoining hotel rooms.

SIBYL:	Are you glad you married me?
ELYOT:	Of course I am.
SIBYL:	How glad?
ELYOT:	Incredibly, magnificently glad.
SIBYL:	How lovely.
ELYOT:	We ought to go in and dress.
SIBYL:	Gladder than before?
ELYOT:	Why do you keep harping on that?
SIBYL:	It's in my mind, and yours too, I expect.
ELYOT:	It isn't anything of the sort.
SIBYL:	She was pretty, wasn't she? Amanda?
ELYOT:	Very pretty.
SIBYL:	Prettier than I am?
ELYOT:	Much.
SIBYL:	Elyot!
ELYOT:	She was pretty and sleek, and her hands were long and slim, and her legs were long and slim, and she danced like an angel. You dance very poorly, by the way.
SIBYL:	Could she play the piano as well as I can?
ELYOT:	She couldn't play the piano at all.
SIBYL:	*(Triumphantly)* Aha! Had she my talent for organisation?
ELYOT:	No, but she hadn't your mother either.

SIBYL:	I don't believe you like mother.
ELYOT:	Like her! I can't bear her.
SIBYL:	Elyot! She's a darling, underneath.
ELYOT:	I never got underneath.
SIBYL:	It makes me unhappy to think you don't like mother.
ELYOT:	Nonsense. I believe the only reason you married me was to get away from her.
SIBYL:	I married you because I loved you.
ELYOT:	Oh dear, oh dear, oh dear, oh dear!
SIBYL:	I love you far more than Amanda loved you. I'd never make you miserable like she did.
ELYOT:	We made each other miserable.
SIBYL:	It was all her fault, you know it was.
ELYOT:	(With vehemence) Yes, it was. Entirely her fault.
SIBYL:	She was a fool to lose you.
ELYOT:	We lost each other.
SIBYL:	She lost you, with her violent tempers and carryings on.
ELYOT:	Will you stop talking about Amanda?
SIBYL:	But I'm very glad, because if she hadn't been uncontrolled, and wicked, and unfaithful, we shouldn't be here now.
ELYOT:	She wasn't unfaithful.
SIBYL:	How do you know? I bet she was. I bet she was unfaithful every five minutes.
ELYOT:	It would take a far more concentrated woman than Amanda to be unfaithful every five minutes.
SIBYL:	(Anxiously) You do hate her, don't you?
ELYOT:	No, I don't hate her. I think I despise her.
SIBYL:	(With satisfaction) That's much worse.
ELYOT:	And yet I'm sorry for her.
SIBYL:	Why?
ELYOT:	Because she's marked for tragedy; she's bound to make a mess of everything.
SIBYL:	If it's all her fault, I don't see that it matters much.
ELYOT:	She has some very good qualities.
SIBYL:	Considering what a hell she made of your life, I think you are very nice about her. Most men would be vindictive.
ELYOT:	What's the use of that? It's all over now, such a long time ago.
SIBYL:	Five years isn't very long.

S

ELYOT:	*(Seriously)* Yes it is.
SIBYL:	Do you think you could ever love her again?
ELYOT:	Now then, Sibyl.
SIBYL:	But could you?
ELYOT:	Of course not, I love you.
SIBYL:	Yes, but you love me differently; I know that.
ELYOT:	More wisely perhaps. . . .
SIBYL:	. . . I should think you needed a little quiet womanliness after Amanda.
ELYOT:	Why will you keep on talking about her?
SIBYL:	It's natural enough, isn't it?
ELYOT:	What do you want to find out?
SIBYL:	Why did you really let her divorce you?
ELYOT:	She divorced me for cruelty, and flagrant infidelity. I spent a whole week-end at Brighton with a lady called Vera Williams. She had the nastiest looking hair brush I have ever seen.
SIBYL:	Misplaced chivalry, I call it. Why didn't you divorce her?
ELYOT:	It would not have been the action of a gentleman, whatever that may mean.
SIBYL:	I think she got off very lightly.
ELYOT:	Once and for all will you stop talking about her.
SIBYL:	Yes, Elli dear.
ELYOT:	I don't wish to see her again or hear her name mentioned.
SIBYL:	Very well, darling.
ELYOT:	Is that understood?
SIBYL:	Yes, darling. Where did you spend your honeymoon?

S

DAPHNE DU MAURIER
REBECCA, 1938

British author Daphne du Maurier (1907–1989) is probably best known today for *Rebecca*, a Gothic novel told by a nameless heroine, essentially the tale of a second marriage haunted by the first. In this scene, the narrator waits while her fiancé, Maxim de Winter, breaks the news of their engagement to the woman with whom she has been traveling as a lady's companion. The narrator's reaction to seeing Rebecca's name is just a hint of things to come.

The ellipses are the author's.

The walls of the suite were thick, I could hear no hum of voices. I wondered what he was saying to her, how he phrased his words. Perhaps he said, "I fell in love with her, you know, the very first time we met. We've been seeing one another every day." And she in answer, "Why, Mr. de Winter, it's quite the most romantic thing I've ever heard." Romantic, that was the word I had tried to remember coming up in the lift. Yes, of course. Romantic. That was what people would say. It was all very sudden and romantic. They suddenly decided to get married and there it was. Such an adventure. I smiled to myself as I hugged my knees on the window seat, thinking how wonderful it was, how happy I was going to be. I was to marry the man I loved. I was to be Mrs. de Winter. It was foolish to go on having that pain in the pit of my stomach when I was so happy. Nerves of course. Waiting like this; the doctor's ante-room. It would have been better, after all, more natural surely to have gone into the sitting-room hand in hand, laughing, smiling at one another and for him to say: "We're going to be married, we're very much in love."

In love. He had not said anything yet about being in love. No time perhaps. It was all so hurried at the breakfast table. Marmalade, and coffee, and that tangerine. No time. The tangerine was very bitter. No, he had not said anything about being in love. Just that we would be married. Short and definite, very original. Original proposals were much better. More genuine. Not like other people. Not like younger men who talked nonsense probably, not meaning half they said. Not like younger men being very incoherent, very passionate, swearing impossibilities. Not like him the first time, asking Rebecca. . . . I must not think of that. Put it away. A thought forbidden, prompted by demons. Get thee behind me, Satan. I must never think about that, never, never, never. He loves me, he wants to show me Manderley. Would they ever have done with their talking, would they ever call me into the room?

There was the book of poems lying beside my bed. He had forgotten he had ever lent them to me. They could not mean much to him then. "Go on," whispered the demon, "open the title-page, that's what you want to do, isn't it? Open the title-page." Nonsense, I said, I'm only going to put the book with the rest of the things. I yawned, I wandered to the table beside the bed. I picked up the book. I caught my foot in the flex of the bedside lamp, and stumbled, the book falling from my hands on to the floor. It fell open, at the title-page. "Max from Rebecca." She was dead, and one must not have thoughts about the dead. They slept in peace, the grass blew over their graves. How alive was her writing though, how full of force. Those curious, sloping letters. The blob of ink. Done yesterday. It was just as if it had been written yesterday. I took my nail scissors from the dressing-case and cut the page, looking over my shoulder like a criminal.

I cut the page right out of the book. I left no jagged edges, and the book looked white and clean when the page was gone. A new book, that had not been touched. I tore the page up in many little fragments and threw them into the wastepaper basket. Then I went and sat on the window seat again. But I kept thinking of the torn scraps in the basket, and after a moment I had to get up and look in the basket once more. Even now the ink stood up on the fragments thick and black, the writing was not destroyed. I took a box of matches and set fire to the fragments. The flame had a lovely light, staining the paper, curling the edges, making the slanting writing impossible to distinguish. The fragments fluttered to grey ashes. The letter R was the last to go, it twisted in the flame, it curled outwards for a moment, becoming larger than ever. Then it crumpled too; the flame destroyed it. It was not ashes even, it was feathery dust. . . . I went and washed my hands in the basin. I felt better, much better. I had the clean, new feeling that one has when the calendar is hung on the wall at the beginning of the year. January the 1st. I was aware of the same freshness, the same gay confidence. The door opened and he came into the room.

PHILIP BARRY
THE PHILADELPHIA STORY, 1939

Philip Barry (1896–1949) wrote the play *The Philadelphia Story* expressly for Katharine Hepburn, and it was a great success, both on Broadway and, the following year, as a film also starring Cary Grant and Jimmy Stewart. The action takes place on the day before the intended wedding of the blue-blooded Tracy Lord to the up-and-comer George Kittredge. C. K. Dexter Haven, husband number one, has arrived just in time to throw a wrench into the works. Margaret, Tracy's mother, is more sanguine about the bad behavior of her own husband, Seth.

TRACY:	I'm not worried, Mother. The only trouble Mr. C. K. Dexter Haven ever gave me was when he married me.—*You* might say the same for one Seth Lord. If you'd just face it squarely as I did—
MARGARET:	That will do! I will allow none of you to criticise your father.
TRACY:	What are we expected to do when he treats you—
MARGARET:	Did you hear me, Tracy?
TRACY:	All right, I give up.
MARGARET:	And in view of this second attempt of yours, it might pay you to remind yourself that neither of us has proved to be a very great success as a wife.
TRACY:	We just picked the wrong first husbands, that's all.

JULIE CONNELLY
"THE CEO'S SECOND WIFE," *FORTUNE*, 1989

Julie Connelly was a senior editor at *Fortune* magazine when she reported on a marital pattern among powerful men that she linked to the growing acceptance of divorce in American society. Along the way, she coined a term that has since made its way into everyday use.

Powerful men are beginning to demand trophy wives. . . . The more money men make, the argument goes, the more self-assured they become, and the easier it is for them to think: I *deserve* a queen.

Enter the second wife: a decade or two younger than her husband, sometimes several inches taller, beautiful, and very often accomplished. The second wife certifies her husband's status and, if possible given the material she has to work with, dispels the notion that men peak sexually at age 18. This trophy does not hang on the wall like a moose head—she works. Hard.

SECRETS

WILLIAM SHAKESPEARE
JULIUS CAESAR, CIRCA 1599

The wife of Brutus, Portia sounds remarkably modern in her desire to know what is troubling her husband—and distinctly annoyed by the prospect of being excluded from his world. She inflicts her "voluntary wound" as she addresses him.

PORTIA: You have some sick offense within your mind,
Which, by the right and virtue of my place,
I ought to know of; and upon my knees
I charm you, by my once commended beauty,
By all your vows of love, and that great vow
Which did incorporate and make us one,
That you unfold to me, yourself, your half,

	Why you are heavy, and what men to-night
	Have had resort to you; for here have been
	Some six or seven, who did hide their faces
	Even from darkness.
BRUTUS:	Kneel not, gentle Portia.
PORTIA:	I should not need, if you were gentle Brutus.
	Within the bond of marriage, tell me, Brutus,
	Is it excepted I should know no secrets
	That appertain to you? Am I yourself
	But, as it were, in sort or limitation.
	To keep with you at meals, comfort your bed,
	And talk to you sometimes? Dwell I but in the suburbs
	Of your good pleasure? If it be no more,
	Portia is Brutus' harlot, not his wife.
BRUTUS:	You are my true and honorable wife,
	As dear to me as are the ruddy drops
	That visit my sad heart.
PORTIA:	If this were true, then should I know this secret.
	I grant I am a woman; but withal
	A woman that Lord Brutus took to wife.
	I grant I am a woman; but withal
	A woman well reputed, Cato's daughter.
	Think you I am no stronger than my sex,
	Being so father'd and so husbanded?
	Tell me your counsels, I will not disclose 'em.
	I have made strong proof of my constancy,
	Giving myself a voluntary wound
	Here, in the thigh; can I bear that with patience,
	And not my husband's secrets?
BRUTUS:	O ye gods!
	Render me worthy of this noble wife!

HEINRICH ZSCHOKKE
"THE EVENING BEFORE THE MARRIAGE," CIRCA 1830

Born in Germany but more closely associated with his adopted country of Switzerland, Johann Heinrich Daniel Zschokke (1771–1848) served in various political and educational posts, wrote novels and history, and edited the *Schweizerbote* (*Swiss Messenger*), a popular liberal weekly. He married a pastor's daughter named Anna Elisabeth Nüsperli in 1805. Together they had twelve sons and a daughter.

The short story from which the following excerpt is taken was translated into English and reprinted in the American magazine *The Ladies' Wreath*.

In the first solitary hour after the ceremony . . . promise each other, sincerely and solemnly, *never to have a secret from each other* under whatever pretext, with whatever excuse it may be. You must continually and every moment, see clearly into each other's bosom. Even when one of you has committed a fault, wait not an instant, but confess it freely—let it cost tears, but confess it. And as you keep *nothing secret from each other,* so, on the contrary, preserve the privacies of your house, marriage state and heart, from *father, mother, sister, brother, aunt, and all the world.* You two, with God's help, build your own quiet world.

COTESWORTH PINCKNEY
THE WEDDING GIFT, TO ALL WHO ARE ENTERING THE MARRIAGE STATE, 1848

The Rev. Charles Cotesworth Pinckney (see In-laws, page 225) was firm in his advice about the airing of marital grievances.

S

Should the fact of your having sought the advice of your friends become known to your husband, that mutual trust which must exist between you to render the married state a happy one, will be forever destroyed. Consider well, therefore, before you impart to a third party any disagreements that may take place in your home. Be rather solicitous to screen them from observation. The human heart is not generally hard, unless it is made so; beware, then, of tampering with it.

G. K. CHESTERTON
CHARLES DICKENS, 1906

Author of some eighty books, Gilbert Keith Chesterton (1874–1936) wrote social, political, and literary criticism, theology, poetry, novels, plays, biographies, and short stories. His book about Dickens was one of the first to rekindle an appreciation of the Victorian writer and his insights into the rich variety of average people. Dickens's great lesson, Chesterton wrote, was: "It is in our own daily life that we are to look for the portents and the prodigies."

Chesterton met his future wife, Frances Blogg, in 1896 and in his proposal letter two years later, described how he'd felt upon meeting her: "If I had anything to do with this girl I should go on my knees to her; if I spoke with her she would never deceive me; if I depended on her she would never deny me; if I loved her she would never play with me: if I trusted her she would never go back on me." They remained married until his death.

A man and a woman cannot live together without having against each other a kind of everlasting joke. Each has discovered that the other is a fool, but a great fool. This largeness, this grossness and gorgeousness of folly is the thing which we all find about those with whom we are in intimate contact; and it is the one enduring basis of affection, and even of respect. . . .

Many of us live publicly with featureless public puppets, images of the small public abstractions. It is when we pass our own private gate, and open our own secret door, that we step into the land of the giants.

MOHANDAS GANDHI
"QUESTION BOX," 1940

Mohandas Gandhi (1869–1948), who led the Indian fight for independence from Britain, was, among countless other things, an effective writer. Fairly late in his life, he founded the English weekly journal *Harijan*, which featured a column called "Question Box." This was his response to a husband who suspected his wife of keeping a secret.

I admit that between husband and wife there should be no secrets from one another. I have a very high opinion of the marriage tie. I hold that husband and wife merge in each other. They are one in two or two in one.

PAUL TOURNIER
THE MEANING OF PERSONS, 1954

The great insight of the Swiss doctor and writer Paul Tournier (1898–1986) sounds perfectly unremarkable today: that one could not know, let alone help heal, a person's body without understanding his or her psychological and spiritual health. In his medical and counseling practices, as in his many books and speeches, Tournier blended Christian theology, modern psychology, and traditional medical training in an attempt to understand the health of the whole person, including the extent to which honesty played a part in marriage.

The true dialogue is not that first easy communion, wonderful though it be—the impression one has of sharing the same feelings, saying the same things and thinking the same thoughts. The true dialogue is inevitably the confrontation of two personalities, differing in their past, their upbringing, their view of life, their prejudices, their idiosyncrasies and failings—and in any case with two distinct psychologies, a man's and a woman's. Sooner or later they will find out that they are less alike than they thought.

Either, one will dominate the other, and there will no longer be a dialogue because one of the persons is eclipsed, his power of self-determination paralysed. Or else the course of the dialogue will take it through some very dangerous waters. One of the partners will find himself saying to the other: "I can't understand why you are acting like this." And then there arises the risk of being judged or betrayed . . . And the temptation to run away from it by keeping back certain confidences. . . .

It is always a denial of love, and to some extent a disavowal of marriage, to begin to calculate what one says and does not say, even when it is done with the excellent motive of safeguarding one's love. It is a contradiction of the law of marriage instituted by God: "They are no more twain, but one flesh" (Matt. 19:6). . . .

But even in the happiest marriage personal contact cannot be a permanent state, acquired once and for all. The windows of our houses have to be cleaned from time to time if the light is to penetrate. They get dirty more quickly in the town, but there is no countryside so remote or so clean that they do not gradually lose their transparency. Between man and wife too, the true dialogue has periodically to be re-established by the confession of some secret; and the higher and more sincere our ideal of marriage, the more irksome it is to admit that we have hidden something.

S

SEPARATION

PLINY THE YOUNGER
LETTER TO CALPURNIA, CIRCA 2ND CENTURY

Roman author, administrator, and lawyer, Pliny the Younger (circa 61–circa 113) wrote hundreds of letters, eventually collected in ten volumes, that provided invaluable glimpses of life in the Roman Empire.

Scholars debate whether Calpurnia was Pliny's second or third wife, and whether this letter was a literary conceit or a legitimate expression of longing. In 1966, critic A. N. Sherwin-White wrote that it is one of three letters by Pliny that "blend together, for the first time in European literature, the role of husband and lover."

The eagerness of my desire to see you is incredible. Love is the first spring of it. The next ariseth from our having been so seldom separated. For these reasons, I pass a great part of the night in thinking of you. In the day too, at those hours, when I used to see you, my feet carry me spontaneously, in the strictest sense of the expression, to your apartment, from whence I constantly return as much out of humour, and dejected, as if I had been refused admittance into your chamber. There is one part of the day only, that affords relief to my misery; I mean the particular time, when I am employed in pleading causes for my friends. Just what a kind of life mine must be, when labour is my rest, and when perplexity and cares are my comfort. Adieu.

THE WIDOW OF EUNG-TAE YI
LETTER TO HER LATE HUSBAND, 1586

This letter was found in 1998 when archaeologists excavated the tomb of a thirty-one-year-old man named Eung-Tae Yi in Andong City, South Korea. Clothing, family letters, and a pair of sandals, woven from hemp and the widow's hair, were also found in the tomb.

You always said, "Dear, let's live together until our hair turns gray and die on the same day." How could you pass away without me? Who should I and our little boy listen to and how should we live? How could you go ahead of me?

How did you bring your heart to me and how did I bring my heart to you? Whenever we lay down together you always told me, "Dear, do other people cherish and love each other like we do? Are they really like us?" How could you leave all that behind and go ahead of me?

I just cannot live without you. I just want to go to you. Please take me to where you are. My feelings toward you I cannot forget in this world and my sorrow knows no limit. Where would I put my heart in now and how can I live with the child missing you?

Please look at this letter and tell me in detail in my dreams. Because I want to listen to your saying in detail in my dreams I write this letter and put it in. Look closely and talk to me.

When I give birth to the child in me, who should it call father? Can anyone fathom how I feel? There is no tragedy like this under the sky.

You are just in another place, and not in such a deep grief as I am. There is no limit and end that I write roughly. Please look closely at this letter and come to me in my dreams and show yourself in detail and tell me. I believe I can see you in my dreams. Come to me secretly and show yourself. There is no limit to what I want to say and I stop here.

NATHANIEL BRASSEY HALHED
A CODE OF GENTOO LAWS, 1781

Edited by Nathaniel Brassey Halhed (1751–1830) and published by the East India Company, *A Code of Gentoo Laws* was a British colonial attempt to create a canon of Hindu law. Based on Brahmin scholars' compilation of beliefs and practices from old Hindu texts, it included some ancient marriage customs—from thousands of years before Christ—that radically curtailed a wife's freedoms (including the right to divorce) and allowed polygamy. Not until 1955 did India's Hindu Marriage Act officially reverse these rules.

If a man goes on a journey, his wife shall not divert herself by play, nor shall see any public show, nor shall laugh, nor shall dress herself in jewels and fine clothes, nor shall see dancing, nor hear music, nor shall sit in the window, nor shall ride out, nor shall behold any thing choice or rare; but shall fasten well the house-door, and remain private; and shall not eat any dainty victuals, and shall not blacken her eyes with eye-powder, and shall not view her face in a mirror; she shall never exercise herself in any such agreeable employment during the absence of her husband.

ABIGAIL ADAMS
LETTER TO JOHN ADAMS, 1782

Few eighteenth-century American marriages are as vivid as that of John and Abigail Adams (1744–1818). Circumstances forced them to spend a great deal of time apart, and the letters they consequently wrote were wonderfully eloquent. The future president was in Paris, helping to negotiate the peace with England, when Abigail sent this one.

Portia was the Adamses' nickname for Abigail, a direct reference to Brutus's faithful wife (see Secrets, page 383). "No man liveth for himself" paraphrases Romans 14:7: "For none of us liveth to himself, and no man dieth to himself."

Look to the date of this Letter—and tell me, what are the thoughts which arise in your mind? Do you not recollect that Eighteen years have run their anual Circuit, since we pledged our mutual Faith to each other, and the Hymeneal torch was Lighted at the Alter of Love. Yet, yet it Burns with unabating fervour, old ocean has not Quenched it, nor old Time smootherd it, in the Bosom of Portia. It cheers her in the Lonely Hour, it comforts her even in the gloom which sometimes possesses her mind.

It is my Friend from the Remembrance of the joys I have lost that the arrow of affliction is pointed. I recollect the untitled Man to whom I gave my Heart, and in the agony of recollection when time and distance present themseves together, wish he had never been any other. Who shall give me back Time? Who shall compensate to me those *years* I cannot recall? How dearly have I paid for a titled Husband; should I wish you less wise, that I might enjoy more happiness? I cannot find that in my Heart. Yet providence has wisely placed the real Blessings of Life within the reach of moderate abilities, and he who is wiser than his Neighbour sees so much more to pitty and Lament, that I doubt whether the balance of happiness is in his Scale.

I feel a disposition to Quarrel with a race of Beings who have cut me of, in the midst of my days from the only Society I delighted in. Yet No Man liveth for himself, says an authority I will not dispute. Let me draw satisfaction from this Source and instead of murmuring and repineing at my Lot consider it in a more pleasing view. Let me suppose that the same Gracious Being who first smiled upon our union and Blessed us in each other, endowed my Friend with powers and talents for the Benifit of Mankind and gave him a willing mind, to improve them for the service of his Country.

ELIZABETH BARRETT BROWNING
SONNET 4, *SONNETS FROM THE PORTUGUESE*, CIRCA 1845

Most of the poems in *Sonnets from the Portuguese* (see Love, page 285) were written between 1845, the year Elizabeth Barrett met Robert Browning, and 1846, the year they married. A combination of ill health, depression over the deaths of several of her siblings, and increasing reticence kept Elizabeth more or less housebound, while Robert moved freely in society. The poem suggests how physical separation can threaten spiritual separation as well.

Thou hast thy calling to some palace floor,
Most gracious singer of high poems! where
The dancers will break footing from the care
Of watching up thy pregnant lips for more,
And dost thou lift this house's latch too poor
For hand of thine? and canst thou think and bear
To let thy music drop here unaware
In folds of golden fulness at my door?
Look up and see the casement broken in,
The bats and owlets builders in the roof!
My cricket chirps against thy mandolin.
Hush, call no echo up in further proof
Of desolation! there's a voice within
That weeps—as thou must sing—alone, aloof.

ABREAM SCRIVEN
LETTER TO DINAH JONES, 1858

Abream Scriven wrote this heartbreaking letter to his wife, Dinah Jones, on the eve of their forced separation. Both slaves on Colonel's Island in Georgia, they had had four children together. Abream was sold to a New Orleans slave trader in Savannah. Despite Dinah's attempts to have Abream bought by a nearby plantation owner and returned, the two never saw each other again.

In 1861, Dinah married again but died of typhoid fever the same year. By 1863, Abream had also remarried.

My Dear Wife,

I take the pleasure of writing you these few with much regret to inform you that I am sold to a man by the name of Peterson a [trader] and Stays in new orleans. I am here yet But I expect to go before long but when I get there I will write and let you know where I am. My Dear I want to Send you some things but I donot know who to Send them by but I will thry to get them to you and my children. Give my love to my father and mother and tell them good Bye for me. and if we Shall not meet in this world I hope to meet in heaven. My Dear wife for you and my children my pen cannot Express the griffe I feel to be parted from you all

I remain your truly husband until death

Abream Scriven

MARCUS SPIEGEL
LETTER TO CAROLINE SPIEGEL, 1862

A German Jew and son of a rabbi, Marcus Spiegel (1829–1864) came to the United States in 1849 and, outfitted by relatives in Chicago, became a peddler of fabrics, thread, and needles on a route in Ohio farm country. There he fell in love with a young Quaker woman named Caroline Hamlin. By 1853, they were married, and she converted to Judaism. He was already in his mid-thirties when he joined the Union army in 1861 and would, as a colonel, become one of its highest-ranking Jewish officers.

Spiegel was able to leave for home the day after writing this letter, though the Spiegels' fourth child, Hattie, wouldn't be born for another month. Their fifth and youngest child, Clara, was also born during the war, only a few months before Spiegel was fatally wounded by an exploding shell in the Red River Campaign. *Gefattershopt* means "godfather."

My good, lovely and abused Wife!

I have no doubt you think that I speak truly when I say "abused Wife"; a Woman as good and lovely, as saving and industrious, as kind a wife and good mother as you are should be left alone hundreds of miles from her husband who loves her more and with more fervor, zeal and devotion than any other man can love, just at this time in your situation, with 3 small children and one coming, or that he should leave her at all. That I went to this War I never yet regretted. I think it helped me in my health, reputation and pecuniary, and if just now I were permitted to go home and stay 30 days, I would gladly stay until Fall in the Service. But it does not make me very kind to military authorities if I do not get a leave of absence for some 20 or 30 days pretty soon. If I should not succeed in getting permission to go, I ask of you if you love me, to be as easy as you possibly can be and spend the fifty Dollars which it would cost me to come home for your own benefit and comfort. Get that Woman from Akron to stay with you during that time and if you should bring us a Son give the "Gefattershopt" to Brother Joseph and mother. Call the Boy "George McClellan Spiegel." Buy everything you want to be happy and just console yourself. Yet it seems to me as though such a thing could not be possible without me being there. I would gladly walk 600 miles to see you if they would only say go.

God bless you my love, my sweet, my all; may the blessings of heaven rest upon you. Ever your true and loving

Marcus

VITA SACKVILLE-WEST
LETTER TO HAROLD NICOLSON, 1929

They married in 1913, embarking on what was essentially an open marriage, with both partners having affairs—for the most part homosexual. But by all accounts, the marriage of writer Vita Sackville-West (1892–1962) and Harold Nicolson was a hugely positive force in both their lives, contributing to their separate but remarkable productivity as writers; to Nicolson's career as a British diplomat; and to their partnership as creators of the amazing Sissinghurst Castle gardens. Nicolson was returning to Berlin, where he was stationed as chargé d'affaires, when Vita wrote him this letter, one of hundreds that passed between them. "Hadji" and "Mar" were Harold and Vita's childhood nicknames. "Coffee cups" were what the couple called reminders. Resht, in what was then called Persia, was one of Nicolson's postings. He resigned from the diplomatic corps three months after this letter was written. Eventually Nicolson outlived Sackville-West by six years.

My darling,

What is so torturing, when I leave you at these London stations and drive off, is the knowledge that you are *still there*—that, for half an hour, or three quarters of an hour, I could still return and find you; come up behind you, take you by the elbow, and say "Hadji."

I came straight home, feeling horribly desolate and sad, driving down that familiar and dreary road. I remembered Resht and our parting there; our parting at Victoria when you left for Persia; till our life seemed made up of partings, and I wondered how long it would continue.

I got home, and all the way was strewn with coffee-cups: specially the road through the beeches on the common. I remembered how you had said that so long as you were alive they were there for you, and when you were dead it wouldn't matter.

Then I came round the corner onto the view—our view—and I thought how you loved it, and how simple you were really, apart from your activity; and how I loved you, for being both simple and active, in one and the same person.

S

Then I came home, and it was no consolation at all. You see, whenever I am unhappy for other reasons . . . the cottage is a real solace to me; but when it is on account of *you* that I am unhappy (because you have gone away), it is an additional pang—it is the same place, but a sort of mockery and emptiness hangs about it—I almost wish that just *once* you could lose me and then come straight back to the cottage and find it still full of me but empty of me—then you would know what I go through after you have gone away.

Anyhow, you will say, it is worse for you who go to a horrible and alien city, whereas *I* stay in the place we both love so much, but really, Hadji, it is *no* consolation to come back to a place full of coffee-cups—there was a cardboard-box-lid full of your rose petals still on the terrace.

Whenever I am unhappy for other reasons, the cottage is a real solace to me; but when it is because you have gone away, it is an additional pang.

You are dearer to me than anybody ever has been or ever could be. If you died I should kill myself as soon as I had made provision for the boys. I really mean this. I could not live if I lost you. Every time I get you to myself you become dearer to me. I do not think one could conceive of a love more exclusive, more tender, or more pure than that I have for you. It is absolutely divorced from physical love—sex—*now*. I feel it is immortal, I am superstitious about it, I feel it is a thing which happens seldom. I suppose that everybody who falls in love feels this about their love, and that for them it is merely a platitude. But then when one falls in love it is all mixed up with physical desire, which is the most misleading of all human emotions, and most readily and convincingly wears the appearance of the real thing. This does not enter at all into my love for you. I simply feel that you are me and I am you—what you meant by saying that you "became the lonely me" when we parted.

Darling, there are not many people who would write such a love letter after nearly sixteen years of marriage, yet who would be saying therein only one-fiftieth of what they were feeling as they wrote it. But you know not only that it is true, every word, but that it represents only a pale version of the real truth—I could not exaggerate, however much I tried—I don't try. I try sometimes to tell you the truth and then I find that I have no words at my command which could possibly convey it to you.

Your Mar

DYLAN THOMAS
LETTER TO CAITLIN THOMAS, 1950

Welsh poet and novelist Dylan Thomas (1914–1953) was thirty-six years old and only three years away from his early death—by some combination of pneumonia and alcohol poisoning—when he made the first of his four trips to the United States and wrote this passionate, evocative letter to his wife, Caitlin, whom he had married in 1937.

Both Thomas and Caitlin were heavy drinkers, and their marriage was bumpy, marked by a number of infidelities on his part—including one during this first U.S. tour. Laugharne was the Welsh town in which they settled in 1949, though their lives together had involved many moves and homes.

Caitlin my own own own dearest love whom God and *my* love and *your* love for me protect, my sweet wife, my dear one, my Irish heart, my wonderful wonderful girl who is with me invisibly every second of these dreadful days, awake or sleepless, who is forever and forever with me and is my own true beloved amen—I love you, I need you, I want, want you, we have never been apart as long as this, never, never, and we will never be again. I am writing to you now, lying in bed, in the Roman Princess's sister's rich social house, in a posh room that is hell on earth. Oh why why, *didn't* we arrange it *somehow* that we came out together to this devastating, insane, demoniacally loud, roaring continent. We *could* somehow have arranged it. Why oh why did I think I could live, I could bear to live, I could think of living, for all these torturing, unending, echoing months without you, Cat, my life, my wife, my wife on earth and in God's eyes, my reason for my blood, breath, and bone. Here, in this vast, mad horror, that doesn't know its size, or its strength, or its weakness, or its barbaric speed, stupidity, din, selfrighteousness, this cancerous Babylon, here we could cling together, sane, safe, & warm & face, together, everything. I LOVE YOU. I have been driven for what seem like, and probably are, thousands of miles, along neoned, jerrybuilt, motel-ed, turbined, ice-cream-salooned, gigantically hoared roads of the lower region of the damned, from town to town, college to college, university to university, hotel to hotel, & all I want, before Christ, before you, is to hold you in my arms in our house in Laugharne, Carmarthenshire . . . Oh, Cat, my beautiful, my love, what am I doing here?

JIM WEATHERLY
"MIDNIGHT TRAIN TO GEORGIA," 1970

Originally titled "Midnight Plane to Houston," the song was written by Jim Weatherly (1943–) after a phone call he had with the actress Farrah Fawcett, who happened to be packing for a flight home. At the time, Fawcett was living with Weatherly's college friend (and Fawcett's future husband), actor Lee Majors. As recorded in 1973 by Gladys Knight and the Pips, "Midnight Train to Georgia" was eventually inducted into the Grammy Hall of Fame.

In 2013 Knight recalled: "While recording that single, I was thinking about my own situation. My husband at the time was a beautiful saxophonist and so gifted. But he was unhappy that we didn't have a more traditional marriage because I was often on the road or recording. Ultimately it all proved too much for him, like the song said, and we divorced . . . I was going through the exact same thing that I was singing about when recording—which is probably why it sounds so personal."

LA proved too much for the man,
So he's leavin' the life he's come to know.
He said he's goin' back to find, ooh,
What's left of his world,
The world he left behind not so long ago.
He's leavin'
On that midnight train to Georgia,
And he's goin' back to a simpler place and time.
And I'll be with him
On that midnight train to Georgia
I'd rather live with him in his world
Than live without him in mine.

S

I'd rather live with him in his world

Than live without him in mine.

SEX

THE CODE OF HAMMURABI, CIRCA 1780 BC

The Babylonian ruler Hammurabi (?–circa 1750 BC) derived his extraordinary code from many long-existing Mesopotamian laws, but he is famous in modern times as a lawgiver because his code was literally written in stone: all 282 laws, covering everything from commerce to slavery to marriage, were inscribed on an eight-foot-tall monument for all to see. It was discovered by a French scholar in 1901 and now is on display in the Louvre.

If a man take a woman to wife, but have no intercourse with her, this woman is no wife to him.

---

1 CORINTHIANS 7:1-9

Often quoted but rarely in context, the Apostle Paul's final injunction in this passage clearly does not refer to outer flames but to inner longings. While there remains some debate about whether Paul (circa 5–circa 67) had once been married himself, it is generally agreed that he was a committed celibate when he wrote the verses below.

1   Now concerning the things whereof ye wrote unto me: It is good for a man not to touch a woman.

2   Nevertheless, to avoid fornication, let every man have his own wife, and let every woman have her own husband.

3   Let the husband render unto the wife due benevolence: and likewise also the wife unto the husband.

4   The wife hath not power of her own body, but the husband: and likewise also the husband hath not power of his own body, but the wife.

5   Defraud ye not one the other, except it be with consent for a time, that ye may give yourselves to fasting and prayer; and come together again, that Satan tempt you not for your incontinency.

6   But I speak this by permission, and not of commandment.

S

7   For I would that all men were even as I myself. But every man hath his proper gift of God, one after this manner, and another after that.

8   I say therefore to the unmarried and widows, It is good for them if they abide even as I.

9   But if they cannot contain, let them marry: for it is better to marry than to burn.

HALY ABBAS
THE PANTEGNI, 10TH CENTURY

A millennium before Viagra altered the equation, impotence captured the attention of practitioners who identified—with scientific-sounding precision—causes and cures rooted in magic. *The Pantegni* was the Latin translation of an influential medical encyclopedia written by the eminent Persian physician Haly Abbas, who died late in the tenth century.

Magical incantations often rhymed. The Latin *avis* means "bird"; *gravis* means "heavy" or "serious"; *seps* means "venomous serpent"; *sipa* doesn't appear in Latin dictionaries, though *sipo* and *sipare* are forms of the verb "to scatter."

There are some people who, impeded by spells, cannot have intercourse with their wives. We do not want to deprive our book of help for them, because the remedy (if I am not wrong) is most sacred. Therefore if this happens to someone, he should put his hope in God, and he will show him kindness. But because there are many kinds of magic, we ought to discuss them.

For some spells are made from animated substances, such as the testicles of a cock which, when put under a bed with the cock's blood, bring it about that those who lie in the bed will not have intercourse. Some are made of characters written in bat's blood. Some are made of inanimate substances, for instance if a nut or acorn is separated, and one half is put on one side of the road where the bride and groom must pass, and the other on the other side. . . .

But because these spells are diabolical, and are especially found among women, they can sometimes be cured by divine methods, sometimes by human ones. . . .

. . . If a nut or acorn is the cause of this spell, someone should take a nut or acorn, and separate it. With one half, the man should proceed on one side of some road, or of that road along which [the bride and groom] went, and put his half there; but the woman should put the other part of the nut on the other side of the road. Then the bride and groom should take both parts of the nut, without taking the shell off, and thus put the whole nut back together and keep it for seven days. Having done this, they should have intercourse. . . .

If magic has been done against a virgin bride and groom, so that the groom cannot have sexual intercourse with the bride, take a dish or a cup. In the middle of it write a cross and these four names on the four sides of the cross: *avis, gravis, seps, sipa,* and on the inside rim of the cup write the entire gospel of St John. Afterwards take holy water, if you can, or wine or other water if you cannot get holy water, and put it in the cup, and with your finger wash all the letters in it, and both [the bride and groom] should drink it devotedly, and in God's name they should have intercourse. It has been proved.

DANIEL DEFOE
CONJUGAL LEWDNESS; OR, MATRIMONIAL WHOREDOM: A TREATISE CONCERNING THE USE AND ABUSE OF THE MARRIAGE BED, 1727

The author of popular novels such as *Robinson Crusoe* and *Moll Flanders,* Daniel Defoe (1660–1731) also wrote hundreds of nonfiction books and essays on a wide range of subjects, including marriage.

Suppose here are two young People, a Man and Woman . . . and the Man solemnly promises to marry her: But, in the mean time, the Fellow (Hell prompting, and his own Wickedness tempting) presses this Woman to let him lie with her. His Arguments are smooth and subtle; *Why should you refuse?* Says he: *We are fairly Man and Wife already* by Agreement (and, in the Sight of God, the Intention is the same thing as the Action) *there is nothing more to be done* but *just a few Words of the Parson, and the formality of repeating it in the Church, and that we will do too as soon as I can get the Licence down,* (suppose it to be in the Country) or as soon as the Asking in the Church is over; and you may take my Word, for I assure you again, *I will be very honest to you,* (and then perhaps he swears to it) and *How can you refuse me? And then he kisses her,* and continues urging and teazing her, and wheadling her to it, and perhaps she as much inclined to it as he, only more for waiting till Marriage than he; so that the Devil takes hold of Inclination on both Sides, to bring about the Wickedness. . . .

On the Man's Part; here is a publick Confession, that you had a wicked filthy ungovernable Inclination, that could not contain your self from a Woman for a few Days. . . .

. . . How absurd a Thing is it to make a Whore of his own Wife; to expose her for a Whore, who he proposes to embrace as an honest Woman ever after; to draw her in to be exposed, to be flouted at, to be jested with, and insulted all her Days, to be the scorn of her Neighbours, slighted and shunned by modest Women, and laughed at by every Body.

MARIA THERESA
LETTER TO MARIE ANTOINETTE, 1775

The powerful Austrian empress Maria Theresa (1717–1780) bore sixteen children, including two future queens, a couple of emperors, and a slew of archdukes and archduchesses. Yet her own marriage had been strained by her husband's infidelities, and she wanted to ensure that her daughter Marie Antoinette make a success of her marriage to the French king Louis XVI. The empress had reason to be concerned: despite many warning letters like this one, it took seven years before the couple consummated their marriage.

During their lifetimes, Louis was rumored to be impotent, Marie Antoinette licentious; in the early twentieth century, author Stefan Zweig put forth the view that Louis had a small deformity but was loath to have it corrected surgically. More recent research suggests that the problem was actually that Louis was so well endowed that it made intercourse excruciating for both parties.

All the letters from Paris say that you sleep separately from the King, and that he does not trust you very much. I must admit that that strikes me even more as in the daytime you are amusing yourself without the King, and therefore this friendship, and custom of being together will end soon, and I can only foresee unhappiness and pain for you in your brilliant position, although Rosenberg assured me that the King loved and esteemed you, and therefore you could easily maintain your position.

Your sole task must be to spend the whole day with him as much as possible, to keep him company, be his best friend and confidante, and to try to know what is happening in order to be able to talk to him and support him; then he will never find more pleasure and comfort elsewhere than in your company. We are not here to amuse ourselves, but to become worthy of heaven. Forgive these sermons, but I tell you, this sleeping apart, and these trips with the comte d'Artois have pained me greatly, as I realize the consequences, and cannot present them to you too dramatically, as I wish to save you from the abyss towards which you are racing. My love requires me to warn you of these matters, do not dismiss my words too hastily.

S

Just as ideas go on increasing indefinitely, so
it ought to be with pleasures.

WILLIAM BLAKE
NOTEBOOK FRAGMENT, CIRCA 1793

Little regarded in his lifetime and often mocked for his eccentric views, the brilliant poet, engraver, and painter William Blake (1757–1827) was acclaimed in later centuries as a pioneer of Romantic poetry and an astonishing visionary. Wife Catherine, to whom he was devoted and who helped him create and print his vividly illustrated works, once said of Blake: "I have very little of Mr. Blake's company; he is always in Paradise."

In a wife I would desire
What in whores is always found
The lineaments of Gratified desire.

HONORÉ DE BALZAC
THE PHYSIOLOGY OF MARRIAGE, 1829

The passage below is from a chapter called "The Fore-Ordained," in which the then-single Balzac (see Fidelity, page 113; Honeymoon, page 172; Power, pages 338–39) offers a series of aphorisms that he describes as the "Matrimonial Catechism."

XXXIII.   The husband's interest, quite as much as his honour, prescribes that he shall never allow himself a pleasure for which he has not had the wit to awake a longing in his wife.

XXXIV.   Pleasure is caused by the union of excitement and affection, hence one can hardly pretend that pleasures are solely material.

XXXV.   Just as ideas go on increasing indefinitely, so it ought to be with pleasures. . . .

XLVI.   Every night should have its own menu.

XLVII.   Marriage should war unceasingly against a monster that is the ruin of everything: the monster custom.

XLVIII.   If a man cannot distinguish the difference between the pleasures of two consecutive nights, he has married too early in life.

XLIX.   It is easier to be a lover than a husband, for the simple reason that it is more difficult to have a ready wit the whole day long than to say a good thing occasionally.

S

SEXUAL AID ADVERTISEMENT
MORNING OREGONIAN, 1896

The forty-eight-page pamphlet described in this ad promised potency and sexual stamina, in not quite so few words. The pamphlet, though free, actually promoted the "Erie Vacuum Appliance" to be purchased by mail order and designed to cause "a vigorous circulation of the blood throughout that part."

The Triumph of Love Is Happy and Fruitful Marriage.

Every Man Who Would Know the Grand Truths, the Plain Facts, the New Discoveries of Medical Science as Applied to Married Life, Who Would Atone for Past Errors and Avoid Future Pitfalls, Should Secure the Wonderful Little Book Called "Complete Manhood, and How to Attain It."

Here at last is information from a high medical source that must work wonders with this generation of men.

The book fully describes a method by which to attain full vigor and manly power.

A method by which to end all unnatural strains on the system.

To cure nervousness, lack of self-control, despondency, &c.

To exchange a jaded and worn nature for one of brightness, buoyancy and power.

To cure forever effects of excesses, overwork, worry, &c.

To give full strength, development and tone to every portion and organ of the body.

Age no barrier. Failure impossible. Two thousand references.

The book is purely medical and scientific, useless to curiosity seekers, invaluable to men only who need it.

A despairing man, who had applied to us, soon after wrote:

"Well, I tell you that first day is one I'll never forget. I just bubbled with joy. I wanted to hug everybody and tell them my old self had died yesterday, and my new self was born to-day. Why didn't you tell me when I first wrote that I would find it this way?"

And another thus:

"If you dumped a cart load of gold at my feet it would not bring such gladness into my life as your method has done."

Write to the ERIE MEDICAL COMPANY, Buffalo, N.Y., and ask for the little book called "COMPLETE MANHOOD." Refer to this paper, and the company promises to send the book, in sealed envelope, without any marks, and entirely free, until it is well introduced.

WILLIAM ROBINSON
SEXUAL PROBLEMS OF TO-DAY, 1912

As a team of reviewers wrote of Dr. Robinson (see Grievances, page 144) in a 1924 issue of the *Journal of Social Forces*: "More than any other comparable writer . . . [Robinson] has freed his medical writing from those considerations and implications of conventional mysticism, prudery and supernaturalistic ethics which surround even most of the medical and semi-medical writings on sexual problems."

Quite often, when a married woman is ailing, has a pasty, dingy complexion, lusterless eyes, suffers from lack of appetite and insomnia, is irritable and cranky, wants she-does-not-know-what, is in a mood varying from black to the deepest azure, has been given dozens of kinds of drugs, and treated by massage, baths, electricity, etc., and has not been improved in the least, quite often we say, such a woman needs no treatment at all—it is her husband who needs it. And very

> *O*ften, when a married woman is ailing, has a pasty complexion, lusterless eyes, is irritable and has been treated by drugs, massage, baths, etc.—she needs no treatment at all—it is her husband who needs it.

often he needs no treatment either—merely a little advice. And just a little advice frankly and plainly given does the work. The wife's complexion clears up, her eyes acquire a luster, her walk has a spring to it which it did not possess before, her appetite is fine, she is jolly and happy, life has a new interest which it did not possess before—in short, she is thoroly permeated with the *joie de vivre*. And what did it all?

The *cognoscenti* know; as to the others, we must let them do some guessing, for we regret to say, our censors will not let us discuss such things frankly in print.

MARIE STOPES
MARRIED LOVE: A NEW CONTRIBUTION TO THE SOLUTION OF SEX DIFFICULTIES, 1918

A British botanist and outspoken advocate of sexual freedom, birth control, and early eugenics, Marie Stopes (1880–1958) earned praise and condemnation for her extraordinarily frank bestseller on sex and fulfillment. Among the subjects she explored were the differences between men and women when it came to the subject of sleep after sex, which for men "falls like a soft curtain of oblivion and saves the man's consciousness from the jar and disappointment of an anti-climax." Stopes's first marriage was annulled in 1916 on the uncontested grounds that it had never been consummated.

How fare women in this event? When they too have had complete satisfaction they similarly relax and slumber.

But as things are to-day it is scarcely an exaggeration to say that the majority of wives are left wakeful and nerve-racked to watch with tender motherly brooding, or with bitter and jealous envy, the slumbers of the men who, through ignorance and carelessness, have neglected to see that they too had the necessary resolution of nervous tension.

Many married women have told me that after they have had relations with their husbands they are restless, either for some hours or for the whole night; and I feel sure that the prevalent failure on the part of many men to effect orgasms for their wives at each congress, must be a very common source of the sleeplessness and nervous diseases of so many married women.

The relation between the completion of the sex-act and sleep in woman is well indicated in the case of Mrs. A., who is typical of a large class of wives. She married a man with whom she was passionately in love. Neither she nor her husband had ever had connection with any one else, and, while they were both keen and intelligent people with some knowledge of biology, neither knew anything of the details of human sex-union. For several years her husband had unions with her which gave him some satisfaction and left him ready at once to sleep. Neither he nor she knew that women should have an orgasm, and after every union she was left so "on edge" and sleepless that never less than several hours would elapse before she could sleep at all, and often she remained wakeful the whole night.

After her husband's death her health improved, and in a year or two she entered into a new relation with a man who was aware of women's needs and spent sufficient time and attention to them to ensure a successful completion for her as well as for himself. The result was that she soon became a good sleeper, with the attendant benefits of restored nerves and health.

Sleep is so complex a process, and sleeplessness the resultant of so many different malad-justments, that it is, of course, possible that the woman may sleep well enough, even if she be deprived of the relief and pleasure of perfect union. But in so many married women sleeplessness and a consequent nervous condition are coupled with a lack of the complete sex-relation, that one of the first questions a physician *should* put to those of his women patients who are worn and sleepless is: Whether her husband really fulfills his marital duty in their physical relation.

W. F. ROBIE
SEX AND LIFE: WHAT THE EXPERIENCED SHOULD TEACH AND WHAT THE INEXPERIENCED SHOULD LEARN, 1920

Writing boldly on sexual technique and satisfaction for both genders, Massachusetts physician Walter Franklin Robie (1866–1928) managed to get his book published by agreeing that it would be sold "only to members of the recognized professions." But he and his publishers also put out pamphlets of separate chapters, so that doctors would be able to disseminate the information to their patients as well.

Robie slightly misquotes Shakespeare's epic poem "Venus and Adonis." The actual line is "Graze on my lips, and if those hills be dry . . ."

Young husband, . . . Don't say much; but slowly and carefully feel your way. Your hands were made to use; your wife's rounded form, her protuberances and depressions were largely made for hands and lips. The final act of love's drama with the man and wife in mutual orgasm in love's embrace, alone and without preliminaries, is like a banquet served on bare boards, without the accompaniments of light, heat, china, linen, silver, or conversation.

Kiss without shame, for she desires it, your wife's lips, tongue, neck; and, as Shakespeare says: "If these founts be dry, stray lower where the pleasant fountains lie." There is good instruction to young married people in good literature, but it is often unknown or ignored. Kiss her nipples, arms, and abdomen. Hold tenderly and manipulate softly her breasts, and delicately, when she yields nestlingly, caress her nipples.

. . . If her mind has not been freed from the ancient notion that a married woman should be cold and unresponsive toward her husband, gentleness and care and explanation will lead her to be properly responsive in time. Always remember this truth, that no woman lives who is so glacial that she will not respond to the tactful insistence of the right man. If you are sure that you are the right man at the time of marriage and do your part tenderly and faithfully, you need have no fears for the outcome.

S

LEWIS TERMAN
PSYCHOLOGICAL FACTORS IN MARITAL HAPPINESS, 1938

For background on Terman, see Happiness, page 161.

It seems almost incredible that intercourse should be almost as frequent in the most unhappily mated couples as in the most happily mated, but such seems to be the case. One can only conclude that in this group sexual intercourse is to only a slight extent an expression of the sentiments of love and affection. It also bears little relation to the number of sexual complaints. . . . That is, spouses who claim that they have much to complain of with regard to the sexual unsatisfactoriness of their mates nevertheless have intercourse only a little less frequently than others.

A possible explanation of the unexpectedly high frequency of intercourse in unhappy marriages is that in such cases sex is the one type of communion between husband and wife which is mutually satisfying. "Any port in a storm," as one of our friends has expressed it. Doubtless, too, there are marriages in which one of the mates consciously employs the stratagem of sexual enticement in the hope of reviving the waning affection of the other.

MARIE ROBINSON
THE POWER OF SEXUAL SURRENDER, 1959

Though her book was a huge bestseller in a prefeminist age, American psychiatrist and psychoanalyst Marie Nyswander Robinson (1919–1986) was later excoriated for her support of traditional sex roles and her claim that, for women, "excitement comes from the act of surrender."

A woman suffering from frigidity will be very relieved if her husband will make a gentle but blanket announcement to her that she is to drop her entire concern with orgasm until it happens. I have pointed out before that this indeed must be her working attitude before she has her first orgasmic experience. For a husband to affirm that this attitude is also his can be a great reassurance to her. She will then allow herself to really enjoy his "selfish" ecstasy without neurotically fixing on her own localized sensations. Indulging the deeply feminine role of *giving* pleasure can be more exciting to her than any other thing.

NENA O'NEILL AND GEORGE O'NEILL
OPEN MARRIAGE: A NEW LIFE STYLE FOR COUPLES, 1972

For background on the O'Neills, see Expectations, page 107. The authors diagramed what they called "the expanding spiral of open marriage." In its somewhat cryptic format, this spiral detailed the limitless possibilities inherent in open marriage. To clarify, however, the authors wrote: "We are not recommending outside sex, but we are not saying that it should be avoided, either. The choice is entirely up to you, and can be made only upon your own knowledge of the degree to which you have achieved, within your marriage, the trust, identity, and open communication necessary to the eradication of jealousy."

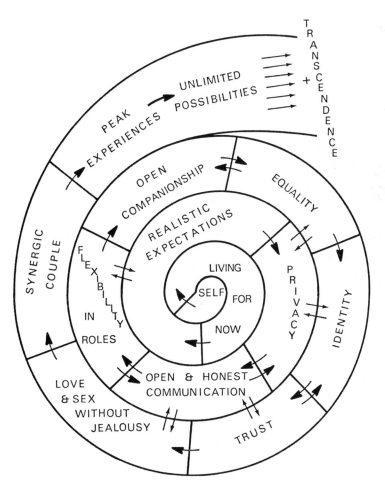

Expanding Spiral of Open Marriage

ERICA JONG
FEAR OF FLYING, 1973

In her first and most famous novel, Erica Jong (1942–) created a married protagonist, Isadora Wing, who sets out, despite her fear of flying, to pursue adventures both sexual and geographical. "This book," the novelist Henry Miller correctly predicted at the time, "will make literary history." To date, it has sold about twenty million copies worldwide, and the phrase defined in the excerpt below has endured as a slogan of female liberation.

I was not against marriage. I believed in it in fact. It was necessary to have one best friend in a hostile world, one person you'd be loyal to no matter what, one person who'd always be loyal to you. But what about all those other longings which after a while marriage did nothing much to appease? The restlessness, the hunger, the thump in the gut, the thump in the cunt, the longing to be filled up, to be fucked through every hole, the yearning for dry champagne and wet kisses, for the smell of peonies in a penthouse on a June night, for the light at the end of the pier in *Gatsby*. . . .

Five years of marriage had made me itchy for all those things: itchy for men, and itchy for solitude. Itchy for sex and itchy for the life of a recluse. I knew my itches were contradictory—and that made things even worse. I knew my itches were un-American—and that made things *still* worse. It is heresy in America to embrace any way of life except as half of a couple. Solitude is un-American. It may be condoned in a man—especially if he is a "glamorous bachelor" who "dates starlets" during a brief interval between marriages. But a woman is always presumed to be alone as a result of abandonment, not choice. And she is treated that way: as a pariah. There is simply no dignified way for a woman to live alone. Oh, she can get along financially perhaps (though not nearly as well as a man), but emotionally she is never left in peace. Her friends, her family, her fellow workers never let her forget that her husbandlessness, her childlessness—her *selfishness*, in short—is a reproach to the American way of life.

Even more to the point, the woman (unhappy though she knows her married friends to be) can never let *herself* alone. She lives as if she were constantly on the brink of some great fulfillment. As if she were waiting for Prince Charming to take her away "from all this." All what? The solitude of living inside her own soul? The certainty of being herself instead of half of something else?

My response to all this was not (not yet) to have an affair and not (not yet) to hit the open road, but to evolve my fantasy of the Zipless Fuck. The zipless fuck was more than a fuck. It was a platonic ideal. Zipless because when you came together zippers fell away like rose petals, underwear blew off in one breath like dandelion fluff. Tongues intertwined and turned liquid. Your whole soul flowed out through your tongue and into the mouth of your lover.

For the true, the ultimate zipless A-1 fuck, it was necessary that you never get to know the man very well. . . .

. . . The zipless fuck is absolutely pure. It is free of ulterior motives. There is no power game. The man is not "taking" and the woman is not "giving." No one is attempting to cuckold a husband or humiliate a wife. No one is trying to prove anything or get anything out of anyone. The zipless fuck is the purest thing there is. And it is rarer than the unicorn. And I have never had one.

GAY TALESE
THY NEIGHBOR'S WIFE, 1980

Gay Talese (1932–) first gained fame for practicing the genre-bending New Journalism, essentially employing the techniques of literary fiction to convey fact. Talese was rigorous, patient, and immersive in his reporting, whether revealing the workings of the Mafia in *Honor Thy Father* or exploring America's secret sexual life in *Thy Neighbor's Wife*. The book was a bombshell—popular with readers and controversial among critics, many of whom decried Talese's explicitness as well as his participation in plenty of the behavior he was reporting. Central to the book was the narrative of Judith and John Bullaro, an LA couple who were drawn to visit Sandstone, the swingers' retreat started by John Williamson and Barbara Cramer. In the scene below, Cramer explained the philosophy of marriage that she and her husband shared.

Talese's marriage to the publisher Nan Talese passed the half-century mark in 2009.

In the room she hastily removed her clothes, and Bullaro saw again her remarkable body, and soon felt her aggressive touch as he lay naked on the bed and she mounted him. The ease with which she achieved her satisfaction, and the agile manner with which she pulled him on top of her without disengaging him, reminded him of a tumbling act in a circus, and confirmed as well that her marriage had neither altered her sportive style nor diminished her desire for supplementary sex.

After they had finished and were relaxing on the bed, Bullaro asked if she was happily married. She answered that she was, adding that her husband was the most remarkable man she had ever known; he was sensitive and self-assured and was not intimidated by her individuality.

In fact, she went on, he was encouraging her to become more independent than she was already, hoping that as she attained higher levels of fulfillment and self-awareness she would reinvest these assets into their marriage. A marriage should promote personal growth instead of limitations and restrictions, she went on, and as Bullaro listened with a certain cynicism he assumed that she was paraphrasing her husband. He had never heard her speak this way before, and while he was still bewildered by her husband's motives, and pondered what her husband would do if he knew what had just transpired in this bedroom, he remained silent as Barbara Williamson continued to explain for his benefit, and perhaps for her own, the kind of marriage she now had.

Most married people, she said, had "ownership problems": They wanted to totally possess their spouse, to expect monogamy, and if one partner admitted an infidelity to the other it would most likely be interpreted as a sign of a deteriorating marriage. But this was absurd, she said—a husband and wife should be able to enjoy sex with other people without threatening their primary relationship, or lying or feeling guilty about their extramarital experiences. People cannot expect all of their needs to be satisfied by a spouse, and Barbara said that her relationship with John Williamson was enhanced by their mutual respect for freedom, and they both felt sufficiently secure in their love to admit openly to one another that they sometimes made love to other people.

JOHN UPDIKE
RABBIT IS RICH, 1981

In the third of his four novels featuring everyman Harry "Rabbit" Angstrom, John Updike (see Power, page 341) follows Harry and wife Janice through a financially comfortable, if maritally complicated, middle age. In Updike's work, sex and money frequently intertwine—here more explicitly than usual.

[Rabbit] has locked their bedroom door and arranged himself in his underpants on the bed. He calls in a husky and insinuating voice. "Hey, Janice. Look. I bought us something today."

Her dark eyes are glazed from all that drinking and parenting downstairs; she took the shower to help clear her head. Slowly her eyes focus on his face, which must show an intensity of pleasure that puzzles her.

He tugs open the sticky drawer and is himself startled to see the two tinted cylinders sliding toward him, still upright, still there. He would have thought something so dense with preciousness would broadcast signals bringing burglars like dogs to a bitch in heat. He lifts one roll out and places it in Janice's hand; her arm dips with the unexpected weight, and her robe, untied, falls open. Her thin brown used body is more alluring in this lapsed sheath of rough bright cloth than a girl's; he wants to reach in, to where the shadows keep the damp fresh.

"What is it, Harry?" she asks, her eyes widening.

"Open it," he tells her, and when she fumbles too long at the transparent tape holding on the toilet-seat-shaped little lid he pries it off for her with his big fingernails. He removes the wad of tissue paper and spills out upon the quilted bedspread the fifteen Krugerrands. Their color is redder than gold in his mind had been. "Gold," he whispers, holding up close to her face, paired in his palm, two coins, showing the two sides, the profile of some Boer on one and a kind of antelope on the other. "Each of these is worth about three hundred sixty dollars," he tells her. "Don't tell your mother or Nelson or anybody."

She does seem bewitched, taking one into her fingers. Her nails scratch his palm as she lifts the coin off. . . .

. . . "Where are you going to keep them?" she asks. Her tongue sneaks forward in thought, and rests on her lower lip. He loves her when she tries to think.

"In your great big cunt," he says, and pulls her down by the lapels of her rough robe. Out of deference to those around them in the house—Ma Springer just a wall's thickness away, her television a dim rumble, the Korean War turned into a joke—Janice tries to suppress her cries as he strips the terrycloth from her willing body and the coins on the bedspread come in contact with her skin. The cords of her throat tighten; her face darkens as she strains in the grip of indignation and glee. His underwear off, the overhead light still on, his prick up like a jutting piece of pink wreckage, he calms her into lying motionless and places a Krugerrand on each nipple, one on her navel, and a number on her pussy, enough to mask the hair with a triangle of unsteady coins overlapping like snake scales. If she laughs and her belly moves the whole construction will collapse. Kneeling at her hips, Harry holds a Krugerrand by the edge as if to insert it in a slot. *"No!"* Janice protests, loud enough to twitch Ma Springer awake through the wall, loud enough to jar loose the coins so some do spill between her legs. He hushes her mouth with his and then moves his mouth south, across the desert, oasis to oasis, until he comes to the ferny jungle, which his wife lays open to him with a humoring toss of her thighs. A kind of interest compounds as, seeing red, spilled gold pressing on his forehead, he hunts with his tongue for her clitoris.

S

STEPHEN DUNN
"THE NIGHT THE CHILDREN WERE AWAY," 1986

Pulitzer Prize–winning poet Stephen Dunn (1939–), author of more than a dozen poetry collections, writes of the struggles and joys of the American middle class. A *New York Times* review of a later work described his voice as that of "a regular guy cursed with an understanding of human nature more subtle than he'd prefer."

When she comes home he's waiting for her
      on the secluded deck, naked,
            the wine open,

her favorite cheese already sliced.
      Though he hasn't done anything
            like this in years

he knows she'll laugh at his nakedness
      as one laughs at seeing
            an old friend

at a dirty movie. Then she'll take off
      her clothes, join him.
            Tonight

he wants to make love profanely
      as if the profane
            were the only way

to disturb, to waken, the sacred.
      But neither is in a hurry.
            They sip wine,

touch a little, nothing much needs
      to be said. That glacial
            intolerable drift

S

toward quietude and habit, he was worried
      that he'd stopped worrying
            about it.

It's time, a kiss says, to stop time
      by owning it, transforming it
            into body-time, hip-sway

and heartbeat, though really the kiss says
      now, the now he trusts
            is both history

and this instant, reflexive, the good past
      brought forward in a rush.

KENNETH LONERGAN, PETER TOLAN, AND HAROLD RAMIS
ANALYZE THIS, 1999

In this broad parody of such Mafia films as *The Godfather* and *Goodfellas*, nebbishy psychiatrist Ben Sobel (played by Billy Crystal) is conscripted to treat menacing but panic-prone mob chief Paul Vitti (Robert De Niro).

SOBEL: What happened with your wife last night?

VITTI: I wasn't with my wife, I was with my girlfriend.

SOBEL: Are you having marriage problems?

VITTI: No.

SOBEL: Then why do you have a girlfriend?

VITTI: What, are you gonna start moralizing on me?

SOBEL: No, I'm not. I'm just trying to understand. Why do you have a girlfriend?

VITTI: I do things with her I can't do with my wife.

SOBEL: Why can't you do them with your wife?

VITTI: Hey, that's the mouth she kisses my kids good night with! What are you, crazy?

S

ISADORA ALMAN
"TWO LIVES," 2005

The California marriage therapist (1940–) has written a syndicated sex and relationship column, "Ask Isadora," for more than a quarter century. Here she describes meeting a coworker from the 1960s for the first time in four decades.

Mike is the husband of Isadora's friend Mavis. The ellipsis is the author's.

I plunged right into pressing for details of her life and, most specifically, her feelings. She painted what I saw as a dismal picture. Neither she nor Mike had worked at a paying job for some years. She went to parties, to political functions, to her various volunteer causes, and Mike sat at home consuming at least one book and two six-packs of beer a day. "Girl," she laughed, "I bet I am the only individual in the history of humanity who went to a drive-in movie by herself. And then I had to get back early to fix his supper. I mean, he doesn't do one damn thing for himself. Sometimes I just hate that man."

"But why are you still married, then?"

She gave me a variety of "good" reasons—embers of old affection, the comfort of habit, companionship of a sort, no attractive alternatives, inertia, and ended with a casual . . . "and, of course, he doesn't ever bother me for his husband's rights in bed."

I was stunned into silence. She filled it with a barrage of questions about my life. I thought I presented a truthful and upbeat picture of a single working woman in the big city, but as I spoke I could see she was appalled. Having to meet bills and mortgage payments on my own? Sole responsibility for a child all those years? Coming home to an empty house after a disappointing date? Midnight heebie-jeebies faced alone in a solitary bed? "But you two got along so well. He never even drank. I don't understand why you left."

So I gave her my variety of "good" reasons—boredom, growing differences between us, different interests and friends, the call of imagined possibilities elsewhere. "And," I finished. "I wanted more intimacy in my life, more sex."

She couldn't hide her shock. "Whatever for?"

ESTHER PEREL
"MATING IN CAPTIVITY," 2007

A New York–based psychotherapist with gifts for both insight and provocation, Esther Perel (1958–) struck a chord in 2006 when her first book offered the somewhat challenging sugges-tion that in order for their marital sex lives to survive, husbands and wives had to confront the tension between the separate lures of domestic security and erotic adventure. Perel's explora-tion of this paradox hit people where they lived—and loved. *Mating in Captivity* was translated into two dozen languages, and Perel has become a familiar figure on television talk shows, in TED Talks, and on the *Huffington Post*, where this article by the same title appeared.

As a couples therapist in New York, I've seen young and old, married or not and gay, bi and straight, with passports from all over the world. Plenty has changed in my 20 years of private practice, but not my patients' opening lines.

They tend to go something like this: "We love each other very much, but we have no sex."

Next they'll move into describing relationships that are open and loving, yet sexually dull. Time and again they tell me that, though they treasure the stability, security and predictability of a committed relationship, they miss the excitement, novelty and mystery that eroticism thrives on.

Sophia's gripe says it all. She wants the comfort of familiarity, but misses the edge of the unknown. "We get along really well; [Jeff] is warm and reliable, and even though he's not the type to gush, I feel cozy with him. I know we're lucky. We have a nice place, enough money, three great kids. So what is it I miss? I want to feel some of the intensity of the beginning, the butterflies in the stomach, the feeling of anticipation. I know that the excitement was bound up with insecurity, with not knowing if he would call or not. I don't want that insecurity at this time in my life. But I would like to feel something. . . ."

So, there you have it: the human species design flaw. Exactly the caring and coddling that nurture love snuff out the unselfconsciousness of desire. When we love, we worry about our partner and feel responsible. Desire is more wolfish. Selfish. Beast-like.

Funny thing, desire. You'd think you'd need to throw more intimacy at it to keep it in pink health. But you'd be wrong. Withered desire is all too often the unanticipated side effect of a growing intimacy, not one that's cooled. In fact, the very qualities that nurture closeness can be sexually deflating. Sophia points to the familiarity between Jeff and her, the protectiveness she feels. She talks about the shared rituals that make their days more predictable, the security of knowing that Jeff checks in with her four times a day. But in their attempts to secure love, Jeff and Sophia have squeezed out the very erotic ingredients that spurred the relationship into being: novelty, spontaneity, curiosity, surprise.

Popular psychology tells us sexual problems come from relationship problems. Poor communication, lack of intimacy and accumulated resentments are some of the boxes checked off to explain this numbing of desire. If troubled relationship = no sex, then it flows that if we improve the relationship, hot sex should follow.

But my practice suggests otherwise. I've helped plenty of couples buff up their relationship and it did nothing for the sex. Because the rules of desire are not the same as the rules of good citizenship.

I t isn't always the lack of closeness that stifles desire, but too much closeness. And while love seeks closeness, desire needs space to thrive.

It isn't always the lack of closeness that stifles desire, but too much closeness. And while love seeks closeness, desire needs space to thrive. That's because love is about having, and desire is about wanting.

Here's the nut of it: Eroticism occurs in the space between self and other.

Now, most of us don't want that uncertainty in the very place where we seek consistency. We prefer to experience the thrill of the unknown elsewhere.

But there's no way around it. Learn to love the unknown right here with your honey. To want, you've got to have a synapse to cross. In short, fire needs air, and many couples don't leave enough air.

SEXES, THE

BAN ZHAO
LESSONS FOR WOMEN, CIRCA 100

Ban Zhao (circa 45–circa 120) is considered to have been the first female historian in China, but there doesn't seem to have been a lot of competition for the title. The exceptionally well educated daughter and sister of brilliant scholars, she was eventually asked to complete their official history of the Han Dynasty. At roughly the same time, she wrote the book that would make her most famous. *Lessons for Women*, though short, was clear in its rules for women's conduct, which essentially involved subjugating oneself to one's husband. As a book of etiquette, it is considered to have had a greater influence on the conduct of women in China than virtually any source. While drawing clear distinctions between the sexes, Ban argued, almost paradoxically, that women needed to be educated in order to serve their husbands best.

If a husband be unworthy, then he possesses nothing by which to control his wife. If a wife be unworthy, then she possesses nothing with which to serve her husband. If a husband does not control his wife, then the rules of conduct manifesting his authority are abandoned and broken. If a wife does not serve her husband, then the proper relationship between men and women and the natural order of things are neglected and destroyed. As a matter of fact the purpose of these two [roles] is the same.

Now examine the gentlemen of the present age. They only know that wives must be controlled, and that the husband's rules of conduct manifesting his authority must be established. They therefore teach their boys to read books and study histories. But they do not in the least understand that husbands and masters must also be served, and that the proper relationship and the rites should be maintained. Yet only to teach men and not to teach women—is that not ignoring the essential relation between them? According to the "Rites," it is the rule to begin to teach children to read at the age of eight years, and by the age of fifteen years they ought then to be ready for cultural training. Only why should it not be that girls' education as well as boys' be according to this principle?

As Yin and Yang are not of the same nature, so man and woman have different characteristics. The distinctive quality of the Yang is rigidity; the function of the Yin is yielding. Man is honored for strength; a woman is beautiful on account of her gentleness. Hence there arose the common saying: "A man though born like a wolf may, it is feared, become a weak monstrosity; a woman though born like a mouse may, it is feared, become a tiger."

WILLIAM GOUGE
OF DOMESTICALL DUTIES, EIGHT TREATISES, 1622

A graduate of Eton and King's College, Cambridge, William Gouge (1578–1653) was ordained as a minister at the age of thirty-two, and for the next forty-five years was both a lecturer at Cambridge and a pastor at London's Blackfriars Church. *Of Domesticall Duties* was one of his most famous and influential works, though even he admitted that when he introduced his precepts about female submission and inferiority, he often encountered among his women parishioners what he called "squirming" and "murmuring."

PARTICULAR DUTIES OF WIVES.

Subjection, the generall head of all wives duties,

1. Acknowledgment of an husbands superioritie,
2. A due esteeme of her owne husband to be the best for her, and worthy of honour on her part,
3. An inward wive-like feare,
4. An outward reverend cariage towards her husband, which consisteth in a wive-like so-brietie, mildnesse, courtesie, and modestie in apparell,
5. Reverend speech to, and of her husband,
6. Obedience,
7. Forbearing to doe without or against her husbands consent, such things as he hath power to order, as, to dispose and order the common goods of the familie, and the allowance for it, or children, servants, cattel, guests, journies, &c.
8. A ready yeelding to what her husband would have done. This is manifested by her willingnesse to dwell where he will, to come when he calls, and to doe what he requireth,
9. A patient bearing of any reproofe, and a ready redressing of that for which she is justly reproved,
10. Contentment with her husbands present estate,
11. Such a subjection as may stand with her subjection to Christ.
12. Such a subjection as the Church yeeldeth to Christ, which is sincere, pure, cheerefull, constant, for conscience sake, &c.

PARTICULAR DUTIES OF HUSBANDS

Wisdom and love, the generall heads of all husbands duties,

1. Acknowledgment of a wives neere conjunction, and fellowship with her husband,

2. A good esteeme of his owne wife to be the best for him, and worthy of love on his part,

3. An inward intire affection,

4. An outward amiable cariage towards his wife, which consisteth in an husband-like gravitie, mildnesse, courteous acceptance of her courtesie, and allowing her to weare fit apparell,

5. Milde and loving speech to and of his wife,

6. A wise maintaining his authoritie, and forbearing to exact all that is in his power,

7. A ready yielding to his wives request, and giving a generall consent and libertie unto her to order the affaires of the house, children, servants, &c And a free allowing her something to bestow as she seeth occasion,

8. A forbearing to exact more than his wife is willing to doe, or to force her to dwell where it is not meet, or to enjoyne her to doe things unmeet in themselves, or against her minde,

9. A wise ordering of reproofe: not using it without just and weighty cause, and then privatly, and meekly,

10. A provident care for his wife, according to his abilitie,

11. A forbearing to exact any thing which stands not with a good conscience,

12. Such a love, as Christ beareth to the Church, and man to himselfe, which is first free, in deed, and truth, pure, chaste, constant &c.

GEORGE SAVILE
THE LADY'S NEW-YEARS GIFT: OR, ADVICE TO A DAUGHTER, 1688

George Savile, Marquis of Halifax (1633–1695), was an influential member first of Britain's House of Commons and then of the House of Lords. As an advocate of moderation and compromise, he was known as "The Trimmer," and his best-known books took on religious tolerance, foreign affairs, and the politics of his own country. *The Lady's New-Years Gift*, however, was a highly personal attempt to give his daughter a realistic view of the proper conduct of women in light of what he admitted was injustice between the sexes.

You must first lay it down for a Foundation in general, That there is *Inequality* in the *Sexes*, and that for the better Oeconomy of the World, the *Men*, who were to be the Law-givers, had the larger share of *Reason* bestow'd upon them; by which means your Sex is the better prepar'd for the *Compliance* that is necessary for the better performance of those *Duties* which seem'd to be most properly assign'd to it. This looks a little uncourtly at the first appearance; but upon examination it will be found, that *Nature* is so far from being unjust to you, that she is partial on your side: She hath made you such large *Amends* by other Advantages, for the seeming *Injustice* of the first Distribution, that the Right of Complaining is come over to our Sex; you have it in your power not only to free your selves, but to subdue your Masters, and without violence throw both their *Natural* and *Legal Authority* at your Feet. We are made of differing *Tempers*, that our *Defects* might be mutually supplied: Your *Sex* wanteth our *Reason* for your *Conduct*, and our *Strength* for your *Protection*: *Ours* wanteth your *Gentleness* to soften, and to entertain us. The first part of our Life is a good deal of it subjected to you in the *Nursery*, where you Reign without Competition, and by that means have the advantage of giving the first *Impressions*; afterwards you have stronger Influences, which, well manag'd, have more force in your behalf, than all our *Priviledges* and *Jurisdictions* can pretend to have against you. You have more strength in your *Looks*, than we have in our *Laws*; and more power by your *Tears*, than we have by our *Arguments*.

KENNETH WALKER
PREPARATION FOR MARRIAGE, 1933

Kenneth Walker (1882–1966) was a British surgeon who wrote extensively on procedures and diseases of the male sexual organs. He minced no words in his assertions about the differences between the sexes, and the importance for men and women of accepting and understanding them.

Walker, in this same book, debunked the notion that women could control the future gender of their children, presciently writing: "The control of the sex *in utero* is still beyond our power, although at the present rate of advancement it does not seem impossible that some day it may be attained. Whether we shall benefit by this or not is a debatable point."

Many of the misunderstandings that arise between married couples and between those who have not yet married arise from an ignorance of the differences between the sexes. Woman is as different from man in her intellectual and emotional make-up as she is in her physical line, and the sooner this is understood by those who intend to marry the better. As a broad generalisation it may be said that the emotions play a far greater part in the life of a woman than they do in that of a man. The idea of emotional understanding has not yet found a place in conventional psychology, but that a woman may arrive at a truth by a process in which the intellect appears to play but little part is undoubtedly a fact. It is useless for the man to dispute her conclusions simply because she cannot justify them by means of logic. She knows that what she says is true and he may argue till he is tired without making any impression. So when the man attempts to prove that what he says is reasonable let him realize that to the woman his arguments are useless. They are but the dressed up puppets with which men (like little boys playing at soldiers) amuse themselves. Men move slowly along the road of reason; women, like arrows, fly straight to the mark. . . . Who shall not say that the emotions sometimes succeed where reasoning fails? In any case, they move on different planes, and to combat intuition by reason is a vain beating of the air.

JESS OPPENHEIMER, MADELYN PUGH, AND BOB CARROLL JR.
"THE ADAGIO," *I LOVE LUCY*, 1951

A classic of television comedy, *I Love Lucy* (see Work, page 496–98) featured Lucille Ball as Lucy Ricardo, tirelessly pushing the boundaries of the good wife's role.
Ethel was Lucy's best friend and frequent co-conspirator.

LUCY: Oh, Ethel, do you ever wish there was something else to marry besides men?

GERMAINE GREER
THE FEMALE EUNUCH, 1970

For background on Greer, see Expectations, page 106.

Every wife must live with the knowledge that she has nothing else but home and family, while her house is ideally a base which her tired warrior-hunter can withdraw to and express his worst manners, his least amusing conversation, while he licks his wounds and is prepared by laundry and toilet and lunch-box for another sortie.

    Obviously any woman who thinks in the simplest terms of liberating herself to enjoy life and create expression for her own potential cannot accept such a role. And yet marriage is based upon this filial relationship of a wife who takes her husband's name, has her tax declared on his return, lives in a house owned by him and goes about in public as his companion wearing his ring on her finger at all times.

S

HANNA ROSIN
"THE END OF MEN," 2010

In an *Atlantic* magazine article (later a book by the same title), Hanna Rosin (1970–) argued that women had become the dominant sex in modern society—better educated, employable, and suited than men for leadership in a world in which physical strength has become nearly irrelevant. With women holding a majority of jobs in the United States, men like Mustafaa El-Scari and his students—about whom Rosin wrote in this passage—struggled to cope with the startling role reversal and its implications for family dynamics.

El-Scari, a teacher and social worker, taught a weekly class on fathering for Kansas City men who had failed to pay child support and had been given the choice of taking this class or serving jail time.

Like them, [El-Scari] explains [in class], he grew up watching Bill Cosby living behind his metaphorical "white picket fence"—one man, one woman, and a bunch of happy kids. "Well, that check bounced a long time ago," he says. "Let's see," he continues, reading from a worksheet.

> He writes on the board: $85,000. "This is her salary." Then: $12,000. "This is your salary. Who's the damn man?"

What are the four kinds of paternal authority? Moral, emotional, social, and physical. "But you ain't none of those in that house. All you are is a paycheck, and now you ain't even that. And if you try to exercise your authority, she'll call 911. How does that make you feel? You're supposed to be the authority, and she says, 'Get out of the house, bitch.' She's calling you 'bitch'!"

. . . "What is our role? Everyone's telling us we're supposed to be head of a nuclear family, so you feel like you got robbed. It's toxic, and poisonous, and it's setting us up for failure." He writes on the board: $85,000. "This is her salary." Then: $12,000. "This is your salary. Who's the damn man? Who's the man now?" A murmur arises. "That's right. She's the man."

SICKNESS AND HEALTH

"A DEATH-BED MARRIAGE"
SAN FRANCISCO DAILY EVENING BULLETIN, 1866

On our third page will be found the notice of a marriage which took place in this city on Wednesday last, followed by the announcement of the death of the bridegroom on the following day. The circumstances of this case make it one of sad and peculiar interest. It not unfrequently happens that a bride or groom, soon after the performance of that rite which knits the dearest and holiest of bonds, is suddenly taken away in the midst of health and a new-found happiness. Then the affliction is indeed terrible to the bereaved, because unanticipated. But in the present instance, the young man having returned recently from the army, was confined to his bedroom from a disease contracted in the service. Day by day he sank visibly, and it was evident that his end was not far distant. In this extremity his affianced asked that the marriage ceremony might be no longer delayed, in order that she might be his bride, though but a few short hours, that for a lifetime she might be the widow of one who had so bravely served his country. Under these circumstances the marriage was consummated; and so it comes to pass that between the wedding and the burial there lies but the breadth of a single day.

CYRIL CONNOLLY
THE UNQUIET GRAVE, 1944

British author Cyril Connolly (1903–1974) cofounded the magazine *Horizon*, contributed influential essays and criticism to various publications, and published a novel. But some of his best-known works are no longer than a sentence, mainly because he collected his aphorisms in his book *The Unquiet Grave*.

The true index of a man's character is the health of his wife.

S

DANA REEVE
LETTER TO CHRISTOPHER REEVE, 1996

Dana Morosini Reeve (1961–2006) wrote this letter on the fourth anniversary of her marriage to actor Christopher Reeve, most famous for playing Superman in a series of successful films. In 1995, a horse-riding accident left him a quadriplegic, but his resolve to persevere and hers to support him as they raised money for stem-cell research brought the couple a different kind of renown. He died in 2004 of cardiac arrest; she, two years later of lung cancer.

My darling Toph,

This path we are on is unpredictable, mysterious, profoundly challenging, and yes, even fulfilling. It is a path we chose to embark on together and for all the brambles and obstructions that have come our way of late, I have no regrets. In fact, all of our difficulties have shown me how deeply I love you and how grateful I am that we can follow this path together. Our future will be bright, my darling one, because we have each other and our young 'uns.

> With all my heart and soul,
> I love you,
> Dana

JOHN GOTTMAN AND NAN SILVER
THE SEVEN PRINCIPLES FOR MAKING MARRIAGE WORK, 1999

For background on Gottman and Silver, see Friendship, page 138.

When we tested the immune system responses of the fifty couples who stayed overnight in the Love Lab, we found a striking difference between those who were very satisfied with their marriages and those whose emotional response to each other was neutral or who were unhappy. Specifically, we used blood samples from each subject to test the response of certain of their white blood cells—the immune system's major defense weapons. In general, happily married men and women showed a greater proliferation of these white blood cells when exposed to foreign invaders than did the other subjects.

We also tested the effectiveness of other immune system warriors—the natural killer cells, which, true to their name, destroy body cells that have been damaged or altered (such as infected or cancerous ones) and are known to limit the growth of tumor cells. Again, subjects who were satisfied with their marriage had more effective natural killer cells than did the others.

It will take more study before scientists can confirm that this boost in the immune system is one of the mechanisms by which a good marriage benefits your health and longevity. But what's most important is that we know for certain that a good marriage does.

RICHARD COHEN
BLINDSIDED, 2004

Journalist Richard Cohen (1948–) was diagnosed with multiple sclerosis in his twenties and with colon cancer in his fifties. A former CBS news producer and three-time Emmy Award winner, he married the TV host Meredith Vieira in 1986; they have three children.

Smiling your way through sickness is a preposterous plan, though it can work wonders from time to time. My rose-colored glasses went into a drawer long ago. They are gathering dust, lying next to Meredith's cracked lenses of the same hue. Meredith had to discard dreams too soon in her life. She cannot have bargained for a relationship so defined by diseases. But that is what she got.

When Meredith learned in the spring of 2002 that *Ladies' Home Journal* was planning another cover story about her for the following September, the black humor around our kitchen table ignited spontaneously. I started the pointed jokes about being cast as Richard, the house cripple. Meredith likes *LHJ,* but she half joined in. I could smell tragedy in the oven, just baking away.

Here we go again was all I could think. An *LHJ* cover story in October 2000 had been a sob story, the tale of the rising star and her crumpling husband, portraying me as physically devastated and Meredith as all-suffering. The magazine's cover and index chose the words "heartbreaking" and "devastating" to highlight my condition. Neither applied.

"Meredith Vieira's tears begin without warning," the magazine wrote back then. That was the opening line. The tears are real and occasionally present in our house. Meredith has her emotional threshold, frequently different from mine. The tears are tempered with strength, however, and to lead this article with this maudlin suggestion that Meredith is only a weeping willow is misleading. Meredith can be one tough broad.

Now I was certain I would be portrayed in this next profile as even more of a wreck. Colon cancer had struck again, and I had written a series of very candid, personal essays in the *New York Times* about my health struggles, so I had already gone public. Meredith's life would be presented as even more of a soap opera. I did not like what I saw coming. "You should pose for the cover, sitting, perched on the arm of a wheelchair," I suggested. "Or maybe you should lie next to me in an oxygen tent." Meredith had a better idea. "How about if I just get out that cute little black dress I bought for your funeral, you know, just before the cancer surgery," she offered with a giggle. "I was so disappointed I never got to wear it."

My pessimistic scenario did not play out. The article was okay, only because Meredith headed off the martyr mania at the pass. I happened to call Meredith on her cellphone while she was lunching with the writer for the *Journal* piece. "Yeah, I am being interviewed," Meredith is quoted in the article as saying to me. "I am just at the part when I say I have to take care of you because you're a shadow of a man." Notes the interviewer, "My terminally pleasant interviewer's face freezes into what I suspect is a gargoyle-like grimace." I believe she got the point.

JESSICA AND ANTHONY VILLARREAL
STORYCORPS RECORDING, 2013

A Marine corporal serving in Afghanistan, Anthony Villarreal was just twenty-two years old in 2008 when his truck was hit by a roadside bomb. He suffered third-degree burns that covered his face and most of his body and eventually led to the amputation of his left arm and several fingers on his right hand. He and his wife, Jessica, twenty-one, had only recently married. For a StoryCorps project, they talked to each other about what it was like to be reunited.

JESSICA: I remember when I first saw you. The doctors wanted me to identify you, like you had died or something. You were covered in bandages, and I can only see your eyes and your lips. And then they showed me the extent of the burn, how it went straight to the bone. They told me, "We can't salvage the tissue," so I had to sign papers saying that it was OK for them to amputate.

ANTHONY: When I woke up from that three-month drug-induced coma, having to learn everything that a baby has to learn, I didn't even recognize myself. After the first time I saw myself in the mirror, that's when I just broke down. I really thought that my life was over. Kept thinking what was I going to do? How am I going to get a job?
What did you think about?

JESSICA: I just knew that you needed me and I was going to be there.
Were you ever scared that I'd leave you?

ANTHONY: Yeah. I mean, it's hard not to think about that, because a lot of people, they don't want to be seen with someone that was ugly. What was it, like seventy-plus surgeries, skin grafts? I really didn't want to leave the house. I just thought to myself, man, people don't know how to ask questions. They just want to stare and point. I'm just glad that you're here to help me.

JESSICA: The crazy thing is I'm still more self-conscious about what I look like than you are. But I have grown so much over the past five years. Didn't ever think that I'd be as strong as I am today and most of it is from you. I can't imagine you not being in my life.

ANTHONY: We've been through so much in so little time. Shouldn't be anything that could tear us apart besides death itself.

S

TOASTS

MEL BROOKS, 1985

Offering a toast at the wedding of our friends Kate Lear and Jon LaPook, Carl Reiner and Mel Brooks reprised their famous *2000 Year Old Man* routine. In character as the interviewer, Reiner asked Brooks: "Sir, you have lived a long time, you've seen many marriages. What advice would you give to this young couple to live a happy and fruitful life?" This was the pseudo-sage's advice.

Ignore each other.

No, I say that with love and spirit and spirit and love and in feeling and sentiment and romance and spirit and love. I'm saying that all in love. Ignore each other.

Because the more you find out about each other, the more disenchanted, the more disgusted, the more you realize you're just plain people like each other, and you'll hate each other because the same hatred you feel for yourselves you're going to throw on each other. So keep the mystery alive.

When Dr. LaPook comes home at night, Kate should say, "Who is it?" and Dr. LaPook should say, "It's Irving."

Never give your real name in marriage. Never. Once they know your real name in a marriage, you're finished.

. . . No seriously. Let me be serious. Don't give away too much. You'll be married a long time.

TRIUMPHS

SAMUEL JOHNSON, CIRCA 1770

This was the comment that Dr. Johnson (see Devotion, page 55; Infidelity, page 203) made in regard to a widower who had remarried right after his first wife's death.

[A second marriage is] the triumph of hope over experience.

H. L. MENCKEN AND GEORGE JEAN NATHAN
HELIOGABALUS, 1920

Mencken (see Adam and Eve, page 3; Expectations, page 105; Jealousy, page 240) and drama critic George Jean Nathan (1882–1958) were founders of *The American Mercury* magazine.

Love is the triumph of imagination over intelligence.

CARRIE FISHER
WISHFUL DRINKING, 2008

Daughter of Debbie Reynolds, star of *Star Wars*, screenwriter, novelist, and recovering alcoholic, Carrie Fisher (1956–) wrote and performed *Wishful Drinking* as a one-woman show before publishing it in book form. She was married to singer/songwriter Paul Simon for two years but with him on and off for more than a dozen.

Remarrying the same person is the triumph of nostalgia over judgment.

UNMARRIED

ELIZABETH I, 1563

For Queen Elizabeth I (1533–1603), being unmarried was a tool, sometimes a weapon, as she astutely played one would-be suitor against another, all the while maintaining her power as British sovereign and staking her reputation as "the Virgin Queen." She is supposed to have said the following when an envoy from the Holy Roman court was sent to negotiate a marriage with the Austrian archduke.

If I am to disclose to you what I should prefer if I followed the inclination of my nature, it is this: Beggar-woman and single, far rather than Queen and married.

"THE OLD MAID'S APOLOGY," 1801

Unsigned, this poem appeared in a short-lived American periodical called *The Lady's Magazine and Musical Repository.*

"They that die maids, lead apes in hell," is a proverb mentioned in several of Shakespeare's plays, although its original source is subject to debate.

I determin'd the moment I left off my bib,
I would never become any man's crooked rib,
And think you to fright me, when gravely you tell
That Old Maids will surely lead apes when in hell?

I'll take the reversion, and grant 'twill be so
But yet I shall keep to my vow,
For I'd rather lead apes in the regions below,
Than be led by a foolish ape now.

"THE OLD MAID'S DIARY"
FREEDOM'S JOURNAL, 1827

The first newspaper owned and run by African-Americans in the United States, *Freedom's Journal* was published in New York City starting in 1827, the year that New York State officially abolished slavery. It was a weekly with a commitment to antebellum reform but featured, in addition to serious editorials and news reports, a fine complement of human interest pieces, travelogues, and, as in the two examples below, social commentary.

In this context, the word *chit* means "child" or "young woman."

YEARS

15.	Anxious for coming out, and the attention of the men.
16.	Begins to have some idea of the tender passion.
17.	Talks of love in a cottage, and disinterested affection.
18.	Fancies herself in love with some handsome man, who has flattered her.
19.	Is a little more difficult, in consequence of being noticed.
20.	Commences fashionable, and dashes.
21.	Still more confidence in her own attractions, and expects a brilliant establishment.
22.	Refuses a good offer, because he is not a man of fashion.
23.	Flirts with every young man she meets.
24.	Wonders she is not married.
25.	Rather more circumspect in her conduct.
26.	Begins to think a large fortune not quite so indispensable.
27.	Prefers the company of rational men to flirting.

28.   Wishes to be married in a quiet way, with a comfortable income.
29.   Almost despairs of entering the married state.
30.   Rather fearful of being called an old maid.
31.   An additional love of dress.
32.   Professes to dislike balls, finding it difficult to get good partners.
33.   Wonders how men can leave the society of sensible men to flirt with chits.
34.   Affects good humour in her conversation with men.
35.   Jealous of the praises of women.
36.   Quarrels with her friend, who is lately married.
37.   Thinks herself slighted in society.
38.   Likes talking of her acquaintance who are married unfortunately, and finds consolation in their misfortune.
39.   Ill-nature increases.
40.   Very meddling and officious . . . A growing penchant.
41.   If rich, as a dernier resort makes love to a young man without fortune.
42.   Not succeeding, rails against the sex.
43.   Partiality for cards, and scandal commences.
44.   Severe against the manners of the age.
45.   Strong predilection for a Methodist parson.
46.   Enraged at his desertion.
47.   Becomes desponding, and takes snuff.
48.   Turns all her sensibility to cats and dogs.
49.   Adopts a dependent relation to attend on dogs.
50.   Becomes disgusted with the world. Vents all her ill-humour on this unfortunate relation.

"A BACHELOR'S THERMOMETER"
FREEDOM'S JOURNAL, 1827

The counterpart to the column above appeared one week later.

YEARS
16.   Incipient palpitations towards the young ladies.
17.   Blushing and confusion in conversing with them.

18. Confidence in conversing with them much increased.

19. Angry if treated by them as a boy.

20. Very conscious of his own charms and manliness.

21. A looking glass, indispensable in his room, to admire himself.

22. Insufferable puppyism.

23. Thinks no woman good enough for him.

24. Caught unawares by the snares of Cupid.

25. The connexion broken off, from self-conceit on his part.

26. Conducts himself with much superiority towards her.

27. Pays his addresses to another lady, not without hope of mortifying the first.

28. Mortified and frantic at being refused.

29. Rails against the fair sex in general.

30. Morose and out of humour in all conversations on matrimony.

31. Contemplates matrimony more under the influence of interest than formerly.

32. Considers personal beauty in a wife not so indispensable as formerly.

33. Still retains a high opinion of his attractions as a husband.

34. Consequently has no idea but he may still marry a chicken.

35. Falls deeply and violently in love with one of seventeen.

36. *Au dernier desespoir* another refusal.

37. Indulges in every kind of dissipation.

38. Shuns the best part of the female sex.

39. Suffers much remorse and mortification in so doing.

40. A fresh budding of matrimonial ideas, but no spring shoots.

41. A nice young widow perplexes him.

42. Ventures to address her with mixed sensations of love and interest.

43. Interest prevails, which causes much cautious reflection.

44. The widow jilts him, being as cautious as himself.

45. Becomes every day more averse to the fair sex.

46. Gouty and nervous symptoms begin to appear.

47. Fears what may become of him when old and infirm.

48. Thinks living alone quite irksome.

49. Resolves to have a prudent young woman as house keeper and companion.

50. A nervous affection about him, and frequent [attacks] of the gout.

51. Much pleased with his new house keeper as nurse.

52. Begins to feel some attachment to her.

53.   His pride revolts at the idea of marrying her.

54.   Is in great distress how to act.

55.   Completely under her influence and very miserable.

56.   Many painful thoughts about parting with her.

57.   She refuses to live any longer with him *solo*.

58.   Gouty, nervous, and billious to excess.

59.   Feels very ill, sends for her to his bedside, and intends espousing her.

60.   Grows rapidly worse, has his will made in her favour, and makes his exit.

CHARLES DICKENS
GREAT EXPECTATIONS, 1861

Charles Dickens (1812–1870) wrote fifteen novels, but the scene below has to be among the top two or three most memorable in all his work. It is narrated by the orphan Pip upon encountering for the first time the terrifying Miss Havisham, a woman abandoned on her wedding day and more than slightly crazy as a result.

Pumblechook is Pip's brother-in-law's uncle and the person who has arranged to have Pip visit Miss Havisham.

In an arm-chair, with an elbow resting on the table and her head leaning on that hand, sat the strangest lady I have ever seen, or shall ever see.

She was dressed in rich materials—satins, and lace, and silks—all of white. Her shoes were white. And she had a long white veil dependent from her hair, and she had bridal flowers in her hair, but her hair was white. Some bright jewels sparkled on her neck and on her hands, and some other jewels lay sparkling on the table. Dresses, less splendid than the dress she wore, and half-packed trunks, were scattered about. She had not quite finished dressing, for she had but one shoe on—the other was on the table near her hand—her veil was but half arranged, her watch and chain were not put on, and some lace for her bosom lay with those trinkets, and with her handkerchief, and gloves, and some flowers, and a Prayer-book, all confusedly heaped about the looking-glass.

It was not in the first moments that I saw all these things, though I saw more of them in the first moments than might be supposed. But, I saw that everything within my view which ought to be white, had been white long ago, and had lost its lustre, and was faded and yellow. I saw that the bride within the bridal dress had withered like the dress, and like the flowers, and had no brightness left but the brightness of her sunken eyes. I saw that the dress had been put

U

upon the rounded figure of a young woman, and that the figure upon which it now hung loose, had shrunk to skin and bone. Once, I had been taken to see some ghastly waxwork at the Fair, representing I know not what impossible personage lying in state. Once, I had been taken to one of our old marsh churches to see a skeleton in the ashes of a rich dress, that had been dug out of a vault under the church pavement. Now waxwork and skeleton seemed to have dark eyes that moved and looked at me. I should have cried out, if I could.

"Who is it?" said the lady at the table.

"Pip, ma'am."

"Pip?"

"Mr. Pumblechook's boy, ma'am. Come—to play."

"Come nearer; let me look at you. Come close."

It was when I stood before her, avoiding her eyes, that I took note of the surrounding objects in detail, and saw that her watch had stopped at twenty minutes to nine, and that a clock in the room had stopped at twenty minutes to nine.

"Look at me," said Miss Havisham. "You are not afraid of a woman who has never seen the sun since you were born?"

I regret to state that I was not afraid of telling the enormous lie comprehended in the answer "No."

"Do you know what I touch here?" she said, laying her hands, one upon the other, on her left side.

"Yes, ma'am." (It made me think of the young man.)

"What do I touch?"

"Your heart."

"Broken!"

P. G. WODEHOUSE
"THE RUMMY AFFAIR OF OLD BIFFY," 1924

Bertie Wooster is a recurring protagonist in the nearly hundred books penned by the British humorist Sir Pelham Grenville Wodehouse (1881–1975). Through Bertie's long-suffering yet good-natured travels through the British upper class, he often finds himself trying to extricate himself from marital plans that repeatedly seem to be made on his behalf. As Wodehouse wrote in 1960's *Jeeves in the Offing*: "I don't know anything that braces one up like finding you haven't got to get married after all." In this story, Honoria Glossop is the fate Bertie has most recently escaped, and Wodehouse's inimitable valet, Jeeves, takes the news in stride.

"Great Scott!" I exclaimed.

"Sir?" said Jeeves, turning at the door.

"Jeeves, you remember Miss Glossop?"

"Very vividly, sir."

"She's engaged to Mr. Biffen!"

"Indeed, sir?" said Jeeves. And, with not another word, he slid out. The blighter's calm amazed and shocked me. It seemed to indicate that there must be a horrible streak of callousness in him. I mean to say, it wasn't as if he didn't know Honoria Glossop.

I read the paragraph again. A peculiar feeling it gave me. I don't know if you have ever experienced the sensation of seeing the announcement of the engagement of a pal of yours to a girl whom you were only saved from marrying yourself by the skin of your teeth. It induces a sort of—well, it's difficult to describe it exactly; but I should imagine a fellow would feel much the same if he happened to be strolling through the jungle with a boyhood chum and met a tigress or a jaguar, or what not, and managed to shin up a tree and looked down and saw the friend of his youth vanishing into the undergrowth in the animal's slavering jaws. A sort of profound, prayerful relief, if you know what I mean, blended at the same time with a pang of pity. What I'm driving at is that, thankful as I was that I hadn't had to marry Honoria myself, I was sorry to see a real good chap like old Biffy copping it. I sucked down a spot of tea and began to brood over the business. . . .

"I must say, Jeeves," I said, "I'm dashed disappointed in you."

"I am sorry to hear that, sir."

"Well, I am. Dashed disappointed. I do think you might rally round. Did you see Mr. Biffen's face?"

"Yes, sir."

"Well, then."

"If you will pardon my saying so, sir, Mr. Biffen has surely only himself to thank if he has entered upon matrimonial obligations which do not please him."

"You're talking absolute rot, Jeeves. You know as well as I do that Honoria Glossop is an Act of God. You might just as well blame a fellow for getting run over by a truck."

U

ESTONIAN PROVERB

Better be an honest old spinster than a worthless husband's wife.

HELEN GURLEY BROWN
SEX AND THE SINGLE GIRL, 1962

In many ways an unlikely feminist, Helen Gurley Brown (1922–2012) was both a pioneer in championing women's sexual independence and a traditionalist in expressing women's desire for the validation of men. Brown began her career as an advertising copywriter and, later, executive. She married David Brown (producer of such films as *The Sting* and *Jaws*) three years before writing *Sex and the Single Girl*, an overnight bestseller that tapped into young women's needs to navigate a new landscape of work, love, sex, fashion, and culture. The book made Brown famous, spawned many others, and led to her being named editor-in-chief of *Cosmopolitan* magazine, which she remade into a hugely successful monthly. Her fifty-one-year marriage to Brown lasted until his death in 2010.

The passage below is from the introduction to Brown's first book.

WOMEN ALONE? OH COME NOW!

I married for the first time at thirty-seven. I got the man I wanted. It *could* be construed as something of a miracle considering how old *I* was and how eligible *he* was.

David is a motion picture producer, forty-four, brainy, charming and sexy. He was sought after by many a Hollywood starlet as well as some less flamboyant but more deadly types. And *I* got him! We have two Mercedes-Benzes, one hundred acres of virgin forest near San Francisco, a Mediterranean house overlooking the Pacific, a full-time maid and a good life.

I am not beautiful, or even pretty. I once had the world's worst case of acne. I am not bosomy or brilliant. I grew up in a small town. I didn't go to college. My family was, and is, desperately poor and I have always helped support them. I'm an introvert and I am sometimes mean and cranky.

But *I* don't think it's a miracle that I married my husband. I think I deserved him! For seventeen years I worked hard to become the kind of woman who might interest him. And when he finally walked into my life I was just worldly enough, relaxed enough, financially secure enough (for I also worked hard at my job) and adorned with enough glitter to attract him. He wouldn't have looked at me when I was twenty, and I wouldn't have known what to do with *him*.

There is a tidal wave of misinformation these days about how many more marriageable women there are than men (that part is true enough) and how tough is the plight of the single woman—spinster, widow, divorcee.

I think a single woman's biggest problem is coping with the people who are trying to marry her off! She is so driven by herself and her well-meaning but addlepated friends to become married that her whole existence seems to be an apology for *not* being married. Finding *him* is all she can think about or talk about when (a) she may not be psychologically ready for marriage; (b) there is no available husband for every girl at the time she wants one; and (c) her years as a single woman can be too rewarding to rush out of.

Although many's the time I was sure I would die alone in my spinster's bed, I could never bring myself to marry just to get married. If I had, I would have missed a great deal of misery along the way, no doubt, but also a great deal of fun.

I think marriage is insurance for the *worst* years of your life. During your best years you don't need a husband. You do need a man of course every step of the way, and they are often cheaper emotionally and a lot more fun by the dozen. . . .

Frankly, the magazines and their marriage statistics give me a royal pain.

There is a more important truth that magazines never deal with, that single women are too brainwashed to figure out, that married women know but won't admit, that married men *and* single men endorse in a body, and that is that the single woman, far from being a creature to be pitied and patronized, is emerging as the newest glamour girl of our times.

She is engaging because she lives by her wits. She supports herself. She has had to sharpen her personality and mental resources to a glitter in order to survive in a competitive world and the sharpening looks good. Economically she is a dream. She is not a parasite, a dependent, a scrounger, a sponger or a bum. She is a giver, not a taker, a winner and not a loser. . . .

SEX—WHAT OF IT?

Theoretically a "nice" single woman has no sex life. What nonsense! She has a better sex life than most of her married friends. She need never be bored with one man per lifetime. Her choice of partners is endless and they seek *her*. They never come to her bed duty-bound. Her married friends refer to her pursuers as wolves, but actually many of them turn out to be lambs—to be shorn and worn by her.

Sex of course is more than the act of coitus. It begins with the delicious feeling of attraction between two people. It may never go further, but sex it is. And a single woman may promote the attraction, bask in the sensation, drink it like wine and pour it over her like blossoms, with never a guilty twinge. She can promise with a look, a touch, a letter or a kiss—and she doesn't have to deliver. She can be maddeningly hypocritical and, after arousing desire, insist that it be shut off by stating she wants to be chaste for the man she marries. Her pursuer may strangle her with his necktie, but he can't *argue* with her. A flirtatious married woman is expected to Go Through With Things.

U

Since for a female getting there is at *least* half the fun, a single woman has reason to prize the luxury of taking long, gossamer, attenuated, pulsating trips before finally arriving in bed. . . .

Yet, while indulging her libido, which she has plenty of if she is young and healthy, it is still possible for the single woman to be a lady, to be highly respected and even envied if she is successful in her work.

I did it. So have many of my friends.

Perhaps this all sounds like bragging. I do not mean to suggest for a moment that being single is not often hell. But I do mean to suggest that it can also be quite heavenly, whether you choose *it* or it chooses *you.*

There is a catch to achieving single bliss. You have to work like a son of a bitch.

PAUL MAZURSKY
AN UNMARRIED WOMAN, 1978

Being unmarried is the last thing that Erica Benton, played by Jill Clayburgh, imagines or wants at the start of *An Unmarried Woman,* which was written and directed by Paul Mazursky (1930–2014). The film, which was in many ways a feminist landmark, tells the story of Erica's gradual liberation after being left by her husband for a younger woman. Alone, Erica experiences friendships with other women, self-exploration through therapy, casual sex with a colleague, and finally a love affair with a British artist, Saul, played by Alan Bates.

SAUL: I know you want to get out on your own and I approve—

ERICA: I don't need your approval.

SAUL: Let me finish—. But taking two months off to be with someone you like very much—that's not really out of line.

ERICA: How do you know? How do you know what I need? What I have to do for myself?

SAUL: *(Wryly)* Maybe we should see a marriage counselor.

ERICA: Saul, you're free to see other women.

SAUL: I don't want other women. I want you. Do you want to see other men?

ERICA: Not today—I don't know about tomorrow.

(They sit on a bench.)

ERICA: I don't know what's going to happen—I may move to a smaller apartment—I may get another job—Am I in love with you?—I don't think about it like that.—I like you very much.—It's nice.—But I want my own space.—My own self. Do you understand?

NANCY MEYERS, CHARLES SHYER, HARVEY MILLER
PRIVATE BENJAMIN, 1980

Goldie Hawn coproduced and starred in this comedy about a privileged young woman, Judy Benjamin, who goes from her wedding to her husband's funeral to the U.S. army in the course of several days. In this scene, she is holed up in a hotel room, talking to a radio hotline host.

If I'm not going to be married—I don't know what I'm supposed to do with myself. Did you happen to see that movie, *Unmarried Woman*? Well, I didn't get it. I mean, I would've been Mrs. Alan Bates so fast that guy wouldn't have known what hit him.

HELEN FIELDING
BRIDGET JONES'S DIARY, 1996

In her popular column-turned-novel-turned-high-grossing-movie, British writer Helen Fielding (1958–) captured the joys and frustrations—in work, friendship, dating, and dieting—of a single woman surrounded by smug young-marrieds who seem to want to impose their questionable bliss on others. Bumbling toward love and self-realization through a maze of missteps and embarrassments, Bridget defends her "singleton" turf with winning strength and humor.

Frankie Howerd was a British comedian famous for his double entendres.

Humph. Incensed by patronizing article in the paper by Smug Married journalist. It was head-lined, with subtle-as-a-Frankie-Howerd-sexual-innuendo-style irony: "The Joy of Single Life."

"They're young, ambitious and rich but their lives hide an aching loneliness . . . When they leave work a gaping emotional hole opens up before them . . . Lonely style-obsessed individuals seek consolation in packeted comfort food of the kind their mother might have made."

Huh. Bloody nerve. How does Mrs. Smug Married-at-twenty-two think she knows, thank you very much?

U

I'm going to write an article based on "dozens of conversations" with Smug Marrieds: "When they leave work, they always burst into tears because, though exhausted, they have to peel potatoes and put all the washing in while their porky bloater husbands slump burping in front of the football demanding plates of chips. On other nights they plop, wearing unstylish pinnies, into big black holes after their husbands have rung to say they're working late again, with the sound of creaking leatherware and sexy Singletons tittering in the background."

JENNY BICKS
"A WOMAN'S RIGHT TO SHOES," *SEX AND THE CITY*, 2003

Based on the book by Candace Bushnell, the HBO television series *Sex and the City* ran for six years, showcasing the intimate lives of four Manhattan women in their thirties (in one case forties) as they grappled with the challenges of dating, sex, work, fashion, friendship, and marriage. Carrie, the Bushnell-based narrator of the show, was played by Sarah Jessica Parker, and Charlotte, the sweetest and most romantic of the four, by Kristin Davis. This scene occurs in an episode from the sixth season, when Carrie's expensive shoes have disappeared from her friend Kyra's baby shower. After Kyra questions the extravagance of Carrie's lifestyle, Carrie debates with Charlotte her "right to shoes."

CARRIE: I did a little mental addition, and over the years I have bought Kyra an engagement gift, a wedding gift, then there was the trip to Maine for the wedding, the three baby gifts—in toto, I have spent over $2,300 celebrating her choices, and she is shaming me for spending a lousy 485 bucks on myself? Yes, I did the math.

CHARLOTTE: But those were gifts. I mean, if you got married or had a child, she would spend the same on you.

CARRIE: And if I don't ever get married or have a baby, I get what? Bupkis? Think about it. If you are single, after graduation there isn't one occasion where people celebrate you.

CHARLOTTE: We have birthdays.

CARRIE: Oh no no no no. We all have birthdays. That's a wash. I am talking about the single gal. Hallmark doesn't make a "congratulations, you didn't marry the wrong guy" card. And where's the flatware for going on vacation alone?

OPRAH WINFREY
JAIPUR LITERATURE FESTIVAL INTERVIEW, 2012

One of the most powerful women in the world, Oprah Winfrey (1954–) is an actress, entrepreneur, philanthropist, and—most famously—talk-show host, with a magazine and a cable TV network of her own. Though for many years she was publicly if loosely engaged to author and educator Stedman Graham, they didn't marry, a decision she discussed during an interview in India.

I live in a country that allows me to have the choice of not marrying. If I would have married, he would have been a wonderful husband, but I'll be honest that we would have been divorced by now. I'm my own person, and I find it difficult to conform to other people's ideas about me. And being married does call for some conformity. I respect the women of India who were in arranged marriages, which later turned into love marriages.

But that's just not a part of the way I think because I wasn't brought up in this culture. And I think I'm too old now. I was engaged once in my 30s for a while, and like most women I just wanted to see if he cared enough to want to marry me. And then I told my friend that I don't just have cold feet, my feet are in a bucket of cement.

U

VIOLENCE

BRITISH CHURCH COURT RECORD, 1300

The fourteenth century in England was not exactly a liberated time for wives; grave injury or grave risk usually had to be proven for divorces to be granted. Nonetheless, according to this fragment (originally written in Latin) from a church court in Droitwich, there were some consequences for violent behavior.

Thomas Louchard ill treated his wife with a rod. The man appears, confesses, and is whipped in the usual manner once through the market.

SAMUEL ROWLANDS
"A WHOLE CREW OF KIND GOSSIPS, ALL MET TO BE MERRY," 1609

Not much appears to be known about the British author Samuel Rowlands (circa 1565–circa 1630) except that he wrote a considerable number of pamphlets and what were called "jest books." In the one from which this passage is taken, Rowlands purports to record the chatter of six women in a tavern, all unloading complaints about their husbands. The faults range from cheapness to drunkenness to sexual incompetence and, in the case of the "second Gossip," below, constant disagreement. The upshot: Then as now, marital violence is not always a male act.

The original meaning of *faggot* is "a bundle of sticks."

At first (indeed) he put me in a feare,
When as I heard him but begin to sweare:
Then spake I faire, and to him was right kinde,
Thinking to put him in a better minde.
I tride him thus a while, but t'was a wonder
How he would dominiere, and keepe me under.
Nay then (quoth I) Ile try my Mothers tricke,
And valiantly tooke up a Faggot-sticke.
(For he had given me a blow or twaine)
But as he likes it, let him strike againe,

When a Wife goes astray, 'tis safe to use a sympathetick Remedy, such as the rebuke of a Kiss.

The blood ran downe about his eares apace,
I brake his head, and all bescratch't his face:
Then got him downe, and with my very fist
I did bepommell him untill he pist.
So from that houre unto this present day,
He never durst begin another fray:
But is content to let all fighting cease,
A Faggot-sticke hath bound him to the peace.

BRITISH PROVERB, 1678

Leaving aside the women and the animals, walnut trees were beaten because they were believed to flourish best when their nuts were shaken down, rather than gathered from the ground.

Another version: "A woman, an ass, and a walnut tree . . ."

A spaniel, a woman, and a walnut tree,
The more they're beaten the better still they be!

JOHN DUNTON
THE POST-ANGEL, 1701

A bookseller and author with an eccentric and broad range of interests, John Dunton (1659–1733) formed the Athenian Society in London as a "society of experts" and in 1691 started publishing the twice-weekly *Athenian Mercury*, using his experts to produce what was essentially the first advice column. A women's version soon followed, and then, in 1701, a short-lived British periodical, *The Post-Angel: or, Universal Entertainment*, which featured legal cases, obituaries, book news, and a section called "A New Athenian Mercury: Resolving the most Nice and Curious Questions propos'd by the Ingenious of either Sex." This was one of those questions.

Quest. 27. Whether tis lawful for a Man to beat his Wife.

Answ. The affirmative would be very disobliging to that Sex, without adding any more to it, therefore I ought to be as cautious and tender as may be asserting such an ill natur'd Position. I allow a Wife to be naturaliz'd into, and part of her Husband, and yet Nature sometimes wars against part of itself, in ejecting by Sweat, Urine, &c. what otherwise would be destructive to its very Frame; nay, sometimes there is occasion of greater Violences to Nature; so there are but few Husbands that know how to correct a Wife. To do it in a Passion, and pretend Justice, is ridiculous; because the Passion incapacitates the Judgment from its Office; and to do it when one is pleas'd, is a harder Task; so that I conclude, as the Legality is questionable, so the Time and Measure are generally too critical for a *Calculation;* when a Wife goes astray, 'tis safe to use a sympathetick Remedy, as the rebuke of a Kiss: The Antipathetick may prove worse than the Disease.

V

V

JUDGE THUMB.
or _ *Patent Sticks for Family Correction; Warranted Lawful!*

JAMES GILLRAY
JUDGE THUMB, 1782

Francis Buller is the central figure in this caricature by British printmaker James Gillray (circa 1756–1815). Buller earned the nickname "Judge Thumb" for his supposed court ruling (records are unclear) that a man had the legal right to beat his wife, as long as the stick he used was no wider than a man's thumb. This, by the way, is one of many suggested origins of the phrase "rule of thumb."

In the cartoon, the judge is saying: "Who wants a cure for a nasty Wife? Here's your nice Family Amusement for Winter Evenings! Who buys here?" The wife is saying: "Help! Murder, for God sake, Murder!" The husband is saying: "Murder, hey? It's Law, you Bitch: it's not bigger than my Thumb!"

TENNESSEE WILLIAMS
A STREETCAR NAMED DESIRE, 1947

Winner of the 1948 Pulitzer Prize for Drama, *A Streetcar Named Desire* made a luminary of author Tennessee Williams (1911–1983) and a star of Marlon Brando. Eventually a movie as well, the play tells the story of Blanche DuBois, an aging southern belle, who—out of money, luck, and almost hope—comes to New Orleans to stay with her sister and brother-in-law, Stella and Stanley Kowalski. The conflict between the feral Stanley and the self-deluded Blanche is at the heart of the play, and Stella is torn between her love for her husband and the desire to protect her sister from his violent nature. The conflict is clear when Stella and Blanche arrive home to find a poker game in full swing.

Mitch, one of Stanley's friends, courts Blanche until Stanley tells him about her past. Eunice is the Kowalskis' upstairs neighbor. "The blue piano" is Williams's term for the jazz music that wafts through New Orleans—and through the play. What separates the two excerpts below is a scene of the poker players forcing Stanley into a shower to try to sober him up, then hastily leaving.

STELLA:	Drunk—drunk—animal thing, you! *(She rushes through to the poker table.)* All of you—please go home! If any of you have one spark of decency in you—
BLANCHE:	*(Wildly)* Stella, watch out, he's—
	(Stanley charges after Stella.)
MEN:	*(Feebly)* Take it easy, Stanley. Easy, fellow.—Let's all—
STELLA:	You lay your hands on me and I'll—

V

(She backs out of sight. He advances and disappears. There is the sound of a blow. Stella cries out. Blanche screams and runs into the kitchen. The men rush forward and there is grappling and cursing. Something is overturned with a crash.)

BLANCHE: *(Shrilly)* My sister is going to have a baby!

MITCH: This is terrible.

BLANCHE: Lunacy, absolute lunacy!

MITCH: Get him in here, men.

(Stanley is forced, pinioned by the two men, into the bedroom. He nearly throws them off. Then all at once he subsides and is limp in their grasp.

(They speak quietly and lovingly to him and he leans his face on one of their shoulders.)

STELLA: *(In a high, unnatural voice, out of sight)* I want to go away, I want to go away!

MITCH: Poker shouldn't be played in a house with women. . . .

. . . *(Stanley comes out of the bathroom dripping water and still in his clinging wet polka dot drawers.)*

Stell-lahhhhh!

STANLEY: Stella! *(There is a pause.)* My baby doll's left me!

(He breaks into sobs. Then he goes to the phone and dials, still shuddering with sobs.) Eunice? I want my baby! *(He waits a moment; then he hangs up and dials again.)* Eunice! I'll keep on ringin' until I talk with my baby!

(An indistinguishable shrill voice is heard. He hurls phone to floor. Dissonant brass and piano sounds as the rooms dim out to darkness and the outer walls appear in the night light. The "blue piano" plays for a brief interval.

(Finally, Stanley stumbles half-dressed out to the porch and down the wooden steps to the pavement before the building. There he throws back his head like a baying hound and bellows his wife's name: "Stella! Stella, sweetheart! Stella!")

STANLEY: Stell-lahhhhh!

EUNICE:	*(Calling down from the door of her upper apartment)* Quit that howling out there an' go back to bed!
STANLEY:	I want my baby down here. Stella, Stella!
EUNICE:	She ain't comin' down so you quit! Or you'll git th' law on you!
STANLEY:	Stella!
EUNICE:	You can't beat on a woman an' then call 'er back! She won't come! And her goin' t' have a baby!—You stinker! You whelp of a Polack, you! I hope they do haul you in and turn the fire hose on you, same as the last time!
STANLEY:	*(Humbly)* Eunice, I want my girl to come down with me!
EUNICE:	Hah! *(She slams her door.)*
STANLEY:	*(With heaven-splitting violence)* STELL-LAHHHHH!
	(The low-tone clarinet moans. The door upstairs opens again. Stella slips down the rickety stairs in her robe. Her eyes are glistening with tears and her hair loose about her throat and shoulders. They stare at each other. Then they come together with low, animal moans. He falls to his knees on the steps and presses his face to her belly, curving a little with maternity. Her eyes go blind with tenderness as she catches his head and raises him level with her. He snatches the screen door open and lifts her off her feet and bears her into the dark flat.
	(Blanche comes out on the upper landing in her robe and slips fearfully down the steps.)
BLANCHE:	Where is my little sister? Stella? Stella?
	(She stops before the dark entrance of her sister's flat. Then catches her breath as if struck. She rushes down to the walk before the house. She looks right and left as if for a sanctuary.)
	(The music fades away. Mitch appears from around the corner.)
MITCH:	Miss DuBois?
BLANCHE:	Oh!
MITCH:	All quiet on the Potomac now?
BLANCHE:	She ran downstairs and went back in there with him.
MITCH:	Sure she did.
BLANCHE:	I'm terrified!
MITCH:	Ho-ho! There's nothing to be scared of. They're crazy about each other.

V

RUTH GORDON AND GARSON KANIN
ADAM'S RIB, 1949

Ruth Gordon (1896–1985) and Garson Kanin (1912–1999) wrote the movie *Adam's Rib* for Katharine Hepburn and Spencer Tracy, who play married lawyers going head-to-head in a courtroom trial. As Amanda Bonner, Hepburn makes the case that the female defendant, having shot at her husband and his lover, is being subjected to a double standard that makes a husband more entitled to violence than a wife. The conflict between defense and prosecution gets personal for the Bonners when, back at home, Adam gives Amanda a massage—and a questionable slap on the backside.

ADAM:	What's a matter? Don't you want your rub-down? What are ya? Sore about a little slap?
AMANDA:	No.
ADAM:	Well, what then?
AMANDA:	*(Outraged)* You meant that, didn't you? You really meant that.
ADAM:	Why, no, I—
AMANDA:	Yes, you did. I can tell. I know your type. I know a slap from a slug.
ADAM:	Well, OK, OK.
AMANDA:	I'm not sure it is. I'm not so sure I care to expose myself to typical instinctive masculine brutality.
ADAM:	Oh, come now.
AMANDA:	And it felt not only as though you meant it, but as though you felt you had a right to. I can tell.
ADAM:	What've you got back there? Radar equipment?

V

WEDDINGS

RUMI
"THIS MARRIAGE," 13TH CENTURY

Renowned Persian Sufi mystic Mevlána Jaláluddin Rumi (circa 1207–1273) (the spelling of his full name differs widely) wrote rhythmic, spiritually inspired poetry, often intended to be sung and accompanied by a whirling dance. His deep connection to a charismatic holy man named Shams al Din, and Shams's murder (probably by Rumi's resentful family), were said to inspire his most passionate poems of love and loss. The universality of his work has led to its wide translation and broad appeal over centuries and continents.

May these vows and this marriage be blessed.
May it be sweet milk,
this marriage, like wine and halvah.
May this marriage offer fruit and shade
like the date palm.
May this marriage be full of laughter,
our every day a day in paradise.
May this marriage be a sign of compassion,

a seal of happiness here and hereafter.
May this marriage have a fair face and a good name,
an omen as welcome
as the moon in a clear blue sky.
I am out of words to describe
how spirit mingles in this marriage.

MARRIAGE BUREAU, CIRCA 1900

EMILY HOLT
EVERYMAN'S ENCYCLOPÆDIA OF ETIQUETTE, 1901

In her oft-reprinted book of etiquette, the pseudonymous author Emily Holt wrote about what foods should be eaten with fingers, what cards to leave after a funeral, how to achieve noise-less eating, and what to do at a ball about "the guest who does not dance." Engagements and weddings merited their own section, and the groom's and best man's special challenges did not escape her attention.

A question that calls for consideration—What is the proper disposition for the best man to make of his own and the groom's hat? One of the best man's most obvious duties is supposed to be the guardianship of the groom's hat and gloves during the ceremony. It stands to reason that if he takes his own hat and gloves into the chancel and also assumes the care of his friend's belongings, he will not only present a ludicrous spectacle as he stands through the service with a silk hat in either hand, but when the moment for presentation of the ring arrives he will be unable, without awk-

> ## What is the proper disposition for the best man to make of his own and the groom's hat?

wardly laying aside at least one hat and one pair of gloves, to fulfill his allotted and most important office in the programme. In recent seasons, at well-ordered weddings, hats have not been carried into the chancel. In the vestry the best man takes charge of his friend's hat and, placing it with his own, sends them by a trusty person to the door of the church, so that when the bridal procession files out they may be delivered back to the owners just as they are passing to their respective carriages. This is especially the course when the best man on coming out is to walk down the aisle with a maid of honor on his arm. At a wedding where there is no maid of honor the best man can, if he prefers, leave his own hat and gloves in the vestry room, and when the ceremony is over make his exit from the church through the vestry, to find his carriage awaiting him at a side door. This leaves him free to hold the groom's hat and gloves and still present the ring and the fee.

W

MYRA PIPKIN
ORAL HISTORY INTERVIEW, 1941

A migrant worker named Myra Pipkin, interviewed for an oral history of the Dust Bowl, recalled these maxims on marriage attire. There have been many others, by far the most famous today being the adage that originated in Victorian England: "Something old, something new, something borrowed, something blue." The usually forgotten last line: "And a silver sixpence in her shoe."

Marry in white
You're sure to be right.
Marry in blue
You're sure to be true.
Marry in green
You're ashamed to be seen.
Marry in brown
You'll live in town.
Marry in red
You'll wish yourself dead.
Marry in black
You'll wish yourself back.

FRANCES GOODRICH AND ALBERT HACKETT
FATHER OF THE BRIDE, 1950

Written by Frances Goodrich (1890–1984) and Albert Hackett (1900–1995) and based on the bestselling 1949 novel by Edward Streeter, the film *Father of the Bride* began with an endearing, long-suffering Spencer Tracy taking off a shoe, rubbing his foot, and then emptying the shoe of rice.

The bride was played by an effervescent Elizabeth Taylor.

W

I would like to say a few words about weddings. I've just been through one. Not my own. My daughter's. Someday in the far future I may be able to remember it with tender indulgence, but not now. I always used to think that marriage was a simple affair. Boy and girl meet. They fall in love, get married. They have babies. Eventually the babies grow up and meet other babies. And they fall in love and get married. And so on and on and on. Looked at that way, it's not only simple, it's downright monotonous. But I was wrong. I figured without the wedding.

JOHN KENNEDY AND JACQUELINE BOUVIER, 1953

W

SHARON McDONALD
"WHAT MOTHER NEVER TOLD ME," 1979

Twenty-five years before Massachusetts became the first state to legalize same-sex marriage, author Sharon McDonald (1951–) described her proposal to and wedding with Jeanne Cordova, then publisher of *The Lesbian Tide*, where this piece first appeared. In the article, McDonald gave Cordova the pseudonym "Louise" in an attempt to universalize the experience beyond the well-known publication and publisher. Their marriage lasted four years and was eventually followed, in Cordova's case, by a second marriage. (Regrettably, we've been unable to track McDonald down.) It would be decades before gay weddings were called "weddings," not "commitment ceremonies." This one was called a "tryst" in the ancient Goddess tradition.

The couple had been together four years before they married. The Greek actress Irene Papas had starred as Helen in a film of *The Trojan Women*.

PROLOGUE: UNNATURAL DESIRES

With several years of love, lust, and irreconcilable differences behind us, Louise and I had become aware that we were drifting into that strange uncharted territory known as "long term." They had been tumultuous years, but our dismay at each other's failings had more often than not been matched by our delight in each other's company. Having seen many models of love that start out strong and weaken over time, I was shocked to find the reverse dynamic with Louise.

Now when heterosexuals get to this point they tend to get married, a custom which I have envied for its sentimental symbolism while disdaining its more odious political aspects. I myself had never wanted to get married, but Mother always told me that when I really fell in love I'd change my mind. Imagine my chagrin twenty years later and a whole lifestyle different to find out once *again* that Mother is always right.

Of course, I pondered my desire in secret. I am politically unsophisticated enough to know that I can squeak by being monogamous, and even in some tolerant circles being femme, but my Radical Lesbian License would be revoked for sure if word got out that I wanted to "settle down" with the woman of my dreams.

The more I thought about it, the more ironic it seemed. I was free to explore my wildest fantasies of unnatural acts with Fido and a few dozen close friends, but I was supposed to feel constrained about wanting to shout, "Hallelujah, she's the one!" I finally decided to hell with Convention (Women Have to Marry Men) and to hell with Unconvention (Women Have to Not Marry at All). Who says this lesbian can't live happily ever after?

W

POPPING THE QUESTION

I took her out to dinner, fancy gay restaurant, table in the corner, soft candlelight, gay waiters wafting by. I sat terrified, drinking like there was no tomorrow, as might well be true if she said no. She wasn't drinking, and, as I sank lower and lower in my chair, she started leaning over the table and asking solicitously, "Are you all right?"

After our boy had taken away my untouched pork chop and filled my glass for the fifth time, I lurched, er, launched into a rambling preamble. She listened intently, looking concerned. About the tenth time I heard myself stutter, "I, uh, you see, I think we, uh . . ." I shoved a ring box in front of her and just like in the movies blurted, "Will you marry me?" And with that, I was off on what has proven to be the most politically controversial and personally rewarding thing I've done since coming out.

SHARING OR SHACKLING?

Louise and I quickly found out that an event of this nature in a feminist community is much like a natural disaster; it brings out the best and the worst in people. Community reactions broke down into three categories: The Aghast, The Amused, and The Admiring. The Aghast, of course, were radical lesbian feminists. So were the Amused. So were The Admiring.

Longtime friends took us out to ask if perhaps we weren't working too hard, maybe the stress had affected our better judgment. Less delicate acquaintances snorted openly, one summing it up by asking, "Why don't you two just shackle yourselves together?"

But here and there other lesbian couples popped up, delighted at the news. They called us up, some women we barely knew, and said in a rush how they thought it was wonderful and brave and how they'd wanted to have a ceremony for years. We congratulated each other conspiratorially and invited them.

WICCA TO THE RESCUE!

Not wanting to march down any heterosexist aisles, we set about looking for a lesbian ceremony and hit upon the tryst. A Witch friend explained that it was an ancient ritual of bonding that was not the ownership contract of conventional marriage, but rather a mutual coming together of two equals to bond in love and friendship. She offered to help us do it. "We'll take it!"

We called our mothers and sisters and invited them. We sent invitations to our friends, painfully resisting our initial excited impulse to send them to every lesbian west of the Rockies.

One night as the date was drawing near, I sat in bed flipping through a book on witchcraft rituals. I came across a passage that made my hair stand on end. It described how women

W

standing in a circle at a Sabbat turn to each other and give each other "the fivefold kiss," kissing the forehead, eyes, lips, breasts, and genitals. I nearly fell off the bed. "LOUISE!" I shrieked. "We've got to get ALL the details on this ceremony!"

The next morning I called our Witch friend and asked for a blow-by-blow account of what was going to happen. I was all right until she got to the part about "anointing the genitals with water."

"We can't *do* that," I said. "Our mothers are going to be there. Besides, I think Louise would faint."

The Witch was horrified. "You can't drop it! This is a very important part of the ceremony! I just can't imagine what the spiritual repercussions might be! It could be terrible!"

"I'll risk it."

"You don't understand. The genitals are very involved in what you're doing here . . ."

"You're telling ME!"

". . . and it could be *tragic* to omit this protective blessing on your sexual union!"

"Do it like the Catholics do—offer up a silent blessing."

In the end, Witch tradition won out, but only if done with ex-Catholic subtlety.

The women of both our families jumped into the preparations for the tryst with enthusiasm, this being the first tryst in both families' history. The fathers and brothers took a somewhat dimmer view of the proceedings. Because of their customary lack of enthusiasm for events of a lesbian nature, and because of the customary lack of enthusiasm of many of our guests for men in general, they had not been invited. They reacted to this with customary outrage, half of them "threatening" not to come, the other half threatening to come.

CHECKING OUR CLOSETS

But Louise and I had no time for family squabbles; we busied ourselves with weightier issues, like the What-to-Wear argument. I had always wanted to see her in a tuxedo, and this seemed the perfect time, but she had other plans and could not be moved. When I wailed, "But when will I ever get to see you in a tuxedo if not on this day?" she replied, "The day you bury me." End of discussion.

Louise's idea was that we should be "outside of time and fashion and contemporary limitations—we should wear stately robes!"

"Robes?"

"Yeah, you know, like Ben-Hur, El Cid, Diana the Goddess, Helen of Troy."

"Jesus!"

W

"That's RIGHT! Roman togas!"

"Good lord, the witches want to bless my genitals, you want me to dress up like Irene Papas, why did I ever start this thing?"

And with that it hit us: that period of reflection and kicking ourselves known as Prenuptial Jitters. This malady expresses itself in many different forms, all of them desperate. Lesbians, it turned out, are not immune to any of them.

Louise went scurrying off to her shrink to babble, "I love her, *but . . .*" Meanwhile, I surveyed the preparations for the coming tryst, which were in a shambles. Half the women we'd invited weren't speaking to the other half. The men were still threatening to come. Louise's aunt, who had promised to help, suddenly decided to get divorced, and so spent all the time she should have been whipping up Roman togas crying instead. Louise and I looked at each other and saw the face of a haunted stranger. We retired to separate gay bars to think things over.

Drinking alone, we missed each other. Coming home to bed, we found again some common ground. Revitalized, we remembered that while neither of us wanted to be a groom, we couldn't pass up this once in a lifetime chance to both get a bride.

While neither of us wanted to be a groom, we couldn't pass up this once in a lifetime chance to both get a bride.

THE DAY OF RECKONING

Faster than you can say "public commitment," the day of the tryst had arrived. The ceremony itself was short, sweet, and to the point. There were no dramatic surprises, no one popping up to yell, "Stop! She's got a wife and four kids in Des Moines!" There was just us and the goddess and our families and friends, standing there doing what every lesbian has the right to do: be proud and public about her love. I cannot vouch for my appearance, but Louise looked like a dyke angel, shining from the inside out. We held hands, jumped the broom, and it was done! Applause broke out and the party was on.

W

WILLIAM GOLDMAN
THE PRINCESS BRIDE, 1987

The vows in this scene are being hurried by an impending disruption from the bride's true love. We will forgo any other introductory explanation to say, simply, that if you have never seen this movie, please put this book down and go do so.

IMPRESSIVE CLERGYMAN:	*(Clears his throat, begins to speak.)*
	Mawidge . . . Mawidge is what bwings us togewer tooday.
	(He has an impediment that would stop a clock.)
	Mawidge, that bwessed awwangment, that dweam wiffim a dweam . . .
	(And now, from outside the castle, there begins to come a commotion.)
	Ven wuv, twoo wuv, wiw fowwow you fowever . . .
	(Prince Humperdinck, turning quickly, gives a sharp nod to Count Rugen.)
	So tweasure your wuv—
HUMPERDINCK:	Skip to the end.
IMPRESSIVE CLERGYMAN:	Have you the wing?

Mawidge is what bwings us togewer tooday.

Mawidge, that bwessed awwangment,

that dweam wiffim a dweam . . .

W

IRA GLASS
"NIAGARA," *THIS AMERICAN LIFE*, 1998

Long known as a romantic honeymoon destination, Niagara Falls has also become a favorite for quickie nuptials, with numerous chapels springing up within a bouquet's throw of the roaring falls. The popular public radio show *This American Life*, hosted by Ira Glass (1959–), presented this account by documentary producer Alix Spiegel of one such wedding.

SPIEGEL: It's Catherine and A.J.'s first time, which is a little unusual for the Niagara wedding chapel. Most of their market is second marriages. Catherine and A.J. have driven to Niagara from Pittsburgh with 30 of their friends and family, and are now waiting together with their maid of honor in the welcome area outside the chapel. They all look happy and nervous. They're laughing and joking, talking about the kinds of things you talk about right before you get married.

WOMAN 1: A.J., you still have time to back out.

WOMAN 2: No.

CATHERINE: He's calmer than me.

WOMAN 1: I know. He's so calm. That's cool.

CATHERINE: I should have gone to the bathroom.

SPIEGEL: Chris, the owner and manager of the Niagara chapel, comes in to tell Catherine and A.J. that even though two of their guests haven't arrived, the wedding must start. He's got a 4:30. He can't wait anymore. Everyone hurries to their places while Chris makes a brief announcement to their guests. They're allowed to take pictures, but everyone must remain in their seats until the end of the ceremony. I barely have time to wonder why this last instruction is necessary before—
(Music: "Bridal Chorus" by Richard Wagner)

Catherine starts crying as soon as she enters the chapel. She cries her way to the altar, cries as she takes her place beside A.J., cries as the justice reads through the opening of the ceremony, cries more when the justice asks her if she'll love her husband through sickness and through health. The bareness of her emotion infects everyone in the room.

I see three people in the front row hunch their shoulders and bring their hands to their

W

faces, then the man in the second row next to the wall, then the woman sitting next to him. It jumps the 12-year-old boy sitting next to her and moves to the third row, then the fourth. Now I am crying. We are all in the room crying. Everyone happy and flushed and sure that everything, everywhere is going to be OK after all.

And then, six minutes and 47 seconds after it begins, it's finished. A.J. and Catherine are now husband and wife.

CHIP BROWN
"THE WAITING GAME," 2005

Chip Brown has written two nonfiction books, as well as hundreds of articles for national magazines including *Esquire*, *Men's Journal*, *Vogue*, *Harper's*, and *National Geographic*. He contributed this essay to an anthology of men's stories about love and commitment. Brown married fashion writer and editor Kate Betts in 1996.

I remember the sense of a larger force at work when my younger brother, Toby, got married at age twenty-five. Waiting for the ceremony to begin on the altar of an Episcopal church in Connecticut, he seemed relaxed, laughing when the young organist wove the theme from *The Flintstones* into the prelude. But when Anne appeared at the end of the aisle, he began to tremble. Maybe it was the rustle of the organ, but the sound in the church was like the clamor of surf, as if we were all standing by the ocean or inside a giant shell. You could feel the presence of the life force shuddering in its traces, impatient to get the ceremony out of the way so the real work of minting fresh DNA could begin. It seemed at that moment, free will notwithstanding, my brother and his wife were but the means to an end, the instruments of their genes, clapped together by a design much more consequential than their personalities, or their ostensible reasons for getting married. The machinery of life proceeds independently of vows.

The machinery of life proceeds independently of vows.

WHEN

TRADITIONAL RHYME

If you're wondering about weekdays . . .

Monday for wealth,
Tuesday for health,
Wednesday the best of all,
Thursday for crosses,
Friday for losses,
Saturday no luck at all.

TRADITIONAL RHYME

Or months . . .

Married in January's hoar and rime,
Widowed you'll be before your prime.
Married in February's sleety weather,
Life you'll tread in tune together.
Married when March winds shrill and roar,
Your home will lie on a foreign shore.
Married 'neath April's changeful skies,
A chequered path before you lies.
Married when bees o'er May blooms flit,
Strangers around your board will sit.
Married in month of roses—June—
Life will be one long honeymoon.
Married in July, with flowers ablaze,
Bitter-sweet memories in after days.
Married in August's heat and drowse,

W

Lover and friend in your chosen spouse.
Married in golden September's glow,
Smooth and serene your life will flow.
Married when leaves in October thin,
Toil and hardship for you begin.
Married in veils of November mist,
Dame Fortune your wedding ring has kissed.
Married in days of December's cheer,
Love's star burns brighter from year to year.

Marry'd in haste, we oft repent at leisure.

BENJAMIN FRANKLIN
POOR RICHARD'S ALMANACK, 1734

Franklin (see also Rings, page 372; Why, page 477) proposed to his wife, Deborah Read, when he was just seventeen and she was fifteen. Her mother refused the offer, partly because he was about to leave for England and partly because he had already fathered a child with another woman. Deborah married in Franklin's absence, but her husband robbed and left her. Her ensuing common-law marriage with Franklin took place in 1730, when he was twenty-four, and lasted until her death in 1774.

Wedlock, as old men note, hath likened been,
Unto a public crowd or common rout;
Where those that are without would fain get in,
And those that are within, would fain get out.
Grief often treads upon the heels of pleasure,
Marry'd in haste, we oft repent at leisure;
Some by experience find these words missplaced,
Marry'd at leisure, they repent in haste.

SHEET MUSIC COVER, 1906

GULIELMA ALSOP AND MARY McBRIDE
SHE'S OFF TO MARRIAGE, 1942

Physician and educator, founder of Barnard College's medical department in 1917, Gulielma Alsop (1881–1978) was its head for thirty-five years. The responsibilities of that job did not stop her from writing voluminously on subjects pertaining to women in war, at college, at work, and in marriage. Mary Frances McBride (1900–1959), a longtime private-school teacher in the New York area, was Alsop's coauthor on this and a number of other books and articles.

[A] girl may not know whether she wants to marry the man she is going out with or not. She enjoys him as a friend. She likes to be with him. His manners are good, and he does not annoy her with too much affection. He is a rising young man in the community. But she does not think she wants to marry him. The truth is, although she may not know it, she is not ready for marriage. She wants neither its physical nor emotional impact; nor does she want her life disturbed and upset. Deep within her, she wants children, and she knows that a young mother is the best. Theoretically, she agrees that she ought to marry Jim and marry him now, while he is beseeching her to. But she is still reluctant, not being sure whether she loves him or not, not being sure whether he is the sort of person she wants for her husband or not. The reason is, she doesn't want to be disturbed.

But a girl should know that men do not wait; that if she does not marry her Jim, he, like a sensible man, will find himself a girl who will marry him, and marry him now. Not by too much introspection nor too much weighing of pros and cons will a girl find her heart and its dictates, but by making up her mind resolutely that, since she does want to be married, she will have to say yes to the man of the moment.

WHO

PITTACUS, CIRCA 600 BC

Credited with such sayings as "The measure of a man is what he does with power" and "Forgiveness is better than revenge," Pittacus of Mytilene (circa 640–circa 568 BC) was considered one of the Seven Wise Men of Greece. In his advice about marriage—compiled in 1825 by the Archbishop of Cambray—he was downright playful.

The little congeniality that existed between [Pittacus] and his wife inspired him . . . with the liveliest aversion to ill-assorted matches. A man went to him one day to ask his advice as to which wife he should choose from two that were offered to him, one of whom was nearly on an equality with himself, the other much his superior both in birth and fortune. "Go," said Pittacus, pointing with the stick on which he was leaning to the place he meant to describe, "go to the corner where you see the children assembling together to play, join them a while, and follow the advice they will presently give you." Accordingly the young man went among them; the little ones directly began to laugh and push him about, and to call out to him, "Get away; go among your equals." This determined him to think no more of the lady who was so much above himself, but to be contented with her who was in his own rank.

MANU
CODE OF LAW, CIRCA 500 BC

In the ancient Hindu text the Manava-Dharma Shastra, or laws of Manu, the great Brahmin teacher Manu laid out the rules of family and religious life. Some believed he had received the laws from Lord Brahma himself. The text was written by multiple authors and added to over time. The passage quoted below is from the chapter titled "Marriage."

He must not marry a girl who has red hair or an extra limb; who is sickly; who is without or with too much bodily hair; who is a blabbermouth or jaundiced-looking; who is named after a constellation, a tree, a river, a very low caste, a mountain, a bird, a snake, or a servant; or who has a frightening name. He should marry a woman who is not deficient in any limb; who has a pleasant name; who walks like a goose or an elephant; and who has fine body and head hair, small teeth, and delicate limbs.

AFRICAN PROVERB

W

Never marry a woman with bigger feet than your own.

AESOP
"THE FATAL MARRIAGE," CIRCA 6TH CENTURY BC

There have always been questions about the identity of Aesop, a Greek figure credited with the writing of hundreds of fables. So much confusion surrounds his background that, though a man named Aesop is believed to have lived in the sixth or seventh century BC, his name is now assumed to be a catchall signature for the moralistic tales that came either from oral traditions or from a variety of writers. Under the title of *Aesop's Fables*, however, are such famous tales as "The Tortoise and the Hare" and "Androcles and the Lion" and such morals as "One person's meat is another's poison," and "Beware the wolf in sheep's clothing."

The Lion, touched with gratitude by the noble procedure of a Mouse, and resolving not to be outdone in generosity by any wild beast whatsoever, desired his little deliverer to name his own terms, for that he might depend upon his complying with any proposal he should make. The Mouse, fired with ambition at this gracious offer, did not so much consider what was proper for him to ask, as what was in the powers of his prince to grant; and so demanded his princely daughter, the young lioness, in marriage. The Lion consented; but, when he would have given the royal virgin into his possession, she, like a giddy thing as she was, not minding how she walked, by chance set her paw upon her spouse, who was coming to meet her, and crushed him to pieces.

Moral: Beware of unequal matches. Alliances prompted by ambition often prove fatal.

CHODERLOS DE LACLOS
LES LIAISONS DANGEREUSES, 1782

Pierre Choderlos de Laclos (1741–1803) was a French statesman and military officer, but his expressed ambition was to write something that would outlast him. He succeeded with *Les Liaisons Dangereuses*, an epistolary novel that explored the scandalous intrigues of French society. Rumors and advice flew back and forth in the letters, including this kernel of wisdom from the scheming Marquise de Merteuil to the virginal Cécile de Volanges.

W

As far as husbands are concerned, one is as good as another; and even the most inconvenient is less of a trial than a mother.

"THE CHOICE OF A HUSBAND, BY A LADY"
MASSACHUSETTS MAGAZINE, 1794

A man that's neither high nor low
In party nor in stature,
No rake, no rattle, and no beau,
But not unus'd to flatter.

Let him not be a learned fool
That nods o'er musty books,
That eats, and drinks, and lives by rule,
And weighs our words and looks.

Let him be easy, free, and gay,
Of dancing never tir'd,
Have always something smart to say,
Yet silent when requir'd.

Let him be rich, not covetous,
Nor generous to excess,
Willing that I should keep the purse,
And please myself in dress.

A little courage let him have
From insults to protect me,
Provided that he's not so brave
To dare to contradict me.

Ten thousand pounds a year I like,
But if so much can't be,
You seven from the ten may strike,
I'll be content with three.

His face—no matter if 'tis plain,
But let it not be fair—

W

The man my heart is sure to gain,
Who can with this compare.

And if some lord should chance t'agree
With the above description,
Though I'm not fond of quality,
It shall be no objection.

"HOW TO AVOID A BAD HUSBAND"
ROCKLAND COUNTY MESSENGER, 1853

When the *Christian Observer* reprinted this article five months after its first publication, an editor added one sentence: "In the choice of a wife, take the obedient daughter of a good mother."

1. Never marry for wealth. A woman's life consisteth not in the things he possesseth.
2. Never marry a fop, or one who struts about, dandy like, in his silk gloves and ruffles, with silvered cane, and rings on his fingers. Beware! there is a trap!
3. Never marry a niggard, a close-fisted, mean, sordid wretch, who saves every penny, or spends it grudgingly. Take care, least he stint you to death!
4. Never marry a stranger, or one whose character is not known or tested. Some females jump right into the fire with their eyes wide open!
5. Never marry a mope, or a drone, one who drawls through life, one foot after another, and lets things take their own course!
6. Never marry a man who treats his mother or sister unkindly or indifferently. Such treatment is a sure indication of a mean and wicked beast!
7. Never, on any account, marry a gambler, profane person, one who in the least speaks lightly of God, or religion! Such a man can never make a good husband!
8. Never marry a sloven, a man who is negligent of his person, or his dress, and is filthy in his habits! The external appearance is an index to the heart!
9. Shun the rake as a snake! a viper! a demon!
10. Finally, never marry a man who uses tobacco in any form, or who is addicted to the use of ardent spirits. Depend upon it, you are better off alone than you would be were you tied to a man whose breath is polluted, and whose vitals are being gnawed by alcohol.

FRANCES HARPER
"ADVICE TO THE GIRLS," 1855

Frances Ellen Watkins Harper (1825–1911) was an abolitionist, a member of the Women's Christian Temperance Union, and a cofounder of the National Association of Colored Women.

Wed not a man whose merit lies
In things of outward show,
In raven hair or flashing eyes,
That please your fancy so.

But marry one who's good and kind,
And free from all pretence;
Who, if without a gifted mind,
At least has common sense.

HENRY STANTON
SEX: AVOIDED SUBJECTS DISCUSSED IN PLAIN ENGLISH, 1922

In his list of who should *not* marry, Henry Stanton was echoing themes popularized in the 1920s by eugenicists, many of them mainstream scientists who believed that factors including poor mental and physical health should rule out some candidates for marriage and procreation.

We have been unable to locate any information about the author of this sixty-two-page book, part of a series published by "Social Culture Publications"; all we know is that he is *not* the Henry B. Stanton who was married to Elizabeth Cady. Possibly the topic made the use of a pseudonym seem necessary.

Men suffering with diseases which may be communicated by contagion or heredity should not marry. These diseases include: tuberculosis, syphilis, cancer, leprosy, epilepsy and some nervous disorders, some skin diseases and insanity. A worn-out rake has no business to marry, since marriage is not a hospital for the treatment of disease, or a reformatory institution for moral lepers. Those having a marked tendency to disease must not marry those of similar tendency. The marriage of cousins is not to be advocated. The blood relation tends to bring together persons with similar morbid tendencies. Where both are healthy, however, there seems to be no special liability to mental incompetency, though such marriages are accused of producing defective or idiot

W

children. Men suffering from congenital defects should not marry. Natural blindness, deafness, muteness, and congenital deformities of limb are more or less likely to be passed on to their children. There are cases of natural blindness, though, to which this rule does not apply. Criminals, alcoholics, and persons disproportionate in size should not marry. In the last-mentioned, lack of mutual physical adaptability may produce much unhappiness, especially on the part of the wife. Serious local disease, sterility, and great risk in childbirth may result. Disparity of years, disparity of race, a poverty which will not permit the proper raising of children, undesirable moral character are all good reasons for not marrying.

There's lots of good fish in the sea, but the vast masses seem to be mackerel or herring, and if you're not mackerel or herring yourself, you are likely to find very few good fish in the sea.

D. H. LAWRENCE
LADY CHATTERLEY'S LOVER, 1928

For background on Lawrence, see Fidelity, page 114.
The ellipses are the author's.

The world is supposed to be full of possibilities, but they narrow down to pretty few in most personal experience. There's lots of good fish in the sea . . . maybe . . . but the vast masses seem to be mackerel or herring, and if you're not mackerel or herring yourself, you are likely to find very few good fish in the sea.

W

EXHIBIT CARD, 1938

Sometimes they were used to sell actual products, but in the 1930s and 1940s, "exhibit cards" were a thing in themselves, available in vending machines and offering everything from jokes to sports memorabilia to bathing beauties to the occasional message for women.

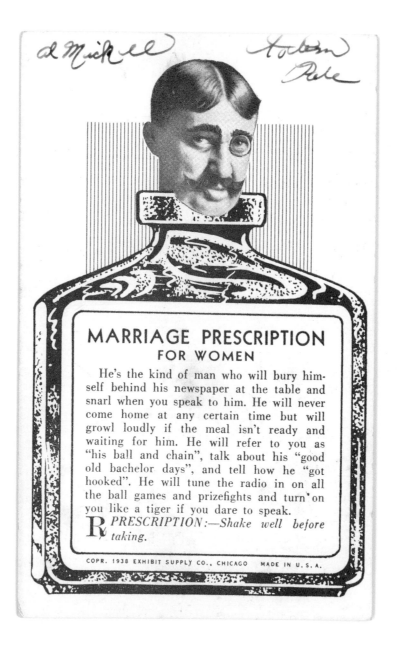

MARRIAGE PRESCRIPTION
FOR WOMEN

He's the kind of man who will bury himself behind his newspaper at the table and snarl when you speak to him. He will never come home at any certain time but will growl loudly if the meal isn't ready and waiting for him. He will refer to you as "his ball and chain", talk about his "good old bachelor days", and tell how he "got hooked". He will tune the radio in on all the ball games and prizefights and turn on you like a tiger if you dare to speak.
℞ *PRESCRIPTION:—Shake well before taking.*

COPR. 1938 EXHIBIT SUPPLY CO., CHICAGO   MADE IN U.S.A.

W

MARTHA GELLHORN
LETTER TO SANDY MATTHEWS, 1969

Journalist, novelist, and third wife of Ernest Hemingway, Martha Gellhorn (1908–1998) offered this bit of advice to the son she had adopted in 1949 from an Italian orphanage, adding a tentative corollary that men who were too close to their mothers might consequently "turn out to be fairies."

Now I know enough to know that no woman should ever marry a man who hated his mother.

LIBERTY GODSHALL
"NO PROMISES," *THIRTYSOMETHING*, 1989

Between 1987 and 1991, Baby Boomers tuned in weekly to watch as their television counterparts, a group of eight friends living in Philadelphia, passed through the milestones of early midlife in the hour-long ABC drama *thirtysomething*. The show touched many chords—and set off some controversy—with its exploration of changing sex roles, women's careers, and marital fidelity.

Ellyn Warren is the childhood friend of main character Hope Steadman; Marjorie is Ellyn's mother. This episode was written by actress/writer/producer Liberty Godshall, wife of series cocreator Edward Zwick.

MARJORIE: You see, there are two kinds of boys in high school. There are the good-looking ones, the ones on every team, the ones everyone wants. They're the greatest dancers too. And then there are the others—the boys who look as if they'd always rather be somewhere else reading a book, who are shy and awkward. I think you'd call them "nerds" now. Those are the boys to marry, Ellyn. Those are the boys who tell you secrets, who hold you when you cry in the middle of the night, who want to grow old with you.

ELLYN: How do you know about this, Mom?

MARJORIE: Because—I married a great dancer.

W

WHY

BENJAMIN FRANKLIN
"THE OLD MISTRESSES' APOLOGUE," 1745

Apparently a friend had written to Franklin (see Rings, page 372; When, page 466) seeking a kind of blessing for premarital sex. In this letter, Franklin defended the institution of marriage. Later in the letter, Franklin advised the friend that if he absolutely had to engage in "Commerce with the Sex," he should choose an old rather than a young woman because, among other reasons, "in the dark all cats are gray."

My dear Friend,

I know of no Medicine fit to diminish the violent natural Inclinations you mention; and if I did, I think I should not communicate it to you. Marriage is the proper Remedy. It is the most natural State of Man, and therefore the State in which you are most likely to find solid Happiness. Your Reasons against entring into it at present, appear to me not well-founded. The circumstantial Advantages you have in View by postponing it, are not only uncertain, but they are small in comparison with that of the Thing itself, the being *married and settled*. It is the Man and Woman united that make the compleat human Being. Separate, she wants his Force of Body and Strength of Reason; he, her Softness, Sensibility and acute Discernment. Together they are more likely to succeed in the World. A single Man has not nearly the Value he would have in that State of Union. He is an incomplete Animal. He resembles the odd Half of a Pair of Scissars.

CHARLES DARWIN
"THIS IS THE QUESTION," 1838

Through his five-year, around-the-world voyage on the H.M.S. *Beagle* and his intense studies of flora, fauna, and fossils, Charles Darwin (1809–1882) developed the modern theory of natural selection. He had just returned from the trip, in fact, and was twenty-nine years old when he sat down to consider the arguments for and against marriage. That same year, he wrote to a friend: "As for a wife, that most interesting specimen in the whole series of vertebrate animals, Providence only knows whether I shall ever capture one or be able to feed her if caught." The following year, Darwin married his cousin Emma Wedgwood. They went on to have ten children together.

W

This is the Question

MARRY

Children—(if it Please God)—Constant companion, (& friend in old age) who will feel interested in one—object to be beloved & played with.— —better than a dog anyhow.— Home, & someone to take care of house—Charms of music & female chitchat.—These things good for one's health. ~~Forced to visit and receive relations~~—.

My God, it is intolerable to think of spending ones whole life, like a neuter bee, working, working, & nothing after all. No, no won't do.—Imagine living all one's day solitarily in smoky dirty London House.— Only picture to yourself a nice soft wife on a sofa with good fire, & books & music perhaps—Compare this vision with the dingy reality of Grt Marlboro' St. Marry— Marry—Marry Q.E.D.

NOT MARRY

No children, (no second life), no one to care for one in old age.—

What is the use of working without sympathy from near & dear friends—who are near & dear friends to the old, except relatives

Freedom to go where one liked—choice of Society & <u>little of it</u>. Conversation of clever men at clubs Not forced to visit relatives, & to bend in every trifle.—to have the expense & anxiety of children—perhaps quarreling—

<u>Loss of time.</u>—cannot read in the Evenings—fatness & idleness—Anxiety & responsibility—less money for books &c— if many children forced to gain one's bread.—(But then it is very bad for ones health to work too much)

Perhaps my wife wont like London; then the sentence is banishment & degradation into indolent idle fool—

It being proved necessary to Marry—When? Soon or Late

The Governor says soon for otherwise bad if one has children—one's character is more flexible—one's feelings more lively & if one does not marry soon, one misses so much good pure happiness.—

But then if I married tomorrow: there would be an infinity of trouble & expense in getting & furnishing a house,—fighting about no Society—morning calls—awkwardness—loss of time every day. (without one's wife was an angel, & made one keep industrious).—Then how should I manage all my business if I were obliged to go every day walking with my wife.— Eheu!! I never should know French,—or see the Continent—or go to America, or go up in a Balloon, or take solitary trip in Wales—poor slave.—you will be worse than a negro—And then horrid poverty, (without one's wife was better than an angel & had money)—Never mind my boy—Cheer up—One cannot live this solitary life, with groggy old age, friendless & cold & childless staring one in one's face, already beginning to wrinkle.—Never mind, trust to chance— keep a sharp look out—There is many a happy slave—

EMILY BRONTË
WUTHERING HEIGHTS, 1847

Wuthering Heights was the only novel written by Emily Brontë (1818–1848), who died of tuber-culosis a year after its publication. Like her sister Charlotte's *Jane Eyre* (see pages 279 and 348–50) it is a classic tale of love and heartache on the Yorkshire moors. In this scene, the hero-ine, Catherine Earnshaw, describes her fateful decision to marry the wealthy, respectable Edgar Linton instead of her true love and former childhood companion, the orphaned and penniless Heathcliff. Nelly, the wise housekeeper and Catherine's confidante, tells the story.

"Nelly, will you keep a secret for me?" she pursued, kneeling down by me, and lifting her win-some eyes to my face with that sort of look which turns off bad temper, even when one has all the right in the world to indulge it.

"Is it worth keeping?" I inquired, less sulkily.

"Yes, and it worries me, and I must let it out! I want to know what I should do. To-day, Edgar Linton has asked me to marry him, and I've given him an answer. Now, before I tell you whether it was a consent or denial, you tell me which it ought to have been."

"Really, Miss Catherine, how can I know?" I replied. "To be sure, considering the exhibi-tion you performed in his presence this afternoon, I might say it would be wise to refuse him: since he asked you after that, he must either be hopelessly stupid or a venturesome fool."

"If you talk so, I won't tell you any more," she returned, peevishly, rising to her feet. "I ac-cepted him, Nelly. Be quick, and say whether I was wrong!"

"You accepted him! then what good is it discussing the matter? You have pledged your word, and cannot retract."

"But, say whether I should have done so—do!" she exclaimed in an irritated tone; chafing her hands together, and frowning.

W

"There are many things to be considered before that question can be answered properly," I said, sententiously. "First and foremost, do you love Mr Edgar?"

"Who can help it? Of course I do," she answered.

Then I put her through the following catechism: for a girl of twenty-two, it was not injudicious.

"Why do you love him, Miss Cathy?"

"Nonsense, I do—that's sufficient."

"By no means; you must say why?"

"Well, because he is handsome, and pleasant to be with."

"Bad!" was my commentary.

"And because he is young and cheerful."

"Bad, still."

"And because he loves me."

"Indifferent, coming there."

"And he will be rich, and I shall like to be the greatest woman of the neighbourhood, and I shall be proud of having such a husband."

"Worst of all. And now, say how you love him?"

"As everybody loves—You're silly, Nelly."

"Not at all—Answer."

"I love the ground under his feet, and the air over his head, and everything he touches, and every word he says. I love all his looks, and all his actions, and him entirely and altogether. There now!"

"And why?"

"Nay; you are making a jest of it: it is exceedingly ill-natured! It's no jest to me!" said the young lady scowling, and turning her face to the fire.

"I'm very far from jesting, Miss Catherine," I replied. "You love Mr Edgar because he is handsome, and young, and cheerful, and rich, and loves you. The last, however, goes for nothing: you would love him without that, probably; and with it you wouldn't, unless he possessed the four former attractions."

"No, to be sure not: I should only pity him—hate him, perhaps, if he were ugly, and a clown."

"But there are several other handsome, rich young men in the world: handsomer, possibly, and richer than he is. What should hinder you from loving them?"

"If there be any, they are out of my way: I've seen none like Edgar."

"You may see some; and he won't always be handsome, and young, and may not always be rich."

"He is now; and I have only to do with the present. I wish you would speak rationally."

"Well, that settles it: if you have only to do with the present, marry Mr Linton."

"I don't want your permission for that—I *shall* marry him: and yet you have not told me whether I'm right."

"Perfectly right; if people be right to marry only for the present. And now, let us hear what you are unhappy about. Your brother will be pleased; the old lady and gentleman will not object, I think; you will escape from a disorderly, comfortless home into a wealthy, respectable one; and you love Edgar, and Edgar loves you. All seems smooth and easy: where is the obstacle?"

"*Here!* and *here!*" replied Catherine, striking one hand on her forehead, and the other on her breast: "in whichever place the soul lives. In my soul and in my heart, I'm convinced I'm wrong!"

"That's very strange! I cannot make it out." . . .

He's more myself than I am.
Whatever our souls are made of,
his and mine are the same.

. . . "I've no more business to marry Edgar Linton than I have to be in heaven; and if the wicked man in there had not brought Heathcliff so low, I shouldn't have thought of it. It would degrade me to marry Heathcliff now; so he shall never know how I love him: and that, not because he's handsome, Nelly, but because he's more myself than I am. Whatever our souls are made of, his and mine are the same; and Linton's is as different as a moonbeam from lightning, or frost from fire. . . .

. . . "Nelly, I see now, you think me a selfish wretch; but did it never strike you that if Heathcliff and I married, we should be beggars? whereas, if I marry Linton, I can aid Heathcliff to rise, and place him out of my brother's power."

W

"With your husband's money, Miss Catherine?" I asked. "You'll find him not so pliable as you calculate upon: and, though I'm hardly a judge, I think that's the worst motive you've given yet for being the wife of young Linton."

"It is not," retorted she; "it is the best! The others were the satisfaction of my whims: and for Edgar's sake, too, to satisfy him. This is for the sake of one who comprehends in his person my feelings to Edgar and myself. I cannot express it; but surely you and everybody have a notion that there is or should be an existence of yours beyond you. What were the use of my creation, if I were entirely contained here? My great miseries in this world have been Heathcliff's miseries, and I watched and felt each from the beginning: my great thought in living is himself. If all else perished, and *he* remained, *I* should still continue to be; and if all else remained, and he were annihilated, the universe would turn to a mighty stranger: I should not seem a part of it. My love for Linton is like the foliage in the woods: time will change it, I'm well aware, as winter changes the trees. My love for Heathcliff resembles the eternal rocks beneath: a source of little visible delight, but necessary. Nelly, I *am* Heathcliff! He's always, always in my mind: not as a pleasure, any more than I am always a pleasure to myself, but as my own being."

C. H. FOWLER AND W. H. DE PUY
HOME AND HEALTH AND HOME ECONOMICS, 1880

Methodist ministers Charles Henry Fowler (1837–1908) and William Harrison De Puy (1821–1901) took on everything from dirty socks to tight-lacing when they published their very popular handbook (see Wives, How to Keep, page 489). Touchingly, they dedicated their volume to their mothers, wives, daughters, readers, and "to those who have good homes and to those who need them."

The authors listed thirty-seven reasons why and why not to marry. What follows is a selection.

Do not marry to please any third party. You must do the living and enduring.

Do not marry to spite any body. It would add wickedness to folly.

Do not marry because some one else may seek the same hand. One glove may not fit all hands equally well.

Do not marry to get rid of any body. The coward who shot himself to escape from being drafted was insane.

Do not marry merely for the impulse love. Love is a principle as well as an emotion. So far as it is a sentiment it is a blind guide. It does not wait to test the presence of exalted character in its object before breaking out into a flame. Shavings make a hot fire, but hard coal is better for the winter.

Do not marry without love. A body without a soul soon becomes offensive.

Do not regard marrying as absolutely necessary. While it is the general order of Providence that people should marry, yet Providence may have some other plan for you.

Do not marry simply because you have promised to do so. If a seam opens between you now it will widen into a gulf. It is less offensive to retract a mistaken promise than to perjure your soul before the altar. Your intended has a right to absolute integrity.

Do not marry the wrong object. Themistocles said he would rather marry his daughter to a man without money, than to money without a man. It is well to have both. It is fatal to have neither.

Never marry as a missionary deed. If one needs saving from bad habits he is not suitable for you.

CYRIL CONNOLLY
THE UNQUIET GRAVE, 1944

For background on Connolly, see Sickness and Health, page 423.

Two fears alternate in marriage, the one of loneliness and the other of bondage. The dread of loneliness is greater than the fear of bondage, so we get married.

AVA GARDNER
TO A CONCERT AUDIENCE MEMBER, 1952

In 1951, Frank Sinatra left his wife Nancy for actress Ava Gardner (1922–1990) and a marriage that was famously combustible. They were intermittently separated in 1952, but both were scheduled to appear at a rally for Democratic presidential hopeful Adlai Stevenson. Seeing Sinatra from the wings, Ava was apparently seized with an unexpected wave of affection that carried over to her interaction with an audience member after the show.

"Hey, Ava, Sinatra's career is over, he can't sing anymore. . . . What do you see in this guy? He's just a hundred-and-nineteen-pound has-been."

"Well, I'll tell you—nineteen pounds is cock."

W

STANLEY SHAPIRO AND MAURICE RICHLIN
PILLOW TALK, 1959

Jonathan was played by needy, nerdy Tony Randall, Brad by box office idol Rock Hudson, and the love interest by Hudson's frequent screen partner Doris Day. The plot involves a reluctantly shared party phone line (there were such things); flaring tempers; a false identity; and, of course, romance, even as Brad remains seemingly immune to Jonathan's arguments in favor of marriage.

Screenwriters Stanley Shapiro (1925–1990) and Maurice Richlin (1920–1990) shared the 1960 Oscar for best original screenplay with Russell Rouse and Clarence Greene, who were credited with the story.

JONATHAN:	As a friend, I only hope one day you find a girl like this. You oughta quit all this chasing around, get married.
BRAD:	Why?
JONATHAN:	Why? You're not getting any younger, fella. Oh, sure, it's fun, it's exciting, dancing, nightclubbing with a different doll every night. But there comes a time when a man wants to give up that kind of life.
BRAD:	Why?
JONATHAN:	Because he wants to create a stable, lasting relationship with one person. Brad, believe me, there is nothing in this world so wonderful, so fulfilling, as coming home to the same woman every night.
BRAD:	Why?
JONATHAN:	Because! That's what it means to be adult! A wife, a family, a house. A mature man wants those responsibilities.
BRAD:	Why?
JONATHAN:	Well, if you want to, you can find tricky arguments against anything.

Because a man wants to create a stable, lasting relationship with one person.

LINDA PASTAN
"BECAUSE," 1982

Winner of a Pushcart Prize and a Dylan Thomas Award, among other honors, New York native Linda Pastan (1932–) has published some dozen volumes of poetry and for several decades was on the faculty of the Bread Loaf Writers' Conference.

Pastan married molecular biologist Ira Pastan in 1958 and had three children, putting her writing career temporarily on hold but gaining insight and material for the work that followed, much of it about love and family life.

Because the night you asked me,
the small scar of the quarter moon
had healed—the moon was whole again;
because life seemed so short;
because life stretched before me
like the darkened halls of nightmare;
because I knew exactly what I wanted;
because I knew exactly nothing;
because I shed my childhood with my clothes—
they both had years of wear left in them;
because your eyes were darker than my father's;
because my father said I could do better;
because I wanted badly to say no;
because Stanley Kowalski shouted "Stella . . .";
because you were a door I could slam shut;
because endings are written before beginnings;
because I knew that after twenty years
you'd bring the plants inside for winter
and make a jungle we'd sleep in naked;
because I had free will;
because everything is ordained;
I said yes.

W

AUDREY WELLS
SHALL WE DANCE?, 2004

A high point of the American version of the 1996 Japanese film by Masayuki Suo is Susan Sarandon's scene with a private eye (played by Richard Jenkins). Having found out that her husband's unusual behavior has involved dancing lessons, not adultery, Beverly tells the detective she won't be wanting him to investigate further.

Screenwriter Audrey Wells (1960–) has also been a producer and director. Among her other credits are *Under the Tuscan Sun*, *George of the Jungle*, and *The Truth About Cats & Dogs*.

BEVERLY:	All these promises that we make and we break. Why is it, do you think, that people get married?
DETECTIVE:	Passion.
BEVERLY:	No.
DETECTIVE:	That's interesting, because I would have taken you for a romantic. Why then?
BEVERLY:	Because we need a witness to our lives. There's a billion people on the planet. I mean, what does any one life really mean? But in a marriage, you're promising to care about everything. The good things, the bad things, the terrible things, the mundane things. All of it, all the time, every day. You're saying, "Your life will not go unnoticed because I will notice it. Your life will not go unwitnessed because I will be your witness."

Because we need a witness to our lives.
There's a billion people on the planet. What
does any one life really mean? But in a marriage,
you're promising to care about everything.

JASON REITMAN, SHELDON TURNER
UP IN THE AIR, 2009

In the popular movie written by Jason Reitman and Sheldon Turner, Ryan Bingham and Natalie Keener (played by George Clooney and Anna Kendrick) travel the country firing people on behalf of companies that are downsizing and don't want to do the dirty work themselves. In due course, the older, commitment-free Ryan ends up being grilled about his life choices by the younger, more hopeful Natalie.

The screenplay was an adaptation of a 2001 novel by Walter Kirn.

NATALIE:	Never?
RYAN:	No.
NATALIE:	Ever?
RYAN:	No.
NATALIE:	You never wanna get married?
RYAN:	Nope.
NATALIE:	Never want kids?
RYAN:	Not a chance.
NATALIE:	Ever.
RYAN:	Never. Is that so bizarre?
NATALIE:	Yes. Yes, it is.
RYAN:	I just don't see the value in it. All right, sell it to me.
NATALIE:	What?
RYAN:	Sell me marriage.
NATALIE:	Okay. How about love?
RYAN:	(*Scoffs.*) Okay.
NATALIE:	Stability. Just somebody you can count on.
RYAN:	How many stable marriages do you know?
NATALIE:	Somebody to talk to, someone to spend your life with.
RYAN:	I'm surrounded by people to talk to. I doubt that's gonna change.
NATALIE:	How about just not dying alone?
RYAN:	Starting when I was twelve, we moved each one of my grandparents into a nursing facility. My parents went the same way. Make no mistake, we all die alone. Now those cult members in San Diego, with the sneakers and the Kool-Aid, they didn't die alone. I'm just saying there are options.

W

WIVES, HOW TO KEEP

"THE FAMILY CIRCLE"
THE LADIES' REPOSITORY, 1866

Starting in 1841, *The Ladies' Repository* was published monthly by the Methodist Episcopal Church. Just before the end of the Civil War, "The Family Circle" was added as a popular column addressing manners, morals, prayer, and family relationships of all sorts.

How to Treat a Wife—

First, get a wife; secondly, be patient. You may have great trials and perplexities in your business with the world; but do not, therefore, carry to your home a cloudy or contracted brow. Your wife may have many trials, which, though of less magnitude, may have been as hard to bear. . . . You encounter your difficulties in open air, fanned by heaven's cool breezes; but your wife is often shut in from these healthful influences, and her health fails, and her spirits lose their elasticity. But O! bear with her; she has trials and sorrows to which you are a stranger; but which your tenderness can deprive of all their anguish. Notice kindly her efforts to promote your comfort. Do not take them all as a matter of course, and pass them by, at the same time being very sure to observe any omission of what you may consider duty to you. Do not treat her with indifference, if you would not scar and palsy her heart, which, watered by kindness, would, to the last day of your existence, throb with constant and sincere affection. Sometimes yield your wishes to hers. She has preferences as strong as you, and it may be just as trying to her to yield her choice as to you. Do you think it hard to yield sometimes? Think you it is not as difficult for her to give up always? If you never yield to her wishes, there is danger that she will think you are selfish, and care only for yourself; and with such feelings she can not love as she might. Again, show yourself manly, so that your wife may look up to you, and feel that you will act nobly, and that she can confide in your judgment.

How to treat a wife—First, get a wife.

C. H. FOWLER AND W. H. DE PUY
HOME AND HEALTH AND HOME ECONOMICS, 1880

For background on Fowler and De Puy, see Why, page 482.

Many a noble man toils early and late to earn bread and position for his wife. He hesitates at no weariness for her sake. He justly thinks that such industry and providence give a better expression of his love than he could give by caressing her and letting the grocery bills go unpaid. He fills the cellar and pantry. He drives and pushes his business. He never dreams that he is actually starving his *wife* to death. He may soon have a *woman* left to superintend his home, but his *wife* is dying. She must be kept alive by the same process that called her into being. Recall and repeat the little attentions and delicate compliments that once made you so agreeable, and that fanned her love into a consuming flame. . . . It is good work for a husband to cherish his wife.

"DON'TS FOR HUSBANDS"
DETROIT FREE PRESS, 1891

Don't think your wife is a servant.
Don't forget that your wife was once your sweetheart.
Don't try to run the household your way.
Don't think your wife can't keep your secrets.
Don't imagine you are a superior person.
Don't neglect to compliment your wife whenever opportunity offers.
Don't withhold your confidence.
Don't dole out a dollar as if it were a tax.
Don't stay out late at night.
Don't grumble at your wife and the work she does.
Don't think love has come to stay anyhow.

W

DORA SUTTON
HOUSEHOLD COMMANDMENTS, 1902

The case of Dora Sutton, a resident of Wilkes-Barre, Pennsylvania, drew attention from numerous papers around the country. Fed up with the behavior of her husband, Byron, she left him, then sent him the following list with the note: "If you want to live with me, you must comply with these rules." Byron refused. Dora had him arrested and charged with desertion. Byron argued that she was the one who had left him. The judge agreed with Byron, and he was let off.

1. Get up at 5 without my calling you.
2. Provide material for one cake a week.
3. Provide material for pies each week.
4. Twenty-five cents worth of beef Tuesdays and Saturdays.
5. Clothes for you that will make you look attractive and clean.
6. You will not use vulgar or profane language at all.
7. You will go to church and Sunday-school . . . and not make my life a burden to get you there in time.
8. Remove all mother's things and her cow, as I cannot tend the latter.
9. Buy us one quart of milk a day.
10. Will you take a bath all over once a week?
11. Ruth must not peddle, buy or carry things.
12. Wipe your feet clean when you come into the house.

BLANCHE EBBUTT
DON'TS FOR HUSBANDS, 1913

A selection of the hundreds of "don'ts" included in the companion book to Ebbutt's pre–World War I *Don'ts for Wives* (see Food, page 122; Husbands, How to Keep, pages 190–91).

Don't sit down to breakfast in your shirt-sleeves in hot weather on the ground that "only your wife" is present. She is a woman like any other woman. The courtesies you give to womankind are her due, and she will appreciate them.

Don't be too grave and solemn. Raise a bit of fun in the home now and then.

Don't keep all your best jokes for your men friends. Let your wife share them.

Don't shelter her from every wind that blows. You will kill her soul that way, if you save her body.

Don't rush out of the house in such a hurry that you haven't time to kiss your wife "good-bye." She will grieve over the omission all day.

Don't belittle your wife before visitors. You may think it a joke to speak of her little foibles, but she will not easily forgive you.

Don't keep your wife outside your business interests. It is foolish to say that she knows nothing about the business, and therefore it can't interest her. You will often find, too, that her fresh mind will see a way out of some little difficulty that has not occurred to you.

Don't expect to understand every detail of the working of your wife's mind. A woman arrives at things by different ways, and it is useless to worry her with "Why?" does she think this or that.

Don't think you can live your lives apart under the same roof and still be happy. Marriage is a joint affair, and cannot comfortably be worked along separate lines.

Don't insist upon having the last word. If you know when to drop an argument, you are a wise man.

Don't throw your mother's perfections at her head, or you needn't be surprised if she suggests that you might as well return to your mother's wing.

Don't forget to trust your wife in everything—in money matters; in her relations with other men; in her correspondence. Trust her to the utmost, and you will rarely find your trust misplaced.

WALTER GALLICHAN
HOW TO LOVE, 1915

In his several dozen books, Walter Matthew Gallichan (1861–1946) wrote about fishing, travel, birds, health, and, most controversially, sex. In such volumes as *Modern Woman and How to Manage Her*, *Women Under Polygamy*, and *Sexual Apathy and Coldness in Women*, he was decidedly against women's equality yet forward-thinking in his belief that women and men should be educated about one another. In the passage below, he suggested that husbands have a responsibility to keep their wives happy, if only by a kind of romantic noblesse oblige.

Gallichan outlived his first wife, was divorced by his second, and was outlived by his third.

W

True marriage based upon love and esteem is a prolongation courtship. . . .

. . . There is a conventional British view that making love is somewhat ridiculous after the honey-moon. Courtship is abandoned as a sort of necessary folly preliminary to complete union. . . .

The common use of the phrase "conjugal rights" shows that the reciprocal altruisms of wooing often tend to disappear in Western marriage. The husband is no longer the supplicant or pleader for privileges. He is a citizen with the law behind him, insisting upon "rights." This conception of matrimony is a source of the deepest discontent among women. It entirely negates the art of marriage, and reduces the wife in theory, if not always in absolute practice, to the status of a serf. It annihilates the spiritual element in conjugal love, and fatally accentuates the masculine tendency to exert force in place of tender suasion.

There is no hope for widespread married happiness till men learn that love is the art of understanding and pleasing women. Wives in revolt are the natural result of man's neglect of the art of courtship in marriage. It is the woman more often than the man who is disappointed in married life. After marriage it is the husband's part to show his aptitude in arousing and maintaining the responsiveness of the wife.

OGDEN NASH
"ADVICE OUTSIDE A CHURCH," 1935

For American author Ogden Nash (see Conflict, page 41), a master of joyously rhyming poetry that at times rose above nonsense and doggerel to good sense and even wisdom, marriage was a frequent topic. Nash wrote from experience; he married Frances Leonard in 1931 and remained married to her until his death forty years later.

Dear George, behold the portentous day
When bachelorhood is put away.
Bring camphor balls and cedarwood
For George's discarded bachelorhood;
You, as the happiest of men,
Wish not to wear it ever again.
Well, if you wish to get your wish,
Mark well my words, nor reply "Tush-pish."
Today we fly, tomorrow we fall,

And lawyers make bachelors of us all.
If you desire a noisy nursery
And a golden wedding anniversary,
Scan first the bog where thousands falter:
They think the wooing ends at the altar,
And boast that one triumphant procession
Has given them permanent possession.
They simply desist from further endeavor,
And assume that their wives are theirs forever.
They do not beat them, they do no wrong to them,
But they take it for granted their wives belong to them.
Oh, every trade develops its tricks,
Marriage as well as politics;
Suspense is silk and complacence is shoddy,
And no one belongs to anybody.
It is pleasant, George, and necessary
To pretend the arrangement is temporary.
Thank her kindly for favors shown:
She is the lender, and she the loan;
Nor appear to notice the gradual shift
By which the loan becomes a gift.
Strong are the couples who resort
More to courtship and less to court.
And I warn you, George, for your future good,
That ladies don't want to be understood.
Women are sphinxes, Woman has writ it;
It you understand her, never admit it.
Tell her that Helen was probably beautifuller,
Call, if you will, Penelope dutifuller,
Sheba charminger, Guinevere grander,
But never admit that you understand her.
Hark to the strains of Lohengrin!
Heads up, George! Go in and win!

W

WORK

GUSTAV MAHLER
LETTER TO ALMA MAHLER, 1910

Austrian composer Gustav Mahler (1860–1911) was in Munich, preparing for the premiere of his Eighth Symphony, when he wrote this letter to his wife, Alma. The well-received work coincided, however, with his discovery of an affair between the alluring Alma and architect Walter Gropius. A distressed Mahler consulted Freud for advice and didn't end the marriage.

Alma's high-profile romantic adventures continued after Mahler died the following year. She married and divorced Gropius, then married writer Franz Werfel.

Today the first rehearsal. Went quite well and my physique held out quite gallantly. With every beat, I looked round and thought how lovely it would be if my divinity were seated down there and I could brush her dear face with a stolen glance—then I'd know what I was alive for and why I was doing it all.

GULIELMA ALSOP AND MARY McBRIDE
SHE'S OFF TO MARRIAGE, 1942

For background on Alsop and McBride, see When, page 468.

The girl who is interested in her work, in getting on in her chosen profession, should realize that there is no real and devastating choice between work and marriage. In the past, there was such a choice, and women thought they would have the leisure and opportunity to solve the problem on a high ethical and emotional plane; that they would be able to take their time to decide between being wonderful mothers and darling wives . . . and going on with their work. But only in very few instances is there a choice to be made, for that great power of our times, economic pressure, has decided the matter for most girls. If a girl wants a husband, home, and children, she has to do her part in getting and in keeping them, and in the majority of cases she will have to go on working after marriage. So a girl should not put off her decision to marry the man of the moment for reasons of economy.

W

SIMONE DE BEAUVOIR
THE SECOND SEX, 1949

Some scholars feel it was the French philosopher and author Simone de Beauvoir (1908–1986) who was the mother of the twentieth century's second wave of feminism. In her sweeping history of women, she traced the origins of women's subservience to men, calling on women to see themselves, marriage, and motherhood in a new and harsher light.

The situation has to be changed in their common interest by prohibiting marriage as a "career" for the woman. Men who declare themselves antifeminist with the excuse that "women are already annoying enough as it is" are not very logical: it is precisely because marriage makes them "praying mantises," "bloodsuckers," and "poison" that marriage has to be changed and, as a consequence, the feminine condition in general. Woman weighs so heavily on man because she is forbidden to rely on herself; he will free himself by freeing her, that is, by giving her something *to do* in this world.

JOSEPH MANKIEWICZ
ALL ABOUT EVE, 1950

With his unforgettable screenplay for *All About Eve*, Joseph Mankiewicz (1909–1993) introduced the world to the brilliant but aging actress Margo Channing (played by Bette Davis) and to the sycophantic assistant Eve Harrington (Anne Baxter), the would-be usurper of Margo's professional and personal life. Never married, jealous of Eve, and suspicious of her director and lover, Bill, Margo in this scene ponders the personal sacrifices that have come with her professional success.

Karen is Margo's best friend.

MARGO: More than anything in this world I love Bill. And I want Bill. And I want him to want me. But me, not Margo Channing. And if I can't tell them apart, how can he?

KAREN: Well, why should he, and why should you?

MARGO: Bill's in love with Margo Channing. He's fought with her, worked with her, and loved her. But ten years from now Margo Channing will cease to exist. And what's left will be—what?

KAREN:	Margo, Bill is all of eight years younger than you.
MARGO:	Those years stretch as the years go on. I've seen it happen too often.
KAREN:	Not to you. Not to Bill.
MARGO:	Isn't that what they always say? . . . About Eve. I've acted pretty disgracefully toward her too.
KAREN:	Well—
MARGO:	Don't fumble for excuses, not here and now with my hair down. At best let's say I've been oversensitive to—well, to the fact that she's so young, so feminine, and so helpless, to so many things I want to be for Bill. Funny business a woman's career, the things you drop on your way up the ladder so you can move faster. You forget you'll need them again when you get back to being a woman. That's one career all females have in common, whether we like it or not. Being a woman. Sooner or later, we've got to work at it, no matter how many other careers we've had or wanted. And in the last analysis nothing's any good unless you can look up just before dinner or turn around in bed and there he is. Without that you're not a woman. You're something with a French Provincial office or a book full of clippings. But you're not a woman. Slow curtain, the end.

JESS OPPENHEIMER, MADELYN PUGH, AND BOB CARROLL JR. "JOB SWITCHING," *I LOVE LUCY*, 1952

I Love Lucy head writer Jess Oppenheimer (1913–1988) and writers Madelyn Pugh (1921–2011) and Bob Carroll Jr. (1918–2007) had a simple premise for a classic episode: the husbands and wives disagree about whose work is harder, and they swap roles for the day, each trying to prove their point. At home, Ricky and Fred come close to destroying the Ricardos' apartment in the course of cooking and cleaning. As for Lucy and Ethel, they land jobs coating and wrapping chocolates, and in one of TV comedy's most famous scenes, try desperately to keep up with a fast-moving conveyor belt. The dialogue below represents the "before" and "after" of the day.

RICKY:	Brother, if they had to make the dough, they would think twice before spending it that fast.
FRED:	Yeah.
ETHEL:	What's so tough about earning a living?
LUCY:	Yeah.

RICKY:	Have you ever done it?
LUCY:	No. But I could.
RICKY:	Hah!
ETHEL:	I could too.
FRED:	Hah!
RICKY:	Listen, holding down a job is a lot more difficult than lying around the house all day long.
LUCY:	Lying around the house! Is that all you think we do?
RICKY:	Yeah.
FRED:	Now, let's be fair, Rick. Every once in a while they get up and play canasta.
LUCY:	Who do you think does the housework?
ETHEL:	And who do you think cooks all the meals?
LUCY:	Yeah.
RICKY:	Oh, anybody can cook and do the housework.
LUCY:	Ha! I'd just like to see you two try it for a week.
RICKY:	Okay, we will.
FRED:	We will?
RICKY:	Yeah.
LUCY:	This I've got to see.
ETHEL:	I wanna get a load of this too.
RICKY:	Yeah, but wait a minute. You will have to go out and earn a living.
LUCY:	Okay, we will.
ETHEL:	We will?
LUCY:	Yeah. We'll change places. We'll get jobs, and you take care of the house for a week. Okay?
RICKY:	Okay.
ETHEL:	Okay?
FRED:	Okay.

· · · ·

RICKY:	Listen, we don't know how you girls feel about it, but we'd like to forget the whole thing. We're lousy housewives.
FRED:	Hideous.
LUCY:	Well, we're not so good at bringing home the bacon, either.
ETHEL:	We got fired off our first job.
LUCY:	Yeah.

W

RICKY:	Well, let's say we go back to the way we were. We'll make the money and you spend it.
LUCY:	Well, that's great with me.
RICKY:	And listen, girls. We never realized how tough it was to run a house before. So just to show you our appreciation, we brought you a little present.
LUCY:	Really?
ETHEL:	You did?
RICKY:	For each one of you, a five-pound box of chocolates.

Vivian Vance, Elvia Allman (as the factory foreman), and Lucille Ball

W

DAVID SIPRESS, 2011

It took David Sipress twenty-five years before one of his cartoons was accepted by *The New Yorker*. Since then, more than five hundred have appeared, on topics ranging from international to household politics.

"You make a very compelling case, Jeffrey,
but I still maintain that my day was worse than yours."

W

SHERYL SANDBERG
LEAN IN: WOMEN, WORK, AND THE WILL TO LEAD, 2013

As the chief operating officer of Facebook, Sheryl Sandberg (1969–) became both role model and lightning rod with her publication of *Lean In*, a bestselling exhortation to women to overcome personal and cultural barriers and reach for leadership opportunities. A key chapter, "Make Your Partner a Real Partner," cites her own marriage to SurveyMonkey chief executive Dave Goldberg in emphasizing how much a professionally successful woman needs a supportive husband who does his fair share of child rearing and household work.

I truly believe that the single most important career decision that a woman makes is whether she will have a life partner and who that partner is. I don't know of one woman in a leadership position whose life partner is not fully—and I mean fully—supportive of her career. No exceptions. . . .

. . . The image of a happy couple still includes a husband who is more professionally successful than the wife. If the reverse occurs, it's perceived as threatening to the marriage. People frequently pull me aside to ask sympathetically, "How *is* Dave? Is he okay with, you know, all your (*whispering*) *success*?" Dave is far more self-confident than I am, and given his own professional success, these comments are easy for him to brush off. More and more men will have to do the same, since almost 30 percent of U.S. working wives now outearn their husbands. As that number continues to grow, I hope the whispering stops.

Dave and I can laugh off concerns about his supposedly fragile ego, but for many women, this is no laughing matter. Women face enough barriers to professional success. If they also have to worry that they will upset their husbands by succeeding, how can we hope to live in an equal world?

W

X-WIVES AND HUSBANDS

CHARLES LEDERER, BEN HECHT, AND CHARLES MacARTHUR
***HIS GIRL FRIDAY*, 1940**

The Front Page, a popular play—and later film—written in 1928 by Ben Hecht and Charles MacArthur, told the story of two hardened newsmen in the heyday of print journalism. In 1940, director Howard Hawks had the inspired idea of changing the gender of one of the lead characters, thus creating one of the great screwball comedies of all time. In this version, Walter Burns (played by Cary Grant) and Hildy Johnson (played by Rosalind Russell) are colleagues who married, then divorced. On the eve of Hildy's remarriage (to an insurance salesman), she stops in at her old office, and Walter, with the help of a huge news story, attempts to lure her back to the work (and the man) she loves.

WALTER:	Whaddaya want?
HILDY:	Your ex-wife is here, do you want to see her?
WALTER:	Well, hello, Hildy!
HILDY:	Hello Walter. . . .
WALTER:	Well, well. How long is it?
HILDY:	How long is what?

WALTER:	You know what. How long is it since we've seen each other?
HILDY:	Oh well, let's see, I spent six weeks in Reno, then Bermuda, oh about four months, I guess. Seems like yesterday to me.
WALTER:	Maybe it was yesterday, Hildy. Been seeing me in your dreams?
HILDY:	Oh no—Mama doesn't dream about you anymore, Walter. You wouldn't know the old girl now.
WALTER:	Oh, yes I would. I'd know you any time—
WALTER AND HILDY:	—Any place, anywhere—
HILDY:	Aw, you're repeating yourself, Walter! That's the speech you made the night you proposed.
WALTER:	Well, I notice you still remember it.
HILDY:	Of course I remember it. If I didn't remember it, I wouldn't have divorced you.
WALTER:	Yeah, I sort of wish you hadn't done that, Hildy.
HILDY:	Done what?
WALTER:	Divorced me. Makes a fellow lose all faith in himself. Gives him a—almost gives him a feeling he wasn't wanted.
HILDY:	Oh, now, look, Junior, that's what divorces are for.
WALTER:	Nonsense. You've got an old-fashioned idea divorce is something that lasts forever—"till death do us part." Why, a divorce doesn't mean anything nowadays, Hildy. Just a few words mumbled over you by a judge. We've got something between us nothing can change. . . .
HILDY:	. . . Look, now, Walter. What I came up here to tell you is that you must stop phoning me a dozen times a day—sending me twenty telegrams—
WALTER:	I write a beautiful telegram, don't I? Everybody says so.
HILDY:	Are you gonna listen to what I have to say?
WALTER:	Look, look, what's the use of fighting, Hildy? I'll tell you what you do. You come back to work on the paper—if we find we can't get along in a friendly fashion, we'll get married again.

X

YOUTH AND AGE

THALES OF MILETUS, CIRCA 6TH CENTURY BC

Thales of Miletus (circa 624 BC–circa 547 BC) was one of the earliest Greek philosophers and a pioneer in mathematics. His view below, about when to marry, was supposed to have been expressed to his mother, Cleobulina, when he was still in his early twenties. According to the historian Diogenes Laërtius, Thales nonetheless was said to have married, although when is not clear.

When a man is young, it is too early for him to marry; when he is old, it is too late; and between these two periods he ought not to be able to command leisure enough to choose a wife.

DECIMUS MAGNUS AUSONIUS
"TO HIS WIFE," CIRCA 350

Ausonius was a Roman poet and teacher born in Bordeaux around 310. The best known of his works is a long poem called *Mosella*, which describes the countryside. But his *Epigrams* have also survived and are frequently translated. Epigram 20 is notable for its beauty; it is also, according to one scholar, unusual in that it applies the conventions of Latin erotic poetry to the state of marriage.

In Greek mythology, both the warrior Nestor and the prophetess Sibyl were famous for their advanced ages.

Love, let us live as we have lived, nor lose
The little names that were the first night's grace,
And never come the day that sees us old,
I still your lad, and you my little lass.
Let me be older than old Nestor's years,
And you the Sibyl, if we heed it not.
What should we know, we two, of ripe old age?
We'll have its richness, and the years forgot.

Then be not coy, but use your time,

And while ye may, go marry;

For having lost but once your prime,

You may for ever tarry.

ROBERT HERRICK
"TO THE VIRGINS, TO MAKE MUCH OF TIME," 1648

English poet Robert Herrick (1591–1674), though a lifelong bachelor, wrote glowingly of sensuality, love, and—when it came to marriage—the virtues of seizing the day.

Gather ye rosebuds while ye may,
Old time is still a-flying;
And this same flower that smiles to-day,
To-morrow will be dying.

The glorious lamp of heaven, the sun,
The higher he's a-getting,

Y

The sooner will his race be run,
And nearer he's to setting.

That age is best which is the first,
When youth and blood are warmer;
But being spent the worse and worst
Times still succeed the former.

Then be not coy, but use your time,
And while ye may, go marry;
For having lost but once your prime,
You may for ever tarry.

ARNOT BAGOT
LEARN TO LYE WARM, 1672

Like most proverbs, the one referred to in the title of this thirty-five-page pamphlet is undated, and the author is identified only as "a person of Honour." We have been unable to locate any information about Arnot Bagot, except that he was a lawyer.

In Ovid's *Metamorphosis*, Phaeton is reluctantly allowed by his father, the sun god Phoebus, to drive the chariot of the sun for a day. Phaeton is unable to control the horses, with the result that the earth is nearly frozen, then nearly burned up. To stop total disaster, Zeus kills Phaeton with a thunderbolt.

You say, that you cannot beleive that I, who have seen so many rare, excelent, and incomparable peices of nature; viewed them with so crittical an Eye; and set them forth with more than ordinary Commendations, should now fix my affection upon one, whose face in all probability must needs looke like the trees which mourne in October. . . . [I]n Common reason and prudence it is most proper, for a young man to marry a woman endowed with a larger flock of years than himself: . . . for youth to marry youth, what is it in nature but to add fuell to fire; to set a Giddy and Unexperienced *Phaeton* to guide the flaming Steeds of *Phoebus?* it is an old Proverb among horsmen, an old Horse to a young Man, and an old Man to a young Horse . . . that the staiedness and sobriety of the old Horse may prevent the precipitency and rashness of the young Man; and the discretion and moderation of the old Man, may correct the Fury and Wildness of the young Horse.

Y

ROBERT BURNS
"JOHN ANDERSON MY JO," 1798

Known as Scotland's national poet, Robert Burns (1759–1796) started writing as a teenager, mostly love poems inspired by his many crushes. Son of a farmer, he was always poor, which did not stop him from writing, marrying, having affairs, and eventually fathering fourteen children, including nine by his wife, Jean Armour. In addition to succeeding with his many original poems, Burns was well known for publishing and/or rewriting traditional Scottish songs, including "Auld Lang Syne" and the once-bawdy "John Anderson, My Jo." His two-stanza version is a beautiful ode to marriage in old age, ironic because the poet died at thirty-seven.

Burns wrote—and spoke—in the language known as Old Scots. *Jo* means "sweetheart"; *acqent* is "acquainted"; *brent* is "smooth"; *beld* is "bald"; *snaw* is "snow"; *pow* is "head"; *canty* is "merry"; and *maun* is "must."

John Anderson my jo, John
When we were first acqent;
Your locks were like the raven,
Your bonnie brow was brent;
But now your brow is beld, John,
Your locks are like the snaw;
But blessings on your frosty pow,
John Anderson my jo.

John Anderson my jo, John,
We clamb the hill thegither;
And mony a canty day John,
We've had wi' ane anither:
Now we maun totter down, John,
But hand in hand we'll go;
And sleep thegither at the foot,
John Anderson my jo.

DUTCH PROVERB

Two cocks in one house, a cat and a mouse, an old man and young wife, are always in strife.

E.B.B.
"A LETTER TO YOUNG LADIES ON MARRIAGE," 1837

Almost as popular a subject as whom and how to marry has been the question of the optimum age. For the almost certainly fictional "E.B.B.," there was no mincing words for the recipient of this letter, his supposed ward. *Now* was clearly much better than *soon* or *later*.

Of one thousand married women, taken without selection, it has been ascertained, by a long and tedious investigation, that the number of females married at each age is as follows: or if, by arithmetical license, we call a woman's chance of marriage in her whole life 1000, her chances in each two years will be shown below:

Age.	Chances.	Age.	Chances.
14 } 15 }	32	28 } 29 }	45
16 } 17 }	101	30 } 31 }	18
18 } 19 }	219	32 } 33 }	14
20 } 21 }	230	34 } 35 }	8
22 } 23 }	165	36 } 37 }	4
24 } 26 }	205	38 } 39 }	1
26 } 27 }	60		1000

Now, my dear Sarah, do lay this table to heart. It tells you that one *half* of a woman's chances of marriage are gone when she has completed her *twentieth* year. And mind you what the consequence of this is,—she must then, as the sailors say, carry less sail and limit her views.

Y

At twentythree years of age, she ought to be *very reasonable*; for *three-fourths* of the golden opportunities are gone, never to return. At *twentysix*, you will see at a glance that sauciness is out of the question, for your hopes, if the case should, unfortunately, be yours, will be reduced to the small fraction of *an eighth*. Possibly you may then think Rhyming Sandy a handsome fellow. At *thirtyone*, despair should begin to wrinkle your brow; for when that age comes and finds you single, pray remember that if you have in the whole circle of your acquaintances forty marrying men (a rare contingency), you have just one solitary chance amongst them all! When you stand on the dread verge of *thirtysix*, it is quite killing to reflect, that out of the thousand chances with which you started, *three*—a miserable remnant of *three*—only remains! . . . I am not of stern stuff, and can pursue the melancholy subject no farther, but again I entreat you, my dear Sarah, to lay the matter to heart. *Carpe diem* . . . or in plain English, *improve your time*.

STEPHEN CONRAD
THE SECOND MRS. JIM, 1904

American author Stephen Conrad (1875–1918) created the engaging character of Mrs. Jim, the second wife of a well-to-do farmer and the devoted stepmother to his two sons. As chatty narrator, she dispenses wisdom on everything from courting to budgeting to baking—and, of course, marriage.

I tell you it pays to start right when you're gettin' married. That's one trouble with gettin' married young, 'specially for girls. They don't know what they want, nor how to get it if they do know. But you take a middle-aged woman an' let her get married, an' she's a might poor stick if she don't know just what she wants, an' get it. I'll admit there's one advantage in gettin' married young. If you're goin' to be happy, you'll be happy lots longer, but then, there's this disadvantage, if you ain't goin' to be happy, you've got that much more time to be miserable in. But when you get married at middle age, if you're goin' to be happy, you can be twice as happy, 'cause you know better how to be happy, an' you know enough to have an easier time, an' if you ain't goin' to be happy, you won't be quite so miserable as if you didn't know how to have an easy time, an' you won't be miserable so long.

Y

W. B. YEATS
"THE YOUNG MAN'S SONG," 1910

William Butler Yeats (see Encouragement, page 83) was famously and futilely in love with the actress and activist Maud Gonne. By the time he wrote this poem, it had been more than a decade since she had rejected the last of his several marriage proposals.

In 1916, at the age of fifty-one, Yeats proposed to Gonne one last hopeless time, then swiftly, if creepily, proposed to her twenty-two-year-old daughter, Iseult, who also turned him down. In the same year, he married the twenty-five-year-old Georgie Hyde Lees, with whom he eventually had two children.

I whispered, "I am too young,"
And then, "I am old enough,"
Wherefore I threw a penny
To find out if I might love;
"Go and love, go and love, young man,
If the lady be young and fair,"
Ah, penny, brown penny, brown penny,
I am looped in the loops of her hair.

Oh love is the crooked thing,
There is nobody wise enough
To find out all that is in it,
For he would be thinking of love
Till the stars had run away,
And the shadows eaten the moon;
Ah, penny, brown penny, brown penny,
One cannot begin it too soon.

Y

PHILIP LEVINE
"FOR FRAN," 1961

Philip Levine (1928–2015) once selected this poem for an anthology of poets' favorites, explaining, "it says in an acceptable form what no man has a right to say to his wife." Acknowledging the toll that marriage, time, and the work of raising three sons were taking on his wife, Levine spent months working on this poem. When he finally read it to her, he wrote, "She wept with gratitude. She who never cried in pain wept real tears for these twenty inept lines that celebrate the curse of being a wife."

Levine won the Pulitzer Prize for Poetry in 1994 and was named the United States Poet Laureate in 2011.

She packs the flower beds with leaves,
Rags, dampened paper, ties with twine
The lemon tree, but winter carves
Its features on the uprooted stem.

I see the true vein in her neck
And where the smaller ones have broken
Blueing the skin, and where the dark
Cold lines of weariness have eaten

Out through the winding of the bone.
On the hard ground where Adam strayed,
Where nothing but his wants remain,
What do we do to those we need,

To those whose need of us endures
Even the knowledge of what we are?
I turn to her whose future bears
The promise of December air—

My living wife, Frances Levine,
Mother of Theodore, John, and Mark,
Out of whatever we have been
We will make something for the dark.

Y

ELOISE SALHOLZ
"TOO LATE FOR PRINCE CHARMING?," *NEWSWEEK*, 1986

One hundred fifty years and several intense waves of women's rights movements after "E.B.B." wrote to "his ward Sarah" (see page 507), *Newsweek* took its readers through what was essentially the same exercise. "Too Late for Prince Charming?" was one of the magazine's most controversial stories, inspiring reactions that *Newsweek* itself later described as "fury, anxiety, and skepticism." Revisiting the piece in 2006, the magazine reported: "Those odds-she'll-marry statistics turned out to be too pessimistic: today it appears that about ninety percent of baby-boomer men and women either have married or will marry." Of the eleven single women in the original story whom *Newsweek* was able to find, eight had married.

The traumatic news came buried in an arid demographic study titled, innocently enough, "Marriage Patterns in the United States." But the dire statistics confirmed what everybody suspected all along: that many women who seem to have it all—good looks and good jobs, advanced degrees and high salaries—will never have mates. According to the report, white, college-educated women born in the mid-'50s who are still single at 30 have only a 20 percent chance of marrying. By the age of 35 the odds drop to 5 percent. Forty-year-olds are more likely to be killed by a terrorist: they have a minuscule 2.6 percent probability of tying the knot.

Y

ZOLOFT

DANIEL AMEN
IMAGES OF HUMAN BEHAVIOR, 2004

Selective serotonin reuptake inhibitors, best known by brand names including Zoloft, Prozac, and Paxil, became the go-to antidepressants when they were introduced in the 1990s. Effective for many in easing symptoms of depression, obsessive-compulsive behavior, and social phobias, they also came, for many, at the cost of decreased sexual desire. Their wide use in the last two decades has thus rendered them either hero or villain in countless marriages.

Dr. Daniel Amen (1954–) is a psychiatrist and bestselling author whose application of brain imaging to psychiatry has been highly controversial. His scan technique, SPECT, stands for single proton emission computer tomography. The cingulate cortex is a part of the brain involved with emotion and learning.

On the outside, Gail was normal. She went to work every day, she was married to her high school sweetheart, and she had two small children. On the inside, Gail felt like a mess. Her husband was ready to leave her[,] and her children were often withdrawn and upset. Gail was distant from her family and locked into the private hell of obsessive-compulsive disorder. She cleaned her house for hours every night after work. She screamed at her husband and children when anything was out of place. She would become especially hysterical if she saw a piece of hair on the floor, and she was often at the sink washing her hands. She also made her husband

and children wash their hands more than ten times a day. She stopped making love to her husband because she couldn't stand the feeling of being messy.

On the verge of divorce, Gail and her husband came to see me. At first, her husband was very skeptical about the biological nature of her illness. Gail's brain SPECT study showed marked increased activity in the anterior cingulate system, demonstrating that she really did have trouble shifting her attention.

With this information, I placed Gail on Zoloft. Within six weeks, she had significantly relaxed, her ritualistic behavior had diminished and she stopped making her kids wash their hands every time they turned around. Her husband couldn't believe the change. Gail was more like the woman he married.

MESSAGE BOARD USER
"ANYONE TAKING ANXIETY DRUGS?," 2005

As is often the case online, a message board devoted to one subject created a community of users who felt trusting enough to delve into other areas. In this case, the message board was about rubber stamps; the topic, however, was antidepressants.

Zoloft saved my marriage!

I was waaaay anxious, always too careful, obsessed about cleanliness, and worried about EVERYTHING! I would cry at the drop of a hat if my husband (or anyone for that matter) did not agree with me. I could not sleep at night—I would get up multiple times throughout the night just to check if the doors in my house were still locked (knowing that they really were!). I would check on my children in their beds CONSTANTLY making sure they were still breathing!!!

Since on Zoloft, I no longer worry about the small stuff. This can be bad in some cases especially where money is concerned. While I am still "concerned" about cleanliness, it does not consume me. If the children have a toy mess it does not just drive me crazy. While I still have crying spell (mostly pre-menstrual) I do not cry near as often.

Pre-Zoloft, my husband and I fought—a lot!

Post-Zoloft we are more in love with each other than when we first met.

Z

ACKNOWLEDGMENTS

For his gracious, gifted eye and mind, we would like to thank Darrel Frost, who helped wrestle this project down, proving once again that he can do absolutely anything. We are grateful also to Michael Solomon, whose few weeks of research provided some of the most memorable entries in this anthology. We are indebted as well to Colin Kinniburgh, who came late to the game to assist us in tracking down sources and information; his efforts made us wish we'd had him with us all along. Sophia Jimenez kept the wheels turning, Fred Courtright secured rights, Michael Bierut gave inspiration, and Chris Jerome and her magic pencil answered our prayers. In addition to them, we are grateful to our children, Elizabeth and Jonathan; our friends Susie Bolotin, Betsy Carter, Cathy Cramer, Lee Eisenberg, and Dan Okrent for various suggestions and contributions; and our late beloved friend and advisor, Barb Burg. As in the past, agents Liz Darhansoff and Kathy Robbins represented us with faith and forethought. We will always be grateful.

This book could not have been written without the many people who have helped to keep the machines and machinery of our lives running, especially Donna Ash, Valerie Barber, Dr. Richard Cohen, Marcus Forman, Dr. Alexandra Heerdt, Milena Jelic, Dr. Jon LaPook, Eden Maningas, Isabel Pickett, Danny Radakovic, Dr. Saud Sadiq, and Dr. Paresh Shah.

Above all, we owe our thanks to Simon & Schuster's Priscilla Painton, lasting proof that great friends can be great editors, and great editors great friends. Her patience, skill, and insight throughout this long process have been a blessing, and her marriage along the way to the wonderful Andrew Heyward has provided yet more evidence that hope and love spring eternal.

SOURCES, PERMISSIONS, AND INDEX

NOTE: Text permissions are included in the list below.

    Bold numbers indicate the page numbers of the relevant text in this book.

Abbas, Haly. *The Pantegni*, 10th century, trans. Henry E. Sigerist. In Catherine Rider, *Magic and Impotence in the Middle Ages*, appendix 1. New York: Oxford University Press, 2006, pp. 224–25, 227. **398–399**

Adams, Abigail. Letter to John Adams, October 25, 1782. In C. James Taylor, ed., The Adams Papers (Digital Edition). Charlottesville: University of Virginia Press, 2008. Online at http://www.masshist.org/publications/apde/portia.php ?id=ADMS-04-05-02-0013. **390**

Adams, Clifford R. *Preparing for Marriage: A Guide to Marital and Sexual Adjustment.* New York: E. P. Dutton, 1951, pp. 179, 180. Copyright © 1951 by Clifford Adams. Reprinted with permission of the estate of Clifford Adams. **44, 153–54**

Adams, John. Diary, January?, 1761. In C. James Taylor, ed., The Adams Papers (Digital Edition). Charlottesville: University of Virginia Press, 2008. Online at http://www.masshist.org/publications/apde/portia.php?mode=p&id=DJA01p193#193. **180–82**

Addison, Joseph. "Wedlock's an Ill Men Eagerly Embrace." *The Spectator*, December 29, 1711. In *The Works of Joseph Addison: The Spectator, no. 1–314*, vol. 1. New York: Harper & Brothers, 1837, p. 377. Online at Google Books. **159**

"Advice to Prospective Mothers-in-Law." *The Baltimore Sun*, May 10, 1908, p. 4. Online at ProQuest Historical Newspapers. **228**

"Advice to Unmarried Ladies." *New-York Daily Gazette*, February 18, 1789, p. 178. Online at America's Historical Newspapers (NewsBank). **182–83**

"Advice to Young Wives." *Chicago Daily Tribune*, November 1, 1895, p. 12. Online at ProQuest Historical Newspapers. **227**

Aesop. "The Fatal Marriage," circa 6th century BC. In *Aesop's Fables*. Online at www.readbookonline.net/readOnLine/6589/. **470**

African proverb. In Mineke Schipper, *Never Marry a Woman with Big Feet: Women in Proverbs From Around the World*. Amsterdam: Amsterdam University Press, 2006, p. 66. **469**

Albee, Edward. *Who's Afraid of Virginia Woolf?*, 1962. New York: Pocket Books, 1964, pp. 16, 158–59. **47, 73**

Alcott, Louisa May. *Little Women*, 1867. New York: Aladdin Classics, 2000, p. 151. **298**

Alcott, William A. *The Young Wife, or Duties of Woman in the Marriage Relation*. Boston: George W. Light, 1838, pp. 306–7. **164–65**

Alexander, Stephany. "Cheating Husbands: Top 10 Ways on How to Catch a Cheating Husband," 2009. Online at www.womansavers.com/cheating-husbands.asp. Reprinted by permission of the author. **217–19**

Allen, Woody. *Love and Death*, dir. Woody Allen. United Artists, 1975. **290–91**

———. "My Marriage," 1964. On *Woody Allen: Stand-up Comic, 1964–1968*. Rhino CD, 1999. **73–74**

Alman, Isadora. "Two Lives," 2005. In *Single Woman of a Certain Age*. Hawaii: Inner Ocean Publishing, 2005, p. 156. Copyright © 2005 by Isadora Alman. Reprinted by permission of New World Library, Novato, CA, www.newworldlibrary.com. **414**

Alsop, Gulielma Fell and Mary F. McBride. *She's Off to Marriage: A Guide to Success and Happiness in Married Life*. New York: Vanguard, 1942, pp. 25–26. **468, 494**

Amen, Daniel G. *Images of Human Behavior: A Brain SPECT Atlas*. Newport Beach, CA: Mindworks Press, 2004. Reprinted with the permission of the Sanford J. Greenburger Associates. **513–14**

Andelin, Helen. *The Fascinating Girl*, 1969. Santa Barbara, CA: Pacific Press, 1975, pp. 289–92. Copyright © 1970 by Helen Andelin. Reprinted by permission of the estate of Helen Andelin. **187–88**

Arnold, Danny. "Mother, Meet What's His Name." *Bewitched*, season 1, episode 4, air date October 8, 1964. **232–33**

Auden, W. H. "Leap Before You Look," 1940. In *The Collected Poetry of W. H. Auden*. New York: Random House, 1945, p. 123–24. Copyright © 1945 and renewed © 1973 by W. H. Auden. Reprinted by permission of Random House, an imprint and division of Random House LLC and Curtis Brown, Ltd. All rights reserved. **260–62**

Ausonius, Decimus Magnus. "To his Wife," circa 350. In Helen Waddell, *Mediaeval Latin Lyrics*. New York: Henry Holt, 1948, p. 33. Copyright © 1929 by Helen Waddell. Reprinted by permission of Constable Publishers/Little Brown Book Group (UK). **503**

Austen, Jane. *Pride and Prejudice*, 1813. New York: Penguin Books, 1996, pp. 102–7. **344–48**

Austin, John Mather. *A Voice to the Married; Being a Compendium of Social, Moral, and Religious Duties, Addressed to Husbands and Wives*. Boston: A. Tompkins, 1847, pp. 56, 276–77. Online at Google Books. **278, 339**

Bach, George R., and Peter Wyden. *The Intimate Enemy: How to Fight Fair in Love and Marriage*. New York: William Morrow, 1969, pp. 59–66 passim. **48**

"A Bachelor's Thermometer." *Freedom's Journal*. November 9, 1827, p. 1. Online at America's Historical Newspapers (NewsBank). **433–35**

Bacon, Francis. "Of Marriage and Single Life," 1612. In Alfred S. West, ed., *Bacon's Essays*. Cambridge: Cambridge University Press, 1908, pp. 19, 20. Online at HathiTrust. **236, 315**

Bagot, Arnot. *Learn to Lye Warm, or, An Apology for that Proverb, "Tis good Sheltering under an old Hedge"; containing Reasons, Wherefore a Young Man should Marry an Old Woman*. London: W. Gilbert, 1672, pp. 21, 37. Online at ProQuest. **505**

Ballou, Sullivan. Letter to Sarah Ballou, July 14, 1861. In Robin Young, *For Love & Liberty: The Untold Civil War Story of Major Sullivan Ballou & His Famous Love Letter*. New York: Thunder's Mouth Press, 2006, pp. xxiv–vii. **93–94**

Balzac, Honoré de. *The Marriage Contract*, 1835, trans. Katharine Prescott Wormeley. Boston: Roberts Brothers, 1895, pp. 127–28. Online at Google Books. **338–39**

———. *The Physiology of Marriage*, 1829. London: Strangeways & Sons, 1904, p. 61, 63–64. **113, 172–73, 401**

Barreca, Gina. "Jealousy: How Do You Solve a Problem Like Medea?" *Psychology Today*, July 30, 2009. Online at www.psychologytoday.com/node/31518. **242**

Barry, Philip. *The Philadelphia Story: A Comedy in Three Acts*, 1939. New York: Samuel French, 1969, p. 13. **382**

Bates, Jerome Paine. *The Imperial Highway; or, the Road to Fortune and Happiness*, 1880. Chicago: The National Library Association, 1886, p. 478. **83**

Beauvoir, Simone de. *The Second Sex*, 1949, trans. Constance Borde and Sheila Malovany-Chevalier. New York: Alfred A. Knopf, 2009, p. 523. **495**

Beecher, Henry Ward. *Proverbs from Plymouth Pulpit: Selected from the Writings and Sayings of Henry Ward Beecher*, ed. William Drysdale. New York: D. Appleton, 1887, p. 93. **130**

Behrendt, Greg, and Liz Tuccillo. *He's Just Not That Into You: The No-Excuses Truth to Understanding Guys*. New York: Simon Spotlight Entertainment, 2004, pp. 79, 84. Copyright © 2004 Greg Behrendt and Liz Tuccillo. Reprinted with the permission of Simon Spotlight, a division of Simon & Schuster, Inc. **247–48**

Benton, Robert. *Kramer vs. Kramer*, based on the novel by Avery Corman, dir. Robert Benton. Columbia Pictures, 1979. **28–29**

Bergen, Candice. *Knock Wood*, 1984. New York: Simon & Schuster, 2014, p. 291. **244–45**

Bicks, Jenny. "A Woman's Right to Shoes." *Sex and the City*, season 6, episode 9, air date August 17, 2003. **442**

Bierce, Ambrose. *The Devil's Dictionary*, 1911. In David E. Schultz and S. T. Joshi, eds., *The Unabridged Devil's Dictionary*. Athens: University of Georgia Press, 2000, p. 162. **295**

"Bintel Brief" editor and The Unhappy Fool. Letters, 1908. In Isaac Metzker, ed. and trans., *A Bintel Brief: Sixty Years of Letters from the Lower East Side to the* Jewish Daily Forward. New York: Schocken Books, 1971, pp. 73–74. **362**

Blackwell, Henry, and Lucy Stone. Marriage protest, 1855. In "A Marriage Under Protest." *New York Times*, May 4, 1855, p. 2. **267–68**

Blake, William. Notebook fragment, circa 1793. In *The Complete Poems*. New York: Penguin, 1977, p. 153. **401**

Blakely, Mary Kay. "Hers." *New York Times*, April 16, 1981, p. C2. Copyright © 1982 by The New York Times Company. Reprinted by permission of the author. **125–26**

Bloggers. "Is Facebook a Cyber Threat to Your Marriage?" *Techlationships* (blog), January 22, 2010. http://techlationships.com/2009/01/22/is-facebook-a-cyber-threat-to-your-marriage/. **118–19**

Bonaparte, Napoleon. Letter to Josephine, November 13, 1796. In Arthur Levy, *The Private Life of Napoleon*, vol. 1, trans. Stephen Louis Simeon. New York: Scribner's, 1894, pp. 181–82. **238**

British church court record, 1300. In P. J. P. Goldberg, ed. and trans., *Women in England, c. 1275–1525: Documentary Sources*. Manchester and New York: Manchester University Press, 1995, p. 140. **445**

British proverb. In John R. Wise, *The New Forest: Its History and Its Scenery*. London: Gibbings, 1895, p. 179. **228**

Brome, Alexander. "To a Jealous Husband," 1664. In *Songs and Poems: Drinking Songs: Love Poems of the Cavaliers of Cromwell's Time*. Louisville, KY: privately printed, 1924, p. 77. Online at HathiTrust. **236**

Brontë, Charlotte. *Jane Eyre*, 1847. New York: Puffin Books, pp. 267–69 and 429–30. Online at Google Books. **279, 348–50**

Brontë, Emily. *Wuthering Heights*, 1847. London: Smith, Elder, 1870, pp. 63–67. Online at Google Books. **479–82**

Brooks, Mel. Wedding toast, 1985. Printed by permission of Mel Brooks. **429–30**

"Brother Jonathan's Wife's Advice to Her Daughter on the Day of Her Marriage." *New England Farmer* (Boston), May 1, 1833. Online at Google Books. **190**

Brown, Chip. "The Waiting Game." In Chris Knutsen and David Kuhn, eds., *Committed: Men Tell Stories of Love, Commitment, and Marriage*, 2005. London: Bloomsbury, 2006, pp. 200–201. **464**

Brown, Helen Gurley. *Sex and the Single Girl*. New York: Bernard Geis, 1962, pp. 3–8. Copyright © 1962 by Helen Gurley Brown. Reprinted by permission of Barricade Books. **438–40**

Browning, Elizabeth Barrett. Sonnets 4 and 43, circa 1845. In *Sonnets from the Portuguese*. New York: Harper & Row, n.d., pp. 4 and 43. **285, 391**

Bülbül. "My Name Was Helen," 1979. In Gloria Kaufman and Mary Kay Blakely, eds., *Pulling Our Own Strings: Feminist Humor & Satire*. Bloomington: Indiana University Press, 1980, p. 186. **309**

Burns, Robert. "John Anderson My Jo," 1798. In *The Works of Robert Burns; with An Account of His Life, and a Criticism on his Writings*. London: T. Cadell, Jun, and W. Davies, 1801, pp. 302–3. **506**

Burton, Richard. Letter to Elizabeth Taylor, June 25, 1973. In Sam Kashner and Nancy Schoenberger, *Furious Love: Elizabeth Taylor, Richard Burton, and the Marriage of the Century*. New York: HarperCollins, 2010, pp. 360–61. Copyright © 2010 by Sam Kashner and Nancy Schoenberger. Reprinted by permission of HarperCollins Publishers. **76–77**

Butler, Samuel. Letter to Eliza Mary Ann Savage, November 21, 1884. In Henry Festing Jones, *Samuel Butler, Author of Erewhon (1835–1902): A Memoir*, vol. 1. London: Macmillan, 1919, p. 429. **294**

Butterfield, Oliver M. *Planning for Marriage*, 1956. Princeton, NJ: D. Van Nostrand, 1957, p. 295. **154**

Calof, Rachel. *My Story*, 1936. In Jacob Calof and Molly Shaw, trans., *Rachel Calof's Story: Jewish Homesteader on the Northern Plains*. Bloomington: Indiana University Press, 1995, pp. 41–43. Reprinted by permission of Indiana University Press. **122–24**

Campbell, Beatrice. Quoted in Alexander Woollcott, *While Rome Burns*. New York: Grosset & Dunlap, 1934, p. 140. **13**

Campbell, Joseph, 1988. Quoted in Joseph Campbell and Bill Moyers, *The Power of Myth*. New York: Random House, 2011, p. 7. **29–30**

Capon, Robert Farrar. *Bed and Board: Plain Talk About Marriage*. New York: Simon & Schuster, 1965, pp. 70–71. Copyright © 1965 by Robert Farrar Capon. Reprinted by permission of the Estate of Robert Capon. **14–15**

Carpenter, Edward. *Love's Coming of Age*, 1896. New York: Modern Library, 1911, pp. 99–101. **324**

Carter, Jimmy. Quoted in "Jimmy Carter: A Candid Conversation with the Democratic Candidate for President." *Playboy*, November 1976, p. 86. **52**

Carville, James, and Mary Matalin. Interview by John King, *State of the Union with John King*, CNN, December 27, 2009. Online at http://www.youtube.com/watch?v=LGL6eaIe3kM. **49–50**

Cary, Phoebe. "The Wife." In *Poems and Parodies*. Boston: Ticknor, Reed, and Fields, 1854, p. 192. Online at Google Books. **165**

Casanova, Giacomo. *History of My Life*, 1797. New York: Alfred A. Knopf, 2006, p. 880. **316**

Catharine of Aragon. Letter to Henry VIII, January 7, 1536. In "Catherine of Aragon: In Her Own Words," *The Six Wives of Henry VIII* (PBS). Online at www.pbs.org/wnet/sixwives/inherwords/ca_words2.html. **54**

Cervantes, Miguel de. "The Divorce Court Judge," 1615. In Dawn L. Smith, trans., *Eight Interludes*. London: J. M. Dent, 1996, pp. 13–14. **63–64**

Chesterton, G. K. *Charles Dickens: A Critical Study*, 1906. New York: Dodd, Mead, 1913, pp. 264, 265. **386**

Childfreeeee. "The Top 100 Reasons Not to Have Kids (and Remain Childfree)." *Childfreedom: Musings on the Childfree Lifestyle and our Child-Centric Society* (blog), March 17, 2009. http://childfreedom.blogspot.com/2009/03/top-100-reasons-not-to-have-kids-and.html. Reprinted by permission. **31**

"The Choice of a Husband, By a Lady." *Massachusetts Magazine, or, Monthly Museum of Knowledge & Rational Entertainment*, February 1, 1794, p. 120. **471–72**

Chopin, Kate. "The Story of An Hour," 1894. In *Kate Chopin: A Re-Awakening* (PBS). Online at http://www.pbs.org/katechopin/library/storyofanhour.html. **131–34**

Churchill, Clementine. Letter to Winston Churchill, September 12, 1909. In Mary Soames, ed., *Winston and Clementine: The Personal Letters of the Churchills*. Boston: Houghton Mifflin, 1998, p. 28. Copyright © 1998 by the Lady Soames. Reprinted by permission of Curtis Brown, London, on behalf of the Estate of Winston S. Churchill and the Master, Fellows and Scholars of Churchill College, Cambridge. **5–6**

Churchill, Winston. Letters to Clementine Churchill, September 12, 1909 and September 12, 1948. In Mary Soames, ed., *Winston and Clementine: The Personal Letters of the Churchills*. Boston: Houghton Mifflin, 1998, pp. 29, 549. Copyright © 1998 by the Lady Soames. Reprinted by permission of Curtis Brown, London, on behalf of the Estate of Winston S. Churchill and the Master, Fellows and Scholars of Churchill College, Cambridge. **6–7**

Cibber, Colley. *The Double Gallant; or, The Sick Lady's Cure: A Comedy*, 1707. London: John Bell, 1792, p. 18. **371**

C.K., Louis. *Shameless*, dir. Steven J. Santos. HBO Studios, 2007. **30–31**

Clinton, Bill. Grand Jury testimony, August 17, 1998. Transcript online at www.washingtonpost.com/wp-srv/politics/special/clinton/stories/bctest092198_2.htm. **216**

Clinton, Bill, and Hillary Clinton. Interview by Steve Kroft, *60 Minutes*, CBS, January 26, 1992. **62**

Code of Hammurabi. Circa 1780 BC. Trans. L. W. King. Online at Ancient History Sourcebook, Fordham University. **397**

Cohen, Richard M. *Blindsided: Lifting a Life Above Illness, A Reluctant Memoir*. New York: HarperCollins, 2004, pp. 198–201. Copyright © 2004 by Richard Cohen. Reprinted by permission of HarperCollins Publishers. **425–26**

Coleridge, Samuel Taylor. *Table Talk of Samuel Taylor Coleridge*, 1824. London: George Routledge, 1884, p. 50. **297, 329**

Connell, Evan. *Mrs. Bridge*, 1959. Berkeley, CA: Counterpoint, 2010, p. 69. **35**

Connelly, Julie. "The CEO's Second Wife." *Fortune*, August 28, 1989, p. 53. **383**

Connolly, Cyril. *The Unquiet Grave: A Word Cycle by Palinurus*, 1944. New York: Harper & Brothers, 1945, pp. 12, 67. **423, 489**

Conrad, Stephen. *The Second Mrs. Jim*. Boston: L. C. Page, 1904, pp. 59–60. Online at Internet Archive. **508**

1 Corinthians 7:1–9 and 13:1–8. *The Holy Bible, Containing the Old and New Testaments*, King James Version. **282, 397**

Coward, Noël. "Private Lives," 1930. In *Play Parade*. New York: Doubleday, 1948, pp. 184–86, 188–89. Copyright © 1930 by Noël Coward. Reprinted by permission of William Heinemann, Ltd. and Bloomsbury Publishing Plc. **378**

Cowper, Ernest. Letter to Elbert Hubbard II, 1916. In *The Selected Writings of Elbert Hubbard: His Mintage of Wisdom, Coined from a Life of Love, Laughter and Work*, ed. Elbert Hubbard II. New York: Wm. H. Wise, 1922, pp. 16–18. **97–98**

Cramer, Richard Ben. *Joe DiMaggio: The Hero's Life*. New York: Simon & Schuster, 2000, pp. 367–68. Copyright 2000 by Richard Ben Cramer. Reprinted by permission of Simon & Schuster, Inc. **241–42**

Crane, George W. "Marital Rating Scale, Husband's Chart," and "Marital Rating Scale, Wife's Chart." In *Tests for Husbands and Wives* (pamphlet), 1939, pp. 1–8. Online at http://www.scribd.com/doc/3086410/Tests-for-Husbands-and-Wives. **146–53**

Curtis, Richard. *Four Weddings and a Funeral*, dir. Mike Newel. Channel Four Films, 1994. **358**

Damon, Matt, and Ben Affleck. *Good Will Hunting*, dir. Gus Van Sant. Miramax Films, 1997. **245–46**

Darwin, Charles. "This is the Question," 1838. In John van Wyhe, ed., *The Complete Work of Charles Darwin Online*. Online at http://darwin-online.org.uk/content/record?itemID=CUL-DAR210.8.2. **477–79**

David, Hal, and Burt Bacharach. "Wives and Lovers," 1963. Copyright © 1963. Reprinted by permission of Sony Music Publishing. **194**

David, Larry. "The Engagement." *Seinfeld*, season 7, episode 1, air date September 21, 1995. **319–20**

"A Death-Bed Marriage." *Daily Evening Bulletin* (San Francisco), March 15, 1866, col. C. Online at Gale 19th Century U.S. Newspapers. **423**

De Botton, Alain. "A Point of View: Why Books Do Not Prepare Us for Real Love." *BBC News Magazine*, February 11, 2011. Online at www.bbc.co.uk/news/magazine-12404332. **291**

"Declares Her Husband Was Jealous of Dog." *Pittsburgh Press*, November 13, 1916, p. 8. Online at Google News. **240–41**

De Cleyre, Voltairine. "Sex Slavery," 1890. Online at Molinari Institute Online Library. http://praxeology.net/VC-SS.htm. **131**

Defoe, Daniel. *Conjugal Lewdness; or, Matrimonial Whoredom: A Treatise concerning the Use and Abuse of the Marriage Bed*, 1727. Gainesville, FL: Scholars' Facsimiles & Reprints, 1967, pp. 280–82. **399**

Derenzy, Margaret Graves. *A Whisper to a Newly-Married Pair, from a Widowed Wife*, 1824. London: Wellington, Salop, 1824, pp. 97–98. **277–78**

Diana, Princess of Wales. Interview by Martin Bashir, *Panorama*, BBC1, November 1995, p. 198. Transcript online at http://www.bbc.co.uk/news/special/politics97/diana/panorama.html. **214–215**

Dickens, Charles. *Great Expectations*, 1861. Mineola, N.Y.: Dover Publications, 2001, pp. 43–45. **435–36**

Didion, Joan. Interview by Sara Davidson, "Playing It as It Lays." *O: The Oprah Magazine*, November 2005. Online at ProQuest. **49**

Dix, Dorothy. "Dorothy Dix Talks." *Times-Picayune* (New Orleans), May 3, 1922, p. 12. **184–85**

Dixie Cup Advertisement, *Ladies' Home Journal*, September, 1970 **170**

The Don't Sweat Guide for Newlyweds. New York: Hyperion Books, 2003, p. 110. **314**

"Don'ts for Husbands." *Detroit Free Press*, November 22, 1891, p. 4. Online at ProQuest Historical Newspapers. **489**

Douglass, Frederick. Finsbury Chapel speech, 1846. In *My Bondage and My Freedom*. New York: Miller, Orton & Mulligan, 1855, p. 409 **266**.

Dryden, John. "Why Should a Foolish Marriage Vow," 1673. In Talia Felix, ed., *Marriage à la Mode: With Original Music Restored*. Talia Felix, 2010, p. 5. **112–13**

Du Maurier, Daphne. *Rebecca*, 1938. New York: Avon Books, 1971, pp. 56–57. Copyright © 1938 and renewed © 1965 by Daphne du Maurier. Used by permission of Curtis Brown, Ltd. and Doubleday, an imprint of the Knopf Doubleday Publishing Group, a division of Random House, LLC. All rights reserved. **380–82**

Dunbar, William. "Upon the Midsummer Eve, Merriest of Nights," 15th century. In Conor McCarthy, ed. and trans., *Love, Sex and Marriage in the Middle Ages: A Sourcebook*. New York: George Routledge, 2004, pp. 251–52. **141–42**

Duncan, Isadora. *My Life*. New York: Boni and Liveright, 1927, p. 187. **269**

"Dunmow Oath," 1510. In Francis Grose and Thomas Astle, eds., *The Antiquarian Repertory: A Miscellaneous Assemblage of Topography, History, Biography, Customs, and Manners Intended to Illustrate and Preserve Several Valuable Remains of Old Times*, vol. 3. London: Edward Jeffery, 1808, p. 343. **53–54**

Dunn, Stephen. "The Night the Children Were Away." In *Local Time*. New York: William Morrow, 1986, pp. 42–43. Copyright © 1986 by Stephen Dunn. Reprinted by permission of the author. **412–13**

Dunton, John, ed. *The Post-Angel: Or, Universal Enlightenment,* vol. 1, March 1701, p. 200. Online at Eighteenth Century Journals: A Portal to Newspapers and Periodicals, c1685–1835 (Adam Matthew). **447**

Dutch proverb, n.d. In Jon R. Stone, ed., *The Routledge Book of World Proverbs*. New York: George Routledge, 2006, p. 447. **506**

Duvall, Evelyn, and Sylvanus Duvall. *Saving Your Marriage*. New York: Public Affairs Pamphlets, 1954, p. 13. **231**

Duvall, Evelyn Millis, and Reuben Hill. "Ways of Handling Conflict." In *When You Marry*. Boston: D. C. Heath, 1945, p. 190. **43–44**

Earhart, Amelia. Letter to George Palmer Putnam, February 7, 1931. In *Letters From Amelia, 1901–1937*, ed. Jean L. Backus, pp. 104–5. Boston: Beacon Press, 1982. Copyright © 1982 by Jean L. Backus. Reprinted by permission of Beacon Press, Boston. **364**

E.B.B., Esq. *A Letter to Young Ladies on Marriage*. Boston: Tuttle, Dennett & Chisholm, 1837, pp. 8–9. **507–8**

Ebbutt, Blanche. *Don'ts for Husbands,* 1913. London: A & C Black, 2007, pp. 2–34 passim. **490–91**

———. *Don'ts for Wives*, 1913. London: A & C Black, 2007, pp. 1–69 passim. **122, 190–91**

Eddy, Mary Baker. *Science and Health*. Boston: Christian Scientist Publishing, 1875, p. 325. **239**

Editorial, *The National Advocate*, November 25, 1817, col. A. Online at Gale 19th Century U.S. Newspapers. **296–97**

Editorial, *The Raleigh Register*, June 22, 1850, col. B. Online at Gale 19th Century U.S. Newspapers. **308**

Edward VIII. Abdication speech, December 11, 1936. Online at http://www.historyplace.com/speeches/edward.htm. **57**

Egyptian marriage contract, 200 BC. In "Trial Marriages 200 BC: Ancient Contracts Unearthed Reveal Curious Matrimonial Laws of Egypt." *The Washington Post*, May 22, 1910, p. 10. **264**

Einstein, Albert. "Conditions" for Mileva Marić, 1914. In Walter Isaacson, *Einstein: His Life and Universe*. New York: Simon & Schuster, 2007, pp. 185–86. **268–69**

Eliot, George. *Middlemarch: A Study of Provincial Life*, 1874. New York: Modern Library, 2000, p. 186. **103**

———. *Romola*, vol. 3, 1863. New York: Croscup, 1896, p. 22. Online at Google Books. **340**

Elizabeth I, 1563. Quoted in J. E. Neale, *Queen Elizabeth I*, 1934. London: Jonathan Cape, 1971, p. 143. **431**

Ephron, Nora. *Heartburn*. New York: Alfred A. Knopf, 1983, pp. 12–13. **213–14**

Estonian Proverb, date unknown. In Mineke Schipper, *Never Marry a Woman with Big Feet: Women in Proverbs from Around the World*. Amsterdam: Amsterdam University Press, 2006, p. 99. **437**

Eubanks, Bob, and contestants. *The Newlywed Game*, air date circa 1972. Online at http://www.youtube.com/watch?v=qT4Xo3CAC0M. **313–14**

Euripides. *Medea*, 5th century BC, trans. Edward P. Coleridge, *Great Books of the Western World*, vol. 5. Chicago: Encyclopaedia Britannica, 1952, pp. 218–19. **235–36**

Exodus 20:14. The Holy Bible, Containing the Old and New Testaments. King James Version. **200**

"The Family Circle." *Ladies' Repository,* September 1866, pp. 563–64. **488**

"A Father's Advice to His Daughter." *Pennsylvania Inquirer and National Gazette*, August 24, 1843, col. C. Online at Gale 19th Century U.S. Newspapers. **297–98**

Faulkner, William. *Go Down, Moses*, 1940. New York: Vintage Books, 1973, pp. 107–8. **244**

———. Letter to the *New Orleans Item-Tribune*, April 4, 1925. In James G. Watson, "Faulkner's 'What Is the Matter with Marriage.'" *The Faulkner Journal*, vol. 5, no. 2 (Spring 1990), p. 7. **335**

Feynman, Richard. Letter to Arline Feynman, October 17, 1946. In James Gleick, *Genius: The Life and Science of Richard Feynman*. New York: Vintage Books, 1992, pp. 221–22. Copyright © 1992 by James Gleick. Reprinted by permission of the Melanie Jackson Agency. **58–59**

Fielding, Helen. *Bridget Jones's Diary*. London: Macmillan, 1996, p. 244. **441–42**

Fisher, Carrie. *Wishful Drinking*, 2008. New York: Simon & Schuster, 2009, p. 94. **430**

Fitzgerald, F. Scott. Letter to Zelda Fitzgerald, April 26, 1934. In Jackson R. Bryer and Cathy W. Barks, eds., *Dear Scott, Dearest Zelda: The Love Letters of F. Scott and Zelda Fitzgerald*. New York: St. Martin's Press, 2002, pp. 193–94. Copyright © 1994 by the Trustees Under Agreement dated July 3, 1975, created by Frances Scott Fitzgerald Smith. Printed by permission of Scribner Publishing Group, an imprint of Simon & Schuster, Inc. **86–87**

Fleming, Ian. *Diamonds Are Forever*, 1956. In *A James Bond Omnibus: Containing Live and Let Die, Diamonds Are Forever, Dr. No*. London: Jonathan Cape, 1973, p. 455. **295**

Fowler, C. H., and W. H. De Puy. *Home and Health and Home Economics: A Cyclopedia of Facts and Hints for All Departments of Home Life, Health, and Domestic Economy*. New York: Phillips & Hunt, 1880, pp. 14–15, 17. Online at Google Books. **482–83, 489**

Franklin, Benjamin. "The Old Mistresses' Apologue," June 25, 1745. The Papers of Benjamin Franklin, sponsored by the American Philosophical Society and Yale University. Online at http://franklinpapers.org. **477**

———. *Poor Richard's Almanack: Being the choicest Morsels of Wit and Wisdom, written during the thirty Years of the Almanack's Publication*, 1734. Mount Vernon, NY: Peter Pauper Press, 1936, p. 21. Online at HathiTrust. **466**

———. "Rules and Maxims for Promoting Matrimonial Happiness. Addressed to All Widows, Wives and Spinsters." *The Pennsylvania Gazette*, October 8, 1730. In Walter Isaacson, ed., *A Benjamin Franklin Reader*. New York: Simon & Schuster, 2003, p. 55. **372**

Friedan, Betty. *The Feminine Mystique*. New York: W. W. Norton, 1963, pp. 15–16. Copyright © 1963 by Betty Friedan. Used by permission of W. W. Norton, Inc. **135–36**

Frost, Robert. "The Master Speed," 1936. In Edward Connery Lathem, ed., *The Complete Poetry of Robert Frost*. New York: Macmillan, 2002, p. 300. Copyright © 1936 by Robert Frost. Copyright © 1969 by Henry Holt and Company, LLC. Reprinted by permission of Henry Holt and Company, LLC, and Random House (UK) Ltd. **325**

Gallichan, Walter M. *How to Love: The Art of Courtship and Marriage*, 1915. As quoted in *Sex Searchlights and Sane Sex Ethics*. Chicago: Science, 1922, pp. 108–10. Online at Google Books. **491–92**

Gandhi, Mohandas. "Question Box." *Harijan*, March 9, 1940. In *The Collected Works of Mahatma Gandhi*, vol. 78 (23 February–15 July, 1940). Delhi: Publication Division, Ministry of Information & Broadcasting, Govt. of India, 1994, p. 22. **386**

Gardner, Ava, 1952. Quoted in Lee Server, *Ava Gardner: "Love is Nothing."* New York: St. Martin's Press, 2006, p. 249. **483**

Gardner, Ralph, Jr. "Alpha Women, Beta Men." *New York*, November 17, 2013. Online at http://nymag.com/nymetro/news/features/n_9495/. **303**

Gautama Buddha. *The Dhammapada*, circa 3rd Century BC. In F. Max Muller, ed. and trans., *Wisdom of the Buddha: The Unabridged Dhammapada*. New York: Dover, 2000, p. 38. Online at Google Books. **51**

Gauvain, Jennifer. "The Shocking Truth for Thirty Percent of Divorced Women." *Huffington Post*, August 6, 2011. Online at http://www.huffingtonpost.com/jennifer-gauvain/doubts-before-marriage_b_919868.html. Reprinted by permission of the author. **368–69**

Gellhorn, Martha. Letter to Sandy Matthews, October 31, 1969. In Caroline Moorehead, ed., *Selected Letters of Martha Gellhorn*. London: Chatto & Windus, 2006, p. 356. **476**

Genesis 2:18–24. *The Holy Bible, Containing the Old and New Testaments*. King James Version. **1–2**

G.I. Roundtable Series. *Can War Marriages Be Made to Work?*, ed. American Historical Association, November 1944. Online at http://www.historians.org/about-aha-and-membership/aha-history-and-archives/gi-roundtable-series/. **230**

Gibran, Kahlil. *The Prophet*, 1923. New York: Alfred A. Knopf, 1968, pp. 15–16. Copyright © 1923 by Kahlil Gibran, renewed © 1951 by Administrators C.T.A. of Kahlil Gibran Estate and Mary G. Gibran. Used by permission of Alfred A. Knopf, an imprint of the Knopf Doubleday Publishing Group, a division of Random House, LLC. All rights reserved. **198–99**

Gilbert, Elizabeth. *Eat, Pray, Love: One Woman's Search for Everything Across Italy, India and Indonesia*. New York: Viking, 2006, pp. 10–11. **320–21**

Glass, Ira. "Niagara." *This American Life* (podcast), May 1, 1998. Online at http://www.thisamericanlife.org/radio-archives/episode/101/niagara. Copyright © 1998. Used by permission. **463–64**

Glyn, Elinor. *Three Things*. New York: Hearst's International Library, 1915, pp. 49–50. **324–25**

Godshall, Liberty. "No Promises." *thirtysomething*, season 2, episode 5, air date January 10, 1989. **476**

Goethe, Johann Wolfgang von, 1823. Quoted in P. Hume Brown, *The Youth of Goethe*. New York: E. P. Dutton, 1913, p. 101. **99**

Goldman, Emma. *Marriage and Love*. New York: Mother Earth Publishing Association, 1911, pp. 13, 15. **287–89**

Goldman, William. *The Princess Bride*, dir. Rob Reiner. Based on the novel by William Goldman. Twentieth Century Fox, 1987. **462**

Goodman, David. *A Parents' Guide to the Emotional Needs of Children*. New York: Hawthorn Books, 1959, p. 33. **28**

Goodrich, Frances, and Albert Hackett. *Father of the Bride*, dir. Vincente Minnelli. Based on the novel by Edward Streeter. Metro-Goldwyn-Mayer, 1950. **456–457**

Gordon, Ruth, and Garson Kanin. *Adam's Rib*, dir. George Cukor. Metro-Goldwyn-Mayer, 1949. **452**

Gottman, John M., and Nan Silver. *The Seven Principles for Making Marriage Work*. New York: Three Rivers Press, 1999, pp. 5–6, 19–21. Copyright © 1999 by John M. Gottman, Ph.D, and Nan Silver. Reprinted by permission of Crown Books, an imprint of the Crown Publishing Group, a division of Random House, LLC, and the Orion Publishing Group, Ltd. All rights reserved. **138–39, 424–25**

Gouge, William. *Of Domesticall Duties, Eight Treatises*. London: William Bladen, 1622, n.p. Online at Early English Books Online. **418–19**

Graham, Billy. Quoted in Jon Meacham, "Pilgrim's Progress." *Newsweek*, August 14, 2006. Online at http://www.newsweek.com /2006/08/13/pilgrim-s-progress.html. **257**

Graham, John. *Opening Speech of John Graham, Esq. to the Jury, on the Part of the Defence, on the Trial of Daniel E. Sickles in the Criminal Court of the District of Columbia, Judge Thomas H. Crawford, Presiding*. New York: T. R. Dawley, 1859, pp. 6, 40. Online at HeinOnline. **205–6**

Graves, Ellen Coile. Letter to Henry Graves, October 13, 1844. Chester County Archives, West Chester, PA. **66–67**

Greer, Germaine. *The Female Eunuch*, 1970. London: MacGibbon & Kee, 1971, pp. 214–15, 232–33. Copyright © 1970 by Germaine Greer. Reprinted by permission of HarperCollins Publishers and Aitken Alexander Associates Ltd. **106, 421**

Gregg, Natalie. "Divorce Readiness Questionnaire." *Huffington Post*, August 4, 2012. Online at http://www.huffingtonpost.com /natalie-gregg/divorce_b_1739302.html. Reprinted by permission of the author. **81**

Groves, Ernest R. *Marriage*, 1933. New York: Henry Holt, 1934, p. 10. **160**

Haines, T. L., and L., W. Yaggy. *The Royal Path of Life: Aims and Aids to Success and Happiness*. Chicago: A. P. T. Elder, 1882, pp. 428–29. Online at HathiTrust. **104**

Halhed, Nathaniel Brassey, ed. *A Code of Gentoo laws, or, Ordinations of the Pundits. From a Persian translation, made from the original, written in the Shanscrit language*. London: 1781, p. 253. Online at Gale Eighteenth Century Collections. **389**

Hamlisch, Marvin, and Terre Blair Hamlisch. Interviews on *Marvin Hamlisch: What He Did for Love*, American Masters, PBS, air date December 27, 2013. Online at www.pbs.org/wnet/americanmasters. Printed by permission. **248–49**

Hardwick, Elizabeth. "Amateurs: Jane Carlyle." *The New York Review of Books*, December 14, 1972. Online at www.nybooks.com /issues/1972/dec/14/?insrc=wai. **302**

Hardy, Edward J. *How to Be Happy Though Married: Being a Handbook to Marriage by a Graduate in the University of Matrimony*, 1885. New York: Scribner's, 1886, pp. 6, 82–83. **174, 227**

Harper, Frances. "Advice to the Girls," 1854. In *Poems on Miscellaneous Subjects*. Boston: J. B. Yerrinton, 1855, p. 21. **473**

Harris, Neil Patrick. Interview by Ryan Seacrest, "Neil Patrick Harris Talks 'HIMYM' Wedding . . . and His Own!," July 30, 2013. Online at www.ryanseacrest.com/2013/07/30/neil-patrick-harris-talks-himym-wedding-and-his-own. **311**

Harrison, Olivia. Interviewed in *George Harrison: Living in the Material World*, dir. Martin Scorsese. Grove Street Pictures, Spitfire Pictures, Sikelia Productions, 2011. **257**

Hawthorne, Nathaniel. Note to Sophia Hawthorne, 1843. In Philip McFarland, *Hawthorne in Concord*. New York: Grove Press, 2004, p. 88, and in Robert Miller, *Hawthorne's Habitations: A Literary Life*. Oxford University Press, 2013, p. 76. **5**

———. *The Scarlet Letter*, 1850. Boston: Houghton Mifflin, 1889, pp. 72–74. Online at Google Books. **204–5**

Hayes, John Michael. *Rear Window*, dir. Alfred Hitchcock. Paramount Pictures, 1954. **336–37**

Haywood, Eliza. Book X, 1745. In Patricia Meyer Spacks, ed., *Selections from The Female Spectator*. New York: Oxford University Press, 1999, p. 116. **237**

Heine, Heinrich. "Thoughts and Fancies," circa 1840. In *Wit, Wisdom, and Pathos from the Prose of Heinrich Heine, with a Few Pieces from the "Book of Songs,"* ed. and trans. J. Snodgrass. London: Alexander Gardner, 1888, p. 297. **361**

Hekker, Terry Martin. "Paradise Lost (Domestic Division)." Modern Love, *New York Times*, January 1, 2006. Online at www.ny times.com/2006/01/01/fashion/sundaystyles/01LOVE.html. Copyright © 2006 by the New York Times Company. Reprinted by permission. **304–5**

Héloïse. Letter to Abelard, 12th century. In *Letters of Abelard and Heloise, To which is prefix'd a Particular Account of their Lives, Amours, and Misfortunes*, ed. Pierre Bayle, trans. John Hughes. London: James Rivington et al., 1760, p. 94. Online at Google Books. **296**

Herbert, A. P. "Twenty-five Years Happily Married." *News Chronicle* (London), January 1, 1940, p. 6. **43**

Herrick, Robert. "To the Virgins, to Make Much of Time," 1648. In Herbert P. Horne, ed., *Hesperides: Poems by Robert Herrick*. London: Walter Scott, 1887, p. 179. **504–5**

Heywood, John. Proverbs, 1546. In Julian Sharman, ed., *The Proverbs of John Heywood, Being the "Proverbes" of That Author Printed 1546*. London: George Bell, 1874, pp. 9, 32. **13, 259**

Hill, Thomas E. *Hill's Manual of Social and Business Forms: Guide to Correct Writing*. Chicago: Moses Warren, 1879, pp. 159, 161. Online at Google Books. **40, 329**

Holt, Emily. *Everyman's Enclopaedia of Etiquette: A Book of Manners for Everyday Use*, vol. 1. New York: Doubleday, 1920, pp. 240–41. **455**

Homer. *The Odyssey*, circa 8th century BC, trans. Robert Fitzgerald. New York: Anchor Books, 1963, pp. 21–22. Copyright © 1963 by Robert Fitzgerald. Reprinted by permission of Farrar, Straus & Giroux, LLC. **111–12**

Honorius of Autun. Sermon, 12th century. Quoted in Michael Sheehan, "*Maritalis Affectio* Revisited." In Robert R. Edwards and Stephen Spector, eds., *The Olde Daunce: Love, Friendship, Sex, and Marriage in the Medieval World*. New York: State University of New York Press, 1991, p. 42. **322**

"The Householder of Paris." *The Good Wife's Guide: A Medieval Household Book*, circa 1392, trans. Gina L. Greco and Christine M. Rose. Ithaca, NY: Cornell University Press, 2009, pp. 138–140. Copyright © 2009 by Gina L. Greco and Christine M. Rose. Reprinted by permission of Cornell University Press. **163–64**

"How To Avoid a Bad Husband." *The Rockland County Messenger* (Haverstraw, NY), June 16, 1853, p. 1. **472**

How to Be a Good Husband (originally *Do's and Don'ts for Husbands*), 1936. Oxford: Bodleian Library, 2008, pp. 13, 29–33 passim. **146, 229**

Howe, Julia Ward. Letter to Ann Eliza Ward, 1846. In Laura E. Richards, Maud Howe Elliott, and Florence Howe Hall, eds., *Julia Ward Howe, 1819–1910*, vol. 1. Boston: Houghton Mifflin, 1915, pp. 117–18. Online at North American Women's Letters and Diaries: Colonial to 1950. **16–17**

Hubbard, Elbert. *Hollyhocks and Goldenglow*. Erie County, NY: The Roycrofters, 1912, pp. 71–75 passim. **137–38**

———. *Love, Life, and Work*. Erie County, NY: The Roycrofters, 1906, p. 108. **160**

Hudson, Virginia Cary. *O Ye Jigs & Juleps*, 1904. New York: Macmillan, 1962, p. 41. **361**

Hugo, Victor. Letter to Adèle Foucher, October 20, 1821. In Elizabeth W. Latimer, trans., *The Love Letters of Victor Hugo, 1820–1822*. New York: Harper & Bros., 1901, p. 56. **243–44**

Hutton, Isabel Emslie. *The Sex Technique in Marriage*, 1932. New York: Emerson Books, 1936, pp. 52–53. **177**

Ibsen, Henrik. *A Doll House*, 1879. In *Four Major Plays*, trans. Rolf Fjelde. New York: Signet, 1965, pp. 110–14. Note: Rolf Fjelde translated the title without the apostrophe "s" because, he said, "the house is not Nora's." Copyright © 1965, 1992 by Rolf Fjelde. Reprinted by permission of Dutton Signet, a division of Penguin Group (USA) Inc. **128–30**

Iovine, Vicki. "Seven Habits of Really Happy Wives." *Redbook*, June 1998, p. 88. **10**

Islamic Shari'ah Council. Muslim marriage contract, 2008. Online at www.lapidomedia.com/downloads/Muslim_Marriage_Contract .pdf. **272–74**

Italian mother. Advice to her daughter, circa 1300. In Diane Bornstein, *The Lady in the Tower: Medieval Courtesy Literature for Women*. Hamden, CT: Archon Books, 1983, p. 63. **189–90**

James, Henry. *What Maisie Knew*. Chicago: Herbert S. Stone, 1897, pp. 3–5. Online at Google Books. **25**

Jefferis, B. G., and J. L. Nichols. *Safe Counsel: Search Lights on Health*, 1897. In Karen Yvonne Hamilton, ed., *Safe Counsel: Advice on Love & Marriage from the Late 19th Century*. Port St. Lucie, FL: Double-Roads Publishing, 2007, p. 25. **280–81**

A Jeweler. "Men's Marriage Rings," editorial reprinting *St. Louis Globe-Democrat* item, *Bangor Daily Whig & Courier* (Bangor, ME), December 10, 1889, col A. **372–73**

Johnson, Lady Bird. Letter to Lyndon Johnson, August 25, 1964. In *A White House Diary*. Austin: University of Texas Press, 2007, p. 192. Copyright © 1970. Printed courtesy of the LBJ Library, Austin, Texas. **87**

Johnson, Nunnally. *How to Marry a Millionaire*, dir. Jean Negulesco. Twentieth Century Fox, 1953. **186–87**

Johnson, Samuel. Letter to Thomas Lawrence, 1780. In Myrtle Reed, *Love Affairs of Literary Men*. New York: G. P. Putnam's Sons, 1907, p. 51. **55**

———, 1768 and circa 1770. Quoted in James Boswell, *The Life of Samuel Johnson, LL.D.*, vol. 2, 1791. London: G. Walker, 1820, pp. 41, 119. **203, 430**

Jong, Erica. *Fear of Flying*. New York: Holt, Rinehart and Winston, 1973, pp. 9, 11–12, 14–15. Copyright © 1973 by Erica Jong. Reprinted by permission of Henry Holt and Company, LLC; and the author. All rights reserved. **408–9**

Just, Ward. "Honor, Power, Riches, Fame, and the Love of Women" (novella), 1973. In *Honor, Power, Riches, Fame, and the Love of Women*. New York: E. P. Dutton, 1979, p. 151. **251–52**

Juvenal. "The Ways of Women," 1st–2nd century. In Mary R. Lefkowitz and Maureen B. Fant, eds., *Women's Life in Greece and Rome*. Baltimore: Johns Hopkins University Press, 2005, pp. 32–33. Copyright © 1982, 1992, 2005 by M. B. Fant and M. R. Lefkowitz. Reprinted by permission of the Johns Hopkins University Press. **224–25**

Kafka, Franz. Diary, 1913. In Max Brod, ed., and Joseph Kresh, trans., *The Diaries of Franz Kafka, 1910–1913*. New York: Schocken Books, 1965, pp. 292–93. Copyright © 1948–1949 by Joseph Kresh. Reprinted by permission of Schocken Books, an imprint of the Knopf Doubleday Publishing Group, a division of Random House, LLC. All rights reserved. **363**

Kaufman, George S., Morrie Ryskind, Bert Kalmar, and Harry Ruby. *Animal Crackers*, dir. Victor Heerman. Paramount Pictures, 1930. **351**

Keillor, Garrison. "How to Improve Your Marriage in Just One Day." The Old Scout, *A Prairie Home Companion*, April 11, 2006. Online at http://prairiehome.publicradio.org/features/deskofgk/2006/old_scout/04/18.shtml. Copyright © 2006 by Minnesota Public Radio. Reprinted by permission. **255–57**

King, Stephen. "Proust Questionnaire." *Vanity Fair*, October 2013, p. 376. **259**

Klaus, Marley. "25 Years." *The Heathen Learns* (blog), May 9, 2012. http://marleytheheathen.blogspot.com/2012/05/25-years.html. Copyright © 2012 by Marley Klaus. Reprinted by permission of the author. **199–200**

Kunitz, Stanley. "Route Six," 1978. In *Passing Through: The Later Poems, New and Selected*. New York: W. W. Norton, 1995, pp. 105–6. Copyright © 1995 by Stanley Kunitz. Reprinted by permission of W. W. Norton & Company, Inc. **252–53**

Kwei-Li. Letter to her husband, circa 1886. In Elizabeth Cooper, *The Love Letters of a Chinese Lady*. Edinburgh: T. N. Foulis, 1919, pp. 19–20. Online at Open Library. **18–19**

Laclos, Choderlos de. *Les Liaisons Dangereuses*, 1782. In *Valmont*, trans. P. W. K. Stone. New York: Penguin, 1989, p. 251. **470**

Lady Shigenari. Letter to Kimura Shigenari, 1615. In Robert Ramsey and Randall Toye, eds., *The Goodbye Book*. New York: Van Nostrand Reinhold, 1979, p. 51. **92**

Lane, Harriet. *The Book of Culture*. New York: Social Mentor Publications, 1922, p. 34. **373**

Lattimore, Richmond. "Anniversary." *The New Yorker*, June 16, 1956, p. 35. Reprinted by permission. **7**

Lavner, Justin A., Benjamin R. Karney, and Thomas N. Bradbury. "Do Cold Feet Warn of Trouble Ahead? Premarital Uncertainty and Four-Year Marital Outcomes." *Journal of Family Psychology*, vol. 26, no. 6 (December 2012), p. 1012. **369**

Lawrence, D. H. *Lady Chatterley's Lover*, 1928. New York: The Modern Library, 1959, pp. 33, 48–49. **114, 474**

Lear, Edward. "The Owl and the Pussy-Cat," 1871. In *Nonsense Songs, Stories, Botany, and Alphabets*. London: Robert John Bush, 1872, pp. 2–4. Online at Google Books. **285–86**

Lederer, Charles, Ben Hecht, and Charles MacArthur. *His Girl Friday*, dir. Howard Hawks. Columbia Pictures, 1940. **501–2**

"A Letter of Advice, From a Father to His Only Daughter, Immediately after Her Marriage." *Weekly Visitor and Ladies' Museum*, October 12, 1822, p. 374. Online at ProQuest. **39**

Levine, Philip. "For Fran," 1961. *Poetry*. January 1961, p. 214. Reprinted in *New Selected Poems*. Copyright © 1963, 1991 by Philip Levine. Used by permission of Alfred A. Knopf, an imprint of the Knopf Doubleday Publishing Group, a division of Random House, LLC. All rights reserved. **510**

Levinson, Barry. *Diner*, dir. Barry Levinson. Metro-Goldwyn-Mayer, 1982. **36–37**

Levy, David M. *Maternal Overprotection*. New York: Columbia University Press, 1943, pp. 121–22. **27**

Levy, John, and Ruth Munroe. *The Happy Family*, 1938. New York: Alfred A. Knopf, 1939, pp. 94–96. **207**

Lewis, C. S. *The Pilgrim's Regress: An Allegorical Apology for Christianity, Reason and Romanticism*, 1933. Grand Rapids, MI: Wm. B. Eerdmans, 2014, p. 163. **335–36**

Lilley, Stephen. "How to Propose on the Yankee Stadium Big Screen," 2011. Online at http://www.ehow.com/how_81716 01_propose-yankee-stadium-big-screen.html. Copyright © 2011 by Demand Media, Inc. Reprinted by permission. All rights reserved. **358–59**

Lindbergh, Anne Morrow. *Gift From the Sea*. New York: Pantheon Books, 1955, pp. 70–71. **124**

Loesser, Frank. "Marry the Man Today," 1949. From *Guys and Dolls*. Reprinted by permission. All rights reserved. **185–86**

Lonergan, Kenneth, Peter Tolan, and Harold Ramis. *Analyze This*, dir. Harold Ramis. Warner Brothers, 1999. **413**

Long, H. W. *Sane Sex Life and Sane Sex Living: Some Things That All Sane People Ought to Know About Sex Nature and Sex Functioning; Its Place in the Economy of Life, Its Proper Training and Righteous Exercise*. New York: Eugenics Publishing, 1919, pp. 63–64. Online at Project Gutenberg. **176**

Luce, Clare Boothe. "A Doll's House 1970." *Life*, October 16, 1970, p. 63. **136**

Mackenzie, Sir George. *Moral Gallantry: A Discourse*. Edinburgh: Robert Broun, 1667, pp. 68–79, passim. Online at Early English Books Online. **202**

Mahler, Gustav. Letter to Alma Mahler, September 5, 1910. In Henry-Louis De La Grange, *Gustav Mahler*, vol. 4. New York: Oxford University Press, 2008, p. 936. **494**

Mainardi, Pat. "The Politics of Housework," *New England Free Press* pamphlet, 1968, reprinted in *Redstockings*, 1970. In Rosalyn Baxandall and Linda Gordon, eds., *Dear Sisters: Dispatches from the Women's Liberation Movement*. New York: Basic Books, 2000, pp. 255–57. Reprinted by permission of the author. **168–70**

Manchester, William. *The Death of a President: November 20–November 25, 1963*. New York: Harper & Row, 1967, pp. 293–94. Copyright © 1967 and renewed © 1995 by William Manchester. Reprinted by permission of HarperCollins Publishers and Don Congdon Associates, Inc. **374–75**

Mankiewicz, Joseph L. *All About Eve*, dir. Joseph L. Mankiewicz. Twentieth Century Fox, 1950. **495–96**

Manu. *Manu's Code of Law*, circa 500 BC, trans. Patrick Olivelle. Oxford: Oxford University Press, 2005, p. 108. **469**

Maria Theresa. Letter to Marie Antoinette, June 2, 1775. In Margaret Anne Macleod, ed., *There Were Three of Us in the Relationship: The Secret Letters of Marie Antoinette*, vol. 1. Irvine, Scotland: Isaac MacDonald, 2008, pp. 244–45. **400**

Márquez, Gabriel García. *Love in the Time of Cholera*, 1985, trans. Edith Grossman. New York: Vintage, 2003, p. 224. **328**

"Marriage and Cookery." *New-York Tribune*, May 23, 1890, p. 6. Online at ProQuest Historical Newspapers. **120**

"Marriage and Health." *The Milwaukee Sentinel*, June 25, 1893, p. 12. Online at Gale 19th Century U.S. Newspapers. **143–44**

"The Marriage Colors," circa 1933. In "Voices from the Dust Bowl: The Charles L. Todd and Robert Sonkin Migrant Worker Collection, 1940–1942." Online at American Memory Project. **456**

A Married Man. "The Marriage Injunction to Obey," letter to the editor. *St. Louis Globe-Democrat*, June 7, 1886, p. 4. Online at Gale 19th Century U.S. Newspapers. **340–41**

Marshall, Margaret. Massachusetts Supreme Judicial Court decision, 2003. *Goodridge v. Department of Public Health*, 440 Mass. 309 (2003). Online at http://masscases.com/cases/sjc/440/440mass309.html. **269–70**

Martin, Martin. *A Voyage to Saint Kilda, The Remotest of all the Hybrides or Western Isles of Scotland*, 1698. Glasgow: John Wylie, 1818, pp. 59–60. **342**

Marx, Groucho. *Memoirs of a Mangy Lover*, 1963. New York: Fireside Books, 1989, p. 197. **20**

Marx, Marvin and Walter Stone. "A Woman's Work is Never Done." *The Honeymooners*, season 1, episode 4, air date October 22, 1955. **46**

Maupin, Armistead. *Tales of the City*, 1978. New York: HarperCollins, 2007, pp. 115–16. **21**

Mazursky, Paul. *An Unmarried Woman*, dir. Paul Mazursky. Twentieth Century Fox, 1978. **440–41**

McDonald, Sharon. "What Mother Never Told Me." In *The Lesbian Tide*, March/April, 1979, pp. 4–5. **458–61**

McEwan, Ian. *On Chesil Beach*. New York: Doubleday, 2007, pp. 186–91 passim. Copyright © 2007 by Ian McEwan. Used by permission of Nan A. Talese, an imprint of the Knopf Doubleday Publishing Group, a division of Random House, LLC. All rights reserved. **179–80**

McGinley, Phyllis. "The 5:32." *The New Yorker*, October 25, 1941, p. 19. Reprinted in *Times Three: Selected Verse From Three Decades*. Copyright © 1960 by Phyllis McGinley. Used by permission of Viking Penguin, a division of Penguin Books (USA) Inc. and Random House (UK) Ltd. **167**

McGraw, Phil. "Marriage Meltdown." *Dr. Phil*, season 10, episode 49, air date November 17, 2011. Online at https://www.youtube.com/watch?v=LzijZtF5h_A. **50**

"Men, Women and Affairs." *Springfield Sunday Republican* (Springfield, MA), November 10, 1901, p. 4. Online at America's Historical Newspapers (NewsBank). **308**

Mencken, H. L. *A Book of Burlesques*, 1916. New York: Alfred A. Knopf, 1924, pp. 214, 216, 218. Online at Google Books. **3, 105, 240**

Mencken, H. L., and George Jean Nathan. *Heliogabalus: A Buffoonery in Three Acts*. New York: Alfred A. Knopf, 1920, p. 131. **430**

Menninger, Karl. Letter to a *Ladies' Home Journal* reader, "Mrs. P.," 1930. In Howard J. Faulkner and Virginia D. Pruitt, eds., *Dear Dr. Menninger: Women's Voices from the Thirties*. Columbia, MO: University of Missouri Press, 1997, pp. 135–36. Copyright © 1930. Reprinted by permission. **84–86**

Merwin, W. S. "Anniversary on the Island." In *Poems by W. S. Merwin*. New York: Alfred A. Knopf, 1988, p. 34. Copyright © 1988 by W. S. Merwin. Used by permission of the Wylie Agency, LLC; and Alfred A. Knopf, an imprint of the Knopf Doubleday Publishing Group, a division of Random House, LLC. All rights reserved. **9–10**

Mesopotamian marriage contract, Reign of Shamshu-ilu-na, circa 2200 BC. In "A Collection of Contracts from Mesopotamia, circa 2300–426 BCE." Online at Ancient History Sourcebook, Fordham University. **264**

Message board user. Comment on "Anyone taking anxiety drugs," March 4, 2005. Splitcoaststampers, the Stampers Community. Online at http://www.splitcoaststampers.com/forums/everyday-chit-chat-f10/anyone-taking-anxiety-drugs-t33145.html#post361705#ixzz2tsnurMXG. **514**

Meyers, Nancy, Charles Shyer, and Harvey Miller. *Private Benjamin*, dir. Howard Zieff. Warner Bros., 1980. **441**

Michelet, Jules. *Love*, trans. J. W. Palmer. New York: Rudd & Carlton, 1859, p. 103. Online at Google Books. **67**

Milton, John. *Paradise Lost*, 1667, ed. Merritt Y. Hughes. New York: Odyssey Press, 1962, p. 227. **2**

Miner's wife. Letter to unknown recipient, 1914. In *The Vagabond Path*, ed. Iris Origo. London: Chatto & Windus, 1972, p. 103. **96**

Mitchell, Margaret. *Gone With the Wind*, 1936. New York: Macmillan, 1986, pp. 760–62. Copyright © 1936 by Margaret Mitchell. Reprinted by permission of William Morris Endeavor Entertainment, LLC. **351–53**

Montaigne, Michel de. "On Some Verses of Virgil," 1588. In Donald M. Frame, ed. and trans., *The Complete Works of Montaigne*. Stanford: Stanford University Press, 1957, p. 647. Copyright © 2007 by Donald M. Frame. Reprinted by permission of Stanford University Press. **127, 136–37**

Montand, Yves. Quoted in "Conversation with Yves Montand." *Oui* (USA), November 1973, p. 70. **210**

More, Sir Thomas. *Utopia*, 1516, ed. and trans. Robert M. Adams. New York: W. W. Norton, 1975, p. 66. **275–76**

Morgan, Marabel. *The Total Woman*, 1973. New York: Pocket Books, 1975, pp. 114–17. Reprinted by permission of the author. **195–96**

Morley, Christopher. "Washing the Dishes." In *Songs for a Little House*. New York: George H. Doran, 1917, p. 36. **166**

Morrison, Toni. *Jazz*. New York: Alfred A. Knopf, 1992, p. 228. **16**

"The Motion Picture Production Code of 1930." The History of American Film: Primary Sources. Online at http://www.digitalhistory.uh.edu/historyonline/film_censorship.cfm. **206–7**

Mount, M. W. "The Ticklish Art of Proposing Marriage: Many Difficulties Encountered Both By Man and Maid." *New-York Tribune*, October 6, 1907, p. C3. Online at ProQuest Historical Newspapers. **350**

Mozart, Wolfgang Amadeus. Letter to Leopold Mozart, December 22, 1781. In Robert Spaethling, ed. and trans., *Mozart's Letters, Mozart's Life: Selected Letters*. New York: W. W. Norton, 2000, pp. 298–99. Copyright © 2000 by Robert Spaethling. Reprinted by permission of W. W. Norton & Co. **265–66**

Mula, Frank. "The Last Temptation of Homer." *The Simpsons*, season 5, episode 9, air date December 9, 1993. **117**

Napheys, George H. *The Physical Life of Woman*, 1869. Philadelphia: David McKay, 1890, pp. 106–8. **172–73**

Nash, Ogden. "Advice Outside a Church." *The Saturday Evening Post*, November 16, 1935, p. 29. Copyright © 1935 by Ogden Nash. Reprinted by permission of Curtis Brown, Ltd. **492–93**

———. "A Word to Husbands," 1931. In *Marriage Lines: Notes of a Student Husband*. Boston: Little, Brown, 1964, p. 79. Copyright © 1964 by Ogden Nash. Reprinted by permission of Curtis Brown, Ltd. **41**

Navey, Hayley. "The 5 best things about being married." *A Beautiful Exchange* (blog), May 25, 2013. http://beautifulxchange.blogspot.com/2013/05/the-5-best-things-about-being-married.html. Copyright © 2013 by Hayley Navey. Reprinted by permission. **108–9**

Nemerov, Howard. "The Common Wisdom," 1975. In *The Collected Poems of Howard Nemerov*. Chicago: University of Chicago Press, 1977, p. 463. Copyright © 1977 by Howard Nemerov. Reprinted by permission of the University of Chicago Press. **98**

Neumann, Henry. *Modern Youth and Marriage*. New York: D. Appleton, 1928, pp. 18–19. **84**

Newman, Paul. Quoted in Richard Warren Lewis, "Playboy Interview: Paul Newman," *Playboy*, July 1968, p. 72. **115**

Nichols, Mike, and Elaine May. "Adultery," 1960. On *In Retrospect*. Polygram CD, 1996. **208–10**

Nietzsche, Friedrich. *Daybreak: Thoughts on the Prejudices of Morality*, 1881, trans. R. J. Hollingdale. Cambridge: Cambridge University Press, 1982, p. 98. **334**

———. *Human, All Too Human: A Book for Free Spirits*, 1878, trans. R. J. Hollingdale. Cambridge: Cambridge University Press, 1986, p. 152. **33**

Obama, Michelle. Quoted in Joy Bennett Kinnon, "Michelle Obama: Not Just the Senator's Wife." *Ebony*, March 2006, pp. 62–63. **117**

"Of Divorces," circa 6th century AD. In Katherine Fisher Drew, ed. and trans., *The Burgundian Code: Book of Constitutions or Law of Gundobad: Additional Enactments*. Philadelphia: University of Pennsylvania Press, 1996, pp. 45–46. **63**

"The Old Maid's Apology." *The Lady's Magazine and Musical Repository*, August 1801, p. 107. Online at ProQuest Historical Newspapers. **431–32**

"The Old Maid's Diary." *Freedom's Journal*, November 2, 1827, p. 2. Online at America's Historical Newspapers (NewsBank). **432–33**

O'Neill, Eugene. Letter to Agnes Boulton O'Neill, December 26?, 1927. In Travis Bogard and Jackson R. Bryer, eds., *Selected Letters of Eugene O'Neill*. New York: Limelight Editions, 1994, pp. 270–71. Printed in *The Unknown O'Neill: Unpublished or Unfamiliar Writings of Eugene O'Neill*. Copyright © 1988. Reprinted by permission of Yale University Press. **68–69**

O'Neill, Nena, and George O'Neill. *Open Marriage: A New Life Style for Couples*. New York: M. Evans, 1972, pp. 84–86. Copyright © 1972 by Nena O'Neill and George O'Neill. Reprinted by permission of Rowman & Littlefield Publishing Group. **107, 407**

Oppenheimer, Jess, Madelyn Pugh, and Bob Carroll, Jr. "The Adagio," *I Love Lucy*, season 1, episode 12, air date December 31, 1951. **421**

———. "Job Switching," *I Love Lucy*, season 2, episode 39, air date September 15, 1952. **496–98**

Ovid. *The Art of Love*, book 3, circa 1 BC. In J. Lewis May, trans., *The Love Books of Ovid*. New York: Rarity Press, 1930, p. 172. Online at http://www.sacred-texts.com/cla/ovid/lboo/lboo60.htm. **189**

Owenson, Sydney, Lady Morgan. Letter to Alicia de Fanu, February 1812. In *Lady Morgan's Memoirs: Autobiography, Diaries and Correspondence*, vol. 2. London: Wm. H. Allen, 1863, pp. 4–5. Online at http://lordbyron.cath.lib.vt.edu/monograph.php?doc=LyMorga.1863. **98–99**

Oxford, Kelly (@kellyoxford). Tweet, April 8, 2011. Online at https://twitter.com/kellyoxford/status/56230328133627904. **126**

Painter, William. "Novel 29: Marriage of Widow and Widower." In *The Palace of Pleasure: Beautiful, adorned and well furnished, with Pleasant Histories and excellent Nouelles, selected out of diuers good and commendable Authors*, 1566. London: Henry Denham, p. 114. Online at Project Gutenberg. **377–78**

Pastan, Linda. "Because." In *PM/AM: New and Selected Poems*. New York: W. W. Norton, 1982, p. 79. Copyright © 1982 by Linda Pastan. Reprinted by permission of W. W. Norton & Company, Inc. **485**

Patent medicine advertisement. "A Childless Marriage." *The Atchison Daily Globe* (Atchison, KS), December 1, 1896, p. 3. Online at Gale 19th Century U.S. Newspapers. **24**

Patent medicine advertisement. "The Triumph of Love." *Morning Oregonian* (Portland, OR), May 5, 1896, p. 2. Online at Gale 19th Century U.S. Newspapers. **402**

Pease, Sarah. Brilliant Event Planning website, 2013. Online at http://www.brillianteventplanning.com/nyc-proposal/nyc-proposal-facts.html and http://www.brillianteventplanning.com/blog/scavenger-hunt-marriage-proposal. Copyright © 2014 Brilliant Event Planning. Reprinted by permission. **359–60**

Penn, William. *Some Fruits of Solitude, in Reflections and Maxims Relating to the Conduct of Human Life*, 1682. London: Thomas Northcott, 1693, pp. 27–28, 32–34, 36–37. Online at Early English Books Online. **284**

Perel, Esther. "Mating in Captivity." Healthy Living, *Huffington Post,* May 28, 2007. Online at http://www.huffingtonpost.com /esther-perel/mating-in-captivity_b_49653.html. Reprinted by permission of the author. **415–16**

Personal ad. *Boston Evening Post,* February 23, 1759. In Margaret Baker, *Wedding Customs and Folklore.* Totowa, NJ: Rowman and Littlefield, 1977, p. 27. **344**

Philp, Robert Kemp. *Enquire Within Upon Everything.* London: Boulston and Stoneman, 1856, p. 213. Online at Google Books. **372**

Pinckney, Cotesworth, ed. *The Wedding Gift, to All Who are Entering the Marriage State*, 1848. Buffalo, NY: Geo. H. Derby, 1849, pp. 19–21, 25. Online at HathiTrust. **225–26, 385**

Pipkin, Myra. Oral history interview, 1941. In Voices from the Dust Bowl: The Charles L. Todd and Robert Sonkin Migrant Worker Collection, 1940–1941. Online at memory.loc.gov. **456**

Pittacus, circa 600 BC. Quoted in M. De La Motte Fenelon, Archbishop of Cambray, *Lives of the Philosophers.* London: Knight and Lacey, 1825, p. 70. Online at Google Books. **468–69**

Plath, Sylvia. Letter to Aurelia Plath, October 8, 1956. In Aurelia Schober Plath, ed., *Letters Home: Correspondence 1950–1963.* New York: Bantam, 1977, pp. 315–16. Copyright © 1975. Reprinted by permission of Faber and Faber, Ltd. and HarperCollins Publishers. **327**

Plato. *The Symposium,* 360 BC, trans. Benjamin Jowett. Online at classics.mit.edu/Plato/symposium.html. **321–22**

Pliny the Younger. Epistle V, letter to Calpurnia, circa 2nd century. In John Earl of Orrery, ed., *The Letters of Pliny the Younger, with Observations on Each Letter,* vol. 2. Dublin: George Faulkner, 1751, pp. 110–11. Online at Google Books. **388**

Plump, Wendy. "A Roomful of Yearning and Regret." Modern Love, *New York Times,* December 9, 2010. Online at http://www .nytimes.com/2010/12/12/fashion/12Modern.html. Copyright © 2010 by The New York Times Company. Reprinted by permission. **219–22**

Plutarch. *Advice to the Bride and Groom,* 1st century. In Sarah B. Pomeroy, ed., *Plutarch's Advice to the Bride and Groom and A Consolation to His Wife.* New York: Oxford University Press, 1999, p. 10. Copyright © 1999. Reprinted by permission of Oxford University Press, Ltd. **224, 322**

Pope, Alexander. "The Wife of Bath, Her Prologue, From Chaucer," ca. 1704. In *The Poetical Works of Alexander Pope,* vol. 2. London: William Pickering, 1831, p. 284. **142–43**

Pound, Ezra. "The River-Merchant's Wife: A Letter." In *Lustra of Ezra Pound with Earlier Poems.* New York: Alfred A. Knopf, 1917, pp. 77–79. Online at Google Books. **56–57**

Proverb. "A spaniel, a woman . . ." In J. Ray, *A Collection of English Proverbs.* Cambridge: John Hayes, 1678, p. 59. Online at Google Books. **447**

Proverb. "As your wedding ring . . ." n.d. In *The Antiquary: A Magazine Devoted to the Study of the Past,* vol. XVII. London: Elliot Stock, 1888, p. 253. **371**

Proverb. "Choose a wife . . ." n.d. In Thomas Fuller, ed., *Gnomologia: Adagies and Proverbs; Wise Sentences and Witty Sayings, Ancient and Modern, Foreign and British.* London: B. Barker, 1762, p. 41, no. 1107. **276**

Proverb. "Love is a flower . . ." n.d. *The Penguin Dictionary of Proverbs.* London: Market House Books, 2000, p. 113. **119**

Proverb. "Marry first . . ." n.d. *The Penguin Dictionary of Proverbs.* London: Market House Books, 2000, p. 113. **282**

Proverb. "Why buy a cow . . ." n.d. *The Penguin Dictionary of Proverbs.* London: Market House Books, 2000, p. 113. **315**

Queen Victoria. Letter to Vicky, the Princess Royal, March 15, 1858. In Roger Fulford, ed., *Dearest Child: Letters between Queen Victoria and the Princess Royal, 1858–1861.* New York: Holt, Rinehart and Winston, 1965, pp. 77–78. **127–28**

Raleigh, Sir Walter. Letter to Elizabeth Throckmorton, 1603. In "Walter Raleigh Bids Farewell to His Wife," *Luminarium: Anthology of English Literature*: online at www.luminarium.org/renlit/raleghfarewell.htm. **91–92**

———. "Sir Walter Raleigh's Instructions to His Son, and to Posterity." In *Remains of Sir Walter Raleigh: Maxims of State.* London: Henry Mortlock, 1702, pp. 62–63. Online at Google Books. **276–77**

Rank, Otto. Diary, circa 1904. Quoted in E. James Lieberman, *Acts of Will: The Life and Work of Otto Rank.* New York: The Free Press, 1985, p. 7. **52**

Rauch, Jonathan. "Gay Marriage Is Good for America." *The Wall Street Journal,* June 21, 2008. Online at ProQuest. Reprinted by permission of the author. **271–72**

Readers' comments. "A Roomful of Yearning and Regret." Modern Love, *New York Times,* December 10, 11, and 12, 2010. Online at http://community.nytimes.com/comments/www.nytimes.com/2010/12/12/fashion/12Modern.html?sort=newest&offset=1. **222–23**

Reagan, Ronald. Letter to Michael Reagan, June 1971. In Kiron K. Skinner, Annelise Anderson, and Martin Anderson, eds., *Reagan: A Life in Letters.* New York: Free Press, 2004, pp. 60–61. Ronald Reagan's writings copyright © 2003 by the Ronald Reagan Presidential Foundation. Reprinted by permission of Simon & Schuster Publishing Group from the Free Press edition. All rights reserved. **115–17**

———. Letter to Nancy Reagan, 1972. In Nancy Reagan, ed., *I Love You, Ronnie: The Letters of Ronald Reagan to Nancy Reagan.* New York: Random House, 2000. Copyright © 2000, 2002 by the Ronald Reagan Presidential Foundation. Reprinted by permission of Random House, an imprint and division of Random House, LLC. All rights reserved. **8–9**

The Real Tolerance. London: A. C. Fifield, 1913, pp. 37–43. **239–240**

Reddit users, "Will you/have you hyphenated your last name . . . ? ," TwoXChromosomes subreddit, 2011. Online at http://www
.reddit.com/r/TwoXChromosomes/comments/ibnto/will_youhave_you_hyphenated_your_last_name_or/. **310–11**

Reeve, Dana. Letter to Christopher Reeve, April 11, 1996. In Dana Reeve, *Care Packages*. New York: Random House, 1999, n.p.
424

Reiner, Carl, R. S. Allen, and Harvey Bullock. "Bank Book 6565696." *The Dick Van Dyke Show*, season 2, episode 4, air date October 17, 1962. **300–302**

Reitman, Jason, and Sheldon Turner. *Up in the Air*, dir. Jason Reitman. Based on the novel by Walter Kirn. Paramount Pictures,
2009. **487**

Rilke, Rainer Maria. Letter to Emanuel von Bodman, August 17, 1901. In F. W. van Heerikhuizen, *Rainer Maria Rilke: His Life and
Work*. New York: The Philosophical Library, 1952, pp. 137–38. Online at Google Books. Used by permission of the Philosophical Library. **197–98**

Robie, W. F. *Sex and Life: What the Experienced Should Teach and What the Inexperienced Should Learn*. Boston: Richard G. Badger,
1920, pp. 358–59. **405**

Robinson, Marie N. *The Power of Sexual Surrender*. New York: Signet, 1959, p. 177. **406**

Robinson, William J. *Sexual Problems of To-day*. New York: Critic and Guide, 1912, pp. 252–53, 254. **144, 403**

Rock, Chris. "Intercourse," 2007. On *Cheese and Crackers: The Greatest Bits*. Geffen Records CD, 2007. **79**

Roman husband. "Laudatio Turiae," 1st century BC, trans. Erik Wistrand. In Mary R. Lefkowitz and Maureen B. Fant, eds.,
Women's Life in Greece and Rome: A Source Book in Translation. Baltimore: Johns Hopkins University Press, 1992, pp. 135–39.
89–90

Roosevelt, Eleanor. *This Is My Story*. New York: Harper & Brothers, 1937, p, 162. **229**

Rose, William. *Guess Who's Coming to Dinner*, dir. Stanley Kramer. Columbia Pictures, 1967. **289–90**

Rosin, Hanna. "The End of Men." *The Atlantic*, July/August, 2010. Online at http://www.theatlantic.com/magazine/archive/2010
/07/the-end-of-men/308135/. **422**

Roth, Philip. *Portnoy's Complaint*, 1967. New York: Ballantine Books, 1985, pp. 116–17. **318**

Routledge, George. *Routledge's Manual of Etiquette*. London: George Routledge, 1860, pp. 150–51. Online at the Internet Archive.
119

Rowlands, Samuel. "A whole crew of kind Gossips, all met to be merry," 1609. In *The Complete Works of Samuel Rowlands, 1598–
1628*, vol. 2. London: The Hunterian Club, 1880, p. 9. Online at Google Books. **445–46**

Rufus, Anneli. "15 Signs You'll Get Divorced." *The Daily Beast*, July 6, 2010. Online at www.thedailybeast.com/articles/2010/07/06
/unhappy-marriage-signs-youll-get-divorced.html. Reprinted by permission. **79–80**

Rumi. "This Marriage," 13th century. In Kabir Helminski, ed. and trans., *The Rumi Collection*. Boston: Shambhala Publications,
1998, pp. 6–7. Copyright © 1998 by Kabir Helminski. Reprinted by arrangement with The Permissions Company, Inc., on
behalf of Shambhala Publications, Inc., Boston, MA. www.shambhala.com. **453–54**

Rutherford, H. Dean. Letter to Pattie Rutherford, circa 2012. "A letter my dad wrote to my mother for their 59th Anniversary."
Compelled to Tell (blog), February 7, 2012. http://dudleyrutherford.blogspot.com/2012/02/letter-my-dad-wrote-to-my-mother
-for.html. Reprinted by permission. **10–12**

Ryan, Christopher, and Cacilda Jethá. *Sex at Dawn: How We Mate, Why We Stray, and What It Means for Modern Relationships*. New
York: Harper Perennial, 2010, pp. 97–98. **223–24**

Saarinen, Eero. Letter to Aline Bernstein Saarinen, 1954. Aline and Eero Saarinen papers, Archives of American Art, Smithsonian
Institution. Online at http://www.aaa.si.edu/collections/images/detail/eero-saarinen-letter-to-aline-b-aline-bernstein-saarinen
-8766. **19–20**

Sackville-West, Vita. Letter to Harold Nicolson, June 25, 1929. In Nigel Nicolson, ed., *Vita and Harold: The Letters of Vita
Sackville-West and Harold Nicolson*. London: Weidenfeld & Nicolson, 1992, pp. 215–16. Copyright © 1992. Reprinted by permission. **393–95**

"The Sale of Wives," *The Whitehaven Herald and Cumberland Advertiser* (Liverpool), 1832. In *Chambers's Journal of Popular Literature,
Science and Arts* (London), October 12, 1861, p. 238. Online at WikiSource. **65–66**

Salholz, Eloise. "Too Late for Prince Charming?" *Newsweek*, June 2, 1986, p. 54. Online at LexisNexis. **511**

Salinger, J. D. "Zooey," 1957. In *Franny and Zooey*. New York: Little, Brown, 1991, p. 106. **318**

Sand, George. *Jacques*, vol. 1, 1833, trans. Anna Blackwell. New York: J. S. Redfield, 1847, p. 122. Online at Google Books. **203–4**

Sandberg, Sheryl, with Nell Scovell. *Lean In: Women, Work, and the Will to Lead*. New York: Alfred A. Knopf, 2013, pp. 110, 115. **500**

Sanger, Margaret. *Happiness in Marriage*, 1926. Elmsford, NY: Maxwell Reprint, 1969, pp. 87–88. **176**

Savile, George. *The Lady's New-years Gift, or, Advice to a Daughter*. London: Printed for Matthew Gillyflower in Westminster-Hall
and James Partridge at Charing-Cross, 1688, pp. 26–28. Online at Open Library. **419–20**

Schopenhauer, Arthur. "Of Women," 1851. In *Studies in Pessimism: A Series of Essays*, ed. and trans. Thomas Bailey Saunders. London: Swan Sonnenschein, 1908, p. 117. **293**

Scriven, Abream. Letter to Dinah Jones, September 19, 1858. In Frances Smith Foster, ed., *Love and Marriage in Early African America*. Boston: Northeastern University Press, 2008, p. 238. **391–392**

Seinfeld, Jerry. White House tribute to Paul McCartney, 2010. Online at http://www.whitehouse.gov/photos-and-video/video/2010/06/01/jerry-seinfeld-performs-gershwin-prize-paul-mccartney. **38**

Sexual aid advertisement. "The Triumph of Love," *Morning Oregonian* (Portland, OR), May 5, 1896, p. 2. Online at Gale 19th Century U.S. Newspapers. **402**

Shakespeare, William. *Julius Caesar*, circa 1599. In G. Blakemore Evans, ed., *The Riverside Shakespeare*. Boston: Houghton Mifflin, 1974, p. 1114. **383–84**

———. Sonnet 116, 1609. In Douglas Bush and Alfred Harbage, eds., *Shakespeare's Sonnets*. Baltimore: Penguin Books, 1972, p. 136. **283**

———. *The Taming of the Shrew*, circa 1592, ed. David Bevington. New York: Bantam Books, 1988, p. 103. **337–38**

Shanley, John Patrick. *Moonstruck*, dir. Norman Jewison. Metro-Goldwyn-Mayer, 1987. **3**

Shapiro, Stanley, and Maurice Richlin. *Pillow Talk*, dir. Michael Gordon. Universal Pictures, 1959. **484**

Shaw, Elizabeth Smith. Letter to Abigail Adams Smith, November 27, 1786. In C. James Taylor, ed., The Adams Papers (Digital Edition). Charlottesville: University of Virginia Press, Rotunda 2008. Online at www.masshist.org/publications/apde/portia.php?id=ADMS-04-07-02-0152. **38**

Shaw, George Bernard. *Getting Married*, 1908. New York: Brentano's, 1920, pp. 25–26. **334**

"Should This Marriage Be Saved?" *Ladies' Home Journal*, August 1970, pp. 68–69. Subject to national and international intellectual property laws and treaties. **74–75**

Simon, Neil. *The Odd Couple: A Comedy in Three Acts*, 1966. New York: Samuel French, Inc., 1998, p. 36. **74**

Sizer, Nelson, and H. S. Drayton. *Heads and Faces and How to Study Them: A Manual of Phrenology and Physiognomy for the People*, 1885. New York: Fowler & Wells, 1897, pp. 180–81. **330–31**

Sondheim, Stephen. "Getting Married Today" (from *Company*), 1970. Copyright © Herald Square Music o/b/o Range Road Music/Quartet Music. All rights administered by WB Music Corp (Publishing) and Alfred Publishing Company, Inc. (Print). All rights reserved. **365–67**

Spiegel, Marcus. Letter to Caroline Spiegel, May 8, 1862. In Frank L. Byrne and Jean Powers Soman, eds., *Your True Marcus: The Civil War Letters of a Jewish Colonel*. Ohio: Kent State University Press, 1985, pp. 107–8. Reprinted courtesy of the Jacob Rader Marcus Center of the American Jewish Archives, Cincinnati, OH. americanjewisharchives.org. **392–93**

Stanton, Elizabeth Cady, Susan B. Anthony, and Matilda Joslyn Gage, eds. *History of Woman Suffrage*, vol. 2. New York: Fowler & Wells, 1882, p. 643. **299**

Stanton, Henry. *Sex: Avoided Subjects Discussed in Plain English*. New York: Social Culture Publications, 1922, pp. 43–44. **473–74**

Steinbeck, John. Letter to Gwyndolyn Steinbeck, July 4, 1943. In Elaine Steinbeck and Robert Wallsten, eds., *Steinbeck: A Life in Letters*. New York: Penguin Books, 1975, pp. 256–57. Copyright © 1975 by Elaine A. Steinbeck and Robert Wallsten. Reprinted by permission of Penguin Group (UK), Ltd. and Viking Penguin, a division of Penguin Group (USA), Inc. **326**

Stevenson, Robert Louis. *"Virginibus Puerisque" and Other Papers*, 1876. New York: Current Literature, 1916, pp. 15–16. Online at Google Books. **32**

Stopes, Marie Carmichael. *Married Love: A New Contribution to the Solution of Sex Difficulties*, 1918. London: G. P. Putnam's Sons, 1921, pp. 100–102. **404–405**

Stoppard, Tom. *The Real Thing*, 1982. New York: Faber & Faber, 1984, pp. 69–71. Copyright © 1984 by Tom Stoppard. Reprinted by permission of Faber & Faber, Ltd. **210–12**

Stowe, Harriet Beecher. *Pink and White Tyranny: A Society Novel*. Boston: Roberts Brothers, 1871, p. 45. Online at Google Books. **102–3**

Strindberg, August. *Getting Married*, Parts I and II, 1884, ed. and trans. Mary Sandbach. London: Victor Gollancz, 1972, pp. 38–39, 40–41. Copyright © 1972 by Mary Sandback. Reprinted by permission of Victor Gollancz, Ltd. and Viking, a division of Penguin Group (USA), Inc. **23–24, 317–18**

Sutton, Dora. Household commandments, 1902. In "Too Much for Sutton: His Wife Formulated 12 Household Commandments—He Bucked, Was Arrested and Then Discharged." *Boston Globe*, September 20, 1902, p. 10. Online at ProQuest Historical Newspapers. **490**

Swan, Annie S. *Courtship and Marriage and the Gentle Art of Home-Making*. London: Hutchinson, 1894, pp. 35–37. Online at Google Books. **299–300**

Talese, Gay. *Thy Neighbor's Wife*. New York: Doubleday, 1980, pp. 154–55. Copyright © 1980 by Gay Talese. Reprinted by permission of the author. **409–10**

Taylor, Richard. *Having Love Affairs*. Buffalo, NY: Prometheus Books, 1982, pp. 11–12. Copyright © 1982 by Richard Taylor. Reprinted by courtesy of Prometheus Books. **212–13**

Tennyson, Alfred, Lord. "Marriage Morning," circa 1867, and "The Princess," 1847. In *Tennyson: Poems and Plays*. London: Oxford University Press, 1975, pp. 199, 229–30. **17–18, 323**

Terman, Lewis. *Psychological Factors in Marital Happiness*. New York: McGraw-Hill, 1938, pp. 277–78, 372. **161, 406**

Thales of Miletus, circa 6th century BC. Quoted in M. de La Motte Fenelon, Archbishop of Cambray, *Lives of the Ancient Philosophers*. London: Knight and Lacy, 1825, p. 33. **503**

Thayer, Ella Cheever. *Wired Love: A Romance of Dots and Dashes*. New York: W. J. Johnston, 1880, p. 57. Online at Google Books. **33**

Thomas, Dylan. Letter to Caitlin Thomas, circa March 11, 1950. In Paul Ferris, ed. *The Collected Letters of Dylan Thomas*. London: J. M. Dent, 2000, pp. 836–37. Copyright © 1957, 1966, 1985 the Trustees for the Estate of Dylan Thomas. Reprinted by permission. **395**

Thompson, Dorothy. Letter to Sinclair Lewis, 1938. Dorothy Thompson Papers, Syracuse University. Reprinted by permission of William Morris Endeavor. **70–72**

Thompson, Ernest. *On Golden Pond*, dir. Mark Rydell. Universal Pictures, 1981. **88–89**

Tournier, Paul. *The Meaning of Persons*, 1954, trans. Edwin Hudson. New York: Harper & Row, 1957, pp. 136–38. Copyright © 1954 by Paul Tournier, renewed, © 1985 by SCM Press, Ltd. Reprinted by permission of HarperCollins Publishers and SCM—Canterbury Press, Ltd. **387**

Traditional rhyme. "Monday for wealth," n.d. *Galveston Daily News* (Houston, TX), August 4, 1878, col. H. Online at Gale 19th Century U.S. Newspapers. **465**

Traditional rhyme. "Ponder This Ye Brides-To-Be," n.d. *The Presbyterian Banner* (Pittsburgh, PA), April 2, 1903, pp. 20–21. Online at Google Books. **465–66**

Traditional rhyme. "Some wed for gold," 19th century. In Christine Bloxham and Mollie Picken, *Love and Marriage*. Devon, England: Webb & Bower, 1990, p 27. **259**

Twain, Mark. "Extracts From Adam's Diary," 1893. In W. D. Howells, Mark Twain, Nathaniel S. Shaler, et al., *The Niagara Book*. New York: Doubleday Page, 1901, p. 234. Online at Google Books. **3**

———. Notebook, 1894 and 1904. In Albert Bigelow Paine, ed., *Mark Twain's Notebook*. New York: Harper & Bros., 1935, pp. 235, 387–89. Copyright © 1935. Reprinted by permission of HarperCollins Publishers. **251, 95–96**

Updike, John. *Couples*. New York: Fawcett Books, 1968, p. 60. **341**

———. *Rabbit Is Rich*, 1981. New York: Random House, 2012, pp. 245, 247–248. Copyright © 1981 by John Updike. Reprinted by permission of Penguin Group (UK) Ltd. and Alfred A. Knopf, an imprint of the Knopf Doubleday Group, a division of Random House, LLC. All rights reserved. **410–11**

Vardalos, Nia. *My Big Fat Greek Wedding*, dir. Joel Zwick. Gold Circle Films, 2002. **341**

Villarreal, Jessica and Anthony. Storycorps recording, November 9, 2013. Online at http://www.npr.org/2013/11/09/244000145/severely-burned-marine-finds-strength-in-nascent-marriage. Reprinted by permission. **426–27**

Viorst, Judith. *Love and Shrimp*. New York: Samuel French, 1993, pp. 27–30. Copyright ©1993 by Judith Viorst. Reprinted by permission. **154–57**

Vonnegut, Kurt. *Cat's Cradle*, 1963. New York: Dial Press, 2010, pp. 86–87. **327–28**

Walker, Kenneth M. *Preparation for Marriage*. New York: W. W. Norton, 1933, pp. 86–88. **420–21**

Walker, Mary Richardson. Letter to unknown recipient, March 12, 1838. In Clifford M. Drury, *Elkanah and Mary Walker: Pioneers Among the Spokanes*. Caldwell, ID: Caxton Printers, 1940, pp. 68–69. Online in North American Women's Letters and Diaries: Colonial to 1950. **307**

Ward, Emily. Letter to Sallie Ward Lawrence, April 1849. In Timothy Bigelow Lawrence, *An Exposition of the Difficulties Between T. B. Lawrence, and his wife, Sallie Ward Lawrence, Which Led to Their Divorce*. Boston: W. Little, circa 1850, p. 8. **279–80**

Waugh, Evelyn. Letter to Laura Herbert, February 1936. In Alexander Waugh, *Fathers and Sons: The Autobiography of a Family*. New York: Doubleday, 2004, pp. 238–39. Copyright © 2004 by the Evelyn Waugh Trust. Reprinted verbatim by permission of The Wylie Agency, LLC. **354–55**

Weatherly, Jim. "Midnight Train to Georgia," 1970. Copyright © 1971, 1973 by Keca Music, Inc., International copyright secured. All rights reserved. **396**

Wells, Audrey. *Shall We Dance?*, dir. Peter Chelsom. Based on the 1997 screenplay by Masayuki Suo. Miramax Films, 2004. **486**

Wharton, Edith. *The Age of Innocence*. New York: D. Appleton, 1920, pp. 358–60. Online at Google Books. **33–35**

"What Do Young Men Marry?" *Eliza Cook's Journal*, October 7, 1854, p. 370. Online at Google Books. **101–2**

Whitty, Edward M. *Knaves and Fools; or, Friends of Bohemia: A Satirical Novel of London Life*. New York: Rudd & Carleton, 1857, pp. 399–400. Online at Google Books. **102**

Widow of Eung-Tae Yi. Letter to her late husband, 1586. In Hyung-Eun Kim, "Korean Love Affair." *Archaeology*, March/April 2010, p. 29. **388–89**

Wilde, Oscar. *The Importance of Being Earnest*, 1895. London: Leonard Smithers, 1899, pp. 17–18. Online at Google Books. **294–95**

Wilder, Billy, and I. A. L. Diamond. *Some Like It Hot*, dir. Billy Wilder. United Artists, 1959. **355–57**

Wilder, Thornton. *The Matchmaker: A Farce in Four Acts*, 1954. New York: Samuel French, 1985, p. 37. **45**

Wile, Ira S., and Mary Day Winn. *Marriage in the Modern Manner*. New York: Century, 1929, pp. 160–62, 181–84. Copyright © 1929 by Ira S. Wile and Mary Day Winn. Reprinted by permission of Viking, a division of Penguin (USA), Inc. **145, 193**

Williams, Joan. "Are Children Necessary to a Successful Marriage?" *The Times of India*, June 20, 1932, p. 14. Online at ProQuest Historical Newspapers: Times of India (1838–2003). **26–27**

Williams, Robin. Interview by Johnny Carson, *The Tonight Show*, NBC, January 10, 1991. Online at http://www.youtube.com/watch?v=ofgYq59QZck. **78**

Williams, Tennessee. *A Streetcar Named Desire*. New York: New American Library, 1947, pp. 57–61. Copyright © 1947, 1953 by the University of the South. Reprinted by permission of New Directions Publishing Corp. and George Borchardt, Inc. for the Estate of Tennessee Williams. All rights reserved. **449–51**

Winfrey, Oprah. Quoted in Jaipur Literature Festival interview, 2012. Online at www.arabiaweddings.com/news/oprah-winfrey-marriage. **443**

Winger, Debra. Quoted in Nancy Collins, "Debra Winger: Making It." *Esquire*, December 1986, p. 250. **375**

Winthrop, John. Journal entry, 1644. In James Kendall Hosmer, ed., *Winthrop's Journal, "History of New England," 1630 to 1649*, vol. 2. New York: Scribner's, 1908, pp. 161–63. Online at Sabin Americana, 1500–1926. **201**

Wodehouse, P. G. "The Rummy Affair of Old Biffy," 1924. In *The World of Jeeves*. New York: Harper & Row, 1989, pp. 282, 292–93. Reprinted by permission. **436–37**

Wolcott, James. "Noises On," 2005. In Chris Knutsen and David Kuhn, eds., *Committed: Men Tell Stories of Love, Commitment, and Marriage*. New York: Bloomsbury, 2005, pp. 140–42. Copyright © 2005 by Chris Knutsen and David Kuhn. Reprinted by permission of Bloomsbury Publishing. **254–55**

Wolfe, Tom. *The Right Stuff*. New York: Farrar, Straus and Giroux, 1979, pp. 154–56, 291–92. Copyright © 1979 by Tom Wolfe. Reprinted by permission of Farrar, Straus & Giroux, LLC. and the Random House Group Limited. **60–61**

Woodhull, Victoria. "What I Oppose in Marriage." *Boston Investigator*, May 10, 1876, p. 2. Online at Gale 19th Century U.S. Newspapers. **316–17**

Woolf, Virginia, circa 1936. Quoted in Anne Olivier Bell with Andrew McNeillie, eds., *The Diary of Virginia Woolf*, vol. 5: 1936–1941. London: Hogarth Press, 1984, p. 275. **160**

———. *To the Lighthouse*, 1927. New York: Oxford University Press, 2006, pp. 60–61. **26**

Wordsworth, William. Letter to Mary Wordsworth, August 11, 1810. In Beth Darlington, ed., *The Love Letters of William and Mary Wordsworth*. Ithaca, NY: Cornell University Press, 1981, p. 60. **333**

Wycherly, William. *The Country Wife*, 1675, ed. Thomas H. Fujimura. Lincoln: University of Nebraska Press, 1966, p. 13. **202**

Wynette, Tammy, and Billy Sherrill. "Stand By Your Man," 1968. Copyright © 1968 by Tammy Wynette and Billy Sherrill. Reprinted by permission. All rights reserved. **59–60**

Xenophon. *On Household Management* [*Oeconomics*], 4th century BC. In Mary R. Lefkowitz and Maureen B. Fant, eds., *Women's Life in Greece & Rome: A Source Book in Translation*. Baltimore: Johns Hopkins University Press, 1992, pp. 202–3. Copyright © 1982 by Mary R. Lefkowitz and Maureen B. Fant. Reprinted by permission of The Johns Hopkins University Press and Bristol Classical Press, an imprint of Bloomsbury Publishing Plc. **274–75**

Yeats, John Butler. Letter to Oliver Elton, January 21, 1917. In Joseph Hone, ed., *J. B. Yeats: Letters to His Son W. B. Yeats and Others, 1869–1922*. New York: E. P. Dutton, 1946, p. 236. **55**

Yeats, W. B. Journal, 1909. In Denis Donoghue, ed., *W. B. Yeats: Memoirs*. London: Macmillan, 1972, p. 145. **83**

———. "The Young Man's Song," 1910. In *The Green Helmet and Other Poems*. New York: Macmillan, 1912, p. 37. **509**

Yiddish proverb. "When two divorced people . . ." In Jon R. Stoe, ed. *The Routledge Book of World Proverbs*. New York: Routledge, 2006, p. 107. **377**

Zhao, Ban. "Lessons for Women," circa 100. In Nancy Lee Swann, ed., *Pan Chao: Foremost Woman Scholar of China*. New York: The Century Co., 1932, pp. 84–85. Copyright © 1932 by Nancy Lee Swann. Reprinted by permission. **417–18**

Zschokke, Heinrich. "The Evening Before the Marriage: A Story, From the German of Zschokke," 1830. In Mrs. S. T. Martyn, ed., *The Ladies' Wreath: A Magazine Devoted to Literature Industry and Religion*, vol. 1. New York: J. H. Martyn, 1847, pp. 378–79. **385**

ILLUSTRATIONS

Cartoon, Bülbül, "My name was Helen . . ." 1979. In Gloria Kaufman and Mary Kay Blakely, eds., *Pulling Our Own Strings: Feminist Humor & Satire*. Bloomington: Indiana University Press, 1980, p. 186. Copyright © 1979 Bülbül (Genevieve Leland Guracar). **309**

Cartoon, Bruce Eric Kaplan, "Sometimes I think . . ." *The New Yorker*, November 15, 1999. Copyright © Bruce Eric Kaplan/The New Yorker Collection/The Cartoon Bank. **37**

Cartoon, Lee Lorenz, "Your wife gets the house . . ." *The New Yorker*, March 20, 2006. Copyright © Lee Lorenz/The New Yorker Collection/The Cartoon Bank. **78**

Cartoon, David Sipress, "You make a very compelling case . . ." *The New Yorker*, October 24, 2011. Copyright © David Sipress/The New Yorker Collection/The Cartoon Bank. **499**

Cartoon, Mick Stevens, "Well, it was original . . ." *The New Yorker*, September 3, 2012. Copyright © Mick Stevens/The New Yorker Collection/The Cartoon Bank. **4**

Cartoon, James Thurber, "Have it your way . . ." *The New Yorker*, January 30, 1932, p. 11. Copyright © 1932 by Rosemary A. Thurber. Reprinted by arrangement with Rosemary A. Thurber and the Barbara Hogenson Agency. All rights reserved. **42**

Exhibit card, "Marriage prescription." Exhibit Supply Card, 1938. **475**

Honeymoon photo, John Lennon and Yoko Ono, Bed-in, Montreal, 1969. Copyright © Bettmann/CORBIS. **178**

Honeymoon photo, Queen Elizabeth and Prince Phillip, 1947. Copyright © Topical Press Agency / Hulton Royals Collection / Getty Images. **258**

Illustration, "Harmonious Man" and "Harmonious Woman." In Nelson Sizer and H. S. Drayton, *Heads and Faces and How to Study Them*, New York: Fowler & Wells, 1897, p.181. **331**

Illustration, "Expanding Spiral of Open Marriage." In Nena and George O'Neill, *Open Marriage: A New Life Style for Couples*. New York: M. Evans, 1972, p. 266. **407**

Illustration, "Love Will Survive." Clara Elsene Peck. In Minna Thomas Antrim, *Phrases, Mazes and Crazes of Love*. Philadelphia: George W. Jacobs, 1904, n.p. **287**

Illustration, "Woman's Chance of Marriage" chart. In E.B.B., *A Letter to Young Ladies on Marriage*. Boston: Tuttle, Dennett & Chisholm, 1837, p. 9. **507**

Movie still, Henry Fonda and Katharine Hepburn. *On Golden Pond*, 1981. Copyright © Rex USA/TV. **88**

Movie still, Joe E. Brown and Jack Lemmon, *Some Like It Hot*, 1959. Reprinted by permission of MGM. **357**

Painting, William Hogarth, "Marriage a La Mode, Scene II: Shortly After the Marriage," 1743. Courtesy of the National Gallery, London. **312**

Photograph, baseball cap. Irony Designs, 2013. **51**

Photograph, the Mistress Stone, by Anna Hanlon. Courtesy of the Royal Scottish Geographical Society. **343**

Photograph, the Marriage Bureau, circa 1900. Courtesy of the Library of Congress. **454**

Photograph, Queen Elizabeth and Prince Phillip, 2007. Copyright © Tim Graham / Getty Images News / Getty Images. **258**

Postcards, authors' collection. **8, 14, 72, 105, 121, 134, 192, 208, 260**

Poster, "Predicting Happiness in Marriage." In Evelyn Millis Duvall and Reuben Hill, *When You Marry*. Boston: D. C. Heath, 1945, p. 119. **162**

Print, Currier and Ives, "The Day before Marriage," 1847. Courtesy of the Library of Congress. **100**

Print, "Judge Thumb," by James Gilray, 1782. Courtesy of the Library of Congress. **448**

Prints, British mezzotints, "The Wedding Day," and "6 Weeks After;" 1777. Copyright © The Trustees of the British Museum. All rights reserved. **171**

Sheet music, "Don't You Think It's Time to Marry?" 1906. **467**

Sheet music, "Honey on Our Honeymoon," 1909. **175**

Trade card, "My Wife and my mother-in-law," 1885. **226**

TV still, Audrey Meadows and Jackie Gleason, *The Honeymooners*. By permission of the Everett Collection. **46**

TV still, Vivian Vance, Elvia Allman, and Lucille Ball, *I Love Lucy*, Copyright © CBS Broadcasting Inc. **498**

Wedding photo, Jacqueline Bouvier and John Kennedy, 1953. Courtesy of the JFK Library. Copyright © 1953 Toni Frissell. **457**

Wedding photo, Croatia couple, by Zvonimir Barisin. Reprinted with the permission of the photographer. **262–263**

Wedding photo, Neil Patrick Harris and David Burtka, 2014. Photographed by Danielle Levitt. Reprinted by permission. **311**

Wedding photo, Marley Klaus and Kevin Dowling, 1987. From "25 Years," *The Heathen Learns* blog, May 9, 2012: http://marley thetheathen.blogspot.com. Courtesy of Marley Klaus. **199**

Wedding photo, Elizabeth Taylor and Richard Burton, 1973. Copyright © William Lovelace / Hulton Archive / Getty Images. **77**

ABOUT THE AUTHORS

LISA GRUNWALD and **STEPHEN ADLER** collaborated on two bestselling anthologies: *Women's Letters: America from the Revolutionary War to the Present* and *Letters of the Century: America 1900–1999*. Grunwald is the author of the novels *The Irresistible Henry House, Whatever Makes You Happy, New Year's Eve, The Theory of Everything*, and *Summer*. Adler is president and editor in chief of Reuters and author of *The Jury: Trial and Error in the American Courtroom*. Grunwald and Adler have two children and live in New York City. The authors have been married to each other since 1988 and plan to stay that way. Visit them at TheMarriageBook.com.